DEMOCRACY IN AMERICA

论美国的民主

上

（经典文库 汉英对照）

（法）托克维尔⊙著

吴　睿⊙译

台海出版社

图书在版编目（CIP）数据

论美国的民主：汉英对照 /（法）托克维尔著；吴
睿译 . -- 北京：台海出版社，2017.2（2022.7重印）
　　ISBN 978-7-5168-1268-6

Ⅰ．①论… Ⅱ．①托… ②吴… Ⅲ．①民主—研究—
美国—汉、英 Ⅳ．① D771.209

中国版本图书馆CIP数据核字（2017）第030757号

论美国的民主：汉英对照

著　　者：	（法）托克维尔	译　　者：	吴　睿
责任编辑：	刘　峰	装帧设计：	同人阅文化传媒·书装设计
版式设计：	同人阅文化传媒·书装设计	责任印制：	蔡　旭

出版发行：台海出版社
地　　址：北京市东城区景山东街 20 号　　　邮政编码：100009
电　　话：010 — 64041652（发行，邮购）
传　　真：010 — 84045799（总编室）
网　　址：www.taimeng.org.cn/thcbs/default.htm
E - m a i l：thcbs@126.com

经　　销：全国各地新华书店
印　　刷：香河县宏润印刷有限公司
本书如有破损、缺页、装订错误，请与本社联系调换

开　　本：	787mm×1092mm	1/16	
字　　数：	1024 千字	印　　张：	46.75
版　　次：	2017年5月第1版	印　　次：	2022年7月第4次印刷
书　　号：	ISBN 978-7-5168-1268-6		
定　　价：	148.00元（上、下册）		

C 目录
ontents

Volume I

Introductory Chapter ·· 2

Chapter I: Exterior Form Of North America ······························ 16

Chapter II: Origin Of The Anglo–Americans ···························· 24

Chapter III: Social Conditions Of The Anglo–Americans ········· 41

Chapter IV: The Principle Of The Sovereignty Of The People In America ·········· 50

Chapter V: Necessity Of Examining The Condition Of The States ············· 54

Chapter VI: Judicial Power In The United States ······················ 88

上 卷

前　言 ··· 2

第一章　北美的外貌 ·· 16

第二章　英裔美国人的起源 ·· 24

第三章　英裔美国人的社会情况 ··· 41

第四章　美国人民主权的原则 ··· 50

第五章　研究各州过去的必要性 ··· 54

第六章　美国的司法权 ·· 88

Chapter VII: Political Jurisdiction In The United States ·············· 96

Chapter VIII: The Federal Constitution ·············· 102

Chapter IX: Why The People May Strictly Be Said To Govern In The United States ·········· 160

Chapter X: Parties In The United States ·············· 162

Chapter XI: Liberty Of The Press In The United States ·············· 170

Chapter XII: Political Associations In The United States ·············· 180

Chapter XIII: Government Of The Democracy In America—Part I ·············· 189

Chapter XIV: Advantages American Society Derive From Democracy ·············· 226

Chapter XV: Unlimited Power Of Majority, And Its Consequences ·············· 244

Chapter XVI: Causes Mitigating Tyranny In The United States ·············· 261

Chapter XVII: Principal Causes Maintaining The Democratic Republic ·············· 277

Chapter XVIII: Future Condition Of Three Races In The United States ·············· 320

Conclusion ·············· 408

第七章　美国的政治审判·············· 96

第八章　联邦宪法·············· 102

第九章　为什么严格地说美国是由人民进行统治的·············· 160

第十章　美国的政党·············· 162

第十一章　美国的出版自由·············· 170

第十二章　美国的政治社团·············· 180

第十三章　美国的民主政府·············· 189

第十四章　民主制带给美国社会的好处·············· 226

第十五章　多数的无限力量及其后果·············· 244

第十六章　美国如何削弱多数的暴政·············· 261

第十七章　民主共和制度得以维持的主要原因·············· 277

第十八章　美国境内三个种族的未来·············· 320

结论·············· 408

Volume 2

De Tocqueville's Preface To The Second Part ················· 416

Section I: Influence of Democracy on the Action of Intellect in The United States. ··········· 419

Section 2: Influence of Democracy on the Feelings of Americans ·············· 499

Book Three: Influence Of Democracy On Manners, Properly So Called ············ 556

Book Four: Influence Of Democratic Opinions On Political Society ············ 665

APPENDIX ·· 706

下　卷

前　言··· 416

第一篇　民主对美国观念进步的影响·············· 419

第二篇　民主对美国人情感的影响················ 499

第三篇　民主对所谓民情的影响·················· 556

第四篇　民主观念对政治社会的影响·············· 665

附录··· 706

Volume I

上　卷

Introductory Chapter

Amongst the novel objects that attracted my attention during my stay in the United States, nothing struck me more forcibly than the general equality of conditions. I readily discovered the prodigious influence which this primary fact exercises on the whole course of society, by giving a certain direction to public opinion, and a certain tenor to the laws; by imparting new maxims to the governing powers, and peculiar habits to the governed. I speedily perceived that the influence of this fact extends far beyond the political character and the laws of the country, and that it has no less empire over civil society than over the Government; it creates opinions, engenders sentiments, suggests the ordinary practices of life, and modifies whatever it does not produce. The more I advanced in the study of American society, the more I perceived that the equality of conditions is the fundamental fact from which all others seem to be derived, and the central point at which all my observations constantly terminated.

I then turned my thoughts to our own hemisphere, where I imagined that I discerned something analogous to the spectacle which the New World presented to me. I observed that the equality of conditions is daily progressing towards those extreme limits which it seems to have reached in the United States, and that the democracy which governs the American communities appears to be rapidly rising into power in Europe. I hence conceived the idea of the book which is now before the reader.

It is evident to all alike that a great democratic revolution is going on amongst us; but there are two opinions as to its nature and consequences. To some it appears to be a novel accident, which as such may still be checked; to others it seems irresistible, because it is the most uniform, the

前　言

在美国逗留的这段时间，有很多新鲜事物都引起了我的注意，其中最打动我的莫过于人与人的平等。我轻轻松松就发现这一基本事实对整个社会进程产生的重大影响：它为公众舆论指出特定的方向，为法律定下特定的方针，向执政当局传授新的箴言，让被统治者养成特定的习惯。

不久我便意识到，这一事实影响的远远不止这个国家的政治特征和法律，它对于政府的绝对权威一点也不亚于对公民社会的权威；它制造舆论，激发情感，倡议日常生活行为规范，并修正非它所产生的一切。对美国社会的研究越是深入，我就越意识到平等是根本大事，似乎所有的一切都源于此，而且往往是我所有观察最终归结的中心点。

接着，当我把思绪转向我们半球的时候，觉得我们这里的某些情形和新世界呈现在我眼前的景象类似。我注意到在我们这里平等尽管没有达到美国那种极端的程度，不过正日益朝着这个方向前进；而且在美国社会处于支配地位的民主，似乎在欧洲正在迅速崛起掌权。

从那时起，我便萌发了撰写读者面前这本书的念头。

显而易见，对所有人都一样，一场伟大的民主革命正在我们中间进行，但是人们对它的看法却各异。对有些人来说，它似乎新奇而偶然，而且想要加以遏制；而对另外一些

most ancient, and the most permanent tendency which is to be found in history. Let us recollect the situation of France seven hundred years ago, when the territory was divided amongst a small number of families, who were the owners of the soil and the rulers of the inhabitants; the right of governing descended with the family inheritance from generation to generation; force was the only means by which man could act on man, and landed property was the sole source of power. Soon, however, the political power of the clergy was founded, and began to exert itself: the clergy opened its ranks to all classes, to the poor and the rich, the villein and the lord; equality penetrated into the Government through the Church, and the being who as a serf must have vegetated in perpetual bondage took his place as a priest in the midst of nobles, and not infrequently above the heads of kings.

The different relations of men became more complicated and more numerous as society gradually became more stable and more civilized. Thence the want of civil laws was felt; and the order of legal functionaries soon rose from the obscurity of the tribunals and their dusty chambers, to appear at the court of the monarch, by the side of the feudal barons in their ermine and their mail. Whilst the kings were ruining themselves by their great enterprises, and the nobles exhausting their resources by private wars, the lower orders were enriching themselves by commerce. The influence of money began to be perceptible in State affairs. The transactions of business opened a new road to power, and the financier rose to a station of political influence in which he was at once flattered and despised. Gradually the spread of mental acquirements, and the increasing taste for literature and art, opened chances of success to talent; science became a means of government, intelligence led to social power, and the man of letters took a part in the affairs of the State. The value attached to the privileges of birth decreased in the exact proportion in which new paths were struck out to advancement. In the eleventh century nobility was beyond all price; in the thirteenth it might be purchased; it was conferred for the first time in 1270; and equality was thus introduced into the Government by the aristocracy itself.

In the course of these seven hundred years it sometimes happened that in order to resist the authority of the Crown, or to diminish the power of their rivals, the nobles granted a certain share

人来说，它似乎根本不可抗拒，因为它是有史以来最一致、最古老也最持久的趋势。让我们重新追忆一下七百年前法国的情形。那时，法国被一小撮家族瓜分，他们拥有土地、统治居民，统治权世代相传；武力是人对付人的唯一手段；地产是权力的唯一来源。可是，不久教士的政治权力开始崛起，并不断壮大。教士阶层对所有的人都敞开大门：穷人和富人，属民和领主；通过教会平等开始向政府渗透；原先终身受奴役的农奴摇身一变成为神父，加入到贵族的行列，而且时不时地还会凌驾于国王之上。

随着社会逐渐变得稳定开化，人们之间的关系变得越来越复杂多样。因此，人们开始觉得需要民法，于是法律人士走出阴森的法庭，离开布满灰尘的办公室，出现在君主的宫廷，与穿貂皮披盔甲的封建贵族肩并肩。当国王因为野心勃勃而濒临破产，贵族因为私人战争而倾家荡产的时候，下层阶级靠着商业积累起财富。金钱对国家事务的影响力开始显现出来。商业成为通向权力大门的一条新路。金融家成为一股政治势力，既受到人们的奉迎，却又被鄙视。渐渐地随着知识的普及，人们对文学艺术的兴趣渐浓，人才有了成功的机会，科学成为为政的手段，智慧成为一种社会力量，文人开始参与国家政事。随着通往权力大门的新路不断出现，与生俱来的特权的价值降低了。11世纪贵族头衔是无价之宝，到13世纪用钱就可以买到，贵族头衔的出售始于1270年，结果平等也由贵族亲自带进政府。

在这七百年里，为了对抗国王的权威，削弱对手的权力，贵族将一部分特定的权利赋予人民。而更常见的情形是，为了达到抑制贵族的目的，国王允许下层阶级享有一定的权力。在法国，国王一直都是最积极、最彻底的平等主义者。当他们力量强大、野心勃勃的

of political rights to the people. Or, more frequently, the king permitted the lower orders to enjoy a degree of power, with the intention of repressing the aristocracy. In France the kings have always been the most active and the most constant of levellers. When they were strong and ambitious they spared no pains to raise the people to the level of the nobles; when they were temperate or weak they allowed the people to rise above themselves. Some assisted the democracy by their talents, others by their vices. Louis XI and Louis XIV reduced every rank beneath the throne to the same subjection; Louis XV descended, himself and all his Court, into the dust.

As soon as land was held on any other than a feudal tenure, and personal property began in its turn to confer influence and power, every improvement which was introduced in commerce or manufacture was a fresh element of the equality of conditions. Henceforward every new discovery, every new want which it engendered, and every new desire which craved satisfaction, was a step towards the universal level. The taste for luxury, the love of war, the sway of fashion, and the most superficial as well as the deepest passions of the human heart, co-operated to enrich the poor and to impoverish the rich.

From the time when the exercise of the intellect became the source of strength and of wealth, it is impossible not to consider every addition to science, every fresh truth, and every new idea as a germ of power placed within the reach of the people. Poetry, eloquence, and memory, the grace of wit, the glow of imagination, the depth of thought, and all the gifts which are bestowed by Providence with an equal hand, turned to the advantage of the democracy; and even when they were in the possession of its adversaries they still served its cause by throwing into relief the natural greatness of man; its conquests spread, therefore, with those of civilization and knowledge, and literature became an arsenal where the poorest and the weakest could always find weapons to their hand.

In perusing the pages of our history, we shall scarcely meet with a single great event, in the lapse of seven hundred years, which has not turned to the advantage of equality. The Crusades and the wars of the English decimated the nobles and divided their possessions; the erection of communities introduced an element of democratic liberty into the bosom of feudal monarchy; the invention of fire-

时候，不费吹灰之力便可以让平民与贵族平起平坐；而当他们平庸无能的时候，竟允许平民凌驾于自己之上。有些国王凭借他们的才能帮助了民主，而另一些国王则因为他们的昏庸而成就了民主。路易十一和路易十四让王位之下的全体臣民保持平等，而路易十五则将自己连同王室一同埋葬在灰烬之中。

一旦土地不再受到封建土地所有制的制约，动产反过来开始产生影响和制造权势，商业和制造业上的每一次改进，都成为平等的新因素。自此之后，每一个新发现，每一个新需求，以及渴望得到满足的每一个新愿望，都是向普遍平等迈进的一步。喜好奢侈，穷兵黩武，追求时髦，以及人们内心最肤浅也最高尚的热情，携起手来让穷人变富，让富人变穷。

从智慧变成力量和财富的源泉之时起，每一个科学发明，每一个新的真理，每一个新思想，都无法不被视作人民触手可及的权力胚芽。诗情、口才、记忆力、智慧的魅力、想象力的光辉、思想的深邃，以及上天平等之手所赋予的一切才华，都在促进民主。甚至当它们落入民主敌人之手时，依然会通过彰显人天性的伟大来为民主服务。因此，随着文明和知识所征服的领域不断扩大，被民主征服的领域也将扩大。而文学则成为兵工厂，穷人和弱者在这里总能找到应手的武器。

翻阅一下我们的历史，在逝去的七百年里，几乎没有一个伟大的事件不曾推动平等的发展。十字军东征和几次对英战争消灭了十分之一的贵族，并分化了他们的土地。地方自治制度的确立给封建君主政体引进了民主自由的元素。火器的发明让平民和贵族在战场上变得平等。印刷术的出现将同样的精神食粮平等地呈现在所有阶级面前。邮政制度的开

arms equalized the villein and the noble on the field of battle; printing opened the same resources to the minds of all classes; the post was organized so as to bring the same information to the door of the poor man's cottage and to the gate of the palace; and Protestantism proclaimed that all men are alike able to find the road to heaven. The discovery of America offered a thousand new paths to fortune, and placed riches and power within the reach of the adventurous and the obscure. If we examine what has happened in France at intervals of fifty years, beginning with the eleventh century, we shall invariably perceive that a twofold revolution has taken place in the state of society. The noble has gone down on the social ladder, and the roturier has gone up; the one descends as the other rises. Every half century brings them nearer to each other, and they will very shortly meet.

Nor is this phenomenon at all peculiar to France. Whithersoever we turn our eyes we shall witness the same continual revolution throughout the whole of Christendom. The various occurrences of national existence have everywhere turned to the advantage of democracy; all men have aided it by their exertions: those who have intentionally labored in its cause, and those who have served it unwittingly; those who have fought for it and those who have declared themselves its opponents, have all been driven along in the same track, have all labored to one end, some ignorantly and some unwillingly; all have been blind instruments in the hands of God.

The gradual development of the equality of conditions is therefore a providential fact, and it possesses all the characteristics of a divine decree: it is universal, it is durable, it constantly eludes all human interference, and all events as well as all men contribute to its progress. Would it, then, be wise to imagine that a social impulse which dates from so far back can be checked by the efforts of a generation? Is it credible that the democracy which has annihilated the feudal system and vanquished kings will respect the citizen and the capitalist? Will it stop now that it has grown so strong and its adversaries so weak? None can say which way we are going, for all terms of comparison are wanting: the equality of conditions is more complete in the Christian countries of the present day than it has been at any time or in any part of the world; so that the extent of what already exists prevents us from foreseeing what may be yet to come.

启不但可以把消息传送到华丽的宫殿门前，也同样送抵穷人的草庐门口。基督教新教宣布所有人都一样均能找到通往天堂之路。美洲大陆的发现提供了上千条发财致富的新路，一文不名的冒险家也有机会染指财富和权力。如果从11世纪开始对法国每50年的变化加以考察，我们必然会发现，每50年法国的社会体制都会发生一次双重革命。贵族会从社会的阶梯上走下来，而平民则升上去。就这样一个向下，一个向上。每半个世纪他们之间的距离就会缩短一点，不久之后他们就能彼此相遇。

而且这样的现象并非法国所独有。无论我们将目光投向何处，都能看到同样的革命在整个基督教世界进行。各地人民生活中发生的各种事件，都促进了民主的发展。所有的人，不管他们是自愿促进民主事业还是无意之举；或是为民主而战，乃至自称是民主的敌人，都助了民主一臂之力。他们走上了同一条路，奔向同一目标，殊途同归，尽管有些人身不由己，有些人不知不觉。所有的人都成为了上帝手中驯服的工具。

因此身份平等的逐步发展是大势所趋，顺应天意。它的发展是普遍持久的，可以不断挣脱人为的阻挠，所有的事、所有的人都在推动它的发展。一个由来已久的社会原动力会被一代人的努力所绊住，这样的想法难道会是明智的吗？摧毁封建制度并将国王打倒的民主会在资产者和有钱人面前卑躬屈膝，这样的想法难道不是异想天开？在民主已经如此壮大，其敌人变得虚弱的今天，它又怎会裹足不前？没有人能说得清我们正在走向何方，因为对比的办法已经无法对此做出回答。在今天的基督教徒之间，身份平等已经发展到以往任何时候和世界上任何地方都前所未有的程度。所以已经实现的巨大成果让我们无法预见

The whole book which is here offered to the public has been written under the impression of a kind of religious dread produced in the author's mind by the contemplation of so irresistible a revolution, which has advanced for centuries in spite of such amazing obstacles, and which is still proceeding in the midst of the ruins it has made. It is not necessary that God himself should speak in order to disclose to us the unquestionable signs of His will; we can discern them in the habitual course of nature, and in the invariable tendency of events: I know, without a special revelation, that the planets move in the orbits traced by the Creator's finger. If the men of our time were led by attentive observation and by sincere reflection to acknowledge that the gradual and progressive development of social equality is at once the past and future of their history, this solitary truth would confer the sacred character of a Divine decree upon the change. To attempt to check democracy would be in that case to resist the will of God; and the nations would then be constrained to make the best of the social lot awarded to them by Providence.

The Christian nations of our age seem to me to present a most alarming spectacle; the impulse which is bearing them along is so strong that it cannot be stopped, but it is not yet so rapid that it cannot be guided: their fate is in their hands; yet a little while and it may be so no longer. The first duty which is at this time imposed upon those who direct our affairs is to educate the democracy; to warm its faith, if that be possible; to purify its morals; to direct its energies; to substitute a knowledge of business for its inexperience, and an acquaintance with its true interests for its blind propensities; to adapt its government to time and place, and to modify it in compliance with the occurrences and the actors of the age. A new science of politics is indispensable to a new world. This, however, is what we think of least; launched in the middle of a rapid stream, we obstinately fix our eyes on the ruins which may still be described upon the shore we have left, whilst the current sweeps us along, and drives us backwards towards the gulf.

In no country in Europe has the great social revolution which I have been describing made such rapid progress as in France; but it has always been borne on by chance. The heads of the State have never had any forethought for its exigencies, and its victories have been obtained without their

未来还会有什么出现。

呈现给大家的这本书，全篇都是在唯恐受到上帝责罚的心境下完成。作者之所以会这样，是因为已经看到这样一场无法阻挡的革命尽管遭遇重重障碍，但是依然进行了几个世纪；而如今它仍旧在它所制造的废墟上前进。上帝完全没有必要将其意志亲自昭告天下。我们只需看一看自然界年复一年的正常运作和事件无可逆转的发展趋势便可。没有造物主的启示，我也知道天上的恒星是按照它手指画出的轨道运行。如果说今天的人们是通过细心地观察和认真地思索，才认识到持续向前发展的社会平等既是人类历史的过去，又是人类历史的未来，那么单单是发现这一事实本身就可以为这一变化附上神的意旨。所以，试图阻止民主就是违抗上帝的旨意。因此，各个国家只能顺应上苍为他们安排的社会情况。

在我看来，我们这个时代信奉基督教的国家呈现出一种非常可怕的状况。席卷它们的革命运动已经强大到无法遏止，但是它的速度还没有快到无法驾驭；它们的命运依旧掌握在自己手中，但是过不了多久就会失去控制。所以此时领导社会的人所肩负的首要责任就是要教化民主，如果可能要唤起对民主的信仰，纯洁民主的风尚，规范民主的行动，用治世的科学取代民情的经验，用对民主真正利益的认识取代盲目的本能，让民主的治理与时间和地方相协调，并依据环境和人事加以修正。一个崭新的社会必然要有一个全新的政治科学。然而我们几乎没有这么想过。我们身处湍急的河流之中，顽强地注视着河岸上依稀可见的断壁残垣，然而水流又将我们卷回到漩涡之中。

我刚刚所描述的伟大的社会革命，在欧洲任何一个国家都不曾像在法国一般高歌猛

consent or without their knowledge. The most powerful, the most intelligent, and the most moral classes of the nation have never attempted to connect themselves with it in order to guide it. The people has consequently been abandoned to its wild propensities, and it has grown up like those outcasts who receive their education in the public streets, and who are unacquainted with aught but the vices and wretchedness of society. The existence of a democracy was seemingly unknown, when on a sudden it took possession of the supreme power. Everything was then submitted to its caprices; it was worshipped as the idol of strength; until, when it was enfeebled by its own excesses, the legislator conceived the rash project of annihilating its power, instead of instructing it and correcting its vices; no attempt was made to fit it to govern, but all were bent on excluding it from the government.

The consequence of this has been that the democratic revolution has been effected only in the material parts of society, without that concomitant change in laws, ideas, customs, and manners which was necessary to render such a revolution beneficial. We have gotten a democracy, but without the conditions which lessen its vices and render its natural advantages more prominent; and although we already perceive the evils it brings, we are ignorant of the benefits it may confer.

While the power of the Crown, supported by the aristocracy, peaceably governed the nations of Europe, society possessed, in the midst of its wretchedness, several different advantages which can now scarcely be appreciated or conceived. The power of a part of his subjects was an insurmountable barrier to the tyranny of the prince; and the monarch, who felt the almost divine character which he enjoyed in the eyes of the multitude, derived a motive for the just use of his power from the respect which he inspired. High as they were placed above the people, the nobles could not but take that calm and benevolent interest in its fate which the shepherd feels towards his flock; and without acknowledging the poor as their equals, they watched over the destiny of those whose welfare Providence had entrusted to their care. The people never having conceived the idea of a social condition different from its own, and entertaining no expectation of ever ranking with its chiefs, received benefits from them without discussing their rights. It grew attached to them when they

进。然而在法国，这场革命则进行得毫无章法肆意而为。国家的领导人从来没有对这样的紧急事件深谋远虑，在没有得到他们认可并在他们不知不觉之中，革命便取得了胜利。这个国家最强有力、最有知识以及最有道德的阶级根本未曾染指其间试图将其驾驭。结果，人民被遗弃而民主则任由其狂野的本性支配，如同流浪街头只知道社会弊端和悲惨的野孩子一般成长起来。当民主突然之间取得至高无上权力的时候，其存在似乎还无人知晓，但是在其掌权之后，人们便对它的反复无常唯命是从，将其视为力量的象征顶礼膜拜。而后来，由于它的过分的行为而声势渐微的时候，立法者非但没有要对其进行引导和纠正的想法，反而匆忙设计出法案妄图将其置于死地。立法者并不想让它学会治国之道，而是竭尽所能要将它从政府中排挤出去。

结果，民主革命只是对于社会自身层面来说发生了，而作为使这场革命意义重大的必要的法律、思想、民情和道德方面的变化则根本没有发生。我们虽然已经有了民主，但是缺少能够让它扬长避短的东西。尽管我们已经意识到它所带来的弊端，而对它所能带来的益处视而不见。

当贵族支持下的王权平安无事地统治着欧洲各国的时候，身处不幸的人们还享受一些我们这个时代人们看来难以想象和理解的幸福。某些臣子所拥有的权力成为王亲国戚施暴难以逾越的障碍。而于国王，由于他觉得自己在众人面前犹如神一般的存在，所以当他在受到神一样的尊重后，绝不愿意滥用自己的权力。在人民面前高高在上的贵族，对待人民的命运根本无动于衷，只不过是同情心而已，就好像牧人对待自己的牲口一样。他们并不

were clement and just, and it submitted without resistance or servility to their exactions, as to the inevitable visitations of the arm of God. Custom, and the manners of the time, had moreover created a species of law in the midst of violence, and established certain limits to oppression. As the noble never suspected that anyone would attempt to deprive him of the privileges which he believed to be legitimate, and as the serf looked upon his own inferiority as a consequence of the immutable order of nature, it is easy to imagine that a mutual exchange of good-will took place between two classes so differently gifted by fate. Inequality and wretchedness were then to be found in society; but the souls of neither rank of men were degraded. Men are not corrupted by the exercise of power or debased by the habit of obedience, but by the exercise of a power which they believe to be illegal and by obedience to a rule which they consider to be usurped and oppressive. On one side was wealth, strength, and leisure, accompanied by the refinements of luxury, the elegance of taste, the pleasures of wit, and the religion of art. On the other was labor and a rude ignorance; but in the midst of this coarse and ignorant multitude it was not uncommon to meet with energetic passions, generous sentiments, profound religious convictions, and independent virtues. The body of a State thus organized might boast of its stability, its power, and, above all, of its glory.

But the scene is now changed, and gradually the two ranks mingle; the divisions which once severed mankind are lowered, property is divided, power is held in common, the light of intelligence spreads, and the capacities of all classes are equally cultivated; the State becomes democratic, and the empire of democracy is slowly and peaceably introduced into the institutions and the manners of the nation. I can conceive a society in which all men would profess an equal attachment and respect for the laws of which they are the common authors; in which the authority of the State would be respected as necessary, though not as divine; and the loyalty of the subject to its chief magistrate would not be a passion, but a quiet and rational persuasion. Every individual being in the possession of rights which he is sure to retain, a kind of manly reliance and reciprocal courtesy would arise between all classes, alike removed from pride and meanness. The people, well acquainted with

认为穷人与他们平等，他们关注穷人的命运不过就是完成上帝交托给他们的任务。人民从来没有奢望自己的社会地位会有什么不同，也从没想过要跟首领平起平坐，觉得自己从他们那里得到恩惠根本不会计较自己的权利。当首领仁慈而公正的时候，人民爱戴他，对首领的严厉统治逆来顺受，卑躬屈膝，如同接受上帝的摆布。而且当时的习俗和民情也为暴政做出限定，对暴力的实施进行约束。因为贵族从来没有想过谁会将其自以为合法的特权剥夺，而奴隶也将自己低下的地位视作是无法更改的自然规律，所以人们很容易地想到在这样命运如此悬殊的两个阶级间建立起相互照顾的关系。进而，不平等和苦难便在社会中应运而生，所幸的是双方的灵魂都没有堕落。不论是执政者践行他的权力还是人民习惯性的服从，都没有让人堕落；而人们之所以堕落是因为掌权者行使了被认为不合法的权力而人民则服从了被视作篡夺和压迫的强权。一方面，一些人集财富、权力、享乐于一身，过着奢华的生活，品位优雅，寻欢作乐，崇尚艺术；而另一些人则终生劳碌，粗鲁无知。然而正是在这群粗鲁无知的群众中，也常常能发现活力四射的激情，高尚的情操，虔诚的宗教信仰以及独立的美德。这样组建起的社会或许可以为其稳定、强大特别是辉煌自吹自擂。

但是这样的社会面貌现在则发生了变化，各个阶级开始渐渐相互融合，曾经将人们分隔开的屏障开始纷纷倒塌，财富分散到更多的人手中，权力也由更多的人共享，知识得到传播，各阶级可以平等地接受教育，国家变得民主，最终，民主渐渐和平地渗透到国家的法律和民情之中。于是我想象着这样一个社会，在这里人人都将自己视为法律的缔造者，对法律有着同样的热爱和尊重，人们对于政府权威的尊重是出于必要而不是它的神圣，而臣民对于国家首脑的忠诚也不是出于热情，而是冷静且理智的信念。人人都拥有权利并得

its true interests, would allow that in order to profit by the advantages of society it is necessary to satisfy its demands. In this state of things the voluntary association of the citizens might supply the individual exertions of the nobles, and the community would be alike protected from anarchy and from oppression.

I admit that, in a democratic State thus constituted, society will not be stationary; but the impulses of the social body may be regulated and directed forwards; if there be less splendor than in the halls of an aristocracy, the contrast of misery will be less frequent also; the pleasures of enjoyment may be less excessive, but those of comfort will be more general; the sciences may be less perfectly cultivated, but ignorance will be less common; the impetuosity of the feelings will be repressed, and the habits of the nation softened; there will be more vices and fewer crimes. In the absence of enthusiasm and of an ardent faith, great sacrifices may be obtained from the members of a commonwealth by an appeal to their understandings and their experience; each individual will feel the same necessity for uniting with his fellow-citizens to protect his own weakness; and as he knows that if they are to assist he must co-operate, he will readily perceive that his personal interest is identified with the interest of the community. The nation, taken as a whole, will be less brilliant, less glorious, and perhaps less strong; but the majority of the citizens will enjoy a greater degree of prosperity, and the people will remain quiet, not because it despairs of amelioration, but because it is conscious of the advantages of its condition. If all the consequences of this state of things were not good or useful, society would at least have appropriated all such as were useful and good; and having once and for ever renounced the social advantages of aristocracy, mankind would enter into possession of all the benefits which democracy can afford.

But here it may be asked what we have adopted in the place of those institutions, those ideas, and those customs of our forefathers which we have abandoned. The spell of royalty is broken, but it has not been succeeded by the majesty of the laws; the people has learned to despise all authority, but fear now extorts a larger tribute of obedience than that which was formerly paid by reverence and by love.

到保障，因而各阶级间形成一种不卑不亢的坚定的相互信赖和相互尊重的关系。人民对自己的真正利益有清楚的认识，自然能理解，要想享受社会公益，必须要对社会履行自己的义务。在这样的情况下，公民自发的联合会取代贵族个人权威，那么同样地国家也就不会出现暴政和专横。

我认为在以此方式建立的一个民主国家里，社会不会停滞不前，而社会的前进也将会是有规律的循序渐进的。即使民主社会不会像贵族社会那样璀璨夺目，但是苦难不会那么强烈。在民主社会享乐不会过度，但是舒适的生活会更加普遍；科学也许不会那么突出，但是无知会大为减少；情感不会过分冲动，而且行为则更加稳健；恶习也许不会更少，但是犯罪率将大大降低。即使缺少狂热的激情和虔诚的信仰，理解和经验也会让公民勇于献身做出巨大牺牲。因为每个人都很弱小，每个公民都同样感到有必要和其他同胞团结起来。而且他们知道只有向同胞伸出援手才能得到同胞的支援。人们不难发现他们的个人利益与公众利益是一致的。作为一个整体国家可能不再那么辉煌荣耀，也可能不再那么强大，然而大多数公民则能够享受到更大的幸福，人民不会再闹事，而这并不是因为人们不希望变得更好，而是因为他们觉得已经过得够好。在这样的情形下，虽然并不是所有的事物都尽善尽美，但至少社会已经拥有变得善与美的所有条件。而且人们一旦永远拒绝接受贵族政治带来的社会利益，便开始享有民主制度带来的所有好处。

但是在这里，我们也许要问自己在抛弃祖先所有的制度、观念和民情以后，又该拿什么来填补它们留下的空白呢？王室的魔咒被打破，而法律的权威尚未确立，现在人们便开始藐视一切权威，可是同时又惧怕它，而这种惧怕给他们带来的损失远远超过原先尊崇权

I perceive that we have destroyed those independent beings which were able to cope with tyranny single-handed; but it is the Government that has inherited the privileges of which families, corporations, and individuals have been deprived; the weakness of the whole community has therefore succeeded that influence of a small body of citizens, which, if it was sometimes oppressive, was often conservative. The division of property has lessened the distance which separated the rich from the poor; but it would seem that the nearer they draw to each other, the greater is their mutual hatred, and the more vehement the envy and the dread with which they resist each other's claims to power; the notion of Right is alike insensible to both classes, and Force affords to both the only argument for the present, and the only guarantee for the future. The poor man retains the prejudices of his forefathers without their faith, and their ignorance without their virtues; he has adopted the doctrine of self-interest as the rule of his actions, without understanding the science which controls it, and his egotism is no less blind than his devotedness was formerly. If society is tranquil, it is not because it relies upon its strength and its well-being, but because it knows its weakness and its infirmities; a single effort may cost it its life; everybody feels the evil, but no one has courage or energy enough to seek the cure; the desires, the regret, the sorrows, and the joys of the time produce nothing that is visible or permanent, like the passions of old men which terminate in impotence.

We have, then, abandoned whatever advantages the old state of things afforded, without receiving any compensation from our present condition; we have destroyed an aristocracy, and we seem inclined to survey its ruins with complacency, and to fix our abode in the midst of them.

The phenomena which the intellectual world presents are not less deplorable. The democracy of France, checked in its course or abandoned to its lawless passions, has overthrown whatever crossed its path, and has shaken all that it has not destroyed. Its empire on society has not been gradually introduced or peaceably established, but it has constantly advanced in the midst of disorder and the agitation of a conflict. In the heat of the struggle each partisan is hurried beyond the limits of his opinions by the opinions and the excesses of his opponents, until he loses sight of the end of his

威时候所带来的损失。

我认为我们已经破坏了那些可以独自对抗暴政的个体。但是，我也注意到政府继承了所有从家庭、组织和个人那里剥夺的所有特权。这样，少数几个公民掌握的权力，尽管时而具有压迫性但往往又是保守的，但却使全体公民成为弱者。财富的分化缩小了贫富差距，可是随着贫富差距的缩小，他们更加憎恨彼此，对彼此所拥有权力的嫉妒和恐惧也更加强烈。无论是富人还是穷人对权力都没有概念，双方都认为势力是目前唯一的话语权以及未来的不二保障。穷人保留了祖辈的偏见，却没有了祖辈的信仰；如祖辈一般无知却没有祖辈的德行；他们将利己主义视为行动的准则，却不懂得这一主义的科学，而且他们现在的利己主义如同他们与以往的牺牲精神一样都很盲目。社会之所以稳定，并非仰仗其自身的强大和繁荣，而是因为它了解自己的弱点和弊端，稍一折腾就可能赔上性命。每个人都能感到恶的存在，却没有人有足够的勇气和能力去寻找救世之方。在这个时代，无论是渴望、遗憾、悲伤还是喜悦都无法得出显著而永久的满意结果，就如同老年人的冲动一般虚弱无力。

于是，在我们放弃旧时制度所带来所有好处之后，并没有能够从现在体制中获得任何的补偿。我们已经把贵族制度摧毁，却又恋恋不舍地看着它的断壁残垣，似乎想要在那里找到自己的居所。

知识界所呈现出的状况似乎同样的悲惨。法国的民主在前进过程中尽管备受阻挠，却依旧肆意发展无法无天，横扫了前进路上的一切障碍，即便是无法将其摧毁也动摇了它的根基。其帝国根本不是采用循序渐进的和平方式建立起来，而是在混乱和冲突中不断前

exertions, and holds a language which disguises his real sentiments or secret instincts. Hence arises the strange confusion which we are witnessing. I cannot recall to my mind a passage in history more worthy of sorrow and of pity than the scenes which are happening under our eyes; it is as if the natural bond which unites the opinions of man to his tastes and his actions to his principles was now broken; the sympathy which has always been acknowledged between the feelings and the ideas of mankind appears to be dissolved, and all the laws of moral analogy to be abolished.

Zealous Christians may be found amongst us whose minds are nurtured in the love and knowledge of a future life, and who readily espouse the cause of human liberty as the source of all moral greatness. Christianity, which has declared that all men are equal in the sight of God, will not refuse to acknowledge that all citizens are equal in the eye of the law. But, by a singular concourse of events, religion is entangled in those institutions which democracy assails, and it is not unfrequently brought to reject the equality it loves, and to curse that cause of liberty as a foe which it might hallow by its alliance.

By the side of these religious men I discern others whose looks are turned to the earth more than to Heaven; they are the partisans of liberty, not only as the source of the noblest virtues, but more especially as the root of all solid advantages; and they sincerely desire to extend its sway, and to impart its blessings to mankind. It is natural that they should hasten to invoke the assistance of religion, for they must know that liberty cannot be established without morality, nor morality without faith; but they have seen religion in the ranks of their adversaries, and they inquire no further; some of them attack it openly, and the remainder are afraid to defend it.

In former ages slavery has been advocated by the venal and slavish-minded, whilst the independent and the warm-hearted were struggling without hope to save the liberties of mankind. But men of high and generous characters are now to be met with, whose opinions are at variance with their inclinations, and who praise that servility which they have themselves never known. Others, on the contrary, speak in the name of liberty, as if they were able to feel its sanctity and its majesty,

行。在热火朝天的斗争中，在其对手言论和暴行的逼迫下，每个人的言论都超越了自己的极限，忘记了自己行动的目的，发表着不符合自己真实情感和天性的言论。因此，我们眼前呈现出异乎寻常的混乱。我一再回忆，始终没有找到比如今呈现在眼前的景象更让人感到可悲和可怜的场景；似乎将人们的观点和其趣味及行动准则联系起来的天然纽带已经崩断，在任何时代都可以看到的人类情感和思想上的共鸣似乎正在消失，所有的道德规范都形同虚设。

在我们身边依然可以看到虔诚的基督徒，他们相信有来世，用宗教精神指导自己的生活，拥护人类的自由，将其视为所有高尚行为的基础。基督教宣称上帝面前人人平等，而且也不反对法律面前人人平等。但是，在异常事件同时并发的情况下，宗教与民主所要推翻的阵营为伍，不断压制它所钟爱的平等，咒骂自由是敌人，但是如果它与自由联手，会让自由变得神圣且不可侵犯。

在这些教徒的身边，我注意到一些人与其说仰望天堂，不如说面对尘世。他们是自由的虔诚信徒，不仅因为自由是一切最高贵品德的源泉，更重要的是因为自由是一切绝对福利的根本。他们真心得希望自由能够得到传播惠及所有人。自然而然的这些人在情急之下，便投向宗教寻求帮助，因为他们一定知道没有道德规范自由就无法确立，而没有宗教信仰道德规范亦无从谈起；而他们也看到当宗教投入到敌人的怀抱后，便裹足不前。于是，一些人开始公开攻击宗教，而另一些人也不敢再拥护它。

以前，唯利是图卑躬屈膝的小人为奴性大唱颂歌，而思想独立品德高尚之士则为毫无希望的人类自由不懈斗争。而现如今我们见到的一些出身高贵的大方雅士，他们所持的观

and loudly claim for humanity those rights which they have always disowned. There are virtuous and peaceful individuals whose pure morality, quiet habits, affluence, and talents fit them to be the leaders of the surrounding population; their love of their country is sincere, and they are prepared to make the greatest sacrifices to its welfare, but they confound the abuses of civilization with its benefits, and the idea of evil is inseparable in their minds from that of novelty.

Not far from this class is another party, whose object is to materialize mankind, to hit upon what is expedient without heeding what is just, to acquire knowledge without faith, and prosperity apart from virtue; assuming the title of the champions of modern civilization, and placing themselves in a station which they usurp with insolence, and from which they are driven by their own unworthiness. Where are we then? The religionists are the enemies of liberty, and the friends of liberty attack religion; the high-minded and the noble advocate subjection, and the meanest and most servile minds preach independence; honest and enlightened citizens are opposed to all progress, whilst men without patriotism and without principles are the apostles of civilization and of intelligence. Has such been the fate of the centuries which have preceded our own? and has man always inhabited a world like the present, where nothing is linked together, where virtue is without genius, and genius without honor; where the love of order is confounded with a taste for oppression, and the holy rites of freedom with a contempt of law; where the light thrown by conscience on human actions is dim, and where nothing seems to be any longer forbidden or allowed, honorable or shameful, false or true? I cannot, however, believe that the Creator made man to leave him in an endless struggle with the intellectual miseries which surround us: God destines a calmer and a more certain future to the communities of Europe; I am unacquainted with His designs, but I shall not cease to believe in them because I cannot fathom them, and I had rather mistrust my own capacity than His justice.

There is a country in the world where the great revolution which I am speaking of seems nearly to have reached its natural limits; it has been effected with ease and simplicity, say rather that this country has attained the consequences of the democratic revolution which we are undergoing without having experienced the revolution itself. The emigrants who fixed themselves on the shores of

点则和其身份大相径庭，开始褒奖起卑躬屈膝来了。与此相反，另一些人言必称自由，似乎他们亲身感受过自由的圣洁与庄严，并大声疾呼，为人类要求一些连他们自己也不知为何物的一些权利。有一些品德高尚爱好和平的人，他们正派、沉稳、富裕、博学，便顺理成章地被周围的人推举为领袖。他们对祖国的热爱出自真心，时刻准备为之做出最大的牺牲。但是，他们却分不清文明的弊端和好处，在他们的头脑中，恶总是和新纠缠在一起。

在这些人身边还有另一种人，他们的目的旨在把人唯物化，追求罔顾正义的利益，脱离信仰的知识，摒弃美德的幸福。他们自诩是现代文明的战士，高傲地占据着他们本不配拥有的位置。然而我们现在处于什么样的状态呢？宗教信徒与自由为敌；自由的伙伴对宗教大肆攻击；品格高贵的高尚之士鼓吹卑躬屈膝；最卑微的人大谈独立；诚实开明的公民却反对一切进步事物；然而既不爱国又毫无原则的人却担当起了文明和开化的使徒。难道我们之前的所有世纪也有着与我们这个世纪一样的命运吗？难道人们一直都生活在与现在一样的世界？在这里所有的一切都不正常，有德者无才，有才者无名，把热爱秩序和压迫混为一谈，把自由的神圣视为对法律的蔑视，投射在人们行为之上的良知之光灰暗惨淡；所有事物无论荣辱对错好像都无所谓。可是，造物主造人就是为了让人们在有如今天一般的知识贫困中做无尽的挣扎，这一点我无法相信。因为它已经为欧洲社会安排了一个更为平静更为安定的未来。对于上帝的意图我无法探知，但我不会因此而失去对它的信仰，我宁愿怀疑自己的智慧而不是上帝的公正。

世界上有这样一个国家在那里我所说的这场伟大革命似乎马上就要接近它的自然极

America in the beginning of the seventeenth century severed the democratic principle from all the principles which repressed it in the old communities of Europe, and transplanted it unalloyed to the New World. It has there been allowed to spread in perfect freedom, and to put forth its consequences in the laws by influencing the manners of the country.

It appears to me beyond a doubt that sooner or later we shall arrive, like the Americans, at an almost complete equality of conditions. But I do not conclude from this that we shall ever be necessarily led to draw the same political consequences which the Americans have derived from a similar social organization. I am far from supposing that they have chosen the only form of government which a democracy may adopt; but the identity of the efficient cause of laws and manners in the two countries is sufficient to account for the immense interest we have in becoming acquainted with its effects in each of them.

It is not, then, merely to satisfy a legitimate curiosity that I have examined America; my wish has been to find instruction by which we may ourselves profit. Whoever should imagine that I have intended to write a panegyric will perceive that such was not my design; nor has it been my object to advocate any form of government in particular, for I am of opinion that absolute excellence is rarely to be found in any legislation; I have not even affected to discuss whether the social revolution, which I believe to be irresistible, is advantageous or prejudicial to mankind; I have acknowledged this revolution as a fact already accomplished or on the eve of its accomplishment; and I have selected the nation, from amongst those which have undergone it, in which its development has been the most peaceful and the most complete, in order to discern its natural consequences, and, if it be possible, to distinguish the means by which it may be rendered profitable. I confess that in America I saw more than America; I sought the image of democracy itself, with its inclinations, its character, its prejudices, and its passions, in order to learn what we have to fear or to hope from its progress.

In the first part of this work I have attempted to show the tendency given to the laws by the democracy of America, which is abandoned almost without restraint to its instinctive propensities, and to exhibit the course it prescribes to the Government and the influence it exercises on affairs.

限。在那里这场革命轻而易举的简简单单的便得以实现，甚至可以说，这个国家没有经历过我们的民主革命就得到了这场革命的成果。十七世纪初，这些移民踏上了美国的土地定居下来，从他们在欧洲旧社会所反对的所有原则中将民主原则分离出来，独自将它移植到这个新世界。在这里，民主原则可以随意生长，并随着民情一起最终发展成为法律。

在我看来，毋庸置疑，我们迟早能够像美国人一样，实现身份的几乎完全平等。但是我却无法从中断定我们必然会从与美国相似的社会情况中取得同样的政治成果。我也绝不认为美国人采用的政府形式是民主可以采用的唯一样式。但是，两个国家法律和民情产生的原因既然相同，那么弄清这个原因在两个国家所产生的各自不同结果足以引起人们的兴趣。

然而，对美国进行考察，并不仅仅是要满足我的好奇心，我的初衷是要从美国找到我们可以借鉴的经验教训。谁要是认为我就是要写一篇颂词，那就大错而特错了，而且我的目的也不是要鼓吹任何一种形式的政府，因为我认为几乎没有任何法制能够体现绝对的优秀。我甚至没有想这样评论一场不可抗拒的革命对人类到底是有利还是有害。我承认这场革命已经完成或即将完成这一事实，而且想从已经经历过它的众多国家中找到一个国家，在那里，这场革命进行的最和平最完整，从而证明革命的自然选择的结果。而且如果可能的话，进一步探讨人类能够从中获益的方法。我承认，我在美国所看到的超过了美国本身。我探寻民主本身的形象，以及它的意向、特性、偏见以及热情，目的就是要了解在民主发展的过程中我们应该对什么表示担忧又对什么抱有希望。

因此，在本书的第一部分，我尝试说明完全按照自己意志发展几乎完全不受限制按

I have sought to discover the evils and the advantages which it produces. I have examined the precautions used by the Americans to direct it, as well as those which they have not adopted, and I have undertaken to point out the causes which enable it to govern society. I do not know whether I have succeeded in making known what I saw in America, but I am certain that such has been my sincere desire, and that I have never, knowingly, moulded facts to ideas, instead of ideas to facts.

Whenever a point could be established by the aid of written documents, I have had recourse to the original text, and to the most authentic and approved works. I have cited my authorities in the notes, and anyone may refer to them. Whenever an opinion, a political custom, or a remark on the manners of the country was concerned, I endeavored to consult the most enlightened men I met with. If the point in question was important or doubtful, I was not satisfied with one testimony, but I formed my opinion on the evidence of several witnesses. Here the reader must necessarily believe me upon my word. I could frequently have quoted names which are either known to him, or which deserve to be so, in proof of what I advance; but I have carefully abstained from this practice. A stranger frequently hears important truths at the fire-side of his host, which the latter would perhaps conceal from the ear of friendship; he consoles himself with his guest for the silence to which he is restricted, and the shortness of the traveller's stay takes away all fear of his indiscretion. I carefully noted every conversation of this nature as soon as it occurred, but these notes will never leave my writing-case; I had rather injure the success of my statements than add my name to the list of those strangers who repay the generous hospitality they have received by subsequent chagrin and annoyance.

I am aware that, notwithstanding my care, nothing will be easier than to criticise this book, if anyone ever chooses to criticise it. Those readers who may examine it closely will discover the fundamental idea which connects the several parts together. But the diversity of the subjects I have had to treat is exceedingly great, and it will not be difficult to oppose an isolated fact to the body of facts which I quote, or an isolated idea to the body of ideas I put forth. I hope to be read in the spirit which has guided my labors, and that my book may be judged by the general impression it leaves, as I have formed my own judgment not on any single reason, but upon the mass of evidence. It must

照本能行事的美国民主所指出的法制发展方向，对政府工作留下的印记，以及对国家事务产生的影响，同时也要探寻由此而来的利弊。对于美国人引导民主所采用的预防措施我已经进行了研究，甚至他们没有用到的也没有遗漏。而且我也考察了民主得以统治社会的原因。我不确定是否已经将自己在美国的所见所闻说清，但是可以肯定的是，这是我真心想要做到的事情，绝没有让事实迁就观点，而是观点以事实为依据。

但凡发现需要借助文字资料来确立观点的地方，我都会找来原文比对并参考最具权威最受认可的著作。材料的来源都有注释，任何人都可以核对。只要涉及舆论、政治习惯和风土民情的评述，我都会向最为见多识广的人进行请教。如果存在质疑的问题非常重要又存有疑窦，一个人的证言便无法令我满足，我会综合几个证人的意见得出结论。这一点请读者务必相信我。我本可以引用一些权威人士或是称得上权威人士的话来证实我的观点，而我却故意不这么做。因为一个外国人，往往会在接待他的主人家的壁炉旁听到一些内情，而这些通常甚至不会透露给他的亲朋好友，因为他要保持必要的沉默；而一个外国人只在这里做短暂停留，这便将他对自己轻率之举的担忧一扫而空。每每听到这样的见闻，我就小心翼翼地记录下来，但是这样的记录却只会待在文件箱里。因为我宁可让自己的著作少些光彩，也不愿将自己的名字列入受到主人热情款待后却让主人在客人回国后感到后悔和讨厌的黑名单。

我意识到尽管我已经尽心尽力，但是如果有人想要对这本书指手画脚简直易如反掌。认真阅读本书的读者将会发现一个贯穿各个部分的中心思想。但是我所要探讨的对象差异巨大，所以无论是用一个孤立的事实反驳我所引用的成组事实，抑或是用一个孤立的观点

not be forgotten that the author who wishes to be understood is obliged to push all his ideas to their utmost theoretical consequences, and often to the verge of what is false or impracticable; for if it be necessary sometimes to quit the rules of logic in active life, such is not the case in discourse, and a man finds that almost as many difficulties spring from inconsistency of language as usually arise from inconsistency of conduct.

I conclude by pointing out myself what many readers will consider the principal defect of the work. This book is written to favor no particular views, and in composing it I have entertained no designs of serving or attacking any party; I have undertaken not to see differently, but to look further than parties, and whilst they are busied for the morrow I have turned my thoughts to the Future.

反驳我所提出的成组观点，都会是轻而易举之事。因此我希望读者能采用指导我完成本书的相同精神来阅读，也希望能够依据本书留给大家的总印象加以品评，因为本人是根据大量的证据来立论的而不是孤证。务必不要忘记，作者希望读者能够理解他必须要对每个观点进行的理论上的总结，尽管这样的总结往往会出现错误又不切实际。因为在行动中人们有时会偏离逻辑，但是在论述时则不行。而且人们发现言语上的前后矛盾和行动上的前后矛盾几乎一样困难。

最后，我要自己指出一个许多读者认为本书所有的一个重要缺陷：这本书并不是要迎合某些人的观点。在写作本书时并不是要服务或攻击任何特定的政党，也不是要标新立异；而只是想比各政党看得更远一点；当各政党还在为明天忙忙碌碌的时候，我已经开始遥想未来。

Chapter I: Exterior Form Of North America

Chapter Summary

North America divided into two vast regions, one inclining towards the Pole, the other towards the Equator—Valley of the Mississippi—Traces of the Revolutions of the Globe—Shore of the Atlantic Ocean where the English Colonies were founded—Difference in the appearance of North and of South America at the time of their Discovery—Forests of North America—Prairies—Wandering Tribes of Natives—Their outward appearance, manners, and language—Traces of an unknown people.

Exterior Form Of North America

North America presents in its external form certain general features which it is easy to discriminate at the first glance. A sort of methodical order seems to have regulated the separation of land and water, mountains and valleys. A simple, but grand, arrangement is discoverable amidst the confusion of objects and the prodigious variety of scenes. This continent is divided, almost equally, into two vast regions, one of which is bounded on the north by the Arctic Pole, and by the two great oceans on the east and west. It stretches towards the south, forming a triangle whose irregular sides meet at length below the great lakes of Canada. The second region begins where the other terminates, and includes all the remainder of the continent. The one slopes gently towards the Pole, the other towards the Equator.

The territory comprehended in the first region descends towards the north with so imperceptible

第一章　北美的外貌

本章提要

北美分为两大地区，一个延伸向北极，一个延伸向赤道——密西西比河大河谷——地球变迁的痕迹——建立起英国殖民地的大西洋沿岸——北美和南美在被发现之时呈现的不同外貌——北美森林——大草原——四处漂泊的土著部落——这些部落的外貌、习俗和语言——一个早已消失的民族遗迹。

北美的外貌

北美的外形呈现出的总的特点只要一眼便可以轻松分辨出来。土地、河流、山川和峡谷都分布得井井有条。这样简单大气的布置既有景物的杂陈又有景色的多变。这片大陆几乎被整齐的一分为二。一个地区北接北极，东西毗邻两大洋，并向南延伸，形成一个三角形，这个三角形长短不等的两边最终在加拿大五大湖地区下方与底边交汇。另外的一个地区自第一个地区的终点起，疆域囊括北美大陆其余所有的土地。一个地区微微斜向北极，另一个则朝向赤道。

a slope that it may almost be said to form a level plain. Within the bounds of this immense tract of country there are neither high mountains nor deep valleys. Streams meander through it irregularly: great rivers mix their currents, separate and meet again, disperse and form vast marshes, losing all trace of their channels in the labyrinth of waters they have themselves created; and thus, at length, after innumerable windings, fall into the Polar Seas. The great lakes which bound this first region are not walled in, like most of those in the Old World, between hills and rocks. Their banks are flat, and rise but a few feet above the level of their waters; each of them thus forming a vast bowl filled to the brim. The slightest change in the structure of the globe would cause their waters to rush either towards the Pole or to the tropical sea.

The second region is more varied on its surface, and better suited for the habitation of man. Two long chains of mountains divide it from one extreme to the other; the Alleghany ridge takes the form of the shores of the Atlantic Ocean; the other is parallel with the Pacific. The space which lies between these two chains of mountains contains 1,341,649 square miles. Its surface is therefore about six times as great as that of France. This vast territory, however, forms a single valley, one side of which descends gradually from the rounded summits of the Alleghanies, while the other rises in an uninterrupted course towards the tops of the Rocky Mountains. At the bottom of the valley flows an immense river, into which the various streams issuing from the mountains fall from all parts. In memory of their native land, the French formerly called this river the St. Louis. The Indians, in their pompous language, have named it the Father of Waters, or the Mississippi.

The Mississippi takes its source above the limit of the two great regions of which I have spoken, not far from the highest point of the table-land where they unite. Near the same spot rises another river, which empties itself into the Polar seas. The course of the Mississippi is at first dubious: it winds several times towards the north, from whence it rose; and at length, after having been delayed in lakes and marshes, it flows slowly onwards to the south. Sometimes quietly gliding along the argillaceous bed which nature has assigned to it, sometimes swollen by storms, the Mississippi waters 2,500 miles in its course. At the distance of 1,364 miles from its mouth this river attains an

第一个地区整体地势向北缓缓下降，其斜度几乎无法察觉，几乎可以说就是一片平原。在这片广袤的土地上既没有高山也没有深谷。河流弯弯曲曲肆意流淌，一些大河不断地交汇分开，然后再交汇再分开，分流并形成沼泽，在它们自己制造的水乡迷宫中消失了踪影，就这样百转千回，最终汇入北极海域。在第一个地区边界附近的各大湖与旧大陆的大多数湖泊不同，周围没有群山的环绕，怪石嶙峋。这里的湖泊周边地势平坦，只比湖面高出几米而已，因此每个湖就像一个盛满水的大碗。所以地球构造任何一点轻微的变化都会使得湖水不是流向北极就是汇入热带海洋。

第二个地区的地貌变化更为多样，也更适宜人类居住。两条长长的山脉各自盘踞一方：阿勒格尼山脉沿大西洋沿岸延伸，另外的一条（落基山脉）则与太平洋并行。两条大山脉之间的广袤地域总计约有1,341,649平方英里，其面积大约相当于六个法国。然而在这片广大的区域形成一个大河谷，大河的一头自阿勒格尼山脉圆形的峰顶蜿蜒而下，而后逐渐上升，一直爬上落基山脉各个山峰。在这个大河谷的谷底一条大河奔腾而过其间，自群山而下条条河流从四面八方汇入其中。以前法国人为了纪念他们的祖国，曾把这条大河称为圣路易斯河。当地的印第安人则夸张地把它称作"诸河之父"或是密西西比河。

密西西比河发源于刚刚我所提到的两大地区的交汇之处，与将这两大地区分隔开的高原地区最高点相距不远。在这附近还有另外一条河流流淌，最终汇入北极海域。起初密西西比河河道走向并不稳定，曾几度蜿蜒向北，最终在从湖区和沼泽地带缓缓流出之后，终于缓缓向南流去。密西西比河有时沿着大自然造化出的黏土质河道静静流淌，有时因暴雨

average depth of fifteen feet; and it is navigated by vessels of 300 tons burden for a course of nearly 500 miles. Fifty-seven large navigable rivers contribute to swell the waters of the Mississippi; amongst others, the Missouri, which traverses a space of 2,500 miles; the Arkansas of 1,300 miles, the Red River 1,000 miles, four whose course is from 800 to 1,000 miles in length, viz., the Illinois, the St. Peter's, the St. Francis, and the Moingona; besides a countless multitude of rivulets which unite from all parts their tributary streams.

The valley which is watered by the Mississippi seems formed to be the bed of this mighty river, which, like a god of antiquity, dispenses both good and evil in its course. On the shores of the stream nature displays an inexhaustible fertility; in proportion as you recede from its banks, the powers of vegetation languish, the soil becomes poor, and the plants that survive have a sickly growth. Nowhere have the great convulsions of the globe left more evident traces than in the valley of the Mississippi; the whole aspect of the country shows the powerful effects of water, both by its fertility and by its barrenness. The waters of the primeval ocean accumulated enormous beds of vegetable mould in the valley, which they levelled as they retired. Upon the right shore of the river are seen immense plains, as smooth as if the husbandman had passed over them with his roller. As you approach the mountains the soil becomes more and more unequal and sterile; the ground is, as it were, pierced in a thousand places by primitive rocks, which appear like the bones of a skeleton whose flesh is partly consumed. The surface of the earth is covered with a granite sand and huge irregular masses of stone, among which a few plants force their growth, and give the appearance of a green field covered with the ruins of a vast edifice. These stones and this sand discover, on examination, a perfect analogy with those which compose the arid and broken summits of the Rocky Mountains. The flood of waters which washed the soil to the bottom of the valley afterwards carried away portions of the rocks themselves; and these, dashed and bruised against the neighboring cliffs, were left scattered like wrecks at their feet. The valley of the Mississippi is, upon the whole, the most magnificent dwelling-place prepared by God for man's abode; and yet it may be said that at present it is but a mighty desert.

On the eastern side of the Alleghanies, between the base of these mountains and the Atlantic

而泛滥，绵延约2500英里。从密西西比河河口绵延1364英里，这一段河流平均水深达15英尺，载重300吨的船舶可以通行的航道长约500英里。57条可以通航的大河向其供水，其中密苏里河横贯2500英里地域，阿肯色河1300英里，红河1000英里，以及伊利诺伊河、圣皮尔河、圣弗兰西斯河、得梅因河，这四条长度均在800到1000英里，除此之外还有不计其数的小河从四面八方汇入其中。

密西西比河流经的山谷，似乎是为其量身打造，它既会为善也会作恶，犹如上帝的遗珠。在河岸的附近，大自然幻化出一片永不枯竭的沃土。距离河岸越远，植被就变得越稀疏，土地就变得越贫瘠，植物生长得也就越羸弱。地壳的巨变在密西西比河河谷留下了最为清晰可见的痕迹。整个密西西比河流域都是水强大力量的最好证明，无论是丰收还是歉收之年。在谷底，古代海洋厚厚的积淀为植物生长提供了温床，而且在水退去之时把它冲得平平坦坦。在密西西比河的右岸是一望无际的平原，平坦得就好像农夫用磙子轧过一样。而越是靠近大山，土地就变得越发的不平坦和贫瘠，可以说，嶙峋的古老岩石随处可见，就如同一具具骷髅立在那里，其皮肉早已被侵蚀不见踪影。地表覆盖着一层花岗岩风化而成的沙子，一些形状怪异的岩石立于其间，一些植物费尽气力才从其中冒出芽来，看上去就是一片布满巨大建筑断壁残垣的沃野。仔细地观察这些岩石和沙砾，不难发现它们的成分和落基山光秃秃峰顶上的沙石一般无二。将沙土冲到谷底的洪水也连同山上的一些岩石一起冲下来，这些岩石你推我挤互相碰撞，最终在山脚下停了下来。总的来说，密西西比河河谷是上帝为人类打造的最好居处，但是目前它还是一大片蛮荒之地。

Ocean, there lies a long ridge of rocks and sand, which the sea appears to have left behind as it retired. The mean breadth of this territory does not exceed one hundred miles; but it is about nine hundred miles in length. This part of the American continent has a soil which offers every obstacle to the husbandman, and its vegetation is scanty and unvaried.

Upon this inhospitable coast the first united efforts of human industry were made. The tongue of arid land was the cradle of those English colonies which were destined one day to become the United States of America. The centre of power still remains here; whilst in the backwoods the true elements of the great people to whom the future control of the continent belongs are gathering almost in secrecy together.

When the Europeans first landed on the shores of the West Indies, and afterwards on the coast of South America, they thought themselves transported into those fabulous regions of which poets had sung. The sea sparkled with phosphoric light, and the extraordinary transparency of its waters discovered to the view of the navigator all that had hitherto been hidden in the deep abyss. Here and there appeared little islands perfumed with odoriferous plants, and resembling baskets of flowers floating on the tranquil surface of the ocean. Every object which met the sight, in this enchanting region, seemed prepared to satisfy the wants or contribute to the pleasures of man. Almost all the trees were loaded with nourishing fruits, and those which were useless as food delighted the eye by the brilliancy and variety of their colors. In groves of fragrant lemon-trees, wild figs, flowering myrtles, acacias, and oleanders, which were hung with festoons of various climbing plants, covered with flowers, a multitude of birds unknown in Europe displayed their bright plumage, glittering with purple and azure, and mingled their warbling with the harmony of a world teeming with life and motion. Underneath this brilliant exterior death was concealed. But the air of these climates had so enervating an influence that man, absorbed by present enjoyment, was rendered regardless of the future.

North America appeared under a very different aspect; there everything was grave, serious, and solemn: it seemed created to be the domain of intelligence, as the South was that of sensual delight.

在阿勒格尼山的东面，一条由岩石和沙子构成的山脊卧在这条山脉的群山和大西洋之间，看上去似乎是海水消退后遗留的杰作。这个狭长地带的平均宽度不超过100英里，但是长度足有900英里。美洲大陆这一地区的土地给农夫们带来无尽的烦恼，这里不仅植被稀疏品种也单一。

正是在这样一片荒无人烟的海岸，一群强人率先聚集到这里。正是这样不毛的沙嘴地带恰恰成为孕育出美利坚合众国的英国殖民地的摇篮。今天，实力的中心依旧在这里。同时，在它的西面，即将掌握这个大陆的伟大人民的真正的能量正在悄悄聚集。

当欧洲人首先在西印度群岛，而后不久又在南美海岸登陆的时候，他们认为自己来到了诗歌里曾颂扬的圣地。海水泛着粼光，清澈透明，航海者一眼便可看到海底。一些小岛星罗棋布，上面的植物散发着芬芳的香气，如同在静谧的海面上漂浮的花篮一般。在这迷人的地方，所能看到的一切好像就是为满足人们需要而准备，为人们享受而安排。几乎所有的树木硕果累累，这些果实并不适宜食用，但其色彩缤纷令人赏心悦目。生长着芬芳的柠檬树，野生无花果树，圆叶桃金娘树，带刺的金合欢树和夹竹桃树的果林里，长满花朵的条条藤蔓将树木连接起来，在欧洲从未见过的群群鸟儿炫耀着它们紫色和碧蓝色的华丽羽衣，它们悦耳的鸣叫充满活力，和生命的大自然浑然一体。在这辉煌外表下隐藏的是死亡，对此人们丝毫没有察觉，完全沉浸在那时的喜悦之中，这样的环境让人们只顾现在不管未来。

北美则呈现出另外一番景象，在那里一切都威严而庄重，似乎就是为让智力有用武

A turbulent and foggy ocean washed its shores. It was girt round by a belt of granite rocks, or by wide tracts of sand. The foliage of its woods was dark and gloomy, for they were composed of firs, larches, evergreen oaks, wild olive-trees, and laurels. Beyond this outer belt lay the thick shades of the central forest, where the largest trees which are produced in the two hemispheres grow side by side. The plane, the catalpa, the sugar-maple, and the Virginian poplar mingled their branches with those of the oak, the beech, and the lime. In these, as in the forests of the Old World, destruction was perpetually going on. The ruins of vegetation were heaped upon each other; but there was no laboring hand to remove them, and their decay was not rapid enough to make room for the continual work of reproduction. Climbing plants, grasses, and other herbs forced their way through the mass of dying trees; they crept along their bending trunks, found nourishment in their dusty cavities, and a passage beneath the lifeless bark. Thus decay gave its assistance to life, and their respective productions were mingled together. The depths of these forests were gloomy and obscure, and a thousand rivulets, undirected in their course by human industry, preserved in them a constant moisture. It was rare to meet with flowers, wild fruits, or birds beneath their shades. The fall of a tree overthrown by age, the rushing torrent of a cataract, the lowing of the buffalo, and the howling of the wind were the only sounds which broke the silence of nature.

To the east of the great river, the woods almost disappeared; in their stead were seen prairies of immense extent. Whether Nature in her infinite variety had denied the germs of trees to these fertile plains, or whether they had once been covered with forests, subsequently destroyed by the hand of man, is a question which neither tradition nor scientific research has been able to resolve.

These immense deserts were not, however, devoid of human inhabitants. Some wandering tribes had been for ages scattered among the forest shades or the green pastures of the prairie. From the mouth of the St. Lawrence to the delta of the Mississippi, and from the Atlantic to the Pacific Ocean, these savages possessed certain points of resemblance which bore witness of their common origin; but at the same time they differed from all other known races of men: they were neither white like the Europeans, nor yellow like most of the Asiatics, nor black like the negroes. Their skin was

之地而造，而南美则是为愉悦感官而设。狂暴多雾的海水冲刷着海岸。花岗岩的石块和沙粒犹如为海岸系上了一条腰带。海岸的树林幽暗阴郁，因为这里生长着红松、落叶松、常绿树，野橄榄树和桂树。这条腰带的外面是茂密的中央森林，在这里，东西半球的巨大乔木并肩生长。法国梧桐、梓树、糖枫、弗吉尼亚白杨和栎树、山毛榉、椴树枝叶交错。在这里，如同"旧世界"的森林一样，砍伐从未停止。砍伐后的断枝残叶无人收拾，层层叠叠，而它们的腐烂也不够迅速无法为新树木的生长腾出地方。藤蔓、杂草和其他的草木在这些断枝残叶间杀出路来，爬上枯木，在朽木上汲取营养，顶穿盖在它们上面的干枯树皮。因此，死亡带来了生命，它们彼此交换着自己的成果。这些森林的深处昏暗阴郁，未经人们疏导的条条溪流让森林常保湿润。花朵、野果和鸟儿在这里难觅踪影。老朽树木倒地的声音，潺潺水流的声音，野牛的叫声，风的呼啸声是打破大自然沉寂的声响。

在这条大河以东，树林几乎已经消失，取而代之的是无边无际的大草原。到底是自然在其无尽的幻化中不肯在这富饶的平原洒下树种，还是曾经的郁郁葱葱的森林遭到了人为的毁坏，这是个问题，而且无论是传说还是科学都无法解答。

但是这无垠的荒地并非渺无人烟。许多世纪以来，许多游牧部落曾出没在森林的树阴下和绿色的大草原。从圣劳伦斯河河口到密西西比河三角洲，从大西洋到太平洋，分布的这些野人有着相似之处，足以证明他们有着共同的祖先。但同时他们又不同于所有已知人种。他们既不像欧洲人一样白，又不像大多数亚洲人一样黄，也不像黑人那样黑。他们有着棕红色的皮肤，光亮的长发，薄薄的嘴唇和高高的颧骨。北美各部落的语言就用词而言

reddish brown, their hair long and shining, their lips thin, and their cheekbones very prominent. The languages spoken by the North American tribes are various as far as regarded their words, but they were subject to the same grammatical rules. These rules differed in several points from such as had been observed to govern the origin of language. The idiom of the Americans seemed to be the product of new combinations, and bespoke an effort of the understanding of which the Indians of our days would be incapable.

The social state of these tribes differed also in many respects from all that was seen in the Old World. They seemed to have multiplied freely in the midst of their deserts without coming in contact with other races more civilized than their own. Accordingly, they exhibited none of those indistinct, incoherent notions of right and wrong, none of that deep corruption of manners, which is usually joined with ignorance and rudeness among nations which, after advancing to civilization, have relapsed into a state of barbarism. The Indian was indebted to no one but himself; his virtues, his vices, and his prejudices were his own work; he had grown up in the wild independence of his nature.

If, in polished countries, the lowest of the people are rude and uncivil, it is not merely because they are poor and ignorant, but that, being so, they are in daily contact with rich and enlightened men. The sight of their own hard lot and of their weakness, which is daily contrasted with the happiness and power of some of their fellow-creatures, excites in their hearts at the same time the sentiments of anger and of fear: the consciousness of their inferiority and of their dependence irritates while it humiliates them. This state of mind displays itself in their manners and language; they are at once insolent and servile. The truth of this is easily proved by observation; the people are more rude in aristocratic countries than elsewhere, in opulent cities than in rural districts. In those places where the rich and powerful are assembled together the weak and the indigent feel themselves oppressed by their inferior condition. Unable to perceive a single chance of regaining their equality, they give up to despair, and allow themselves to fall below the dignity of human nature.

This unfortunate effect of the disparity of conditions is not observable in savage life: the Indians, although they are ignorant and poor, are equal and free. At the period when Europeans first came

各不相同，但是他们的语法规则相同。这些语法规则在某些方面和已知规范人们语言的语法规则有所不同。美国土著人的土语似乎是新的组合的产物，表明有新成分的人融入，其智力是现代美国印第安人所无法达到的。

这些部落的社会状况在诸多方面与我们在旧世界的所见并不相同。他们似乎在自己的蛮荒之地自由繁衍，从未与比他们更为文明的世界有过接触。因此，他们对是非善恶的看法清晰而一致，不会像有些民族那样在曾经的文明过后再次变回野蛮的状态，并因为无知和粗野而腐化堕落。

美国的印第安人从未受惠于他人，他们自生自长，他们的美德、恶行和偏见都是自身的产物，他们在大自然独立的成长。

在文明的国度，如果社会最底层的人们粗野无理，这并不仅仅因为他们贫穷和无知，而是因为他们终日与富人和文明人接触。他们苦难的命运和劣势，每天都在不断和某些同胞幸福而权势的生活形成对照，同时在他们的内心激起了愤怒和恐慌，而他们的自卑感和依附感也让他们发愤图强的同时感到羞愧难当。这样的内心状态便反映到言谈举止上，他们一下子变得傲慢又卑微。只要稍作观察，这样的事实显而易见，在实行贵族制度的国家人们比别的地方的人更为粗野，在富裕城市里的人又比农村人粗野。在那些富人和权贵人士聚居的地方，软弱而贫穷的人因为他们地位低下而倍感压迫。因为找不到机会让自己获得平等，他们堕入绝望，践踏自己作为人的尊严。

这种不平等所带来的恶果在蛮夷社会则不会出现。尽管印第安人无知而贫穷，但是他

among them the natives of North America were ignorant of the value of riches, and indifferent to the enjoyments which civilized man procures to himself by their means. Nevertheless there was nothing coarse in their demeanor; they practised an habitual reserve and a kind of aristocratic politeness. Mild and hospitable when at peace, though merciless in war beyond any known degree of human ferocity, the Indian would expose himself to die of hunger in order to succor the stranger who asked admittance by night at the door of his hut; yet he could tear in pieces with his hands the still quivering limbs of his prisoner. The famous republics of antiquity never gave examples of more unshaken courage, more haughty spirits, or more intractable love of independence than were hidden in former times among the wild forests of the New World. The Europeans produced no great impression when they landed upon the shores of North America; their presence engendered neither envy nor fear. What influence could they possess over such men as we have described? The Indian could live without wants, suffer without complaint, and pour out his death-song at the stake. Like all the other members of the great human family, these savages believed in the existence of a better world, and adored under different names, God, the creator of the universe. Their notions on the great intellectual truths were in general simple and philosophical.

Although we have here traced the character of a primitive people, yet it cannot be doubted that another people, more civilized and more advanced in all respects, had preceded it in the same regions.

An obscure tradition which prevailed among the Indians to the north of the Atlantic informs us that these very tribes formerly dwelt on the west side of the Mississippi. Along the banks of the Ohio, and throughout the central valley, there are frequently found, at this day, tumuli raised by the hands of men. On exploring these heaps of earth to their centre, it is usual to meet with human bones, strange instruments, arms and utensils of all kinds, made of metal, or destined for purposes unknown to the present race. The Indians of our time are unable to give any information relative to the history of this unknown people. Neither did those who lived three hundred years ago, when America was first discovered, leave any accounts from which even an hypothesis could be formed. Tradition—that

们平等而自由。当欧洲人最初来到北美的时候，他们对于财富的价值一无所知，对于文明人通过财富所获得的享乐毫不在意。然而，他们的举止并不粗鲁，相反，他们矜持谦让，表现出贵族风范。印第安人平时温和好客，但是战争中所表现的残忍又超越人们对凶残已有的认知度。他们甘愿冒着饿死的风险，去搭救深夜来到门前求助的陌生人；但也会只手把浑身颤抖的战俘撕个粉碎。古代一些最著名的共和国都没能像生活在新世界蛮荒之地的人们那样，对独立显示出更为坚定的勇气，更为高傲的精神或是更为倔强的热爱。欧洲人最初登陆北美的时候，当地人并未大惊小怪，欧洲人的到来既没有引起他们的嫉妒也没有引起他们的恐慌。他们会与自己的同类人打架争吵吗？印第安人可以活得无欲无求，受苦而无怨言，载歌而死。像伟大的人类大家庭中其他的成员一样，这些野蛮人相信有美好世界的存在，用不同的名字称呼宇宙的造物主——上帝，并对他顶礼膜拜。他们对于伟大知识真理的看法总的来说简单且富有哲理。

尽管在这里我们赘述的是未开化民族的性格特点，但是毋庸置疑，另外的民族也就是一个在各方面更为文明先进的民族，曾在他们之前在这片土地上繁荣昌盛。

一个含糊却广泛流传于大西洋沿岸印第安部落的传说告诉我们，这个民族的一些部落曾经生活在密西西比河西岸。沿着俄亥俄河两岸，穿过中央峡谷，今天依然可以常常看得到一些人造土丘。挖开这些土丘，往往会发现人骨、奇怪的器皿、武器、各类金属器物或是一些如今人们已无法说清用途的一些东西。现在的印第安人无法提供任何有关这个早已消失民族的信息。300年前当美洲大陆首次被发现时便生活在那里的人们，也没有留下

perishable, yet ever renewed monument of the pristine world—throws no light upon the subject. It is an undoubted fact, however, that in this part of the globe thousands of our fellow-beings had lived. When they came hither, what was their origin, their destiny, their history, and how they perished, no one can tell. How strange does it appear that nations have existed, and afterwards so completely disappeared from the earth that the remembrance of their very names is effaced; their languages are lost; their glory is vanished like a sound without an echo; though perhaps there is not one which has not left behind it some tomb in memory of its passage! The most durable monument of human labor is that which recalls the wretchedness and nothingness of man.

Although the vast country which we have been describing was inhabited by many indigenous tribes, it may justly be said at the time of its discovery by Europeans to have formed one great desert. The Indians occupied without possessing it. It is by agricultural labor that man appropriates the soil, and the early inhabitants of North America lived by the produce of the chase. Their implacable prejudices, their uncontrolled passions, their vices, and still more perhaps their savage virtues, consigned them to inevitable destruction. The ruin of these nations began from the day when Europeans landed on their shores; it has proceeded ever since, and we are now witnessing the completion of it. They seem to have been placed by Providence amidst the riches of the New World to enjoy them for a season, and then surrender them. Those coasts, so admirably adapted for commerce and industry; those wide and deep rivers; that inexhaustible valley of the Mississippi; the whole continent, in short, seemed prepared to be the abode of a great nation, yet unborn.

In that land the great experiment was to be made, by civilized man, of the attempt to construct society upon a new basis; and it was there, for the first time, that theories hitherto unknown, or deemed impracticable, were to exhibit a spectacle for which the world had not been prepared by the history of the past.

任何可以用来提出假说的只言片语。那些容易遭到破坏又不断发现的遗迹也没能提供任何线索。但是有一个事实千真万确，我们千千万万的同类曾经在这里生活过。他们什么时候来到这里？他们的起源、命运、历史以及他们的消亡，没有人能够说得清。一个好端端的民族，竟然在世界上消失得无影无踪，真是怪哉！他们民族的名字已经从人们的记忆中抹去，语言也已失传，他们的荣耀如没有回响的声音一般消失。尽管如此，他们身后留下的坟墓还可以用来纪念他们过去的存在，是人类劳作最经久的纪念，也是人类可悲和虚无的纪念。

尽管我们谈论的这片广袤的土地居住着许多土著部落，但是完全有理由说在欧洲人发现它的时候这里还只不过是一片蛮荒。印第安人在这里居住，但是并没拥有这里。人靠农耕占有土地，而北美的先民靠游猎为生。他们根深蒂固的偏见，他们不可遏止的热情，他们的恶习，也许还有他们野蛮人的品德，注定会让他们走上毁灭之路。从欧洲人登上这片大陆的第一天起，这些民族便开始灭亡，并一直继续，而现在我们正见证着它的大功告成。上帝把他们安置在富饶的新世界，似乎只提供给他们暂时享用。适合贸易和工业发展的海岸，深水河流，永不枯竭的密西西比河大河谷，简而言之，整个大陆就如同等待着一个伟大民族诞生的空摇篮。

在这片土地上，文明人试图在新的基础上构建新社会，并第一次应用那时尚不为人知或是注定无法实践的理论，让世界呈现过往历史里从未出现过的恢宏。

Chapter II: Origin Of The Anglo-Americans

Chapter Summary

Utility of knowing the origin of nations in order to understand their social condition and their laws—America the only country in which the starting-point of a great people has been clearly observable—In what respects all who emigrated to British America were similar—In what they differed—Remark applicable to all Europeans who established themselves on the shores of the New World—Colonization of Virginia—Colonization of New England—Original character of the first inhabitants of New England—Their arrival—Their first laws—Their social contract—Penal code borrowed from the Hebrew legislation—Religious fervor—Republican spirit—Intimate union of the spirit of religion with the spirit of liberty.

Origin Of The Anglo-Americans, And Its Importance In Relation To Their Future Condition.

After the birth of a human being his early years are obscurely spent in the toils or pleasures of childhood. As he grows up the world receives him, when his manhood begins, and he enters into contact with his fellows. He is then studied for the first time, and it is imagined that the germ of the vices and the virtues of his maturer years is then formed. This, if I am not mistaken, is a great error. We must begin higher up; we must watch the infant in its mother's arms; we must see the first images which the external world casts upon the dark mirror of his mind; the first occurrences which he witnesses; we must hear the first words which awaken the sleeping powers of thought, and stand by his earliest efforts, if we would understand the prejudices, the habits, and the passions which will

第二章　英裔美国人的起源

本章提要

了解民族的起源，有利于理解其社会状况及法律——美洲是唯一一个可以清楚追溯一个民族起源的地区——移民到英属美洲地区人们的相似之处——他们的不同之处——评述当初在新大陆海岸定居的欧洲人——向弗吉尼亚殖民——向新英格兰殖民——他们到达新英格兰——他们的首部法律——社会契约——借用摩西立法的刑法典——宗教狂热——共和精神——宗教精神和自由精神的紧密结合

英裔美国人的起源，以及对他们未来的重大影响

一个人出生后，他的童年在嬉戏和玩耍中默默无闻地度过，接着他逐渐地长大，到了成年，世界开始接纳他，便开始了和成年人交往。从那时开始，他第一次被人观察研究，被人仔细观察成人以后才出现的恶性和品德。如果我没弄错的话，这种观点实际上是一个极大的错误。我们应当追溯他更早的过去，应当从他婴儿时期还在妈妈的臂弯里开始考察，从观察外在世界投射在他懵懂小脑袋里的第一个影像开始，应当观察他最初所见的事

rule his life. The entire man is, so to speak, to be seen in the cradle of the child.

The growth of nations presents something analogous to this: they all bear some marks of their origin; and the circumstances which accompanied their birth and contributed to their rise affect the whole term of their being. If we were able to go back to the elements of states, and to examine the oldest monuments of their history, I doubt not that we should discover the primal cause of the prejudices, the habits, the ruling passions, and, in short, of all that constitutes what is called the national character; we should then find the explanation of certain customs which now seem at variance with the prevailing manners; of such laws as conflict with established principles; and of such incoherent opinions as are here and there to be met with in society, like those fragments of broken chains which we sometimes see hanging from the vault of an edifice, and supporting nothing. This might explain the destinies of certain nations, which seem borne on by an unknown force to ends of which they themselves are ignorant. But hitherto facts have been wanting to researches of this kind: the spirit of inquiry has only come upon communities in their latter days; and when they at length contemplated their origin, time had already obscured it, or ignorance and pride adorned it with truth-concealing fables.

America is the only country in which it has been possible to witness the natural and tranquil growth of society, and where the influences exercised on the future condition of states by their origin is clearly distinguishable. At the period when the peoples of Europe landed in the New World their national characteristics were already completely formed; each of them had a physiognomy of its own; and as they had already attained that stage of civilization at which men are led to study themselves, they have transmitted to us a faithful picture of their opinions, their manners, and their laws. The men of the sixteenth century are almost as well known to us as our contemporaries. America, consequently, exhibits in the broad light of day the phenomena which the ignorance or rudeness of earlier ages conceals from our researches. Near enough to the time when the states of America were founded, to be accurately acquainted with their elements, and sufficiently removed from that period to judge of some of their results, the men of our own day seem destined to see further than their predecessors into the series of human events. Providence has given us a torch which our forefathers

物，听一听最初唤醒他沉睡思维能力的话语，还应该看一看显示他顽强性的最初努力。只有这样，我们才能理解支配他一生的偏见、习惯和热情。所以说，一个人是从褓襁开始的。

一个民族的成长也是大同小异。每个民族身上始终留着他们起源的烙印，而且伴随他们出生成长的环境，也影响着他们往后的一切。如果我们能够追溯到社会成员的来历，考察他们最古老的历史遗迹，我一点都不怀疑我们一定能够发现这些偏见、习俗、主要情感以及构成所谓民族特征的所有原因。接着我们还能找到似乎和当今流行风尚不协调的特定习俗的解说，找到与现有原则对立的法律的解说，以及社会上处处可见的前后不一观点的解说，这些观点就好像挂在大厦穹顶上什么都禁不住的一段段破链子。这也许能够用来解释某些民族的命运，他们被莫名的力推向自己也一无所知的结局。但是，时至今日仍然缺乏对于事物的这种研究。直到这个民族暮暮老去的时候这样的探究精神才显现出来，而当他们最终开始回顾其由来，时间已经将它磨得模糊不清，或是已用一些无知傲慢的传说将真相掩盖起来。

美国是唯一一个有可能看到其社会自然而宁静成长的国家，而且在这里还可以明白地看到各州起源不同对于其未来的影响。当欧洲各国人民在新大陆登陆的时候，他们的民族个性已经完全形成，拥有各自面貌，而且他们已经达到能够自我研究的文明程度，于是便为我们留下了他们观点、风俗和法律的忠实画卷。我们对于16世纪人的了解，几乎和我们对今天人们的了解一样多。因此，美国让早先无知和野蛮所隐匿的真相大白于天下。美国建成距今不久，能够准确知晓其各项因素，但是对于其结果的判定还为时尚早。对于人世

did not possess, and has allowed us to discern fundamental causes in the history of the world which the obscurity of the past concealed from them. If we carefully examine the social and political state of America, after having studied its history, we shall remain perfectly convinced that not an opinion, not a custom, not a law, I may even say not an event, is upon record which the origin of that people will not explain. The readers of this book will find the germ of all that is to follow in the present chapter, and the key to almost the whole work.

The emigrants who came, at different periods to occupy the territory now covered by the American Union differed from each other in many respects; their aim was not the same, and they governed themselves on different principles. These men had, however, certain features in common, and they were all placed in an analogous situation. The tie of language is perhaps the strongest and the most durable that can unite mankind. All the emigrants spoke the same tongue; they were all offsets from the same people. Born in a country which had been agitated for centuries by the struggles of faction, and in which all parties had been obliged in their turn to place themselves under the protection of the laws, their political education had been perfected in this rude school, and they were more conversant with the notions of right and the principles of true freedom than the greater part of their European contemporaries. At the period of their first emigrations the parish system, that fruitful germ of free institutions, was deeply rooted in the habits of the English; and with it the doctrine of the sovereignty of the people had been introduced into the bosom of the monarchy of the House of Tudor.

The religious quarrels which have agitated the Christian world were then rife. England had plunged into the new order of things with headlong vehemence. The character of its inhabitants, which had always been sedate and reflective, became argumentative and austere. General information had been increased by intellectual debate, and the mind had received a deeper cultivation. Whilst religion was the topic of discussion, the morals of the people were reformed. All these national features are more or less discoverable in the physiognomy of those adventurers who came to seek a new home on the opposite shores of the Atlantic.

Another remark, to which we shall hereafter have occasion to recur, is applicable not only to

的沧桑，今天的人们似乎注定要比他们的先辈看得更加透彻。上帝给了我们先辈不曾拥有的火炬，让我们能够领悟由于过去的蒙昧所未能察觉到的决定各民族命运的基本原因。在研究了美国的历史之后，如果我们再仔细地考察其社会政治状况，便可以完全肯定：在美国，每一个观念，每一个习俗，每一条法律，我甚至可以说每一个事件，都可以从这个国家的起源中找到解释。本书的读者将在本章发现后面所要叙述的一切的萌芽，这几乎就是开启全书的钥匙。

现如今美国境内不同时代到来的移民，彼此间有着诸多不同之处。他们有不同的目标，并依照不同的原则进行自我治理。然而，这些人又有着特定的共同点，都有着类似的遭遇。语言也许是将人们联合起来的最强韧最持久的纽带。所有的移民说着同样的语言，都是同一民族的儿女。他们出生在一个几个世纪以来由于派别斗争一直纷争不断的国家，而在这里各派别不得不轮番把自己置于法律的保护之下，他们的政治教育在这里得以完善，而且他们比当时大部分的欧洲人更熟悉权利观念和真正的自由原则。在移民之初，地方自治即自由制度的苗壮萌芽，已深植于英国人的习惯之中。人民主权的信条也随着地方自治制度引入都铎王朝的核心。

宗教纷争在基督教世界风起云涌。英格兰也近乎狂热地投身到这轮角逐之中。性格原本一直审慎持重的英国人变得严苛好斗。在这场智力竞赛中人们的知识得到了加强，头脑接受了深入的训练。当宗教成为人们热议话题的时候，人们的品德也得到了升华。英国人所有这些民族特点都可以在前往大西洋彼岸寻找新家园的人们身上或多或少的看到。

the English, but to the French, the Spaniards, and all the Europeans who successively established themselves in the New World. All these European colonies contained the elements, if not the development, of a complete democracy. Two causes led to this result. It may safely be advanced, that on leaving the mother-country the emigrants had in general no notion of superiority over one another. The happy and the powerful do not go into exile, and there are no surer guarantees of equality among men than poverty and misfortune. It happened, however, on several occasions, that persons of rank were driven to America by political and religious quarrels. Laws were made to establish a gradation of ranks; but it was soon found that the soil of America was opposed to a territorial aristocracy. To bring that refractory land into cultivation, the constant and interested exertions of the owner himself were necessary; and when the ground was prepared, its produce was found to be insufficient to enrich a master and a farmer at the same time. The land was then naturally broken up into small portions, which the proprietor cultivated for himself. Land is the basis of an aristocracy, which clings to the soil that supports it; for it is not by privileges alone, nor by birth, but by landed property handed down from generation to generation, that an aristocracy is constituted. A nation may present immense fortunes and extreme wretchedness, but unless those fortunes are territorial there is no aristocracy, but simply the class of the rich and that of the poor.

All the British colonies had then a great degree of similarity at the epoch of their settlement. All of them, from their first beginning, seemed destined to witness the growth, not of the aristocratic liberty of their mother-country, but of that freedom of the middle and lower orders of which the history of the world had as yet furnished no complete example.

In this general uniformity several striking differences were however discernible, which it is necessary to point out. Two branches may be distinguished in the Anglo-American family, which have hitherto grown up without entirely commingling; the one in the South, the other in the North.

Virginia received the first English colony; the emigrants took possession of it in 1607. The idea that mines of gold and silver are the sources of national wealth was at that time singularly prevalent in Europe; a fatal delusion, which has done more to impoverish the nations which adopted it, and

　　另外，在后面我们还有机会再提到这一特点，还会谈到这不仅适用于英国人，也适用于法国人、西班牙人以及前赴后继来到新大陆的所有欧洲人。在所有的欧洲殖民地，即使民主元素没有得到发展，至少被完全保留下来。这样的结果产生的原因有两个。完全有理由认为一般来说背井离乡的移民没有相对于别人的优越感。幸福和有权势的人不会选择流亡，而且贫穷和不幸是人人平等最有力的保障。可是，有些时候一些显贵也会因为受到政治宗教的迫害来到美洲，在这里制定一些贵贱有别的法律，但是不久他们就会发现贵族制度在美洲大陆水土不服。为了征服这块桀骜不驯的土地，只能依靠土地所有者本人不断地努力和付出。而且即便有了土地，其产出也并不足以使地主和农民同时富裕起来。因此，自然而然的土地就被分成许多小块，所有者为自己辛苦劳作。土地是贵族制度的基础，贵族需要土地供养才能生存，贵族制度并不是单独依靠特权或是血统来维系，而是依靠世代承袭的土地来实现。一个民族可能会有大量富人或是穷人，但是这些财富如果不是来自土地，就不能说有贵族，他们只是单纯的穷人和富人。

　　在殖民时代，所有的英国殖民地有很大程度的相似性。从一开始，它们似乎注定要见证史无前例的平民和民主自由的发展，而并非它们祖国贵族阶级的自由。

　　在这样普遍一致的情况下，还是可以看到一些有必要指出的明显区别。英裔的美国人的大家庭有两大分支：一支在南，一支在北，时至今日依然各自发展没有完全融合。

　　1607年，英国移民占据弗吉尼亚并建立了第一个殖民地。那时候，欧洲沉迷于开采金银使国家富强的思想。这是致命的错误想法，会掏空醉心于这种思想国家的财富。在美

has cost more lives in America, than the united influence of war and bad laws. The men sent to Virginia were seekers of gold, adventurers, without resources and without character, whose turbulent and restless spirit endangered the infant colony, and rendered its progress uncertain. The artisans and agriculturists arrived afterwards; and, although they were a more moral and orderly race of men, they were in nowise above the level of the inferior classes in England. No lofty conceptions, no intellectual system, directed the foundation of these new settlements. The colony was scarcely established when slavery was introduced, and this was the main circumstance which has exercised so prodigious an influence on the character, the laws, and all the future prospects of the South. Slavery, as we shall afterwards show, dishonors labor; it introduces idleness into society, and with idleness, ignorance and pride, luxury and distress. It enervates the powers of the mind, and benumbs the activity of man. The influence of slavery, united to the English character, explains the manners and the social condition of the Southern States.

In the North, the same English foundation was modified by the most opposite shades of character; and here I may be allowed to enter into some details. The two or three main ideas which constitute the basis of the social theory of the United States were first combined in the Northern English colonies, more generally denominated the States of New England. The principles of New England spread at first to the neighboring states; they then passed successively to the more distant ones; and at length they imbued the whole Confederation. They now extend their influence beyond its limits over the whole American world. The civilization of New England has been like a beacon lit upon a hill, which, after it has diffused its warmth around, tinges the distant horizon with its glow.

The foundation of New England was a novel spectacle, and all the circumstances attending it were singular and original. The large majority of colonies have been first inhabited either by men without education and without resources, driven by their poverty and their misconduct from the land which gave them birth, or by speculators and adventurers greedy of gain. Some settlements cannot even boast so honorable an origin; St. Domingo was founded by buccaneers; and the criminal courts of England originally supplied the population of Australia.

国，它夺走的性命比战争和糟糕的法律加起来夺走的性命还要多。寻金者、冒险家被送到弗吉尼亚，这些人无才无德，暴躁不安给这个初建的殖民点带来多混乱，使得这里的发展忽快忽慢。手工业者和农民随后而来，尽管这些人比较讲究道德和纪律，他们也不过是英国的下等阶级。既没有崇高的观念又没有知识体系来指导殖民地的建设，所以在殖民地建立之初便引入蓄奴制。正是这一事件对后来整个南方的性格、法律和未来产生了重大影响。奴隶，正如我们后面所述，是对劳动的玷污。它在社会上制造好逸恶劳的恶习，而随着好逸恶劳而来的便是无知、高傲、奢靡和不幸。它让人们的思想颓废，变得懒散麻木不仁。蓄奴制的影响加上英国人的性格特点，对南方各州的风俗和社会状况做出了解释。

尽管都是来自英国，但是在北方则呈现出完全相反的情况。请允许我在这里对此略作详细说明。美国社会学说的几个主要基础思想最先产生在北方诸州，也就是人们普遍所说的新英格兰诸州。新英格兰地区的这些思想首先传播到周边各州，接着又扩散到更远的地方，最后散播到整个联邦。现在它们的影响已经远远跨出国门波及整个美洲。新英格兰的文明就像高山上燃起的烽火，不但温暖了周围地区，并用它的光辉照耀了远方。

新英格兰的建立呈现出一片新气象，这里发生的一切都独一无二。绝大多数殖民地的最初居民不是没受过教育、毫无家产由于贫穷和行为不端被赶出家乡的人，就是些贪婪的投机者和冒险者。有些殖民地居民还称不上有这样的出身。比如圣多明戈就是海盗建立的，而且英格兰的刑事法庭不也在向澳大利亚输送人口吗。

在新英格兰登陆的移民在他们的祖国都属于自由派。所以当他们在美洲的土地上联合

The settlers who established themselves on the shores of New England all belonged to the more independent classes of their native country. Their union on the soil of America at once presented the singular phenomenon of a society containing neither lords nor common people, neither rich nor poor. These men possessed, in proportion to their number, a greater mass of intelligence than is to be found in any European nation of our own time. All, without a single exception, had received a good education, and many of them were known in Europe for their talents and their acquirements. The other colonies had been founded by adventurers without family; the emigrants of New England brought with them the best elements of order and morality—they landed in the desert accompanied by their wives and children. But what most especially distinguished them was the aim of their undertaking. They had not been obliged by necessity to leave their country; the social position they abandoned was one to be regretted, and their means of subsistence were certain. Nor did they cross the Atlantic to improve their situation or to increase their wealth; the call which summoned them from the comforts of their homes was purely intellectual; and in facing the inevitable sufferings of exile their object was the triumph of an idea.

The emigrants, or, as they deservedly styled themselves, the Pilgrims, belonged to that English sect the austerity of whose principles had acquired for them the name of Puritans. Puritanism was not merely a religious doctrine, but it corresponded in many points with the most absolute democratic and republican theories. It was this tendency which had aroused its most dangerous adversaries. Persecuted by the Government of the mother-country, and disgusted by the habits of a society opposed to the rigor of their own principles, the Puritans went forth to seek some rude and unfrequented part of the world, where they could live according to their own opinions, and worship God in freedom.

A few quotations will throw more light upon the spirit of these pious adventures than all we can say of them. Nathaniel Morton, the historian of the first years of the settlement, thus opens his subject:

"Gentle Reader,—I have for some length of time looked upon it as a duty incumbent, especially on the immediate successors of those that have had so large experience of those many memorable and signal demonstrations of God's goodness, viz., the first beginners of this Plantation in New

起来，社会便立即呈现出独特的气象，在这个社会无所谓领主和属民，也无所谓穷人和富人。按照人数比例来讲，这些人中知识分子所占比例比如今欧洲任何国家都要多。无一例外所有人都接受过良好教育，其中还有许多人才学出众闻名欧洲。其他的殖民地则由没有携带家眷的冒险家们建立。新英格兰移民带来良好的秩序和道德因素，和他们的妻儿一起踏上这片蛮荒。但是，他们与其他居民最大的不同在于目的。他们不是被迫离开自己的祖国，所放弃的社会地位也令人遗憾，也拥有稳定的谋生方式。他们远渡重洋来到这里既不是改善境遇也非发财致富，把他们从温馨家园召唤而来的纯粹是对于知识的追求，他们甘愿受流离之苦，使理想得以实现。

这些移民，或是按照他们自己喜好的称谓——朝圣者，属于英国一个以教义严格而著称的清教徒教派。清教徒教义并不仅仅是宗教学说，在许多方面它还与绝对民主和共和理论相辅相成。正是这样的倾向给自己树立了很多危险的敌人。在祖国他们受到政府的迫害，他们自己也厌弃有悖于他们严格教义的社会习俗，清教徒出发去寻找世界上人迹罕至的地方，在那里，他们可以按照自己的意愿生活，自由地崇拜上帝。

摘录几段文字，比我们所说更能清晰的诠释这些虔诚冒险家们的精神。研究新英格兰早期历史的纳撒尼尔·莫尔顿，在其开篇词中这样说道：

"敬爱的读者，一直以来，我认为把祖辈在建立这块殖民地时所享受的上帝多方面仁慈的关怀用文字记录下来，并让后代永远记住上帝的仁慈，是我们义不容辞的责任。凡是我们所见，我们父辈所言，均应告知我们的子女，让他们懂得赞美上帝，特别是让上

England, to commit to writing his gracious dispensations on that behalf; having so many inducements thereunto, not onely otherwise but so plentifully in the Sacred Scriptures: that so, what we have seen, and what our fathers have told us (Psalm lxxviii. 3, 4), we may not hide from our children, showing to the generations to come the praises of the Lord; that especially the seed of Abraham his servant, and the children of Jacob his chosen (Psalm cv. 5, 6), may remember his marvellous works in the beginning and progress of the planting of New England, his wonders and the judgments of his mouth; how that God brought a vine into this wilderness; that he cast out the heathen, and planted it; that he made room for it and caused it to take deep root; and it filled the land (Psalm lxxx. 8, 9). And not onely so, but also that he hath guided his people by his strength to his holy habitation and planted them in the mountain of his inheritance in respect of precious Gospel enjoyments: and that as especially God may have the glory of all unto whom it is most due; so also some rays of glory may reach the names of those blessed Saints that were the main instruments and the beginning of this happy enterprise."

It is impossible to read this opening paragraph without an involuntary feeling of religious awe; it breathes the very savor of Gospel antiquity. The sincerity of the author heightens his power of language. The band which to his eyes was a mere party of adventurers gone forth to seek their fortune beyond seas appears to the reader as the germ of a great nation wafted by Providence to a predestined shore.

The author thus continues his narrative of the departure of the first pilgrims:—

"So they left that goodly and pleasant city of Leyden, which had been their resting-place for above eleven years; but they knew that they were pilgrims and strangers here below, and looked not much on these things, but lifted up their eyes to Heaven, their dearest country, where God hath prepared for them a city (Heb. xi. 16), and therein quieted their spirits. When they came to Delfs-Haven they found the ship and all things ready; and such of their friends as could not come with them followed after them, and sundry came from Amsterdam to see them shipt, and to take their leaves of them. One night was spent with little sleep with the most, but with friendly entertainment and Christian

帝的仆人亚伯拉罕的后裔和上帝的选民雅各布的子孙永远记住上帝的杰作（《诗篇》第105篇第5、6节）。要让他们知道上帝如何把葡萄带到荒野，如何栽上葡萄赶走异教徒，如何整备出种葡萄的用地，把秧苗的根深深插入土地，以及后来如何让葡萄蔓布满大地（《诗篇》第80篇第13、15节）。不仅如此，还要他们知道上帝如何引导他的子民走向他的圣所，而定居在他遗赐的山间（《出埃及记》第15章第13节）。这些事实一定要使他们知道，以使上帝得到他应得的荣誉，让上帝的荣光也能被及作为工具为他服务的圣徒们的可敬名字。"

读完这段开篇词，一定会让人感受到宗教的庄严，闻到古代福音的馨香。作者的虔诚让他的文字更有力量。在读者眼中，就好像在作者的眼中一样，这并不仅仅是一群漂洋过海撞大运的冒险家，而是上帝亲自播洒在选定土地上的伟大民族的种子。

作者接着对第一批背井离乡清教徒的描述：

"于是他们离开了这座美好舒适的莱顿城，他们休养生息的地方，但是他们知道此生他们是朝圣者是异乡人。他们不留恋尘世的东西，眼望上天，他们离开最亲爱的家乡，上帝已为他们准备好的圣城（《希伯来书》第11章16节），在那里他们获得精神的安宁。当他们来到港口，船只和一切都已准备妥当，不能跟随他们的亲友也赶来为他们送行。大家彻夜未眠，倾吐友情，表达基督徒真正的友爱。第二天他们登船起航，可是亲友不愿离开与他们一起登船道别，在这里看到的是离别的悲伤，听到的是分离的叹息、呜咽以及为他们祝福的祷告，人们泪如雨下，只字片语都会刺痛他们的心扉，站在一边的陌生人也为之

31

discourse, and other real expressions of true Christian love. The next day they went on board, and their friends with them, where truly doleful was the sight of that sad and mournful parting, to hear what sighs and sobs and prayers did sound amongst them; what tears did gush from every eye, and pithy speeches pierced each other's heart, that sundry of the Dutch strangers that stood on the Key as spectators could not refrain from tears. But the tide (which stays for no man) calling them away, that were thus loth to depart, their Reverend Pastor falling down on his knees, and they all with him, with watery cheeks commended them with most fervent prayers unto the Lord and his blessing; and then, with mutual embraces and many tears they took their leaves one of another, which proved to be the last leave to many of them."

The emigrants were about 150 in number, including the women and the children. Their object was to plant a colony on the shores of the Hudson; but after having been driven about for some time in the Atlantic Ocean, they were forced to land on that arid coast of New England which is now the site of the town of Plymouth. The rock is still shown on which the pilgrims disembarked.

"But before we pass on," continues our historian, "let the reader with me make a pause and seriously consider this poor people's present condition, the more to be raised up to admiration of God's goodness towards them in their preservation: for being now passed the vast ocean, and a sea of troubles before them in expectation, they had now no friends to welcome them, no inns to entertain or refresh them, no houses, or much less towns to repair unto to seek for succour: and for the season it was winter, and they that know the winters of the country know them to be sharp and violent, subject to cruel and fierce storms, dangerous to travel to known places, much more to search unknown coasts. Besides, what could they see but a hideous and desolate wilderness, full of wilde beasts, and wilde men? and what multitudes of them there were, they then knew not: for which way soever they turned their eyes (save upward to Heaven) they could have but little solace or content in respect of any outward object; for summer being ended, all things stand in appearance with a weather-beaten face, and the whole country full of woods and thickets, represented a wild and savage hew; if they looked behind them, there was the mighty ocean which they had passed, and was now as

动容。开船的信号催促不舍的人们离开，人们随着牧师一起跪地，泪眼汪汪的向上帝祈福祷告。最后，人们相互拥抱道别，对大多数而言这将是他们的永别。"

这批移民大约150人，其中还有一些妇女儿童。他们的目的是要在赫德森河岸建立一个殖民点，但是在大西洋漂泊很长时间以后，他们被迫在新英格兰的荒芜海岸登陆，也就是今天的普利茅斯镇。当时清教徒上岸时登上的那块巨石今天依然在那里。

"在我们长篇大论之前，"我们的历史学家接着说，"让读者与我一起稍停片刻，说一说这些苦命人上岸后的情景，赞美上帝拯救他们的恩德。现在他们已经渡过广阔的海洋，到达目的地，但是既没有亲友的迎候，又没有暖屋栖身解乏。当时正值隆冬时节，了解这个国家气候的人都知道这里冬天的凛冽，暴风雪的残酷暴虐，即使去熟悉的地方旅行都困难重重，更不要说在一无所知的海岸安家。除此之外，他们满目荒凉，遍地野兽和野人。他们不知道有多少野人，他们到底有多凶残。他们环顾四周，没有什么能让他们感到安慰满意。夏天已经远离，一切都已枯萎变得干瘪，到处是树木和灌木丛，一片荒蛮。回头望是来时横渡的无际大海，现在已然成为他们和文明世界的阻隔。"

千万不要认为清教徒的虔诚只停留在嘴上，也不要认为他们不谙世事。清教徒的学说，如我前面所说，既是政治学说，又是宗教教义。移民们一登上纳撒尼尔·莫尔顿描述的不毛海岸，他们所关心的第一要务不是建立自己的社会，而是通过下面的这个公约：

"以上帝的名义，阿门。我们，下面的签名人，我们敬畏的主耶和华詹姆斯国王，等等，为了给上帝增光，发扬基督教信仰和祖国的荣誉，航行至此在这里建立第一个殖民

a main bar or gulph to separate them from all the civil parts of the world."

It must not be imagined that the piety of the Puritans was of a merely speculative kind, or that it took no cognizance of the course of worldly affairs. Puritanism, as I have already remarked, was scarcely less a political than a religious doctrine. No sooner had the emigrants landed on the barren coast described by Nathaniel Morton than it was their first care to constitute a society, by passing the following Act:

"In the name of God. Amen. We, whose names are underwritten, the loyal subjects of our dread Sovereign Lord King James, etc., etc., Having undertaken for the glory of God, and advancement of the Christian Faith, and the honour of our King and country, a voyage to plant the first colony in the northern parts of Virginia; Do by these presents solemnly and mutually, in the presence of God and one another, covenant and combine ourselves together into a civil body politick, for our better ordering and preservation, and furtherance of the ends aforesaid: and by virtue hereof do enact, constitute and frame such just and equal laws, ordinances, acts, constitutions, and officers, from time to time, as shall be thought most meet and convenient for the general good of the Colony: unto which we promise all due submission and obedience," etc.

This happened in 1620, and from that time forwards the emigration went on. The religious and political passions which ravaged the British Empire during the whole reign of Charles I drove fresh crowds of sectarians every year to the shores of America. In England the stronghold of Puritanism was in the middle classes, and it was from the middle classes that the majority of the emigrants came. The population of New England increased rapidly; and whilst the hierarchy of rank despotically classed the inhabitants of the mother-country, the colony continued to present the novel spectacle of a community homogeneous in all its parts. A democracy, more perfect than any which antiquity had dreamt of, started in full size and panoply from the midst of an ancient feudal society.

The English Government was not dissatisfied with an emigration which removed the elements of fresh discord and of further revolutions. On the contrary, everything was done to encourage it, and great exertions were made to mitigate the hardships of those who sought a shelter from the rigor of their country's laws on the soil of America. It seemed as if New England was a region given up to the

点。谨在上帝面前，面对在场的众位，彼此庄严地表示同意，约定共同组成政治社会，以管理我们自己并致力于实现我们的目标。我们会根据这个契约颁布法律、法令和命令，并根据需要任命需要的官员。我们承诺遵守服从这个契约。"等等。

这发生在1620年。此后，移民络绎不绝来到这里。查理一世在位期间，令大不列颠帝国动荡不已的宗教和政治热情，每年把一批批各教派赶到美洲大陆。在英国，清教徒是中产阶级的主力，而大部分移民也是来自这个阶级。新英格兰的人口快速增长，而当等级制度在祖国强行把人们划分为不同阶级的时候，殖民地继续全方位呈现出均一化的全新景象。民主发展的比过往所梦想的都要完美，已从古老的封建社会中无比强大全副武装地冲了出来。

这样的移民可以驱逐不安因素和革命分子，所以英国政府对此甚为满意，对移民大加鼓励，而对于那些到美洲寻求避难来逃脱本国严苛刑法人们的命运则无需在意。似乎新英格兰成了梦幻乐园，革新者的试验田。

英国殖民地（而且这是英国繁荣的主要因素之一）与其他国家的殖民地相比，一直享有更多的内政自由和更大的政治独立。但是，任何地方都不能像新英格兰那样把自由原则应用得那么广泛。

那时的普遍观点是，新大陆的各片土地，哪个欧洲国家最先发现，就属于哪个国家。因此，到16世纪末，几乎整个北美海岸都被英国占据。英国政府对这些新领地采用了几种

dreams of fancy and the unrestrained experiments of innovators.

The English colonies (and this is one of the main causes of their prosperity) have always enjoyed more internal freedom and more political independence than the colonies of other nations; but this principle of liberty was nowhere more extensively applied than in the States of New England.

It was generally allowed at that period that the territories of the New World belonged to that European nation which had been the first to discover them. Nearly the whole coast of North America thus became a British possession towards the end of the sixteenth century. The means used by the English Government to people these new domains were of several kinds; the King sometimes appointed a governor of his own choice, who ruled a portion of the New World in the name and under the immediate orders of the Crown; this is the colonial system adopted by other countries of Europe. Sometimes grants of certain tracts were made by the Crown to an individual or to a company, in which case all the civil and political power fell into the hands of one or more persons, who, under the inspection and control of the Crown, sold the lands and governed the inhabitants. Lastly, a third system consisted in allowing a certain number of emigrants to constitute a political society under the protection of the mother-country, and to govern themselves in whatever was not contrary to her laws. This mode of colonization, so remarkably favorable to liberty, was only adopted in New England.

In 1628 a charter of this kind was granted by Charles I to the emigrants who went to form the colony of Massachusetts. But, in general, charters were not given to the colonies of New England till they had acquired a certain existence. Plymouth, Providence, New Haven, the State of Connecticut, and that of Rhode Island were founded without the co-operation and almost without the knowledge of the mother-country. The new settlers did not derive their incorporation from the seat of the empire, although they did not deny its supremacy; they constituted a society of their own accord, and it was not till thirty or forty years afterwards, under Charles II. that their existence was legally recognized by a royal charter.

This frequently renders its it difficult to detect the link which connected the emigrants with the land of their forefathers in studying the earliest historical and legislative records of New England. They exercised the rights of sovereignty; they named their magistrates, concluded peace or declared war,

不同的统治方式。有时，国王亲选总督治理新大陆的部分地区，按照他的名义和命令行事。欧洲其他国家也都所采用这样的殖民管理体系。有时候国王会将大片土地授权给个人或是公司，在这种情况下所有的民事和政治权利都落入一个或是多个人手中，在国王的监督和控制下出售土地管理居民。最后，第三种体系允许一定数量的移民在母国的保护下组成政治社会并在不违背母国法律的前提下自我统治。这种殖民模式对自由特别有利，只曾经在新英格兰实行。

1628年，查理一世为前往马萨诸塞殖民地的移民颁发一份这种特许状。但是，一般来说，新英格兰的殖民地只有既成事实后才获得这样的特许状。普利茅斯、普罗维登斯、纽黑文、康涅狄格州以及罗得岛州都是在没有母国帮助，并几乎不为母国知晓的情况下建立起来。尽管新移民并不否认宗主国的至高无上的权威，却也不会从宗主国寻求权利之源。他们自行组建社会，直到三四十年后查理二世统治时期，他们的存在才依据皇家特许状变得合法。

因此，在研究新英格兰早期历史立法文献的时候，往往很难察觉移民和其母国的纽带的存在。他们行使主权，任命地方官，自行缔约或是宣战，制定治安条例，并自行立法，似乎他们只听命于上帝。那个时候的立法最独特，同时也是最具启发性。今天美国呈现在世界面前的主要社会问题的谜底，刚好可以在那时的立法中找到答案。

在这些文献中我们应该注意到，1650年康涅狄格州颁布的一部独具特色的法典。康涅

made police regulations, and enacted laws as if their allegiance was due only to God. Nothing can be more curious and, at the same time more instructive, than the legislation of that period; it is there that the solution of the great social problem which the United States now present to the world is to be found.

Amongst these documents we shall notice, as especially characteristic, the code of laws promulgated by the little State of Connecticut in 1650. The legislators of Connecticut begin with the penal laws, and, strange to say, they borrow their provisions from the text of Holy Writ. "Whosoever shall worship any other God than the Lord," says the preamble of the Code, "shall surely be put to death." This is followed by ten or twelve enactments of the same kind, copied verbatim from the books of Exodus, Leviticus, and Deuteronomy. Blasphemy, sorcery, adultery, and rape were punished with death; an outrage offered by a son to his parents was to be expiated by the same penalty. The legislation of a rude and half-civilized people was thus applied to an enlightened and moral community. The consequence was that the punishment of death was never more frequently prescribed by the statute, and never more rarely enforced towards the guilty.

The chief care of the legislators, in this body of penal laws, was the maintenance of orderly conduct and good morals in the community: they constantly invaded the domain of conscience, and there was scarcely a sin which was not subject to magisterial censure. The reader is aware of the rigor with which these laws punished rape and adultery; intercourse between unmarried persons was likewise severely repressed. The judge was empowered to inflict a pecuniary penalty, a whipping, or marriage on the misdemeanants; and if the records of the old courts of New Haven may be believed, prosecutions of this kind were not unfrequent. We find a sentence bearing date the first of May, 1660, inflicting a fine and reprimand on a young woman who was accused of using improper language, and of allowing herself to be kissed. The Code of 1650 abounds in preventive measures. It punishes idleness and drunkenness with severity. Innkeepers are forbidden to furnish more than a certain quantity of liquor to each consumer; and simple lying, whenever it may be injurious, is checked by a fine or a flogging. In other places, the legislator, entirely forgetting the great principles of religious toleration which he had himself upheld in Europe, renders attendance on divine service compulsory, and goes so far as to visit with severe punishment, and even with death, the Christians who chose to

狄格的立法者们首先制定刑法典，而且奇怪的是，他们借用了《圣经》中的一些条文。这部法典的序文中写道："任何人不得崇拜上帝以外的神明，违者将被处死。"接着还有十到十二条法令逐字抄录《出埃及记》《利未记》和《申命记》。亵渎神灵，巫术，通奸和强奸都将处以死刑，儿子虐待父母也将施以相同刑罚。就这样，野蛮和半开化民族的立法竟然应用到开化文明的社会。结果就是法律规定的死刑惩罚多的前所未有，也从未如此多的应用到微不足道的罪行。

在这部刑法中，立法者主要关心的是维护社会的行为规范和良好的德行。他们注重良心问题，几乎每一件恶行都被列入惩戒范围。读者已经意识到法律对于强奸和通奸的惩罚过于严苛，同样未婚男女的私通也将受到严厉惩处。法官有权对罪犯处以罚金、鞭刑和强令结婚。如果纽黑文旧法庭的记录可信，这类的判决为数不少。我们注意到一个日期标为1660年5月1日的一份判决，一位年轻女子因为言语不当和让人吻了一下被判处罚款和申斥。1650年法典中载有很多预防性措施。这部法典对懒惰、酗酒施以重罚。小酒馆的店主向每个顾客兜售的酒不得超过一定限度。而且一个谎言，只要有害就会处以罚款和鞭笞。在其他方面，立法者完全忘记在欧洲他所支持的宗教自由的伟大原则，用罚款强迫人们参加宗教活动，甚至对反对者施以重刑，而且往往对采用不同仪式祭拜上帝的基督徒处以死刑。有时立法者的热情还让他们管起不该管的事情。就在这部法典里还有禁止吸烟的条款。当然一定不要忘记，这种奇怪无厘头的法律并不是强加于民，而是全体当事人自由投

worship God according to a ritual differing from his own. Sometimes indeed the zeal of his enactments induces him to descend to the most frivolous particulars: thus a law is to be found in the same Code which prohibits the use of tobacco. It must not be forgotten that these fantastical and vexatious laws were not imposed by authority, but that they were freely voted by all the persons interested, and that the manners of the community were even more austere and more puritanical than the laws. In 1649 a solemn association was formed in Boston to check the worldly luxury of long hair.

These errors are no doubt discreditable to human reason; they attest the inferiority of our nature, which is incapable of laying firm hold upon what is true and just, and is often reduced to the alternative of two excesses. In strict connection with this penal legislation, which bears such striking marks of a narrow sectarian spirit, and of those religious passions which had been warmed by persecution and were still fermenting among the people, a body of political laws is to be found, which, though written two hundred years ago, is still ahead of the liberties of our age. The general principles which are the groundwork of modern constitutions—principles which were imperfectly known in Europe, and not completely triumphant even in Great Britain, in the seventeenth century—were all recognized and determined by the laws of New England: the intervention of the people in public affairs, the free voting of taxes, the responsibility of authorities, personal liberty, and trial by jury, were all positively established without discussion. From these fruitful principles consequences have been derived and applications have been made such as no nation in Europe has yet ventured to attempt.

In Connecticut the electoral body consisted, from its origin, of the whole number of citizens; and this is readily to be understood, when we recollect that this people enjoyed an almost perfect equality of fortune, and a still greater uniformity of opinions. In Connecticut, at this period, all the executive functionaries were elected, including the Governor of the State. The citizens above the age of sixteen were obliged to bear arms; they formed a national militia, which appointed its own officers, and was to hold itself at all times in readiness to march for the defence of the country.

In the laws of Connecticut, as well as in all those of New England, we find the germ and gradual development of that township independence which is the life and mainspring of American liberty at the present day. The political existence of the majority of the nations of Europe commenced in the

票通过的，而且居民的习俗比政府的法律来得更加苛刻更富于清教徒色彩。1649年，在波士顿成立了一个劝诫人们蓄留长发浮华行为的庄严协会。

这样的错误无疑有辱人类的理性，它们证明了人类天性的低劣，不具备牢牢地掌握真理和正义的能力，而且往往容易走向两个极端。这部刑法被深深打上了狭隘的宗教主义烙印，以及由于迫害而激荡起来并在人们中间持续发酵的宗教热情的烙印。此外，还有一部政治法律，尽管它成文在200年前，仍然大大先进于我们现在的自由精神。一些普遍原则成为现代宪法的基础，也就是在17世纪还不为欧洲所知，而且也尚未在大不列颠取得完胜的原则，然而它们却得到新英格兰法律的完全认可并纳入法律条款。人民参与公共事务，自由投票决定捐税，行政官员责任制，个人自由，陪审团制度，这些都未经讨论确立下来。这些原则已经在新英格兰得到发展应用，而在欧洲还没有一个国家敢于尝试。

在康涅狄格，从开始所有公民就都是选民团成员，人们对于这种做法的意义也马上就能领会。回想当初，这些移民的财富几乎完全相等，而且观点高度一致。在那个时候的康涅狄格，所有的州行政官员都由选举产生，包括总督在内。年满16岁的公民有义务拿起武器，组建州国民军，自行委任军官，并时刻准备开赴前线保家卫国。

在康涅狄格以及所有新英格兰的法律中，我们可以看到地方自主的萌芽和发展，而这仍然是今天美国自由的生命和动力。欧洲大多数国家的政治生活始于社会上层，然后逐渐不完全地蔓延到社会其他阶层成员。在美国，可以说事情刚好相反，乡镇建立的比县早，

superior ranks of society, and was gradually and imperfectly communicated to the different members of the social body. In America, on the other hand, it may be said that the township was organized before the county, the county before the State, the State before the Union. In New England townships were completely and definitively constituted as early as 1650. The independence of the township was the nucleus round which the local interests, passions, rights, and duties collected and clung. It gave scope to the activity of a real political life most thoroughly democratic and republican. The colonies still recognized the supremacy of the mother-country; monarchy was still the law of the State; but the republic was already established in every township. The towns named their own magistrates of every kind, rated themselves, and levied their own taxes. In the parish of New England the law of representation was not adopted, but the affairs of the community were discussed, as at Athens, in the market-place, by a general assembly of the citizens.

In studying the laws which were promulgated at this first era of the American republics, it is impossible not to be struck by the remarkable acquaintance with the science of government and the advanced theory of legislation which they display. The ideas there formed of the duties of society towards its members are evidently much loftier and more comprehensive than those of the European legislators at that time: obligations were there imposed which were elsewhere slighted. In the States of New England, from the first, the condition of the poor was provided for; strict measures were taken for the maintenance of roads, and surveyors were appointed to attend to them; registers were established in every parish, in which the results of public deliberations, and the births, deaths, and marriages of the citizens were entered; clerks were directed to keep these registers; officers were charged with the administration of vacant inheritances, and with the arbitration of litigated landmarks; and many others were created whose chief functions were the maintenance of public order in the community. The law enters into a thousand useful provisions for a number of social wants which are at present very inadequately felt in France.

But it is by the attention it pays to Public Education that the original character of American civilization is at once placed in the clearest light. "It being," says the law, "one chief project of Satan to keep men from the knowledge of the Scripture by persuading from the use of tongues, to the end

县比州早，州又比联邦早。在新英格兰，早在1650年乡镇就已经完全建成。独立的乡镇就是人们自己组织团结起来，为了自己的利益、情感、权利和义务而共同奋斗，这就为真正的政治生活和完全民主的共和生活提供了空间。殖民地仍然认可宗主国的无上权力，君主政体依然写在各州的法律条文之中，但是共和制已经在各乡镇确立。乡镇自行任命各类官员，进行评估，自行征税。新英格兰的乡镇的法律没有规定采用代议制。但是涉及居民利益的事务，会像在雅典一样，在公共场所召开公民大会进行讨论。

对美国共和之初的法律进行仔细研究之后，一定会对其展现的政府科学和先进的立法理论异常诧异。他们所形成的社会应该对其成员负责的思想，显然要比当时欧洲立法者们的想法更崇高更全面，他们规定社会应承担的义务，在其他的地方被完全忽视。在新英格兰各州，从建立之初，便立法对穷人做出保障，采取严格的措施对道路进行养护，并任命监督员检查执行。每个乡镇还设有登记簿，对公共审议结果，以及公民的出生、死亡、婚姻进行记录，任命文书对这些记录进行管理，设置官员负责管理无人继承的财产和有关地产边界界定的仲裁，还有许多其他官员负责维护乡镇内部的公共秩序。法律条文添加了数以千计的实施细则以便满足社会的大量需要，这些甚至令今天的法国依然感到自愧不如。

但是，对于国民教育的重视程度是美国文明最为突出的特征。法律明文规定："为了人类不被撒旦的巧舌如簧蛊惑背弃圣经，为了不让我们祖先的禀赋被埋没，兹依靠上帝的帮助……"接着列出一些条款规定，每个乡镇必须建立学校，责成居民出资办学，对拒不

that learning may not be buried in the graves of our forefathers, in church and commonwealth, the Lord assisting our endeavors. . . ." Here follow clauses establishing schools in every township, and obliging the inhabitants, under pain of heavy fines, to support them. Schools of a superior kind were founded in the same manner in the more populous districts. The municipal authorities were bound to enforce the sending of children to school by their parents; they were empowered to inflict fines upon all who refused compliance; and in case of continued resistance society assumed the place of the parent, took possession of the child, and deprived the father of those natural rights which he used to so bad a purpose. The reader will undoubtedly have remarked the preamble of these enactments: in America religion is the road to knowledge, and the observance of the divine laws leads man to civil freedom.

If, after having cast a rapid glance over the state of American society in 1650, we turn to the condition of Europe, and more especially to that of the Continent, at the same period, we cannot fail to be struck with astonishment. On the Continent of Europe, at the beginning of the seventeenth century, absolute monarchy had everywhere triumphed over the ruins of the oligarchical and feudal liberties of the Middle Ages. Never were the notions of right more completely confounded than in the midst of the splendor and literature of Europe; never was there less political activity among the people; never were the principles of true freedom less widely circulated; and at that very time those principles, which were scorned or unknown by the nations of Europe, were proclaimed in the deserts of the New World, and were accepted as the future creed of a great people. The boldest theories of the human reason were put into practice by a community so humble that not a statesman condescended to attend to it; and a legislation without a precedent was produced offhand by the imagination of the citizens. In the bosom of this obscure democracy, which had as yet brought forth neither generals, nor philosophers, nor authors, a man might stand up in the face of a free people and pronounce the following fine definition of liberty.

"Nor would I have you to mistake in the point of your own liberty. There is a liberty of a corrupt nature which is effected both by men and beasts to do what they list, and this liberty is inconsistent with authority, impatient of all restraint; by this liberty 'sumus omnes deteriores': 'tis the grand enemy of truth and peace, and all the ordinances of God are bent against it. But there is a civil, a moral, a

出资者施以巨额罚款。在人口稠密的乡镇，以同样的方式建立高一级的学校。城市行政当局应敦促家长保证子女入学，并有权对违抗者进行罚款，对拒不履行义务的家长，社会将承担其父母的责任，对孩子进行收容，并剥夺其父上天赋予却被其用作不良目的之权利。读者一定能够从这项法律的序言里注意到，在美国，宗教是通往知识之路，而对神圣法律的仰视则将人们引向自由。

在对1650年美国社会状况的匆匆一瞥之后，回过头再看看欧洲，特别是欧洲大陆的情况，我们无疑会大吃一惊。在17世纪初的欧洲大陆，君主专制在各地与中世纪寡头和封建政治自由废墟的对决中取得全面胜利。在光彩夺目和文艺复兴中的欧洲，权利的概念从来没有像此时一样被完全忽略，人们的政治生活也从来没有像此时一样少，真正自由的思想也从来没有像此时一样不为人了解。而且正是在这一时期，欧洲人不屑一顾或是一无所知的这些原则，已经在新大陆的荒芜之地宣告其存在，并成为一个伟大民族的未来信条。人类理性最大胆设想的理论竟由一个毫不起眼以致都没有政治家愿意屈尊其间的社会付诸实践，想象力丰富的公民创造了史无前例的立法。在这样一个一文不名的民主国家，甚至还未出过将军、哲学家和作家，但是却有人能够站在一群自由人的面前，给自由做出如下精妙的定义：

"我们不应该有认为自己已经拥有自由的错误想法。有一种自由是为所欲为，人如同动物一样随心所欲，其本质是堕落的自由。这种自由不服从权威，无法忍受一切约束。

federal liberty which is the proper end and object of authority; it is a liberty for that only which is just and good: for this liberty you are to stand with the hazard of your very lives and whatsoever crosses it is not authority, but a distemper thereof. This liberty is maintained in a way of subjection to authority; and the authority set over you will, in all administrations for your good, be quietly submitted unto by all but such as have a disposition to shake off the yoke and lose their true liberty, by their murmuring at the honor and power of authority."

The remarks I have made will suffice to display the character of Anglo-American civilization in its true light. It is the result (and this should be constantly present to the mind of two distinct elements), which in other places have been in frequent hostility, but which in America have been admirably incorporated and combined with one another. I allude to the spirit of Religion and the spirit of Liberty.

The settlers of New England were at the same time ardent sectarians and daring innovators. Narrow as the limits of some of their religious opinions were, they were entirely free from political prejudices. Hence arose two tendencies, distinct but not opposite, which are constantly discernible in the manners as well as in the laws of the country.

It might be imagined that men who sacrificed their friends, their family, and their native land to a religious conviction were absorbed in the pursuit of the intellectual advantages which they purchased at so dear a rate. The energy, however, with which they strove for the acquirement of wealth, moral enjoyment, and the comforts as well as liberties of the world, is scarcely inferior to that with which they devoted themselves to Heaven.

Political principles and all human laws and institutions were moulded and altered at their pleasure; the barriers of the society in which they were born were broken down before them; the old principles which had governed the world for ages were no more; a path without a turn and a field without an horizon were opened to the exploring and ardent curiosity of man: but at the limits of the political world he checks his researches, he discreetly lays aside the use of his most formidable faculties, he no longer consents to doubt or to innovate, but carefully abstaining from raising the curtain of the sanctuary, he yields with submissive respect to truths which he will not discuss. Thus, in the moral

实行这种自由，我们就会自行堕落。它是真理与和平的敌人，上帝也认为应该反对它。然而，还有一种公民的、道德的和圣约的自由，是政权的使命终极目标。这种自由支持的是公正和善良。这样神圣的自由，我们应当用生命为代价来捍卫它。"

我所陈述的足以说明英裔美国人文明的真正特点。这种文明是两种不同因素作用的结果（这一点人们应该牢记），而在其他地方这两种因素总是相互敌对，但是在美国它们完美融合。我这里提到的两个因素分别指的是宗教精神和自由精神。

新英格兰的居民既是狂热的信徒，又是大胆的革新者。尽管他们有些宗教观点过于狭隘，但是他们丝毫没有政治偏见。因此出现了两种虽不同也不抵触的趋势。这两种趋势既表现在民情上也表现在法律上。

可以想象人们为了宗教信仰牺牲他们的朋友、家人和祖国，完全沉迷于对这种精神享受的追求，这样的代价非常巨大。然而，我们也可以看到，他们为获得物质财富，精神享乐以及自由世界所付出的努力丝毫不亚于他们对于天堂的奉献。

政治原则以及所有人类法律和机构都可以按照他们的意愿进行改造。在他们面前，束缚社会前进的障碍被打破，几个世纪以来统治世界的旧原则一去不返，一条康庄大道一片无尽的天地展现在热情、充满好奇心的人们面前。但当他们到达政治世界的极限，开始反思过去，他们谨慎地把最为强大的能力放在一边，不再怀疑不敢革新，而是小心翼翼地掀起圣殿的帷幔，恭敬地拜倒在未加争辩即全部接受的真理面前。因此，在精神世界，一切都已分门别类，有条不紊，预定并预知。而在政治世界，一切则是动荡不定，喋喋不休。

world everything is classed, adapted, decided, and foreseen; in the political world everything is agitated, uncertain, and disputed: in the one is a passive, though a voluntary, obedience; in the other an independence scornful of experience and jealous of authority.

These two tendencies, apparently so discrepant, are far from conflicting; they advance together, and mutually support each other. Religion perceives that civil liberty affords a noble exercise to the faculties of man, and that the political world is a field prepared by the Creator for the efforts of the intelligence. Contented with the freedom and the power which it enjoys in its own sphere, and with the place which it occupies, the empire of religion is never more surely established than when it reigns in the hearts of men unsupported by aught beside its native strength. Religion is no less the companion of liberty in all its battles and its triumphs; the cradle of its infancy, and the divine source of its claims. The safeguard of morality is religion, and morality is the best security of law and the surest pledge of freedom.

Reasons Of Certain Anomalies Which The Laws And Customs Of The Anglo-Americans Present

Remains of aristocratic institutions in the midst of a complete democracy—Why?—Distinction carefully to be drawn between what is of Puritanical and what is of English origin.

The reader is cautioned not to draw too general or too absolute an inference from what has been said. The social condition, the religion, and the manners of the first emigrants undoubtedly exercised an immense influence on the destiny of their new country. Nevertheless they were not in a situation to found a state of things solely dependent on themselves: no man can entirely shake off the influence of the past, and the settlers, intentionally or involuntarily, mingled habits and notions derived from their education and from the traditions of their country with those habits and notions which were exclusively their own. To form a judgment on the Anglo-Americans of the present day it is therefore necessary to distinguish what is of Puritanical and what is of English origin.

Laws and customs are frequently to be met with in the United States which contrast strongly with

一个世界消极且自愿服从，另一个世界则是鄙视经验蔑视权威的独立。

明显相互矛盾的两种倾向，非但没有斗争，它们共同携手向前，相互扶持。宗教认为公民自由是人才能的崇高实践，而政治世界是造物主为人类智慧活动开辟的一片天地。宗教满足于在其领域内所获得的自由和权力，满足于所获得的地位，并认识到只有依靠自己的原生力量而不是压制人心，它的帝国才能稳如泰山。宗教是自由的战友胜利的伙伴，是幼时的摇篮，还是权利的神圣源泉。宗教是道德的卫道士，而道德是法律的最佳保障，也是自由最持久的保证。

现在英裔美国人法律和习惯的某些特点产生的原因

完全民主制度中的贵族制度残余——其存在的原因何在？——仔细区分哪些来自清教派哪些来自英国人。

读者应该小心避免根据前面所述内容做出过于笼统和绝对的结论。早期移民的社会条件、宗教和风俗无疑会对他们新国家的命运产生重大影响。然而，新社会的建立并不仅仅依靠这些东西。没有人能够完全摆脱过去的影响，而且无论是有心还是无心，移民已经将来自祖国教育和传统的习惯及观念与其个人的习惯及观念混为一体。为了能够对今天英裔美国人做出评价，因此有必要对来自清教徒的东西和来自英国人的东西加以区分。

在美国，人们经常会看到法律和习俗往往与周边事物形成反差。一些法律的制定依据

all that surrounds them. These laws seem to be drawn up in a spirit contrary to the prevailing tenor of the American legislation; and these customs are no less opposed to the tone of society. If the English colonies had been founded in an age of darkness, or if their origin was already lost in the lapse of years, the problem would be insoluble.

I shall quote a single example to illustrate what I advance. The civil and criminal procedure of the Americans has only two means of action—committal and bail. The first measure taken by the magistrate is to exact security from the defendant, or, in case of refusal, to incarcerate him: the ground of the accusation and the importance of the charges against him are then discussed. It is evident that a legislation of this kind is hostile to the poor man, and favorable only to the rich. The poor man has not always a security to produce, even in a civil cause; and if he is obliged to wait for justice in prison, he is speedily reduced to distress. The wealthy individual, on the contrary, always escapes imprisonment in civil causes; nay, more, he may readily elude the punishment which awaits him for a delinquency by breaking his bail. So that all the penalties of the law are, for him, reducible to fines. Nothing can be more aristocratic than this system of legislation. Yet in America it is the poor who make the law, and they usually reserve the greatest social advantages to themselves. The explanation of the phenomenon is to be found in England; the laws of which I speak are English, and the Americans have retained them, however repugnant they may be to the tenor of their legislation and the mass of their ideas. Next to its habits, the thing which a nation is least apt to change is its civil legislation. Civil laws are only familiarly known to legal men, whose direct interest it is to maintain them as they are, whether good or bad, simply because they themselves are conversant with them. The body of the nation is scarcely acquainted with them; it merely perceives their action in particular cases; but it has some difficulty in seizing their tendency, and obeys them without premeditation. I have quoted one instance where it would have been easy to adduce a great number of others. The surface of American society is, if I may use the expression, covered with a layer of democracy, from beneath which the old aristocratic colors sometimes peep.

的好像是相悖于美国普遍立法宗旨的精神，而这些习俗也总是和社会氛围格格不入。如果英国殖民地的建立是在暗黑时代，又或者他们的起源随着岁月的流逝而无从考证，那么这个问题会无法解决。

我将引用一个例子来说明我的观点。美国的民事和刑事诉讼程序，对被告人只有两种处置办法——收监和保释。首先治安官要求被告缴纳保证金，如果遭到拒绝，就将其收监。然后对其被控事实和量刑进行讨论。显而易见，这样的立法对于穷人并不公平，只对富人有利。穷人总是拿不起保证金，甚至在民事案件中也是如此。如果他不得不在监狱中等待公正的到来，那么他很快就会因此而变得不幸。相反，有钱人在民事案件中总是躲过牢狱之苦，更有甚者，还会在保释期外逃，从而轻而易举地逃脱应有惩罚。因此，对于富人而言，法律上的惩罚不过是缴纳罚金罢了。这是最具贵族特征的立法体系。然而在美国法律是由穷人来制定，通常来说他们会考虑保留最大的社会利益。我们可以在英国找到针对这种现象的解释。因为我所说的法律本就是英国法律，尽管它和美国的立法主旨及美国人的普遍思想南辕北辙，而他们还是将其保留下来。对一个民族而言，最难改变的就是习惯，而民法则紧随其后。只有法律人士才熟知民法，也就是那些因为精通民法而能够通过维护法律获得直接利益的人，他们可以把法律解释成好法或是坏法。大部分国民并不谙于此道，仅能从个别案例中看到法律的作用，也无从抓住其倾向，只是盲目服从。这只是一个例子，我还可以轻松的举出许多其他的例子。美国社会，如果我可以这样说的话，包裹着一层民主的外衣，在其之下，旧贵族的色彩时不时地若隐若现。

Chapter III: Social Conditions Of The Anglo-Americans

Chapter Summary

A Social condition is commonly the result of circumstances, sometimes of laws, oftener still of these two causes united; but wherever it exists, it may justly be considered as the source of almost all the laws, the usages, and the ideas which regulate the conduct of nations; whatever it does not produce it modifies. It is therefore necessary, if we would become acquainted with the legislation and the manners of a nation, to begin by the study of its social condition.

The Striking Characteristic Of The Social Condition Of The Anglo-Americans In Its Essential Democracy.

The first emigrants of New England—Their equality—Aristocratic laws introduced in the South—Period of the Revolution—Change in the law of descent—Effects produced by this change—Democracy carried to its utmost limits in the new States of the West—Equality of education.

Many important observations suggest themselves upon the social condition of the Anglo-Americans, but there is one which takes precedence of all the rest. The social condition of the Americans is eminently democratic; this was its character at the foundation of the Colonies, and is still more strongly marked at the present day. I have stated in the preceding chapter that great equality

第三章　英裔美国人的社会情况

本章提要

一般而言，社会状况是环境的产物，有时候也是法律的产物，而大多数时候是这两者共同作用的结果。然而，只要它确立下来，便会成为几乎所有法律、惯例以及规范国民行为的重要因素，只要不源自于它，便要对其进行改变。因此，如果我们想要了解一个民族的立法和风俗，就要从研究其社会状况开始。

英裔美国人社会状况的最突出特点在于其民主的本质

新英格兰的第一批移民——他们之间的平等——南方推行的贵族法律——革命时期——继承法的改革——由此项改革引发的变化——西部新成立的各州将民主推向极致——教育平等。

针对英裔美国人的社会状况有许多不同的看法，但是其中有一种尤为重要。美国人最突出的社会状况就是民主化，而且这也是殖民地建立的基础，时至今日仍然尤为显著。在

existed among the emigrants who settled on the shores of New England. The germ of aristocracy was never planted in that part of the Union. The only influence which obtained there was that of intellect; the people were used to reverence certain names as the emblems of knowledge and virtue. Some of their fellow-citizens acquired a power over the rest which might truly have been called aristocratic, if it had been capable of transmission from father to son.

This was the state of things to the east of the Hudson: to the south-west of that river, and in the direction of the Floridas, the case was different. In most of the States situated to the south-west of the Hudson some great English proprietors had settled, who had imported with them aristocratic principles and the English law of descent. I have explained the reasons why it was impossible ever to establish a powerful aristocracy in America; these reasons existed with less force to the south-west of the Hudson. In the South, one man, aided by slaves, could cultivate a great extent of country: it was therefore common to see rich landed proprietors. But their influence was not altogether aristocratic as that term is understood in Europe, since they possessed no privileges; and the cultivation of their estates being carried on by slaves, they had no tenants depending on them, and consequently no patronage. Still, the great proprietors south of the Hudson constituted a superior class, having ideas and tastes of its own, and forming the centre of political action. This kind of aristocracy sympathized with the body of the people, whose passions and interests it easily embraced; but it was too weak and too short-lived to excite either love or hatred for itself. This was the class which headed the insurrection in the South, and furnished the best leaders of the American revolution.

At the period of which we are now speaking society was shaken to its centre: the people, in whose name the struggle had taken place, conceived the desire of exercising the authority which it had acquired; its democratic tendencies were awakened; and having thrown off the yoke of the mother-country, it aspired to independence of every kind. The influence of individuals gradually ceased to be felt, and custom and law united together to produce the same result.

But the law of descent was the last step to equality. I am surprised that ancient and modern jurists have not attributed to this law a greater influence on human affairs. It is true that these laws belong

前面的章节中我已经提到，在新英格兰海岸定居的移民享有很高程度的平等。贵族制度从未在合众国的这个地方生根发芽。能对这里产生影响的只有知识。人们习惯于对某几个姓氏表现出尊重，因为它们代表的是知识和美德。某些公民由于自己的声望而获得权力，如果这样的权力能够由父亲传给儿子，那么也能称得上贵族化。

赫德森河东岸就是这样的情况。从这条河的西南直到佛罗里达，情况就截然不同。定居在赫德森河西南大部分各州的有来自英国的大地主，他们将贵族制度及英国的继承法带到这里。我已经解释过在美国无法建立强有力的贵族制度的原因。这些原因对于赫德森河西南地区作用不大。在南方，人们利用奴隶可以耕作大片土地，因此可以见到很多富有的大地主。但是他们的影响不同于欧洲贵族的影响，因为他们没有特权，而且他们的土地也是奴隶进行耕种，没有依附于他们的佃户，当然也就不用给酬劳。不过，赫德森河以南的大地主们却依旧形成一个上层阶级，拥有自己的观点和品位，并形成当地政治活动的核心。这些贵族能够与人们大众产生共鸣，容易对群众的感情和利益表示认同，而且他们很脆弱生命力不强不足以激起人们对它的爱或恨。正是这样的一个阶级领导了南方的起义，为美国革命提供了最伟大的领袖。

在我们所谈论的这个时期，整个社会都处于大动荡之中。以人民名义进行的斗争，让人民产生了当家做主的想法，民主意识被唤醒，想要打破宗主国的束缚，渴望各种形式的独立。个人的影响力逐渐下降，习俗和法律共同作用起到同样的效果。

继承法是迈向平等的最后一步。令我感到惊讶的是，无论是古代还是现代的立法者都

to civil affairs; but they ought nevertheless to be placed at the head of all political institutions; for, whilst political laws are only the symbol of a nation's condition, they exercise an incredible influence upon its social state. They have, moreover, a sure and uniform manner of operating upon society, affecting, as it were, generations yet unborn.

Through their means man acquires a kind of preternatural power over the future lot of his fellow-creatures. When the legislator has regulated the law of inheritance, he may rest from his labor. The machine once put in motion will go on for ages, and advance, as if self-guided, towards a given point. When framed in a particular manner, this law unites, draws together, and vests property and power in a few hands: its tendency is clearly aristocratic. On opposite principles its action is still more rapid; it divides, distributes, and disperses both property and power. Alarmed by the rapidity of its progress, those who despair of arresting its motion endeavor to obstruct it by difficulties and impediments; they vainly seek to counteract its effect by contrary efforts; but it gradually reduces or destroys every obstacle, until by its incessant activity the bulwarks of the influence of wealth are ground down to the fine and shifting sand which is the basis of democracy. When the law of inheritance permits, still more when it decrees, the equal division of a father's property amongst all his children, its effects are of two kinds: it is important to distinguish them from each other, although they tend to the same end.

In virtue of the law of partible inheritance, the death of every proprietor brings about a kind of revolution in property; not only do his possessions change hands, but their very nature is altered, since they are parcelled into shares, which become smaller and smaller at each division. This is the direct and, as it were, the physical effect of the law. It follows, then, that in countries where equality of inheritance is established by law, property, and especially landed property, must have a tendency to perpetual diminution. The effects, however, of such legislation would only be perceptible after a lapse of time, if the law was abandoned to its own working; for supposing the family to consist of two children (and in a country people as France is the average number is not above three), these children, sharing amongst them the fortune of both parents, would not be poorer than their father or mother.

没有让继承法对人类事务产生重大影响。的确，这些法律属于民法范畴，但是却是所有政治制度的重中之重，因为，它会对社会产生难以估量的影响，而政治法律只是社会状况的表现。此外，继承法对社会的影响确定无疑始终如一，甚至会影响到尚未出生的子孙后代。

依靠继承法，人获得可以左右他人未来的神奇力量。当立法者将继承法订立完成，便可以高枕无忧。这项法律如同机器一般，在随后的数个世纪可自行运转，自我引导，朝着预定的目标前进。按照一定方式制定的这种法律，会将财产和权力聚集并集中到一些人的手中，其趋势必然是贵族化。如果按照相反的原则进行制定，它起作用的速度会变得更快，不过是对财产和权力进行分化、分裂和分割。因为对它的快速发展感到惊恐，无法抑制其前进的人们想方设法地给它制造困难和障碍。人们试图采用相反措施去抵消其作用，但却徒劳无功。它慢慢地将所有障碍的影响削弱摧毁，直到通过它的不断努力，财富影响力的堡垒被磨碎成细细的流沙，成为民主的积淀。当继承法允许并理由充分的判定父辈的财产在子女中平均分配的时候，会产生两种效果。尽管其目标一致，但是有必要对它们加以区分。

通过继承法的分割，每个财产所有人的死亡都会引发对其财产的一场革命。不但他的财产易手，而且财产的性质也会发生改变。通过每次分割，财产被划分成许多块，变得越来越小。这就是这项法律的直接影响，或者说有形影响。所以，在法律规定进行平均继承的国家，私人财产特别是地产，必定呈现不断缩小的趋势。可是，如果任这种法律自行发展，其作用需要一定的时间才能发挥出来。因为如果在一个育有两个子女的家庭（像法国

But the law of equal division exercises its influence not merely upon the property itself, but it affects the minds of the heirs, and brings their passions into play. These indirect consequences tend powerfully to the destruction of large fortunes, and especially of large domains. Among nations whose law of descent is founded upon the right of primogeniture landed estates often pass from generation to generation without undergoing division, the consequence of which is that family feeling is to a certain degree incorporated with the estate. The family represents the estate, the estate the family; whose name, together with its origin, its glory, its power, and its virtues, is thus perpetuated in an imperishable memorial of the past and a sure pledge of the future.

When the equal partition of property is established by law, the intimate connection is destroyed between family feeling and the preservation of the paternal estate; the property ceases to represent the family; for as it must inevitably be divided after one or two generations, it has evidently a constant tendency to diminish, and must in the end be completely dispersed. The sons of the great landed proprietor, if they are few in number, or if fortune befriends them, may indeed entertain the hope of being as wealthy as their father, but not that of possessing the same property as he did; the riches must necessarily be composed of elements different from his.

Now, from the moment that you divest the landowner of that interest in the preservation of his estate which he derives from association, from tradition, and from family pride, you may be certain that sooner or later he will dispose of it; for there is a strong pecuniary interest in favor of selling, as floating capital produces higher interest than real property, and is more readily available to gratify the passions of the moment.

Great landed estates which have once been divided never come together again; for the small proprietor draws from his land a better revenue, in proportion, than the large owner does from his, and of course he sells it at a higher rate. The calculations of gain, therefore, which decide the rich man to sell his domain will still more powerfully influence him against buying small estates to unite them into a large one.

What is called family pride is often founded upon an illusion of self-love. A man wishes to

平均每个家庭的子女不超过三个）中平分父母的遗产，孩子们独立生活以后并不会比他们的父母穷多少。

但是平分遗产法律的影响并不仅限于财产本身，还会影响到继承者们的思想，激发他们对于这项法律的热情。这些间接作用对大宗财产特别是地产，产生巨大的破坏力。而在继承法以长子继承权为基础的国家，地产往往不会遭到分割，代代相传。这样就会在一定程度上将家族声望与地产整合起来，家族代表地产，地产代表家族。因此，家族的姓氏与起源，以及荣誉、权力和美德依靠土地永久的流传下去，成为过去不朽的纪念，未来可靠的保障。

而当遗产继承法以平均分配为原则，家族声望与土地完整性之间的紧密联系遭到破坏。土地不再代表家族，因为一两代人之后它一定会被分割，而且显然会越分越小，最终会变得分无可分。如果大地主的子孙人数很少，或是运气好有希望像其父辈一样富有，但是也并非完全拥有其父辈财产。这些富人除了继承来的财产之外，一定还有其他财产。

现在，如果地主因拥有土地而得到的情感记忆、传统以及家族荣誉的好处被剥夺，可以断定，他们迟早会把土地处理掉。因为卖掉土地会给他们带来巨大的金钱上的利益，而与不动产相比流动资本会带来更高的利润，还能更大程度的满足他们现实的欲望。

大地产一旦被分割，便不会再聚合起来，因为从比例上来讲，小的地主会从其土地上获得比大地主更丰厚的回报，当然其土地售价也会更高。因此，通过计算收益，已将土地售出的富人必定不会以高价购买小块地产来恢复大地产。

perpetuate and immortalize himself, as it were, in his great-grandchildren. Where the esprit de famille ceases to act individual selfishness comes into play. When the idea of family becomes vague, indeterminate, and uncertain, a man thinks of his present convenience; he provides for the establishment of his succeeding generation, and no more. Either a man gives up the idea of perpetuating his family, or at any rate he seeks to accomplish it by other means than that of a landed estate. Thus not only does the law of partible inheritance render it difficult for families to preserve their ancestral domains entire, but it deprives them of the inclination to attempt it, and compels them in some measure to co-operate with the law in their own extinction.

The law of equal distribution proceeds by two methods: by acting upon things, it acts upon persons; by influencing persons, it affects things. By these means the law succeeds in striking at the root of landed property, and dispersing rapidly both families and fortunes.

Most certainly it is not for us Frenchmen of the nineteenth century, who daily witness the political and social changes which the law of partition is bringing to pass, to question its influence. It is perpetually conspicuous in our country, overthrowing the walls of our dwellings and removing the landmarks of our fields. But although it has produced great effects in France, much still remains for it to do. Our recollections, opinions, and habits present powerful obstacles to its progress.

In the United States it has nearly completed its work of destruction, and there we can best study its results. The English laws concerning the transmission of property were abolished in almost all the States at the time of the Revolution. The law of entail was so modified as not to interrupt the free circulation of property. The first generation having passed away, estates began to be parcelled out, and the change became more and more rapid with the progress of time. At this moment, after a lapse of a little more than sixty years, the aspect of society is totally altered; the families of the great landed proprietors are almost all commingled with the general mass. In the State of New York, which formerly contained many of these, there are but two who still keep their heads above the stream, and they must shortly disappear. The sons of these opulent citizens are become merchants, lawyers, or physicians. Most of them have lapsed into obscurity. The last trace of hereditary ranks

　　所谓的家族荣誉通常建立在利己主义的错觉之上。人都希望流传千古，永远被子孙怀念。凡是在家族荣誉不再起作用的地方，个人私心就开始登上舞台。当家族荣誉变得模糊、含混以及变化无常，人们便会只追求当下的享乐，一心想把自己这一生过好，不再去考虑其他。人们会放弃让家族流芳百世的想法，或无论如何不是通过不动产而是其他方式来实现这一目标。因此，平分继承法不但会让完整保留祖先土地变得困难重重，而且还剥夺了人们尝试这样做的愿望，并迫使他们采取某种方式配合法律消灭自己。

　　平分遗产的法律采用两种方式执行：一个是由物及人，另一个是由人及物。通过这些方法，法律成功地打击了土地所有制的根基，并迅速地将家族和财富分散。

　　可以肯定，19世纪的法国人，尽管他们每天都在见证继承法给政治和法律带来的变化，却仍然质疑它的效力。这个法律在我们的国土上特别引人注目，它让人们推倒自家的宅院，拆掉自家土地的围栏。但是尽管它在法国产生巨大的效果，但仍然有很多工作有待处理。我们的回忆、观念和习惯给它的推进带来极大的阻碍。

　　在美国，继承法几乎已经完成了它的破坏工作，而正是在这里，我们能对其结果进行最充分的研究。在独立战争时期，几乎美国各州都废除了有关财产继承的英国法律。限嗣继承法经过改变已经无法阻碍财产的自由流通。第一代人去世后，地产开始遭到分割，而且随着时间的流逝这一进程不断加速。如今，只过了60年多一点，社会面貌便发生了翻天覆地的改变。拥有大片土地家族的后人们几乎与普通大众无异。在原本大地主数量最多的纽约州，如今只有两个家族能在这样的洪流中垂死挣扎，而且不久他们必将消失。这些有

and distinctions is destroyed—the law of partition has reduced all to one level.

I do not mean that there is any deficiency of wealthy individuals in the United States; I know of no country, indeed, where the love of money has taken stronger hold on the affections of men, and where the profounder contempt is expressed for the theory of the permanent equality of property. But wealth circulates with inconceivable rapidity, and experience shows that it is rare to find two succeeding generations in the full enjoyment of it.

This picture, which may perhaps be thought to be overcharged, still gives a very imperfect idea of what is taking place in the new States of the West and South-west. At the end of the last century a few bold adventurers began to penetrate into the valleys of the Mississippi, and the mass of the population very soon began to move in that direction: communities unheard of till then were seen to emerge from the wilds: States whose names were not in existence a few years before claimed their place in the American Union; and in the Western settlements we may behold democracy arrived at its utmost extreme. In these States, founded off-hand, and, as it were, by chance, the inhabitants are but of yesterday. Scarcely known to one another, the nearest neighbors are ignorant of each other's history. In this part of the American continent, therefore, the population has not experienced the influence of great names and great wealth, nor even that of the natural aristocracy of knowledge and virtue. None are there to wield that respectable power which men willingly grant to the remembrance of a life spent in doing good before their eyes. The new States of the West are already inhabited, but society has no existence among them.

It is not only the fortunes of men which are equal in America; even their requirements partake in some degree of the same uniformity. I do not believe that there is a country in the world where, in proportion to the population, there are so few uninstructed and at the same time so few learned individuals. Primary instruction is within the reach of everybody; superior instruction is scarcely to be obtained by any. This is not surprising; it is in fact the necessary consequence of what we have advanced above. Almost all the Americans are in easy circumstances, and can therefore obtain the first elements of human knowledge.

钱人的子孙如今变成商人、律师或医生，而且大部分已默默无闻。最后世袭等级和世袭特权的最后一丝残留已经消失，平分继承法让一切变得平均。

这并不是说美国的有钱人比其他地方少。据我所知，还没有哪个国家的人比美国人更视财如命，对永久的财产平等更不屑一顾。但是在这里，财富流通的速度快得惊人，而且根据经验，几乎没有持续两代的富人。

这幅承载过多的图画，依旧不足以呈现出西部及西南部新建各州正在发生的事情。在上个世纪末，一些大胆的冒险家开始深入密西西比河流域，不久之后大量的人口开始涌入，一些从未听说过的乡镇开始出现在这片荒天野地。一些连名字都没有的州，出现不久后便要求加入美联邦，而且，在西部，我们可以看到民主被推向极致。在这些随性建立起来的州里，居民不过是昨天才踏上这片土地。人们彼此之间刚刚认识，距离最近的邻居对彼此的家史也一无所知。因此，在美洲大陆的这个地方，人们没有受到家族声誉和财富的影响，甚至也没有受到因知识和德行而被奉为贵族人们的影响。在这里，没有人被授予受人尊敬的权力，以纪念他毕生在人前做的好事。美国西部新兴各州虽然已经建立起来，但是还没有形成社会。

在美国，人们不仅在财富上平等，甚至在学识上也达成某种程度的平等。从人口比例上看，我不认为世界上任何一个国家会像美国一样，未受教育的人数如此之少，同时学识渊博人数又如此不多。每个人都受过初等教育，却几乎没什么人受过高等教育。这并不奇怪，事实上这是我们前面所述内容的必然结果。几乎所有的美国人都生活得舒适安逸，所

In America there are comparatively few who are rich enough to live without a profession. Every profession requires an apprenticeship, which limits the time of instruction to the early years of life. At fifteen they enter upon their calling, and thus their education ends at the age when ours begins. Whatever is done afterwards is with a view to some special and lucrative object; a science is taken up as a matter of business, and the only branch of it which is attended to is such as admits of an immediate practical application. In America most of the rich men were formerly poor; most of those who now enjoy leisure were absorbed in business during their youth; the consequence of which is, that when they might have had a taste for study they had no time for it, and when time is at their disposal they have no longer the inclination.

There is no class, then, in America, in which the taste for intellectual pleasures is transmitted with hereditary fortune and leisure, and by which the labors of the intellect are held in honor. Accordingly there is an equal want of the desire and the power of application to these objects.

A middle standard is fixed in America for human knowledge. All approach as near to it as they can; some as they rise, others as they descend. Of course, an immense multitude of persons are to be found who entertain the same number of ideas on religion, history, science, political economy, legislation, and government. The gifts of intellect proceed directly from God, and man cannot prevent their unequal distribution. But in consequence of the state of things which we have here represented it happens that, although the capacities of men are widely different, as the Creator has doubtless intended they should be, they are submitted to the same method of treatment.

In America the aristocratic element has always been feeble from its birth; and if at the present day it is not actually destroyed, it is at any rate so completely disabled that we can scarcely assign to it any degree of influence in the course of affairs. The democratic principle, on the contrary, has gained so much strength by time, by events, and by legislation, as to have become not only predominant but all-powerful. There is no family or corporate authority, and it is rare to find even the influence of individual character enjoy any durability.

America, then, exhibits in her social state a most extraordinary phenomenon. Men are there

以获得最起码的教育不成问题。

在美国，富人很少，几乎每个人都需要一个职业。每个职业都要经过学徒期，这就使得年轻时接受教育的时间受到限制。从十五岁他们开始加入一个行业，所以他们的学校教育在法国教育开始的时候戛然而止。此后无论他们做什么一定出于某种特殊和赚钱的目的。他们把科学当作一门生意，重视的是立竿见影的效益。在这里，大多数的有钱人以前都很穷，大多数生活悠闲的人，年轻的时候都很忙。于是就会产生这样的结果，当他们想要学习的时候没有时间，而当时间充裕的时候又没了学习的意愿。

所以，在美国，并不存在这样的阶层，使对知识的爱好能随着财富和悠闲的传承而得到传承，并以脑力劳动为荣。于是，美国人既没有专心从事脑力劳动的意愿，也没有专心从事脑力劳动的意志。

在美国，人们的知识普遍处于中等水平。所有人都在这个水平上下，有些人高一点，有些人低一点。当然，绝大多数人在宗教、历史、科学、政治经济、立法及政府方面都有着大致相同的观点。智力天赋直接来自上帝的恩赐，人们对此毫无办法。但是，我刚才所说的一切，并不妨碍做出这样的结论：尽管人们的智力不同，而这正是造物主的意图，但是他们受到的待遇相同。

从美国诞生之初，贵族因素便岌岌可危，而今天，即使它没有被完全摧毁，至少已经完全变成废物，无法对事物的进程产生任何影响。相反，民主原则随着时间、事件和立法变得越来越强大，不仅具有支配地位而且无所不能。这里没有权威的家庭或团体，甚至没

seen on a greater equality in point of fortune and intellect, or, in other words, more equal in their strength, than in any other country of the world, or in any age of which history has preserved the remembrance.

Political Consequences Of The Social Condition Of The Anglo-Americans

The political consequences of such a social condition as this are easily deducible. It is impossible to believe that equality will not eventually find its way into the political world as it does everywhere else. To conceive of men remaining forever unequal upon one single point, yet equal on all others, is impossible; they must come in the end to be equal upon all. Now I know of only two methods of establishing equality in the political world; every citizen must be put in possession of his rights, or rights must be granted to no one. For nations which are arrived at the same stage of social existence as the Anglo-Americans, it is therefore very difficult to discover a medium between the sovereignty of all and the absolute power of one man: and it would be vain to deny that the social condition which I have been describing is equally liable to each of these consequences.

There is, in fact, a manly and lawful passion for equality which excites men to wish all to be powerful and honored. This passion tends to elevate the humble to the rank of the great; but there exists also in the human heart a depraved taste for equality, which impels the weak to attempt to lower the powerful to their own level, and reduces men to prefer equality in slavery to inequality with freedom. Not that those nations whose social condition is democratic naturally despise liberty; on the contrary, they have an instinctive love of it. But liberty is not the chief and constant object of their desires; equality is their idol: they make rapid and sudden efforts to obtain liberty, and if they miss their aim resign themselves to their disappointment; but nothing can satisfy them except equality, and rather than lose it they resolve to perish.

On the other hand, in a State where the citizens are nearly on an equality, it becomes difficult for them to preserve their independence against the aggressions of power. No one among them being strong enough to engage in the struggle with advantage, nothing but a general combination can

有任何人拥有持久的影响力。

所以，美国的社会状况呈现出非常独特的现象。与世界上任何国家，或是历史上记录下的任何时代相比，这里的人们在财富和学识上更加平等，或者说是力量上更加平等。

英裔美国人社会状况的政治后果

这样一种社会状况的政治后果不难推断。不能认为平等最终在政治世界无法像它在其他领域那样发挥作用。认为人们在各方面取得平等后，还能永远接受在某一方面的不平等，这根本毫无可能，他们最后一定会要求全部的平等。据我所知，只有两种方法能够实现政治世界的平等，不是让每个公民都享有权利，就是不给予他们任何权利。对于社会状况已经到达英裔美国人这样程度的国家而言，很难在人人有权和个人专权之间找到折中的办法。而且，无法否认的是对于我已经谈到的社会状况，这两种后果产生的可能性一样大。

实际上，有一种对平等豪迈合法的热情鼓舞人们希望每个人都能变得强大并受到尊重。这种热情希望小人物能加入伟人的行列。但是在人们的心中还有一种对于平等的变态爱好，驱使弱者想要把强者拉到与他们同样的水平，宁可退化到奴隶制的平等，也不要自由的不平等。这并不意味着民主社会国家天生鄙视自由，相反，他们对自由有着本能的热爱。但是自由并非他们主要的一成不变的渴望，平等才是他们崇拜的对象。他们朝自由快速猛冲，而如果没能达到目的便心灰意冷。但是，除了平等，什么也不会令他们满足，他们宁死也不愿意失去平等。

protect their liberty. And such a union is not always to be found.

From the same social position, then, nations may derive one or the other of two great political results; these results are extremely different from each other, but they may both proceed from the same cause.

The Anglo-Americans are the first nations who, having been exposed to this formidable alternative, have been happy enough to escape the dominion of absolute power. They have been allowed by their circumstances, their origin, their intelligence, and especially by their moral feeling, to establish and maintain the sovereignty of the people.

但从另一方面来说，如果一个国家所有的公民几乎完全平等，人们很难在权力全面入侵的时候保持独立。因为他们当中没有人足够强大与它对抗，只有团结起来才能捍卫他们的自由。而这样的团结并非总是存在。

因此，不同的民族，在同样的社会状况下，会得到两种不同的政治后果。这两种后果截然不同，但又系出同门。

英裔美国人是面对这种艰难抉择的民族中，第一个幸运地避开专制政权统治的民族。他们的环境、起源、智慧而且特别是民情，使得人民主权得以建立和保持下来。

Chapter IV: The Principle Of The Sovereignty Of The People In America

Chapter Summary

It predominates over the whole of society in America—Application made of this principle by the Americans even before their Revolution—Development given to it by that Revolution—Gradual and irresistible extension of the elective qualification.

The Principle Of The Sovereignty Of The People In America

Whenever the political laws of the United States are to be discussed, it is with the doctrine of the sovereignty of the people that we must begin. The principle of the sovereignty of the people, which is to be found, more or less, at the bottom of almost all human institutions, generally remains concealed from view. It is obeyed without being recognized, or if for a moment it be brought to light, it is hastily cast back into the gloom of the sanctuary. "The will of the nation" is one of those expressions which have been most profusely abused by the wily and the despotic of every age. To the eyes of some it has been represented by the venal suffrages of a few of the satellites of power; to others by the votes of a timid or an interested minority; and some have even discovered it in the silence of a people, on the supposition that the fact of submission established the right of command.

In America the principle of the sovereignty of the people is not either barren or concealed, as it

第四章　美国人民主权的原则

本章提要

人民主权原则主宰整个美国社会——美国人早在革命之前便已开始应用这种原则——革命使人民主权原则得到发展——选举资格逐步不可抑制地扩大。

美国人民主权的原则

无论何时，只要谈到美国政治法律，一定会从人民主权原则开始。人们发现，在几乎所有人类制度的深处或多或少都有人民主权原则的存在，只是它往往隐藏起来。人们服从它，又不认可它，只要它出现在光天化日，人们便匆忙把它塞回到圣殿的阴暗角落。"民族的意志"是被每个时代狡猾的暴君滥用的最多的字眼之一。一些人在大人物贿选活动中听到过它，另一些人则在胆小又有兴趣的少数人投票的时候听到过它，还有一些人把人民的沉默看作对它的认可，认为服从的事实就是对他们发号施令权利的默认。

在美国，人民主权原则并没有像在其他国家那样空洞或是隐蔽，它得到习俗的认可，

is with some other nations; it is recognized by the customs and proclaimed by the laws; it spreads freely, and arrives without impediment at its most remote consequences. If there be a country in the world where the doctrine of the sovereignty of the people can be fairly appreciated, where it can be studied in its application to the affairs of society, and where its dangers and its advantages may be foreseen, that country is assuredly America.

I have already observed that, from their origin, the sovereignty of the people was the fundamental principle of the greater number of British colonies in America. It was far, however, from then exercising as much influence on the government of society as it now does. Two obstacles, the one external, the other internal, checked its invasive progress. It could not ostensibly disclose itself in the laws of colonies which were still constrained to obey the mother-country: it was therefore obliged to spread secretly, and to gain ground in the provincial assemblies, and especially in the townships.

American society was not yet prepared to adopt it with all its consequences. The intelligence of New England, and the wealth of the country to the south of the Hudson (as I have shown in the preceding chapter), long exercised a sort of aristocratic influence, which tended to retain the exercise of social authority in the hands of a few. The public functionaries were not universally elected, and the citizens were not all of them electors. The electoral franchise was everywhere placed within certain limits, and made dependent on a certain qualification, which was exceedingly low in the North and more considerable in the South.

The American revolution broke out, and the doctrine of the sovereignty of the people, which had been nurtured in the townships and municipalities, took possession of the State: every class was enlisted in its cause; battles were fought, and victories obtained for it, until it became the law of laws.

A no less rapid change was effected in the interior of society, where the law of descent completed the abolition of local influences.

At the very time when this consequence of the laws and of the revolution was apparent to every eye, victory was irrevocably pronounced in favor of the democratic cause. All power was, in fact, in

进行法律宣告，它可以自由传播，毫无阻碍地实现最终目的。如果世界上有一个国家，在那里人民主权的原则可以得到公正的评价，可以对人民主权原则在社会事务方面的应用加以研究，而且能够预见它的危险和优势，这个国家一定是美国。

我已经注意到，从一开始，人民主权就是美国绝大多数英属殖民地的基本原则。可是，那时人民主权对社会制度的影响远远不及现在。有两个障碍，一个来自外部，一个来自内部，阻碍了它的快速发展。当时人民主权之所以未能公然写入法律，是因为殖民地要服从宗主国。所以，只能在各地人民大会上特别是乡镇政府中，秘密普及。

当时，美国社会还没有准备好接受人民主权所带来的一切后果。新英格兰地区的文化知识，以及赫德森河以南地区的财富（正如我前面章节中提到的），使得一种贵族影响长期存在，这使得社会权力落入少数人手中。公职人员并非都经选举产生，而选举人也并非全体公民。选举权在各处受到限制，而且必须具备一定条件。对于选举资格的要求在北方过低而在南方又太高。

美国革命爆发以后，曾经在乡镇养精蓄锐的人民主权制度，开始占领各州。每个阶级都被卷入其中，人们为它而战，又靠着它取得胜利，最终人民主权成为法中之法。

在社会内部，改变同样迅速地发生，继承法粉碎了地方势力。

正当大家清楚地看到法律和革命结果的时候，民主庄严宣告了彻底的胜利。实际上，所有的权力都已经落入民主的手中，抵抗已毫无意义。上层阶级乖乖投降等待从今往后不可避免的悲惨境遇。失去权势的命运在等待着他们，因为其成员都只顾自己的私利。因为

its hands, and resistance was no longer possible. The higher orders submitted without a murmur and without a struggle to an evil which was thenceforth inevitable. The ordinary fate of falling powers awaited them; each of their several members followed his own interests; and as it was impossible to wring the power from the hands of a people which they did not detest sufficiently to brave, their only aim was to secure its good-will at any price. The most democratic laws were consequently voted by the very men whose interests they impaired; and thus, although the higher classes did not excite the passions of the people against their order, they accelerated the triumph of the new state of things; so that by a singular change the democratic impulse was found to be most irresistible in the very States where the aristocracy had the firmest hold. The State of Maryland, which had been founded by men of rank, was the first to proclaim universal suffrage, and to introduce the most democratic forms into the conduct of its government.

When a nation modifies the elective qualification, it may easily be foreseen that sooner or later that qualification will be entirely abolished. There is no more invariable rule in the history of society: the further electoral rights are extended, the greater is the need of extending them; for after each concession the strength of the democracy increases, and its demands increase with its strength. The ambition of those who are below the appointed rate is irritated in exact proportion to the great number of those who are above it. The exception at last becomes the rule, concession follows concession, and no stop can be made short of universal suffrage.

At the present day the principle of the sovereignty of the people has acquired, in the United States, all the practical development which the imagination can conceive. It is unencumbered by those fictions which have been thrown over it in other countries, and it appears in every possible form according to the exigency of the occasion. Sometimes the laws are made by the people in a body, as at Athens; and sometimes its representatives, chosen by universal suffrage, transact business in its name, and almost under its immediate control.

In some countries a power exists which, though it is in a degree foreign to the social body, directs it, and forces it to pursue a certain track. In others the ruling force is divided, being partly within and partly without the ranks of the people. But nothing of the kind is to be seen in the United States; there

无法从人民手中夺回权力，也不敢冒天下之大不韪，他们只能不惜一切代价讨好人民。最民主的法律正是那些利益受到损害的人们投票通过的。因此，上层阶级非但没有成为人民的众矢之的，反而加速了新秩序的胜利。事情真是瞬息万变，曾经贵族因素最为根深蒂固的州一跃成为民主发展最不可遏制的州。曾经由大地主们建立起来的马里兰州，第一个宣布普选，第一个成为采用最民主形式进行政府管理。

当一个国家对选举资格进行改变，便可预见迟早那样的资格会被完全废除。在社会历史上没有一成不变的制度：选举权越是扩大，就越需要扩大。因为在每次妥协之后，民主的力量就得到壮大，它的要求随着力量的壮大而不断增加。没有选举资格的努力争取选举资格，其劲头和已取得选举资格的人数成正比。最后，例外成为规定，妥协接二连三，直到实行普选为止。

现在，人民主权原则在美国已经取得所能想到的一切实际进展。它没有像在其他国家那样被谎言架空，并根据情况的需要以各种不同的形式出现。有时好像在雅典一样，全体人民共同制定法律，有时又由普选的代表以它的名义并在人民几乎直接监督下处理工作。

在某些国家，一股来自社会之外的力量对社会进行管理，并迫使它朝着特定的轨迹前进。在其他的一些国家，统治力量被分化，部分属于人民而部分不属于人民。但是没有任何一种与我们在美国看到的一样，在这里，社会自我管理。所有的权力都属于社会，没有

society governs itself for itself. All power centres in its bosom; and scarcely an individual is to be meet with who would venture to conceive, or, still less, to express, the idea of seeking it elsewhere. The nation participates in the making of its laws by the choice of its legislators, and in the execution of them by the choice of the agents of the executive government; it may almost be said to govern itself, so feeble and so restricted is the share left to the administration, so little do the authorities forget their popular origin and the power from which they emanate.

人胆敢去想到处谋求权力，更别提说了。人民通过选择立法人员参与法律制定，通过选择政府行政人员参与执政。几乎可以说人民在进行自我管理，而留给政府的权力脆弱而且非常有限，而且政府还要受到人民的监督，并服从建立政府的人民的权力。

Chapter V: Necessity Of Examining The Condition Of The States

Necessity Of Examining The Condition Of The States Before That Of The Union At Large

It is proposed to examine in the following chapter what is the form of government established in America on the principle of the sovereignty of the people; what are its resources, its hindrances, its advantages, and its dangers. The first difficulty which presents itself arises from the complex nature of the constitution of the United States, which consists of two distinct social structures, connected and, as it were, encased one within the other; two governments, completely separate and almost independent, the one fulfilling the ordinary duties and responding to the daily and indefinite calls of a community, the other circumscribed within certain limits, and only exercising an exceptional authority over the general interests of the country. In short, there are twenty-four small sovereign nations, whose agglomeration constitutes the body of the Union. To examine the Union before we have studied the States would be to adopt a method filled with obstacles. The form of the Federal Government of the United States was the last which was adopted; and it is in fact nothing more than a modification or a summary of those republican principles which were current in the whole community before it existed, and independently of its existence. Moreover, the Federal Government is, as I have just observed, the exception; the Government of the States is the rule. The author who should attempt to exhibit the picture as a whole before he had explained its details would necessarily fall into obscurity and repetition.

第五章　研究各州过去的必要性

在叙述联邦政府之前，研究各州过去的必要性

在这一章节中，将对建立在人民主权原则之上的美国政府的形式、行动手段、障碍、优势及危险加以研究。美国纷繁复杂的宪法是摆在面前的第一个难题。美国社会有两个截然不同的社会结构，它们彼此相连嵌入对方。美国还有两个政府，彼此毫不相干，几乎完全独立。一个政府负责处理社会的日常需要，另一个政府只管辖有关国家利益的重大问题。简而言之，美国有24个小的主权国家，它们构成联邦的主体。如果没有对各州进行研究，便开始对联邦进行考察，一定会困难重重。美国联邦政府的形式是最后形成的，事实上，它不过是共和原则的优化总结，而这些原则早在它存在之前就已经在各地通行，并不依它的存在而存在。而且，正如我刚刚所说，联邦政府是特例，而州政府才是常态。想要在说明细节前展示这幅画作全景的作者，必然有些地方说不清和不断重复。

今天统治美国社会的伟大政治原则无疑都是在各州产生和发展起来的。因此为了能够掌握解决所有其他问题的关键，有必要先对它们进行了解。就制度的外在形式而言，组成

The great political principles which govern American society at this day undoubtedly took their origin and their growth in the State. It is therefore necessary to become acquainted with the State in order to possess a clue to the remainder. The States which at present compose the American Union all present the same features, as far as regards the external aspect of their institutions. Their political or administrative existence is centred in three focuses of action, which may not inaptly be compared to the different nervous centres which convey motion to the human body. The township is the lowest in order, then the county, and lastly the State; and I propose to devote the following chapter to the examination of these three divisions.

The American System Of Townships And Municipal Bodies

Why the Author begins the examination of the political institutions with the township—Its existence in all nations—Difficulty of establishing and preserving municipal independence—Its importance—Why the Author has selected the township system of New England as the main topic of his discussion.

It is not undesignedly that I begin this subject with the Township. The village or township is the only association which is so perfectly natural that wherever a number of men are collected it seems to constitute itself.

The town, or tithing, as the smallest division of a community, must necessarily exist in all nations, whatever their laws and customs may be: if man makes monarchies and establishes republics, the first association of mankind seems constituted by the hand of God. But although the existence of the township is coeval with that of man, its liberties are not the less rarely respected and easily destroyed. A nation is always able to establish great political assemblies, because it habitually contains a certain number of individuals fitted by their talents, if not by their habits, for the direction of affairs. The township is, on the contrary, composed of coarser materials, which are less easily fashioned by the legislator. The difficulties which attend the consolidation of its independence rather augment than diminish with the increasing enlightenment of the people. A highly civilized community spurns

美联邦的各州都呈现出相同的特点。它们的政治和行政管理活动中心集中在三个地方，就好比指挥人体行动的神经中枢一样。按照由低到高的顺序来说依次是：乡镇、县和州。下面我要对它们进行分别研究。

美国乡镇组织

作者为何要从乡镇开始考察政治制度——乡镇存在于所有国家——实现和保持乡镇独立的困难——实现和保持乡镇独立的重要性——作者选择新英格兰乡镇作为讨论对象的原因。

从乡镇开始考察并非随意之举。乡镇是自然界只要有一定数量的人聚集便可自然形成的唯一联合体。

因此，任何国家无论其法律风俗如何，必然会有乡镇的存在。如果建立君主政体和共和政体的是人，那么人类最初的联合体乡镇似乎出自上帝之手。尽管乡镇自人类存在之初便已存在，但其自由则鲜获尊重，而且常常被毁。一个国家经常可以举行盛大的政治集会，一般而言因为它拥有相当数量的文化水平发展到可以在一定程度上处理公务的人民。相反，乡镇则是一群粗人组成，不大容易听从立法者的教化。随着民智的开化，巩固乡镇独立的难度非但没有缩小反而增大。一个高度文明的社会，对于地方独立的尝试不屑一顾，厌弃乡镇离经叛道的做法，而且在其尝试完成前就已经认定他们毫无成功的希望。而且，一般来说，乡镇自由也最难于避免国家政权的侵犯。他们无法赤手空拳与孔

the attempts of a local independence, is disgusted at its numerous blunders, and is apt to despair of success before the experiment is completed. Again, no immunities are so ill protected from the encroachments of the supreme power as those of municipal bodies in general: they are unable to struggle, single-handed, against a strong or an enterprising government, and they cannot defend their cause with success unless it be identified with the customs of the nation and supported by public opinion. Thus until the independence of townships is amalgamated with the manners of a people it is easily destroyed, and it is only after a long existence in the laws that it can be thus amalgamated. Municipal freedom is not the fruit of human device; it is rarely created; but it is, as it were, secretly and spontaneously engendered in the midst of a semi-barbarous state of society. The constant action of the laws and the national habits, peculiar circumstances, and above all time, may consolidate it; but there is certainly no nation on the continent of Europe which has experienced its advantages. Nevertheless local assemblies of citizens constitute the strength of free nations. Town-meetings are to liberty what primary schools are to science; they bring it within the people's reach, they teach men how to use and how to enjoy it. A nation may establish a system of free government, but without the spirit of municipal institutions it cannot have the spirit of liberty. The transient passions and the interests of an hour, or the chance of circumstances, may have created the external forms of independence; but the despotic tendency which has been repelled will, sooner or later, inevitably reappear on the surface.

In order to explain to the reader the general principles on which the political organization of the counties and townships of the United States rests, I have thought it expedient to choose one of the States of New England as an example, to examine the mechanism of its constitution, and then to cast a general glance over the country. The township and the county are not organized in the same manner in every part of the Union; it is, however, easy to perceive that the same principles have guided the formation of both of them throughout the Union. I am inclined to believe that these principles have been carried further in New England than elsewhere, and consequently that they offer greater facilities to the observations of a stranger. The institutions of New England form a complete and regular whole; they have received the sanction of time, they have the support of the laws, and the still stronger support of the manners of the community, over which they exercise the most prodigious

武有力的中央政府斗争，而且如果他们的事业不符合国家风俗得不到舆论的支持根本无法确保成功。因此，在乡镇独立成为民情风尚之前，很容易就会被摧毁，只有在长期写入法律之后，才能成为风俗的一部分。所以说乡镇自由并非人为所能创造，而是悄悄自发地在半野蛮社会产生，而在法律的不断作用以及民族习惯，特定的环境因素，尤其是时间的共同影响下，得到日益地巩固。然而在欧洲大陆，并没有哪个国家曾经体验过它的好处。乡镇国民大会是自由人民的力量源泉。乡镇大会之于自由，就好像小学之于科学。它们把自由带给人民，教会人们如何使用、享受自由。一个国家也许可以建立一个自由的政府，但是如果没有乡镇机构就不会拥有自由精神。瞬间的激情和暂时的利益或是偶然的机遇也许可以创造出独立的外表，但是潜伏在社会体制内部的专制倾向迟早会浮出表面。

为了能向读者说明美国乡镇和县得以建立的一般原则，我认为最好选择新英格兰州为例，来说明其体制，然后再对其余各州进行总览。尽管合众国各州乡镇和县建立的方式并不一致，但是人们很容易发现，在整个合众国，是相同的原则在发挥着作用。我倾向于认为这些原则在新英格兰比其他地方推行得更深入，也就给人们提供了更便利的观察条件。新英格兰的乡镇组织是一个完整有序的整体，经历了时间的洗礼，得到了法律的扶持，以及更强有力的民情支持，靠着这些它对社会产生了最为巨大的影响，最终引起我们的注意。

influence; they consequently deserve our attention on every account.

Limits Of The Township

The township of New England is a division which stands between the commune and the canton of France, and which corresponds in general to the English tithing, or town. Its average population is from two to three thousand; so that, on the one hand, the interests of its inhabitants are not likely to conflict, and, on the other, men capable of conducting its affairs are always to be found among its citizens.

Authorities Of The Township In New England

The people the source of all power here as elsewhere—Manages its own affairs—No corporation—The greater part of the authority vested in the hands of the Selectmen—How the Selectmen act—Town-meeting—Enumeration of the public officers of the township—Obligatory and remunerated functions.

In the township, as well as everywhere else, the people is the only source of power; but in no stage of government does the body of citizens exercise a more immediate influence. In America the people is a master whose exigencies demand obedience to the utmost limits of possibility.

In New England the majority acts by representatives in the conduct of the public business of the State; but if such an arrangement be necessary in general affairs, in the townships, where the legislative and administrative action of the government is in more immediate contact with the subject, the system of representation is not adopted. There is no corporation; but the body of electors, after having designated its magistrates, directs them in everything that exceeds the simple and ordinary executive business of the State.

This state of things is so contrary to our ideas, and so different from our customs, that it is necessary for me to adduce some examples to explain it thoroughly.

The public duties in the township are extremely numerous and minutely divided, as we shall see further on; but the larger proportion of administrative power is vested in the hands of a small

乡镇的规模

新英格兰的乡镇介于法国的乡和区之间，大体上和英国的镇相同，人口数量一般是两三千。所以，一方面，居民们的利益不大容易发生矛盾，另一方面，居民的人数足以能够从中选出有能力处理政务的管理人员。

新英格兰的乡镇政权

与其他地方一样，人民是乡镇一切权力的源泉——乡镇自行处理自己的事务——没有乡镇议会——乡镇大权主要掌握在行政委员手中——行政委员如何工作——乡镇居民大会——乡镇官员名称列举——义务官职和带薪官职。

无论是乡镇还是其他行政区，人民是权力的唯一源泉，但是公民对任何行政区的影响都没有这里来的直接。在美国，人民是各级政府需要极力讨好的主人。

在新英格兰，大多数人通过代表参与州公共事务。在乡镇，立法和行政活动在被统治者面前完成，所以没有采用代议制。没有乡镇议会，行政官员上任后接受选举团的全面领导，其执行之简便，远超州行政事务的处理。

这种制度与我们的观念相左，与我们的习俗不同，因而有必要提出几个例子进行详细说明。

number of individuals, called "the Selectmen." The general laws of the State impose a certain number of obligations on the selectmen, which they may fulfil without the authorization of the body they represent, but which they can only neglect on their own responsibility. The law of the State obliges them, for instance, to draw up the list of electors in their townships; and if they omit this part of their functions, they are guilty of a misdemeanor. In all the affairs, however, which are determined by the town-meeting, the selectmen are the organs of the popular mandate, as in France the Maire executes the decree of the municipal council. They usually act upon their own responsibility, and merely put in practice principles which have been previously recognized by the majority. But if any change is to be introduced in the existing state of things, or if they wish to undertake any new enterprise, they are obliged to refer to the source of their power. If, for instance, a school is to be established, the selectmen convoke the whole body of the electors on a certain day at an appointed place; they explain the urgency of the case; they give their opinion on the means of satisfying it, on the probable expense, and the site which seems to be most favorable. The meeting is consulted on these several points; it adopts the principle, marks out the site, votes the rate, and confides the execution of its resolution to the selectmen.

The selectmen have alone the right of calling a town-meeting, but they may be requested to do so: if ten citizens are desirous of submitting a new project to the assent of the township, they may demand a general convocation of the inhabitants; the selectmen are obliged to comply, but they have only the right of presiding at the meeting.

The selectmen are elected every year in the month of April or of May. The town-meeting chooses at the same time a number of other municipal magistrates, who are entrusted with important administrative functions. The assessors rate the township; the collectors receive the rate. A constable is appointed to keep the peace, to watch the streets, and to forward the execution of the laws; the town-clerk records all the town votes, orders, grants, births, deaths, and marriages; the treasurer keeps the funds; the overseer of the poor performs the difficult task of superintending the action of the poor-laws; committee-men are appointed to attend to the schools and to public instruction; and the road-surveyors, who take care of the greater and lesser thoroughfares of the township, complete

下面我们会看到，在乡镇里公务繁多而且分类极细，但是，行政权力很大程度上落入一些个别人手中，他们就是"行政委员"。州的法律给行政委员规定了一定职责，无须乡镇居民的授权便可行使这些职权，但如果他们玩忽职守，只能由他们个人负责。例如，州法律规定由他们起草本乡镇选民名单，而如果他们未能履行这一职责，他们就犯有渎职罪。但是，在由乡镇处理的一切行政事务中，行政委员是民意的执行者，就像法国市长是市议会法令的执行者一样。通常他们处理公务自行负责，只是在执行居民早先通过的原则办事。但是如果他们要对州现有事项做出任何的改变，或是拟办一项新事业，必须要向其权力之源进行请示。比如，如果想要兴建一所学校，行政委员需要选定一天将全体选民召集到指定地点，向大家说明这件事的迫切程度，并提出执行方案，所需资金以及最合适的选址。会上人们对此进行讨论，采纳后制定原则，确定地点，对筹措资金的方式进行投票，并委托行政委员执行大会决议。

只有行政委员有权召开镇居民大会，但是人们也可以要求他们召开这样的会议。如果十名居民共同提出一项新的计划并希望能够得到乡镇的认可，他们可以要求行政委员召开乡镇居民大会。而行政委员必须答应他们的要求，并有权主持会议。

每年四月或五月对行政委员进行选举，同时乡镇大会还会选出其他一些担任乡镇重要职务的官员，有多名财产估价员和收税员；一名治安官，负责维护治安，巡逻街道并执行法律；一名乡镇文书，负责记录乡镇所有投票、决议以及出生、死亡和婚姻情况；一名司库，负责管理乡镇财务；一名乡镇济贫工作视察员，承担执行济贫法的艰巨任务；几名校

the list of the principal functionaries. They are, however, still further subdivided; and amongst the municipal officers are to be found parish commissioners, who audit the expenses of public worship; different classes of inspectors, some of whom are to direct the citizens in case of fire; tithing-men, listers, haywards, chimney-viewers, fence-viewers to maintain the bounds of property, timber-measurers, and sealers of weights and measures.

There are nineteen principal officers in a township. Every inhabitant is constrained, on the pain of being fined, to undertake these different functions; which, however, are almost all paid, in order that the poorer citizens may be able to give up their time without loss. In general the American system is not to grant a fixed salary to its functionaries. Every service has its price, and they are remunerated in proportion to what they have done.

Existence Of The Township

Every one the best judge of his own interest—Corollary of the principle of the sovereignty of the people—Application of those doctrines in the townships of America—The township of New England is sovereign in all that concerns itself alone: subject to the State in all other matters—Bond of the township and the State—In France the Government lends its agent to the Commune—In America the reverse occurs.

I have already observed that the principle of the sovereignty of the people governs the whole political system of the Anglo-Americans. Every page of this book will afford new instances of the same doctrine. In the nations by which the sovereignty of the people is recognized every individual possesses an equal share of power, and participates alike in the government of the State. Every individual is, therefore, supposed to be as well informed, as virtuous, and as strong as any of his fellow-citizens. He obeys the government, not because he is inferior to the authorities which conduct it, or that he is less capable than his neighbor of governing himself, but because he acknowledges the utility of an association with his fellow-men, and because he knows that no such association can exist without a regulating force. If he be a subject in all that concerns the mutual relations of citizens, he is free and responsible to God alone

董，管理学校和国民教育；以及几名道路管理员，负责大小道路的管理工作。这些就是乡镇主要行政管理官员。当然官员还有进一步分工，乡镇官员中还有几名负责教区管理，以及各种监察员，他们有人负责组织公民救火，有人组织人力看青护秋，有人协助公民解决修建庭院时可能遇到的困难，还有人负责测量森林，也有人负责检查度量衡器具。

一个乡镇中有19名主要官员。每个居民都必须承担一些不同的职责，违者罚款。而且这些职务大多数都有酬劳，以便贫困的公民能够拿出时间而不受损失。通常情况下，在美国官员没有固定的工资。每项工作都标有酬劳，并按照官员工作的完成程度计算酬劳。

乡镇生活

每个人都是自己利益最好的裁判员——人民主权原则的必然结果——这些信条在美国乡镇的应用——新英格兰的乡镇只在与本州利益相关的所有事务享有主权，其他事务服从于州——乡镇对州的义务——在法国政府把官员借给村镇——在美国乡镇把官员借给政府。

我已经说过，人民主权原则支配整个英裔美国人的政治制度。这本书的每一页都会让读者看到这同一原则的新应用。在践行人民主权原则的国家，每个人都享有同等的权利，平等地参与国家管理。因此，每个个人也应该具备相同的文化水准、道德修养以及和其他同胞一样的能力。个人要服从政府，但这并不是因为他比那些管理社会的人差，也不是因为自己的管理能力不及他人，而是因为他认识到与同胞的这种联合对自己有利，而缺少制

for all that concerns himself. Hence arises the maxim that every one is the best and the sole judge of his own private interest, and that society has no right to control a man's actions, unless they are prejudicial to the common weal, or unless the common weal demands his co-operation. This doctrine is universally admitted in the United States. I shall hereafter examine the general influence which it exercises on the ordinary actions of life; I am now speaking of the nature of municipal bodies.

The township, taken as a whole, and in relation to the government of the country, may be looked upon as an individual to whom the theory I have just alluded to is applied. Municipal independence is therefore a natural consequence of the principle of the sovereignty of the people in the United States: all the American republics recognize it more or less; but circumstances have peculiarly favored its growth in New England.

In this part of the Union the impulse of political activity was given in the townships; and it may almost be said that each of them originally formed an independent nation. When the Kings of England asserted their supremacy, they were contented to assume the central power of the State. The townships of New England remained as they were before; and although they are now subject to the State, they were at first scarcely dependent upon it. It is important to remember that they have not been invested with privileges, but that they have, on the contrary, forfeited a portion of their independence to the State. The townships are only subordinate to the State in those interests which I shall term social, as they are common to all the citizens. They are independent in all that concerns themselves; and amongst the inhabitants of New England I believe that not a man is to be found who would acknowledge that the State has any right to interfere in their local interests. The towns of New England buy and sell, sue or are sued, augment or diminish their rates, without the slightest opposition on the part of the administrative authority of the State.

They are bound, however, to comply with the demands of the community. If the State is in need of money, a town can neither give nor withhold the supplies. If the State projects a road, the township cannot refuse to let it cross its territory; if a police regulation is made by the State, it must

约力量就无法实现这种联合。因此，作为国民，在与公民间关系有关的所有事务上，必须服从；而在仅与自己相关的一切事务上，完全自由，只需向上帝负责。所以，出现了这样的说法：个人是自身利益最好也是唯一的裁判，而社会无权干涉个人行为，除非其行为侵害社会利益或是社会需要其协助。这样的学说在美国得到普遍认可。至于它对日常生活产生的普遍影响，我想留待以后再去考察，现在我要谈谈它对乡镇产生的影响。

乡镇作为一个整体，从与国家政府的关系上看，跟我刚才谈到的个人行使权利的理论一脉相承。因此，乡镇独立是美国人民主权原则产生的必然结果：对此，所有美国各州都或多或少表示认可，而新英格兰各州的环境对这一学说的发展特别有利。

在联邦的这一部分，政治活动始于乡镇，而且几乎可以说每个乡镇最初都是一个独立的国家。当英格兰的国王们要求行使主权的时候，他们满足于州一级的权力。新英格兰的乡镇保持原状，尽管现在它们隶属于州，但是原先他们之间几乎没有依附关系。值得注意的是它们非但没有得到什么好处，反而把一部分的独立让与州。乡镇只在那些与公共利益相关的利益方面服从于州，而与其自身利益相关的方面则是独立的。我认为，对于新英格兰的居民而言，没有人认为州有权干涉乡镇地方的利益。新英格兰的乡镇无论是其买或卖，控告或是被告，提高或是降低预算，州当局完全没有任何的意见。

然而，对于全州性的义务，他们则必须遵守。如果州缺钱，乡镇就没有同意或拒绝的自由。如果州计划建设一条道路，乡镇也无权要求其经过或是绕过其境内。如果州制定了治安条例，乡镇也必须执行。州要在全州推行统一的教育制度，乡镇就要按照法律规定建设学校。在谈到美国行政制度的时候，我还会指出上述情形是通过何种方式迫使乡镇服从

be enforced by the town. A uniform system of instruction is organized all over the country, and every town is bound to establish the schools which the law ordains. In speaking of the administration of the United States I shall have occasion to point out the means by which the townships are compelled to obey in these different cases: I here merely show the existence of the obligation. Strict as this obligation is, the government of the State imposes it in principle only, and in its performance the township resumes all its independent rights. Thus, taxes are voted by the State, but they are levied and collected by the township; the existence of a school is obligatory, but the township builds, pays, and superintends it. In France the State-collector receives the local imposts; in America the town-collector receives the taxes of the State. Thus the French Government lends its agents to the commune; in America the township is the agent of the Government. This fact alone shows the extent of the differences which exist between the two nations.

Public Spirit Of The Townships Of New England

How the township of New England wins the affections of its inhabitants—Difficulty of creating local public spirit in Europe—The rights and duties of the American township favorable to it—Characteristics of home in the United States—Manifestations of public spirit in New England—Its happy effects.

In America, not only do municipal bodies exist, but they are kept alive and supported by public spirit. The township of New England possesses two advantages which infallibly secure the attentive interest of mankind, namely, independence and authority. Its sphere is indeed small and limited, but within that sphere its action is unrestrained; and its independence gives to it a real importance which its extent and population may not always ensure.

It is to be remembered that the affections of men generally lie on the side of authority. Patriotism is not durable in a conquered nation. The New Englander is attached to his township, not only because he was born in it, but because it constitutes a social body of which he is a member, and

的，在此，我只想指出这种义务的存在。这些义务必须尽到，州政府只规定其原则，至于如何执行，乡镇又拥有了独立权。比如，赋税由州议会投票决定，但计征税款的是乡镇。学校的设立是州制定的义务，但花钱兴建进行管理的是乡镇。在法国，国家税务员到地方乡镇收税，而在美国，乡镇税务员为州收税。所以说法国政府把官员借给乡镇，而在美国，乡镇是政府的代理人。仅这一个事实就足以说明两个国家的差别如此之大。

新英格兰乡镇精神

新英格兰乡镇如何赢得居民的热爱——欧洲形成乡镇精神的困难——美国乡镇的权利和义务有利于形成乡镇精神——故乡在美国的特点——乡镇精神在新英格兰的表现——乡镇精神产生的可喜效果。

在美国，乡镇不仅有自己的制度，还有支持和鼓励其存在的乡镇精神。新英格兰的乡镇占据必定能够确保人们利益的两大优势，即独立和权力。尽管乡镇的范围很小而有限，但是在其范围之内，乡镇的活动不受限制。而当人口和面积不足以使乡镇独立的时候，乡镇的独立性给了它很重要的地位。

应当承认，一般来说人们喜欢依附权势。在一个被侵占的国家爱国主义不会长久。新英格兰人热爱他们的乡镇，不仅仅因为他们出生在这里，而是因为乡镇是一个社会集体，自己是其中的一分子，因而值得他们尽心尽力。而在欧洲，很遗憾的是当权者往往缺乏地方精神，他们只是承认地方精神是维护安定的最好的保障，但却不知道该如何培养它。如

whose government claims and deserves the exercise of his sagacity. In Europe the absence of local public spirit is a frequent subject of regret to those who are in power; everyone agrees that there is no surer guarantee of order and tranquility, and yet nothing is more difficult to create. If the municipal bodies were made powerful and independent, the authorities of the nation might be disunited and the peace of the country endangered. Yet, without power and independence, a town may contain good subjects, but it can have no active citizens. Another important fact is that the township of New England is so constituted as to excite the warmest of human affections, without arousing the ambitious passions of the heart of man. The officers of the country are not elected, and their authority is very limited. Even the State is only a second-rate community, whose tranquil and obscure administration offers no inducement sufficient to draw men away from the circle of their interests into the turmoil of public affairs. The federal government confers power and honor on the men who conduct it; but these individuals can never be very numerous. The high station of the Presidency can only be reached at an advanced period of life, and the other federal functionaries are generally men who have been favored by fortune, or distinguished in some other career. Such cannot be the permanent aim of the ambitious. But the township serves as a centre for the desire of public esteem, the want of exciting interests, and the taste for authority and popularity, in the midst of the ordinary relations of life; and the passions which commonly embroil society change their character when they find a vent so near the domestic hearth and the family circle.

In the American States power has been disseminated with admirable skill for the purpose of interesting the greatest possible number of persons in the common weal. Independently of the electors who are from time to time called into action, the body politic is divided into innumerable functionaries and officers, who all, in their several spheres, represent the same powerful whole in whose name they act. The local administration thus affords an unfailing source of profit and interest to a vast number of individuals.

The American system, which divides the local authority among so many citizens, does not scruple to multiply the functions of the town officers. For in the United States it is believed, and with truth, that patriotism is a kind of devotion which is strengthened by ritual observance. In this manner the

果地方变得强大独立，国家就会四分五裂，国家的和平就变得岌岌可危。但是，没有权力和独立，乡镇也许能够成为好的臣民，但却无法得到好公民。另外一个很重要的事实是，新英格兰的乡镇组织得如此之好，不但能够激发人们的热爱，还不会刺激人们的野心。县官员不经选举，权力有限。即使是州也只有次要的权限，其存在无关紧要，不能吸引人们离开自己的利益圈，打乱自己的生活去州里做官。联邦政府授予管理人员以权力和荣誉，但靠这些发财的人并不多。总统是在达到一定年龄之后才能染指的最高职位，而联邦政府的其他高级官员多为任职前已经发财或是事业有成的人员担任。这样他们就不会把当官作为其抱负的终极目标。而乡镇才是日常生活关系中，满足人们追名逐利需要的中心。而当他们能在家里的暖炉边也就是家庭内部找到发泄口，这种让社会变得混乱的冲动也会改变属性。

在美国，权力得以被巧妙的分散，为了能让大多数的人参与公共事务。结果，选民常常被召集起来参与管理，而形形色色的官员则独立于选民之外，在各自的职权范围代表强有力的乡镇，并以它的名义行动。因此，无须操心乡镇政府，人民群众便会自觉的关心乡镇管理。

美国的这套将乡镇权力分散给公民的制度，并不担心扩大乡镇官员的职权。因为在美国，人们这样认为而且的确如此，爱国主义是通过实践进行强化的一种奉献精神。这样，乡镇活动时时刻刻都可以看到，每天通过履行一项职责实行一次权利来实现，因此社会得以缓慢稳步前进，生机勃勃又不会造成混乱。

activity of the township is continually perceptible; it is daily manifested in the fulfilment of a duty or the exercise of a right, and a constant though gentle motion is thus kept up in society which animates without disturbing it.

The American attaches himself to his home as the mountaineer clings to his hills, because the characteristic features of his country are there more distinctly marked than elsewhere. The existence of the townships of New England is in general a happy one. Their government is suited to their tastes, and chosen by themselves. In the midst of the profound peace and general comfort which reign in America the commotions of municipal discord are unfrequent. The conduct of local business is easy. The political education of the people has long been complete; say rather that it was complete when the people first set foot upon the soil. In New England no tradition exists of a distinction of ranks; no portion of the community is tempted to oppress the remainder; and the abuses which may injure isolated individuals are forgotten in the general contentment which prevails. If the government is defective (and it would no doubt be easy to point out its deficiencies), the fact that it really emanates from those it governs, and that it acts, either ill or well, casts the protecting spell of a parental pride over its faults. No term of comparison disturbs the satisfaction of the citizen: England formerly governed the mass of the colonies, but the people was always sovereign in the township where its rule is not only an ancient but a primitive state.

The native of New England is attached to his township because it is independent and free: his co-operation in its affairs ensures his attachment to its interest; the well-being it affords him secures his affection; and its welfare is the aim of his ambition and of his future exertions: he takes a part in every occurrence in the place; he practises the art of government in the small sphere within his reach; he accustoms himself to those forms which can alone ensure the steady progress of liberty; he imbibes their spirit; he acquires a taste for order, comprehends the union or the balance of powers, and collects clear practical notions on the nature of his duties and the extent of his rights.

The Counties Of New England

The division of the countries in America has considerable analogy with that of the arrondissements

美国人对祖国的依恋就如同山民对大山的依附一样，因为他们的祖国有着与其他地方截然不同的特点。总的来说，新英格兰乡镇的生活很幸福。他们的政府由他们亲自选择符合他们的趣味。在生活安稳舒适的美国，乡镇骚乱难得一见。地方事务的管理轻而易举。人民的政治教育早已完成，可以说在他们踏上这片土地之前就已完成。在新英格兰没有等级之分，也没有一部分人压迫另一部分人的现象，而会对孤立个人施加的暴行也在征得全体居民同意后遭到废除。如果这样的政府有什么缺陷（而且毫无疑问指出它的缺陷易如反掌），人们也会对此表示宽容大度，因为事实上管理的根据来源于被统治者，所以不管好坏他们都要接受，以此来表示他们做主人的自豪感。没有什么能跟这种自豪感相比。从前尽管英格兰统治所有殖民地，但是人们依然在乡镇自己行使主权，所以人民主权制度不仅古老而且原生态。

新英格兰当地人热爱他们的乡镇，因为它独立而自由；他们关心乡镇的利益，因为他们参与其事务的管理；乡镇的兴旺也确保了他们的热爱，乡镇的福祉就是他们的目标和未来。他们参与乡镇的一切事务，在能力所及的范围管理社会，已经习惯于确保自由得以实现的形式。他们接受了乡镇精神，产生了遵守秩序的兴趣，领悟了权力的平衡，并对义务的本质和权利的范围有了清晰的概念。

新英格兰的县

美国的县划分与法国很相似。县被随意划分，而且其各个地区没有什么必然的联系，

of France. The limits of the counties are arbitrarily laid down, and the various districts which they contain have no necessary connection, no common tradition or natural sympathy; their object is simply to facilitate the administration of justice.

The extent of the township was too small to contain a system of judicial institutions; each county has, however, a court of justice, a sheriff to execute its decrees, and a prison for criminals. There are certain wants which are felt alike by all the townships of a county; it is therefore natural that they should be satisfied by a central authority. In the State of Massachusetts this authority is vested in the hands of several magistrates, who are appointed by the Governor of the State, with the advice of his council. The officers of the county have only a limited and occasional authority, which is applicable to certain predetermined cases. The State and the townships possess all the power requisite to conduct public business. The budget of the county is drawn up by its officers, and is voted by the legislature, but there is no assembly which directly or indirectly represents the county. It has, therefore, properly speaking, no political existence.

Administration In New England

Administration not perceived in America—Why?—The Europeans believe that liberty is promoted by depriving the social authority of some of its rights; the Americans, by dividing its exercise—Almost all the administration confined to the township, and divided amongst the town-officers—No trace of an administrative body to be perceived, either in the township or above it—The reason of this—How it happens that the administration of the State is uniform—Who is empowered to enforce the obedience of the township and the county to the law—The introduction of judicial power into the administration—Consequence of the extension of the elective principle to all functionaries—The Justice of the Peace in New England—By whom appointed—County officer: ensures the administration of the townships—Court of Sessions—Its action—Right of inspection and indictment disseminated like the other administrative functions—Informers encouraged by the division of fines.

Nothing is more striking to an European traveller in the United States than the absence of what we

共同的传统或是天然的感情。县的划分完全出于行政考虑。

乡镇很小，小到无法建立成套的司法体系。可是每个县都有法院，负责执行法令的治安官和一所羁押犯人的监狱。有些设施是一个县几乎所有乡镇都需要的，因此自然地一个满足他们需要的中央机构应运而生。在马萨诸塞州，这个机构的大权落入几个个人的手中，他们由州长咨议会提议最后经州长任命。县的官员只有临时的有限的权力，只能在预定的事项中行使。乡镇和州拥有处理公共事务必需的一切权利。县的官员只负责起草预算并交由立法机关投票表决。县并没有直接或间接代表其自身的议会。因此，确切地说县没有政治生活。

新英格兰的行政

在美国感觉不到行政——为什么——欧洲人认为自由要靠在公权方面剥夺某些人的权力来建立，美国人则认为需要通过分散某些人的权力来建立——几乎全部的行政工作都划归乡镇，由乡镇官员分管——无论是在乡镇还是其上级机构，感觉不到行政等级森严的痕迹——这一现象的原因——州如何一律成为行政单位——谁迫使乡镇和县服从法律——司法权进入行政部门——选举权扩展到一切官职的后果——新英格兰的治安法官——由谁任命——县官员保障乡镇的行政——地方法院——其办案方式——同其他行政职务一样，侦讯权和起诉权由多人掌管——以分得罚款的办法鼓励举报。

term the Government, or the Administration. Written laws exist in America, and one sees that they are daily executed; but although everything is in motion, the hand which gives the impulse to the social machine can nowhere be discovered. Nevertheless, as all peoples are obliged to have recourse to certain grammatical forms, which are the foundation of human language, in order to express their thoughts; so all communities are obliged to secure their existence by submitting to a certain dose of authority, without which they fall a prey to anarchy. This authority may be distributed in several ways, but it must always exist somewhere.

There are two methods of diminishing the force of authority in a nation: The first is to weaken the supreme power in its very principle, by forbidding or preventing society from acting in its own defence under certain circumstances. To weaken authority in this manner is what is generally termed in Europe to lay the foundations of freedom. The second manner of diminishing the influence of authority does not consist in stripping society of any of its rights, nor in paralyzing its efforts, but in distributing the exercise of its privileges in various hands, and in multiplying functionaries, to each of whom the degree of power necessary for him to perform his duty is entrusted. There may be nations whom this distribution of social powers might lead to anarchy; but in itself it is not anarchical. The action of authority is indeed thus rendered less irresistible and less perilous, but it is not totally suppressed.

The revolution of the United States was the result of a mature and dignified taste for freedom, and not of a vague or ill-defined craving for independence. It contracted no alliance with the turbulent passions of anarchy; but its course was marked, on the contrary, by an attachment to whatever was lawful and orderly.

It was never assumed in the United States that the citizen of a free country has a right to do whatever he pleases; on the contrary, social obligations were there imposed upon him more various than anywhere else. No idea was ever entertained of attacking the principles or of contesting the rights of society; but the exercise of its authority was divided, to the end that the office might be powerful and the officer insignificant, and that the community should be at once regulated and free. In no country in the world does the law hold so absolute a language as in America, and in no country is the right of applying it vested in so many hands. The administrative power in the United States

让到美国旅行的欧洲人最感到惊讶是发现在这里没有我们所说的政府或衙门。美国有成文的法律，而且人们每天都在按照法律行事，尽管每件事都按部就班，可是却看不到操纵社会机器的推手。然而，正如人们需要依赖特定的语法结构表达自己的思想一样，所有的社会也必须服从某个特定的权威以保障自身的生存，而没有这个权威，社会就会成为无政府状态的猎物。这个权威可能有不同的表现形式，但是它一定会在某个地方存在。

一个国家可以采用两种方法来削弱权威的影响。第一种方式是通过禁止或阻止当局在特定情况下进行自卫，从而从根本上减弱当局的权力。采用这种方法削弱当局通常是欧洲自由建立的基础。另外一种方式是减小当局的影响力，此种方法既不会剥夺当局的任何权利也不会导致其瘫痪，而是将它的特权分散到不同人手中，并增设官职，从而使每个官员只有履行职务所需的权限。也许在有些国家这样的权力分化会引发混乱，但就其本身而言并非如此。这种做法无疑会降低权威活动的不可抗性和危险性，但是对权威完全没有产生任何抑制作用。

美国革命是对自由的一种成熟高贵的热爱使然，而不是对独立盲目的追求。这场革命并没有与暴动的激情为伍，相反，它是以法制和秩序而著称。

所以，在美国这个自由国家公民没有权力为所欲为，相反，加诸在人们身上的社会义务比起任何地方都要多。人们从未抱有攻击当局权力或否定其权限的想法，而是将其权力分化，以此达到加强权威削弱官员权力的目的，而社会也必然会变得自由而有序。世界上没有一个国家的法律像美国一样铁面无私，也没有任何一个国家将公权分散到如此多的人

presents nothing either central or hierarchical in its constitution, which accounts for its passing, unperceived. The power exists, but its representative is not to be perceived.

We have already seen that the independent townships of New England protect their own private interests; and the municipal magistrates are the persons to whom the execution of the laws of the State is most frequently entrusted. Besides the general laws, the State sometimes passes general police regulations; but more commonly the townships and town officers, conjointly with justices of the peace, regulate the minor details of social life, according to the necessities of the different localities, and promulgate such enactments as concern the health of the community, and the peace as well as morality of the citizens. Lastly, these municipal magistrates provide, of their own accord and without any delegated powers, for those unforeseen emergencies which frequently occur in society.

It results from what we have said that in the State of Massachusetts the administrative authority is almost entirely restricted to the township, but that it is distributed among a great number of individuals. In the French commune there is properly but one official functionary, namely, the Maire; and in New England we have seen that there are nineteen. These nineteen functionaries do not in general depend upon one another. The law carefully prescribes a circle of action to each of these magistrates; and within that circle they have an entire right to perform their functions independently of any other authority. Above the township scarcely any trace of a series of official dignitaries is to be found. It sometimes happens that the county officers alter a decision of the townships or town magistrates, but in general the authorities of the county have no right to interfere with the authorities of the township, except in such matters as concern the county.

The magistrates of the township, as well as those of the county, are bound to communicate their acts to the central government in a very small number of predetermined cases. But the central government is not represented by an individual whose business it is to publish police regulations and ordinances enforcing the execution of the laws; to keep up a regular communication with the officers of the township and the county; to inspect their conduct, to direct their actions, or to reprimand their faults. There is no point which serves as a centre to the radii of the administration.

手中。美国的行政权力既不代表中央集权也不代表逐级分权，这也正是在其行使时不为人所察觉的原因所在。权力虽然存在，但是它的代表却不知道在哪里。

我们已经看到独立的新英格兰乡镇捍卫了他们自己的利益，而且乡镇的行政委员们往往亲自执行全州性的法律。除了通用法律以外，州有时候还会颁布州通用的治安条例。但是更惯常的做法是，乡镇当局和乡镇官员会连同治安官，根据当地的需要制定社会生活细则，发布有关公共卫生、地方安定以及公民道德方面的规定。最后，乡镇行政委员也可以在没有授权的情况下自行处理那些经常出现而又不可预见的紧急情况。

根据上面所述可以知道在马萨诸塞州，行政权几乎完全属于乡镇，并由大量个人分掌。在法国的乡镇，确切的来说只有一位行政官员即乡长，而在新英格兰则有19名行政官员。一般来说，这些行政官员彼此独立，法律也对每个人的职权范围做出详细的规定，在其职权范围内他们独立行事不受制于任何权威。在乡镇之上，几乎看不到任何行政等级的蛛丝马迹。有时候县里的官员会对乡镇或是乡镇行政委员们做出的决定进行修改，但是一般来说除非是与县里相关的事务，否则县当局没有权力干涉乡镇活动。

乡镇行政官员和县里的行政官员必须要向州政府通报那些极少数的预定事项的执行情况。

但是，州政府并不会指派专门人员去制定全州性的治安条例和颁布执行法律的法令，却经常和县及乡镇的官员保持联系，视察他们的政绩，指导他们的行动或谴责他们的错误。所以，并不存在以行政权力为半径的中心。

What, then, is the uniform plan on which the government is conducted, and how is the compliance of the counties and their magistrates or the townships and their officers enforced? In the States of New England the legislative authority embraces more subjects than it does in France; the legislator penetrates to the very core of the administration; the law descends to the most minute details; the same enactment prescribes the principle and the method of its application, and thus imposes a multitude of strict and rigorously defined obligations on the secondary functionaries of the State. The consequence of this is that if all the secondary functionaries of the administration conform to the law, society in all its branches proceeds with the greatest uniformity: the difficulty remains of compelling the secondary functionaries of the administration to conform to the law. It may be affirmed that, in general, society has only two methods of enforcing the execution of the laws at its disposal: a discretionary power may be entrusted to a superior functionary of directing all the others, and of cashiering them in case of disobedience; or the courts of justice may be authorized to inflict judicial penalties on the offender: but these two methods are not always available.

The right of directing a civil officer presupposes that of cashiering him if he does not obey orders, and of rewarding him by promotion if he fulfils his duties with propriety. But an elected magistrate can neither be cashiered nor promoted. All elective functions are inalienable until their term is expired. In fact, the elected magistrate has nothing either to expect or to fear from his constituents; and when all public offices are filled by ballot there can be no series of official dignities, because the double right of commanding and of enforcing obedience can never be vested in the same individual, and because the power of issuing an order can never be joined to that of inflicting a punishment or bestowing a reward.

The communities therefore in which the secondary functionaries of the government are elected are perforce obliged to make great use of judicial penalties as a means of administration. This is not evident at first sight; for those in power are apt to look upon the institution of elective functionaries as one concession, and the subjection of the elected magistrate to the judges of the land as another. They are equally averse to both these innovations; and as they are more pressingly solicited to grant the former than the latter, they accede to the election of the magistrate, and leave him independent

那么，如何按照一个统一的计划来指导社会，又如何让县及其行政官员和乡镇及其行政官员来执行呢？在新英格兰各州，立法当局所涉及的范围比法国要大得多。立法者已经深入到行政当局的核心。法律的规定事无巨细，一条法律既规定原则又规定其应用方法。因此，这就给下一级官员施加了众多细致严密的义务。

这样做的结果就是，如果下一级的官员都能够依法行事，整个社会的各部分都能够协调一致的前进。而问题就在于如何能够让下一级的官员依法行事。可以断言，社会一般只有两种方法保证官员按照其意愿执行法律。一种是让一名官员能够凌驾于其他官员之上对他们加以指导，并拥有决断权，能够在他们不服从的时候将其罢黜，另一种是授权法院对违法官员进行惩治。但是这两种方法用起来并不总能得心应手。

拥有官员指导权的前提是：如果这名官员不能尽忠职守就要将其罢黜，而如果能够做到这一点就应该得到升迁。但是民选的官员既不能被罢黜也不能得到提拔。所有经选举产生的官员在任期未满前不能被撤换。实际上，选举产生的官员只会对选民有所期待和畏惧，而当所有的公职都经投票产生的时候，官员之间就不会有真正的等级差别，因为命令权和惩戒权不会落入一人之手，而且颁布命令的权力和奖惩权也不会合并一处。

因此，通过选举任用下级政府官员的国家必然会充分利用司法惩处作为行政管理手段。乍看起来这并不容易被发现，因为当权者们往往把实行选举制度视为一次妥协，而把许可法官对选举产生的官员进行惩处视为又一次妥协。他们对这两种革新都讨厌，但当不得不做出选择的时候，他们更愿意选择前者，他们认可了官员选举制，并让选举产生的官

of the judicial power. Nevertheless, the second of these measures is the only thing that can possibly counterbalance the first; and it will be found that an elective authority which is not subject to judicial power will, sooner or later, either elude all control or be destroyed. The courts of justice are the only possible medium between the central power and the administrative bodies; they alone can compel the elected functionary to obey, without violating the rights of the elector. The extension of judicial power in the political world ought therefore to be in the exact ratio of the extension of elective offices: if these two institutions do not go hand in hand, the State must fall into anarchy or into subjection.

It has always been remarked that habits of legal business do not render men apt to the exercise of administrative authority. The Americans have borrowed from the English, their fathers, the idea of an institution which is unknown upon the continent of Europe: I allude to that of the Justices of the Peace. The Justice of the Peace is a sort of mezzo termine between the magistrate and the man of the world, between the civil officer and the judge. A justice of the peace is a well-informed citizen, though he is not necessarily versed in the knowledge of the laws. His office simply obliges him to execute the police regulations of society; a task in which good sense and integrity are of more avail than legal science. The justice introduces into the administration a certain taste for established forms and publicity, which renders him a most unserviceable instrument of despotism; and, on the other hand, he is not blinded by those superstitions which render legal officers unfit members of a government. The Americans have adopted the system of the English justices of the peace, but they have deprived it of that aristocratic character which is discernible in the mother-country. The Governor of Massachusetts appoints a certain number of justices of the peace in every county, whose functions last seven years. He further designates three individuals from amongst the whole body of justices who form in each county what is called the Court of Sessions. The justices take a personal share in public business; they are sometimes entrusted with administrative functions in conjunction with elected officers, they sometimes constitute a tribunal, before which the magistrates summarily prosecute a refractory citizen, or the citizens inform against the abuses of the magistrate. But it is in the Court of Sessions that they exercise their most important functions. This court meets twice a

员独立于司法权力。然而，只有后者才能制衡前者，而且人们会发现不受司法权监督的选举权迟早会失控或毁灭。法院是中央政权和行政单位之间唯一可能的调停者。能在不侵害选民权力的前提下，迫使民选官员俯首听命的只有法院。因此，司法权力向政治领域的延伸应该和民选官员的扩大协调起来。如果它们不能同步进行，国家必定陷入混乱或是一部分人压迫另一部分人的窘境。

一直以来人们认为司法习惯并没有很好的培养公民行使行政权力。美国人从他们的祖先英国人那里学到了不为欧洲大陆所了解的一种制度。我所指的就是设置治安法官。治安法官是官员与普通民众和行政机关与法院之间的中立者。治安法官通常由见识广博的公民担任，但并不一定要精通律法。他的职责就是要维持治安，在工作中良知和公正的重要性远胜于法律知识。当治安法官参与行政管理的时候，会让管理工作变得循规蹈矩透明化，而这就让他能够成为防止独裁最强有力的工具。但是，从另一方面来说，也不能迷信法律，这会让律政官员无法胜任政府工作。美国人采用了英国的治安法官制度，但摒弃了它在宗主国所具有的鲜明的贵族特性。马萨诸塞的州长为本州每个县任命一定数量的任期为7年的治安法官。而且，他还会从各县的全体治安法官中选出三名组成地方法院。个别的治安法官也会参与公共事务，有时候他们也被委以行政职务，协同民选官员工作；还有时候组成临时法庭，处理行政官员对拒不履行义务公民的诉讼或是公民对滥用职权官员的控告。但是，他们行使最主要职责的场所还是地方法庭。地方法庭每年在县里两次开庭，在马萨诸塞州，它有权迫使大多数的公职人员服从。必须指出的是，在马萨诸塞州地方法庭

year in the county town; in Massachusetts it is empowered to enforce the obedience of the greater number of public officers. It must be observed, that in the State of Massachusetts the Court of Sessions is at the same time an administrative body, properly so called, and a political tribunal. It has been asserted that the county is a purely administrative division. The Court of Sessions presides over that small number of affairs which, as they concern several townships, or all the townships of the county in common, cannot be entrusted to any one of them in particular. In all that concerns county business the duties of the Court of Sessions are purely administrative; and if in its investigations it occasionally borrows the forms of judicial procedure, it is only with a view to its own information, or as a guarantee to the community over which it presides. But when the administration of the township is brought before it, it always acts as a judicial body, and in some few cases as an official assembly.

The first difficulty is to procure the obedience of an authority as entirely independent of the general laws of the State as the township is. We have stated that assessors are annually named by the town-meetings to levy the taxes. If a township attempts to evade the payment of the taxes by neglecting to name its assessors, the Court of Sessions condemns it to a heavy penalty. The fine is levied on each of the inhabitants; and the sheriff of the county, who is the officer of justice, executes the mandate. Thus it is that in the United States the authority of the Government is mysteriously concealed under the forms of a judicial sentence; and its influence is at the same time fortified by that irresistible power with which men have invested the formalities of law.

These proceedings are easy to follow and to understand. The demands made upon a township are in general plain and accurately defined; they consist in a simple fact without any complication, or in a principle without its application in detail. But the difficulty increases when it is not the obedience of the township, but that of the town officers which is to be enforced. All the reprehensible actions of which a public functionary may be guilty are reducible to the following heads:

He may execute the law without energy or zeal;
He may neglect to execute the law;

即是纯粹的行政主体又是政治法庭。正如已经说过的县只是一个行政区划。地方法庭主持的工作，只是为数不多的一些与几个乡镇或是县里所有乡镇有关而又不能由任何一个乡镇单独处理的事务。当涉及与全县有关的所有事务时，地方法院的职能纯属行政性质，而地方法院工作时之所以时不时地借用司法程序，只是为了让被审官员明白处理的法律依据，或是只为工作便利。但是对乡镇行政官员进行审理的时候，它几乎总是以司法机关的性质进行工作，只在极少的情况下才以行政机关的身份出现。

在这里需要克服的第一个困难就是，如何让乡镇这个几乎完全独立的政体服从于州的一般法律。前面已经说过，乡镇每年都会任命一些财产评估员来征税。但是如果一个乡镇妄图以不任命财产评估员的方法来逃避纳税义务，地方法庭会对其处以巨额罚款。这笔罚款会均摊到全体居民身上，县治安官作为执法人员负责执行判决。因此，在美国，行政当局神秘地悄然藏身于司法判决之后，而与此同时，凭借人们赋予法律的不可抗拒的权力，行政当局的影响力得以加强。

这些做法便于推行易于理解。一般来说，对于乡镇的要求都有明文规定，清清楚楚。这些规定要不是内容单一，简单明了，要不就是只给出原则不对具体实行细则进行规定。但是困难并不仅仅是让乡镇服从，迫使负责执行命令的乡镇官员服从则是难上加难。公职人员应受斥责的行为可归纳为下列几种：

执法时不积极不卖力

He may do what the law enjoins him not to do.

The last two violations of duty can alone come under the cognizance of a tribunal; a positive and appreciable fact is the indispensable foundation of an action at law. Thus, if the selectmen omit to fulfil the legal formalities usual at town elections, they may be condemned to pay a fine; but when the public officer performs his duty without ability, and when he obeys the letter of the law without zeal or energy, he is at least beyond the reach of judicial interference. The Court of Sessions, even when it is invested with its official powers, is in this case unable to compel him to a more satisfactory obedience. The fear of removal is the only check to these quasi-offences; and as the Court of Sessions does not originate the town authorities, it cannot remove functionaries whom it does not appoint. Moreover, a perpetual investigation would be necessary to convict the officer of negligence or lukewarmness; and the Court of Sessions sits but twice a year and then only judges such offences as are brought before its notice. The only security of that active and enlightened obedience which a court of justice cannot impose upon public officers lies in the possibility of their arbitrary removal. In France this security is sought for in powers exercised by the heads of the administration; in America it is sought for in the principle of election.

Thus, to recapitulate in a few words what I have been showing: If a public officer in New England commits a crime in the exercise of his functions, the ordinary courts of justice are always called upon to pass sentence upon him. If he commits a fault in his official capacity, a purely administrative tribunal is empowered to punish him; and, if the affair is important or urgent, the judge supplies the omission of the functionary. Lastly, if the same individual is guilty of one of those intangible offences of which human justice has no cognizance, he annually appears before a tribunal from which there is no appeal, which can at once reduce him to insignificance and deprive him of his charge. This system undoubtedly possesses great advantages, but its execution is attended with a practical difficulty which it is important to point out.

I have already observed that the administrative tribunal, which is called the Court of Sessions, has

未能执行法律规定

做出法律禁止的行为

法院只对官员的后两种失职行为进行追究，而且要有确凿的事实作为审理的依据。因此，如果乡镇行政委员在乡镇选举时未能履行法定程序，有可能会被处以罚款。但是如果官员在履行职责时表现出能力不足或是执行法律规定时不积极卖力，则起码不会受到法律的惩处。在这样的情形下，尽管地方法庭已经拥有行政权，仍然不能让这些官员完全俯首听命。只有对于被罢黜的担忧可能对这些轻微的犯罪有震慑作用，而由于乡镇政权并非源自地方法庭，它自然无权对并非其任命的乡镇官员进行罢免。此外，为了查处玩忽职守消极怠工的官员，长效的监督机制必不可少。但是，地方法院每年只开庭两次且只对提起诉讼的犯罪行为进行审理。促使官员积极服从的唯一保障就在于公职人员的罢免权，而一般的司法机构并没有这样的权力。在法国，我们可以从行政等级制度里得到这样的保障，而在美国，则是通过选举制度得以实现。

因此，依据前面所述内容可以简要概括为：

如果新英格兰的官员在执行公务时有犯罪行为，普通法庭可以对他们惩处；但是如果他们出现行政过错时，只有纯行政法庭有权对其进行处分；而当情节严重或是事态紧急时，法官可以弥补这一缺陷对其进行处罚。最后，如果一名公职人员所犯罪行难以认定，同时法庭也无法确定其有罪与否的时候，会将其提交当年不准上诉的法庭进行审理，这一

no right of inspection over the town officers. It can only interfere when the conduct of a magistrate is specially brought under its notice; and this is the delicate part of the system. The Americans of New England are unacquainted with the office of public prosecutor in the Court of Sessions, and it may readily be perceived that it could not have been established without difficulty. If an accusing magistrate had merely been appointed in the chief town of each county, and if he had been unassisted by agents in the townships, he would not have been better acquainted with what was going on in the county than the members of the Court of Sessions. But to appoint agents in each township would have been to centre in his person the most formidable of powers, that of a judicial administration. Moreover, laws are the children of habit, and nothing of the kind exists in the legislation of England. The Americans have therefore divided the offices of inspection and of prosecution, as well as all the other functions of the administration. Grand jurors are bound by the law to apprise the court to which they belong of all the misdemeanors which may have been committed in their county. There are certain great offences which are officially prosecuted by the States; but more frequently the task of punishing delinquents devolves upon the fiscal officer, whose province it is to receive the fine: thus the treasurer of the township is charged with the prosecution of such administrative offences as fall under his notice. But a more special appeal is made by American legislation to the private interest of the citizen; and this great principle is constantly to be met with in studying the laws of the United States. American legislators are more apt to give men credit for intelligence than for honesty, and they rely not a little on personal cupidity for the execution of the laws. When an individual is really and sensibly injured by an administrative abuse, it is natural that his personal interest should induce him to prosecute. But if a legal formality be required, which, however advantageous to the community, is of small importance to individuals, plaintiffs may be less easily found; and thus, by a tacit agreement, the laws may fall into disuse. Reduced by their system to this extremity, the Americans are obliged to encourage informers by bestowing on them a portion of the penalty in certain cases, and to insure the execution of the laws by the dangerous expedient of degrading the morals of the people. The only administrative authority above the county magistrates is, properly speaking, that of

法庭可以即刻剥夺他的权力，罢免他的官职。这一体制无疑好处多多，但同时也必须指出其实际执行起来困难重重。

我已经注意到称之为地方法庭的行政性法院对于乡镇官员没有监督权。只有对行政官员的行为提起诉讼的时候，它才能进行干预，这正是这一体制的缺陷所在。新英格兰的美国人没有为地方法院设置检察官，而且也应该注意到这样的设置对他们也绝非易事。如果只在县设置检察官，而在乡镇没有他的助理，那么他对县情况的了解也并不会比地方法院的人员更多。但是要在每个乡镇都为他设置助理，其必然要将行政和司法大权独揽。法律是习惯的产物，况且在英国法律也没有类似的规定。因此，美国人将侦讯权和司法权分开，就好像他们将所有行政权分开一样。大陪审团的成员依法将本县内可能发生的各类犯罪行为向其所属法庭进行通报。一些重大的渎职行为须提交高级检察机关起诉，但在大多时候，对于失职人员的处罚交由财务官员执行，由其负责收纳被处的罚款。所以，乡镇司库有违法行为的时候，大部分直接由他进行起诉。但是，美国的立法特别重视公民个人权益，这是在对美国法律进行研究时经常能够见到的重要原则。美国的立法者更愿意相信人的理智而不是诚信，因此在执行法律的时候他们丝毫不会依赖人的贪欲。当个人感到行政处罚带来的伤害的时候，个人利益会促使他们提出诉讼。但是不管法律如何对全社会有利，要是对个人没有任何利益而言，那也不会有人愿意去做原告。因此，通过一种默契，法律就会被弃之一边。美国人的这种体制让他们走上极端，所以美国人不得不对检举者加以鼓励，在某些特定案件中，他们能够从中分得一部分罚款。美国人不得不以伤风败俗为

the Government.

General Remarks On The Administration Of The United States

Differences of the States of the Union in their system of administration—Activity and perfection of the local authorities decrease towards the South—Power of the magistrate increases; that of the elector diminishes—Administration passes from the township to the county—States of New York, Ohio, Pennsylvania—Principles of administration applicable to the whole Union—Election of public officers, and inalienability of their functions—Absence of gradation of ranks—Introduction of judicial resources into the administration.

I have already premised that, after having examined the constitution of the township and the county of New England in detail, I should take a general view of the remainder of the Union. Townships and a local activity exist in every State; but in no part of the confederation is a township to be met with precisely similar to those of New England. The more we descend towards the South, the less active does the business of the township or parish become; the number of magistrates, of functions, and of rights decreases; the population exercises a less immediate influence on affairs; town meetings are less frequent, and the subjects of debate less numerous. The power of the elected magistrate is augmented and that of the elector diminished, whilst the public spirit of the local communities is less awakened and less influential. These differences may be perceived to a certain extent in the State of New York; they are very sensible in Pennsylvania; but they become less striking as we advance to the northwest. The majority of the emigrants who settle in the northwestern States are natives of New England, and they carry the habits of their mother country with them into that which they adopt. A township in Ohio is by no means dissimilar from a township in Massachusetts.

We have seen that in Massachusetts the mainspring of public administration lies in the township. It forms the common centre of the interests and affections of the citizens. But this ceases to be the case as we descend to States in which knowledge is less generally diffused, and where the township

代价来确保法律的执行。确切地说，县行政官员之上的行政当局没有行政权只有统治权。

美国行政概况

联邦各州行政制度的差异——越往南方，乡镇当局的活动越不积极充分——随着官员权力变大，选民的权力反而变小——行政权由乡镇向县转移——纽约州、俄亥俄州、宾夕法尼亚州——适用于整个联邦的行政原则——公职人员的选举及其职位的不可剥夺性——等级制度的缺位——司法手段介入行政。

前面我已经说过，在对新英格兰乡镇和县体制进行详细考察后，要对联邦其余部分进行概述。每个州都有乡镇以及地方活动，但是无论哪个州都没有一个乡镇跟新英格兰的乡镇一模一样。越往南，乡镇和教区的活力越差，乡镇官员的职能和权限越少，居民对乡镇事务的直接影响越小，乡镇大会的次数也越少，而且讨论的议题也越有限。随着民选官员权力的增大，选民权力的变小，乡镇的自治精神变得更萎靡不振。这些差异在纽约州已经能够看出一些端倪，而到了宾夕法尼亚州便已十分明显，但是如果你到过西北部，这些差异就不足为奇了。定居在西北各州的移民，大部分来自新英格兰，他们把故乡的行政习惯带到这里。俄亥俄州的乡镇跟马萨诸塞州的乡镇如出一辙。

我们已经注意到，在马萨诸塞州公共行政的大权主要握在乡镇手里。因而，乡镇成为公民利益和情感的中心。但是越靠近教育不够普及的各州，乡镇便不再成为这样的中心，

consequently offers fewer guarantees of a wise and active administration. As we leave New England, therefore, we find that the importance of the town is gradually transferred to the county, which becomes the centre of administration, and the intermediate power between the Government and the citizen. In Massachusetts the business of the county is conducted by the Court of Sessions, which is composed of a quorum named by the Governor and his council; but the county has no representative assembly, and its expenditure is voted by the national legislature. In the great State of New York, on the contrary, and in those of Ohio and Pennsylvania, the inhabitants of each county choose a certain number of representatives, who constitute the assembly of the county. The county assembly has the right of taxing the inhabitants to a certain extent; and in this respect it enjoys the privileges of a real legislative body: at the same time it exercises an executive power in the county, frequently directs the administration of the townships, and restricts their authority within much narrower bounds than in Massachusetts.

Such are the principal differences which the systems of county and town administration present in the Federal States. Were it my intention to examine the provisions of American law minutely, I should have to point out still further differences in the executive details of the several communities. But what I have already said may suffice to show the general principles on which the administration of the United States rests. These principles are differently applied; their consequences are more or less numerous in various localities; but they are always substantially the same. The laws differ, and their outward features change, but their character does not vary. If the township and the county are not everywhere constituted in the same manner, it is at least true that in the United States the county and the township are always based upon the same principle, namely, that everyone is the best judge of what concerns himself alone, and the most proper person to supply his private wants. The township and the county are therefore bound to take care of their special interests: the State governs, but it does not interfere with their administration. Exceptions to this rule may be met with, but not a contrary principle.

The first consequence of this doctrine has been to cause all the magistrates to be chosen either by or at least from amongst the citizens. As the officers are everywhere elected or appointed for a certain period, it has been impossible to establish the rules of a dependent series of authorities;

正是因为教育的普及性差，所以难以保障行政的智慧和活力。因此，当我们离开新英格兰，便会看到乡镇的重心开始渐渐向县转移，乃至其成为行政工作的中心，以及政府和公民之间的权力中枢。在马萨诸塞州，县事务由地方法庭打理。地方法院由州长及其咨议会任命的数名官员组成。县不设议会，其预算由州立法机关投票决定。然而，在纽约州这样的大州以及俄亥俄州和宾夕法尼亚州，县里的居民会选出一定数量的代表，组成县议会。县议会有权利在一定范围内向居民征税，就这一方面而言，它享有立法机关的特权，同时它还拥有县行政权，领导乡镇的行政管理，并将其权力限制在比马萨诸塞州乡镇权力小得多的范围内。

这就是联邦各州在县和乡镇体制上表现出的主要差异。如果我的意图旨在详细考察美国的行政权，一定能够在具体的执行方式上找到更多的不同。但是我所陈述的内容足以说明美国行政工作所依据的主要原则。这些原则的应用方式不同，其成果也随地域的差异而有大有小，但是其实质相同。法律条文不同，其面貌也有差异，但是其根本没有变化。尽管在各地乡镇和县并非采用同样的方式建立，但是至少它们都建立在相同的原则之上，即每个人都是与个人利益相关事务的最好裁判以及满足个人需要的最佳人选。因此，乡镇和县只负责照管人们的共同利益。州只负责统治，不介入行政管理。在应用这一原则的时候也有例外，但是不能与这一原则发生抵触。

这一原则造就的第一个结果便是，行政官员全部经选举产生，或至少从自己人中产生。当各地官员都经选举产生并不能随意罢免，等级制度就无法建立。所以，有多少官职

there are almost as many independent functionaries as there are functions, and the executive power is disseminated in a multitude of hands. Hence arose the indispensable necessity of introducing the control of the courts of justice over the administration, and the system of pecuniary penalties, by which the secondary bodies and their representatives are constrained to obey the laws. This system obtains from one end of the Union to the other. The power of punishing the misconduct of public officers, or of performing the part of the executive in urgent cases, has not, however, been bestowed on the same judges in all the States. The Anglo-Americans derived the institution of justices of the peace from a common source; but although it exists in all the States, it is not always turned to the same use. The justices of the peace everywhere participate in the administration of the townships and the counties, either as public officers or as the judges of public misdemeanors, but in most of the States the more important classes of public offences come under the cognizance of the ordinary tribunals.

The election of public officers, or the inalienability of their functions, the absence of a gradation of powers, and the introduction of a judicial control over the secondary branches of the administration, are the universal characteristics of the American system from Maine to the Floridas. In some States (and that of New York has advanced most in this direction) traces of a centralized administration begin to be discernible. In the State of New York the officers of the central government exercise, in certain cases, a sort of inspection or control over the secondary bodies.

At other times they constitute a court of appeal for the decision of affairs. In the State of New York judicial penalties are less used than in other parts as a means of administration, and the right of prosecuting the offences of public officers is vested in fewer hands. The same tendency is faintly observable in some other States; but in general the prominent feature of the administration in the United States is its excessive local independence.

Of The State

I have described the townships and the administration; it now remains for me to speak of the State and the Government. This is ground I may pass over rapidly, without fear of being misunderstood;

就有多少独立的官员，行政权也就分散到众人之手。因此，司法对于行政权的控制以及罚款制度便不可或缺，这样便可迫使下属机构及其代表服从法律的约束。美国上下从南到北从东到西都采用这样的制度。然而，在美国各州，惩处公职人员犯罪行为的权力或是紧急情况下的执行权并不由一名法官掌控。英裔美国人的治安法官制度都出自同一来源。尽管这一制度在各州普遍存在，但是其目的并不相同。各地的治安法官均参与乡镇和县的行政管理，既是公职人员又是审理行政犯罪行为的法官。但是在大多数州，重大的行政犯罪案件则由普通法院进行审理。

行政官员选举制或者说是任期结束前不可罢免的制度，行政等级制度的不存在，以及司法手段对下级行政部门的干预，这就是美国从缅因州到弗洛里达州所实行的行政制度的普遍特点。在某些州，开始出现行政管理权集中的迹象，纽约州在这方面走的最远。在纽约州，州政府的官员在特定的情形下可以对下级部门进行监督和控制。有时，州官员会成立一个上诉法庭对事务进行仲裁。与其他州相比，在纽约州采用司法处分作为行政管理手段的情形更少，而对于行政犯罪行为的起诉则掌握在少数的人手中。在其他各州，同样的趋势也露出了苗头，但是总的来说，美国行政管理的突出特点是过度的地方独立。

关于州

前面已经对乡镇及其行政管理进行了描述，接下来我要说一说州及其政府。有关州的内容我会一笔带过，而且并不担心人们会对此产生误解。因为我所述的都可以在宪法里找

for all I have to say is to be found in written forms of the various constitutions, which are easily to be procured. These constitutions rest upon a simple and rational theory; their forms have been adopted by all constitutional nations, and are become familiar to us. In this place, therefore, it is only necessary for me to give a short analysis; I shall endeavor afterwards to pass judgment upon what I now describe.

Legislative Power Of The State

Division of the Legislative Body into two Houses—Senate—House of Representatives—Different functions of these two Bodies.

The legislative power of the State is vested in two assemblies, the first of which generally bears the name of the Senate. The Senate is commonly a legislative body; but it sometimes becomes an executive and judicial one. It takes a part in the government in several ways, according to the constitution of the different States; but it is in the nomination of public functionaries that it most commonly assumes an executive power. It partakes of judicial power in the trial of certain political offences, and sometimes also in the decision of certain civil cases. The number of its members is always small. The other branch of the legislature, which is usually called the House of Representatives, has no share whatever in the administration, and only takes a part in the judicial power inasmuch as it impeaches public functionaries before the Senate. The members of the two Houses are nearly everywhere subject to the same conditions of election. They are chosen in the same manner, and by the same citizens. The only difference which exists between them is, that the term for which the Senate is chosen is in general longer than that of the House of Representatives. The latter seldom remain in office longer than a year; the former usually sit two or three years. By granting to the senators the privilege of being chosen for several years, and being renewed seriatim, the law takes care to preserve in the legislative body a nucleus of men already accustomed to public business, and capable of exercising a salutary influence upon the junior members.

The Americans, plainly, did not desire, by this separation of the legislative body into two branches,

到明文规定。这些宪法都建立在一个简单而合理的理论之上，其形式为所有的立宪国家所采用，所以我们对此非常熟悉。因此，在这里，我只需做以简单分析，后面会再对我现在的所有叙述进行评判。

州立法权

立法机构分两院——参议院——众议院——两院的不同职能。

州立法权分属两院。一个一般称为参议院，通常是立法机关，有时也变身为行政和司法机关。依据各州的宪法，参议院会采用不同方式参与政府行政管理，通常是在官员竞选得到任命时获得行政权。在对某些特定的政治案件和民事案件进行审理时，它还会分享司法权。参议院成员的人数一般很少。另一个立法机关通常被称为众议院，不享有任何的行政权，仅在向参议院控告公职人员的时候享有司法权。两院议员的当选条件在各州几乎相同，按照相同的方式由相同的公民选出。两者的唯一不同之处就是任期，通常参议员的任期比众议员要更长。后者的任期往往不超过一年，前者的任期通常为两到三年。法律之所以赋予参议员长任期和连选连任的特权，是希望能够在立法机构保留一部分熟知公务并对新当选的参议员产生积极影响的核心人员。

显而易见，美国人在将立法机关分成两院时，并没有打算把一个建成世袭制，另一个建成选举制，一个贵族制一个民主制。他们的目的也不是让一个成为政权的保护伞，让另

to make one house hereditary and the other elective; one aristocratic and the other democratic. It was not their object to create in the one a bulwark to power, whilst the other represented the interests and passions of the people. The only advantages which result from the present constitution of the United States are the division of the legislative power and the consequent check upon political assemblies; with the creation of a tribunal of appeal for the revision of the laws.

Time and experience, however, have convinced the Americans that if these are its only advantages, the division of the legislative power is still a principle of the greatest necessity. Pennsylvania was the only one of the United States which at first attempted to establish a single House of Assembly, and Franklin himself was so far carried away by the necessary consequences of the principle of the sovereignty of the people as to have concurred in the measure; but the Pennsylvanians were soon obliged to change the law, and to create two Houses. Thus the principle of the division of the legislative power was finally established, and its necessity may henceforward be regarded as a demonstrated truth. This theory, which was nearly unknown to the republics of antiquity—which was introduced into the world almost by accident, like so many other great truths—and misunderstood by several modern nations, is at length become an axiom in the political science of the present age.

The Executive Power Of The State

Office of Governor in an American State—The place he occupies in relation to the Legislature—His rights and his duties—His dependence on the people.

The executive power of the State may with truth be said to be represented by the Governor, although he enjoys but a portion of its rights. The supreme magistrate, under the title of Governor, is the official moderator and counsellor of the legislature. He is armed with a veto or suspensive power, which allows him to stop, or at least to retard, its movements at pleasure. He lays the wants of the country before the legislative body, and points out the means which he thinks may be usefully employed in providing for them; he is the natural executor of its decrees in all the undertakings which interest the nation at large. In the absence of the legislature, the Governor is bound to take all necessary steps to guard the State against violent shocks and unforeseen dangers. The whole military

一个代表人民的利益和民意。美国现行的两院制唯一优势在于：立法权分开后，抑制了国会的活动，并建立了对法律进行修订的上诉法庭。

时间和经验让美国人相信，如果这是唯一的优势，那么立法权的分割就是最为必要的原则。宾夕法尼亚州是美国唯一一个在最初尝试建立单一议会的州，而富兰克林在人民主权原则的推动下，赞成了这一方案。但是，不久宾夕法尼亚人被迫对法律做出修改，并设立两院。最终，立法权分散的原则确立起来，所以自此之后，这一原则被认为是已经证明的真理。这个几乎不为古老共和国所知的理论，就像其他许多真理一样，几乎是偶然的来到这个世界，尽管曾经被一些现代国家所误解，最终成为如今政治科学的公理。

州行政权

一个美国州的州长——他在立法机构的地位——他的权利和义务——他对人民的依靠。

实事求是地说，州的行政权以州长为代表，尽管他只行使其权利的一部分。顶着州长头衔的最高官员既是立法机构的主宰也是它的顾问。拥有否决权这一武器，他可以随意阻止至少是拖延司法机构的活动。他会在立法机构面前说明州的需要，并提出他认为能够满足这些需要最行之有效的方法。他是与全州利益相关的所有法令的当然执行人。在立法机关休会期，州长必须采用一切必要措施保护州免遭动乱和意外的危险。州长握有全州军事

power of the State is at the disposal of the Governor. He is the commander of the militia, and head of the armed force. When the authority, which is by general consent awarded to the laws, is disregarded, the Governor puts himself at the head of the armed force of the State, to quell resistance, and to restore order. Lastly, the Governor takes no share in the administration of townships and counties, except it be indirectly in the nomination of Justices of the Peace, which nomination he has not the power to cancel. The Governor is an elected magistrate, and is generally chosen for one or two years only; so that he always continues to be strictly dependent upon the majority who returned him.

Political Effects Of The System Of Local Administration In The United States

Necessary distinction between the general centralization of Government and the centralization of the local administration—Local administration not centralized in the United States: great general centralization of the Government—Some bad consequences resulting to the United States from the local administration—Administrative advantages attending this order of things—The power which conducts the Government is less regular, less enlightened, less learned, but much greater than in Europe— Political advantages of this order of things—In the United States the interests of the country are everywhere kept in view—Support given to the Government by the community—Provincial institutions more necessary in proportion as the social condition becomes more democratic—Reason of this.

Centralization is become a word of general and daily use, without any precise meaning being attached to it. Nevertheless, there exist two distinct kinds of centralization, which it is necessary to discriminate with accuracy. Certain interests are common to all parts of a nation, such as the enactment of its general laws and the maintenance of its foreign relations. Other interests are peculiar to certain parts of the nation; such, for instance, as the business of different townships. When the power which directs the general interests is centred in one place, or vested in the same persons, it constitutes a central government. In like manner the power of directing partial or local interests, when brought together into one place, constitutes what may be termed a central administration.

Upon some points these two kinds of centralization coalesce; but by classifying the objects which fall more particularly within the province of each of them, they may easily be distinguished.

大权，既是国民军的司令又是武装力量的首脑。当依法得到认可的州的权威遭到践踏的时候，州长可以统领州的武装力量镇压反抗恢复秩序。最后，除通过任命治安法官间接参与行政工作以外，州长无权参与乡镇和县的行政管理，而且尽管治安法官由其任命但是他并没有罢免权。州长是民选官员，一般任期只有一到两年，从而将其一直置于选举他的大多数选民的严密监控之下。

美国行政分权的政治效果

政府集权和地方行政集权的差别——美国地方行政权并不集中，政府更为集权——地方行政分权带给美国的一些害处——这种做法的行政优势——运作政府的权力尽管不够正规、文明和博学，但是比欧洲要大——这种做法的政治好处——在美国，国家意识表现在各个方面——被统治者对政府的支持——社会越民主越需要完备的地方组织——其原因何在。

"集权"已经成为一个常用的词，但是人们并没有给它一个精准的定义。实际上，存在两种性质非常不同的集权，因此要对此进行准确区分。有些利益关乎整个国家，例如全国性法律的制定和对外关系的维护。还有一些利益只关乎部分群体，诸如不同乡镇的地方事业。当用来管理共同利益的权力集中到同一个地方或是掌握在同一群人手中时，政府集权形成。以同样的方式，当管理地方利益的权力集中起来，便称之为行政集权。

It is evident that a central government acquires immense power when united to administrative centralization. Thus combined, it accustoms men to set their own will habitually and completely aside; to submit, not only for once, or upon one point, but in every respect, and at all times. Not only, therefore, does this union of power subdue them compulsorily, but it affects them in the ordinary habits of life, and influences each individual, first separately and then collectively.

These two kinds of centralization mutually assist and attract each other; but they must not be supposed to be inseparable. It is impossible to imagine a more completely central government than that which existed in France under Louis XIV.; when the same individual was the author and the interpreter of the laws, and the representative of France at home and abroad, he was justified in asserting that the State was identified with his person. Nevertheless, the administration was much less centralized under Louis XIV. than it is at the present day.

In England the centralization of the government is carried to great perfection; the State has the compact vigor of a man, and by the sole act of its will it puts immense engines in motion, and wields or collects the efforts of its authority. Indeed, I cannot conceive that a nation can enjoy a secure or prosperous existence without a powerful centralization of government. But I am of opinion that a central administration enervates the nations in which it exists by incessantly diminishing their public spirit. If such an administration succeeds in condensing at a given moment, on a given point, all the disposable resources of a people, it impairs at least the renewal of those resources. It may ensure a victory in the hour of strife, but it gradually relaxes the sinews of strength. It may contribute admirably to the transient greatness of a man, but it cannot ensure the durable prosperity of a nation.

If we pay proper attention, we shall find that whenever it is said that a State cannot act because it has no central point, it is the centralization of the government in which it is deficient. It is frequently asserted, and we are prepared to assent to the proposition, that the German empire was never able to bring all its powers into action. But the reason was, that the State was never able to enforce obedience to its general laws, because the several members of that great body always claimed the right, or found the means, of refusing their co-operation to the representatives of the common authority, even in the

这两种集权在某些点上有些重合，但是从其各自管辖的对象来看，两者的区别便显而易见。当政府集权和行政集权联手，中央政府就会拥有无限权力。这样就会让人们习惯性的完全将个人意志放到一边，并不是一次在一件事上表示服从，而是在所有事情上时时刻刻表示服从。因此，这种联合起来的权力不但将人们制服，而且还会影响人们的习惯，进而影响每一个人。它先将人民孤立起来，然后各个击破让他们变成顺民。

这两种集权相互扶持，彼此吸引，但它们绝非不可分割。路易十四统治时期，在法国建立起最为强大的中央政府，以至于当时人们认为他既是法律的制定者也是法律的解说着，还是法国内政外交的代表，他还有理有据的宣称自己就是国家。然而，在路易十四统治时期，行政集权远比不上现在。

在英国，政府集权达到巅峰。政府就好像是一个精力充沛的人，只要其愿意便能仅凭一己之力让国家机器这个庞然大物运转起来，还能将所有的权力投向它所想的任何地方。我的确无法想象没有强有力的政府集权一个国家能够存在或是繁荣昌盛。但是我也秉持这样的观点：行政集权会让国家变得萎靡不振，因为它的存在会不断消磨国民精神。的确，在特定的时间和特定的地点，这样的集权能够成功地将所有的力量都集结起来，但它至少会对这些力量的再生造成损害。它也许可以保证一时得胜，但会让绷紧的力量渐渐放松。它会成就一个转瞬即逝的伟人，但是无法保证一个国家长久的繁荣。

如果我们给予适当的关注，就会发现当我们说一个国家由于未能实行集权而碌碌无为的时候，总是指向未能真正理解的政府集权。人们一再指出，而我也很赞成这样的说法，

affairs which concerned the mass of the people; in other words, because there was no centralization of government. The same remark is applicable to the Middle Ages; the cause of all the confusion of feudal society was that the control, not only of local but of general interests, was divided amongst a thousand hands, and broken up in a thousand different ways; the absence of a central government prevented the nations of Europe from advancing with energy in any straightforward course.

We have shown that in the United States no central administration and no dependent series of public functionaries exist. Local authority has been carried to lengths which no European nation could endure without great inconvenience, and which has even produced some disadvantageous consequences in America. But in the United States the centralization of the Government is complete; and it would be easy to prove that the national power is more compact than it has ever been in the old nations of Europe. Not only is there but one legislative body in each State; not only does there exist but one source of political authority; but district assemblies and county courts have not in general been multiplied, lest they should be tempted to exceed their administrative duties, and interfere with the Government. In America the legislature of each State is supreme; nothing can impede its authority; neither privileges, nor local immunities, nor personal influence, nor even the empire of reason, since it represents that majority which claims to be the sole organ of reason. Its own determination is, therefore, the only limit to this action. In juxtaposition to it, and under its immediate control, is the representative of the executive power, whose duty it is to constrain the refractory to submit by superior force. The only symptom of weakness lies in certain details of the action of the Government. The American republics have no standing armies to intimidate a discontented minority; but as no minority has as yet been reduced to declare open war, the necessity of an army has not been felt. The State usually employs the officers of the township or the county to deal with the citizens. Thus, for instance, in New England, the assessor fixes the rate of taxes; the collector receives them; the town-treasurer transmits the amount to the public treasury; and the disputes which may arise are brought before the ordinary courts of justice. This method of collecting taxes is slow as well as inconvenient, and it would prove a perpetual hindrance to a Government whose pecuniary demands

即德意志帝国从未能将所有的力量发动起来。而原因就在于，国家未能强迫人民服从国家通用法律，就因为这个大机体内的几个成员总是声称有权利或是找到方法拒绝与国家当局代表合作，甚至有关人民大众的事务也是如此。换句话说，就是因为没有实行政府集权。这样的说法也适用于中世纪。封建社会的种种混乱之源就在于掌控权被过度分割并落入到太多人手中。因为政府集权的缺失，阻碍欧洲各国生机勃勃地朝着目标前进。

我们已经说过，美国没有行政集权和等级制度的存在。美国地方权力已经到达欧洲国家无可容忍的地步，而且也给美国自身带来许多不利的后果。但是，在美国政府集权已经完成，而且不难证明美国国家权力的集中远超任何欧洲国家。每个州不仅只有一个立法机构，也不仅只有一个政权的来源。而各地区议会和县法庭一般也不允许联合行动，以防他们越权干扰政府工作。在美国，每个州的立法机关至高无上，什么也不能阻挡它的权威，无论是特权还是地方豁免权，抑或是个人影响，甚至是理性的权威。因为它代表了自认为是理性代言人的大多数。所以，它自己的决定是其行动的唯一束缚。与其肩并肩，且直接受其领导的就是行政权的代表，他们的职责就是迫使不满分子就范。政府工作的细节方面还存有一些薄弱环节。美国各州共和国没有可以震慑不满少数派的常备军，但是这些少数派至今也没有发展到发动战争，让州感到军队不可或缺的程度。在与公民打交道的时候，州通常利用乡镇和县里的官员。但是对于像美国那样组建起来的中央政府，往往易于根据自身需要采用新的更为行之有效的行动方式。

所以，并不像人们常说的那样，美国中央集权的缺位导致新世界各共和国的灭亡。美

were large. It is desirable that, in whatever materially affects its existence, the Government should be served by officers of its own, appointed by itself, removable at pleasure, and accustomed to rapid methods of proceeding. But it will always be easy for the central government, organized as it is in America, to introduce new and more efficacious modes of action, proportioned to its wants.

The absence of a central government will not, then, as has often been asserted, prove the destruction of the republics of the New World; far from supposing that the American governments are not sufficiently centralized, I shall prove hereafter that they are too much so. The legislative bodies daily encroach upon the authority of the Government, and their tendency, like that of the French Convention, is to appropriate it entirely to themselves. Under these circumstances the social power is constantly changing hands, because it is subordinate to the power of the people, which is too apt to forget the maxims of wisdom and of foresight in the consciousness of its strength: hence arises its danger; and thus its vigor, and not its impotence, will probably be the cause of its ultimate destruction.

The system of local administration produces several different effects in America. The Americans seem to me to have outstepped the limits of sound policy in isolating the administration of the Government; for order, even in second-rate affairs, is a matter of national importance. As the State has no administrative functionaries of its own, stationed on different points of its territory, to whom it can give a common impulse, the consequence is that it rarely attempts to issue any general police regulations. The want of these regulations is severely felt, and is frequently observed by Europeans. The appearance of disorder which prevails on the surface leads him at first to imagine that society is in a state of anarchy; nor does he perceive his mistake till he has gone deeper into the subject. Certain undertakings are of importance to the whole State; but they cannot be put in execution, because there is no national administration to direct them. Abandoned to the exertions of the towns or counties, under the care of elected or temporary agents, they lead to no result, or at least to no durable benefit.

The partisans of centralization in Europe are wont to maintain that the Government directs the affairs of each locality better than the citizens could do it for themselves; this may be true when the central power is enlightened, and when the local districts are ignorant; when it is as alert as they are

国政府绝非人们所认为的那样不够集权，后面我会证明他们其实非常集权。立法机构每天都在蚕食政府这样或那样的权力，就好像法国国民公会做的一样，妄图把所有权力都揽到手里。因为这样集中起来的社会权力从属于人民，所以会不断易手。它自恃力量强大，经常表现得缺乏智慧和远见。这正是它的危险之处，所以正是它的力量本身而非软弱无能导致自己的灭亡。

行政分权制度在美国产生了几个不同的后果。在我看来，美国人的所作所为似乎已经超出合理的范围，他们把行政完全从政府中独立出来。因为即使是次要的事务，全国也应该有统一的制度。因为州没有在其管辖行政区内设立固定的行政官员，从而无法建立统一的惩罚制度，结果就导致几乎想不到要颁布州统一的治安条例，而对于这些条例的需求实际上则非常迫切。欧洲人往往会注意到这些，美国所表现出的混乱表象会让欧洲人开始误以为美国社会处于无政府状态，只有当他们对美国有了深入了解的时候，才会意识到自己的错误。有些事情关系到整个州，却因为没有全州性行政机构进行管理无法统一行动。而把事情交给各乡镇和县由选举产生的有一定任期的官员执行，结果不是一事无成就是无法长久。

欧洲集权主义的拥护者们秉持这样的观点，由国家对地方行政事务进行领导比交给地方当局自己管理要好得多。这样的做法是正确的，但其前提是中央政权是开明的，而地方当局是无知的，或是前者很积极后者很消极，前者习惯于工作而后者习惯于服从。显然这种两极化的趋势会随着中央集权的加强而加剧，也就是一方的全能和另一方的无能之间的差异会越来越鲜明。但是，我认为当人民如美国人一般的开明、关心自身利益，又习惯于

slow; when it is accustomed to act, and they to obey. Indeed, it is evident that this double tendency must augment with the increase of centralization, and that the readiness of the one and the incapacity of the others must become more and more prominent. But I deny that such is the case when the people is as enlightened, as awake to its interests, and as accustomed to reflect on them, as the Americans are. I am persuaded, on the contrary, that in this case the collective strength of the citizens will always conduce more efficaciously to the public welfare than the authority of the Government. It is difficult to point out with certainty the means of arousing a sleeping population, and of giving it passions and knowledge which it does not possess; it is, I am well aware, an arduous task to persuade men to busy themselves about their own affairs; and it would frequently be easier to interest them in the punctilios of court etiquette than in the repairs of their common dwelling. But whenever a central administration affects to supersede the persons most interested, I am inclined to suppose that it is either misled or desirous to mislead. However enlightened and however skilful a central power may be, it cannot of itself embrace all the details of the existence of a great nation. Such vigilance exceeds the powers of man. And when it attempts to create and set in motion so many complicated springs, it must submit to a very imperfect result, or consume itself in bootless efforts.

Centralization succeeds more easily, indeed, in subjecting the external actions of men to a certain uniformity, which at least commands our regard, independently of the objects to which it is applied, like those devotees who worship the statue and forget the deity it represents. Centralization imparts without difficulty an admirable regularity to the routine of business; provides for the details of the social police with sagacity; represses the smallest disorder and the most petty misdemeanors; maintains society in a status quo alike secure from improvement and decline; and perpetuates a drowsy precision in the conduct of affairs, which is hailed by the heads of the administration as a sign of perfect order and public tranquillity: in short, it excels more in prevention than in action. Its force deserts it when society is to be disturbed or accelerated in its course; and if once the co-operation of private citizens is necessary to the furtherance of its measures, the secret of its impotence is disclosed. Even whilst it invokes their assistance, it is on the condition that they shall act exactly as

为自身利益思考的时候，就不会发生这样的情况。相反，在这样的情况下，公民的集体力量总是能够比政府更有效地促进社会福利。我承认，在某种条件下要找到一种方法去唤醒沉睡民族并赋予他们所不曾拥有的热情和知识并不容易。我也已经充分意识到，说服人们要为自己的事情忙前忙后也非易事。而且，与修缮普通民居相比，宫廷礼仪的繁文缛节往往更能勾起人们的兴趣。但是，无论何时只要中央行政部门想要越俎代庖取代下级机构，在我看来都是自误或是误人的举动。不管一个中央政权多么的精明强干，都无法仅凭一己之力对全国上下的事情了若指掌。因为这绝非凡人能力所及。但是当它想要尝试创建一系列的发条构件并使之连动起来，其结果不是遗憾连连，就是徒劳无益。

集权制的确能够更为轻而易举地实现人们表面行为一定程度的一致。这种一致完全出于人们对中央集权的尊重，而对其目的却一无所知，这就好像那些虔诚的信徒，一心只顾膜拜神灵，却忘记了神灵代表的是什么。中央集权不费吹灰之力就可以让国家日常事务变得规规矩矩，制定出的治安条例详细且英明，能够对最小规模的叛乱和最轻微的犯罪行为进行及时处治，从而让社会能够维持现状，既无法实现真正的进步也不会出现实质的倒退，一直处于昏昏欲睡的循规蹈矩的状态，也就是官员们所称道的秩序良好社会安宁。简而言之，中央集权保守有余创新不足。当它激起社会动荡或是加速社会发展的时候，控制力就会削弱，而且如果一旦各项措施的推进需要公民的配合，其虚弱不堪的弱点就暴露无遗。甚至当中央集权的政府有求于民的时候，也会开出条件要求公民完全按照它的意思和方式行事，只负责细枝末节不要妄想对整个体系指手画脚，只能不闻不问盲目工作，只能

much as the Government chooses, and exactly in the manner it appoints. They are to take charge of the details, without aspiring to guide the system; they are to work in a dark and subordinate sphere, and only to judge the acts in which they have themselves cooperated by their results. These, however, are not conditions on which the alliance of the human will is to be obtained; its carriage must be free and its actions responsible, or (such is the constitution of man) the citizen had rather remain a passive spectator than a dependent actor in schemes with which he is unacquainted.

It is undeniable that the want of those uniform regulations which control the conduct of every inhabitant of France is not unfrequently felt in the United States. Gross instances of social indifference and neglect are to be met with, and from time to time disgraceful blemishes are seen in complete contrast with the surrounding civilization. Useful undertakings which cannot succeed without perpetual attention and rigorous exactitude are very frequently abandoned in the end; for in America, as well as in other countries, the people is subject to sudden impulses and momentary exertions. The European who is accustomed to find a functionary always at hand to interfere with all he undertakes has some difficulty in accustoming himself to the complex mechanism of the administration of the townships. In general it may be affirmed that the lesser details of the police, which render life easy and comfortable, are neglected in America; but that the essential guarantees of man in society are as strong there as elsewhere. In America the power which conducts the Government is far less regular, less enlightened, and less learned, but an hundredfold more authoritative than in Europe. In no country in the world do the citizens make such exertions for the common weal; and I am acquainted with no people which has established schools as numerous and as efficacious, places of public worship better suited to the wants of the inhabitants, or roads kept in better repair. Uniformity or permanence of design, the minute arrangement of details, and the perfection of an ingenious administration, must not be sought for in the United States; but it will be easy to find, on the other hand, the symptoms of a power which, if it is somewhat barbarous, is at least robust; and of an existence which is checkered with accidents indeed, but cheered at the same time by animation and effort.

Granting for an instant that the villages and counties of the United States would be more usefully

根据日后的结果再对其所作所为进行评判。然而，这样的条件人们又怎能愿意与它结为盟友，人们要有充分的自由才能对自己的行为负责，所以人们宁可当一个被动的看客也不愿意做傀儡茫然地按照一无所知的计划行事。

无法否认美国也时常会感到对于那些规范法国人行事的统一规范的需要。社会对人所表现出的冷漠毫不关心屡见不鲜，不时出现的可耻瑕疵与周遭的文明形成了强烈的对比。由于无法得到持久的关注和严格的推进，有益的事业难以成功，最后不得不遭到废弃。因为美国人也和其他国家的人一样，做事情往往出于一时冲动。欧洲人总是习惯于遇事去找几乎可以插手一切事务的官员，无法适应美国那种复杂的乡镇行政制度。总的来说我们可以认定在美国那些能够让生活变得安逸舒适的治安细则被忽视了，但是社会对人的主要保障与其他国家一样强而有力。在美国，各州的权力虽然不及欧洲有条有理，开明豁达，博闻强识，但却要强大一百倍。世界上没有任何一个国家能够让人民对社会福利做出如此的贡献，而且据我所知还没有哪个民族设立的学校如此之多如此之有效，其建筑的宗教场所如此适合居民的需求，其修筑的乡间公路保养得如此之完好。所以，在美国找不到表面的一致性和持久性、细节上的事无巨细以及行政上的精致完美，相反一眼看到的是多少有些野蛮至少也是有点粗犷的权力机构，以及一幅意外频频同时却又活力四射锐意进取的生活图景。

如果让我说，要是美国的乡镇和县城由远离它们并被其视为异己的中央政府进行管理，会比由其在当地自行选举出的官员的管理要更为有效。依我看，如果美国整个的行政权都由一人独揽，一定能够把美国治理的更为安全，其社会资源的利用也会更趋合理。尽

governed by a remote authority which they had never seen than by functionaries taken from the midst of them—admitting, for the sake of argument, that the country would be more secure, and the resources of society better employed, if the whole administration centred in a single arm—still the political advantages which the Americans derive from their system would induce me to prefer it to the contrary plan. It profits me but little, after all, that a vigilant authority should protect the tranquillity of my pleasures and constantly avert all dangers from my path, without my care or my concern, if this same authority is the absolute mistress of my liberty and of my life, and if it so monopolizes all the energy of existence that when it languishes everything languishes around it, that when it sleeps everything must sleep, that when it dies the State itself must perish.

In certain countries of Europe the natives consider themselves as a kind of settlers, indifferent to the fate of the spot upon which they live. The greatest changes are effected without their concurrence and (unless chance may have apprised them of the event) without their knowledge; nay more, the citizen is unconcerned as to the condition of his village, the police of his street, the repairs of the church or of the parsonage; for he looks upon all these things as unconnected with himself, and as the property of a powerful stranger whom he calls the Government. He has only a life-interest in these possessions, and he entertains no notions of ownership or of improvement. This want of interest in his own affairs goes so far that, if his own safety or that of his children is endangered, instead of trying to avert the peril, he will fold his arms, and wait till the nation comes to his assistance. This same individual, who has so completely sacrificed his own free will, has no natural propensity to obedience; he cowers, it is true, before the pettiest officer; but he braves the law with the spirit of a conquered foe as soon as its superior force is removed: his oscillations between servitude and license are perpetual. When a nation has arrived at this state it must either change its customs and its laws or perish: the source of public virtue is dry, and, though it may contain subjects, the race of citizens is extinct. Such communities are a natural prey to foreign conquests, and if they do not disappear from the scene of life, it is because they are surrounded by other nations similar or inferior to themselves: it is because the instinctive feeling of their country's claims still exists in their hearts; and because an

管美国人从其所采用的体制里获益良多，但是我依然认为应该采用截然相反的体制。即使有这样一个警醒的权力当局，无须我操心便会保护我的宁静生活不受烦扰，并会一直帮我排除前进道路上的一切危机，但如果它完全成为我自由和生命的绝对主宰，并将一切置于它的垄断之下，它无精打采周围的一切要随之萎靡不振，它入眠周围的一切必须跟随，它死去周围的一切也必须陪葬，那它对我又会有什么好处呢？

在欧洲的某些国家，当地的居民认为自己是外来的移民定居于此，对他们自己生活的所在漠不关心。他们不曾参与国内的重大变化，要不是偶然的听说，对这些变化全不知情，更有甚者，甚至对他们村子的状况、街道的治安以及教堂教士的处境都无动于衷。因为在他们看来这些事情都与他们无关，应该由被称为政府的强大的第三者进行管理。他们认为自己只是作为拥有用益权的人来享用这些财产，既没有将其据为己有的想法也没有要提高收益的念头。他们对自己利益的这种态度已经发展到了如此一种程度，无论是自己或是子女身处险境，他们非但不排除危险，反而插着手等着国家前来救援。他们这样的人尽管愿意完全牺牲自己的自由意志，但也绝非任由人摆布。的确，在最不起眼的小官吏面前他也会畏畏缩缩，然而一旦脱离了上级的管束便敢于违法乱纪。所以，他们不断在奴颜婢膝和肆意妄为之间来回摇摆。当一个国家到达这步田地时，它必须对民情和法律进行改变，否则便会灭亡。公德之源已经干涸，尽管这样的国家可能还有臣民，但是已经不再拥有公民。这样的国家就会想当然的成为外来征服者的猎物，而如果它还没有从世界舞台消失，那不过是因为周边的国家与它相似或比它还差。正是因为与生俱来的爱国本能依然尚

involuntary pride in the name it bears, or a vague reminiscence of its bygone fame, suffices to give them the impulse of self-preservation.

Nor can the prodigious exertions made by tribes in the defence of a country to which they did not belong be adduced in favor of such a system; for it will be found that in these cases their main incitement was religion. The permanence, the glory, or the prosperity of the nation were become parts of their faith, and in defending the country they inhabited they defended that Holy City of which they were all citizens. The Turkish tribes have never taken an active share in the conduct of the affairs of society, but they accomplished stupendous enterprises as long as the victories of the Sultan were the triumphs of the Mohammedan faith. In the present age they are in rapid decay, because their religion is departing, and despotism only remains. Montesquieu, who attributed to absolute power an authority peculiar to itself, did it, as I conceive, an undeserved honor; for despotism, taken by itself, can produce no durable results. On close inspection we shall find that religion, and not fear, has ever been the cause of the long-lived prosperity of an absolute government. Whatever exertions may be made, no true power can be founded among men which does not depend upon the free union of their inclinations; and patriotism and religion are the only two motives in the world which can permanently direct the whole of a body politic to one end.

Laws cannot succeed in rekindling the ardor of an extinguished faith, but men may be interested in the fate of their country by the laws. By this influence the vague impulse of patriotism, which never abandons the human heart, may be directed and revived; and if it be connected with the thoughts, the passions, and the daily habits of life, it may be consolidated into a durable and rational sentiment.

Let it not be said that the time for the experiment is already past; for the old age of nations is not like the old age of men, and every fresh generation is a new people ready for the care of the legislator.

It is not the administrative but the political effects of the local system that I most admire in America. In the United States the interests of the country are everywhere kept in view; they are an object of solicitude to the people of the whole Union, and every citizen is as warmly attached to them as if they were his own. He takes pride in the glory of his nation; he boasts of its success, to which he

存于他们的内心，对过去声名的盲目自豪依然还在，对以往荣耀的模糊记忆依然未退却，便已足以让他们产生自我保护的冲动。

人们曾经为保卫这个他们作为外来人而居住的国家所付出的巨大努力也不能作为支持这一体制的证据，因为经过深入的调查会发现宗教是他们那时斗争的主要动力。国家的长久、荣耀和富强是其神圣信仰的一部分，他们保卫自己的国家就是保卫他们的圣城，因为他们是圣城的公民。土耳其人从来不积极参与社会事务的管理，但是他们能够完成一些艰巨的任务因为苏丹的胜利就是穆罕默德的胜利。如今，他们的宗教一步步衰落，留下的只有专制制度，所以他们自身也在迅速衰败。孟德斯鸠认为专制制度的特有威信来自其自身，但是我认为它不配享有这样的荣誉。因为专制制度只依靠自我根本无法长久。经过仔细的考察就能发现让专制政府保持长久兴盛的是宗教而不是其自身的威吓力。无论你如何寻找，除了依靠人们意志的自由联合外，再也不可能在人们中间找到真正强大的力量。爱国主义和宗教是世界上唯有的两个动因能够让全体公民永远朝着同一个目标前进。

法律无法重新燃起人们对覆灭信仰的狂热，但是却可以让人们关心自己国家的命运。法律的影响能够唤起人们内心尚存的依然模糊不清的爱国主义并对其加以指导。如果能把它与思想、热情和日常生活习惯结合起来，也许可以巩固成为一种持久理性的情感。

不要说已经错过唤醒这种情感的时机，因为国家不会像人一样衰老。新的一代是一群已经做好充分准备掌管立法的新人。

在美国我最为欣赏的不是其地方分权的行政效果，而是这种分权的政治效果。在美

conceives himself to have contributed, and he rejoices in the general prosperity by which he profits. The feeling he entertains towards the State is analogous to that which unites him to his family, and it is by a kind of egotism that he interests himself in the welfare of his country.

The European generally submits to a public officer because he represents a superior force; but to an American he represents a right. In America it may be said that no one renders obedience to man, but to justice and to law. If the opinion which the citizen entertains of himself is exaggerated, it is at least salutary; he unhesitatingly confides in his own powers, which appear to him to be all-sufficient. When a private individual meditates an undertaking, however directly connected it may be with the welfare of society, he never thinks of soliciting the co-operation of the Government, but he publishes his plan, offers to execute it himself, courts the assistance of other individuals, and struggles manfully against all obstacles. Undoubtedly he is often less successful than the State might have been in his position; but in the end the sum of these private undertakings far exceeds all that the Government could have done.

As the administrative authority is within the reach of the citizens, whom it in some degree represents, it excites neither their jealousy nor their hatred; as its resources are limited, every one feels that he must not rely solely on its assistance. Thus, when the administration thinks fit to interfere, it is not abandoned to itself as in Europe; the duties of the private citizens are not supposed to have lapsed because the State assists in their fulfilment, but every one is ready, on the contrary, to guide and to support it. This action of individual exertions, joined to that of the public authorities, frequently performs what the most energetic central administration would be unable to execute. It would be easy to adduce several facts in proof of what I advance, but I had rather give only one, with which I am more thoroughly acquainted. In America the means which the authorities have at their disposal for the discovery of crimes and the arrest of criminals are few. The State police does not exist, and passports are unknown. The criminal police of the United States cannot be compared to that of France; the magistrates and public prosecutors are not numerous, and the examinations of prisoners are rapid and oral. Nevertheless in no country does crime more rarely elude punishment.

国，人们随处都能感到祖国的存在，它是全体人民关心的对象，每个公民将国家利益视作自己的利益。他们以国家的荣誉为骄傲，对国家的成就赞不绝口，确信自己为国家的成就做出贡献，兴奋于自己随着国家的兴盛而获益良多。他们对于国家的这份感情就好似与家庭的感情一般，而且一种自私的心理会促使他们关心州的福祉。

一般来说，欧洲人认为公职人员代表政府从而对其表现得顺从，但是对美国人而言，他们代表的只是权利。可以说，在美国并非是人服从人，而是人服从正义和法律。如果人们所持有的观点被夸大，至少也是有益的。他们对自己的力量丝毫没有怀疑，认为它可以对付一切。当一个人想要做出一番事业，而又与社会公益没有直接关联的时候，他不会想到要从政府那里得到援助。然而他会将自己的计划公之于众，之后便自己付诸行动，也会向其他个人请求协助，并力排一切困难。毫无疑问，其结果肯定比不上有州政府协助来得好，然而私人事业的最终结果往往比政府所能做的要好的多得多。

因为行政当局只负责民事，所以既不会激起人们的嫉妒也不会激起人们的憎恨。而且，由于它能动用的资源有限，人们认为不能全依靠它的协助。因此，当行政机关打算介入的时候，它不会像在欧洲那样全靠自己。公民不会逃避义务，因为公众代表会采取行动。相反，每个人都准备好要帮助支持行政机关。个人努力连同政府当局的作为，往往能完成最具活力的中央集权行政当局所无法完成的事情。找几个实例来证明我所说的话易如反掌，但是我更愿只举一个我最熟悉的事情。在美国，政府当局可以动用的用来发现罪行缉拿罪犯的手段非常少。美国没有行政警察更不知道护照为何物；美国的司法警察无法跟

The reason is, that every one conceives himself to be interested in furnishing evidence of the act committed, and in stopping the delinquent. During my stay in the United States I witnessed the spontaneous formation of committees for the pursuit and prosecution of a man who had committed a great crime in a certain county. In Europe a criminal is an unhappy being who is struggling for his life against the ministers of justice, whilst the population is merely a spectator of the conflict; in America he is looked upon as an enemy of the human race, and the whole of mankind is against him.

I believe that provincial institutions are useful to all nations, but nowhere do they appear to me to be more indispensable than amongst a democratic people. In an aristocracy order can always be maintained in the midst of liberty, and as the rulers have a great deal to lose order is to them a first-rate consideration. In like manner an aristocracy protects the people from the excesses of despotism, because it always possesses an organized power ready to resist a despot. But a democracy without provincial institutions has no security against these evils. How can a populace, unaccustomed to freedom in small concerns, learn to use it temperately in great affairs? What resistance can be offered to tyranny in a country where every private individual is impotent, and where the citizens are united by no common tie? Those who dread the license of the mob, and those who fear the rule of absolute power, ought alike to desire the progressive growth of provincial liberties.

On the other hand, I am convinced that democratic nations are most exposed to fall beneath the yoke of a central administration, for several reasons, amongst which is the following. The constant tendency of these nations is to concentrate all the strength of the Government in the hands of the only power which directly represents the people, because beyond the people nothing is to be perceived but a mass of equal individuals confounded together. But when the same power is already in possession of all the attributes of the Government, it can scarcely refrain from penetrating into the details of the administration, and an opportunity of doing so is sure to present itself in the end, as was the case in France. In the French Revolution there were two impulses in opposite directions, which must never be confounded—the one was favorable to liberty, the other to despotism. Under the ancient monarchy the King was the sole author of the laws, and below the power of the sovereign

法国相比，地方法官和检察官的数量也不多；对犯人的审讯也很迅速而且只是口头审讯。然而世界上没有哪个国家的漏网之鱼会比这里更少。因为每个人都认为提供犯罪证据缉拿罪犯都跟自身的利益息息相关。在美国逗留期间，我亲眼看到在一个发生重大案件的镇里居民们为了抓获罪犯并把他送交法院惩办，自发组织了一个委员会。在欧洲，逃跑的罪犯要是被官员抓住只能算他倒霉，民众不过是旁观者；而在美国他则被视为全人类的公敌，人人对他横眉冷对。

我相信地方分权制度对所有国家都有好处，而对于讲求民主的人们这样的需求就更为迫切。在贵族体制下，只有维持一定的秩序才能确保自由，而对于统治者来说由于他们害怕失去的东西太多，所以秩序是他们关心的头等大事。同样地，贵族体制之所以能够让人民免受专制的过度压迫，是因为人民往往拥有有组织的力量并时刻准备与暴君做斗争。但是没有地方分权制度的民主政体也就失去了与这种邪恶相对抗的保障。在小事情上尚未学会使用民主的平民百姓又怎可能将其运用到大事情上呢？在一个人人都软弱而且也没有被任何共同利益将他们团结起来的国家，又有什么可以拿来与暴君对抗呢？所以那些害怕人民暴动的人以及惧怕专制制度的人，应该都渴望地方自由的逐步发展。

另一方面来说，我认为民主国家最容易受到行政集权制度的束缚，其原因有很多，主要有下列几个。这些国家一直以来都有一种趋势要把全部的政府权力集中到唯一代表人民的权力机关手中。因为除了人民以外什么都没有，而这些人民不过是一群混在一处的平等的个人。但是当这个权力机关拥有政府属性的时候，它又无法避免去干预行政工作的细

certain vestiges of provincial institutions, half destroyed, were still distinguishable. These provincial institutions were incoherent, ill compacted, and frequently absurd; in the hands of the aristocracy they had sometimes been converted into instruments of oppression. The Revolution declared itself the enemy of royalty and of provincial institutions at the same time; it confounded all that had preceded it—despotic power and the checks to its abuses—in indiscriminate hatred, and its tendency was at once to overthrow and to centralize. This double character of the French Revolution is a fact which has been adroitly handled by the friends of absolute power. Can they be accused of laboring in the cause of despotism when they are defending that central administration which was one of the great innovations of the Revolution? In this manner popularity may be conciliated with hostility to the rights of the people, and the secret slave of tyranny may be the professed admirer of freedom.

I have visited the two nations in which the system of provincial liberty has been most perfectly established, and I have listened to the opinions of different parties in those countries. In America I met with men who secretly aspired to destroy the democratic institutions of the Union; in England I found others who attacked the aristocracy openly, but I know of no one who does not regard provincial independence as a great benefit. In both countries I have heard a thousand different causes assigned for the evils of the State, but the local system was never mentioned amongst them. I have heard citizens attribute the power and prosperity of their country to a multitude of reasons, but they all placed the advantages of local institutions in the foremost rank. Am I to suppose that when men who are naturally so divided on religious opinions and on political theories agree on one point (and that one of which they have daily experience), they are all in error? The only nations which deny the utility of provincial liberties are those which have fewest of them; in other words, those who are unacquainted with the institution are the only persons who pass a censure upon it.

节，这样的机会最终总会到来，就像在法国看到的一样。在法国大革命期间，存在两个混乱不清而且南辕北辙的趋势：一个倾向于自由，而另一个则倾向于专制。在古代君王政体中，国王是法律唯一的制定者，但是在君主专权的时候，已遭到部分摧毁的地方分权制度的残余仍然依稀可见。这些地方分权制度缺少连贯性也不完善，总是让人觉得荒谬可笑。而在贵族政治制度下，它们有时候竟然变成压迫的工具。法国大革命不但宣布反对君主专制，而且也反对地方分权制度。它不分青红皂白，对以前的一切全部否定，既反对专制，又反对可以对其进行抑制的措施，这场革命既有共和又有中央集权的性质。法国大革命的双重特点是专制权力之友们可以巧妙利用的一个事实。当他们捍卫大革命重大成果之一行政集权的时候，你难道能够指责他们是在为专制制度卖命吗？这样，民众和人民权力的敌人握手言和，而且暴君的秘密奴仆也许就是自由的公开爱慕者。

我已经拜访过两个地方自由制度高度发达的国家，也聆听了这些国家不同党派的不同声音。在美国，我遇到过想要秘密颠覆国家民主制度的人；在英国，我也看到对贵族制度公开发起攻击的人，但是在任何地方都没有见过认为地方自由不是大好事的人。在这两个国家，我看到人们将国家的弊端归结到千千万万的原因，但从来没有提到过地方自由。我看到公民为他们国家的繁荣富强找到各种理由，而放在首位的却总是地方自由。我发现，尽管人们宗教观念和政治理论上的差别与生俱来，但是他们在每天经历的能够做出正确判断的唯一事实上却意见一致，这个发现不会错吧？只有那些地方自治制度不发达的国家才会否认它的好处。换句话说，只有那些不了解这个制度的人才会谴责这个制度。

Chapter VI: Judicial Power In The United States

Chapter Summary

The Anglo-Americans have retained the characteristics of judicial power which are common to all nations—They have, however, made it a powerful political organ—How—In what the judicial system of the Anglo-Americans differs from that of all other nations—Why the American judges have the right of declaring the laws to be unconstitutional—How they use this right—Precautions taken by the legislator to prevent its abuse.

Judicial Power In The United States And Its Influence On Political Society.

I have thought it essential to devote a separate chapter to the judicial authorities of the United States, lest their great political importance should be lessened in the reader's eyes by a merely incidental mention of them. Confederations have existed in other countries beside America, and republics have not been established upon the shores of the New World alone; the representative system of government has been adopted in several States of Europe, but I am not aware that any nation of the globe has hitherto organized a judicial power on the principle now adopted by the Americans. The judicial organization of the United States is the institution which a stranger has the greatest difficulty in understanding. He hears the authority of a judge invoked in the political occurrences of every day, and he naturally concludes that in the United States the judges are important political functionaries; nevertheless, when he examines the nature of the tribunals, they offer nothing which is contrary to the usual habits and privileges of those bodies, and the

第六章　美国的司法权

本章提要

英裔美国人保留了各国在司法权上的共通特征——但是他们让司法权成为强有力的政治权力——这是怎么做到的——英裔美国人的司法体系与所有其他国家的不同之处——为什么美国法官有权宣布法律违宪——美国法官如何使用这一权利——立法者为防范这一权利被滥用采取的预防措施。

美国的司法权及其对政治社会的影响

我一直认为有必要拿出一个独立的章节说一说美国的司法权，从而避免因为一笔带过而让读者低估了它重大的政治作用。除了美国以外，其他国家也有联邦制，而且共和政体也不是新世界所独有，欧洲的一些国家也已采用了代议制，但是迄今为止我没有发现世界上任何一个国家按照美国所采用的原则建立起司法权。最让外来人感到无法理解的是美国的司法组织。他看到这里每天的政治事务都要求助于法官的权威，因而他自然得出结论，在美国法官是重要的政治官员。然而，当他对法院的性质进行考察的时候，看到它的通常做

magistrates seem to him to interfere in public affairs of chance, but by a chance which recurs every day.

When the Parliament of Paris remonstrated, or refused to enregister an edict, or when it summoned a functionary accused of malversation to its bar, its political influence as a judicial body was clearly visible; but nothing of the kind is to be seen in the United States. The Americans have retained all the ordinary characteristics of judicial authority, and have carefully restricted its action to the ordinary circle of its functions.

The first characteristic of judicial power in all nations is the duty of arbitration. But rights must be contested in order to warrant the interference of a tribunal; and an action must be brought to obtain the decision of a judge. As long, therefore, as the law is uncontested, the judicial authority is not called upon to discuss it, and it may exist without being perceived. When a judge in a given case attacks a law relating to that case, he extends the circle of his customary duties, without however stepping beyond it; since he is in some measure obliged to decide upon the law in order to decide the case. But if he pronounces upon a law without resting upon a case, he clearly steps beyond his sphere, and invades that of the legislative authority.

The second characteristic of judicial power is that it pronounces on special cases, and not upon general principles. If a judge in deciding a particular point destroys a general principle, by passing a judgment which tends to reject all the inferences from that principle, and consequently to annul it, he remains within the ordinary limits of his functions. But if he directly attacks a general principle without having a particular case in view, he leaves the circle in which all nations have agreed to confine his authority, he assumes a more important, and perhaps a more useful, influence than that of the magistrate, but he ceases to be a representative of the judicial power.

The third characteristic of the judicial power is its inability to act unless it is appealed to, or until it has taken cognizance of an affair. This characteristic is less general than the other two; but, notwithstanding the exceptions, I think it may be regarded as essential. The judicial power is by its nature devoid of action; it must be put in motion in order to produce a result. When it is called upon

法和特权又别无二致，而法官只是偶然插手公共事务，但这样的偶然却每天不断重复出现。

当巴黎最高法院对一项法令提出异议或是拒绝给其备案时，或是当它对渎职官员进行传唤时，司法机构的政治影响便清楚地表现出来，但是在美国我们却看不到这些。美国人保留了司法机关的所有普遍特征，并小心翼翼地将其行动限定在有章可循的范围。

各国司法权的首要特征是对案件的仲裁责任。有提起诉讼的案件，法院才能发挥作用，法官才能裁判。因此只要没有依法提起的争诉案件，司法机关就无计可施，司法权存在却不能发挥作用。当法官在审理一个案件并对与此案相关的法律提出指责的时候，他只不过扩大了自己的职权范围而绝非已越雷池，因为他必须对适用于这一案件的法律进行权衡。但是，如果他在审理案件之前就对一项法律说三道四，就是明显的越界，侵犯了立法权。

司法权的第二个特征是它对个案而非普遍原则进行裁决。如果法官在对一个案件进行判决，并趋向于否定某一一般原则的所有推论进而对其加以破坏的时候，他依然是在职权范围内行事。然而，如果他在没有特定待审案件的前提下，直接对一个一般原则加以指责，那么他就越过所有国家都同意进行限制的法官职权范围，那么他就取得了比一般官员更为重要或是更为有用的权力，也就不再是司法权的代表了。

司法权的第三个特征是没有诉讼就无法审判，或者说只有在审理案件的时候它才能采取行动。这个特点不如前面两个普遍。尽管有一些例外，但我认为还是应该将其视为最重要的特征。司法权的本质缺乏主动，要想让它动起来就要推它一把。当需要它对一宗案件进行惩处的时候，它就会惩罚犯人；需要它纠正非法行为的时候，它就会加以纠正；需要

to repress a crime, it punishes the criminal; when a wrong is to be redressed, it is ready to redress it; when an act requires interpretation, it is prepared to interpret it; but it does not pursue criminals, hunt out wrongs, or examine into evidence of its own accord. A judicial functionary who should open proceedings, and usurp the censorship of the laws, would in some measure do violence to the passive nature of his authority.

The Americans have retained these three distinguishing characteristics of the judicial power; an American judge can only pronounce a decision when litigation has arisen, he is only conversant with special cases, and he cannot act until the cause has been duly brought before the court. His position is therefore perfectly similar to that of the magistrate of other nations; and he is nevertheless invested with immense political power. If the sphere of his authority and his means of action are the same as those of other judges, it may be asked whence he derives a power which they do not possess. The cause of this difference lies in the simple fact that the Americans have acknowledged the right of the judges to found their decisions on the constitution rather than on the laws. In other words, they have left them at liberty not to apply such laws as may appear to them to be unconstitutional.

I am aware that a similar right has been claimed—but claimed in vain—by courts of justice in other countries; but in America it is recognized by all authorities; and not a party, nor so much as an individual, is found to contest it. This fact can only be explained by the principles of the American constitution. In France the constitution is (or at least is supposed to be) immutable; and the received theory is that no power has the right of changing any part of it. In England the Parliament has an acknowledged right to modify the constitution; as, therefore, the constitution may undergo perpetual changes, it does not in reality exist; the Parliament is at once a legislative and a constituent assembly. The political theories of America are more simple and more rational. An American constitution is not supposed to be immutable as in France, nor is it susceptible of modification by the ordinary powers of society as in England. It constitutes a detached whole, which, as it represents the determination of the whole people, is no less binding on the legislator

它解读一项法案的时候，它就进行解释。但是，它不会追捕罪犯、调查非法行为或是查证事实。但是如果它以法律检查者身份公开主动出面，那就违背了其被动的本质特征。

美国人保留了司法权的这三个鲜明特征。只有当有人提起诉讼的时候，美国法官才能对案件进行审理。他只受理私人案件，而且只能在接到起诉书后才能开始行动。因此美国法官与其他国家的司法人员完全相同，然而他们又被赋予了巨大的政治权力。如果他们的权力半径和行动手段跟其他的国家的法官一模一样，那么他们那些其他国家法官所没有的权力又源自哪里呢？这种差异的原因就基于这样一个简单的事实——美国人认为法官的裁定权来源于宪法而不是法律。换句话说，美国人赋予法官自由决定权可以不使用他认为与宪法相悖的法律。

据我所知其他国家的法院也有过类似的要求，但是他们的要求没能得到满足，然而在美国，法官的这一权力得到各方的普遍认可，而且没有一个政党或是个人对此提出异议。这种现象只能通过美国宪法的原则得到解释。在法国宪法是或者说至少应该是不可进行修改的，而且任何权威都无权对宪法做出任何修改，已经是公认的学说。在英国，国会有权修改宪法。因此可以说宪法一直处于变化之中，或者说它根本不存在。国会既是立法机关又是制宪机构。美国的政治理论则更为简单合理。美国的宪法并非像法国宪法一样不可修改，也不会像在英国那样可以被社会普通权力机关随意修改。美国的宪法与众不同，代表全体人民的意志，立法者和普通公民都要遵守，而美国的宪法也可以根据人民的意志并依据现有制度在预先规定的条件下加以修改。因此美国的宪法也是可以改变的，但是只要它

than on the private citizen, but which may be altered by the will of the people in predetermined cases, according to established rules. In America the constitution may therefore vary, but as long as it exists it is the origin of all authority, and the sole vehicle of the predominating force.

It is easy to perceive in what manner these differences must act upon the position and the rights of the judicial bodies in the three countries I have cited. If in France the tribunals were authorized to disobey the laws on the ground of their being opposed to the constitution, the supreme power would in fact be placed in their hands, since they alone would have the right of interpreting a constitution, the clauses of which can be modified by no authority. They would therefore take the place of the nation, and exercise as absolute a sway over society as the inherent weakness of judicial power would allow them to do. Undoubtedly, as the French judges are incompetent to declare a law to be unconstitutional, the power of changing the constitution is indirectly given to the legislative body, since no legal barrier would oppose the alterations which it might prescribe. But it is better to grant the power of changing the constitution of the people to men who represent (however imperfectly) the will of the people, than to men who represent no one but themselves.

It would be still more unreasonable to invest the English judges with the right of resisting the decisions of the legislative body, since the Parliament which makes the laws also makes the constitution; and consequently a law emanating from the three powers of the State can in no case be unconstitutional. But neither of these remarks is applicable to America.

In the United States the constitution governs the legislator as much as the private citizen; as it is the first of laws it cannot be modified by a law, and it is therefore just that the tribunals should obey the constitution in preference to any law. This condition is essential to the power of the judicature, for to select that legal obligation by which he is most strictly bound is the natural right of every magistrate.

In France the constitution is also the first of laws, and the judges have the same right to take it as the ground of their decisions, but were they to exercise this right they must perforce encroach on

存在所有机构就必须服从于它，是绝对的权威。

所以不难看出，这些差别一定会影响到我刚刚所提及的这三个国家司法机关的地位和权力。如果法国的法官可以依据法律违宪为由不服从法律，那么实际上他们手中就掌握了至高无上的权力，因为他们有权对宪法进行解释，而且无须授权就可以对其做出修改，最终会取代国家，进而统治社会，而且司法权固有的弱点也会促使他们这样做。毫无疑问，法国的法官无权宣布法律违宪，修订宪法的权力便间接的赋予立法机关，因为没有合法的障碍对其修改宪法进行阻止。但是如果能够把修改人民宪法的权力，赋予那些哪怕是部分代表人民意志的人也会比赋予那些只代表自己利益的人要更好。

然而，如果赋予英国法官抵制立法机构的权力会更加不合理，因为议会不但制定法律也制定宪法，所以在任何情况下由国家三权（国王、上议院和下议院）制定的法律都不会违宪。但是这两种都不适用于美国。

在美国，宪法就像制约普通公民一样制约着立法者，因为它是根本大法，其他法律不能对其进行修改，所以法院的裁决要优先服从宪法。这一点对于司法权至关重要，因为法官在选择适用的法律时要从中选取与宪法最为契合的法律，这是每个法官的天赋权利。

在法国，宪法也是根本大法，而且法官同样有权将其视为其裁决的依据。但是如果要行使这一权利，他们又必定会侵犯到比其更为神圣的权利，也就是他们所代表的国家的权利。在这样的情况下，国家意愿显然会胜过个人意愿。而在美国，国家总是可以通过修改

rights more sacred than their own, namely, on those of society, in whose name they are acting. In this case the State-motive clearly prevails over the motives of an individual. In America, where the nation can always reduce its magistrates to obedience by changing its constitution, no danger of this kind is to be feared. Upon this point, therefore, the political and the logical reasons agree, and the people as well as the judges preserve their privileges.

Whenever a law which the judge holds to be unconstitutional is argued in a tribunal of the United States he may refuse to admit it as a rule; this power is the only one which is peculiar to the American magistrate, but it gives rise to immense political influence. Few laws can escape the searching analysis of the judicial power for any length of time, for there are few which are not prejudicial to some private interest or other, and none which may not be brought before a court of justice by the choice of parties, or by the necessity of the case. But from the time that a judge has refused to apply any given law in a case, that law loses a portion of its moral cogency. The persons to whose interests it is prejudicial learn that means exist of evading its authority, and similar suits are multiplied, until it becomes powerless. One of two alternatives must then be resorted to: the people must alter the constitution, or the legislature must repeal the law. The political power which the Americans have intrusted to their courts of justice is therefore immense, but the evils of this power are considerably diminished by the obligation which has been imposed of attacking the laws through the courts of justice alone. If the judge had been empowered to contest the laws on the ground of theoretical generalities, if he had been enabled to open an attack or to pass a censure on the legislator, he would have played a prominent part in the political sphere; and as the champion or the antagonist of a party, he would have arrayed the hostile passions of the nation in the conflict. But when a judge contests a law applied to some particular case in an obscure proceeding, the importance of his attack is concealed from the public gaze, his decision bears upon the interest of an individual, and if the law is slighted it is only collaterally. Moreover, although it is censured, it is not abolished; its moral force may be diminished, but its cogency is by no means suspended, and its final destruction can only be accomplished by the reiterated attacks of judicial functionaries. It

宪法的方式使法官服从，所以这样的担忧就会荡然无存。因此，从这点上看，不但政治和逻辑上能够保持一致，而且人民和法官都能保有各自特权。

因此，无论何时，在美国的法院只要是法官认为违宪的法律，他都可以拒绝承认该法则。尽管这是美国法官所特有的权力，但却产生了巨大的政治影响。几乎没有任何一条法律能够长期逃脱法官的验证分析，因为几乎所有的法律都会涉及这样或那样的个人利益，而且在涉及诉讼当事人利益或是出于案情需要的时候，他们也可以或是必然会向法庭提出异议。但是，在办案时，从法官拒绝应用某项法律之时起，该法律的部分道德说服力也会随之消失。结果那些利益受到损害的人知道了有这样的方法可以取消法律的效力，因此这类的诉讼倍增，而这项法律也将变得无力。最后，一定要采用下列的两种方式之一来应对这样的窘境：不是人民修改宪法就是立法机构宣布此项法律无效。所以，美国人把无限地政治权利交付给法院的同时，又通过赋予法院对法律进行抨击的职责来最大限度地减少其弊端。如果法官拥有依靠理论概念对法律进行质疑以及对立法者进行抨击和弹劾的权力，那么他们必然会在政治领域起到举足轻重的作用。这样，他们势必会成为某个党派的支持者或是反对者，从而会激起全国人民纷纷参加斗争。但是，当法官在某个不起眼的诉讼中对适用于该案件的某个法律提出质疑的时候，其做法的重要性就不会被公众注意到。因为他们的判决只影响到某个人的利益，而对法律的这种损害也无关大局。此外，尽管此项法律受到质疑，但是并没有被废除，其道德力量也许被弱化，但是它的效力绝没有受损，而且只有在司法人员通过无数判例进行反复验证后，才能

will readily be understood that by connecting the censorship of the laws with the private interests of members of the community, and by intimately uniting the prosecution of the law with the prosecution of an individual, legislation is protected from wanton assailants, and from the daily aggressions of party spirit. The errors of the legislator are exposed whenever their evil consequences are most felt, and it is always a positive and appreciable fact which serves as the basis of a prosecution.

I am inclined to believe this practice of the American courts to be at once the most favorable to liberty as well as to public order. If the judge could only attack the legislator openly and directly, he would sometimes be afraid to oppose any resistance to his will; and at other moments party spirit might encourage him to brave it at every turn. The laws would consequently be attacked when the power from which they emanate is weak, and obeyed when it is strong. That is to say, when it would be useful to respect them they would be contested, and when it would be easy to convert them into an instrument of oppression they would be respected. But the American judge is brought into the political arena independently of his own will. He only judges the law because he is obliged to judge a case. The political question which he is called upon to resolve is connected with the interest of the suitors, and he cannot refuse to decide it without abdicating the duties of his post. He performs his functions as a citizen by fulfilling the precise duties which belong to his profession as a magistrate. It is true that upon this system the judicial censorship which is exercised by the courts of justice over the legislation cannot extend to all laws indiscriminately, inasmuch as some of them can never give rise to that exact species of contestation which is termed a lawsuit; and even when such a contestation is possible, it may happen that no one cares to bring it before a court of justice. The Americans have often felt this disadvantage, but they have left the remedy incomplete, lest they should give it an efficacy which might in some cases prove dangerous. Within these limits the power vested in the American courts of justice of pronouncing a statute to be unconstitutional forms one of the most powerful barriers which has ever been devised against the tyranny of political assemblies.

最终将其废除。不难理解，通过将法律的审查制度和社会成员的私人利益结合起来，以及对法律的审判和对个人的审判结合起来，立法机构就能免遭无妄的质疑，以及政党的骚扰。立法者所暴露出的错误必须要有据可查，也就是说要有明确切实的事实作为裁决的依据。

我趋向于认为美国法庭的做法不但有利于自由也有利于公共秩序。如果法官只能直接公开的对立法者进行指摘，他们有时可能会因为害怕而不敢这样做，而其他时候又会因为党派精神的不断驱使而敢于这样做。因此，当立法机关处于弱势的时候法律就会遭到攻击，而当其非常强大的时候，就会得到服从。也就是说，当人们觉得尊重法律对他们有好处的时候，法律就会受到质疑，而当其可以被轻而易举的转化成为压迫工具的时候，它们就会受到尊重。然而美国的法官已经被不由分说地拉上政治舞台。他们之所以要审理法律是因为他们必须要审理案件。要求他们解决的政治问题与起诉者利益相关，而因为他们不能放弃自己的职责所以不能拒绝审理。他们履行自己作为法官的职责就是作为一名公民在履行自己的义务。因此在这种制度下，由法庭来实施的对立法机关进行的审查，不能肆意扩展到一切法律。因为有些法律永远也不会引发可以称之为诉讼的法律争端，而且即使这样的争端成为可能，其情况也往往是没有人愿意为此诉诸法律。美国人常常能够感觉到这一做法的问题，但是他们宁愿对其修修补补，唯恐彻底的修正会在某些案件上带来可怕的后果。美国法院获得的这种在一定限度内可以宣布某项法律违宪的权力，也成为迄今为止扼制议会政治专制的最强有力的壁垒之一。

Other Powers Granted To American Judges

The United States all the citizens have the right of indicting public functionaries before the ordinary tribunals—How they use this right—Art. 75 of the French Constitution of the An VIII—The Americans and the English cannot understand the purport of this clause.

It is perfectly natural that in a free country like America all the citizens should have the right of indicting public functionaries before the ordinary tribunals, and that all the judges should have the power of punishing public offences. The right granted to the courts of justice of judging the agents of the executive government, when they have violated the laws, is so natural a one that it cannot be looked upon as an extraordinary privilege. Nor do the springs of government appear to me to be weakened in the United States by the custom which renders all public officers responsible to the judges of the land. The Americans seem, on the contrary, to have increased by this means that respect which is due to the authorities, and at the same time to have rendered those who are in power more scrupulous of offending public opinion. I was struck by the small number of political trials which occur in the United States, but I had no difficulty in accounting for this circumstance. A lawsuit, of whatever nature it may be, is always a difficult and expensive undertaking. It is easy to attack a public man in a journal, but the motives which can warrant an action at law must be serious. A solid ground of complaint must therefore exist to induce an individual to prosecute a public officer, and public officers are careful not to furnish these grounds of complaint when they are afraid of being prosecuted.

This does not depend upon the republican form of American institutions, for the same facts present themselves in England. These two nations do not regard the impeachment of the principal officers of State as a sufficient guarantee of their independence. But they hold that the right of minor prosecutions, which are within the reach of the whole community, is a better pledge of freedom than those great judicial actions which are rarely employed until it is too late.

In the Middle Ages, when it was very difficult to overtake offenders, the judges inflicted the most dreadful tortures on the few who were arrested, which by no means diminished the number of crimes.

美国法官的其他权力

在美国，所有公民均有权在普通法院对公职人员提起诉讼——公民如何使用这一权利——法兰西共和国第八年宪法第七十五条——美国人和英国人对这条法律的意义无法理解。

在一个像美国一样的自由国家，所有公民都应该有权在普通法庭起诉公职人员，而且所有法官也有权力对公职人员进行惩治判决，这是自然而然的事情。当政府行政人员触犯法律是，法院拥有对其进行审判的权利是如此的自然根本称不上特权。在我看来，在美国政府的活力并没有因为让所有官员对法院负责而被削弱。美国政治案件数量之少令我非常惊讶，而其中的原因也不难发现。不管一个案件的性质如何，总归是件困难费钱的事。在报刊上对一个人大加指责很容易，但是要把他送上法庭受审，就必须要有理有据。所以当个人对公职人员提起诉讼的时候，必须要有切实的证据，而公职人员害怕被起诉，就要小心翼翼不要给别人留下这样的把柄。

这并不是美国人所采用的共和制度所决定，因为同样的事情也在英国发生。这两个国家的人民并不认为能够对国家主要官员进行弹劾就能充分保障他们的权利。但是他们坚信，与那些重大而又几乎用不到或是很晚才能用到的诉讼程序相比，全民都可享有的小小诉讼权是他们自由的更好保障。

在很难抓获逃犯的中世纪，法官对那些抓获的为数不多的犯人进行最为残酷的折磨，

It has since been discovered that when justice is more certain and more mild, it is at the same time more efficacious. The English and the Americans hold that tyranny and oppression are to be treated like any other crime, by lessening the penalty and facilitating conviction.

In the year VIII of the French Republic a constitution was drawn up in which the following clause was introduced: "Art. 75. All the agents of the government below the rank of ministers can only be prosecuted for offences relating to their several functions by virtue of a decree of the Conseil d'Etat; in which the case the prosecution takes place before the ordinary tribunals." This clause survived the "Constitution de l'An VIII," and it is still maintained in spite of the just complaints of the nation. I have always found the utmost difficulty in explaining its meaning to Englishmen or Americans. They were at once led to conclude that the Conseil d'Etat in France was a great tribunal, established in the centre of the kingdom, which exercised a preliminary and somewhat tyrannical jurisdiction in all political causes. But when I told them that the Conseil d'Etat was not a judicial body, in the common sense of the term, but an administrative council composed of men dependent on the Crown, so that the king, after having ordered one of his servants, called a Prefect, to commit an injustice, has the power of commanding another of his servants, called a Councillor of State, to prevent the former from being punished; when I demonstrated to them that the citizen who has been injured by the order of the sovereign is obliged to solicit from the sovereign permission to obtain redress, they refused to credit so flagrant an abuse, and were tempted to accuse me of falsehood or of ignorance. It frequently happened before the Revolution that a Parliament issued a warrant against a public officer who had committed an offence, and sometimes the proceedings were stopped by the authority of the Crown, which enforced compliance with its absolute and despotic will. It is painful to perceive how much lower we are sunk than our forefathers, since we allow things to pass under the color of justice and the sanction of the law which violence alone could impose upon them.

尽管如此犯罪率依然无法降低。然而自从法律变得更加明确和温和之后，也同时变得更为有效。英国人和美国人主张，通过简化审讯减轻惩罚，对待专制和压迫应该像对待其他犯罪一样。

在法兰西第八共和国时期起草的一部宪法中，有这样的一条法律："第七十五条，部长级以下的政府官员由于职务关系而犯罪时，只有得到行政法院的批准才能被批捕，并送交普通法院进行审理。"这一条法律在第八共和国宪法遭到废除后一直保留至今，尽管人民对它的声讨此起彼伏。我注意到在向美国人和英国人解释这一点的时候非常困难。因为他们会立即得出结论，认为法国的行政法院是王国中央设立的大法院，而将所有的原告先推向那里是对所有政治案件的暴政。于是我告诉他们行政法院并不是普通意义上的审判机关，而是由直接隶属于国王的人员组成的行政机构，所以在国王钦命的一个叫作省长的奴仆犯罪后，为了能够对他进行偏袒，又钦命另外一个叫作行政法院法官的奴仆前去解救他；并向他们证明由于君主的敕令而受到伤害的人只能向君主本人恳求赔偿。每每此时，他们总是不肯相信天下竟有如此荒谬的事情，有时候还会指责我无知胡说。在大革命之前的法国，通常由最高法院下令批准逮捕犯罪的公职人员，而有时候王权的干涉往往会令诉讼失效，人们则只能在压力之下表示服从。如今我们沦落到甚至不及我们祖先的境地，因为如今的法国依靠暴力而强加于人的事情，被我们披上了合法的外衣，想到此处实在让人痛苦不已。

Chapter VII: Political Jurisdiction In The United States

Chapter Summary

Definition of political jurisdiction—What is understood by political jurisdiction in France, in England, and in the United States—In America the political judge can only pass sentence on public officers—He more frequently passes a sentence of removal from office than a penalty—Political jurisdiction as it exists in the United States is, notwithstanding its mildness, and perhaps in consequence of that mildness, a most powerful instrument in the hands of the majority.

Political Jurisdiction In The United States

I understand, by political jurisdiction, that temporary right of pronouncing a legal decision with which a political body may be invested.

In absolute governments no utility can accrue from the introduction of extraordinary forms of procedure; the prince in whose name an offender is prosecuted is as much the sovereign of the courts of justice as of everything else, and the idea which is entertained of his power is of itself a sufficient security. The only thing he has to fear is, that the external formalities of justice should be neglected, and that his authority should be dishonored from a wish to render it more absolute. But in most

第七章　美国的政治审判

本章提要

作者对政治审判的解读——法国、英国和美国对政治审判的各自理解——在美国，政治法官只审理公职人员——其判决中，撤职往往多于刑罚——美国的政治审判尽管温和，但也正是因为其温和才得以成为大多数人手中握有的最强有力的武器。

美国的政治审判

在我看来，政治审判是由暂时获得审判权的政治团体进行的判决。

在专制政府的统治下，给审判规定专门的程序毫无用处。因为在这里是以君主的名义对犯人进行控诉，而君主是法院及王国所有一切的主人，他认为其自身拥有的权力本身就是最好的保障。唯一令他担忧的事情就是坚持司法制度的表面形式，以及这种坚持对其权威的损害。但是，在大多数自由国家，多数表决无法像专制君主那样对法庭裁决产生同样的影响力，司法权往往由其代表在任期内行使。有人认为，权力的暂时合并比打破国家统一的必要原则要强。

free countries, in which the majority can never exercise the same influence upon the tribunals as an absolute monarch, the judicial power has occasionally been vested for a time in the representatives of the nation. It has been thought better to introduce a temporary confusion between the functions of the different authorities than to violate the necessary principle of the unity of government.

England, France, and the United States have established this political jurisdiction by law; and it is curious to examine the different adaptations which these three great nations have made of the principle. In England and in France the House of Lords and the Chambre des Paris constitute the highest criminal court of their respective nations, and although they do not habitually try all political offences, they are competent to try them all. Another political body enjoys the right of impeachment before the House of Lords: the only difference which exists between the two countries in this respect is, that in England the Commons may impeach whomsoever they please before the Lords, whilst in France the Deputies can only employ this mode of prosecution against the ministers of the Crown.

In both countries the Upper House may make use of all the existing penal laws of the nation to punish the delinquents.

In the United States, as well as in Europe, one branch of the legislature is authorized to impeach and another to judge: the House of Representatives arraigns the offender, and the Senate awards his sentence. But the Senate can only try such persons as are brought before it by the House of Representatives, and those persons must belong to the class of public functionaries. Thus the jurisdiction of the Senate is less extensive than that of the Peers of France, whilst the right of impeachment by the Representatives is more general than that of the Deputies. But the great difference which exists between Europe and America is, that in Europe political tribunals are empowered to inflict all the dispositions of the penal code, while in America, when they have deprived the offender of his official rank, and have declared him incapable of filling any political office for the future, their jurisdiction terminates and that of the ordinary tribunals begins.

Suppose, for instance, that the President of the United States has committed the crime of high treason; the House of Representatives impeaches him, and the Senate degrades him; he must then

英国、法国和美国依据法律已经建立起政治审判制度，对这三个大国对政治审判不同运用的考察，也非常有意思。在英国和法国上议院组织各自国家的最高法庭，而且尽管这个法庭一般来说并不是对所有的政治犯罪进行审理，但是它们拥有这样的权力。跟上议院同样享有此项权力的政治机构是下议院，而在这方面两个国家之间唯一的差别是英国的下议院可以向上院控诉任何它们想要控诉的对象，然而在法国众议院只能向贵族院控诉国王的大臣。

在两个国家中，上议院均可以根据本国刑法的规定惩处犯人。

而在美国和欧洲，立法机构的一个分支握有诉讼权，而另一个则握有审判权，即众议院负责对犯人进行审讯，参议院负责判决。但是参议院只能对众议院送审的人员进行宣判，而且他们还必须是公职人员。因此美国参议院的审判权权限不及法国上议院，而美国众议院的起诉权则比法国众议院更为广泛。然而存在于欧洲和美国之间最大的差别是：欧洲的政治法院有权力动用一切刑法法则，而在美国，当他们宣布撤销犯人职务并不能再担任任何公职之后，他们的任务便宣告结束，而接下来普通法院则开始履行职责。

假设，例如美国总统犯了叛国罪，众议院会对他进行弹劾，接着参议院会对他进行罢免。然后，他才会在陪审团的出席下出庭受审，而唯有陪审团有权剥夺其自由和生命。这是我们正在探讨问题的真实写照。欧洲依据法律所建立起来的政治审判旨在对重大刑事罪犯进行审理，无论其出身、等级以及权力如何。为了达到这一目的，会成立大政治审判团并暂时赋予它法院拥有的一切特权。此时，立法者摇身一变成为了法官，他要对罪行进

be tried by a jury, which alone can deprive him of his liberty or his life. This accurately illustrates the subject we are treating. The political jurisdiction which is established by the laws of Europe is intended to try great offenders, whatever may be their birth, their rank, or their powers in the State; and to this end all the privileges of the courts of justice are temporarily extended to a great political assembly. The legislator is then transformed into the magistrate; he is called upon to admit, to distinguish, and to punish the offence; and as he exercises all the authority of a judge, the law restricts him to the observance of all the duties of that high office, and of all the formalities of justice. When a public functionary is impeached before an English or a French political tribunal, and is found guilty, the sentence deprives him ipso facto of his functions, and it may pronounce him to be incapable of resuming them or any others for the future. But in this case the political interdict is a consequence of the sentence, and not the sentence itself. In Europe the sentence of a political tribunal is to be regarded as a judicial verdict rather than as an administrative measure. In the United States the contrary takes place; and although the decision of the Senate is judicial in its form, since the Senators are obliged to comply with the practices and formalities of a court of justice; although it is judicial in respect to the motives on which it is founded, since the Senate is in general obliged to take an offence at common law as the basis of its sentence; nevertheless the object of the proceeding is purely administrative. If it had been the intention of the American legislator to invest a political body with great judicial authority, its action would not have been limited to the circle of public functionaries, since the most dangerous enemies of the State may be in the possession of no functions at all; and this is especially true in republics, where party influence is the first of authorities, and where the strength of many a reader is increased by his exercising no legal power.

If it had been the intention of the American legislator to give society the means of repressing State offences by exemplary punishment, according to the practice of ordinary justice, the resources of the penal code would all have been placed at the disposal of the political tribunals. But the weapon with which they are intrusted is an imperfect one, and it can never reach the most dangerous offenders, since men who aim at the entire subversion of the laws are not likely to murmur at a political interdict.

行认定，选定适用的法律并对犯人进行惩罚。在他行使法官职责的同时，法律规定他要履行所有职责并按照司法程序的规定办事。当一名公职人员在英国或是法国的政治法庭受审的时候，在确认其有罪之后，要依法免去他的职务，甚至能够宣布他以后也不能再担任任何公职。在这样的案件中，禁令并不是最终的判决，只是判决所附带的结果。在欧洲政治审判与其说是行政措施不如说是司法裁定。在美国，事情刚好相反，尽管参议院的决定采用的是司法形式，这是因为它要和法院保持做法和形式上的一致。尽管从判决依据上看，参议院的判决具有司法性质，因为一般来说参议院的判决必须以普通法律为依据。然而这一过程的目的则是行政性的。如果美国立法者的目的就是要赋予一个政治团体极大的司法权，那么它就不会将其行动限制在公职人员的范围，因为国家最危险的敌人也许根本不担任任何公职，而在共和制国家中情况尤其如此。因为在这样的国家政党的最大利益就是掌权，而势力越大则往往越要非法篡权。

如果美国立法者的初衷是要让社会，以法官的身份，掌握对重大罪行进行惩办以儆效尤的手段，那么政治法院也应该以刑法典的一切规定作为其行事的依据。但是他们手中所握有的武器并不完美，也无法对最危险的犯罪进行打击，因为对于那些妄图颠覆法律的人而言，行政撤职的处分并不能给其致命的一击。

所以，美国政治审判的主要目的就是要剥夺居心叵测的那些官员手中的权力，并让他们无法再获得这种权力。这显然是具有司法裁决形式的行政措施。在这方面，美国人创造

The main object of the political jurisdiction which obtains in the United States is, therefore, to deprive the ill-disposed citizen of an authority which he has used amiss, and to prevent him from ever acquiring it again. This is evidently an administrative measure sanctioned by the formalities of a judicial decision. In this matter the Americans have created a mixed system; they have surrounded the act which removes a public functionary with the securities of a political trial; and they have deprived all political condemnations of their severest penalties. Every link of the system may easily be traced from this point; we at once perceive why the American constitutions subject all the civil functionaries to the jurisdiction of the Senate, whilst the military, whose crimes are nevertheless more formidable, are exempted from that tribunal. In the civil service none of the American functionaries can be said to be removable; the places which some of them occupy are inalienable, and the others are chosen for a term which cannot be shortened. It is therefore necessary to try them all in order to deprive them of their authority. But military officers are dependent on the chief magistrate of the State, who is himself a civil functionary, and the decision which condemns him is a blow upon them all.

If we now compare the American and the European systems, we shall meet with differences no less striking in the different effects which each of them produces or may produce. In France and in England the jurisdiction of political bodies is looked upon as an extraordinary resource, which is only to be employed in order to rescue society from unwonted dangers. It is not to be denied that these tribunals, as they are constituted in Europe, are apt to violate the conservative principle of the balance of power in the State, and to threaten incessantly the lives and liberties of the subject. The same political jurisdiction in the United States is only indirectly hostile to the balance of power; it cannot menace the lives of the citizens, and it does not hover, as in Europe, over the heads of the community, since those only who have submitted to its authority on accepting office are exposed to the severity of its investigations. It is at the same time less formidable and less efficacious; indeed, it has not been considered by the legislators of the United States as a remedy for the more violent evils of society, but as an ordinary means of conducting the government. In this respect it probably exercises more real influence on the social body in America than in Europe. We must not be misled by the apparent

出一种混合制度法，他们的政治审判只能做出撤销行政职务的处罚，无权进行更为严厉的惩罚。不难发现政治审判的各个环节都发乎于这一点，所以我们一下子就能明白，为什么美国宪法规定所有文职官员都要服从参议院的司法管辖，而同时又把可能会犯下更可怕罪行的军人排除在其管辖范围之外。就文职官员而言，可以说美国没有可以被罢免的官员，因为他们中有些官员的任期为终身制，而还有些官员一旦当选任期内不能被罢黜。所以，要想剥夺他们的权力就要对其进行司法审判。但是军队的官员则直接隶属于国家元首，而因为国家元首本人也是文职官员，所以对国家元首的有罪裁定就是等于对全体文武官员予以打击。

如果我们将美国和欧洲的制度加以比较，其差异所产生或是可能产生的不同效果会让人惊讶不已。在法国和英国，政治审判被视为一种特殊的手段，只有在挽救国家免遭重大危险的时候才会启用。无法否认，欧洲实行的这种政治审判违背了国家权力平衡的保护主义原则，并且总会对人民的生命和自由产生威胁。而美国的政治审判对国家权力平衡只会产生间接影响，并不会威胁到人民生命安全，而且也不会像在欧洲那样高悬在人民的头顶之上，因为它只会对那些渎职犯罪的人员进行惩治。它既不可怕也不强效。实际上，美国的立法者并没有把它当成铲除重大社会弊端的万用良方，而只是把它当作政府普通的管理手段。就这一点来看，它在美国可能会产生比在欧洲更为实际的影响。我们一定不要被美国政治审判表面所呈现出的温和态势误导。首先要指出的是，在美国进行政治审判法庭

mildness of the American legislation in all that relates to political jurisdiction. It is to be observed, in the first place, that in the United States the tribunal which passes sentence is composed of the same elements, and subject to the same influences, as the body which impeaches the offender, and that this uniformity gives an almost irresistible impulse to the vindictive passions of parties. If political judges in the United States cannot inflict such heavy penalties as those of Europe, there is the less chance of their acquitting a prisoner; and the conviction, if it is less formidable, is more certain. The principal object of the political tribunals of Europe is to punish the offender; the purpose of those in America is to deprive him of his authority. A political condemnation in the United States may, therefore, be looked upon as a preventive measure; and there is no reason for restricting the judges to the exact definitions of criminal law. Nothing can be more alarming than the excessive latitude with which political offences are described in the laws of America. Article II., Section 4, of the Constitution of the United States runs thus:—"The President, Vice-President, and all civil officers of the United States shall be removed from office on impeachment for, and conviction of, treason, bribery, or other high crimes and misdemeanors." Many of the Constitutions of the States are even less explicit. "Public officers," says the Constitution of Massachusetts, "shall be impeached for misconduct or maladministration;" the Constitution of Virginia declares that all the civil officers who shall have offended against the State, by maladministration, corruption, or other high crimes, may be impeached by the House of Delegates; in some constitutions no offences are specified, in order to subject the public functionaries to an unlimited responsibility. But I will venture to affirm that it is precisely their mildness which renders the American laws most formidable in this respect. We have shown that in Europe the removal of a functionary and his political interdiction are the consequences of the penalty he is to undergo, and that in America they constitute the penalty itself. The consequence is that in Europe political tribunals are invested with rights which they are afraid to use, and that the fear of punishing too much hinders them from punishing at all. But in America no one hesitates to inflict a penalty from which humanity does not recoil. To condemn a political opponent to death, in order to deprive him of his power, is to commit what all the world would execrate as a horrible assassination;

的构成以及所受到的影响与刑事法庭的构成完全相同，而这又为党派间相互报复情绪的高涨提供了一种几乎无法抵抗的动力。尽管美国的政治法官不能像他们的欧洲同行那样对罪犯进行严惩，但是他们做出的无罪裁决也更为鲜见。他们做出的判决尽管不怎么严厉，但却最令人信服。而美国人这样做的主要目的就是要剥夺犯人手里的权力。因此，美国的政治审判可以被看作是一项预防措施，所以法官没有必要严格拘泥于刑法条文的精确定义。没有什么会比看到美国法律给出的模棱两可的政治罪定义而更让人感到诧异。《美利坚合众国宪法》第二条第四项写道："总统、副总统以及合众国一切文职官员，在因犯有叛国罪、贿赂罪以及其他不当行为或重大罪行而受弹劾的时候，应对其免职。"而各州的宪法对政治罪的定义更不明确。《马萨诸塞州宪法》规定："施政不善和渎职官员应遭到弹劾。"《弗吉尼亚州宪法》指出，有施政不善、贪污、失职以及其他重罪轻罪的一切文职官员，都应受到众议院的弹劾。在有些州的宪法里甚至没有明确列举出任何罪名，其目的就是要公职人员承担无限责任。但是我敢肯定，正是由于美国法律的温和性才让它在这一点上显得尤为可怕。正如我前面已经说过的，在欧洲罢免以及剥夺政治权利，是他受到刑法使然；而在美国这本身就是对官员的惩罚。其结果就造成，在欧洲，尽管政治法院拥有可怕的权限，但有时会出于对刑法过重的担心而不敢轻易使用。但是在美国只要是不会对人身造成痛苦的惩罚，人们都会毫不犹豫地予以施行。为了剥夺政敌的权力而将其置于死地会被当成是骇人听闻的谋杀；而宣布政敌不配拥有权力而将其剥夺，同时还不对其造成人身伤害，被认为是最具公正性的斗争。然而这种说起来简单的宣判，对于那些接受判决

but to declare that opponent unworthy to exercise that authority, to deprive him of it, and to leave him uninjured in life and limb, may be judged to be the fair issue of the struggle. But this sentence, which it is so easy to pronounce, is not the less fatally severe to the majority of those upon whom it is inflicted. Great criminals may undoubtedly brave its intangible rigor, but ordinary offenders will dread it as a condemnation which destroys their position in the world, casts a blight upon their honor, and condemns them to a shameful inactivity worse than death. The influence exercised in the United States upon the progress of society by the jurisdiction of political bodies may not appear to be formidable, but it is only the more immense. It does not directly coerce the subject, but it renders the majority more absolute over those in power; it does not confer an unbounded authority on the legislator which can be exerted at some momentous crisis, but it establishes a temperate and regular influence, which is at all times available. If the power is decreased, it can, on the other hand, be more conveniently employed and more easily abused. By preventing political tribunals from inflicting judicial punishments the Americans seem to have eluded the worst consequences of legislative tyranny, rather than tyranny itself; and I am not sure that political jurisdiction, as it is constituted in the United States, is not the most formidable weapon which has ever been placed in the rude grasp of a popular majority. When the American republics begin to degenerate it will be easy to verify the truth of this observation, by remarking whether the number of political impeachments augments.

的大多数人来说也会感到异常痛苦。一些罪大恶极的犯人可能对此不屑一顾，但是对于一般罪犯而言，会将其视为令自己地位不保名誉扫地的可怕判决，让自己过上生不如死碌碌无为的可耻生活的判决。美国政治审判机构对社会生活产生的影响似乎并不可怕，但实际上其威力无穷。它并不直接作用于被治者，而是让大多数人能够对掌权者更为专制。它并不是赋予立法者只能在危急关头才能动用的无限权力，而是要确立适度常规的影响力，并能时时发挥作用。而从另一方面来说，权力不大虽然行使起来很方便，但是也会容易造成权力滥用。美国人不允许政治法庭进行刑事判决要防止的不是立法暴政本身而是立法暴政可能带来的可怕后果。我也不太确定能不能说美国的政治审判是迄今为止人民大众手中掌握过的最为强大的武器。当美国共和政体开始衰退的时候，人们只要看看政治审判的数量有没有增加，就能轻而易举地对我提出的观点进行验证。

Chapter VIII: The Federal Constitution

I have hitherto considered each State as a separate whole, and I have explained the different springs which the people sets in motion, and the different means of action which it employs. But all the States which I have considered as independent are forced to submit, in certain cases, to the supreme authority of the Union. The time is now come for me to examine separately the supremacy with which the Union has been invested, and to cast a rapid glance over the Federal Constitution.

History Of The Federal Constitution
Origin of the first Union—Its weakness—Congress appeals to the constituent authority—Interval of two years between this appeal and the promulgation of the new Constitution.

The thirteen colonies which simultaneously threw off the yoke of England towards the end of the last century professed, as I have already observed, the same religion, the same language, the same customs, and almost the same laws; they were struggling against a common enemy; and these reasons were sufficiently strong to unite them one to another, and to consolidate them into one nation. But as each of them had enjoyed a separate existence and a government within its own control, the peculiar interests and customs which resulted from this system were opposed to a compact and intimate union which would have absorbed the individual importance of each in the general importance of all. Hence arose two opposite tendencies, the one prompting the Anglo-Americans to unite, the other to divide their strength. As long as the war with the mother-country lasted the principle of union was

第八章　联邦宪法

到目前为止，我一直将各州视为单独的整体，并对各州采用的不同机构及拥有的行政手段进行了说明。但是在特定的情况下，在我看来各自为政的各个州必须要服从联邦政府这一最高当局。现在是时候考察联邦政府所拥有的无上权力，并一瞥联邦宪法。

联邦宪法的历史

联邦的起源——联邦的弱点——国会呼吁制宪权——从制宪权的呼吁到新宪法的颁布耗时两年。

在18世纪末，同时挣脱英国束缚的十三个殖民地，正如我所见，拥有相同的宗教、相同的语言、相同的传统以及几乎相同的法律，而且还曾经与共同的敌人进行斗争。这些理由足以将它们联合起来，合并成一个国家。但是因为它们一直独立存在各自为政，故而形成各自特有的利益和习惯，所以它们势必反对建立一个会将其各自重要性埋没在全体重要性中的紧密牢固的联合。进而，就出现了两种完全不同的趋势：一个要将英裔美国人团结

kept alive by necessity; and although the laws which constituted it were defective, the common tie subsisted in spite of their imperfections. But no sooner was peace concluded than the faults of the legislation became manifest, and the State seemed to be suddenly dissolved. Each colony became an independent republic, and assumed an absolute sovereignty. The federal government, condemned to impotence by its constitution, and no longer sustained by the presence of a common danger, witnessed the outrages offered to its flag by the great nations of Europe, whilst it was scarcely able to maintain its ground against the Indian tribes, and to pay the interest of the debt which had been contracted during the war of independence. It was already on the verge of destruction, when it officially proclaimed its inability to conduct the government, and appealed to the constituent authority of the nation. If America ever approached (for however brief a time) that lofty pinnacle of glory to which the fancy of its inhabitants is wont to point, it was at the solemn moment at which the power of the nation abdicated, as it were, the empire of the land. All ages have furnished the spectacle of a people struggling with energy to win its independence; and the efforts of the Americans in throwing off the English yoke have been considerably exaggerated. Separated from their enemies by three thousand miles of ocean, and backed by a powerful ally, the success of the United States may be more justly attributed to their geographical position than to the valor of their armies or the patriotism of their citizens. It would be ridiculous to compare the American was to the wars of the French Revolution, or the efforts of the Americans to those of the French when they were attacked by the whole of Europe, without credit and without allies, yet capable of opposing a twentieth part of their population to the world, and of bearing the torch of revolution beyond their frontiers whilst they stifled its devouring flame within the bosom of their country. But it is a novelty in the history of society to see a great people turn a calm and scrutinizing eye upon itself, when apprised by the legislature that the wheels of government are stopped; to see it carefully examine the extent of the evil, and patiently wait for two whole years until a remedy was discovered, which it voluntarily adopted without having wrung a tear or a drop of blood from mankind. At the time when the inadequacy of the first constitution was discovered America possessed the double advantage

起来，一个则要将他们的力量分裂开。只要和母国的战争持续，现实的需要就会让联合的原则始终存在下去。尽管最初建立这一联合的法律存有缺陷，共同的纽带依然继续存在。但是在迎来和平不久之后，最初立法的缺陷开始显现出来，国家似乎一下子解体了。每个殖民地成为独立的共和国，拥有完全的主权。联邦政府因为其宪法而软弱无力，失去共同的危险作为支柱，只能眼睁睁地看着船舶上悬挂的国旗遭到欧洲大国羞辱，而且也没有力量守卫领土不受印第安部落的骚扰，以及偿还独立战争时欠下的巨额外债的利息。此时联邦政府已经岌岌可危，它正式声明无能为力，并呼吁取得制宪权。如果美国曾经，哪怕是极短的一段时间，达到让其居民向我们显示其引以为豪的幻想的荣誉顶点，那也就到了国家权力退位的严肃时刻。在任何时代，都能看到人们拼尽全力争取独立的恢宏场面，而美国人为摆脱英国人束缚所做的努力则被过分夸大了。他们跟敌人有着3800多英里大洋的阻隔，还有强大的盟国做后盾，也许把美国的胜利归结为地理优势更为客观公正，其次才是军队的士气和公民的爱国热情。把美国独立战争和法国大革命战争相提并论显得很荒谬，或者说美国人为独立战争付出的努力不能跟法国人为大革命所付出的努力同日而语。法国人受到了来自整个欧洲的攻击，一没钱，二没同盟，却能投入二十分之一的人力与敌人斗争，并在国外高举革命的火炬同时还要扑灭国内燃起的大火。但是看到一个伟大的民族在立法者告知他们政府的车轮已经停止后，依旧可以平静客观的审视自身，小心翼翼地自检，发现自己的问题，并耐心地等待整整两年时间去找到疗伤的办法，而且还能不流一滴泪不流一滴血地自愿服从它，这真是社会历史上难得一见的新鲜事。在最初宪法的缺陷被

of that calm which had succeeded the effervescence of the revolution, and of those great men who had led the revolution to a successful issue. The assembly which accepted the task of composing the second constitution was small; but George Washington was its President, and it contained the choicest talents and the noblest hearts which had ever appeared in the New World. This national commission, after long and mature deliberation, offered to the acceptance of the people the body of general laws which still rules the Union. All the States adopted it successively. The new Federal Government commenced its functions in 1789, after an interregnum of two years. The Revolution of America terminated when that of France began.

Summary Of The Federal Constitution

Division of authority between the Federal Government and the States—The Government of the States is the rule, the Federal Government the exception.

The first question which awaited the Americans was intricate, and by no means easy of solution: the object was so to divide the authority of the different States which composed the Union that each of them should continue to govern itself in all that concerned its internal prosperity, whilst the entire nation, represented by the Union, should continue to form a compact body, and to provide for the general exigencies of the people. It was as impossible to determine beforehand, with any degree of accuracy, the share of authority which each of two governments was to enjoy, as to foresee all the incidents in the existence of a nation.

The obligations and the claims of the Federal Government were simple and easily definable, because the Union had been formed with the express purpose of meeting the general exigencies of the people; but the claims and obligations of the States were, on the other hand, complicated and various, because those Governments had penetrated into all the details of social life. The attributes of the Federal Government were therefore carefully enumerated and all that was not included amongst them was declared to constitute a part of the privileges of the several Governments of the States. Thus the

发现的时候，美国占据两大优势，曾经鼓舞他们起来闹革命的政治激情尚未完全褪去，制定宪法的伟大人物依然健在。承担起草第二部宪法的制宪会议虽然人员不多，但会议的主席由华盛顿担任，并且囊括新大陆上所有最出类拔萃的人才和品格最高尚的人。在长期的深思熟虑之后，这个国家委员会要求人民接受这部一直沿用至今的基本大法。所有的州相继表示认可。在两年的空白期之后，新的联邦政府终于在1789年重新开始工作。然而，正当美国独立战争告一段落的时候，法国的大革命之战才刚刚拉开帷幕。

联邦宪法的概述

联邦政府与州当局的权力划分——州政府以制定普通法律为常规——联邦政府以制定普通法律为例外。

美国人面临的第一个棘手的问题就是要使主权的划分不但能够让联邦各州继续可以在有关本州繁荣的一切事务上管理自己，而且还要能够让联邦所代表的国家依旧保持是一个整体，并满足全国性的需要。如果想要事先将分享主权的两个政府各自的权限进行准确全面的划分完全没有可能。因为根本无法预见到一个国家可能会发生的所有事情。

联邦政府的权利和义务简单明确，因为联邦成立的目的就是要满足某些全国性的重大需要；而各州政府的权利和义务就非常复杂，因为州政府要深入到社会生活的方方面面。所以，联邦政府的职责可以清楚地列举出来，并宣布凡是不包括其中的事项皆由州政府负

government of the States remained the rule, and that of the Confederation became the exception.

But as it was foreseen that, in practice, questions might arise as to the exact limits of this exceptional authority, and that it would be dangerous to submit these questions to the decision of the ordinary courts of justice, established in the States by the States themselves, a high Federal court was created, which was destined, amongst other functions, to maintain the balance of power which had been established by the Constitution between the two rival Governments.

Prerogative Of The Federal Government

Power of declaring war, making peace, and levying general taxes vested in the Federal Government—What part of the internal policy of the country it may direct—The Government of the Union in some respects more central than the King's Government in the old French monarchy.

The external relations of a people may be compared to those of private individuals, and they cannot be advantageously maintained without the agency of a single head of a Government. The exclusive right of making peace and war, of concluding treaties of commerce, of raising armies, and equipping fleets, was granted to the Union. The necessity of a national Government was less imperiously felt in the conduct of the internal policy of society; but there are certain general interests which can only be attended to with advantage by a general authority. The Union was invested with the power of controlling the monetary system, of directing the post office, and of opening the great roads which were to establish a communication between the different parts of the country. The independence of the Government of each State was formally recognized in its sphere; nevertheless, the Federal Government was authorized to interfere in the internal affairs of the States in a few predetermined cases, in which an indiscreet abuse of their independence might compromise the security of the Union at large. Thus, whilst the power of modifying and changing their legislation at pleasure was preserved in all the republics, they were forbidden to enact ex post facto laws, or to create a class of nobles in their community. Lastly, as it was necessary that the Federal Government

责。因此，州政府以制定普通法为常规，而联邦政府以制定普通法为例外。

但是正如当时已经预见到的，实际上，有些问题可能超出为这个例外政府所规定的职权范围，而把这些问题交给各州自行建立的普通法院处理会有危险，于是联邦最高法院应运而生，除了其他的功能以外，其作用就是要在相互竞争的两个政府之间对宪法规定的分权加以维护。

联邦政府的职权

联邦政府拥有宣战、讲和以及征收一般赋税的权力——联邦政府可管辖的内政事务——在某些方面联邦政府比旧法兰西王国的国王政府更加集权。

在人民之间，每个人民只是一个个人，而一个国家为了能够取得对外的优势，必须要有一个统一的政府。因此，联邦政府被赋予讲和、宣战、缔结贸易条约以及募集军队和筹建舰队的特权。然而，尽管在内政事务的处理上，对于一个统一政府的需要并不是非常迫切，但是有些跟全国利益相关的事务只能交给一个总的当局才能得到有效处理。所以，联邦得到权力掌控货币体制、管理全国邮政以及开辟交通干线确立国家各地区间的联系。各州政府在本州内自主行事，然而它可能会滥用其独立，并鲁莽地做出危及整个联邦安危的行为，所以对于事先已有明确规定的州内事务，联邦政府有权插手。因此，加入联邦的各州虽然有权修订其立法，但不准颁布追究过往的法律，或是在本州内设立贵族阶级。最

should be able to fulfil its engagements, it was endowed with an unlimited power of levying taxes.

In examining the balance of power as established by the Federal Constitution; in remarking on the one hand the portion of sovereignty which has been reserved to the several States, and on the other the share of power which the Union has assumed, it is evident that the Federal legislators entertained the clearest and most accurate notions on the nature of the centralization of government. The United States form not only a republic, but a confederation; nevertheless the authority of the nation is more central than it was in several of the monarchies of Europe when the American Constitution was formed. Take, for instance, the two following examples.

Thirteen supreme courts of justice existed in France, which, generally speaking, had the right of interpreting the law without appeal; and those provinces which were styled pays d'etats were authorized to refuse their assent to an impost which had been levied by the sovereign who represented the nation. In the Union there is but one tribunal to interpret, as there is one legislature to make the laws; and an impost voted by the representatives of the nation is binding upon all the citizens. In these two essential points, therefore, the Union exercises more central authority than the French monarchy possessed, although the Union is only an assemblage of confederate republics.

In Spain certain provinces had the right of establishing a system of custom-house duties peculiar to themselves, although that privilege belongs, by its very nature, to the national sovereignty. In America the Congress alone has the right of regulating the commercial relations of the States. The government of the Confederation is therefore more centralized in this respect than the kingdom of Spain. It is true that the power of the Crown in France or in Spain was always able to obtain by force whatever the Constitution of the country denied, and that the ultimate result was consequently the same; but I am here discussing the theory of the Constitution.

Federal Powers

After having settled the limits within which the Federal Government was to act, the next point was to determine the powers which it was to exert.

后，为了能够让联邦政府清偿债务，而赋予它无限制征税权。

在对联邦宪法确立的分权制度进行考察的时候，也就是说在一方面要考察保留给各州的那部分主权，另一方面也要考察联邦掌握的那些重大权力的时候，能够清楚地看到联邦立法者对于政府集权的本质有着极为清晰和准确的认识。美国不仅是一个共和国，也是一个联邦。然而当美国宪法形成后，它比一些欧洲君主专制国家还要集权。下面的两个例子可供参考。

法国有13个最高法院。一般来说，它们有权对法律做出解释，而且不准上诉。但是一些称之为"国中国"的省份则有权拒绝承认代表国家的最高当局制定的税款。在美国，就好像只有一个立法机构可以制定法律一样，也只有一个法院可以对法律做出解释。因此，尽管美国只是一些共和国的联盟，但是在这两个主要点上，美国比旧法兰西国王更加集权。

在西班牙，有些省有权制定本省税制，而此项权力就其本质来说属于国家。而在美国，只有国会可以对各州间的商业关系进行调整。因此，就这方面而言，美国联邦政府比西班牙国王更加专制。的确，在法国和西班牙，王权总能够通过武力获得宪法拒绝赋予他们的特权。尽管从结果上看毫无差别可言，但是我这里讨论的是理论上的宪法。

联邦权

在联邦政府的权限明确之后，接下来就要对权力的施行加以规定。

Legislative Powers

Division of the Legislative Body into two branches—Difference in the manner of forming the two Houses—The principle of the independence of the States predominates in the formation of the Senate—The principle of the sovereignty of the nation in the composition of the House of Representatives—Singular effects of the fact that a Constitution can only be logical in the early stages of a nation.

The plan which had been laid down beforehand for the Constitutions of the several States was followed, in many points, in the organization of the powers of the Union. The Federal legislature of the Union was composed of a Senate and a House of Representatives. A spirit of conciliation prescribed the observance of distinct principles in the formation of these two assemblies. I have already shown that two contrary interests were opposed to each other in the establishment of the Federal Constitution. These two interests had given rise to two opinions. It was the wish of one party to convert the Union into a league of independent States, or a sort of congress, at which the representatives of the several peoples would meet to discuss certain points of their common interests. The other party desired to unite the inhabitants of the American colonies into one sole nation, and to establish a Government which should act as the sole representative of the nation, as far as the limited sphere of its authority would permit. The practical consequences of these two theories were exceedingly different.

The question was, whether a league was to be established instead of a national Government; whether the majority of the State, instead of the majority of the inhabitants of the Union, was to give the law: for every State, the small as well as the great, would then remain in the full enjoyment of its independence, and enter the Union upon a footing of perfect equality. If, however, the inhabitants of the United States were to be considered as belonging to one and the same nation, it would be just that the majority of the citizens of the Union should prescribe the law. Of course the lesser States could not subscribe to the application of this doctrine without, in fact, abdicating their existence in relation to the sovereignty of the Confederation; since they would have passed from the condition of

立法权

立法机构分为两支——两院建立的不同方式——州独立原则在参议院设立上取得胜利——国家主权原则在众议院组成上占上风——宪法只在国家初建阶段符合逻辑，由此产生的独特效果。

在联邦权力组建的时候，在许多方面都遵循了各州早已制定的宪法。联邦的立法机构由参议院和众议院组成。调和精神使得两院能够分别按照不同的原则建立。前面已经说过，起草联邦宪法的时候，存在两种利益的对立。这两种利益就导致两种观点的出现。一方希望能够把联邦转化成为独立州的联盟，或是成为代表大会，各州代表聚在一起对有关共同利益的问题进行商讨。另一方则希望将美洲各殖民地全体居民团结起来形成一个单一的国家，并建立一个尽管权力范围有限，却是唯一可以代表国家的政府。这两种理论的实践结果大相径庭。

如果联盟代替全国政府，那么法律的制定将取决于州的多数票而不是联邦居民的多数票。因为每个州无论大小都能充分享有独立，在绝对平等的基础上加入联邦。可是，如果美国居民都被认为属于一个相同国家，法律的制定就必然取决于联邦公民的多数票。较小的州自然不会同意这种主张，因为在涉及联邦主权时，它们实际上就要放弃自己的独立性，并从同联邦平等的政权沦落成为大国的附庸。但是如果采用前一种方法它们的权力就会过大，而采用后一种方法它们又毫无发言权而言。在这样的局势下，当利益和理论发生

a co-equal and co-legislative authority to that of an insignificant fraction of a great people. But if the former system would have invested them with an excessive authority, the latter would have annulled their influence altogether. Under these circumstances the result was, that the strict rules of logic were evaded, as is usually the case when interests are opposed to arguments. A middle course was hit upon by the legislators, which brought together by force two systems theoretically irreconcilable.

The principle of the independence of the States prevailed in the formation of the Senate, and that of the sovereignty of the nation predominated in the composition of the House of Representatives. It was decided that each State should send two senators to Congress, and a number of representatives proportioned to its population. It results from this arrangement that the State of New York has at the present day forty representatives and only two senators; the State of Delaware has two senators and only one representative; the State of Delaware is therefore equal to the State of New York in the Senate, whilst the latter has forty times the influence of the former in the House of Representatives. Thus, if the minority of the nation preponderates in the Senate,. it may paralyze the decisions of the majority represented in the other House, which is contrary to the spirit of constitutional government.

These facts show how rare and how difficult it is rationally and logically to combine all the several parts of legislation. In the course of time different interests arise, and different principles are sanctioned by the same people; and when a general constitution is to be established, these interests and principles are so many natural obstacles to the rigorous application of any political system, with all its consequences. The early stages of national existence are the only periods at which it is possible to maintain the complete logic of legislation; and when we perceive a nation in the enjoyment of this advantage, before we hasten to conclude that it is wise, we should do well to remember that it is young. When the Federal Constitution was formed, the interests of independence for the separate States, and the interest of union for the whole people, were the only two conflicting interests which existed amongst the Anglo-Americans, and a compromise was necessarily made between them.

It is, however, just to acknowledge that this part of the Constitution has not hitherto produced those evils which might have been feared. All the States are young and contiguous; their customs,

冲突的时候，理论要服从现实。最终，立法者找到折中的办法，将理论上原本不能调和的两种制度强行调和在一起。

州独立的原则在参议院组建上获胜，而国家主权原则则在众议院组建上占得先机。其最终结果是每个州向国会派驻两名参议员，而众议院的人数则依照各州人口比例决定。这样的安排就使得今天的纽约州仅有两名参议员而拥有40名众议员；而同样拥有两名参议员的特拉华州却只有一名众议员。所以，在参议院特拉华州和纽约州平起平坐，而在众议院后者的影响力是前者的40倍。因此，如果控制了参议院的多数票，众议院的多数票就变得毫无意义，而这恰恰跟宪法精神相悖。

这些事实充分说明，要将立法部门的各个部分既合理又合逻辑地结合起来是多么困难的事。随着时间的推移，利益纷争不断出现，人们会一直采用不同的原则进行处理。而当要制定宪法的时候，这些利益和原则相互作用的结果就成为严格政治原则施行的天然障碍。只有在国家成立之初，法律才能保有绝对逻辑，而当我们注意到一个国家能够享有这样的好处时，千万不要匆忙下定论认为它很英明，要记得它们还年轻。在联邦宪法确立之后，州各自独立利益和联邦全体利益，成为存在英裔美国人中的唯一一对相冲突的利益关系，所以必须要对它们进行调和。

可是，应当承认宪法的这一部分至今都没有引起人们最初曾经担心发生的不良后果。各州都很年轻，联系密切，有着相同的民情、观念和需要，而大小强弱的差异还不足以让它们产生过大的分歧。所以，参议院里不会出现小州联合起来与大州进行对抗的情形，而

their ideas, and their exigencies are not dissimilar; and the differences which result from their size or inferiority do not suffice to set their interests at variance. The small States have consequently never been induced to league themselves together in the Senate to oppose the designs of the larger ones; and indeed there is so irresistible an authority in the legitimate expression of the will of a people that the Senate could offer but a feeble opposition to the vote of the majority of the House of Representatives.

It must not be forgotten, on the other hand, that it was not in the power of the American legislators to reduce to a single nation the people for whom they were making laws. The object of the Federal Constitution was not to destroy the independence of the States, but to restrain it. By acknowledging the real authority of these secondary communities (and it was impossible to deprive them of it), they disavowed beforehand the habitual use of constraint in enforcing g the decisions of the majority. Upon this principle the introduction of the influence of the States into the mechanism of the Federal Government was by no means to be wondered at, since it only attested the existence of an acknowledged power, which was to be humored and not forcibly checked.

A Further Difference Between The Senate And The House Of Representatives

The Senate named by the provincial legislators, the Representatives by the people—Double election of the former; single election of the latter—Term of the different offices—Peculiar functions of each House.

The Senate not only differs from the other House in the principle which it represents, but also in the mode of its election, in the term for which it is chosen, and in the nature of its functions. The House of Representatives is named by the people, the Senate by the legislators of each State; the former is directly elected, the latter is elected by an elected body; the term for which the representatives are chosen is only two years, that of the senators is six. The functions of the House of Representatives are purely legislative, and the only share it takes in the judicial power is in the

且表达全国人民意志的法律条文具有不可抗的权威性，因此对于众议院的多数表决，参议院的反对显得苍白无力。

另一方面，我们也不能忽视，美国的立法者们只能代表人民制定法律，而没有将美国人民联合起来组成为单一国家的职责。联邦宪法的目的并非是要破坏各州的独立性，而是要对其加以限定。所以，在认可二级政权所持实权的时候（而且也无法再次收回），他们事先就放弃了强迫其服从多数表决的惯常做法。有了这样的原则，州政府能够对联邦政府施以影响就不再是什么新鲜事，因为这只是对既成事实的确认，也就是对已经获得认可的权力只能扶持不能强行压制。

参议院和众议院的其他差别

参议员由立法机关提名，众议员由人民提名选出——参议员采用二级复选制，众议员实行一次选举制——参议员和众议员的不同任期——两院的各自之职责

参议院与众议院的差别不仅体现在代表制度的原则上，而且在选举方式，任期以及根本职能也不尽相同。众议员代表由人民提名，而参议员则由各州立法机构提名；前者经选举直接产生，后者需要经过两阶段选举后方才产生；而且众议员的任期只有两年，参议员的任期则长达六年。众议院只有立法权，而且它所分享的司法权只有弹劾公职人员的时候才能行使。参议院协助立法工作，并对众议院提交上来的政治案件进行审理裁决。同时，

impeachment of public officers. The Senate co-operates in the work of legislation, and tries those political offences which the House of Representatives submits to its decision. It also acts as the great executive council of the nation; the treaties which are concluded by the President must be ratified by the Senate, and the appointments he may make must be definitely approved by the same body.

The Executive Power

Dependence of the President—He is elective and responsible—He is free to act in his own sphere under the inspection, but not under the direction, of the Senate—His salary fixed at his entry into office—Suspensive veto.

The American legislators undertook a difficult task in attempting to create an executive power dependent on the majority of the people, and nevertheless sufficiently strong to act without restraint in its own sphere. It was indispensable to the maintenance of the republican form of government that the representative of the executive power should be subject to the will of the nation.

The President is an elective magistrate. His honor, his property, his liberty, and his life are the securities which the people has for the temperate use of his power. But in the exercise of his authority he cannot be said to be perfectly independent; the Senate takes cognizance of his relations with foreign powers, and of the distribution of public appointments, so that he can neither be bribed nor can he employ the means of corruption. The legislators of the Union acknowledged that the executive power would be incompetent to fulfil its task with dignity and utility, unless it enjoyed a greater degree of stability and of strength than had been granted to it in the separate States.

The President is chosen for four years, and he may be reelected; so that the chances of a prolonged administration may inspire him with hopeful undertakings for the public good, and with the means of carrying them into execution. The President was made the sole representative of the executive power of the Union, and care was taken not to render his decisions subordinate to the vote of a council—a dangerous measure, which tends at the same time to clog the action of the Government and to

它也是全国最高的执行机构，总统缔结的条约必须得到其批准方能生效。此外，总统做出的人员任命也必须得到参议院的认可才能最终生效。

行政权

总统的依靠——总统的选举和责任——总统在职权范围内自主行事，受参议院监督但不受参议院干涉——总统的薪俸在就职时已经确定——搁置否决权。

美国的立法者面临着一项艰巨的任务，就是要建立起一个既依靠多数又充分具备足够力量在其职权范围自主行事的行政权。为维护共和制，行政权代表必须服从全国人民的意志。

总统是经选举产生的最高行政官。在他行使权力期间，自己的荣誉、财产、自由和生命就是他给人民的保障。然而在他行使权力的时候，也并非绝对独立。参议院会对他与国外的关系以及人员任命进行监督，所以他既不能受贿也不能贪污腐败。联邦立法者们认识到行政权获得的稳定性和力量必须要比各州所能给予的要更大，才能威严有效地履行职责。

总统一旦当选任期为四年，当然他可以获得连任，这样他就会热心公益事业，并设法将其付诸实现。总统是联邦行政权的唯一代表，而且要防止他的决定被委员会的意志所左右，因为这样危险的做法不但会阻碍政府的行动，而且还会削弱执政者的权力。参议院有

diminish its responsibility. The Senate has the right of annulling g certain acts of the President; but it cannot compel him to take any steps, nor does it participate in the exercise of the executive power.

The action of the legislature on the executive power may be direct; and we have just shown that the Americans carefully obviated this influence; but it may, on the other hand, be indirect. Public assemblies which have the power of depriving an officer of state of his salary encroach upon his independence; and as they are free to make the laws, it is to be feared lest they should gradually appropriate to themselves a portion of that authority which the Constitution had vested in his hands. This dependence of the executive power is one of the defects inherent in republican constitutions. The Americans have not been able to counteract the tendency which legislative assemblies have to get possession of the government, but they have rendered this propensity less irresistible. The salary of the President is fixed, at the time of his entering upon office, for the whole period of his magistracy. The President is, moreover, provided with a suspensive veto, which allows him to oppose the passing of such laws as might destroy the portion of independence which the Constitution awards him. The struggle between the President and the legislature must always be an unequal one, since the latter is certain of bearing down all resistance by persevering in its plans; but the suspensive veto forces it at least to reconsider the matter, and, if the motion be persisted in, it must then be backed by a majority of two-thirds of the whole house. The veto is, in fact, a sort of appeal to the people. The executive power, which, without this security, might have been secretly oppressed, adopts this means of pleading its cause and stating its motives. But if the legislature is certain of overpowering all resistance by persevering in its plans, I reply, that in the constitutions of all nations, of whatever kind they may be, a certain point exists at which the legislator is obliged to have recourse to the good sense and the virtue of his fellow-citizens. This point is more prominent and more discoverable in republics, whilst it is more remote and more carefully concealed in monarchies, but it always exists somewhere. There is no country in the world in which everything can be provided for by the laws, or in which political institutions can prove a substitute for common sense and public morality.

权使总统的某些法令无效，但是却不能迫使总统采取行动，也不能与总统分享行政权。

立法机构对于行政权所能采用的行动也许是直接的，而且正如我们刚才说过的美国人也在尽量避免这样做。但是，另一方面来说，其行动也可能是间接的。两院有权取消公职人员的薪俸从而剥夺他们部分的权利。而因为两院作为立法机构有权制定法律，这样公职人员又会担心依照宪法赋予他们的那部分权力会慢慢被两院蚕食。总统行政权的依附性是共和国宪法固有的缺陷之一。尽管美国人一直未能打破立法机构想要控制政府的趋势，但是他们却使得这一倾向变得不是那么无法抗拒。在总统就职之时，其整个任期的薪俸已经规定好。此外，总统还拥有搁置否决权，这样，对于那些危害到宪法赋予他的独立性的法律，他便可阻止其获得通过。总统和立法机构之间的斗争总是不平等的，因为只要后者有决心总是能够冲破一切阻碍，但是搁置否决权至少可以让立法机构对提案进行重新考虑，而且在对议案进行重新审议的时候，必须要获得全体三分之二的多数支持才能通过。实际上，搁置否决权是向人民进行呼吁。没有这一保障，行政权可能会受到暗中压迫，而采用这一方式行政权就能进行申辩，并陈述其动机。但是如果立法机构一定要推进其提案，就一定能够成功吗？我的回答是不论任何国家，不管其宪法性质怎样，立法者都必须依靠公民的良知和品德。在共和制国家这一点表现得尤为突出和鲜明，而在君主专制国家则总是遥不可及并被精心隐藏起来，可也从未消失。世界上没有任何一个国家的法律能够对一切做出规定，也没有任何一个国家的制度能够取代情理和公德。

Differences Between The Position Of The President Of The United States And That Of A Constitutional King Of France

Executive power in the Northern States as limited and as partial as the supremacy which it represents—Executive power in France as universal as the supremacy it represents—The King a branch of the legislature—The President the mere executor of the law—Other differences resulting from the duration of the two powers—The President checked in the exercise of the executive authority—The King independent in its exercise—Notwithstanding these discrepancies France is more akin to a republic than the Union to a monarchy—Comparison of the number of public officers depending upon the executive power in the two countries.

The executive power has so important an influence on the destinies of nations that I am inclined to pause for an instant at this portion of my subject, in order more clearly to explain the part it sustains in America. In order to form an accurate idea of the position of the President of the United States, it may not be irrelevant to compare it to that of one of the constitutional kings of Europe. In this comparison I shall pay but little attention to the external signs of power, which are more apt to deceive the eye of the observer than to guide his researches. When a monarchy is being gradually transformed into a republic, the executive power retains the titles, the honors, the etiquette, and even the funds of royalty long after its authority has disappeared. The English, after having cut off the head of one king and expelled another from his throne, were accustomed to accost the successor of those princes upon their knees. On the other hand, when a republic falls under the sway of a single individual, the demeanor of the sovereign is simple and unpretending, as if his authority was not yet paramount. When the emperors exercised an unlimited control over the fortunes and the lives of their fellow-citizens, it was customary to call them Caesar in conversation, and they were in the habit of supping without formality at their friends' houses. It is therefore necessary to look below the surface.

The sovereignty of the United States is shared between the Union and the States, whilst in France

美国总统的地位和法国立宪国王地位的不同之处

美国的行政权与其所代表的主权一样是有限和例外的——法国的行政权与其所代表的主权一样可以无限扩大——国王是立法者之一——总统只是法律的执行者——两种权力任期引起的其他差别——总统被束缚在行政范围内——国王独立自主不受约束——尽管有种种差别，但是法国更像是共和国而美国更像君主国——两个国家依附于行政权的官员人数的比较。

行政权对于一个国家前途命运的影响重大，所以有必要在此先对其在美国所占据的地位进行详细说明。为了能对美国总统的地位有一个准确清晰的认识，可以将其地位与欧洲某一君主立宪国家国王的地位进行比较。在做以比较的时候，我不会将注意力集中在它们的外在标志上，因为这些非但不能引导研究者反而会蒙蔽他们的双眼。当一个君主国逐渐向共和国转化的时候，尽管王权已经消失很久，但是行政权依然能够让国王拥有头衔、荣誉、礼遇甚至财富。英国人虽然将一位国王的头颅砍下，把一位国王从王位上撵走，但是仍然习惯于跪着跟这些君主的继承人们讲话。而另一方面，当共和国落入一个人的独裁之下时，独裁者依然可以保持简朴的生活，谦虚的作风，就好像他不是处在权力之巅一样。当皇帝大权在握，可以随意处置国家财富，掌控臣民生死的时候，人们言谈间习惯地称之为恺撒，而他们也往往能屈尊前往友人家中做客。因此，不能只流于表象，要看到本质。

美国的国家主权由联邦和各州共同分享，而法国的主权则不可分割是一个整体。因

it is undivided and compact: hence arises the first and the most notable difference which exists between the President of the United States and the King of France. In the United States the executive power is as limited and partial as the sovereignty of the Union in whose name it acts; in France it is as universal as the authority of the State. The Americans have a federal and the French a national Government.

This cause of inferiority results from the nature of things, but it is not the only one; the second in importance is as follows: Sovereignty may be defined to be the right of making laws: in France, the King really exercises a portion of the sovereign power, since the laws have no weight till he has given his assent to them; he is, moreover, the executor of all they ordain. The President is also the executor of the laws, but he does not really co-operate in their formation, since the refusal of his assent does not annul them. He is therefore merely to be considered as the agent of the sovereign power. But not only does the King of France exercise a portion of the sovereign power, he also contributes to the nomination of the legislature, which exercises the other portion. He has the privilege of appointing the members of one chamber, and of dissolving the other at his pleasure; whereas the President of the United States has no share in the formation of the legislative body, and cannot dissolve any part of it. The King has the same right of bringing forward measures as the Chambers; a right which the President does not possess. The King is represented in each assembly by his ministers, who explain his intentions, support his opinions, and maintain the principles of the Government. The President and his ministers are alike excluded from Congress; so that his influence and his opinions can only penetrate indirectly into that great body. The King of France is therefore on an equal footing with the legislature, which can no more act without him than he can without it. The President exercises an authority inferior to, and depending upon, that of the legislature.

Even in the exercise of the executive power, properly so called—the point upon which his position seems to be most analogous to that of the King of France—the President labors under several causes of inferiority. The authority of the King, in France, has, in the first place, the advantage of duration over that of the President, and durability is one of the chief elements of strength;

此，这便造就了美国总统和法国君主最大、最主要的差异。所以，美国的行政权与其所代表的主权一样是有限的和例外的，而法国的行政权也与其所代表的主权相同可以无限扩大。美国人有的是一个联邦政府，而法国人的则是全国政府。

这自然成为美国总统的地位比不上法国国王的一个重要原因，但这并不是唯一的原因，下面我们来谈谈第二个重要原因：主权内涵的差异，确切地说，可以把主权定义为制定法律的权利。在法国，法国国王可以真正行使主权，因为未经他的同意法律不能生效。此外，国王也是法律的执行者。尽管总统也是法律的执行者，但是他并不真正参与法律的制定，因为他同意与否并不能左右法律的存在。所以，总统只是主权的代理人。但是，法国的国王不但能够行使主权而且还能参与立法，从中得到一份权力。国王有权任命国会议员，还可以随时结束一个国会议员的任期。可是，美国总统不能参与立法机构的组建，也无权解散立法机构。国王与国会一样拥有法律提案权，而美国总统则没有这样的权利。国王在国会两院中各有一定数量的大臣作为其代表，对其观点加以说明，表示支持并确保他的施政纲领获得胜利。总统和其同僚则一样都被排除在议会之外，他只能采用间接的方式向国会施加影响，表达观点。所以，法国国王与立法机构平起平坐，没有国王立法机构无法活动，反之亦然。而总统则是一个低级的从属的权力，排除在立法机构之外。

甚至是在总统地位与法国国王地位最为相似的行政权上，总统依然因为地位低下的原因而任劳任怨的工作。首先，在任期上，法国国王就比美国总统更有优势，而且任期是权力的重要因素之一。因为，人们只对长期存在的东西表现出爱戴和敬畏。总统是经选举产

nothing is either loved or feared but what is likely to endure. The President of the United States is a magistrate elected for four years; the King, in France, is an hereditary sovereign. In the exercise of the executive power the President of the United States is constantly subject to a jealous scrutiny. He may make, but he cannot conclude, a treaty; he may designate, but he cannot appoint, a public officer. The King of France is absolute within the limits of his authority. The President of the United States is responsible for his actions; but the person of the King is declared inviolable by the French Charter.

Nevertheless, the supremacy of public opinion is no less above the head of the one than of the other. This power is less definite, less evident, and less sanctioned by the laws in France than in America, but in fact it exists. In America, it acts by elections and decrees; in France it proceeds by revolutions; but notwithstanding the different constitutions of these two countries, public opinion is the predominant authority in both of them. The fundamental principle of legislation—a principle essentially republican—is the same in both countries, although its consequences may be different, and its results more or less extensive. Whence I am led to conclude that France with its King is nearer akin to a republic than the Union with its President is to a monarchy.

In what I have been saying I have only touched upon the main points of distinction; and if I could have entered into details, the contrast would have been rendered still more striking. I have remarked that the authority of the President in the United States is only exercised within the limits of a partial sovereignty, whilst that of the King in France is undivided. I might have gone on to show that the power of the King's government in France exceeds its natural limits, however extensive they may be, and penetrates in a thousand different ways into the administration of private interests. Amongst the examples of this influence may be quoted that which results from the great number of public functionaries, who all derive their appointments from the Government. This number now exceeds all previous limits; it amounts to 138,000 nominations, each of which may be considered as an element of power. The President of the United States has not the exclusive right of making any public appointments, and their whole number scarcely exceeds 12,000.

生任期为四年的最高行政官，而法国国王则是世袭君主。在行使行政权力的时候，美国总统自始至终都要受到嫉妒性的监督。他可以缔结但是不能批准条约，可以提名但不能任命官员。法国国王则拥有绝对的行政权力。美国总统要为自己的行为负责，而法国宪章规定国王人身权利不得侵害。

然而，不论是法国国王还是美国总统都要受到公众舆论的影响。尽管这一力量在法国表现的并不明显，也未得到公认，更未写入法国法律，但是它确实存在。在美国，这一力量通过选举和法院判决发挥作用，而在法国，则通过革命发挥作用。所以，尽管两个国家的宪法不同，但是舆论都是具有统治作用的力量。两个国家立法的基本原则根本上来说是相同的，由于这一原则在一个国家的发展过于自由而另一个则不够自由，最终导致结果不尽相同。因此，我认为拥有总统的美国与君主国的相似程度，不及拥有国王的法国与共和国的相似程度。

上面我只谈了两者的主要差别，如果进行深入细致的比较，对比的结果更为惊人。我已经说过，美国总统只能在限定的范围内行使部分主权，然而法国国王则拥有绝对主权。我还可以证明法国国王的统治权已经超越其天然权限，并通过无数渠道深入到私人利益的管理。除了国王统治权的影响力之外，我还可以指出大量任命公职人员所产生的后果。这些人几乎都是代替国王行使行政权的。现在，法国公职人员的数量大大超过以往，总数高达138,000。他们当中的每个人都应该被视为权力的分子。美国总统则没有权利任命公职人员，而且公职人员的总数也不超过12,000人。

Accidental Causes Which May Increase The Influence Of The Executive Government

External security of the Union—Army of six thousand men—Few ships—The President has no opportunity of exercising his great prerogatives—In the prerogatives he exercises he is weak.

If the executive government is feebler in America than in France, the cause is more attributable to the circumstances than to the laws of the country.

It is chiefly in its foreign relations that the executive power of a nation is called upon to exert its skill and its vigor. If the existence of the Union were perpetually threatened, and if its chief interests were in daily connection with those of other powerful nations, the executive government would assume an increased importance in proportion to the measures expected of it, and those which it would carry into effect. The President of the United States is the commander-in-chief of the army, but of an army composed of only six thousand men; he commands the fleet, but the fleet reckons but few sail; he conducts the foreign relations of the Union, but the United States are a nation without neighbors. Separated from the rest of the world by the ocean, and too weak as yet to aim at the dominion of the seas, they have no enemies, and their interests rarely come into contact with those of any other nation of the globe.

The practical part of a Government must not be judged by the theory of its constitution. The President of the United States is in the possession of almost royal prerogatives, which he has no opportunity of exercising; and those privileges which he can at present use are very circumscribed. The laws allow him to possess a degree of influence which circumstances do not permit him to employ.

On the other hand, the great strength of the royal prerogative in France arises from circumstances far more than from the laws. There the executive government is constantly struggling against prodigious obstacles, and exerting all its energies to repress them; so that it increases by the extent of its achievements, and by the importance of the events it controls, without modifying its constitution. If the laws had made it as feeble and as circumscribed as it is in the Union, its influence would very soon become still more preponderant.

可加强行政权影响力的偶然因素

联邦的对外安全——为数六千人的军队——为数不多的军舰——美国总统拥有特权却没有机会行使——即使有机会行使特权，总统依旧显得虚弱无力。

如果说美国的行政权不如法国的强大，主要的原因在于环境而不是两国法律的差别。

主要在与外国打交道的时候，一个国家的行政权才有机会展示其技巧和力量。如果联邦的安危不断受到威胁，重大利益每天都与其他大国交织在一起，那么行政权的重要性就会随着人们对它的期待以及它自己的作为而不断提升。美国总统是军队的统帅，但是这支军队只有区区六千人；他号令舰队，而这舰队舰船的数量却寥寥无几；他负责联邦的对外管理，而美国则是一个没有邻国的国家。海洋把美国和世界分隔开，而且也没有称霸海上的力量。他们没有敌人，与世界上其他国家也几乎没有利益冲突。

美国总统手中的权力几乎和王权一样强大，但是却没有施展的机会，而且目前，他的权力只能在极为有限的范围内行使。法律赋予他强大的权力，而环境并未给他创造机会去施展。

而另一方面，法国王权的巨大力量则主要源于环境而不是法律。在法国，行政权要跟巨大的障碍不断斗争，并用尽全力对其进行打压，所以，根本无须修改宪法，随着其成就的广泛性以及所处理事务的重要性的增加，其力量也随之增强。如果法律让它像在美国一样软弱无力，但是由于环境使然，不久它依旧会变得越来越强大。

Why The President Of The United States Does Not Require The Majority Of The Two Houses In Order To Carry On The Government

It is an established axiom in Europe that a constitutional King cannot persevere in a system of government which is opposed by the two other branches of the legislature. But several Presidents of the United States have been known to lose the majority in the legislative body without being obliged to abandon the supreme power, and without inflicting a serious evil upon society. I have heard this fact quoted as an instance of the independence and the power of the executive government in America: a moment's reflection will convince us, on the contrary, that it is a proof of its extreme weakness.

A King in Europe requires the support of the legislature to enable him to perform the duties imposed upon him by the Constitution, because those duties are enormous. A constitutional King in Europe is not merely the executor of the law, but the execution of its provisions devolves so completely upon him that he has the power of paralyzing its influence if it opposes his designs. He requires the assistance of the legislative assemblies to make the law, but those assemblies stand in need of his aid to execute it: these two authorities cannot subsist without each other, and the mechanism of government is stopped as soon as they are at variance.

In America the President cannot prevent any law from being passed, nor can he evade the obligation of enforcing it. His sincere and zealous co-operation is no doubt useful, but it is not indispensable, in the carrying on of public affairs. All his important acts are directly or indirectly submitted to the legislature, and of his own free authority he can do but little. It is therefore his weakness, and not his power, which enables him to remain in opposition to Congress. In Europe, harmony must reign between the Crown and the other branches of the legislature, because a collision between them may prove serious; in America, this harmony is not indispensable, because such a collision is impossible.

Election Of The President

Dangers of the elective system increase in proportion to the extent of the prerogative—This system

为了领导国务工作，为什么美国总统不需要在两院取得多数

在欧洲人们公认，如果立宪君主遭到作为立法机构的两院的反对，便不能进行统治。但是美国已知的几位总统虽然已经在立法机构失去多数，却依然没有被迫放弃权利，而且也并未对社会产生恶果。据我所知，有人以此为例来证明美国行政权的独立和强势。然而只要稍作思索，就会发现情况恰恰相反，这样的事实只能证明美国行政权的极度虚弱。

欧洲国王之所以需要立法机构的支持来履行宪法赋予他的职责，是因为这些职责海纳百川。欧洲的立宪君主不仅是法律的执行者，而且他们还要让法律条文完全按照他们的意思执行，也就是说如果法律有悖于其制定的初衷，他们有权使之无效。国王需要国会的辅助来制定法律，而国会也需要国王的帮助来实现法律的执行。两者谁也离不开谁，一旦双方意见分歧，政府就要停摆。

在美国，总统无法阻止任何法律的通过，也不能规避执行法律的义务。无疑他热情真诚的配合对政府工作大有裨益，但也并非必不可少。总统的一切行动都要直接或间接的受制于立法机构，摆脱立法机构的束缚，他几乎一事无成。因此，正是他的虚弱而不是权力让其与立法机构作对。在欧洲，国王要和其他立法机构和谐相处，因为他们之间的冲突会产生严重的后果。而在美国，这种和谐则可有可无，因为这样的冲突根本不会产生。

美国总统的选举

总统选举制度的危险随行政权的扩大而增加——这种制度之所以在美国行得通，是因

possible in America because no powerful executive authority is required—What circumstances are favorable to the elective system—Why the election of the President does not cause a deviation from the principles of the Government—Influence of the election of the President on secondary functionaries.

The dangers of the system of election applied to the head of the executive government of a great people have been sufficiently exemplified by experience and by history, and the remarks I am about to make refer to America alone. These dangers may be more or less formidable in proportion to the place which the executive power occupies, and to the importance it possesses in the State; and they may vary according to the mode of election and the circumstances in which the electors are placed. The most weighty argument against the election of a chief magistrate is, that it offers so splendid a lure to private ambition, and is so apt to inflame men in the pursuit of power, that when legitimate means are wanting force may not unfrequently seize what right denied.

It is clear that the greater the privileges of the executive authority are, the greater is the temptation; the more the ambition of the candidates is excited, the more warmly are their interests espoused by a throng of partisans who hope to share the power when their patron has won the prize. The dangers of the elective system increase, therefore, in the exact ratio of the influence exercised by the executive power in the affairs of State. The revolutions of Poland were not solely attributable to the elective system in general, but to the fact that the elected monarch was the sovereign of a powerful kingdom. Before we can discuss the absolute advantages of the elective system we must make preliminary inquiries as to whether the geographical position, the laws, the habits, the manners, and the opinions of the people amongst whom it is to be introduced will admit of the establishment of a weak and dependent executive government; for to attempt to render the representative of the State a powerful sovereign, and at the same time elective, is, in my opinion, to entertain two incompatible designs. To reduce hereditary royalty to the condition of an elective authority, the only means that I am acquainted with are to circumscribe its sphere of action beforehand, gradually to diminish its prerogatives, and to accustom the people to live without its protection. Nothing, however, is further

为他们不需要特别强大的行政权——环境为什么有利于选举制度的建立——为什么总统的改选不会引起政府原则的改变——总统改选对下级官员的影响。

采用选举制选出国家行政首脑，其危险性已经被经验和历史学家充分证明，所以，在这里我要特别针对美国谈一谈这种危险。随着行政权所占的地位及其在国家中的重要性，以及选举方式和国家所处环境的不同，这些危险的可怕程度也或大或小。对国家首脑选举制最为有力的批驳就是，这样的制度对野心家有着致命的吸引力，会激起人们对权力的追逐，而且当权力即将远去时，他们便要诉诸武力。

显然，行政权越大，诱惑力也就越大；觊觎者的野心越强，就越会引得拥护者蜂拥而至，而这些人则希望在他们的候选人获胜后能够一起分享权力。因此，选举制度的危险会和行政权对国家事务的影响成正比。波兰的历次革命不仅应当归因于一般选举制度，还应当归因于当选的官员成为大君主国的首脑。在探讨选举制的绝对优势之前，我们必须预先寻求一些问题的答案，即这个国家的地理位置、法律、习俗、国情以及人们的观念是否允许在这个国家建立一个软弱且受制于人的行政权。因为，在我看来，既要让国家代表拥有强大的权力又要让他经由选举产生根本就互相矛盾。为了将王权世袭制过渡到民主选举制，据我所知的唯一办法就是要先对王权的活动半径做出规定，并逐渐削减其特权，并一步步让人民习惯在没有王权的保护下生活。但是，欧洲的共和主义者们从来没有这样想过，因为他们之于暴政的憎恨源于自身所受到的暴政对他们的欺凌。激起他们反抗的是压迫而不是行

from the designs of the republicans of Europe than this course: as many of them owe their hatred of tyranny to the sufferings which they have personally undergone, it is oppression, and not the extent of the executive power, which excites their hostility, and they attack the former without perceiving how nearly it is connected with the latter.

Hitherto no citizen has shown any disposition to expose his honor and his life in order to become the President of the United States; because the power of that office is temporary, limited, and subordinate. The prize of fortune must be great to encourage adventurers in so desperate a game. No candidate has as yet been able to arouse the dangerous enthusiasm or the passionate sympathies of the people in his favor, for the very simple reason that when he is at the head of the Government he has but little power, but little wealth, and but little glory to share amongst his friends; and his influence in the State is too small for the success or the ruin of a faction to depend upon the elevation of an individual to power.

The great advantage of hereditary monarchies is, that as the private interest of a family is always intimately connected with the interests of the State, the executive government is never suspended for a single instant; and if the affairs of a monarchy are not better conducted than those of a republic, at least there is always some one to conduct them, well or ill, according to his capacity. In elective States, on the contrary, the wheels of government cease to act, as it were, of their own accord at the approach of an election, and even for some time previous to that event. The laws may indeed accelerate the operation of the election, which may be conducted with such simplicity and rapidity that the seat of power will never be left vacant; but, notwithstanding these precautions, a break necessarily occurs in the minds of the people.

At the approach of an election the head of the executive government is wholly occupied by the coming struggle; his future plans are doubtful; he can undertake nothing new, and the he will only prosecute with indifference those designs which another will perhaps terminate. "I am so near the time of my retirement from office," said President Jefferson on the 21st of January, 1809 (six weeks before the election), "that I feel no passion, I take no part, I express no sentiment. It appears to me just to leave to my successor the commencement of those measures which he will have to prosecute,

政权的扩大，因此他们攻击前者而丝毫没有意识到这两者关系是如何的密不可分。

迄今为止，还没有人愿意以荣誉和生命为代价来争当美国总统，因为总统的职位是暂时的且受限制和制约。因为只有赌桌上的赌注够大，才能吸引赌徒不顾一切。至今也没有任何一个候选人能够激起人们以强烈的同情或热烈的激情去支持他，原因非常简单，因为在他当选国家首脑后，他可以和朋友共同分享的权力、财富和荣耀非常有限，而且他在国内的影响力很小，无法在当权时左右本派人事业的成功。

王权世袭制的最大好处在于，因为一个家族的利益与一个国家的利益息息相关，所以一时一刻也不会罔顾国家的利益。所以，在对国家事务的处理上，即使君主国不如共和国，但不管好坏至少会有一个人会尽心尽力主持大局。相反，在实行国家首脑选举制的国家，政府的车轮往往会在临近选举之际，有时甚至是在选举之前的一段时间自动停下来。毫无疑问，法律可以加速选举的进程，经过对这一过程的简化和加速就可以不让行政权出现空位，但是即便是采取了这样的预防措施，人们内心依然会觉得行政权处于空位。

每当临近选举的时候，行政首脑满脑子想的都是即将到来的斗争，未来的计划变得不能确定，他不再提出新的东西，而只会漠然地处理那些也许会由另一个人来结束的工作。1809年1月21日杰弗逊总统曾说过这样的话："我已经如此临近退职期限，以至于不再参加实际工作，而只是提出我的建议。我觉得，应当由我的继任者采取他要实行或是要负责的措施才是合理的。"

and for which he will be responsible."

On the other hand, the eyes of the nation are centred on a single point; all are watching the gradual birth of so important an event. The wider the influence of the executive power extends, the greater and the more necessary is its constant action, the more fatal is the term of suspense; and a nation which is accustomed to the government, or, still more, one used to the administrative protection of a powerful executive authority would be infallibly convulsed by an election of this kind. In the United States the action of the Government may be slackened with impunity, because it is always weak and circumscribed.

One of the principal vices of the elective system is that it always introduces a certain degree of instability into the internal and external policy of the State. But this disadvantage is less sensibly felt if the share of power vested in the elected magistrate is small. In Rome the principles of the Government underwent no variation, although the Consuls were changed every year, because the Senate, which was an hereditary assembly, possessed the directing authority. If the elective system were adopted in Europe, the condition of most of the monarchical States would be changed at every new election. In America the President exercises a certain influence on State affairs, but he does not conduct them; the preponderating power is vested in the representatives of the whole nation. The political maxims of the country depend therefore on the mass of the people, not on the President alone; and consequently in America the elective system has no very prejudicial influence on the fixed principles of the Government. But the want of fixed principles is an evil so inherent in the elective system that it is still extremely perceptible in the narrow sphere to which the authority of the President extends.

The Americans have admitted that the head of the executive power, who has to bear the whole responsibility of the duties he is called upon to fulfil, ought to be empowered to choose his own agents, and to remove them at pleasure: the legislative bodies watch the conduct of the President more than they direct it. The consequence of this arrangement is, that at every new election the fate of all the Federal public officers is in suspense. Mr. Quincy Adams, on his entry into office, discharged the majority of the individuals who had been appointed by his predecessor: and I am not aware that General Jackson allowed a single removable functionary employed in the Federal service

然而，此时全国人民的目光都聚焦于一点，眼睁睁地看着行将开始的分娩的阵痛。行政权的延伸范围越大，要参与的活动越多越重要，这段真空期的致命性就越强。而对于一个已经习惯于行政权领导的国家，或者说一个习惯于强有力的行政权保护的国家，这样的选举制度必然带来强烈的震撼。而在美国，行政权的行使可以优哉游哉而不受谴责，因为它一直都虚弱无力受到限制。

选举制最主要的弊端之一就是，它会给国家的内政外交带来一定程度的不稳定性。而当经选举产生的首脑握有的权力不大的时候，这一问题就不易察觉。在古罗马时期，尽管执政官每年都换，但是政府工作原则始终未变，因为握有指导权的元老院采用世袭制。如果在欧洲采用首脑选举制，大多数君主国的面貌都会因为选举而面目全非。在美国，总统尽管对国家事务具有一定的影响力，但是并不主持国务，压倒性的权力握在全国人民的代表议员手中。因此能够改变政治准则的不是总统而是人民，所以选举制不会对美国政府的稳定性产生重大影响。然而稳定性的不足是选举制的固有缺陷，即使是在美国总统原本就已经非常有限的活动范围内，依然表现得极为明显。

美国人认为，对要履行职责并承担全部责任的行政权首脑而言，他有权亲自选择下属并随时对他们进行撤换，而立法机构则主要进行监督而不能指手画脚。而这一做法的结果就是，只要一进行新的选举，所有联邦官员的命运就会变得悬而未决。在欧洲的立宪君主国，人们往往抱怨行政机关小职员的命运总是取决于大臣们的命运。然而在实行国家首

to retain his place beyond the first year which succeeded his election. It is sometimes made a subject of complaint that in the constitutional monarchies of Europe the fate of the humbler servants of an Administration depends upon that of the Ministers. But in elective Governments this evil is far greater. In a constitutional monarchy successive ministries are rapidly formed; but as the principal representative of the executive power does not change, the spirit of innovation is kept within bounds; the changes which take place are in the details rather than in the principles of the administrative system; but to substitute one system for another, as is done in America every four years, by law, is to cause a sort of revolution. As to the misfortunes which may fall upon individuals in consequence of this state of things, it must be allowed that the uncertain situation of the public officers is less fraught with evil consequences in America than elsewhere. It is so easy to acquire an independent position in the United States that the public officer who loses his place may be deprived of the comforts of life, but not of the means of subsistence.

I remarked at the beginning of this chapter that the dangers of the elective system applied to the head of the State are augmented or decreased by the peculiar circumstances of the people which adopts it. However the functions of the executive power may be restricted, it must always exercise a great influence upon the foreign policy of the country, for a negotiation cannot be opened or successfully carried on otherwise than by a single agent. The more precarious and the more perilous the position of a people becomes, the more absolute is the want of a fixed and consistent external policy, and the more dangerous does the elective system of the Chief Magistrate become. The policy of the Americans in relation to the whole world is exceedingly simple; for it may almost be said that no country stands in need of them, nor do they require the co-operation of any other people. Their independence is never threatened. In their present condition, therefore, the functions of the executive power are no less limited by circumstances than by the laws; and the President may frequently change his line of policy without involving the State in difficulty or destruction.

Whatever the prerogatives of the executive power may be, the period which immediately precedes an election and the moment of its duration must always be considered as a national crisis, which is

脑选举制的国家，这种情况有过之而无不及。在立宪君主国，继任的大臣往往能够很快走马上任，这是因为行政权的主要代表没有改变，革新的精神也没有超越限制，改变只是发生在细枝末节而非行政管理原则，所以这并不是用一种制度取代另一种制度，不会引起革命。而在美国，则每隔四年都会依法进行一场这样的革命。至于这样的立法会给个人带来的不幸，我们得承认在美国官员命运的不确定性还尚未产生在别处已经出现的灾难。在美国找一个自食其力的工作很容易，所以丢官后也许舒适的生活不在，但是不会因此而找不到谋生的手段。

在本章开始的时候，我说过采用首脑选举制国家所面对危险的大小，会因采用这一制度国家所处环境的不同而不同。尽管行政权的权限受到限制，但却始终对国家的外交政策产生重大的影响，因为除非由一人负责，否则谈判无法开始并顺利进行下去。一个国家的形势越是艰难不定，就越是需要一个贯穿始终的外交政策，这样，对于采用首脑选举制的国家而言，危险也就越大。而美国的对外政策非常简单，因为没有哪个国家需要它，而它也不需要与别国合作。他们的独立不会造成任何威胁。因此，在他们目前的状态下，行政权既受到法律的制约又受到环境的制约。总统也许会对政策不断做出改变，但这并不会让国家遭殃或是毁灭。

不管行政权如何，选举前夕以及选举时期始终都是国家危机时期。一个国家的内忧越大外患也就越大，选举制所带来的危险也就越大。在欧洲，每当有国家要选出新的首脑

perilous in proportion to the internal embarrassments and the external dangers of the country. Few of the nations of Europe could escape the calamities of anarchy or of conquest every time they might have to elect a new sovereign. In America society is so constituted that it can stand without assistance upon its own basis; nothing is to be feared from the pressure of external dangers, and the election of the President is a cause of agitation, but not of ruin.

Mode Of Election

Skill of the American legislators shown in the mode of election adopted by them—Creation of a special electoral body—Separate votes of these electors—Case in which the House of Representatives is called upon to choose the President—Results of the twelve elections which have taken place since the Constitution has been established.

Besides the dangers which are inherent in the system, many other difficulties may arise from the mode of election, which may be obviated by the precaution of the legislator. When a people met in arms on some public spot to choose its head, it was exposed to all the chances of civil war resulting from so martial a mode of proceeding, besides the dangers of the elective system in itself. The Polish laws, which subjected the election of the sovereign to the veto of a single individual, suggested the murder of that individual or prepared the way to anarchy.

In the examination of the institutions and the political as well as social condition of the United States, we are struck by the admirable harmony of the gifts of fortune and the efforts of man. The nation possessed two of the main causes of internal peace; it was a new country, but it was inhabited by a people grown old in the exercise of freedom. America had no hostile neighbors to dread; and the American legislators, profiting by these favorable circumstances, created a weak and subordinate executive power which could without danger be made elective.

It then only remained for them to choose the least dangerous of the various modes of election; and the rules which they laid down upon this point admirably correspond to the securities which the

时，几乎都无法逃脱无政府状态或是外来入侵的灾难。在美国，即使没有总统社会依旧可以自立，而且也从未感受过外患带来的压力，所以总统选举是激动人心的大事，而非毁灭性的举动。

选举方式

美国立法者在选择选举方式时所展示出的才华—— 一个独特选举团的创立——选举人分别投票——众议院在什么情况下会应召进行总统选举——自宪法确立以来的十二次选举结果。

除了选举制固有的缺陷外，许多其他的困难都源于选举方式，而这些都可以通过立法者采取预防措施而避免。当人们带着武器来到公开场所进行首脑选举的时候，除了选举本身的危险外，还会暴露出这种尚武的选举方式所带来的内战的危险。波兰的法律规定，有一个人可以拥有国王选举的一票否决权，这无疑就是唆使人民除掉这个人或是预先铺就了通往无政府状态的道路。

在对美国的制度以及政治经济状况进行深入考察后，我们惊讶地发现人们的付出与他们的财富完美匹配。美国国内秩序能够保持安定的两大主要原因是，美国是一个新兴国家，但是人民早已习惯于自由。美国不用担心邻国的敌视，美国的立法者正是凭借着这样

physical and political constitution of the country already afforded. Their object was to find the mode of election which would best express the choice of the people with the least possible excitement and suspense. It was admitted in the first place that the simple majority should be decisive; but the difficulty was to obtain this majority without an interval of delay which it was most important to avoid. It rarely happens that an individual can at once collect the majority of the suffrages of a great people; and this difficulty is enhanced in a republic of confederate States, where local influences are apt to preponderate. The means by which it was proposed to obviate this second obstacle was to delegate the electoral powers of the nation to a body of representatives. This mode of election rendered a majority more probable; for the fewer the electors are, the greater is the chance of their coming to a final decision. It also offered an additional probability of a judicious choice. It then remained to be decided whether this right of election was to be entrusted to a legislative body, the habitual representative assembly of the nation, or whether an electoral assembly should be formed for the express purpose of proceeding to the nomination of a President. The Americans chose the latter alternative, from a belief that the individuals who were returned to make the laws were incompetent to represent the wishes of the nation in the election of its chief magistrate; and that, as they are chosen for more than a year, the constituency they represent might have changed its opinion in that time. It was thought that if the legislature was empowered to elect the head of the executive power, its members would, for some time before the election, be exposed to the manoeuvres of corruption and the tricks of intrigue; whereas the special electors would, like a jury, remain mixed up with the crowd till the day of action, when they would appear for the sole purpose of giving their votes.

It was therefore established that every State should name a certain number of electors, who in their turn should elect the President; and as it had been observed that the assemblies to which the choice of a chief magistrate had been entrusted in elective countries inevitably became the centres of passion and of cabal; that they sometimes usurped an authority which did not belong to them; and that their proceedings, or the uncertainty which resulted from them, were sometimes prolonged so much as to endanger the welfare of the State, it was determined that the electors should all vote upon the same

的环境优势，创立起一个软弱而具有依附性的行政权，这样既能采用选举制，又不会带来危险。

那么接下来他们所要做的，就只剩下从各种选举方式中选出最为妥当的一个，使在这方面制定的制度能够与国家自然条件和政治制度所提供的保障相契合。他们的目的就是要找到最能够表达人民意愿的选举方式，还要尽可能少的激化人们的情绪，并尽可能缩短权力空位感。首先，他们采用简单的多数通过的法律的方式，但是困难依旧存在，因为人们为获得多数通过不惜拖延时间，而这正式立法者想要尽量避免的。在一个大国很难出现只需一轮投票即获得多数通过的情况，而在地方势力强大的共和国联邦，其难度会变得更大。为了能够克服第二个障碍，他们采取的方法是将全国人民选举权委托给一个代表全国人民的机构。这样更便于人们做出明智的决定。接下来要决定的就是，到底是该将选举权委托给代表全国人民的立法机构，还是应该专为总统选举而设立一个选举团呢？美国人选择了后者，因为他们认为法律的制定者不足以代表人民的意志进行最高行政官的选举，而且他们当选为议员的时间已经超过一年，他们所代表的选民此时的想法也可能已经发生变化。所以，美国人断定，如果立法机构有权对行政权首脑进行选举，议员们会在选举前很长一段时间内受贿并参与阴谋活动。然而，特别选举人就好像陪审团的成员一样，直到选举日之前都会混迹于人民之中，只有在投票的时候他们才会露面。

因此，每个州都要提名一定数量的选举人，由他们进行总统选举。但是，正如前面所说，在实行选举制的国家，负责进行政府首脑选举的团体，必然又会成为争吵和阴谋的

day, without being convoked to the same place. This double election rendered a majority probable, though not certain; for it was possible that as many differences might exist between the electors as between their constituents. In this case it was necessary to have recourse to one of three measures; either to appoint new electors, or to consult a second time those already appointed, or to defer the election to another authority. The first two of these alternatives, independently of the uncertainty of their results, were likely to delay the final decision, and to perpetuate an agitation which must always be accompanied with danger. The third expedient was therefore adopted, and it was agreed that the votes should be transmitted sealed to the President of the Senate, and that they should be opened and counted in the presence of the Senate and the House of Representatives. If none of the candidates has a majority, the House of Representatives then proceeds immediately to elect a President, but with the condition that it must fix upon one of the three candidates who have the highest numbers.

Thus it is only in case of an event which cannot often happen, and which can never be foreseen, that the election is entrusted to the ordinary representatives of the nation; and even then they are obliged to choose a citizen who has already been designated by a powerful minority of the special electors. It is by this happy expedient that the respect which is due to the popular voice is combined with the utmost celerity of execution and those precautions which the peace of the country demands. But the decision of the question by the House of Representatives does not necessarily offer an immediate solution of the difficulty, for the majority of that assembly may still be doubtful, and in this case the Constitution prescribes no remedy. Nevertheless, by restricting the number of candidates to three, and by referring the matter to the judgment of an enlightened public body, it has smoothed all the obstacles which are not inherent in the elective system.

In the forty-four years which have elapsed since the promulgation of the Federal Constitution the United States have twelve times chosen a President. Ten of these elections took place simultaneously by the votes of the special electors in the different States. The House of Representatives has only twice exercised its conditional privilege of deciding in cases of uncertainty; the first time was at the election of Mr. Jefferson in 1801; the second was in 1825, when Mr. Quincy Adams was named.

中心。它有时候会篡夺本不属于他们的权力，而且它的议而不决有时还会拖累到国家的福祉。所以美国人决定所有的选举人要在同一天投票，而不必将他们召集到同一地点。这种双重选举制有助于多数票的产生，但也并非绝对。就像这些选举人的委托人会有不同意见一样，他们也会有不同的意见。这样，就有必要从以下三种办法中选出一种，要不就指定新的选举人，或是由原来的选举人再次协商，再或是交给另外一个权力当局进行选举。前两种办法不够可靠，而且很可能会拖延做出最终决定的时间，并必然带来无休止的争吵。因此，他们采用了第三种办法。根据规定，选票要密封送交参议院议长，并当着参众两院的面进行开封清点。如果没有一个候选人获得多数票，众议院会立即进行总统选举，但是总统人选要在得票最高的三名候选人中选出。

所以，只有在不会经常出现和无法预见的情况下，才会把总统选举权交给众议院议员，而他们只能从特别选举人选出的指定候选人中进行选择。这是非常好的权宜之计，能够把对人民意志的尊重和迅速完成选举以及国家对于平稳的需求结合起来。但是，众议院议员参与并不能够解决所有的困难。因为能否在众议院获得多数通过依然无法预料，而对此宪法并没有提出解决办法。但是通过将总统候选人限定在三人之内，并交由毫无偏见的机构进行决定，必然能够克服除选举制本身固有障碍以外的一切障碍。

在联邦宪法生效以来的44年中，已选举出12位总统。其中有10次由各州特别选举人在各州投票后直接选出。众议院只行使过两次它可以分享的这一特殊权力：一次出现在1801年对杰斐逊先生的选举，另一次出现在1825年，当选者是昆西·亚当斯先生。

Crises Of The Election

The Election may be considered as a national crisis—Why?—Passions of the people—Anxiety of the President—Calm which succeeds the agitation of the election.

I have shown what the circumstances are which favored the adoption of the elective system in the United States, and what precautions were taken by the legislators to obviate its dangers. The Americans are habitually accustomed to all kinds of elections, and they know by experience the utmost degree of excitement which is compatible with security. The vast extent of the country and the dissemination of the inhabitants render a collision between parties less probable and less dangerous there than elsewhere. The political circumstances under which the elections have hitherto been carried on have presented no real embarrassments to the nation.

Nevertheless, the epoch of the election of a President of the United States may be considered as a crisis in the affairs of the nation. The influence which he exercises on public business is no doubt feeble and indirect; but the choice of the President, which is of small importance to each individual citizen, concerns the citizens collectively; and however trifling an interest may be, it assumes a great degree of importance as soon as it becomes general. The President possesses but few means of rewarding his supporters in comparison to the kings of Europe, but the places which are at his disposal are sufficiently numerous to interest, directly or indirectly, several thousand electors in his success. Political parties in the United States are led to rally round an individual, in order to acquire a more tangible shape in the eyes of the crowd, and the name of the candidate for the Presidency is put forward as the symbol and personification of their theories. For these reasons parties are strongly interested in gaining the election, not so much with a view to the triumph of their principles under the auspices of the President-elect as to show by the majority which returned him, the strength of the supporters of those principles.

For a long while before the appointed time is at hand the election becomes the most important and the all-engrossing topic of discussion. The ardor of faction is redoubled; and all the artificial passions

选举是紧急时期

总统大选时期被看作全国紧急时期——为什么？——人民的热情——总统的忧虑——选举热潮之后的平静。

我已经说过哪些有利的环境因素促使美国采用国家首脑选举制，并指出立法者为规避这一制度带来的危险所采取的预防措施。美国人已经习惯于各种各样的选举，因为经验丰富，他们知道如何将人们高涨的热情控制在安全范围。美国广袤的疆域和居民的分散，使得这里的党派之争不及其他地方那样显见，那样危险。迄今为止，全国大选期间的政治形势并没有给这个国家带来真正的危险。

然而，美国总统大选时期依然可以被看作全国紧急时期。毫无疑问总统对于公共事务的影响是微小的间接的，而且总统选举之于个人可能无足轻重，但是之于整个民族则是举足轻重。因为不管一项利益多么微不足道，但是只要成为普遍利益其重要性就会陡然而增变得事关重大。跟欧洲国王相比，美国的总统能用来惠及其支持者的手段寥寥无几，但是由他任免的职位则多得足以让成千上万的选民直接或间接地关心他的成败。为了能够得到大众的关注，美国的政党往往会团结在一个人的周围。因此，总统候选人的名字就成为它们的象征，并由他来践行本党的理论。正是由于这些原因，各政党对于赢得选举乐此不疲，他们并不是要用总统的当选来让自家的理论获胜，而是通过这一事实要说明自家的学说获得多数的支持。

在选举日到来之前的很长一段时间，选举成为最为重要而且举国上下关心的唯一大

which the imagination can create in the bosom of a happy and peaceful land are agitated and brought to light. The President, on the other hand, is absorbed by the cares of self-defence. He no longer governs for the interest of the State, but for that of his re-election; he does homage to the majority, and instead of checking its passions, as his duty commands him to do, he frequently courts its worst caprices. As the election draws near, the activity of intrigue and the agitation of the populace increase; the citizens are divided into hostile camps, each of which assumes the name of its favorite candidate; the whole nation glows with feverish excitement; the election is the daily theme of the public papers, the subject of private conversation, the end of every thought and every action, the sole interest of the present. As soon as the choice is determined, this ardor is dispelled; and as a calmer season returns, the current of the State, which had nearly broken its banks, sinks to its usual level: but who can refrain from astonishment at the causes of the storm.

Re-election Of The President

When the head of the executive power is re-eligible, it is the State which is the source of intrigue and corruption—The desire of being re-elected the chief aim of a President of the United States—Disadvantage of the system peculiar to America—The natural evil of democracy is that it subordinates all authority to the slightest desires of the majority—The re-election of the President encourages this evil.

It may be asked whether the legislators of the United States did right or wrong in allowing the re-election of the President. It seems at first sight contrary to all reason to prevent the head of the executive power from being elected a second time. The influence which the talents and the character of a single individual may exercise upon the fate of a whole people, in critical circumstances or arduous times, is well known: a law preventing the re-election of the chief magistrate would deprive the citizens of the surest pledge of the prosperity and the security of the commonwealth; and, by a

事。各党派热情洋溢，凡是能够想象得出的党派激情，此时又在这样一个幸福平静的国家激荡起来。而另一方面，在任的总统则专注于自我保护。他不再为国家的利益处理政务，而是为再次当选而奔走忙碌。为了能获得多数支持，他讨好选民，而且非但没有按照职责的要求抑制自己的激情，而是不断地肆意妄为。当选举接近尾声的时候，各种阴谋活动日益猖獗，公民分化为不同的敌对阵营，而且每个阵营都会高举自己候选人的旗帜。整个国家都处在亢奋的状态。选举成为报纸的头条新闻，私人谈话的话题，以及一切思想和行动的目的，是目前人们唯一关心的事情。然而，选举的结果一经公布，这样的热情便会退却，恢复往日的平静，就好像即将决堤的河水，又静静地淌回原来的河道。但是，看到这样一场本可成为疾风骤雨的风暴就这样销声匿迹，人们又怎会不惊讶呢。

总统的连选连任

允许行政首脑连选连任，便已说明国家已经成为阴谋和腐化的温床——获得连选连任是美国总统的主要目标——连选连任之于美国的特别害处——民主的固有弊端在于一切权力都要服从多数的微小愿望——总统的连选连任助长了这一弊端。

美国的立法者允许总统连选连任是错还是对呢？初看起来，似乎不允许行政首脑连选连任并不合理。一个人的才干和品格对于整个国家命运的影响力不言而喻，特别是在危急时刻紧要关头的时候。然而，禁止行政首脑连选连任就会剥夺公民对于国家繁荣和安全的最有力的保障。因为这种不连贯性的存在，一个人很可能在已经表现出卓越管理才能的时

singular inconsistency, a man would be excluded from the government at the very time when he had shown his ability in conducting its affairs.

But if these arguments are strong, perhaps still more powerful reasons may be advanced against them. Intrigue and corruption are the natural defects of elective government; but when the head of the State can be re-elected these evils rise to a great height, and compromise the very existence of the country. When a simple candidate seeks to rise by intrigue, his manoeuvres must necessarily be limited to a narrow sphere; but when the chief magistrate enters the lists, he borrows the strength of the government for his own purposes. In the former case the feeble resources of an individual are in action; in the latter, the State itself, with all its immense influence, is busied in the work of corruption and cabal. The private citizen, who employs the most immoral practices to acquire power, can only act in a manner indirectly prejudicial to the public prosperity. But if the representative of the executive descends into the combat, the cares of government dwindle into second-rate importance, and the success of his election is his first concern. All laws and all the negotiations he undertakes are to him nothing more than electioneering schemes; places become the reward of services rendered, not to the nation, but to its chief; and the influence of the government, if not injurious to the country, is at least no longer beneficial to the community for which it was created.

It is impossible to consider the ordinary course of affairs in the United States without perceiving that the desire of being re-elected is the chief aim of the President; that his whole administration, and even his most indifferent measures, tend to this object; and that, as the crisis approaches, his personal interest takes the place of his interest in the public good. The principle of re-eligibility renders the corrupt influence of elective government still more extensive and pernicious.

In America it exercises a peculiarly fatal influence on the sources of national existence. Every government seems to be afflicted by some evil which is inherent in its nature, and the genius of the legislator is shown in eluding its attacks. A State may survive the influence of a host of bad laws, and the mischief they cause is frequently exaggerated; but a law which encourages the growth of the canker within must prove fatal in the end, although its bad consequences may not be immediately perceived.

候被排除在政府之外。

尽管这些论点足够有力，但是也许还存在更为有力的观点对其进行反驳。阴谋和腐化是总统选举制的天然弊端，而当首脑可以获得连选连任的时候，这些弊端会无限扩大，并危及国家的存亡。当候选人企图通过阴谋达到目的的时候，其诡计只能在非常有限的范围内施展，而当行政首脑出现在候选人名单中的时候，他则可以借助政府的力量达成自己的目的。在前一种情况下，一个人所能施展的影响力非常微薄，而与后一种情况，则是国家本身运用其强大的影响力进行腐化搞阴谋。采用不道德方式攫取权力的人，只能对国家的繁荣产生间接的损害。然而，如果行政权代表本人要参与角逐，那么其成功当选便会成为头等大事，而政府所要关注的事务则要屈居次席。他应处理的所有法律和对外谈判事宜都不及选举方案来的重要，政府官员已然不是再为国家服务而是在为其上司服务，政府活动如果不能说是违背国家利益，至少已然不是在为国家效劳。

美国总统对于连选连任的渴望，使得其整个施政方针，甚至是最微不足道的举措都服务于这一目的，而且当大选紧要关头来临的时候，其个人利益会取代公共利益。认识不到这一点，就无法认识美国总统处理国务的常规。连选连任的原则让民选政府的腐化影响格外广泛和危险。

在美国，这会对国家存亡的基础产生特别致命的影响。每个政府似乎都会受到其固有弊端的困扰，而立法者的智慧则表现在如何抵挡这些弊端的攻击。一个国家也许可以在革除许多不良法律后继续存在下去，而不良法律所产生的恶劣影响则往往会被夸大。任何可

The principle of destruction in absolute monarchies lies in the excessive and unreasonable extension of the prerogative of the crown; and a measure tending to remove the constitutional provisions which counterbalance this influence would be radically bad, even if its immediate consequences were unattended with evil. By a parity of reasoning, in countries governed by a democracy, where the people is perpetually drawing all authority to itself, the laws which increase or accelerate its action are the direct assailants of the very principle of the government.

The greatest proof of the ability of the American legislators is, that they clearly discerned this truth, and that they had the courage to act up to it. They conceived that a certain authority above the body of the people was necessary, which should enjoy a degree of independence, without, however, being entirely beyond the popular control; an authority which would be forced to comply with the permanent determinations of the majority, but which would be able to resist its caprices, and to refuse its most dangerous demands. To this end they centred the whole executive power of the nation in a single arm; they granted extensive prerogatives to the President, and they armed him with the veto to resist the encroachments of the legislature.

But by introducing the principle of re-election they partly destroyed their work; and they rendered the President but little inclined to exert the great power they had vested in his hands. If ineligible a second time, the President would be far from independent of the people, for his responsibility would not be lessened; but the favor of the people would not be so necessary to him as to induce him to court it by humoring its desires. If re-eligible (and this is more especially true at the present day, when political morality is relaxed, and when great men are rare), the President of the United States becomes an easy tool in the hands of the majority. He adopts its likings and its animosities, he hastens to anticipate its wishes, he forestalls its complaints, he yields to its idlest cravings, and instead of guiding it, as the legislature intended that he should do, he is ever ready to follow its bidding. Thus, in order not to deprive the State of the talents of an individual, those talents have been rendered almost useless; and to reserve an expedient for extraordinary perils, the country has been exposed to daily dangers.

以滋生腐化的法律其危害最终证明都是致命的，尽管人们也许无法马上发现它的恶果。

君主专制国家灭亡的原因是王权不合理地无限扩大。然而为了取消宪法中有关规定所采取的措施，即使其危害性并不会立即显露，但势必会产生极大的危害。基于同样的原因，在人民握有一切权力的民主国家，那些让人民活动日益积极活跃的法律，也会成为政府存亡的直接推手。

美国立法者能力的最好证明是，尽管他们清晰地认识到这一真理，依然有勇气将其付诸实践。他们认识到凌驾于人民之上的权力当局必不可少，它应在一定程度上保持独立自主，但又不能脱离民主的掌控，既要能够服从多数的一致决定，还要有能力阻止多数的肆意妄为并拒绝其危险的要求。为了达到这一目的，立法者们将国家行政权力集中交到一个人手中，让总统拥有大量的特权，并用否决权把总统武装起来，以防范立法机构的干涉。

但是，通过实行连选连任原则，立法者们又部分地破坏了自己的工作，而且他们又打压了大权在握的总统运用特权的意愿。如果总统不能获得连选连任，就不会脱离人民，因为他的责任不会因为竞选而缩水，而且对他来说人民的支持也不再重要，所以也没有必要完全听命于人民。相反，如果允许连选连任，那么美国总统就会沦落成为多数手中俯首听命的工具，特别是在政治道德沦丧伟人难觅的今天，情况尤其如此。他要爱多数之所爱，恨多数之所恨，他要为多数的愿望而奔忙，为多数的不满而疾呼，对于多数的无足轻重的要求也要妥协退让。立法者本来希望他可以对多数加以引导，而现在却变成他对多数唯命是从。立法者的初衷是唯恐国家失去人才，结果却让人才落得几乎毫无用处；本来是应对

Federal Courts

Political importance of the judiciary in the United States—Difficulty of treating this subject—Utility of judicial power in confederations—What tribunals could be introduced into the Union—Necessity of establishing federal courts of justice—Organization of the national judiciary—The Supreme Court—In what it differs from all known tribunals.

I have inquired into the legislative and executive power of the Union, and the judicial power now remains to be examined; but in this place I cannot conceal my fears from the reader. Their judicial institutions exercise a great influence on the condition of the Anglo-Americans, and they occupy a prominent place amongst what are probably called political institutions: in this respect they are peculiarly deserving of our attention. But I am at a loss to explain the political action of the American tribunals without entering into some technical details of their constitution and their forms of proceeding; and I know not how to descend to these minutiae without wearying the curiosity of the reader by the natural aridity of the subject, or without risking to fall into obscurity through a desire to be succinct. I can scarcely hope to escape these various evils; for if I appear too lengthy to a man of the world, a lawyer may on the other hand complain of my brevity. But these are the natural disadvantages of my subject, and more especially of the point which I am about to discuss.

The great difficulty was, not to devise the Constitution to the Federal Government, but to find out a method of enforcing its laws. Governments have in general but two means of overcoming the opposition of the people they govern, viz., the physical force which is at their own disposal, and the moral force which they derive from the decisions of the courts of justice.

A government which should have no other means of exacting obedience than open war must be very near its ruin, for one of two alternatives would then probably occur: if its authority was small and its character temperate, it would not resort to violence till the last extremity, and it would

这种特殊情况的权宜之计，结果却让国家时时处于危险之中。

联邦法院

美国司法权的政治重要性——论述这一问题的难度——司法权在联邦的实行——哪些法院通行于全联邦——设立全联邦性法院的必要性——联邦司法工作的组织——最高法院——最高法院与我们已知其他法院的不同之处。

我已经对美国的立法权和行政权进行了研究，现在还有司法权有待考察，但是，在这里我要直言不讳的向读者表达我的忧虑，唯恐我的讲述会令他们生厌。美国的司法制度对于英裔美国人的处境产生了重大的影响，而且在政治制度中占有重要的地位。就这一方面而言，特别值得我们注意。但是，如果没有深入探究美国法院的组织体系和审判程序的技术细节，就无法理解美国法院的政治作用。而且我也不知道如何不让读者对这一本身枯燥无味的话题感到厌烦，如何进行简单扼要又前后连贯的讲解。我丝毫不想要回避这些问题，因为也许在普通人看来我的讲解拖沓庸长，而另一方面法学家们还会觉得我过于简明扼要呢。而这些正是我无法两全其美的地方，特别是我将要讲述的这一部分，表现得尤为明显。

最大的困难并非是了解联邦政府是怎样组织的，而是找出其推动法律施行的方式。一般来说，政府只有两种方式对付人们的反抗：一是运用手中掌握的物质力量，二是通过法庭判决赋予的道德力量。

connive at a number of partial acts of insubordination, in which case the State would gradually fall into anarchy; if it was enterprising and powerful, it would perpetually have recourse to its physical strength, and would speedily degenerate into a military despotism. So that its activity would not be less prejudicial to the community than its inaction.

The great end of justice is to substitute the notion of right for that of violence, and to place a legal barrier between the power of the government and the use of physical force. The authority which is awarded to the intervention of a court of justice by the general opinion of mankind is so surprisingly great that it clings to the mere formalities of justice, and gives a bodily influence to the shadow of the law. The moral force which courts of justice possess renders the introduction of physical force exceedingly rare, and is very frequently substituted for it; but if the latter proves to be indispensable, its power is doubled by the association of the idea of law.

A federal government stands in greater need of the support of judicial institutions than any other, because it is naturally weak and exposed to formidable opposition. If it were always obliged to resort to violence in the first instance, it could not fulfil its task. The Union, therefore, required a national judiciary to enforce the obedience of the citizens to the laws, and to repeal the attacks which might be directed against them. The question then remained as to what tribunals were to exercise these privileges; were they to be entrusted to the courts of justice which were already organized in every State? or was it necessary to create federal courts? It may easily be proved that the Union could not adapt the judicial power of the States to its wants. The separation of the judiciary from the administrative power of the State no doubt affects the security of every citizen and the liberty of all. But it is no less important to the existence of the nation that these several powers should have the same origin, should follow the same principles, and act in the same sphere; in a word, that they should be correlative and homogeneous. No one, I presume, ever suggested the advantage of trying offences committed in France by a foreign court of justice, in order to secure the impartiality of the judges. The Americans form one people in relation to their Federal Government; but in the

如果一个政府只有采用武力才能迫使人们服从法律的话，那么它就离灭亡不远了。接下来就很可能产生下列两种情形：如果政府软弱而温和，除非万不得已否则不会诉诸武力，就会对局部不断出现的不服从听之任之，这样国家就会渐渐坠入无政府状态。然而，如果政府鲁莽而强大，则会自始至终运用武力并加速向军事专制国家的堕落。因此，无论政府是消极被动还是积极主动都会对被统治者产生同样的危害。

司法工作最重要的目的就是用权利观念取代暴力观念，并在政府力量和物质力量的运用之间设立一道法律屏障。人们普遍认为赋予法院的干预力量强大得惊人，与司法如影随形，并对其产生实际影响。然而法院所带有的道德力量使得物质力量的用武之地少之又少，并可以在大多数情况下取而代之。但是，如果最终不得不诉诸武力的时候，法律的道德力量会让武力如虎添翼。

因此，联邦制政府会比任何其他形式的政府更加渴望司法部门的支持，因为它生来软弱。面临各种可怕的反对，如果它一旦开始诉诸武力，就无法完成自己的任务。因此，联邦需要一个全国性的司法机构来确保公民服从其法律，或是保护公民免遭侵犯。那么，接下来的问题就是应该由什么样的法院来施行这一特权。是应该委托给各州现有的法院？还是应该创建隶属于联邦当局的法院？不难证明，联邦无法让各州的司法当局进行调整以适应它的需求。毋庸置疑，各州司法权与行政权的分离对于每个公民的安全与自由非常重要。但是，各州的几种权力应该来自同一源头，遵循同样地原则，并在同样的范围行事。简而言之，它们应该彼此关联性质统一，这对于一个国家的存亡同样不可或缺。我猜从没有人想过，为了确保法官的公正，而要将在法国境内犯下的罪行交给国外的法院进行审

bosom of this people divers political bodies have been allowed to subsist which are dependent on the national Government in a few points, and independent in all the rest; which have all a distinct origin, maxims peculiar to themselves, and special means of carrying on their affairs. To entrust the execution of the laws of the Union to tribunals instituted by these political bodies would be to allow foreign judges to preside over the nation. Nay, more; not only is each State foreign to the Union at large, but it is in perpetual opposition to the common interests, since whatever authority the Union loses turns to the advantage of the States. Thus to enforce the laws of the Union by means of the tribunals of the States would be to allow not only foreign but partial judges to preside over the nation.

But the number, still more than the mere character, of the tribunals of the States rendered them unfit for the service of the nation. When the Federal Constitution was formed there were already thirteen courts of justice in the United States which decided causes without appeal. That number is now increased to twenty-four. To suppose that a State can subsist when its fundamental laws may be subjected to four-and-twenty different interpretations at the same time is to advance a proposition alike contrary to reason and to experience.

The American legislators therefore agreed to create a federal judiciary power to apply the laws of the Union, and to determine certain questions affecting general interests, which were carefully determined beforehand. The entire judicial power of the Union was centred in one tribunal, which was denominated the Supreme Court of the United States. But, to facilitate the expedition of business, inferior courts were appended to it, which were empowered to decide causes of small importance without appeal, and with appeal causes of more magnitude. The members of the Supreme Court are named neither by the people nor the legislature, but by the President of the United States, acting with the advice of the Senate. In order to render them independent of the other authorities, their office was made inalienable; and it was determined that their salary, when once fixed, should not be altered by the legislature. It was easy to proclaim the principle of a Federal judiciary, but difficulties multiplied when the extent of its jurisdiction was to be determined.

判。就美国人与联邦政府的关系而言，他们是一个统一的国家。但是，这个国家却允许只在某些方面服从全国政府，而在其他一切方面独立自主的这样的政治组织存在，它们的来源不同，宗旨各异，行事方式也各不相同。让这些迥异的政治组织设立的法庭去施行联邦的法律，无异于由外国法官主持国家事务。而且，更有甚者，每个州对于联邦而言不仅形同外国，而且还一直与联邦对立，因为联邦所丧失的权力最终都落入各州之手。所以，将联邦法律交给各州法院执行，不仅是把国家交给外国法官管理，而且还是交给心怀偏见的法官。

除了州法院的性质外，其数量之多也使得其不适合为国家目的服务。在联邦宪法制定的时候，美国已经拥有13个宣判后不得上诉的法院，并且现在这类法院的数目已经飙升至24个。也就是说对于国家的主要法律会同时存在24种解说和应用，这既不合情也不合理，更有违经验。

因此，美国的立法者们创建一个联邦司法当局来执行联邦法律，并在预先精心规定后对涉及全国利益的问题进行处理。所以，联邦的整个司法权都落入一个名为"美国最高法院"的法院手里。但是，为了便于审理案件，这个法院又设立了一些下属法院，对一些不太重要的案件做最终判决，或是对重大的争讼进行初判。最高法院的法官既不由人民也不由立法机构选举产生，而是由美国总统经参议院审核后任命。为了能够确保最高法院法官保持独立，不受其他权力机关的影响，其任期为终身制，并规定薪俸一旦确定，司法机构不能进行变更。联邦司法制度的原则概括地说一说很容易，但是要深入讲解它的职权时，困难就会倍增。

Means Of Determining The Jurisdiction Of The Federal Courts

Difficulty of determining the jurisdiction of separate courts of justice in confederations—The courts of the Union obtained the right of fixing their own jurisdiction—In what respect this rule attacks the portion of sovereignty reserved to the several States—The sovereignty of these States restricted by the laws, and the interpretation of the laws—Consequently, the danger of the several States is more apparent than real.

As the Constitution of the United States recognized two distinct powers in presence of each other, represented in a judicial point of view by two distinct classes of courts of justice, the utmost care which could be taken in defining their separate jurisdictions would have been insufficient to prevent frequent collisions between those tribunals. The question then arose to whom the right of deciding the competency of each court was to be referred.

In nations which constitute a single body politic, when a question is debated between two courts relating to their mutual jurisdiction, a third tribunal is generally within reach to decide the difference; and this is effected without difficulty, because in these nations the questions of judicial competency have no connection with the privileges of the national supremacy. But it was impossible to create an arbiter between a superior court of the Union and the superior court of a separate State which would not belong to one of these two classes. It was, therefore, necessary to allow one of these courts to judge its own cause, and to take or to retain cognizance of the point which was contested. To grant this privilege to the different courts of the States would have been to destroy the sovereignty of the Union de facto after having established it de jure; for the interpretation of the Constitution would soon have restored that portion of independence to the States of which the terms of that act deprived them. The object of the creation of a Federal tribunal was to prevent the courts of the States from deciding questions affecting the national interests in their own department, and so to form a uniform body of jurisprudene for the interpretation of the laws of the Union. This end would not have been accomplished if the courts of the several States had been competent to decide upon cases in their

规定联邦法院管辖权的方法

规定联邦各法院管辖权的困难——联邦法院有权对自己的管辖权做出规定——这一规定在哪些方面侵犯了让与各州的那部分权力——这些州的权力受到法律及法律解释的限制——因此，各州实际上遇到的危险并没有表面上看的那么严重。

由于美国宪法承认两种不同主权的并存，而且在司法制度上，这两种主权又分别以两种不同系统的法院为代表，所以，在对两个系统法院各自审理权进行规定的时候要格外小心，即使如此也难以避免两者之间经常出现的冲突。那么，接下来的问题就是应当确定要把决定法院管辖权的权力交给谁。

在政治制度单一的国家，如果出现两个法院之间的权限之争，通常由另一个法院进行仲裁。这样问题就可以迎刃而解，因为在这些国家司法权限问题和国家主权问题并无联系。但是，在美国无法在联邦最高法院和各州最高法院之上再设立一个既不属于前一体系也不属于后一体系的仲裁机构。因此，必须要让其中一个法院能够进行自行裁定受理或拒绝受理案件。如果把这一特权交给各州法院，就会实际上侵害联邦的主权。因为州法院在获得宪法解释权后，必然很快就会恢复以前被宪法有关条款剥夺的那部分独立性。建立联邦法院的目的就在于防止各州法院在涉及全国利益的问题上自行其是，并成立一个统一的司法机构对联邦法律做出解释。如果各州的法院有权独立行事确定案件的归属，那么这一目的就无法达成。因此，与法院管辖权有关的所有问题的决定权就交到了联邦最高法院手中。

separate capacities from which they were obliged to abstain as Federal tribunals. The Supreme Court of the United States was therefore invested with the right of determining all questions of jurisdiction.

This was a severe blow upon the independence of the States, which was thus restricted not only by the laws, but by the interpretation of them; by one limit which was known, and by another which was dubious; by a rule which was certain, and a rule which was arbitrary. It is true the Constitution had laid down the precise limits of the Federal supremacy, but whenever this supremacy is contested by one of the States, a Federal tribunal decides the question. Nevertheless, the dangers with which the independence of the States was threatened by this mode of proceeding are less serious than they appeared to be. We shall see hereafter that in America the real strength of the country is vested in the provincial far more than in the Federal Government. The Federal judges are conscious of the relative weakness of the power in whose name they act, and they are more inclined to abandon a right of jurisdiction in cases where it is justly their own than to assert a privilege to which they have no legal claim.

Different Cases Of Jurisdiction

The matter and the party are the first conditions of the Federal jurisdiction—Suits in which ambassadors are engaged—Suits of the Union—Of a separate State—By whom tried—Causes resulting from the laws of the Union—Why judged by the Federal tribunals—Causes relating to the performance of contracts tried by the Federal courts—Consequence of this arrangement.

After having appointed the means of fixing the competency of the Federal courts, the legislators of the Union defined the cases which should come within their jurisdiction. It was established, on the one hand, that certain parties must always be brought before the Federal courts, without any regard to the special nature of the cause; and, on the other, that certain causes must always be brought before the same courts, without any regard to the quality of the parties in the suit. These distinctions were therefore admitted to be the basis of the Federal jurisdiction.

Ambassadors are the representatives of nations in a state of amity with the Union, and whatever

这对于州的主权是一个严厉的打击。这样一来，州主权不但要受到法律的约束还要受到司法解释的约束；既要受到已知范围的限制，又要受到未知范围的限制；既要受到明文规定的限制，又要受到模糊不清规定的限制。宪法的确已经对联邦主权做出明确的规定，但同时也规定，一旦联邦主权与州主权发生冲突，则由联邦法院负责对此进行裁定。尽管如此，这一诉讼程序给州主权带来威胁的危险性，实际上并不如表面看上去的那么严重。后面我们会看到，美国各州实际拥有的权力远远大于联邦政府的权力。联邦法官认识到他们以自己名义行使的权力比较薄弱，所以在他们依法有权审理的案件中，如果附带规定了一些不合理的要求，他们宁可放弃其审判权。

联邦法院审理的各种案件

案件与诉讼当事人是联邦法院审判的要件——涉及外国大使的诉讼——涉及联邦的诉讼——涉及一个州的诉讼——由谁审判——因联邦法律而产生的诉讼——为什么交由联邦法院审理——不履行合同的诉讼由联邦法院审理——这种安排产生的后果。

在找到确定联邦法院权限的方式后，美国立法者们又对哪些案件应该交由联邦法院审理做出规定。一方面，他们规定了联邦法院审理的诉讼人的范围，而不考虑案件的性质；另一方面，又规定了联邦法院所审理案件的范围，而不考虑涉案的当事各方。因此，诉讼当事人和案件构成联邦法院审判的要件。

concerns these personages concerns in some degree the whole Union. When an ambassador is a party in a suit, that suit affects the welfare of the nation, and a Federal tribunal is naturally called upon to decide it.

The Union itself may be invoked in legal proceedings, and in this case it would be alike contrary to the customs of all nations and to common sense to appeal to a tribunal representing any other sovereignty than its own; the Federal courts, therefore, take cognizance of these affairs.

When two parties belonging to two different States are engaged in a suit, the case cannot with propriety be brought before a court of either State. The surest expedient is to select a tribunal like that of the Union, which can excite the suspicions of neither party, and which offers the most natural as well as the most certain remedy.

When the two parties are not private individuals, but States, an important political consideration is added to the same motive of equity. The quality of the parties in this case gives a national importance to all their disputes; and the most trifling litigation of the States may be said to involve the peace of the whole Union.

The nature of the cause frequently prescribes the rule of competency. Thus all the questions which concern maritime commerce evidently fall under the cognizance of the Federal tribunals. Almost all these questions are connected with the interpretation of the law of nations, and in this respect they essentially interest the Union in relation to foreign powers. Moreover, as the sea is not included within the limits of any peculiar jurisdiction, the national courts can only hear causes which originate in maritime affairs.

The Constitution comprises under one head almost all the cases which by their very nature come within the limits of the Federal courts. The rule which it lays down is simple, but pregnant with an entire system of ideas, and with a vast multitude of facts. It declares that the judicial power of the Supreme Court shall extend to all cases in law and equity arising under the laws of the United States.

Two examples will put the intention of the legislator in the clearest light:

The Constitution prohibits the States from making laws on the value and circulation of money: If, notwithstanding this prohibition, a State passes a law of this kind, with which the interested parties

外国大使是联邦友好国家的代表，所以与他们相关的案件在某种程度上说就是与全联邦相关。当外国大使成为案件中的一方当事人，该案件必然会涉及国家利益，因此自然就要交给联邦法院审理。

联邦本身也有可能牵涉到诉讼之中。此时，如果它不是向代表联邦主权的法院提起控诉，而是到其他法院进行诉讼，显然有悖于常理和国家惯例。所以，这样的案件只能由联邦法院进行审理。

当案件双方当事人分属于不同州的时候，将案件交给任何一方的州法院都不合适。最可行的做法就是选择一个不会引起双方质疑的法院进行审理，而这个法院自然非联邦法院莫属。

当案件的双方不是个人而是州的时候，除了前面提到的公平初衷外，还要做政治考虑。诉讼双方的性质便使得这一案件具有全国性影响。双方最微不足道的争端都会影响到全国的和平。

诉讼的性质本身往往就能够决定管辖权的归属。例如，与海上贸易有关的所有问题都归联邦法院审理。几乎这类所有问题都会涉及对国际法的解读，而且从这一点来看，这些问题也都会涉及整个联邦与外国的关系。此外，由于并未对海上司法权限归属进行划定，所以要有一个能够对起因于海上的诉讼进行审理的国家法院。

联邦宪法几乎把所有性质上归属联邦法院管辖的案件都归为一类。这项制度的规定虽然简单，但却囊括立法者的整个思想体系以及大量事实。美国宪法宣布联邦最高法院的司

refuse to comply because it is contrary to the Constitution, the case must come before a Federal court, because it arises under the laws of the United States. Again, if difficulties arise in the levying of import duties which have been voted by Congress, the Federal court must decide the case, because it arises under the interpretation of a law of the United States.

This rule is in perfect accordance with the fundamental principles of the Federal Constitution. The Union, as it was established in 1789, possesses, it is true, a limited supremacy; but it was intended that within its limits it should form one and the same people. Within those limits the Union is sovereign. When this point is established and admitted, the inference is easy; for if it be acknowledged that the United States constitute one and the same people within the bounds prescribed by their Constitution, it is impossible to refuse them the rights which belong to other nations. But it has been allowed, from the origin of society, that every nation has the right of deciding by its own courts those questions which concern the execution of its own laws. To this it is answered that the Union is in so singular a position that in relation to some matters it constitutes a people, and that in relation to all the rest it is a nonentity. But the inference to be drawn is, that in the laws relating to these matters the Union possesses all the rights of absolute sovereignty. The difficulty is to know what these matters are; and when once it is resolved (and we have shown how it was resolved, in speaking of the means of determining the jurisdiction of the Federal courts) no further doubt can arise; for as soon as it is established that a suit is Federal—that is to say, that it belongs to the share of sovereignty reserved by the Constitution of the Union—the natural consequence is that it should come within the jurisdiction of a Federal court.

Whenever the laws of the United States are attacked, or whenever they are resorted to in self-defence, the Federal courts must be appealed to. Thus the jurisdiction of the tribunals of the Union extends and narrows its limits exactly in the same ratio as the sovereignty of the Union augments or decreases. We have shown that the principal aim of the legislators of 1789 was to divide the sovereign authority into two parts. In the one they placed the control of all the general interests of the Union, in the other the control of the special interests of its component States. Their chief solicitude

法权可延伸到一切能够在美国法律找到根据的诉讼。

两个例子便可以让立法者的意图一目了然。

例如，宪法禁止州制定与货币流通相关的法律。如果一个州罔顾这项禁令，制定类似的法律，有关方面可以其违宪为由拒不执行。这样就要由联邦法院进行审理，因为打击这种行为的手段存于联邦法律之中。再如，如果国会制定的进口税在征收过程中遇到困难，也必须交由联邦法院裁决，因为诉讼产生的原因在于对联邦法律的解释。

这一制度与联邦宪法的基本原则完美契合。的确，依据1789年宪法建立的联邦只拥有有限的主权，但是宪法又想要使联邦在此限定范围内成为一个单一制的统一国家。即在这一限定范围内，联邦拥有主权。这一点一旦提出并得到认可，其余问题便可迎刃而解。因为如果承认合众国是宪法规定的拥有主权的国家，就必须赋予它一切国家所具有的权力。但是，自从国家形成以来，每个国家就有权通过其法院对与法律执行相关的问题进行裁定。但是有人提出在这一点上联邦处于特殊的地位，从某些方面来说它是一个国家，而就其他方面而言它又算不上是一个国家。由此可以推断出，只是在与特定方面有关的法律上，它能够拥有完全主权国家的所有权利。但是困难在于如何确定这些方面是什么。一旦这一问题得到解决（在前面谈及联邦法院审判权管辖范围划分方式的时候，我们已经说过这是如何解决的），就不会再产生任何疑问。因为一旦确定诉讼归属联邦法院管辖，也就是说根据宪法规定隶属联邦所保有的主权，该诉讼自然应由联邦法院进行审理。

所以，在联邦法律受到侵犯，或要采取手段捍卫这些法律的时候，都应当向联邦法院

was to arm the Federal Government with sufficient power to enable it to resist, within its sphere, the encroachments of the several States. As for these communities, the principle of independence within certain limits of their own was adopted in their behalf; and they were concealed from the inspection, and protected from the control, of the central Government. In speaking of the division of authority, I observed that this latter principle had not always been held sacred, since the States are prevented from passing certain laws which apparently belong to their own particular sphere of interest. When a State of the Union passes a law of this kind, the citizens who are injured by its execution can appeal to the Federal courts.

Thus the jurisdiction of the Federal courts extends not only to all the cases which arise under the laws of the Union, but also to those which arise under laws made by the several States in opposition to the Constitution. The States are prohibited from making ex post facto laws in criminal cases, and any person condemned by virtue of a law of this kind can appeal to the judicial power of the Union. The States are likewise prohibited from making laws which may have a tendency to impair the obligations of contracts. If a citizen thinks that an obligation of this kind is impaired by a law passed in his State, he may refuse to obey it, and may appeal to the Federal courts.

This provision appears to me to be the most serious attack upon the independence of the States. The rights awarded to the Federal Government for purposes of obvious national importance are definite and easily comprehensible; but those with which this last clause invests it are not either clearly appreciable or accurately defined. For there are vast numbers of political laws which influence the existence of obligations of contracts, which may thus furnish an easy pretext for the aggressions of the central authority.

Procedure Of The Federal Courts

Natural weakness of the judiciary power in confederations—Legislators ought to strive as much as possible to bring private individuals, and not States, before the Federal Courts—How the Americans have succeeded in this—Direct prosecution of private individuals in the Federal Courts—

提起诉讼。可见，联邦法院的审判权会随联邦主权的扩大而扩大缩小而缩小。我们已经说过1789年立法者们的主要目的就是要将主权分成两个部分。让一方掌管联邦的所有共同利益，让另一方掌管所有各州独自的利益。立法者们当时最关心的就是要用足够的权力将联邦政府武装起来并在其权限内对抗各州的侵犯。对于各州，立法者们则采取各州在各州范围内独立自主的原则。为了保护其免受控制，中央政府不能对其进行监督检查。在谈及权力划分的时候，我已经提到这一原则并未始终受到尊重，因为一些法律尽管看来只涉及州自身利益，但州依然无权自行制定。当联邦某个州颁布类似的法律，导致公民因此项法律的执行而受害的时候，便可以向联邦法院提起诉讼。

因此，联邦法院的权力不仅涵盖基于联邦法律而提出的所有诉讼，还延伸至各州违宪制定的法律所引发的所有诉讼。各州禁止颁布溯及既往的刑法，任何受到这类法律制裁的人均可以向联邦法院提出上诉。宪法也不允许各州颁布会对合同既得利益有损害趋向的法律。如果公民认为自己的这类权益受到本州法律的侵害，他可以拒绝服从并向联邦法院提起诉讼。

在我看来这一条款是对州主权的最严厉的打击。出于明显的全国目的而赋予联邦政府的这些权力明确且易于理解，但是我所引用的这条宪法既不明确也不易理解。因为有很多的政治法律会对合同的成立产生影响，并为侵害中央当局的主权提供了借口。

联邦法院的诉讼程序

联邦法院的天然弱点——立法者们尽最大努力让个人而不让州出席联邦法院——美国

Indirect prosecution of the States which violate the laws of the Union—The decrees of the Supreme Court enervate but do not destroy the provincial laws.

I have shown what the privileges of the Federal courts are, and it is no less important to point out the manner in which they are exercised. The irresistible authority of justice in countries in which the sovereignty in undivided is derived from the fact that the tribunals of those countries represent the entire nation at issue with the individual against whom their decree is directed, and the idea of power is thus introduced to corroborate the idea of right. But this is not always the case in countries in which the sovereignty is divided; in them the judicial power is more frequently opposed to a fraction of the nation than to an isolated individual, and its moral authority and physical strength are consequently diminished. In federal States the power of the judge is naturally decreased, and that of the justiciable parties is augmented. The aim of the legislator in confederate States ought therefore to be to render the position of the courts of justice analogous to that which they occupy in countries where the sovereignty is undivided; in other words, his efforts ought constantly to tend to maintain the judicial power of the confederation as the representative of the nation, and the justiciable party as the representative of an individual interest.

Every government, whatever may be its constitution, requires the means of constraining its subjects to discharge their obligations, and of protecting its privileges from their assaults. As far as the direct action of the Government on the community is concerned, the Constitution of the United States contrived, by a master-stroke of policy, that the federal courts, acting in the name of the laws, should only take cognizance of parties in an individual capacity. For, as it had been declared that the Union consisted of one and the same people within the limits laid down by the Constitution, the inference was that the Government created by this Constitution, and acting within these limits, was invested with all the privileges of a national government, one of the principal of which is the right of transmitting its injunctions directly to the private citizen. When, for instance, the Union votes an impost, it does not apply to the States for the levying of it, but to every American citizen in proportion

人如何成功做到这一点——联邦法院对私人进行直接审理——联邦法院对违反联邦法律的州进行间接审理——联邦法院的判决会削弱而不是废除地方法律。

我们已经看到联邦法院拥有的特权，现在要来说一说它们如何行使这些权力。在主权没有分成两部分的国家，法院代表整个国家对触犯法律的个人进行惩处，而司法权的不可抗性正是来源于此。在这里，权力观念和权利观念结合起来。但是在主权分为两部分的国家，情况往往并非如此。在这样的国家，与司法当局打交道的往往不是独立的个人而是国家的各个党派。结果，司法当局的道德力量和物质力量都大打折扣。所以在联邦制国家，法官的权力自然减弱，而受审方的力量则很强大。因此，联邦国家立法者的目的应该是确保法院的地位与主权没有被分成两部分的国家的法院相同。换句话说，立法者不断的努力就是维护确保，联邦司法当局代表国家，受审方代表个人利益。

一个政府，不管其性质如何，都要迫使被统治者履行义务，并保护自身特权免受被统治者的侵犯。就政府采取的强迫被统治者服从法律的直接行动而言，美国宪法规定，以法律名义行事的联邦法院只认可个人作为受审主体。因为，正如所宣称的那样联邦是享有宪法规定的那部分主权的单一制统一国家。所以根据宪法创建并依据宪法规定在权限内行事的政府，应该拥有全国政府的所有权利，而向公民发号施令则是其中最为主要的权利。比如，当政府公布征税法令的时候，并不是在向各州征税，而是依照税率向所有应纳税的美国公民进行征税，而取得授权负责执行这项法律的联邦最高法院，并不对抗税的州进行处

to his assessment. The Supreme Court, which is empowered to enforce the execution of this law of the Union, exerts its influence not upon a refractory State, but upon the private taxpayer; and, like the judicial power of other nations, it is opposed to the person of an individual. It is to be observed that the Union chose its own antagonist; and as that antagonist is feeble, he is naturally worsted.

But the difficulty increases when the proceedings are not brought forward by but against the Union. The Constitution recognizes the legislative power of the States; and a law so enacted may impair the privileges of the Union, in which case a collision in unavoidable between that body and the State which has passed the law: and it only remains to select the least dangerous remedy, which is very clearly deducible from the general principles I have before established.

It may be conceived that, in the case under consideration, the Union might have used the State before a Federal court, which would have annulled the act, and by this means it would have adopted a natural course of proceeding; but the judicial power would have been placed in open hostility to the State, and it was desirable to avoid this predicament as much as possible. The Americans hold that it is nearly impossible that a new law should not impair the interests of some private individual by its provisions: these private interests are assumed by the American legislators as the ground of attack against such measures as may be prejudicial to the Union, and it is to these cases that the protection of the Supreme Court is extended.

Suppose a State vends a certain portion of its territory to a company, and that a year afterwards it passes a law by which the territory is otherwise disposed of, and that clause of the Constitution which prohibits laws impairing the obligation of contracts violated. When the purchaser under the second act appears to take possession, the possessor under the first act brings his action before the tribunals of the Union, and causes the title of the claimant to be pronounced null and void. Thus, in point of fact, the judicial power of the Union is contesting the claims of the sovereignty of a State; but it only acts indirectly and upon a special application of detail: it attacks the law in its consequences, not in its principle, and it rather weakens than destroys it.

The last hypothesis that remained was that each State formed a corporation enjoying a separate

罚，而是对违法的纳税人进行惩罚。同其他国家的司法当局一样，联邦司法当局只能处罚个人。要注意到，联邦的对手是自己选择的，而且它所选择的对手软弱，自然总是屈服。

但是，当联邦不是进攻而是防守的时候，困难就会加大。宪法认可各州的立法权，而这项法律的颁布会侵害到联邦的权利。此时，在联邦和制定法律的州之间必然会产生冲突，为了应对这样的情况，唯有采取最稳妥的处理办法。而这一处理办法显然源自我前面已经讲过的总原则。

通常的看法是，碰到我刚才提到的这种案件，联邦必定会到联邦法院对侵权的州提起诉讼，而联邦法院则会裁定废除州制定的这条法律，这样的做法也合情合理。但是这样做联邦司法当局和州就会处于公开的敌对状态，而这正是联邦法院想要千方百计避免发生的事情。美国人认为，执行一项新的法律而不损害到某些私人利益几乎是不可能的。美国的立法者们认为，这种私人利益可以对各州利用立法措施损害联邦起到抵制作用，所以联邦法院要保护这种私人利益。

假设一个州向一个公司出售一块土地，一年之后由于新法律的出台这块土地被收回挪作他用，这就触犯了宪法中有关禁止损害依合同而获得的利益的条款。当依据新法令取得土地的人要求占有土地的时候，依据旧法令占有土地的人可以向联邦法院提起控诉，要求裁定新的占有无效。因此，事实上联邦当局就侵犯了州的主权，但是联邦对州采取的只是间接攻击，而且只援引州所订法令的细节。它攻击的是法令的后果，而不是其原则；是要对其进行削弱而不是彻底摧毁。

existence and distinct civil rights, and that it could therefore sue or be sued before a tribunal. Thus a State could bring an action against another State. In this instance the Union was not called upon to contest a provincial law, but to try a suit in which a State was a party. This suit was perfectly similar to any other cause, except that the quality of the parties was different; and here the danger pointed out at the beginning of this chapter exists with less chance of being avoided. The inherent disadvantage of the very essence of Federal constitutions is that they engender parties in the bosom of the nation which present powerful obstacles to the free course of justice.

High Rank Of The Supreme Court Amongst The Great Powers Of State

No nation ever constituted so great a judicial power as the Americans—Extent of its prerogative— Its political influence—The tranquillity and the very existence of the Union depend on the discretion of the seven Federal Judges.

When we have successively examined in detail the organization of the Supreme Court, and the entire prerogatives which it exercises, we shall readily admit that a more imposing judicial power was never constituted by any people. The Supreme Court is placed at the head of all known tribunals, both by the nature of its rights and the class of justiciable parties which it controls.

In all the civilized countries of Europe the Government has always shown the greatest repugnance to allow the cases to which it was itself a party to be decided by the ordinary course of justice. This repugnance naturally attains its utmost height in an absolute Government; and, on the other hand, the privileges of the courts of justice are extended with the increasing liberties of the people: but no European nation has at present held that all judicial controversies, without regard to their origin, can be decided by the judges of common law.

In America this theory has been actually put in practice, and the Supreme Court of the United States is the sole tribunal of the nation. Its power extends to all the cases arising under laws and treaties made by the executive and legislative authorities, to all cases of admiralty and maritime

最后，再假设一个案例。在美国，各州都是享有公民权的独立存在的自治体，因此，它既可以向法院提起诉讼也会受到法院的指控。所以，一个州可以到法院控告另一个州。在这样的案例中，并不涉及对地方法令的攻击，只不过诉讼的当事方是州而已。在这样的案件中，除了当事人的性质不同外，与其他案件没有任何不同。在这里，本章开头所指出的危险依然存在，而且难以避免。这是联邦体制固有的危险，会使国内出现一些司法当局难以对抗的强大阻力。

最高法院为各州大权之首

没有任何一个国家曾经创建过像美国那样强大的司法权——其职权范围——其政治影响——联邦的安定与存在取决于七位联邦法官的才智。

在对美国最高法院的组织进行详细考察以及对其职权范围进行全面分析后，不难发现从未有任何国家创建过如此强大的司法权。美国的最高法院，无论是从其权利性质还是从其管辖的受审人范围来看，其地位远远高于任何已知的法院。

在欧洲所有的文明国家，政府一直极力反对将涉及自身利益的案件交给司法当局处理。这种不满情绪在专制政府里表现得最为强烈。然而，随着人们自由的与日俱增，法院的权力也在不断扩大。尽管如此，至今还没有一个欧洲国家认为要将所有的司法诉讼，不管其起因如何，都要交给执行普通法的法官审理。

jurisdiction, and in general to all points which affect the law of nations. It may even be affirmed that, although its constitution is essentially judicial, its prerogatives are almost entirely political. Its sole object is to enforce the execution of the laws of the Union; and the Union only regulates the relations of the Government with the citizens, and of the nation with Foreign Powers: the relations of citizens amongst themselves are almost exclusively regulated by the sovereignty of the States.

A second and still greater cause of the preponderance of this court may be adduced. In the nations of Europe the courts of justice are only called upon to try the controversies of private individuals; but the Supreme Court of the United States summons sovereign powers to its bar. When the clerk of the court advances on the steps of the tribunal, and simply says, "The State of New York versus the State of Ohio," it is impossible not to feel that the Court which he addresses is no ordinary body; and when it is recollected that one of these parties represents one million, and the other two millions of men, one is struck by the responsibility of the seven judges whose decision is about to satisfy or to disappoint so large a number of their fellow-citizens.

The peace, the prosperity, and the very existence of the Union are vested in the hands of the seven judges. Without their active co-operation the Constitution would be a dead letter: the Executive appeals to them for assistance against the encroachments of the legislative powers; the Legislature demands their protection from the designs of the Executive; they defend the Union from the disobedience of the States, the States from the exaggerated claims of the Union, the public interest against the interests of private citizens, and the conservative spirit of order against the fleeting innovations of democracy. Their power is enormous, but it is clothed in the authority of public opinion. They are the all-powerful guardians of a people which respects law, but they would be impotent against popular neglect or popular contempt. The force of public opinion is the most intractable of agents, because its exact limits cannot be defined; and it is not less dangerous to exceed than to remain below the boundary prescribed.

The Federal judges must not only be good citizens, and men possessed of that information and integrity which are indispensable to magistrates, but they must be statesmen—politicians, not unread

然而在美国，这一学说得以付诸实践，而且美国的最高法院是全国唯一的最高法院，负责对一切法律和条约进行解释，凡有关海上问题也就是涉及国际法的案件均归其管辖。甚至可以说，尽管最高法院的组织是司法性的，但其职权几乎完全是政治性的。它的唯一宗旨就是执行联邦的法律，而联邦的任务就是要规范政府与公民的关系，以及本国与外国的关系，而公民之间的关系则几乎完全由州主权做出规定。

美国最高法庭之所以举足轻重，还有另外一个重要原因。在欧洲国家，法院只审理私人之间的争讼，而美国的最高法院则甚至可以让州主权蹲监狱。当法院的执达吏走上法院大厅，简单宣告"纽约州状告俄亥俄州"的时候，必然会让人感到这绝非普通法庭。然而当你想起当事双方，一方代表一百万人而另一方代表两百万人的时候，便不禁感叹七位法官担负责任之重大，因为他们的决定会让如此众多的同胞或悲或喜。

美国的安定、繁荣乃至存亡就系在这七位法官之手。没有他们的积极协作，宪法不过就是一纸空文。行政权要依靠他们的帮助来对抗立法权的侵犯，而立法权也同样需要他们抵御行政权的干扰。联邦依靠他们让各州俯首帖耳，而各州则依靠他们对抗联邦的过分要求。公共利益要靠他们去对抗私人利益，而私人利益则靠他们去对抗公共利益。保守派靠他们去抵制民主派的肆意革新，而民主派则靠他们抵制保守派的因循守旧。他们权力巨大，但这是受到舆论支持的权力。人民奉公守法他们就强大无比，人民桀骜不驯他们便虚弱不堪。舆论的力量最难驾驭，因为它没有明确的界限，而且界限内的危险并不比界限外的危险更低。

联邦法官不但必须是好公民，还要为人正直，知识广博，具有一切行政官必备的品

in the signs of the times, not afraid to brave the obstacles which can be subdued, nor slow to turn aside such encroaching elements as may threaten the supremacy of the Union and the obedience which is due to the laws.

The President, who exercises a limited power, may err without causing great mischief in the State. Congress may decide amiss without destroying the Union, because the electoral body in which Congress originates may cause it to retract its decision by changing its members. But if the Supreme Court is ever composed of imprudent men or bad citizens, the Union may be plunged into anarchy or civil war.

The real cause of this danger, however, does not lie in the constitution of the tribunal, but in the very nature of Federal Governments. We have observed that in confederate peoples it is especially necessary to consolidate the judicial authority, because in no other nations do those independent persons who are able to cope with the social body exist in greater power or in a better condition to resist the physical strength of the Government. But the more a power requires to be strengthened, the more extensive and independent it must be made; and the dangers which its abuse may create are heightened by its independence and its strength. The source of the evil is not, therefore, in the constitution of the power, but in the constitution of those States which render its existence necessary.

In What Respects The Federal Constitution Is Superior To That Of The States

In what respects the Constitution of the Union can be compared to that of the States—Superiority of the Constitution of the Union attributable to the wisdom of the Federal legislators—Legislature of the Union less dependent on the people than that of the States—Executive power more independent in its sphere—Judicial power less subjected to the inclinations of the majority—Practical consequence of these facts—The dangers inherent in a democratic government eluded by the Federal legislators, and increased by the legislators of the States.

The Federal Constitution differs essentially from that of the States in the ends which it is intended

质，而且还必须是国务活动家。他们要善于解读时代精神，勇于直面可以征服的困难，并能力挽狂澜排除会践踏联邦主权及其法律尊严的危险。

总统的权力是有限的，所以即使犯错也不会给州造成重大损失。国会也可能会失误，但并不会因此毁了联邦，因为选举出国会的选举团可以通过改选国会议员的方式改变国会。但是如果联邦最高法院是由莽撞腐化分子组成，联邦必会陷入无政府状态或是内战的危险。

然而，这一危险的真正原因并不在于法院的人员构成，而在于联邦政府的本身的性质。我们注意到，联邦制国家特别需要一个强有力的司法当局，因为在其他体制的国家，个人在与国家进行斗争的时候，无法处于较强较有利的地位对抗政府的武力。但是，一个政权越是需要加强，就越是需要扩大和独立，而滥用职权可能也会随着其独立和力量的加强而增大，危险就会随之而来。所以，恶之源并不是政权的组成，而是能够使这个政权存在下去的必不可少的体制本身。

联邦宪法在哪些方面比各州宪法优越

在哪些方面联邦宪法可以和各州宪法进行比较——联邦宪法的优越性应该归功于联邦立法者们的智慧——联邦立法机构对于人民的依赖性要比各州立法机构小——行政权在其行使范围内更为独立——司法权较少屈服于多数意志——其实际后果——联邦立法者将民主政府的固有危险减少，而州立法者却让其增加。

to accomplish, but in the means by which these ends are promoted a greater analogy exists between them. The objects of the Governments are different, but their forms are the same; and in this special point of view there is some advantage in comparing them together.

I am of opinion that the Federal Constitution is superior to all the Constitutions of the States, for several reasons.

The present Constitution of the Union was formed at a later period than those of the majority of the States, and it may have derived some ameliorations from past experience. But we shall be led to acknowledge that this is only a secondary cause of its superiority, when we recollect that eleven new States have been added to the American Confederation since the promulgation of the Federal Constitution, and that these new republics have always rather exaggerated than avoided the defects which existed in the former Constitutions.

The chief cause of the superiority of the Federal Constitution lay in the character of the legislators who composed it. At the time when it was formed the dangers of the Confederation were imminent, and its ruin seemed inevitable. In this extremity the people chose the men who most deserved the esteem, rather than those who had gained the affections, of the country. I have already observed that distinguished as almost all the legislators of the Union were for their intelligence, they were still more so for their patriotism. They had all been nurtured at a time when the spirit of liberty was braced by a continual struggle against a powerful and predominant authority. When the contest was terminated, whilst the excited passions of the populace persisted in warring with dangers which had ceased to threaten them, these men stopped short in their career; they cast a calmer and more penetrating look upon the country which was now their own; they perceived that the war of independence was definitely ended, and that the only dangers which America had to fear were those which might result from the abuse of the freedom she had won. They had the courage to say what they believed to be true, because they were animated by a warm and sincere love of liberty; and they ventured to propose restrictions, because they were resolutely opposed to destruction.

联邦宪法与各州宪法所要达到的目的从根本上不同，但是实现手段上却极为相似。尽管联邦政府和各州政府的目标并不一致，但是组织形式却完全相同。就这一点而言，对我们将两者进行比较也许更有好处。

我之所以认为联邦宪法从整体上优于各州宪法，有下列几点原因。

现行的联邦宪法的制定时间比大多数州宪法要晚，所以能够从过去的经验中吸取教训。但是，当回想起来自从联邦宪法颁布以来，已有11个州加入美利坚合众国，而且这些新加入的州又几乎总是夸大它们对先前各州宪法的缺陷所做的补救的时候，我们也应该认识到制定较晚不过是联邦宪法优越性的一个次要原因。

联邦宪法之所以优越主要原因在于参与宪法制定的立法者们的品格。在联邦宪法制定的时候，各州似乎很难联合起来，当时这一危机可以说有目共睹。在这样的紧要关头，人们坚定地选择了那些最值得他们尊重的人，而不是那些他们最喜欢的人。前面我已经说过，联邦的立法者们几乎个个以智慧著称，而且更以自己的爱国精神而著称。他们都成长在危机时代。在那个时代，自由精神同一个强大而专横的当局进行着持续不断的斗争。当这场斗争结束后，人们与已经不复存在的危机进行斗争的热情依然不减，于是立法者号召人们平静下来。他们用更为平静犀利的目光观察自己的国家。他们认识到国内战争已经完全结束，而美国需要担忧的就是防止他们争取来的自由被滥用。他们有勇气说出他们内心所想，正是因为在他们内心深处怀有对自由真挚热烈的爱。他们敢于为自由设定条条框框，是因为他们绝对不要自由被毁。根据大部分的州宪法规定，众议员任期为一年，参议员为两年。所以两院的议员不断的紧紧受到最微小民愿的桎梏。联邦立法者们认为立法机

The greater number of the Constitutions of the States assign one year for the duration of the House of Representatives, and two years for that of the Senate; so that members of the legislative body are constantly and narrowly tied down by the slightest desires of their constituents. The legislators of the Union were of opinion that this excessive dependence of the Legislature tended to alter the nature of the main consequences of the representative system, since it vested the source, not only of authority, but of government, in the people. They increased the length of the time for which the representatives were returned, in order to give them freer scope for the exercise of their own judgment.

The Federal Constitution, as well as the Constitutions of the different States, divided the legislative body into two branches. But in the States these two branches were composed of the same elements, and elected in the same manner. The consequence was that the passions and inclinations of the populace were as rapidly and as energetically represented in one chamber as in the other, and that laws were made with all the characteristics of violence and precipitation. By the Federal Constitution the two houses originate in like manner in the choice of the people; but the conditions of eligibility and the mode of election were changed, to the end that, if, as is the case in certain nations, one branch of the Legislature represents the same interests as the other, it may at least represent a superior degree of intelligence and discretion. A mature age was made one of the conditions of the senatorial dignity, and the Upper House was chosen by an elected assembly of a limited number of members.

To concentrate the whole social force in the hands of the legislative body is the natural tendency of democracies; for as this is the power which emanates the most directly from the people, it is made to participate most fully in the preponderating authority of the multitude, and it is naturally led to monopolize every species of influence. This concentration is at once prejudicial to a well-conducted administration, and favorable to the despotism of the majority. The legislators of the States frequently yielded to these democratic propensities, which were invariably and courageously resisted by the founders of the Union.

In the States the executive power is vested in the hands of a magistrate, who is apparently placed upon a level with the Legislature, but who is in reality nothing more than the blind agent and the passive instrument of its decisions. He can derive no influence from the duration of his functions,

构的这种过度依赖性会让代议制主要成果的性质发生变化。因为这不仅是将权力之源交给了人民，而且也把政府交给了人民。于是，他们将联邦两院议员任期延长，以便能让他们在更大程度上自由行使职权。

联邦宪法和各州宪法都将立法机构分为两院。但是在各州，两院的人员组成及选举方式完全一样。其结果就是多数的喜好和意愿会同样迅速充分的在两院表现出来，这就使得法律的制定变得粗暴和轻率。联邦宪法同样规定两院经人民的选举产生，但对候选资格和选举方式做出改变。其目的就是要使得两院中的一支能够像其他国家的立法机构那样，即使立法机构中的一支与另一支所代表的利益相同，但至少也能代表优秀的才智。成熟的年龄是参议员当选的资格之一，而参议院则由选举产生的人数有限的选举团选举产生。

民主制度的天然趋势就是要将整个社会的力量集中到立法机构手中。那么，既然立法机构的权力直接来自人民，就自然享有人民享有的一切大权，并自然产生独占所有权力的倾向。这种权力的集中对于良政的推行非常不利，但对多数的专政却极为有利。各州的立法者们不断地向民主的这种倾向妥协，而联邦的创建者们则勇敢坚定地予以抵制。

在各州，行政权掌握在州长的手里。表面上州长与立法机构平起平坐，但实际上他不过是立法机构的盲目代理和被动工具。他无法从任期上获得力量，因为任期会在转年结束，也无法从特权上获得力量，因为特权几乎形同虚设。立法机构可以将制定好的法律委托给其内部成立的特别委员会执行，从而将行政长官架空，还可以采用停薪的方式让其处

which terminate with the revolving year, or from the exercise of prerogatives which can scarcely be said to exist. The Legislature can condemn him to inaction by intrusting the execution of the laws to special committees of its own members, and can annul his temporary dignity by depriving him of his salary. The Federal Constitution vests all the privileges and all the responsibility of the executive power in a single individual. The duration of the Presidency is fixed at four years; the salary of the individual who fills that office cannot be altered during the term of his functions; he is protected by a body of official dependents, and armed with a suspensive veto. In short, every effort was made to confer a strong and independent position upon the executive authority within the limits which had been prescribed to it.

In the Constitutions of all the States the judicial power is that which remains the most independent of the legislative authority; nevertheless, in all the States the Legislature has reserved to itself the right of regulating the emoluments of the judges, a practice which necessarily subjects these magistrates to its immediate influence. In some States the judges are only temporarily appointed, which deprives them of a great portion of their power and their freedom. In others the legislative and judicial powers are entirely confounded; thus the Senate of New York, for instance, constitutes in certain cases the Superior Court of the State. The Federal Constitution, on the other hand, carefully separates the judicial authority from all external influences; and it provides for the independence of the judges, by declaring that their salary shall not be altered, and that their functions shall be inalienable.

The practical consequences of these different systems may easily be perceived. An attentive observer will soon remark that the business of the Union is incomparably better conducted than that of any individual State. The conduct of the Federal Government is more fair and more temperate than that of the States, its designs are more fraught with wisdom, its projects are more durable and more skilfully combined, its measures are put into execution with more vigor and consistency.

I recapitulate the substance of this chapter in a few words: The existence of democracies is threatened by two dangers, viz., the complete subjection of the legislative body to the caprices of the electoral body, and the concentration of all the powers of the Government in the legislative authority. The growth of these evils has been encouraged by the policy of the legislators of the States, but it has

于被罢黜的状态。联邦宪法则将所有特权和全部责任都交到总统一个人手中。总统的任期定为四年，在其任职期间不得扣发其薪俸，还配有护卫保护其安全，并拥有搁置否决权。简而言之，就是尽一切努力要保证总统能够在赋予他的职权范围之内拥有强大而独立的地位。

在各州的立法中，司法权最不受立法机构权力的约束。但是，各州立法机构却保留了制定法官薪俸的权利，这必然会对法官产生直接的影响。在一些州，法官不过是临时任命，这样做就剥夺了法官大部分的权力和自由。在另一些州，立法权和司法权完全混在一起。比如，纽约州的参议院就是该州负责审理某些案件的最高法院。然而，联邦宪法则小心翼翼地将司法权与所有其他权力完全分开，并通过规定法官薪俸和职权不得改变，来保证法官的独立。

这些不同制度产生的实际效果显而易见。细心的观察家不久就会注意到，联邦政务的处理要比任何一个州都好得多得多。联邦政府的行事比各州更加公平和稳妥，它的设计充满智慧，计划更为长久巧妙，措施的执行更为有力连贯。

我可以将本章的内容给概括成几句话：

民主制度的存在受到两个危险的威胁。即立法机构对选举团的反复无常完全顺从，以及政府所有权力向立法权的集中。各州立法者们的政策助长了这些危险，而联邦立法者们则动用手中所有手段对它们进行遏制。

been resisted by the legislators of the Union by every means which lay within their control.

Characteristics Which Distinguish The Federal Constitution Of The United States Of America From All Other Federal Constitutions

American Union appears to resemble all other confederations—Nevertheless its effects are different—Reason of this—Distinctions between the Union and all other confederations—The American Government not a federal but an imperfect national Government.

The United States of America do not afford either the first or the only instance of confederate States, several of which have existed in modern Europe, without adverting to those of antiquity. Switzerland, the Germanic Empire, and the Republic of the United Provinces either have been or still are confederations. In studying the constitutions of these different countries, the politician is surprised to observe that the powers with which they invested the Federal Government are nearly identical with the privileges awarded by the American Constitution to the Government of the United States. They confer upon the central power the same rights of making peace and war, of raising money and troops, and of providing for the general exigencies and the common interests of the nation. Nevertheless the Federal Government of these different peoples has always been as remarkable for its weakness and inefficiency as that of the Union is for its vigorous and enterprising spirit. Again, the first American Confederation perished through the excessive weakness of its Government; and this weak Government was, notwithstanding, in possession of rights even more extensive than those of the Federal Government of the present day. But the more recent Constitution of the United States contains certain principles which exercise a most important influence, although they do not at once strike the observer.

This Constitution, which may at first sight be confounded with the federal constitutions which preceded it, rests upon a novel theory, which may be considered as a great invention in modern political science. In all the confederations which had been formed before the American Constitution of 1789 the allied States agreed to obey the injunctions of a Federal Government; but they reserved

美国联邦宪法与所有其他联邦制国家宪法的不同

美联邦看起来与其他联邦似乎别无二致——但其效果不同——原因何在——美联邦与所有其他联邦的差别——美国政府并不是一个联邦政府，而是一个不完全的全国政府。

美国并不是第一个也不是唯一一个联邦制的例子。即使不谈古代，单就现代欧洲而言，已有过数个联邦制国家存在。瑞士、德意志帝国以及尼德兰共和国都曾经抑或仍然是联邦制国家。如果对这些不同国家的宪法进行研究，政治家会惊讶地发现它们赋予联邦政府的权力几乎与美国宪法授予美国联邦政府的权力完全一致。这些国家同样将议和权、宣战权、收税权、征兵权以及应对全国危机和谋求全国利益的权力交予中央政府。但是，这些不同国家的联邦政府几乎同样的软弱无能，而只有美国的联邦政府能够果断有力地处理政务。而且美国的第一个联邦之所覆灭也是因为它过于软弱，然而这个软弱的政府却曾经拥有比如今联邦政府更为广泛的权利。尽管美国现行宪法的几项新原则没有立即引起人们的注意，但是却产生了极为重要的影响。

初看上去与以往联邦宪法并没有什么不同的这部宪法，源自一套全新的理论。这套全新的理论可以称得上现代政治科学的一项重大发现。在1789年美国联邦之前成立的所有联邦中，加盟的各州同意服从联邦政府的法令，但却将调整和执行这些联邦法令的权利保留下来。1789年联合起来的美国各州认可联邦政府不但可以颁布法律，而且负责亲自执行。

to themselves the right of ordaining and enforcing the execution of the laws of the Union. The American States which combined in 1789 agreed that the Federal Government should not only dictate the laws, but that it should execute it own enactments. In both cases the right is the same, but the exercise of the right is different; and this alteration produced the most momentous consequences.

In all the confederations which had been formed before the American Union the Federal Government demanded its supplies at the hands of the separate Governments; and if the measure it prescribed was onerous to any one of those bodies means were found to evade its claims: if the State was powerful, it had recourse to arms; if it was weak, it connived at the resistance which the law of the Union, its sovereign, met with, and resorted to inaction under the plea of inability. Under these circumstances one of the two alternatives has invariably occurred; either the most preponderant of the allied peoples has assumed the privileges of the Federal authority and ruled all the States in its name, or the Federal Government has been abandoned by its natural supporters, anarchy has arisen between the confederates, and the Union has lost all powers of action.

In America the subjects of the Union are not States, but private citizens: the national Government levies a tax, not upon the State of Massachusetts, but upon each inhabitant of Massachusetts. All former confederate governments presided over communities, but that of the Union rules individuals; its force is not borrowed, but self-derived; and it is served by its own civil and military officers, by its own army, and its own courts of justice. It cannot be doubted that the spirit of the nation, the passions of the multitude, and the provincial prejudices of each State tend singularly to diminish the authority of a Federal authority thus constituted, and to facilitate the means of resistance to its mandates; but the comparative weakness of a restricted sovereignty is an evil inherent in the Federal system. In America, each State has fewer opportunities of resistance and fewer temptations to non-compliance; nor can such a design be put in execution (if indeed it be entertained) without an open violation of the laws of the Union, a direct interruption of the ordinary course of justice, and a bold declaration of revolt; in a word, without taking a decisive step which men hesitate to adopt.

In all former confederations the privileges of the Union furnished more elements of discord than of power, since they multiplied the claims of the nation without augmenting the means of

在这两种情况下，权利没有改变，但是权利的行使发生变化，而这种变化带来的后果则有天壤之别。

在今天美国联邦成立之前的所有联邦制国家中，联邦政府的给养全仰仗各州政府。如果其采取的措施让任何一个州感到负担，这个州总能找到办法规避。如果联邦政府够强大，它可以诉诸武力。而如果它很虚弱，就只能任其抵制而无所作为。在这样的环境下，不是联邦中最具实力的州攫取政权，挟天子以令诸侯，就是联邦政府遭到原有拥护者的遗弃，国家陷入无政府状态以致联邦失去一切行动力。两者必为其一。

在美国，联邦的臣民不是州而是公民。联邦政府征税的对象不是各州而是各州的居民。以往的所有联邦政府都是对加盟各州政府进行统治，而美国联邦政府统治的是个人。它的力量不是借来的而是自己创造的，并拥有自己的文武官员以及军队和法院。不可否认，民族的精神、民众的激情以及各州的地方偏见，依然在削弱如此组成的联邦的权限，并促成一些反联邦的中心，然而严格受到限制的主权的相对弱点正是联邦制的固有弊端。在美国，各州几乎没有反抗的机会和不轨的图谋。而且除非公开抗拒联邦法律、直接介入正常司法程序并胆大的宣布叛乱，否则没有机会反抗。一句话，人们必须要采取果断措施，而对此人们总是犹豫不决。

在以往所有的联邦制国家，联邦政府得到的特权中不和谐的因子总是大于权力因子。因为他们对国家的要求越来越多但是保证其贯彻的措施却没有得到强化。所以，现实情况

enforcing them: and in accordance with this fact it may be remarked that the real weakness of federal governments has almost always been in the exact ratio of their nominal power. Such is not the case in the American Union, in which, as in ordinary governments, the Federal Government has the means of enforcing all it is empowered to demand.

The human understanding more easily invents new things than new words, and we are thence constrained to employ a multitude of improper and inadequate expressions. When several nations form a permanent league and establish a supreme authority, which, although it has not the same influence over the members of the community as a national government, acts upon each of the Confederate States in a body, this Government, which is so essentially different from all others, is denominated a Federal one. Another form of society is afterwards discovered, in which several peoples are fused into one and the same nation with regard to certain common interests, although they remain distinct, or at least only confederate, with regard to all their other concerns. In this case the central power acts directly upon those whom it governs, whom it rules, and whom it judges, in the same manner, as, but in a more limited circle than, a national government. Here the term Federal Government is clearly no longer applicable to a state of things which must be styled an incomplete national Government: a form of government has been found out which is neither exactly national nor federal; but no further progress has been made, and the new word which will one day designate this novel invention does not yet exist.

The absence of this new species of confederation has been the cause which has brought all Unions to Civil War, to subjection, or to a stagnant apathy, and the peoples which formed these leagues have been either too dull to discern, or too pusillanimous to apply this great remedy. The American Confederation perished by the same defects.

But the Confederate States of America had been long accustomed to form a portion of one empire before they had won their independence; they had not contracted the habit of governing themselves, and their national prejudices had not taken deep root in their minds. Superior to the rest of the world in political knowledge, and sharing that knowledge equally amongst themselves, they were little agitated by the passions which generally oppose the extension of federal authority in a nation, and those passions were

跟我们说的一样,联邦政府真正的弱点总是会随着其有名无实权力的增加而增加。然而,在美国事实并非如此,就像其他普通政府一样,美国联邦政府有手段能够保证做到其握有的权力所能做到的一切。

人们对新事物的理解往往要比对新词的理解容易得多,所以我们只能使用一些不确切不全面的表达。一些国家成立永久性的联盟,并成立一个最高当局,而这个最高当局尽管不能像一个全国政府那样对所有公民进行直接管理,但是却可以对每个加盟政府采取直接行动。这样一个与所有其他政府形式完全不同的政府,就被称之为联邦政府。接着,一种新的社会形式应运而生,在这样的社会中,几个政府会在共同利益方面真正结合为一体,而在其他方面依旧各自为政,或者说仅仅是联邦。在这里,中央政府像全国政府一样采用同样的方式直接对被统治者、行政官员和司法官员进行管理,但是其职权范围有限。显然,这不再是原来意义上联邦政府,而是不完全的全国政府,是一种从未出现过的政府形式既非联邦也非全国。现在我们只能解释到此处,因为能够代表这个全新事物的新词目前还没有出现。

这是因为以前没有这种形式的联邦,才导致过去所有的联邦不是陷入内战或征战,就是沦入毫无生气的状态,组成联邦的国家不是因为太迟钝弄不清状况,就是因为太过胆怯不敢采用大胆的措施。

但是美国的联邦各州在独立之前,曾长期属于同一帝国,因此它们没有养成完全自治的习惯,民族偏见也不根深蒂固。正是因为有着超越世界其他国家的政治见识并能够在各

checked by the wisdom of the chief citizens. The Americans applied the remedy with prudent firmness as soon as they were conscious of the evil; they amended their laws, and they saved their country.

Advantages Of The Federal System In General, And Its Special Utility In America

Happiness and freedom of small nations—Power of great nations—Great empires favorable to the growth of civilization—Strength often the first element of national prosperity—Aim of the Federal system to unite the twofold advantages resulting from a small and from a large territory—Advantages derived by the United States from this system—The law adapts itself to the exigencies of the population; population does not conform to the exigencies of the law—Activity, amelioration, love and enjoyment of freedom in the American communities—Public spirit of the Union the abstract of provincial patriotism—Principles and things circulate freely over the territory of the United States— The Union is happy and free as a little nation, and respected as a great empire.

In small nations the scrutiny of society penetrates into every part, and the spirit of improvement enters into the most trifling details; as the ambition of the people is necessarily checked by its weakness, all the efforts and resources of the citizens are turned to the internal benefit of the community, and are not likely to evaporate in the fleeting breath of glory. The desires of every individual are limited, because extraordinary faculties are rarely to be met with. The gifts of an equal fortune render the various conditions of life uniform, and the manners of the inhabitants are orderly and simple. Thus, if one estimate the gradations of popular morality and enlightenment, we shall generally find that in small nations there are more persons in easy circumstances, a more numerous population, and a more tranquil state of society, than in great empires.

When tyranny is established in the bosom of a small nation, it is more galling than elsewhere, because, as it acts within a narrow circle, every point of that circle is subject to its direct influence. It supplies the place of those great designs which it cannot entertain by a violent or an exasperating interference in a multitude of minute details; and it leaves the political world, to which it properly

州得到共识，所以一般来说人民的情绪不会因为联邦权力的延伸而激动，即使这样的情绪出现，联邦的几个大人物也能够运用智慧克服过去。当美国人意识到这些问题的时候立即坚定地采取措施加以克服，他们修订法律并拯救了自己的国家。

联邦制的一般优点及其在美国的特殊效用

小国的自由与幸福——大国的力量——大帝国有利于文明的进步——实力往往是国家繁荣的第一要素——联邦制的目的就是要将领土大和领土小的各自优势叠加起来——美国从联邦制中获取的好处——法律服从人们的需求，人民不服从法律的需要——美国人民的积极性和进取精神，以及对自由的热爱和享受——联邦的公共精神是集地方爱国主义之大成——在美国的土地上思想和事物可以自由流通——联邦如同小国一样自由幸福，却又像大国一样获得尊重。

在小国社会的注意力会遍及方方面面，革新精神会深入到最微小的细节，而人民的野心必然会因为其弱小而受到压制，所以人民的全部努力和资源都会用于国内的福利，而不会浪费在追求转瞬即逝的荣耀。因为在小国一般每个人的才能有限，所以个人的欲望也不大。而且财富的均等使得人民地位均等，所以民风淳朴。所以，尽管人们的道德水准文化水平不同，但是总的来看，大多数人在小国比在大国更容易安居乐业。

当小国出现暴政的时候，会比在其他地方更加肆虐，因为在一个狭小的范围施行暴

belongs, to meddle with the arrangements of domestic life. Tastes as well as actions are to be regulated at its pleasure; and the families of the citizens as well as the affairs of the State are to be governed by its decisions. This invasion of rights occurs, however, but seldom, and freedom is in truth the natural state of small communities. The temptations which the Government offers to ambition are too weak, and the resources of private individuals are too slender, for the sovereign power easily to fall within the grasp of a single citizen; and should such an event have occurred, the subjects of the State can without difficulty overthrow the tyrant and his oppression by a simultaneous effort.

Small nations have therefore ever been the cradle of political liberty; and the fact that many of them have lost their immunities by extending their dominion shows that the freedom they enjoyed was more a consequence of the inferior size than of the character of the people.

The history of the world affords no instance of a great nation retaining the form of republican government for a long series of years, and this has led to the conclusion that such a state of things is impracticable. For my own part, I cannot but censure the imprudence of attempting to limit the possible and to judge the future on the part of a being who is hourly deceived by the most palpable realities of life, and who is constantly taken by surprise in the circumstances with which he is most familiar. But it may be advanced with confidence that the existence of a great republic will always be exposed to far greater perils than that of a small one.

All the passions which are most fatal to republican institutions spread with an increasing territory, whilst the virtues which maintain their dignity do not augment in the same proportion. The ambition of the citizens increases with the power of the State; the strength of parties with the importance of the ends they have in view; but that devotion to the common weal which is the surest check on destructive passions is not stronger in a large than in a small republic. It might, indeed, be proved without difficulty that it is less powerful and less sincere. The arrogance of wealth and the dejection of wretchedness, capital cities of unwonted extent, a lax morality, a vulgar egotism, and a great confusion of interests, are the dangers which almost invariably arise from the magnitude of States. But several of these evils are scarcely prejudicial to a monarchy, and some of them contribute to

政，其影响力会波及这一范围的方方面面。因为它的宏图大志毫无用武之地，所以只能介入一堆小事，而且是通过暴力和骚扰的方式。它的统治从所谓的政治世界渗入到私人生活。从行动到品位都要符合它的意愿，不管是国家大事还是公民的私人生活都由它做主。然而这种权利的入侵并不常见，因为毕竟自由才是小国的天性。小国政府能够给野心家的诱饵实在太少，而且个人的才智又极为有限，所以国家大权特别容易落入一人之手。而且，一旦这样的情况发生，老百姓会很容易联合起来共同努力把暴政和压迫一起推翻。

因此，小国历来都是政治自由的摇篮。然而随着小国疆域的扩大，大多数国家也会失去这种自由。这样的事实恰好说明政治自由来自国家的弱小，而不是国家自身。

世界历史从没有过大国长期实行共和制的先例，所以自然就会得出这样的事情行不通的结论。我认为，如果终日回避现实，对习以为常的事情表示惊讶，却还要妄图限定可能性和判断未来，未免过于荒唐。但可以肯定地说，大共和国比小共和国面对的危险要多。

随着共和国领土的增加，对共和制的所有热情也会随之增长，但是其德行则不会随之增长。随着国家力量的增长公民的野心不断膨胀，政党的力量也会随其目标重要性的增加而增加，但是能够抵制这种破坏性激情的奉献精神，在大国不如小国强烈。的确，要证明奉献精神在大的共和国来的不那么强烈和真诚也许并不难。贫富的悬殊、城市巨大化、风气的败坏、个人的自私自利、利益的冲突，几乎无疑都是国家巨大化带来的恶果。这其中大多数对于君主制国家毫无影响，有些甚至对君主国的存在大有裨益。在君主制国家，政府的力量源于自身，它可以利用人民但并不依赖人民，而且王权也会随国家繁荣而增强。

maintain its existence. In monarchical States the strength of the government is its own; it may use, but it does not depend on, the community, and the authority of the prince is proportioned to the prosperity of the nation; but the only security which a republican government possesses against these evils lies in the support of the majority. This support is not, however, proportionably greater in a large republic than it is in a small one; and thus, whilst the means of attack perpetually increase both in number and in influence, the power of resistance remains the same, or it may rather be said to diminish, since the propensities and interests of the people are diversified by the increase of the population, and the difficulty of forming a compact majority is constantly augmented. It has been observed, moreover, that the intensity of human passions is heightened, not only by the importance of the end which they propose to attain, but by the multitude of individuals who are animated by them at the same time. Every one has had occasion to remark that his emotions in the midst of a sympathizing crowd are far greater than those which he would have felt in solitude. In great republics the impetus of political passion is irresistible, not only because it aims at gigantic purposes, but because it is felt and shared by millions of men at the same time.

It may therefore be asserted as a general proposition that nothing is more opposed to the well-being and the freedom of man than vast empires. Nevertheless it is important to acknowledge the peculiar advantages of great States. For the very reason which renders the desire of power more intense in these communities than amongst ordinary men, the love of glory is also more prominent in the hearts of a class of citizens, who regard the applause of a great people as a reward worthy of their exertions, and an elevating encouragement to man. If we would learn why it is that great nations contribute more powerfully to the spread of human improvement than small States, we shall discover an adequate cause in the rapid and energetic circulation of ideas, and in those great cities which are the intellectual centres where all the rays of human genius are reflected and combined. To this it may be added that most important discoveries demand a display of national power which the Government of a small State is unable to make; in great nations the Government entertains a greater number of general notions, and is more completely disengaged from the routine of precedent and the egotism of

然而一个共和政府的唯一保障就是依靠多数的支持去克服这些恶果。但是这种支持力并不会按共和国大小的比例而增强。所以，当攻击方式和强度不断增加时，抵抗力量依然没变，甚至可以说被减弱，因为随着人口的增长人民的偏好和利益越发多样化，一个牢固的大多数也就越难以成形。此外，还应注意到，人民热情的高涨程度，不仅取决于他们所要达成目标的重要性，而且还取决于同时有多少人受到这一热情的鼓舞。人们都会说，跟形单影只的时候相比，激情会在与志同道合的人相聚中得到迸发。在大的共和国，政治热情的冲力难以遏制，不仅因为其目标崇高，更因为同时会引起数以百万计人们的共鸣。

所以，一般来说，谁也比不上大的帝国对人民幸福和自由的反对。可是，也必须要承认大国有大国特有的优势。就好像普通人的权力欲在大国来得更加强烈一样，出于同样的原因，一些公民内心的荣誉感也特别的炙热，因为他们认为人民的喝彩是对他们努力的莫大奖赏，以及士气的极大鼓舞。我们会发现，在大国思想会得到更为积极迅速的传播，而且大城市是人类理性之光大放异彩和聚集的智慧中心，这就解释了为什么大国对于人类社会进步的推动更为有力。另外还有一点需要补充，重大的发现需要强大的国力，而这是小国所无法给予的。在大国，政府有远大的理想，会更为彻底地打破陈规旧习以及地方本位主义，会有更多的天才为其构思宏图大业，会有更多的有胆有识的人将其完成。

在和平年代，小国的康乐会更为普遍和完全，但是战争带给它们的痛苦也来得更为尖锐。因为对于大国而言，由于其疆域广阔，即使战祸绵延不断，也可以让人民少受痛苦。所以，对人民而言，与其说战争是痛苦之源，不如说是亡国之根。

local prejudice; its designs are conceived with more talent, and executed with more boldness.

In time of peace the well-being of small nations is undoubtedly more general and more complete, but they are apt to suffer more acutely from the calamities of war than those great empires whose distant frontiers may for ages avert the presence of the danger from the mass of the people, which is therefore more frequently afflicted than ruined by the evil.

But in this matter, as in many others, the argument derived from the necessity of the case predominates over all others. If none but small nations existed, I do not doubt that mankind would be more happy and more free; but the existence of great nations is unavoidable.

This consideration introduces the element of physical strength as a condition of national prosperity. It profits a people but little to be affluent and free if it is perpetually exposed to be pillaged or subjugated; the number of its manufactures and the extent of its commerce are of small advantage if another nation has the empire of the seas and gives the law in all the markets of the globe. Small nations are often impoverished, not because they are small, but because they are weak; the great empires prosper less because they are great than because they are strong. Physical strength is therefore one of the first conditions of the happiness and even of the existence of nations. Hence it occurs that, unless very peculiar circumstances intervene, small nations are always united to large empires in the end, either by force or by their own consent: yet I am unacquainted with a more deplorable spectacle than that of a people unable either to defend or to maintain its independence.

The Federal system was created with the intention of combining the different advantages which result from the greater and the lesser extent of nations; and a single glance over the United States of America suffices to discover the advantages which they have derived from its adoption.

In great centralized nations the legislator is obliged to impart a character of uniformity to the laws which does not always suit the diversity of customs and of districts; as he takes no cognizance of special cases, he can only proceed upon general principles; and the population is obliged to conform to the exigencies of the legislation, since the legislation cannot adapt itself to the exigencies and the customs of the population, which is the cause of endless trouble and misery. This disadvantage does not exist in confederations. Congress regulates the principal measures of the national Government,

但是在这里和其他地方一样，最重要的是要研究事物的必然性。如果没有大国只有小国，无疑人类会更加幸福自由，但是大国的存在不可避免。

于是，国家力量成为国家繁荣的一个重要因素。如果一个国家不断遭受劫掠和侵略，空有富足自由之表又有何用？如果别的国家拥有海上霸权并制定世界贸易规则，那么小国的工商业的优势又何在呢？小国往往贫困，并不是因为它小，而是因为它弱。大国之所以繁荣不是因为它大，而是因为它强。因此，力量成为国家幸福甚至存亡的第一要素。因此，除非环境特殊，否则小国最终必会自愿或非自愿地联合起来或是成为大国的一员。依我看，再也没有什么会比一个国家既不能自卫也无法维护自身独立更可悲的事了。

创立联邦制的目的就是要将大国和小国各自具备的优势结合起来，而且只要看一看美国就足以发现他们从联邦制所取得好处。

在中央集权的大国，立法者必须要保持各项法律的一致性，而不能带有习俗和地方差异。因为立法者并不处理具体的案件，所以只依据正常情况立法。人民必须要服从立法的需要，因为立法不能服从人民的习俗和需要。这就成为国家动乱多灾多难的根源。而在联邦制国家就不存在这样的问题。国会只对全国性的主要法令做出规定，而具体的细节则留给各地方立法机构自行制定。这样的主权划分给美联邦各成员州带来的福祉难以想象。对于这些小社会它们既不需要为扩张也不需要为自卫而伤脑筋，全部的公共力量和个人精力都用于内部改进。与本州居民并肩而战的各州中央政府，总是能够了解社会的需要。它每年

and all the details of the administration are reserved to the provincial legislatures. It is impossible to imagine how much this division of sovereignty contributes to the well-being of each of the States which compose the Union. In these small communities, which are never agitated by the desire of aggrandizement or the cares of self-defence, all public authority and private energy is employed in internal amelioration. The central government of each State, which is in immediate juxtaposition to the citizens, is daily apprised of the wants which arise in society; and new projects are proposed every year, which are discussed either at town meetings or by the legislature of the State, and which are transmitted by the press to stimulate the zeal and to excite the interest of the citizens. This spirit of amelioration is constantly alive in the American republics, without compromising their tranquillity; the ambition of power yields to the less refined and less dangerous love of comfort. It is generally believed in America that the existence and the permanence of the republican form of government in the New World depend upon the existence and the permanence of the Federal system; and it is not unusual to attribute a large share of the misfortunes which have befallen the new States of South America to the injudicious erection of great republics, instead of a divided and confederate sovereignty.

It is incontestably true that the love and the habits of republican government in the United States were engendered in the townships and in the provincial assemblies. In a small State, like that of Connecticut for instance, where cutting a canal or laying down a road is a momentous political question, where the State has no army to pay and no wars to carry on, and where much wealth and much honor cannot be bestowed upon the chief citizens, no form of government can be more natural or more appropriate than that of a republic. But it is this same republican spirit, it is these manners and customs of a free people, which are engendered and nurtured in the different States, to be afterwards applied to the country at large. The public spirit of the Union is, so to speak, nothing more than an abstract of the patriotic zeal of the provinces. Every citizen of the United States transfuses his attachment to his little republic in the common store of American patriotism. In defending the Union he defends the increasing prosperity of his own district, the right of conducting its affairs, and the hope of causing measures of improvement to be adopted which may be favorable to his own interest; and these are motives which are wont to stir men more readily than the general interests of

都会提出新的建议，然后提交乡镇议会或是州立法机构进行讨论，并通过媒体的宣传引起民众的普遍关注和兴趣。这种进取精神一直鼓舞着美国各州，而且从来没有引起动乱。追求权力的野心因为对公益的热爱而变得激情澎湃而不那么危险。在美国人们普遍认为，新大陆共和制政府之所以能够长治久安主要仰仗联邦制的存在和持久。而南美新兴国家所建立起的共和国之所以长期沉沦，其不幸的主要原因就在于它们只采用共和制而没有进行主权划分。

无可争辩的事实是美国对共和制政府的热爱和习惯始于乡镇和地方议会。在一些小州，例如康涅狄格，挖掘运河以及铺设道路都成为政治大事，它也不供养军队进行战争，领导人既没有高薪也得不到荣誉。在这里，人们认为共和制是最为自然合理的政府形式。于是，这种共和精神，也就是一个自由民族的行为方式和习俗，在各州产生并成长起来，之后通行于全国。所以说，美联邦的公共精神不过是集地方爱国主义之大成。联邦之内的每个公民都将自己对小共和国的热爱转化成为对共同祖国的爱国主义热情。保卫联邦就是保卫自己州县的繁荣昌盛，保卫参与国家大事的权利，保卫他们的希望，希望联邦可以制定出有利于其自身利益的改进措施。这些念头往往比国家利益和民族荣誉更能打动人心。

另一方面，如果居民的精神和风尚特别适合促进大国的繁荣，那么，联邦制就能将其遇到的困难降到最低。美国各州的共和制度没有出现人们聚集在一起所带来的通常问题。就领土而言，美联邦是一个大共和国，但就其政府管理事务数量之少来看，它又无异于一个小国。它的一举一动举足轻重，但却不常出手。因为联邦的主权有限且不完整，所以主

the country and the glory of the nation.

On the other hand, if the temper and the manners of the inhabitants especially fitted them to promote the welfare of a great republic, the Federal system smoothed the obstacles which they might have encountered. The confederation of all the American States presents none of the ordinary disadvantages resulting from great agglomerations of men. The Union is a great republic in extent, but the paucity of objects for which its Government provides assimilates it to a small State. Its acts are important, but they are rare. As the sovereignty of the Union is limited and incomplete, its exercise is not incompatible with liberty; for it does not excite those insatiable desires of fame and power which have proved so fatal to great republics. As there is no common centre to the country, vast capital cities, colossal wealth, abject poverty, and sudden revolutions are alike unknown; and political passion, instead of spreading over the land like a torrent of desolation, spends its strength against the interests and the individual passions of every State.

Nevertheless, all commodities and ideas circulate throughout the Union as freely as in a country inhabited by one people. Nothing checks the spirit of enterprise. Government avails itself of the assistance of all who have talents or knowledge to serve it. Within the frontiers of the Union the profoundest peace prevails, as within the heart of some great empire; abroad, it ranks with the most powerful nations of the earth; two thousand miles of coast are open to the commerce of the world; and as it possesses the keys of the globe, its flags is respected in the most remote seas. The Union is as happy and as free as a small people, and as glorious and as strong as a great nation.

Why The Federal System Is Not Adapted To All Peoples, And How The Anglo-Americans Were Enabled To Adopt It

Every Federal system contains defects which baffle the efforts of the legislator—The Federal system is complex—It demands a daily exercise of discretion on the part of the citizens—Practical knowledge of government common amongst the Americans—Relative weakness of the Government of the Union, another defect inherent in the Federal system—The Americans have diminished without remedying it—The sovereignty of the separate States apparently weaker, but really stronger, than that of the Union—

权的行使于自由无害，也就不会激起关系到大共和国存亡的那种争权夺利的邪念。因为没有共同的国家中心，所以不会有巨大的城市、巨富、赤贫以及突然爆发的革命。政治热情也没有横扫全国，而是逐渐蔓延对各州的私利和偏见进行遏制。

然而，在美利坚合众国就如同在单一制的国家一样，所有的商品乃至思想都可以在全国自由交流，什么都无法抑制进取精神。政府为所有能服务于国家的人才和知识提供支持。在整个联邦境内，就如同在一个帝国统治之下的国家内部，一片祥和之气；在国外，它和世界上最强大的国家并驾齐驱，有两千英里的海岸线对外商开放。因为拥有通向世界的钥匙，它的旗帜在最遥远的海域也同样受到尊重。美联邦像小国一样幸福自由，又像大国一样耀眼强大。

为什么联邦制不适用于所有国家，以及英裔美国人何以能够采用这一制度

各种联邦制都有立法者无法克服的固有缺陷——联邦制的复杂性——它经常要利用公民的判断力——美国人治国的实际知识——联邦政府的相对软弱是联邦制的另一个固有缺陷——美国人弱化了这一缺陷，但未能消除——各州政府的主权表面上比联邦政府小，但实则更为强大——为什么——除法律因素外，参加联邦各州之所以要求联合还有自然原因——英裔美国人的这种原因是什么——缅因州和佐治亚州相距一千英里，但却比诺曼底和布列塔尼的联合更加自然——战争是联邦制的主要危险——美国本身的例子就是一

Why?—Natural causes of union must exist between confederate peoples besides the laws—What these causes are amongst the Anglo-Americans—Maine and Georgia, separated by a distance of a thousand miles, more naturally united than Normandy and Brittany—War, the main peril of confederations—This proved even by the example of the United States—The Union has no great wars to fear—Why?—Dangers to which Europeans would be exposed if they adopted the Federal system of the Americans.

When a legislator succeeds, after persevering efforts, in exercising an indirect influence upon the destiny of nations, his genius is lauded by mankind, whilst, in point of fact, the geographical position of the country which he is unable to change, a social condition which arose without his co-operation, manners and opinions which he cannot trace to their source, and an origin with which he is unacquainted, exercise so irresistible an influence over the courses of society that he is himself borne away by the current, after an ineffectual resistance. Like the navigator, he may direct the vessel which bears him along, but he can neither change its structure, nor raise the winds, nor lull the waters which swell beneath him.

I have shown the advantages which the Americans derive from their federal system; it remains for me to point out the circumstances which rendered that system practicable, as its benefits are not to be enjoyed by all nations. The incidental defects of the Federal system which originate in the laws may be corrected by the skill of the legislator, but there are further evils inherent in the system which cannot be counteracted by the peoples which adopt it. These nations must therefore find the strength necessary to support the natural imperfections of their Government.

The most prominent evil of all Federal systems is the very complex nature of the means they employ. Two sovereignties are necessarily in presence of each other. The legislator may simplify and equalize the action of these two sovereignties, by limiting each of them to a sphere of authority accurately defined; but he cannot combine them into one, or prevent them from coming into collision at certain points. The Federal system therefore rests upon a theory which is necessarily complicated, and which demands the daily exercise of a considerable share of discretion on the part of those it governs.

A proposition must be plain to be adopted by the understanding of a people. A false notion which

个证明——联邦不惧怕大战——为什么——如果欧洲国家采用美国的联邦制可能会出现的危险。

经过不懈地努力，立法者成功的对本国的命运产生一些间接的影响，此时，人们便会对其大加赞赏。然而，就事实来看，他既无法改变国家的地理位置，又无法改变在他之前业已存在的社会状况，也无从探究国家民情风尚和思想之源泉，更无从了解其国家的起源，而恰恰正是这些往往会对社会的发展产生不可抗拒的影响。而对于这些影响，他的反抗毫无用处，甚至最后自己也会被洪流卷走。就好像领航员一样，他也许可以引领所驾驶的航船，但是改变不了船的结构，而且既不能在海上呼风唤雨，又无法平复船下大海的愤怒。

我们已经谈过美国人从联邦制中所得到的好处，剩下来的，就是要指出是什么能够让他们采用联邦制，因为并不是所有的国家都能从中得益。联邦制中的某些偶然缺陷源自法律，经过立法者的努力可以排除，但是一些其固有的缺陷并不是采用联邦制的人民所能抵制的。因此，这些国家必须要找到必要的力量来包容这种制度的固有缺陷。

所有联邦制最突出的问题就是其应用的手段的多样性。这种制度必然允许两种主权并存。通过对两种主权的权力半径进行精确划分，立法者可以使这两种主权的活动尽量简单平等，但是他们无法将其合二为一，也无法阻止它们在某个方面发生冲突。所以，联邦制必然建立在一套复杂的理论之上，而且需要被统治者每天运用这套理论。

is clear and precise will always meet with a greater number of adherents in the world than a true principle which is obscure or involved. Hence it arises that parties, which are like small communities in the heart of the nation, invariably adopt some principle or some name as a symbol, which very inadequately represents the end they have in view and the means which are at their disposal, but without which they could neither act nor subsist. The governments which are founded upon a single principle or a single feeling which is easily defined are perhaps not the best, but they are unquestionably the strongest and the most durable in the world.

In examining the Constitution of the United States, which is the most perfect federal constitution that ever existed, one is startled, on the other hand, at the variety of information and the excellence of discretion which it presupposes in the people whom it is meant to govern. The government of the Union depends entirely upon legal fictions; the Union is an ideal nation which only exists in the mind, and whose limits and extent can only be discerned by the understanding.

When once the general theory is comprehended, numberless difficulties remain to be solved in its application; for the sovereignty of the Union is so involved in that of the States that it is impossible to distinguish its boundaries at the first glance. The whole structure of the Government is artificial and conventional; and it would be ill adapted to a people which has not been long accustomed to conduct its own affairs, or to one in which the science of politics has not descended to the humblest classes of society. I have never been more struck by the good sense and the practical judgment of the Americans than in the ingenious devices by which they elude the numberless difficulties resulting from their Federal Constitution. I scarcely ever met with a plain American citizen who could not distinguish, with surprising facility, the obligations created by the laws of Congress from those created by the laws of his own State; and who, after having discriminated between the matters which come under the cognizance of the Union and those which the local legislature is competent to regulate, could not point out the exact limit of the several jurisdictions of the Federal courts and the tribunals of the State.

The Constitution of the United States is like those exquisite productions of human industry which ensure wealth and renown to their inventors, but which are profitless in any other hands. This truth is exemplified by the condition of Mexico at the present time. The Mexicans were desirous of

显而易见，人们必须要掌握一些基本概念。一个被表述得清晰准确的错误概念往往会比一个表述得含糊复杂的正确观点有更多的追随者。因此，一些有如大国中小国的政党必然要利用某些原则和名义做幌子，尽管这些根本不能完全代表其所追求的目的和所使用的手段，但是没有它们，这些政党既不能存在也无法开展活动。建立在一个简单或是容易解说的单一学说之上的政府，尽管算不上最好，但是毫无疑问会是世界上最强最持久的政府。

然而，当我们考察美国宪法，这一世界上有史以来最完美的联邦宪法时，会惊叹于其条款之繁多以及对被统治者具备识别能力的要求。联邦政府几乎完全建立在法律的假设之上。联邦只是存在于想象中的理想国，其界限和范围只能意会。

一旦总的理论得到理解，剩下的就是要解决千千万万实际应用方面的难题。因为联邦主权与各州主权盘根错节，一眼看去完全看不到其界限何在。政府中的一切事务都要经过反复协商和复杂的手续，如果不是长期习惯于自治，或是政治科学已经普及到社会最底层的民族，根本无法采用这套办法。跟其他人所采用的精明策略相比，我对于美国人在解决源自联邦宪法的无数难题时所表现出的理智和判断力更加佩服。我遇到的每个美国普通人都可以轻而易举地将国会法律规定的其所应尽的义务和本州法律规定的义务进行区分，而且还能分清哪些案件该由联邦法院处理哪些又该归地方司法机构管辖，并能分别指出联邦法院和州法院的各自管辖权的界限。

美国宪法就好像那些人类工业制造出的精美产品，能够给发明者带来财富和名誉，但

establishing a federal system, and they took the Federal Constitution of their neighbors, the Anglo-Americans, as their model, and copied it with considerable accuracy. But although they had borrowed the letter of the law, they were unable to create or to introduce the spirit and the sense which give it life. They were involved in ceaseless embarrassments between the mechanism of their double government; the sovereignty of the States and that of the Union perpetually exceeded their respective privileges, and entered into collision; and to the present day Mexico is alternately the victim of anarchy and the slave of military despotism.

The second and the most fatal of all the defects I have alluded to, and that which I believe to be inherent in the federal system, is the relative weakness of the government of the Union. The principle upon which all confederations rest is that of a divided sovereignty. The legislator may render this partition less perceptible, he may even conceal it for a time from the public eye, but he cannot prevent it from existing, and a divided sovereignty must always be less powerful than an entire supremacy. The reader has seen in the remarks I have made on the Constitution of the United States that the Americans have displayed singular ingenuity in combining the restriction of the power of the Union within the narrow limits of a federal government with the semblance and, to a certain extent, with the force of a national government. By this means the legislators of the Union have succeeded in diminishing, though not in counteracting the natural danger of confederations.

It has been remarked that the American Government does not apply itself to the States, but that it immediately transmits its injunctions to the citizens, and compels them as isolated individuals to comply with its demands. But if the Federal law were to clash with the interests and the prejudices of a State, it might be feared that all the citizens of that State would conceive themselves to be interested in the cause of a single individual who should refuse to obey. If all the citizens of the State were aggrieved at the same time and in the same manner by the authority of the Union, the Federal Government would vainly attempt to subdue them individually; they would instinctively unite in a common defence, and they would derive a ready-prepared organization from the share of sovereignty which the institution of their State allows them to enjoy. Fiction would give way to reality, and an organized portion of the territory might then contest the central authority. The same observation holds

是到了其他人手里则一文不值。墨西哥的现状就是一个这样的例子。墨西哥人渴望成立一个联邦制政府，并把邻居英裔美国人的联邦宪法做蓝本，几乎完全照搬过来。但是，尽管他们已经照搬了法律条文，但是却无法创建并移植赋予宪法以生命的精神。这使得他们的双重政府机制间不断地出现尴尬。州主权和联邦主权不断地越界，产生冲突，时至今日，墨西哥已经完全落入无政府状态和军事独裁的恶性循环之中。

我所提到的第二个也是我认为联邦制所有固有缺陷中最致命的一个就是联邦政府的相对软弱。一切联邦制所依据的原则就是主权分割。立法者纵然可以让这样的划分不易察觉，甚至在一段时间蒙骗住大众的眼睛，但是无法不让其存在，而且被划分的主权永远都会比完整的主权软弱。读者可以就我对美国宪法所做的论述中看到，美国人是如何巧妙地将联邦政府的权力限定在有限的狭小范围内的同时，又能够让其拥有全国中央政府的外貌，并在一定程度上，握有其所执掌的权力。通过这样的办法，联邦的立法者们尽管未能完全化解但也成功的弱化了联邦制的固有危险。

据说，美国政府并不直接与各州打交道，而是将其法令直接传达给公民，并强制公民个人服从国家要求。但是如果联邦法律和州的利益和惯例发生冲突，难道就不担心在对不服从该项法律的个人进行惩处的时候，该州的所有公民会认为触及了他们自身的利益吗？如果这个州的所有公民同时同样地感受到自己的利益受到联邦当局的侵害，那么联邦政府的分化企图便会落空。因为他们会自发地团结起来共同抵抗，并认为本州所分享的那部分

good with regard to the Federal jurisdiction. If the courts of the Union violated an important law of a State in a private case, the real, if not the apparent, contest would arise between the aggrieved State represented by a citizen and the Union represented by its courts of justice.

He would have but a partial knowledge of the world who should imagine that it is possible, by the aid of legal fictions, to prevent men from finding out and employing those means of gratifying their passions which have been left open to them; and it may be doubted whether the American legislators, when they rendered a collision between the two sovereigns less probable, destroyed the cause of such a misfortune. But it may even be affirmed that they were unable to ensure the preponderance of the Federal element in a case of this kind. The Union is possessed of money and of troops, but the affections and the prejudices of the people are in the bosom of the States. The sovereignty of the Union is an abstract being, which is connected with but few external objects; the sovereignty of the States is hourly perceptible, easily understood, constantly active; and if the former is of recent creation, the latter is coeval with the people itself. The sovereignty of the Union is factitious, that of the States is natural, and derives its existence from its own simple influence, like the authority of a parent. The supreme power of the nation only affects a few of the chief interests of society; it represents an immense but remote country, and claims a feeling of patriotism which is vague and ill defined; but the authority of the States controls every individual citizen at every hour and in all circumstances; it protects his property, his freedom, and his life; and when we recollect the traditions, the customs, the prejudices of local and familiar attachment with which it is connected, we cannot doubt of the superiority of a power which is interwoven with every circumstance that renders the love of one's native country instinctive in the human heart.

Since legislators are unable to obviate such dangerous collisions as occur between the two sovereignties which coexist in the federal system, their first object must be, not only to dissuade the confederate States from warfare, but to encourage such institutions as may promote the maintenance of peace. Hence it results that the Federal compact cannot be lasting unless there exists in the communities which are leagued together a certain number of inducements to union which render their common dependence agreeable, and the task of the Government light, and that system cannot succeed without the presence of favorable circumstances added to the influence of good laws. All

主权能够为他们做主。此时，法律的假设就要向现实让步，地方有组织的权力当局便会向中央主管当局发起挑战。在我看来，联邦的司法权亦是如此。如果在一个私人案件审理中，联邦法院违背了重要的一条州法律，那就会出现以受害公民为代表的州和以联邦法院为代表的联邦之间的争讼。

如果一个人认为，通过法律的帮助，便能够阻止人们找到并使用那些他们唾手可得的并用以满足其激情的手段，只能说明他对这个世界的了解不够。当美国的立法者尽力化解两个主权间冲突的时候，他们并未能摧毁这个不幸的根源，而且甚至可以肯定，在这种冲突出现的时候，他们都无法保证联邦主权取得优势。联邦拥有金钱和军队，州拥有人民的热爱和偏好。联邦的主权是抽象的存在，只与少数的外部事务有关；而州的主权则时刻被人感知，易于被人理解，并一直处于活跃状态。前者是新生事物，后者则是与民同生。联邦主权是人为创造的，州主权则是与生俱来的，如同父权一样，毫不费力便竖立起来。联邦的主权只对社会重大利益产生影响，代表的是幅员辽阔的国家，是一种模糊的难以说清的爱国情感。但是各州主权则时刻照顾到每个公民的方方面面，它会保护公民的财产、自由以及生命的安全。当我们想到与各州主权息息相关的那些人民的传统和习惯，以及地方的偏见和密不可分的联系，也就是能够使人们心中自发生成的对自己祖国的热爱的各种因素，而与这些因素交织在一起的权力所具有的优势又怎能让人对它产生怀疑。

既然立法者们不能消除联邦制中两种并存的主权发生危险的冲突，那么他们的首要目

the peoples which have ever formed a confederation have been held together by a certain number of common interests, which served as the intellectual ties of association.

But the sentiments and the principles of man must be taken into consideration as well as his immediate interests. A certain uniformity of civilization is not less necessary to the durability of a confederation than a uniformity of interests in the States which compose it. In Switzerland the difference which exists between the Canton of Uri and the Canton of Vaud is equal to that between the fifteenth and the nineteenth centuries; and, properly speaking, Switzerland has never possessed a federal government. The union between these two cantons only subsists upon the map, and their discrepancies would soon be perceived if an attempt were made by a central authority to prescribe the same laws to the whole territory.

One of the circumstances which most powerfully contribute to support the Federal Government in America is that the States have not only similar interests, a common origin, and a common tongue, but that they are also arrived at the same stage of civilization; which almost always renders a union feasible. I do not know of any European nation, how small soever it may be, which does not present less uniformity in its different provinces than the American people, which occupies a territory as extensive as one-half of Europe. The distance from the State of Maine to that of Georgia is reckoned at about one thousand miles; but the difference between the civilization of Maine and that of Georgia is slighter than the difference between the habits of Normandy and those of Brittany. Maine and Georgia, which are placed at the opposite extremities of a great empire, are consequently in the natural possession of more real inducements to form a confederation than Normandy and Brittany, which are only separated by a bridge.

The geographical position of the country contributed to increase the facilities which the American legislators derived from the manners and customs of the inhabitants; and it is to this circumstance that the adoption and the maintenance of the Federal system are mainly attributable.

The most important occurrence which can mark the annals of a people is the breaking out of a war. In war a people struggles with the energy of a single man against foreign nations in the defence of its very existence. The skill of a government, the good sense of the community, and the natural fondness which

标必定是，要阻止联邦各州之间发生战争，并鼓励它们采取促进和平的态度。所以，除非各联邦州之间存在将它们紧密联系在一起的因素，否则联邦不可能持久。同样，没有良好的环境和有利的环境，联邦制也无法获得成功。但凡形成联邦的所有成员国原先必然存有某些共同利益，而这些共同利益就形成了他们联合的精神纽带。

但是除了物质利益外，人们的情感以及原则也需要考虑。对于一个联邦的持久性而言，文明的统一性不亚于物质利益对结盟的重要性。在瑞士，沃州和乌里州的文明差距不亚于15世纪和19世纪的差别。所以，严格来说瑞士从来没有过联邦政府。而这两个州的联合只存在于地图上，如果中央政府打算在全国推行同样地法律，它们之间的差异不久就会暴露出来。

对于美国联邦政府的建立最为有利的因素之一就是，各州不但有大致相同的利益、相同的起源和语言，而且文明程度也大致相同。这些因素总是能够让联合变得顺理成章。我不知道有没有一个欧洲小国，其不同区域所表现出的统一性能够高于面积相当于大半个欧洲的美国。从缅因州到佐治亚州，大约有一千英里，但是它们之间文明程度的差异则大大小于诺曼底和布列塔尼。缅因州和佐治亚州分别位于一这个庞大帝国的两端，结果却比仅有一桥之隔的诺曼底和布列塔尼更自然地结为联邦。

国家的地理环境为美国立法者们可以利用来自居民风气和习惯的优势提供更多便利。联邦制之所以得以采用和保持，主要应归功于国家的地理环境。

men entertain for their country, may suffice to maintain peace in the interior of a district, and to favor its internal prosperity; but a nation can only carry on a great war at the cost of more numerous and more painful sacrifices; and to suppose that a great number of men will of their own accord comply with these exigencies of the State is to betray an ignorance of mankind. All the peoples which have been obliged to sustain a long and serious warfare have consequently been led to augment the power of their government. Those which have not succeeded in this attempt have been subjugated. A long war almost always places nations in the wretched alternative of being abandoned to ruin by defeat or to despotism by success. War therefore renders the symptoms of the weakness of a government most palpable and most alarming; and I have shown that the inherent defeat of federal governments is that of being weak.

The Federal system is not only deficient in every kind of centralized administration, but the central government itself is imperfectly organized, which is invariably an influential cause of inferiority when the nation is opposed to other countries which are themselves governed by a single authority. In the Federal Constitution of the United States, by which the central government possesses more real force, this evil is still extremely sensible. An example will illustrate the case to the reader.

The Constitution confers upon Congress the right of calling forth militia to execute the laws of the Union, suppress insurrections, and repel invasions; and another article declares that the President of the United States is the commander-in-chief of the militia. In the war of 1812 the President ordered the militia of the Northern States to march to the frontiers; but Connecticut and Massachusetts, whose interests were impaired by the war, refused to obey the command. They argued that the Constitution authorizes the Federal Government to call forth the militia in case of insurrection or invasion, but that in the present instance there was neither invasion nor insurrection. They added, that the same Constitution which conferred upon the Union the right of calling forth the militia reserved to the States that of naming the officers; and that consequently (as they understood the clause) no officer of the Union had any right to command the militia, even during war, except the President in person; and in this case they were ordered to join an army commanded by another individual. These absurd and pernicious doctrines received the sanction not only of the governors and the legislative

战争的爆发是能够影响一个国家生活的最重要的事件。在战争中，为了保家卫国，所有的国民会团结起来好像一个人一样来共同抗敌。如果只是要维护国内的和平繁荣，只要国家政府勤于政务，人民通情达理并怀有对祖国与生俱来的热爱便已足够。但是如果要打一场大仗，国家就需要更大的牺牲和代价，如果认为大多数人会自愿服从这样的国家需求，这只能说明对人性太不了解。对于所有那些能够将大战持续下去的国家，结果都不由自主地走上强化政府力量的道路；而未能做到这一点的国家，则最终被征服。陷入长期战争的国家最终逃不出两种可悲结局，不是因失败而毁灭，就是因胜利而专制。所以说政府的弱点在战争中最易察觉也最为危险。而且我已经说过联邦制政府的固有缺陷正是软弱。

联邦制不但缺少中央行政集权及其类似的东西，而且其中央政府本身也是不完整的集权，这就是当这样的国家与单一主权国家交战时所必然居于弱势的原因。从美国的联邦宪法来看，其中央政府比其他的联邦政府拥有更多的实权，但是这一缺陷依旧非常明显。下面仅举一例，读者便可了解其情况。

美国宪法授权国会招募军队执行联邦法律，平定暴乱以及抵御入侵，并另有一条宪法规定美国总统为军队的最高统帅。在1812年的战争中，总统下令北部各州民兵开往前线，但是由于康涅狄格州和马萨诸塞州的利益会因为战争而受到损害，于是便拒绝服从命令。它们辩称，宪法规定联邦政府只有在有叛乱或是入侵发生的时候才能召集民兵，而目前的情况既非入侵也非叛乱。而且它们还补充道，尽管宪法规定联邦政府可以召集民兵，但同时也将民兵军官的任命权留给各州，所以根据它们对此条宪法的理解，联邦军官除总统本人外，无权

bodies, but also of the courts of justice in both States; and the Federal Government was constrained to raise elsewhere the troops which it required.

The only safeguard which the American Union, with all the relative perfection of its laws, possesses against the dissolution which would be produced by a great war, lies in its probable exemption from that calamity. Placed in the centre of an immense continent, which offers a boundless field for human industry, the Union is almost as much insulated from the world as if its frontiers were girt by the ocean. Canada contains only a million of inhabitants, and its population is divided into two inimical nations. The rigor of the climate limits the extension of its territory, and shuts up its ports during the six months of winter. From Canada to the Gulf of Mexico a few savage tribes are to be met with, which retire, perishing in their retreat, before six thousand soldiers. To the South, the Union has a point of contact with the empire of Mexico; and it is thence that serious hostilities may one day be expected to arise. But for a long while to come the uncivilized state of the Mexican community, the depravity of its morals, and its extreme poverty, will prevent that country from ranking high amongst nations. As for the Powers of Europe, they are too distant to be formidable.

The great advantage of the United States does not, then, consist in a Federal Constitution which allows them to carry on great wars, but in a geographical position which renders such enterprises extremely improbable.

No one can be more inclined than I am myself to appreciate the advantages of the federal system, which I hold to be one of the combinations most favorable to the prosperity and freedom of man. I envy the lot of those nations which have been enabled to adopt it; but I cannot believe that any confederate peoples could maintain a long or an equal contest with a nation of similar strength in which the government should be centralized. A people which should divide its sovereignty into fractional powers, in the presence of the great military monarchies of Europe, would, in my opinion, by that very act, abdicate its power, and perhaps its existence and its name. But such is the admirable position of the New World that man has no other enemy than himself; and that, in order to be happy and to be free, it suffices to seek the gifts of prosperity and the knowledge of freedom.

指挥其民兵，甚至是在战时亦是如此。对这种荒谬有害的说法表示赞同的不但有两州的政府和立法机构，还有两州的法院。这样，联邦政府只好被迫去别的地方调集所需军队。

只拥有相对完备法律保障的美国联邦为什么能够逃过因战争而致解体的劫难呢，其原因就在于它没有遇到灾难性的战争。美国位于可以让人类无限发展事业的辽阔大陆的中部，两侧的大洋几乎让它与世隔绝。加拿大的人口只有百万，而且由两个相互敌对的民族构成。此外，严寒的天气限制其领土的扩张，并使其不得不封港长达六个月之久。从加拿大到墨西哥湾还有很多的原始部落，面对着六千士兵而处于半灭亡状态。在南方，联邦和墨西哥帝国有点接壤，因此，这里有朝一日也许会发生严重的军事冲突。但是对处于不开化状态、道德沦丧以及极度贫困的墨西哥而言，要想跻身世界强国还需要漫长的时间。至于欧洲列强，它们与美国距离遥远不足为惧。

所以，美国的巨大优势并不在于他们有一部可以顶得住大战的宪法，而是其所处的得天独厚的地理位置不会导致可怕战争的出现。

没有人会比我更加赞赏联邦制的优点。我认为联邦制是最有利于人类繁荣和自由的组织形式。对于那些能够采用联邦制的国家我羡慕不已，但是我并不相信联邦制国家能够在力量相当的条件下，跟一个中央集权的强国进行长期的对抗。在我看来，面对欧洲那些强大的军事君主制国家，敢于将国家主权一分为二，无异于放弃政权，也许还会自取灭亡让国家的名字不复存在。新世界之所以令人向往，是因为在那里人们可以自我奋斗，只要去追求就能获得幸福和自由。

Chapter IX: Why The People May Strictly Be Said To Govern In The United States

I have hitherto examined the institutions of the United States; I have passed their legislation in review, and I have depicted the present characteristics of political society in that country. But a sovereign power exists above these institutions and beyond these characteristic features which may destroy or modify them at its pleasure—I mean that of the people. It remains to be shown in what manner this power, which regulates the laws, acts: its propensities and its passions remain to be pointed out, as well as the secret springs which retard, accelerate, or direct its irresistible course; and the effects of its unbounded authority, with the destiny which is probably reserved for it.

Why The People May Strictly Be Said To Govern In The United States

In America the people appoints the legislative and the executive power, and furnishes the jurors who punish all offences against the laws. The American institutions are democratic, not only in their principle but in all their consequences; and the people elects its representatives directly, and for the most part annually, in order to ensure their dependence. The people is therefore the real directing power; and although the form of government is representative, it is evident that the opinions, the prejudices, the interests, and even the passions of the community are hindered by no durable obstacles from exercising a perpetual influence on society. In the United States the majority governs in the name of the people, as is the case in all the countries in which the people is supreme. The

第九章　为什么严格地说美国是由人民进行统治的

到目前为止，我已经考察了美国的各项制度，历数了其成文法，并描述了美国当前政治社会的特点。但是在这些制度之上以及所有组织之外，还有另外一个最高权力存在，即人民的权力，它可以随心所欲地改变或是废除这些制度和组织。接下来我所要说明的是，这一可以控制法律的权力以何种方式发挥作用，其本性和激情是什么，和那些妨碍、加速或是引导其不可抗拒进程的秘密动力是什么，其无限权威的效力如何，及其未来的命运走向。

为什么严格地说美国是由人民进行统治的

在美国，人民任命立法者和执法者，并组成陪审团对所有违法行为加以惩处。美国的制度是民主的，不但体现在原则上，还体现在其结果上。人民直接选出其代表，而且为了让他们受之于民，基本上每年都会进行改选。因此，人民拥有真正的指导力。尽管政府是

majority is principally composed of peaceful citizens who, either by inclination or by interest, are sincerely desirous of the welfare of their country. But they are surrounded by the incessant agitation of parties, which attempt to gain their co-operation and to avail themselves of their support.

代议制，但是人民的意见、偏好、利益甚至激情都不会遭到持续地抵制，并对社会产生长久的影响。在美国，就像在所有人民至上的国家一样，多数以人民的名义管理国家。多数主要由爱好和平的公民构成，不管是出于爱好还是利益，他们真心地希望国家富强。但是他们不断受到一些党派的滋扰，妄图得到他们的配合和支持。

Chapter X: Parties In The United States

Chapter Summary

Great distinction to be made between parties—Parties which are to each other as rival nations—Parties properly so called—Difference between great and small parties—Epochs which produce them—Their characteristics—America has had great parties—They are extinct—Federalists—Republicans—Defeat of the Federalists—Difficulty of creating parties in the United States—What is done with this intention—Aristocratic or democratic character to be met with in all parties—Struggle of General Jackson against the Bank.

Parties In The United States

A great distinction must be made between parties. Some countries are so large that the different populations which inhabit them have contradictory interests, although they are the subjects of the same Government, and they may thence be in a perpetual state of opposition. In this case the different fractions of the people may more properly be considered as distinct nations than as mere parties; and if a civil war breaks out, the struggle is carried on by rival peoples rather than by factions in the State.

But when the citizens entertain different opinions upon subjects which affect the whole country alike, such, for instance, as the principles upon which the government is to be conducted, then distinctions arise which may correctly be styled parties. Parties are a necessary evil in free governments; but they have not at all times the same character and the same propensities.

第十章　美国的政党

本章提要

要对政党加以区分——政党之间如同敌国——真正的政党——大党与小党的区别——政党何时产生——各政党的特征——美国有过大党——现已不复存在——联邦党——共和党——联邦党的失败——在美国创立政党的困难——为政党的建立所做的事情——所有政党均有贵族性和民主性——杰克逊将军对银行的斗争。

美国的政党

我要对政党进行一次大的分类。在一些幅员辽阔民族杂居的国家，尽管所有居民都隶属同一个政府管辖，但是彼此之间依旧利益冲突不断，所以人民之间长期处于敌对状态。在这样的情况下，同一个国家中不同群体的人们便形成不同的国家，而不仅仅是政党。如果内战爆发，与其说是不同派系之间的斗争，不如说是国家间的冲突。

但是，当公民就一些关系到全国的问题发表不同看法的时候，例如像政府行事的原

At certain periods a nation may be oppressed by such insupportable evils as to conceive the design of effecting a total change in its political constitution; at other times the mischief lies still deeper, and the existence of society itself is endangered. Such are the times of great revolutions and of great parties. But between these epochs of misery and of confusion there are periods during which human society seems to rest, and mankind to make a pause. This pause is, indeed, only apparent, for time does not stop its course for nations any more than for men; they are all advancing towards a goal with which they are unacquainted; and we only imagine them to be stationary when their progress escapes our observation, as men who are going at a foot-pace seem to be standing still to those who run.

But however this may be, there are certain epochs at which the changes that take place in the social and political constitution of nations are so slow and so insensible that men imagine their present condition to be a final state; and the human mind, believing itself to be firmly based upon certain foundations, does not extend its researches beyond the horizon which it descries. These are the times of small parties and of intrigue.

The political parties which I style great are those which cling to principles more than to their consequences; to general, and not to especial cases; to ideas, and not to men. These parties are usually distinguished by a nobler character, by more generous passions, more genuine convictions, and a more bold and open conduct than the others. In them private interest, which always plays the chief part in political passions, is more studiously veiled under the pretext of the public good; and it may even be sometimes concealed from the eyes of the very persons whom it excites and impels.

Minor parties are, on the other hand, generally deficient in political faith. As they are not sustained or dignified by a lofty purpose, they ostensibly display the egotism of their character in their actions. They glow with a factitious zeal; their language is vehement, but their conduct is timid and irresolute. The means they employ are as wretched as the end at which they aim. Hence it arises that when a calm state of things succeeds a violent revolution, the leaders of society seem suddenly to disappear, and the powers of the human mind to lie concealed. Society is convulsed by great parties, by minor

则，那么这种分歧就会造就真正意义上的政党。政党是自由政府的固有不幸，无论何时，它们都不会有相同的特征和相同的偏好。

往往当一个国家处于灾难深重的时期，会产生全面改革其政治体制架构的想法。还有些时候国家灾难更加深重，以致社会的存在都濒临危机。这就是出现大革命和大政党的时代。但是在这样不幸而混乱的时代，似乎也是社会得以休息，人类得以喘息的时代。实际上，这不过是表面的平静，因为无论是对人还是对社会而言，时间不会停止，会向着未知的未来不断前进。然而当国家和人们的活动未被察觉的时候，我们就想象它们停滞不前。这就好像走着的人一样，在那些跑着的人看来，他们似乎站在原地没动。

但是不管怎样，总是有一些特定的时期，国家的社会和政治结构的变化如此的缓慢难以察觉以至于人们认为自己已经处于最佳状态。此时，人类的理性也自以为有了一定的基础，不再将目光投向视野之外。这就是有利于小党和阴谋活动的时代。

我划归为大党的政党是那些关注原则胜于结果，重视一般甚于个别，笃信思想而不是人的党派。与其他政党相比，它们更加高尚，激情四溢，拥有更加虔诚的信仰以及更为大胆的行事。对政治激情产生巨大影响的私人利益被巧妙地掩藏在公共利益的面纱之后，有时候甚至会蒙蔽受其鼓舞而行动起来的人们的双眼。

另一方面，小党则普遍缺乏政治信念。因为没有崇高的目标给它们以支持，所以它们也并不高尚，进而其行事带有明显的利己主义特征。它们装出热情四射的样子，它们的言辞激烈，但是行动起来唯唯诺诺犹豫不决。它们采取的手段跟他们要达成的目标一样猥

ones it is agitated; it is torn by the former, by the latter it is degraded; and if these sometimes save it by a salutary perturbation, those invariably disturb it to no good end.

America has already lost the great parties which once divided the nation; and if her happiness is considerably increased, her morality has suffered by their extinction. When the War of Independence was terminated, and the foundations of the new Government were to be laid down, the nation was divided between two opinions—two opinions which are as old as the world, and which are perpetually to be met with under all the forms and all the names which have ever obtained in free communities—the one tending to limit, the other to extend indefinitely, the power of the people. The conflict of these two opinions never assumed that degree of violence in America which it has frequently displayed elsewhere. Both parties of the Americans were, in fact, agreed upon the most essential points; and neither of them had to destroy a traditionary constitution, or to overthrow the structure of society, in order to ensure its own triumph. In neither of them, consequently, were a great number of private interests affected by success or by defeat; but moral principles of a high order, such as the love of equality and of independence, were concerned in the struggle, and they sufficed to kindle violent passions.

The party which desired to limit the power of the people endeavored to apply its doctrines more especially to the Constitution of the Union, whence it derived its name of Federal. The other party, which affected to be more exclusively attached to the cause of liberty, took that of Republican. America is a land of democracy, and the Federalists were always in a minority; but they reckoned on their side almost all the great men who had been called forth by the War of Independence, and their moral influence was very considerable. Their cause was, moreover, favored by circumstances. The ruin of the Confederation had impressed the people with a dread of anarchy, and the Federalists did not fail to profit by this transient disposition of the multitude. For ten or twelve years they were at the head of affairs, and they were able to apply some, though not all, of their principles; for the hostile current was becoming from day to day too violent to be checked or stemmed. In 1801 the Republicans got possession of the Government; Thomas Jefferson was named President; and he

琐不堪。因此,它们会出现在暴力革命之后的平静时期。这段时期,社会领袖似乎一下子不见了,智慧也自行隐藏起来。社会因为大党而激荡,因为小党而骚动;会因为前者而分裂,因为后者而堕落;前者有时候因为打乱社会秩序而将社会拯救,后者则只会让社会不安毫无益处而言。

美国那些可以让国家分裂的大党已经不复存在。而从中获益最大的是美国这个国家而不是其道德。在独立战争结束之后,新政府即将奠基之时,国家出现了两种意见分歧。这两种意见与世界同样古老,并始终在不同的社会以不同的形式出现,并被冠以不同的名称。一种意见主张限制人民力量,而另一种意见力挺人民力量的无限扩大化。两种意见矛盾在美国自始至终都没有引起不断在其他地方出现的暴力冲突。实际上,美国的政党在最基本的问题上意见一致,任何一方都不会为了取得优胜而想要毁掉社会秩序或是颠覆社会结构。因此,任何一方的私利都不会因其成败而受到什么影响。但是,斗争双方都很关心的更高层次的道德原则,诸如对于平等和独立的热爱足以撩起狂热的激情。

主张限制人民权力的一派,千方百计要将其学说应用于美国宪法,因而得名联邦党。而唯自由独爱的另一派,就被称为共和党。美国是一个民主国家,所以联邦党人一直是少数派,但是独立战争成就的伟大人物几乎都在他们的阵营,而且他们的道德影响力也非常巨大,更何况环境还于他们有利。第一次联合的瓦解让人们对可怕的无政府状态心有余悸,而联邦党人自然不会放过从这个观望倾向中渔利的大好机会。他们支持国家工作已有10年到12年之久,尽管不是全部,他们的部分原则业已得到应用。这是因为敌对潮流日益

increased the influence of their party by the weight of his celebrity, the greatness of his talents, and the immense extent of his popularity.

The means by which the Federalists had maintained their position were artificial, and their resources were temporary; it was by the virtues or the talents of their leaders that they had risen to power. When the Republicans attained to that lofty station, their opponents were overwhelmed by utter defeat. An immense majority declared itself against the retiring party, and the Federalists found themselves in so small a minority that they at once despaired of their future success. From that moment the Republican or Democratic party has proceeded from conquest to conquest, until it has acquired absolute supremacy in the country. The Federalists, perceiving that they were vanquished without resource, and isolated in the midst of the nation, fell into two divisions, of which one joined the victorious Republicans, and the other abandoned its rallying-point and its name. Many years have already elapsed since they ceased to exist as a party.

The accession of the Federalists to power was, in my opinion, one of the most fortunate incidents which accompanied the formation of the great American Union; they resisted the inevitable propensities of their age and of the country. But whether their theories were good or bad, they had the effect of being inapplicable, as a system, to the society which they professed to govern, and that which occurred under the auspices of Jefferson must therefore have taken place sooner or later. But their Government gave the new republic time to acquire a certain stability, and afterwards to support the rapid growth of the very doctrines which they had combated. A considerable number of their principles were in point of fact embodied in the political creed of their opponents; and the Federal Constitution which subsists at the present day is a lasting monument of their patriotism and their wisdom.

Great political parties are not, then, to be met with in the United States at the present time. Parties, indeed, may be found which threaten the future tranquillity of the Union; but there are none which seem to contest the present form of Government or the present course of society. The parties by which the Union is menaced do not rest upon abstract principles, but upon temporal interests.

强大，使他们终于无力反对。1801年，共和党人执政，托马斯·杰斐逊当选为美国总统，凭借其个人的声望、才智以及极好的人缘，将其政党的影响力大大提高。

联邦党人只是凭借一些不可靠的手段和临时决定的对策，才得以保全其地位。他们之所以能够执政，全仰仗其领袖的美德和才能。当共和党人登上这个宝座，其对手便输得一败涂地。拥有绝对优势的多数宣布反对他们，让联邦党人觉得自己是如此微不足道的少数以致立刻陷入对未来成功的绝望之中。从那时起，共和党人或称为民主党步步为营，直至在全国取得绝对优势。于是，已经意识到自己处于孤立无援窘境的联邦党人，分裂成为两部分，一部分加入了共和党，另一些则改旗易帜。他们不再是政党已经有许多年了。

在我看来，联邦党人执政是随美联邦成立而出现的最幸运的偶然事件之一，他们顶住了那个时代那个国家不可改变的潮流。但是且不论其理论好坏，始终有其欠缺，因为它并不适用它要治理的社会，所以这个社会迟早要交到杰斐逊手上。但是联邦党的政府至少为新共和国提供了自我稳定的时间，并促成其所反对学说的迅速成长。实际上，他们的大量原则后来又被纳入对手的政治信条。如今仍在实施的联邦宪法就是他们爱国主义和智慧的不朽丰碑。

因此，在今天的美国依然看不到大党的身影。纵然，还有一些政党的确可能威胁到联邦未来的安定，但是对于目前的政府形式和社会进程，谁也没有异议。而对联邦未来产生威胁的这些党派，并不是建立在原则之上而是暂时利益。在幅员如此辽阔的国家里的这些利益纷争，与其说是党派之争不地说是敌对国家之争。所以就出现了最近的这个例子，北

These interests, disseminated in the provinces of so vast an empire, may be said to constitute rival nations rather than parties. Thus, upon a recent occasion, the North contended for the system of commercial prohibition, and the South took up arms in favor of free trade, simply because the North is a manufacturing and the South an agricultural district; and that the restrictive system which was profitable to the one was prejudicial to the other.

In the absence of great parties, the United States abound with lesser controversies; and public opinion is divided into a thousand minute shades of difference upon questions of very little moment. The pains which are taken to create parties are inconceivable, and at the present day it is no easy task. In the United States there is no religious animosity, because all religion is respected, and no sect is predominant; there is no jealousy of rank, because the people is everything, and none can contest its authority; lastly, there is no public indigence to supply the means of agitation, because the physical position of the country opens so wide a field to industry that man is able to accomplish the most surprising undertakings with his own native resources. Nevertheless, ambitious men are interested in the creation of parties, since it is difficult to eject a person from authority upon the mere ground that his place is coveted by others. The skill of the actors in the political world lies therefore in the art of creating parties. A political aspirant in the United States begins by discriminating his own interest, and by calculating upon those interests which may be collected around and amalgamated with it; he then contrives to discover some doctrine or some principle which may suit the purposes of this new association, and which he adopts in order to bring forward his party and to secure his popularity; just as the imprimatur of a King was in former days incorporated with the volume which it authorized, but to which it nowise belonged. When these preliminaries are terminated, the new party is ushered into the political world.

All the domestic controversies of the Americans at first appear to a stranger to be so incomprehensible and so puerile that he is at a loss whether to pity a people which takes such arrant trifles in good earnest, or to envy the happiness which enables it to discuss them. But when he comes to study the secret propensities which govern the factions of America, he easily perceives that the

方主张采取贸易禁运措施，而南方则要拿起武器捍卫贸易自由，究其原因不过是因为北方是工业区而南方是农业区，所以对一方有利的政策必然会损害到另一方。

尽管没有大党的存在，美国依然存在许多的小争议，而公众舆论也会因为对一些细小问题的意见不同而形成不同的政见。当时党派的创立不会遭遇任何阻碍，而如今则不再是件容易事。在美国，因为所有宗教都受到尊重，并没有任何一个教派占据统治地位，所以没有宗教仇恨；也不存在阶级仇恨，因为人民就是一切，没有人敢挑战他们的权威；最后，也没有大众的贫穷可以给混乱可乘之机，因为国家的物质状况为勤恳开辟了广阔的道路，一个人只要肯干，就可以创造出奇迹。但是，妄图成立政党的野心家们依然存在，因为他们知道，因为自己垂涎当权人的位置而想要把他拉下来非常困难。因此，政治家将全部的伎俩用于建立政党。美国政界的野心家们便开始通过分析自身利益并算计哪些利益可以集中合并起来，努力挖掘一些适用于新组织的学说和原则，从而能让他的政党来到台前确保其知名度。这就好像以前出版书籍的时候要在扉页上印有国王授权出版的字样一样，尽管跟书的内容毫不相干。当这些准备措施完成，新政党便步入政坛。

对于外国人而言，美国人的所有国内争议，乍一看来会感觉难以理解和无所谓，以至于都不知道究竟是该同情这个把琐碎小事当成正经大事的国家，还是该羡慕他们能够参政议政的这份幸福。但是，当他开始仔细研究支配美国各政党的秘密动力的时候，便能轻而易举意识到这些党派或多或少都和自这个自由国家存在以来便将人们分成两派的两大党有关联。我们对这些党派的了解越深，就越能看明白一方的目的是要限制人民权力，另一方

greater part of them are more or less connected with one or the other of those two divisions which have always existed in free communities. The deeper we penetrate into the working of these parties, the more do we perceive that the object of the one is to limit, and that of the other to extend, the popular authority. I do not assert that the ostensible end, or even that the secret aim, of American parties is to promote the rule of aristocracy or democracy in the country; but I affirm that aristocratic or democratic passions may easily be detected at the bottom of all parties, and that, although they escape a superficial observation, they are the main point and the very soul of every faction in the United States.

To quote a recent example. When the President attacked the Bank, the country was excited and parties were formed; the well-informed classes rallied round the Bank, the common people round the President. But it must not be imagined that the people had formed a rational opinion upon a question which offers so many difficulties to the most experienced statesmen. The Bank is a great establishment which enjoys an independent existence, and the people, accustomed to make and unmake whatsoever it pleases, is startled to meet with this obstacle to its authority. In the midst of the perpetual fluctuation of society the community is irritated by so permanent an institution, and is led to attack it in order to see whether it can be shaken and controlled, like all the other institutions of the country.

Remains Of The Aristocratic Party In The United States
Secret opposition of wealthy individuals to democracy—Their retirement—Their taste for exclusive pleasures and for luxury at home—Their simplicity abroad—Their affected condescension towards the people.

It sometimes happens in a people amongst which various opinions prevail that the balance of the several parties is lost, and one of them obtains an irresistible preponderance, overpowers all obstacles, harasses its opponents, and appropriates all the resources of society to its own purposes.

则是要扩大人民权力。我并不是断言美国政的表面的目的，或者甚至是隐秘的目的，就是在美国推动贵族政治和民主政治的制度。但我可以肯定，所有政党内心深处所怀有的贵族政治和民主政治的激情是很容易察觉到的。尽管也许能够避开人们的视线，但是它们始终是美国政党的敏感点和灵魂。

举一个最近的例子。当美国总统攻击银行时，这个国家骚动起来，形成不同的派别。上层阶级站在银行一边，普通大众则围绕在总统身边。即使是经验丰富的政客也会感到棘手的问题，人民又怎能得到有关于此的理性看法。银行是一个独立存在的巨大机构，而习惯于随心所欲的人民，惊讶地发现自己的权威遇到了障碍。在社会不断的跌宕起伏之中，人们受到这样的一个永久机构刺激，对其展开进攻想要看看它到底能不能像国家其它所有机构一样，被动摇被控制。

贵族党在美国的残余
富人对民主的暗中反对——他们的隐退——他们自家一心享乐奢华——他们在外深居简出——他们向人民假献殷勤。

在一个可以众说纷纭的国家，有时候政党间的平衡会被打破，某一个政党会占据绝对优势。此时，它便要摧毁所有障碍，压制政敌，并利用一切社会资源为自己的利益服务。那些受到排挤的政党因为对成功的绝望，而吞下不满的苦果默不作声。整个国家似乎被一

The vanquished citizens despair of success and they conceal their dissatisfaction in silence and in general apathy. The nation seems to be governed by a single principle, and the prevailing party assumes the credit of having restored peace and unanimity to the country. But this apparent unanimity is merely a cloak to alarming dissensions and perpetual opposition.

This is precisely what occurred in America; when the democratic party got the upper hand, it took exclusive possession of the conduct of affairs, and from that time the laws and the customs of society have been adapted to its caprices. At the present day the more affluent classes of society are so entirely removed from the direction of political affairs in the United States that wealth, far from conferring a right to the exercise of power, is rather an obstacle than a means of attaining to it. The wealthy members of the community abandon the lists, through unwillingness to contend, and frequently to contend in vain, against the poorest classes of their fellow citizens. They concentrate all their enjoyments in the privacy of their homes, where they occupy a rank which cannot be assumed in public; and they constitute a private society in the State, which has its own tastes and its own pleasures. They submit to this state of things as an irremediable evil, but they are careful not to show that they are galled by its continuance; it is even not uncommon to hear them laud the delights of a republican government, and the advantages of democratic institutions when they are in public. Next to hating their enemies, men are most inclined to flatter them.

Mark, for instance, that opulent citizen, who is as anxious as a Jew of the Middle Ages to conceal his wealth. His dress is plain, his demeanor unassuming; but the interior of his dwelling glitters with luxury, and none but a few chosen guests whom he haughtily styles his equals are allowed to penetrate into this sanctuary. No European noble is more exclusive in his pleasures, or more jealous of the smallest advantages which his privileged station confers upon him. But the very same individual crosses the city to reach a dark counting-house in the centre of traffic, where every one may accost him who pleases. If he meets his cobbler upon the way, they stop and converse; the two citizens discuss the affairs of the State in which they have an equal interest, and they shake hands before they part.

But beneath this artificial enthusiasm, and these obsequious attentions to the preponderating

个思想所统治，获胜的政党将国家重获和平以及统一的功劳归给自己。但是，表面上的统一之下隐藏的是深刻的分歧和永久的对抗。

美国就是这种情况。当民主党取得优势，它大权独揽，从那时起不断地对法律和民情进行修改以适应自己的想法。在今天的美国，越是富有的阶级越不愿参与政事，财富不能使人们从政治中获得权力，相反还会成为权力的阻碍而不是攫取它的手段。于是富人放弃官场，以免和最贫穷的公民进行不平等的斗争。他们将乐趣集中到家里，在这里他们形成一个不为大众所知的阶层，并在美国社会里形成一个有着自己品味和乐趣的特殊社会。他们将这些看作无可救治的缺陷而逆来顺受，并小心翼翼地不显露出对这种事态给他们的损失所产生的不满，甚至还能常常听到他们在人群中大赞共和政府以及民主制度的好处多多。在憎恨过敌人之后，紧接着人们最常见的做法是向其大献殷勤。

有没有听说过一些跟一个中世纪害怕露富的犹太人一样的人。他们衣着朴素，举止谦逊，但是居所之内十分奢华，而且只有几个跟他有相同趣味的人允许进入这座神殿。没有一个旧欧洲贵族会超越他的享乐程度，而且他还对特权地位带来的哪怕一丁点好处都嫉妒不已。但是当他从家里出来，穿过城市来到一个位于市中心的一个满是灰尘的小房子做生意的时候，人人都可以与他随意交谈。如果途中碰到鞋匠，他也会停下来攀谈几句。他们谈论共同感兴趣的国家大事，而且分手前还会握手道别。

但是，在这种虚情假意的背后，在对权贵之人的谄媚背后，不难看出国家中的有钱人

power, it is easy to perceive that the wealthy members of the community entertain a hearty distaste to the democratic institutions of their country. The populace is at once the object of their scorn and of their fears. If the maladministration of the democracy ever brings about a revolutionary crisis, and if monarchical institutions ever become practicable in the United States, the truth of what I advance will become obvious.

The two chief weapons which parties use in order to ensure success are the public press and the formation of associations.

对民主制度的由衷厌恶。他对人民既看不起又畏惧。假如民主的弊端会招致革命的危机，或是君主制在美国变得可行，人们会立即发现我所说的都是正确的。

为了获得成功，政党所采用的两个主要武器就是：办报和结社。

Chapter XI: Liberty Of The Press In The United States

Chapter Summary

Difficulty of restraining the liberty of the press—Particular reasons which some nations have to cherish this liberty—The liberty of the press a necessary consequence of the sovereignty of the people as it is understood in America—Violent language of the periodical press in the United States—Propensities of the periodical press—Illustrated by the United States—Opinion of the Americans upon the repression of the abuse of the liberty of the press by judicial prosecutions—Reasons for which the press is less powerful in America than in France.

Liberty Of The Press In The United States

The influence of the liberty of the press does not affect political opinions alone, but it extends to all the opinions of men, and it modifies customs as well as laws. In another part of this work I shall attempt to determinate the degree of influence which the liberty of the press has exercised upon civil society in the United States, and to point out the direction which it has given to the ideas, as well as the tone which it has imparted to the character and the feelings, of the Anglo-Americans, but at present I purpose simply to examine the effects produced by the liberty of the press in the political world.

I confess that I do not entertain that firm and complete attachment to the liberty of the press which things that are supremely good in their very nature are wont to excite in the mind; and I approve of it

第十一章　美国的出版自由

本章提要

限制出版自由的困难——某些国家珍视出版自由的特殊原因——出版自由是美国人所理解的人民主权的必然结果——美国期刊使用的言辞激烈——期刊的特有本性——用美国的例子证明——美国人对司法当局惩处违规出版的看法——为什么美国出版界不如法国强大。

美国的出版自由

出版自由的影响力不仅仅波及政治观点，还会扩展到人们对所有一切的看法，不但能改变法律还能改变社会风气。在本书的另一部分，我会试图判定出版自由对美国国内社会的影响程度，并指出它所给出的思想方向，以及给英裔美国人定下的品行和情感的基调。但现在我只想考察一下出版自由对于政界的影响。

我承认本人对出版自由并没有那种因事物本身超棒而产生的坚定完全的热爱，而我之

more from a recollection of the evils it prevents than from a consideration of the advantages it ensures.

If any one could point out an intermediate and yet a tenable position between the complete independence and the entire subjection of the public expression of opinion, I should perhaps be inclined to adopt it; but the difficulty is to discover this position. If it is your intention to correct the abuses of unlicensed printing and to restore the use of orderly language, you may in the first instance try the offender by a jury; but if the jury acquits him, the opinion which was that of a single individual becomes the opinion of the country at large. Too much and too little has therefore hitherto been done. If you proceed, you must bring the delinquent before a court of permanent judges. But even here the cause must be heard before it can be decided; and the very principles which no book would have ventured to avow are blazoned forth in the pleadings, and what was obscurely hinted at in a single composition is then repeated in a multitude of other publications. The language in which a thought is embodied is the mere carcass of the thought, and not the idea itself; tribunals may condemn the form, but the sense and spirit of the work is too subtle for their authority. Too much has still been done to recede, too little to attain your end; you must therefore proceed. If you establish a censorship of the press, the tongue of the public speaker will still make itself heard, and you have only increased the mischief. The powers of thought do not rely, like the powers of physical strength, upon the number of their mechanical agents, nor can a host of authors be reckoned like the troops which compose an army; on the contrary, the authority of a principle is often increased by the smallness of the number of men by whom it is expressed. The words of a strong-minded man, which penetrate amidst the passions of a listening assembly, have more power than the vociferations of a thousand orators; and if it be allowed to speak freely in any public place, the consequence is the same as if free speaking was allowed in every village. The liberty of discourse must therefore be destroyed as well as the liberty of the press; this is the necessary term of your efforts; but if your object was to repress the abuses of liberty, they have brought you to the feet of a despot. You have been led from the extreme of independence to the extreme of subjection without meeting with a single tenable position for shelter or repose.

There are certain nations which have peculiar reasons for cherishing the liberty of the press,

所以会对其表示认可，更多是出于它可以防止弊端，而不是它本身的优点。

如果任何人能够在思想的完全独立和绝对服从之间指出一个中间点，那么我会很乐于站到这样的位置，但是问题是这个点很难找。如果你的目的不过是纠正无证印刷，进行语言规范，那么首先你要将违法者提交陪审团。但是如果陪审团宣判其无罪，于是单个人的意见就扩大为全国人民的意见。所以，你要办的事情太多，而能办成的又太少，但终归还得继续办。如果接着办下去，你必须要将失职人员诉讼至常设法院。但甚至在这里，法官在做出判决前依然需要听取被告的陈述。于是那些不敢公开写进书里的东西便堂而皇之地写进辩护词，原来隐晦的写在一篇文章中的内容要不断重复见诸于其他不同的出版物。搭载思想的语言不过是思想的躯体，而不是思想本身。法院也许可以对其形式加以处罚，但是作品中的道理和精神则逃脱了惩罚。要办的事情依旧很多，可能办成的依旧很少，所以你还要继续。好吧，如果你设立了出版审查制度，演说家依然可以发声，而这不过是徒增苦恼罢了。好像物质力量一样，思想的力量不依赖于宣传者的数量，而也不能把作家当成军队的士兵。相反，思想的威力往往因为表达这样思想的人为数甚少而得到加强。一个意志坚定的人在鸦雀无声的群众大会上的演讲，会比上千个演说家的喋喋不休更有力量。即使只允许在一个公共场所自由演讲，其结果跟允许在每个村庄自由演讲没有不同。因此演讲自由和出版自由都要被破坏。这就是你努力的结果。但是如果你原本的目的是抑制自由的泛滥，可结果却被带到了暴君的脚下。你从极端的独立来到极端的屈从，都没碰到一个

independently of the general motives which I have just pointed out. For in certain countries which profess to enjoy the privileges of freedom every individual agent of the Government may violate the laws with impunity, since those whom he oppresses cannot prosecute him before the courts of justice. In this case the liberty of the press is not merely a guarantee, but it is the only guarantee, of their liberty and their security which the citizens possess. If the rulers of these nations propose to abolish the independence of the press, the people would be justified in saying: Give us the right of prosecuting your offences before the ordinary tribunals, and perhaps we may then waive our right of appeal to the tribunal of public opinion.

But in the countries in which the doctrine of the sovereignty of the people ostensibly prevails, the censorship of the press is not only dangerous, but it is absurd. When the right of every citizen to co-operate in the government of society is acknowledged, every citizen must be presumed to possess the power of discriminating between the different opinions of his contemporaries, and of appreciating the different facts from which inferences may be drawn. The sovereignty of the people and the liberty of the press may therefore be looked upon as correlative institutions; just as the censorship of the press and universal suffrage are two things which are irreconcilably opposed, and which cannot long be retained among the institutions of the same people. Not a single individual of the twelve millions who inhabit the territory of the United States has as yet dared to propose any restrictions to the liberty of the press. The first newspaper over which I cast my eyes, upon my arrival in America, contained the following article:

In all this affair the language of Jackson has been that of a heartless despot, solely occupied with the preservation of his own authority. Ambition is his crime, and it will be his punishment too: intrigue is his native element, and intrigue will confound his tricks, and will deprive him of his power: he governs by means of corruption, and his immoral practices will redound to his shame and confusion. His conduct in the political arena has been that of a shameless and lawless gamester. He succeeded at the time, but the hour of retribution approaches, and he will be obliged to disgorge his winnings, to throw aside his false dice, and to end his days in some retirement, where he may curse his madness at his leisure; for repentance is a virtue with which his heart is likely to remain forever unacquainted.

可以歇歇的落脚之处。

有一些国家之所以珍视出版自由，除了我已经说过的普遍原因外，还有一些特殊原因。在某些标榜自由的国家，政府的公职人员都可以在触犯法律之后免受惩罚，因为宪法没有赋予被压迫者权利到法院对官员进行控告。这样，舆论自由便不仅仅是公民自由安全的保障，而是唯一的保障。如果这些国家的统治者们宣布废除出版自由，人们就会申辩：给我们去法院控告你们罪行的权利，也许我们会放弃到舆论法庭控诉的权利。

但是在那些人民主权学说盛行的国家，出版监查制度不但危险而且荒谬。当每个公民参与政府管理的权利得到认可，那就必然意味其拥有权力对同时代不同观点进行分辨，以及对经认识后能够知道其行动的各种事实加以鉴别。因此，人民主权和出版自由应该被视为紧密联系的两种制度。然而，出版监察制和普遍选举权则是两件相互对立的事情，无法长期在一个国家的政治制度中共存。生活在美国这片土地上的1200万居民中，没有一个人胆敢提出限制出版自由。我来到美国见到的第一份报纸里面有这样一篇文章：

在整件事上，杰克逊所使用的语言，是冷酷无情，一心维护自己权力的暴君的语言。野心就是他的罪行，也将会获罪于此；阴谋是他的爱好，最终不但会自受其乱还会夺走他的权力。他为政腐化堕落，他不道德的行为必将使其名誉扫地遭人唾弃。他在政坛的所作所为无异于无法无天恬不知耻的赌徒。此刻他成功了，但是受审的时刻正在逼近，他必须将他赢到手的东西再吐出来，扔掉他的假赌具，让他赶紧退休，并在退休之后的闲暇时间

It is not uncommonly imagined in France that the virulence of the press originates in the uncertain social condition, in the political excitement, and the general sense of consequent evil which prevail in that country; and it is therefore supposed that as soon as society has resumed a certain degree of composure the press will abandon its present vehemence. I am inclined to think that the above causes explain the reason of the extraordinary ascendency it has acquired over the nation, but that they do not exercise much influence upon the tone of its language. The periodical press appears to me to be actuated by passions and propensities independent of the circumstances in which it is placed, and the present position of America corroborates this opinion.

America is perhaps, at this moment, the country of the whole world which contains the fewest germs of revolution; but the press is not less destructive in its principles than in France, and it displays the same violence without the same reasons for indignation. In America, as in France, it constitutes a singular power, so strangely composed of mingled good and evil that it is at the same time indispensable to the existence of freedom, and nearly incompatible with the maintenance of public order. Its power is certainly much greater in France than in the United States; though nothing is more rare in the latter country than to hear of a prosecution having been instituted against it. The reason of this is perfectly simple: the Americans, having once admitted the doctrine of the sovereignty of the people, apply it with perfect consistency. It was never their intention to found a permanent state of things with elements which undergo daily modifications; and there is consequently nothing criminal in an attack upon the existing laws, provided it be not attended with a violent infraction of them. They are moreover of opinion that courts of justice are unable to check the abuses of the press; and that as the subtilty of human language perpetually eludes the severity of judicial analysis, offences of this nature are apt to escape the hand which attempts to apprehend them. They hold that to act with efficacy upon the press it would be necessary to find a tribunal, not only devoted to the existing order of things, but capable of surmounting the influence of public opinion; a tribunal which should conduct its proceedings without publicity, which should pronounce its decrees without assigning its motives, and punish the intentions even more than the language of an author. Whosoever should have the power of creating and maintaining a tribunal of this kind would waste

咒骂自己当初的疯狂。但是忏悔并不是能够让他良心有所发现的一种德行。

在法国，人们普遍认为出版业的暴力源自社会的不稳，政治的激情以及随之而来的普遍不安。因此，人们认定只要社会在一定程度上重获宁静，出版业就会摒弃暴力。然而依我看上述的原因虽然可以解释这种情形在我国盛行的原因，但是并未对报刊的语言起到什么重大影响。我认为不管在什么情况下，报刊都应保有其特性和激情。而美国目前状况恰好与我的观点不谋而合。

此刻的美国也许是世界上革命萌芽最难以孕育的国家，但是美国出版业的破坏倾向丝毫不逊于法国，尽管它们各自义愤填膺的初衷不同，但是暴力是一样的。跟在法国一样，在美国报刊是奇怪的将善与恶混为一谈的一种力量。没有它自由就不能存在，有了它秩序才得以维持。它的力量在法国肯定比在美国强大。但在美国也很少看到司法惩治报刊的案件。其原因非常简单：美国人在认可人民主权的学说后，必会将其贯彻始终。他们从来没有想过，在不断变化的因素中能够发现永久存在的制度。所以，只要不采用暴力抗法，现行的法律也不会对其进行制裁。此外，他们确信，法律无力管束报刊，而人类语言的精妙之处又可以让其一直逍遥法外，所以这种性质的违法都能从企图加罪于它们的人手中溜走。于是他们认为，要有效地打击报刊，就必须找到一个既可以维持现有秩序又可以不受公众舆论影响的法庭。这个法庭可以不公开审案，不用陈述理由而宣判，而且惩处的是动机而不是语言。无论是谁有权设立和主持这样的法庭，我认为追溯出版自由都是多余

his time in prosecuting the liberty of the press; for he would be the supreme master of the whole community, and he would be as free to rid himself of the authors as of their writings. In this question, therefore, there is no medium between servitude and extreme license; in order to enjoy the inestimable benefits which the liberty of the press ensures, it is necessary to submit to the inevitable evils which it engenders. To expect to acquire the former and to escape the latter is to cherish one of those illusions which commonly mislead nations in their times of sickness, when, tired with faction and exhausted by effort, they attempt to combine hostile opinions and contrary principles upon the same soil.

The small influence of the American journals is attributable to several reasons, amongst which are the following:

The liberty of writing, like all other liberty, is most formidable when it is a novelty; for a people which has never been accustomed to co-operate in the conduct of State affairs places implicit confidence in the first tribune who arouses its attention. The Anglo-Americans have enjoyed this liberty ever since the foundation of the settlements; moreover, the press cannot create human passions by its own power, however skillfully it may kindle them where they exist. In America politics are discussed with animation and a varied activity, but they rarely touch those deep passions which are excited whenever the positive interest of a part of the community is impaired: but in the United States the interests of the community are in a most prosperous condition. A single glance upon a French and an American newspaper is sufficient to show the difference which exists between the two nations on this head. In France the space allotted to commercial advertisements is very limited, and the intelligence is not considerable, but the most essential part of the journal is that which contains the discussion of the politics of the day. In America three-quarters of the enormous sheet which is set before the reader are filled with advertisements, and the remainder is frequently occupied by political intelligence or trivial anecdotes: it is only from time to time that one finds a corner devoted to passionate discussions like those with which the journalists of France are wont to indulge their readers.

It has been demonstrated by observation, and discovered by the innate sagacity of the pettiest as well as the greatest of despots, that the influence of a power is increased in proportion as its direction is rendered

之举，因为他本人已经是国家的主宰，并可以随心所欲地将作家连同其作品一同处决。因此，在出版问题上，没有中庸之道。为了能够充分享受出版自由带来的莫大好处，必须要忍受它所带来的不可避免的痛苦。既要得到好处又要逃避痛苦是国家处于虚弱时期的惯有的错误认识。此时，国家已经疲于斗争，精力耗尽，想要找出一个能够让敌对观念和矛盾理论在同一片土地上共存的方式。

美国报刊的影响力之所以小有许多原因。部分原因列举如下：

与其他自由一样，写作自由在其最初出现之时令国家望而生畏，还不习惯和它一起讨论国家大事，人民盲目信任第一个出现的法院。自殖民地成立之初，英裔美国人一直享有这一自由。此外，尽管报刊可以煽风点火但是凭一己之力根本无法创造激情。在美国，政治生活虽然热烈而多变，但很少触碰因为正当利益受到损害而激起的强烈情绪，而且在美国这种利益最容易获得满足。只需看一眼美国和法国的报纸，就足以发现两国人就这一问题所存在的差异。在法国，商业广告的版面非常有限，商业消息也不多，绝大部分的版面都是有关时政的讨论。而在美国，整版的四分之三都是广告，其余部分则是政治新闻和短小的奇闻轶事。只有在一些不起眼的角落才能时不时地看到那些跟法国媒体呈献给读者的激情昂扬的讨论相同的内容。

通过观察已经证实，而且靠着自身与生俱来的智慧不管是最大还是最微不足道的暴君都已经发现，随着力量向一起集中，其影响力也就越大。在法国，报刊的集中是双重的，

more central. In France the press combines a twofold centralization; almost all its power is centred in the same spot, and vested in the same hands, for its organs are far from numerous. The influence of a public press thus constituted, upon a sceptical nation, must be unbounded. It is an enemy with which a Government may sign an occasional truce, but which it is difficult to resist for any length of time.

Neither of these kinds of centralization exists in America. The United States have no metropolis; the intelligence as well as the power of the country are dispersed abroad, and instead of radiating from a point, they cross each other in every direction; the Americans have established no central control over the expression of opinion, any more than over the conduct of business. These are circumstances which do not depend on human foresight; but it is owing to the laws of the Union that there are no licenses to be granted to printers, no securities demanded from editors as in France, and no stamp duty as in France and formerly in England. The consequence of this is that nothing is easier than to set up a newspaper, and a small number of readers suffices to defray the expenses of the editor.

The number of periodical and occasional publications which appears in the United States actually surpasses belief. The most enlightened Americans attribute the subordinate influence of the press to this excessive dissemination; and it is adopted as an axiom of political science in that country that the only way to neutralize the effect of public journals is to multiply them indefinitely. I cannot conceive that a truth which is so self-evident should not already have been more generally admitted in Europe; it is comprehensible that the persons who hope to bring about revolutions by means of the press should be desirous of confining its action to a few powerful organs, but it is perfectly incredible that the partisans of the existing state of things, and the natural supporters of the law, should attempt to diminish the influence of the press by concentrating its authority. The Governments of Europe seem to treat the press with the courtesy of the knights of old; they are anxious to furnish it with the same central power which they have found to be so trusty a weapon, in order to enhance the glory of their resistance to its attacks.

In America there is scarcely a hamlet which has not its own newspaper. It may readily be imagined that neither discipline nor unity of design can be communicated to so multifarious a host, and each one is consequently led to fight under his own standard. All the political journals of the United

一来其所有的力量都集中于一点，二来因为其机构为数很少，所以它们都掌握在同一些人手里。因此，在一个人人多疑的国家，报刊的影响力必然是无限的。它是政府的敌人，尽管政府也许可以跟它缔结一个临时的停战协定，但是要与其长期共处实属不易。

在美国并不存在我刚提到的任何一种集中。美国没有大城市，人力和物力散落在这片广袤的土地，智慧的光芒并非从一点发出照耀四方，而是交互生辉。美国人并没有为思想规定总的方向，也没有为工作制定总的方针。这些都是不以人们意志为转移的环境使然，而且根据联邦的法律，印刷无须取得执照，报刊也不用像在法国那样进行注册，更不用像在法国和以前的英格兰一样缴纳保证金。其结果就是，创办一份报纸轻而易举，而且只要有少量读者就足以应付其开销，所以美国定期期刊和半定期期刊的数量多得惊人。

最有教养的美国人都将报刊影响力之小归因于这种过度的分散。所以，在美国有这样一条政治学定理，如果想要削弱报刊的影响力，就要无限增加其数量。我无法理解，如此浅显的一个道理，为什么一直以来未能在欧洲得到普遍认可。因此，可以理解，打算借助报刊发动革命的人们自然想要将报刊的数量限制为强大的几种。但是，目前状态的拥护者和法律的天然支持者，想要通过将它们力量集中的方式来削弱其影响力，这样的做法的确让人觉得不可思议。欧洲各国好像在用古老骑士的翩翩风度对付报刊。它们迫不及待地将强有力的武器集中交到敌人手上，为的就是在将其击败之后能够获得更大的荣耀。

在美国，没有哪个小镇没有自己的报纸。所以一定可以想象，根本无法在数量如此

States are indeed arrayed on the side of the administration or against it; but they attack and defend in a thousand different ways. They cannot succeed in forming those great currents of opinion which overwhelm the most solid obstacles. This division of the influence of the press produces a variety of other consequences which are scarcely less remarkable. The facility with which journals can be established induces a multitude of individuals to take a part in them; but as the extent of competition precludes the possibility of considerable profit, the most distinguished classes of society are rarely led to engage in these undertakings. But such is the number of the public prints that, even if they were a source of wealth, writers of ability could not be found to direct them all. The journalists of the United States are usually placed in a very humble position, with a scanty education and a vulgar turn of mind. The will of the majority is the most general of laws, and it establishes certain habits which form the characteristics of each peculiar class of society; thus it dictates the etiquette practised at courts and the etiquette of the bar. The characteristics of the French journalist consist in a violent, but frequently an eloquent and lofty, manner of discussing the politics of the day; and the exceptions to this habitual practice are only occasional. The characteristics of the American journalist consist in an open and coarse appeal to the passions of the populace; and he habitually abandons the principles of political science to assail the characters of individuals, to track them into private life, and disclose all their weaknesses and errors.

Nothing can be more deplorable than this abuse of the powers of thought; I shall have occasion to point out hereafter the influence of the newspapers upon the taste and the morality of the American people, but my present subject exclusively concerns the political world. It cannot be denied that the effects of this extreme license of the press tend indirectly to the maintenance of public order. The individuals who are already in the possession of a high station in the esteem of their fellow-citizens are afraid to write in the newspapers, and they are thus deprived of the most powerful instrument which they can use to excite the passions of the multitude to their own advantage.

The personal opinions of the editors have no kind of weight in the eyes of the public: the only use of a journal is, that it imparts the knowledge of certain facts, and it is only by altering or distorting those facts that a journalist can contribute to the support of his own views.

众多的斗士中建立起秩序和统一的行动。结果，它们只能各自为政各显神通。的确，美国所有的政治期刊不是对政府表示支持就是表示反对，但是它们的攻守方式则千变万化。所以，它们无法形成足以冲垮最牢固堤坝的强大的思想洪流。报刊力量的分散还产生许多其他不容忽视的结果。办报容易，所以人人都办报，而竞争程度之激烈使得无法从办报获得丰厚的利润，所以社会精英很少从事这一行业。但是由于报刊数量众多，即使办报是生财之道，有才的作家也很难靠此发家。美国的报人一般地位卑微，教育程度有限，头脑不灵活。多数的愿望是最通用的法律，能形成特定的习惯，并成为每个特定社会阶层的宗旨，所以不但有律师业的宗旨还有法庭的宗旨。而法国报业的特点就是用猛烈的往往雄辩而又高尚的方式谈论国家大事，尽管也偶有例外。美国的报业特点则是用公开粗暴的方式激起人们的情绪，而且往往不是以理服人而是攻击其个人品德，追踪其私生活，从而将其弱点和错误揭露出来。

没有什么会比滥用思想力量更可悲的事情了。后面，我还有机会说一说报刊对美国人趣味和道德的影响，但目前的专题是政界。不可否认，对出版业采用这种极度放任的方式产生的效果，对维护公共秩序所起到的间接作用。在同胞心中占有崇高地位的人们不敢在报纸上发表文章，唯恐失去可激发起多数热情为其利益服务的最强有力的工具。

所以，报刊上的个人见解在公众眼里无足轻重，而报纸的唯一用处就是了解事实，所以只有通过改变和扭曲事实报道，撰稿人的观点才能产生一些影响。

But although the press is limited to these resources, its influence in America is immense. It is the power which impels the circulation of political life through all the districts of that vast territory. Its eye is constantly open to detect the secret springs of political designs, and to summon the leaders of all parties to the bar of public opinion. It rallies the interests of the community round certain principles, and it draws up the creed which factions adopt; for it affords a means of intercourse between parties which hear, and which address each other without ever having been in immediate contact. When a great number of the organs of the press adopt the same line of conduct, their influence becomes irresistible; and public opinion, when it is perpetually assailed from the same side, eventually yields to the attack. In the United States each separate journal exercises but little authority, but the power of the periodical press is only second to that of the people.

The opinions established in the United States under the empire of the liberty of the press are frequently more firmly rooted than those which are formed elsewhere under the sanction of a censor

In the United States the democracy perpetually raises fresh individuals to the conduct of public affairs; and the measures of the administration are consequently seldom regulated by the strict rules of consistency or of order. But the general principles of the Government are more stable, and the opinions most prevalent in society are generally more durable than in many other countries. When once the Americans have taken up an idea, whether it be well or ill founded, nothing is more difficult than to eradicate it from their minds. The same tenacity of opinion has been observed in England, where, for the last century, greater freedom of conscience and more invincible prejudices have existed than in all the other countries of Europe. I attribute this consequence to a cause which may at first sight appear to have a very opposite tendency, namely, to the liberty of the press. The nations amongst which this liberty exists are as apt to cling to their opinions from pride as from conviction. They cherish them because they hold them to be just, and because they exercised their own free-will in choosing them; and they maintain them not only because they are true, but because they are their own. Several other reasons conduce to the same end.

It was remarked by a man of genius that "ignorance lies at the two ends of knowledge." Perhaps

尽管美国的报刊只能做到这些，但是其影响力依然不容小觑。正是靠着它的力量，政治生活能够传播到这个地域辽阔国家的各处。它瞪大了眼睛查看政治的秘密动力，并将各党派领导关进舆论的监牢。它把人们的兴趣集中到某种主义，并为政党树立旗帜。它能够让彼此从未谋面的党派彼此对话，听到对方的声音。当大量的报纸走在同一条道路上，它们的影响力就变得无法抗拒，而对公共舆论而言，当不断受到来自同一方向的攻击，最终也会在其不断打击下屈服。美国的每一家报纸各自都有一点威力，而期刊的力量则仅次于人民的力量。

在美国出版自由环境下形成的观点往往比其他地方受监查制度影响而形成的观点更加根深蒂固

在美国，民主制度不断推出新人管理国家事务，所以政府的施政措施总是缺乏连贯性并难以按部就班。但是政府的总原则非常稳定，而且支配社会的舆论一般也比在其他国家更持久。当一种思想占据美国人的头脑，不管是对是错，就再也没有比将它们从头脑中赶走更困难的事情了。同样的事情也在英国发生，在过去的一百多年，更大的思想自由和牢不可破的偏见比在欧洲任何其他国家来得更甚。我将这一结果归因于乍看起来应该阻碍这一现象出现的趋势，即出版自由。实行这一自由的国家，自豪往往和信念一样影响着他们的见解。他们支持某种见解不但因为其合理，更因为是他们自己的选择。

it would have been more correct to have said, that absolute convictions are to be met with at the two extremities, and that doubt lies in the middle; for the human intellect may be considered in three distinct states, which frequently succeed one another. A man believes implicitly, because he adopts a proposition without inquiry. He doubts as soon as he is assailed by the objections which his inquiries may have aroused. But he frequently succeeds in satisfying these doubts, and then he begins to believe afresh: he no longer lays hold on a truth in its most shadowy and uncertain form, but he sees it clearly before him, and he advances onwards by the light it gives him.

When the liberty of the press acts upon men who are in the first of these three states, it does not immediately disturb their habit of believing implicitly without investigation, but it constantly modifies the objects of their intuitive convictions. The human mind continues to discern but one point upon the whole intellectual horizon, and that point is in continual motion. Such are the symptoms of sudden revolutions, and of the misfortunes which are sure to befall those generations which abruptly adopt the unconditional freedom of the press.

The circle of novel ideas is, however, soon terminated; the touch of experience is upon them, and the doubt and mistrust which their uncertainty produces become universal. We may rest assured that the majority of mankind will either believe they know not wherefore, or will not know what to believe. Few are the beings who can ever hope to attain to that state of rational and independent conviction which true knowledge can beget in defiance of the attacks of doubt.

It has been remarked that in times of great religious fervor men sometimes change their religious opinions; whereas in times of general scepticism everyone clings to his own persuasion. The same thing takes place in politics under the liberty of the press. In countries where all the theories of social science have been contested in their turn, the citizens who have adopted one of them stick to it, not so much because they are assured of its excellence, as because they are not convinced of the superiority of any other. In the present age men are not very ready to die in defence of their opinions, but they are rarely inclined to change them; and there are fewer martyrs as well as fewer apostates.

Another still more valid reason may yet be adduced: when no abstract opinions are looked upon as

还有一些其他原因会导致同样的结果。

一位伟人曾经说过"无知处于知识的两端。"如果说自信处于两端而怀疑处在中间也许更为正确。因为可以认为人类智力的发展清楚地分成前后衔接的三个阶段。一个人之所以对某事坚定不移，因为他未经探究便接受这一主张，但是当异议出现的时候，便开始怀疑；在成功地将这些怀疑一一克服的时候，又开始重新笃信。这次他不再随便相信真理，他仔细观察并紧随真理之光前进。

当出版自由作用到处于第一阶段的人们身上，并不能立即对他们不经深思熟虑便深信不疑的习惯发挥作用，但却可以逐渐改变他们轻信的对象。在人类智力整个发展过程中，人类只能一次一点的向前发展，而且被认识的那一点也在不断改变。这就是革命突发的征兆，而且不幸必然会降临到最初采纳无条件出版自由的那几代人身上。

然而，不久一批新的思想又接踵而至，人们因为有了经验，怀疑和不确定性带来的不信任开始普遍。我们可以确定，大多数人不是信而不知其所以，就是不知道该信什么。而那些来自真知和敢于冲破怀疑的干扰的深思熟虑的自信，以及对这种自信的主宰，只有寥寥无几的人能够具备。

也有人指出，在宗教狂热的时代，人们有时会改变宗教信仰。然而在人们普遍怀疑的时代，人们则会坚持己见。同样的事情也见于出版自由风行时的政治。在那些所有社会科学理论被轮番质疑的国家，公民会坚持自己所相信的理论。其原因并不是因为笃信它的卓越，而是因为无法确定还有比它更好的理论。当前，人们不会轻易为保卫自己的主张而献

certain, men cling to the mere propensities and external interests of their position, which are naturally more tangible and more permanent than any opinions in the world.

It is not a question of easy solution whether aristocracy or democracy is most fit to govern a country. But it is certain that democracy annoys one part of the community, and that aristocracy oppresses another part. When the question is reduced to the simple expression of the struggle between poverty and wealth, the tendency of each side of the dispute becomes perfectly evident without further controversy.

身，但也不会轻易改变，所以殉道者和变节者都很少见。

还有一个更加强有力的理由需要补充：当人们无法确信任何一个抽象的主张时，便开始只执著于自己的偏好和物质利益，这些自然比世界上任何的主张都更容易感知，更持久。

一个国家究竟是采用民主制还是贵族制更适合，是一个难以解答的问题。但可以肯定的是民主制必然会让一部分人不快，而贵族制必定会使另一部分人受压迫。当这个问题被简单化说成贫富之间的斗争，便成了自行成立无须争辩的真理。

Chapter XII: Political Associations In The United States

Chapter Summary

Daily use which the Anglo-Americans make of the right of association—Three kinds of political associations—In what manner the Americans apply the representative system to associations—Dangers resulting to the State—Great Convention of 1831 relative to the Tariff—Legislative character of this Convention—Why the unlimited exercise of the right of association is less dangerous in the United States than elsewhere—Why it may be looked upon as necessary—Utility of associations in a democratic people.

Political Associations In The United States

In no country in the world has the principle of association been more successfully used, or more unsparingly applied to a multitude of different objects, than in America. Besides the permanent associations which are established by law under the names of townships, cities, and counties, a vast number of others are formed and maintained by the agency of private individuals.

The citizen of the United States is taught from his earliest infancy to rely upon his own exertions in order to resist the evils and the difficulties of life; he looks upon social authority with an eye of mistrust and anxiety, and he only claims its assistance when he is quite unable to shift without it. This habit may even be traced in the schools of the rising generation, where the children in their games are wont to submit to rules which they have themselves established, and to punish misdemeanors which

第十二章　美国的政治社团

本章提要

英裔美国人对结社权的日常应用——三种政治社团——美国人如何将代议制引入社团——这给国家带来的危险——1831年关税问题大会——大会的立法性质——为什么社团权力的无限使用对美国的危险比其他国家小——为什么可以将这样做法视为必要——社团在民主国家的功用。

美国的政治社团

世界上没有任何一个国家能够比美国更便于组党结社，并将这一强大的行动手段用于各种不同目的。除了那些依法以乡镇、城市和郡县名义成立的常设社团外，还有大量其他个人成立并维持的社团。

美国的公民从孩提时代就被教育要依靠自己对抗不幸和生活中的困难。他们对社会当局投以不信任和怀疑的目光，而且只在迫不得已的时候才会向其求助。他们从上小学开始

they have themselves defined. The same spirit pervades every act of social life. If a stoppage occurs in a thoroughfare, and the circulation of the public is hindered, the neighbors immediately constitute a deliberative body; and this extemporaneous assembly gives rise to an executive power which remedies the inconvenience before anybody has thought of recurring to an authority superior to that of the persons immediately concerned. If the public pleasures are concerned, an association is formed to provide for the splendor and the regularity of the entertainment. Societies are formed to resist enemies which are exclusively of a moral nature, and to diminish the vice of intemperance: in the United States associations are established to promote public order, commerce, industry, morality, and religion; for there is no end which the human will, seconded by the collective exertions of individuals, despairs of attaining.

I shall hereafter have occasion to show the effects of association upon the course of society, and I must confine myself for the present to the political world. When once the right of association is recognized, the citizens may employ it in several different ways.

An association consists simply in the public assent which a number of individuals give to certain doctrines, and in the engagement which they contract to promote the spread of those doctrines by their exertions. The right of association with these views is very analogous to the liberty of unlicensed writing; but societies thus formed possess more authority than the press. When an opinion is represented by a society, it necessarily assumes a more exact and explicit form. It numbers its partisans, and compromises their welfare in its cause: they, on the other hand, become acquainted with each other, and their zeal is increased by their number. An association unites the efforts of minds which have a tendency to diverge in one single channel, and urges them vigorously towards one single end which it points out.

The second degree in the right of association is the power of meeting. When an association is allowed to establish centres of action at certain important points in the country, its activity is increased and its influence extended. Men have the opportunity of seeing each other; means of execution are more readily combined, and opinions are maintained with a degree of warmth and energy which written language cannot approach.

Lastly, in the exercise of the right of political association, there is a third degree: the partisans

就培养这种习惯。在游戏中，孩子们不会违背自己制定的规则，并对触犯其制定的规则的行为加以处罚。这种精神遍及社会生活方方面面。假如公路上出现阻塞，车辆行人无法正常通行，周边的人就会立即自行组织起一个审议团体。这些临时聚集起来的人会选出一个执行机构，在没有人向有关主管部门报告之前，就开始自行解决问题。如果是与公众庆祝集会有关，就会成立活动小组，让节目增辉活动规范。还有一些协会组织成立旨在反对各种各样的道德败坏。在美国，协会的成立就是要促进公共秩序、商业、工业、道德以及宗教。人们的愿望必然可以通过私人组织的强大集体的活动得到满足。

后面，我还有机会对社团对公民生活的影响进行说明，而这里我要讲的是政界。当社团的权利一旦被认可，公民就可以用不同的方式去运用。

简单地说，一个社团是由一群对某种学说或主张表示一致赞同的人组成，并约定努力推广他们的学说。结社权同写作自由基本没有什么不同，但是早先成立的社团却拥有比出版业更大的力量。当一个观点由社团做代表，其形式必须简单明确。社团要有自己的追随者，而且他们还要愿意为社团的事业而牺牲。另一方面，支持者们彼此相识后，热情也会随着人数的增加而高涨。社团把人们的精神力量集中起来，并将它们导入同一轨道，让它们朝其指引的同一方向精神饱满地前进。

结社权的第二阶段是集会权。当一个政治社团将其行动中心设立在国内一个重要地点时，其活动会增多，影响力随之扩大。人们有更多的机会碰面，所以各种执行手段能够结

of an opinion may unite in electoral bodies, and choose delegates to represent them in a central assembly. This is, properly speaking, the application of the representative system to a party.

Thus, in the first instance, a society is formed between individuals professing the same opinion, and the tie which keeps it together is of a purely intellectual nature; in the second case, small assemblies are formed which only represent a fraction of the party. Lastly, in the third case, they constitute a separate nation in the midst of the nation, a government within the Government. Their delegates, like the real delegates of the majority, represent the entire collective force of their party; and they enjoy a certain degree of that national dignity and great influence which belong to the chosen representatives of the people. It is true that they have not the right of making the laws, but they have the power of attacking those which are in being, and of drawing up beforehand those which they may afterwards cause to be adopted.

If, in a people which is imperfectly accustomed to the exercise of freedom, or which is exposed to violent political passions, a deliberating minority, which confines itself to the contemplation of future laws, be placed in juxtaposition to the legislative majority, I cannot but believe that public tranquillity incurs very great risks in that nation. There is doubtless a very wide difference between proving that one law is in itself better than another and proving that the former ought to be substituted for the latter. But the imagination of the populace is very apt to overlook this difference, which is so apparent to the minds of thinking men. It sometimes happens that a nation is divided into two nearly equal parties, each of which affects to represent the majority. If, in immediate contiguity to the directing power, another power be established, which exercises almost as much moral authority as the former, it is not to be believed that it will long be content to speak without acting; or that it will always be restrained by the abstract consideration of the nature of associations which are meant to direct but not to enforce opinions, to suggest but not to make the laws.

The more we consider the independence of the press in its principal consequences, the more are we convinced that it is the chief and, so to speak, the constitutive element of freedom in the modern world. A nation which is determined to remain free is therefore right in demanding the unrestrained exercise of this independence. But the unrestrained liberty of political association cannot be entirely

合使用，思想的热度持续不减，这是语言所无法达到的。

最后，政治社团权利的行使还有第三个阶段：同一观点的追随者们，可以团结成为选举团，选出代表到中央立法机构代表本社团。毋庸置疑，这就是在政党中应用代议制。

所以，首先，社团是将拥护同一主张的个人联系起来的形式，其联系纽带就是思想。第二，小团体代表的只是本党的一个派系。第三，他们建立的是国中国，政府中的政府。它们的代表就像真正的多数代表一样，代表其党派的集体力量。它们也享有一定程度的国家荣誉并对其所代表的人民有着巨大的影响力。的确，它们没有权力制定法律，但是它们有权声讨现有法律，并协助起草以后也许会被采纳的法律。

在一个不习惯利用自由的国家，或是政治激情四溢的国家，如果立法多数的身边只有一个负责审议和监督的少数，那么我就必然认为这个国家的公共安宁必然处于极大的危机之中。毫无疑问，证明一条法律优于另一条，和证明一条法律应被另一条取代，有极大的不同。但是人们的想象非常容易忽视这一不同，尽管智者对此看得很明白。所以，有时候一个国家会刚好分成势力均等的两派，每一派都希望自己成为多数的代表。如果在领导力量的身边再出现另一个几乎与其力量相当的道义力量，无法相信它会长此以往的只说不做，或是长期受制于社团的性质，只做抽象思考提出建议而不去制定法律。

对出版自由的成果研究得越深入，就越会感到它是现代世界自由的主要成分，或是说组成要素。因此，一个决心捍卫自由的国家，要求全力尊重自由是正确的。但是政治结社

assimilated to the liberty of the press. The one is at the same time less necessary and more dangerous than the other. A nation may confine it within certain limits without forfeiting any part of its self-control; and it may sometimes be obliged to do so in order to maintain its own authority.

In America the liberty of association for political purposes is unbounded. An example will show in the clearest light to what an extent this privilege is tolerated.

The question of the tariff, or of free trade, produced a great manifestation of party feeling in America; the tariff was not only a subject of debate as a matter of opinion, but it exercised a favorable or a prejudicial influence upon several very powerful interests of the States. The North attributed a great portion of its prosperity, and the South all its sufferings, to this system; insomuch that for a long time the tariff was the sole source of the political animosities which agitated the Union.

In 1831, when the dispute was raging with the utmost virulence, a private citizen of Massachusetts proposed to all the enemies of the tariff, by means of the public prints, to send delegates to Philadelphia in order to consult together upon the means which were most fitted to promote freedom of trade. This proposal circulated in a few days from Maine to New Orleans by the power of the printing-press: the opponents of the tariff adopted it with enthusiasm; meetings were formed on all sides, and delegates were named. The majority of these individuals were well known, and some of them had earned a considerable degree of celebrity. South Carolina alone, which afterwards took up arms in the same cause, sent sixty-three delegates. On October 1, 1831, this assembly, which according to the American custom had taken the name of a Convention, met at Philadelphia; it consisted of more than two hundred members. Its debates were public, and they at once assumed a legislative character; the extent of the powers of Congress, the theories of free trade, and the different clauses of the tariff, were discussed in turn. At the end of ten days' deliberation the Convention broke up, after having published an address to the American people, in which it declared:

I. That Congress had not the right of making a tariff, and that the existing tariff was unconstitutional;

II. That the prohibition of free trade was prejudicial to the interests of all nations, and to that of the American people in particular.

的无限自由，并不完全等同于出版自由。前者的必要性不如后者，而且危险系数也更高。国家应该对结社自由加以约束，让其处于自己的掌控之中。为了要维护自己的权威，国家有时候必须这样做。

在美国，以政治为目的的结社自由是无限的。举一个例子可以清楚地说明其权力被扩大到何种程度。

关税问题，或者说自由贸易在美国曾引发人们极大的冲动。关税不但是人们热议的话题，并对每个州的重大物质利益产生有利或负面的影响。北方将其繁荣的部分原因归功于关税制度，而在南方它则成为灾难的根源。所以很长一段时间以来，关税问题成为让联邦不得安宁的政治敌对的唯一根源。

1831年，当这一争端处在最激烈的时刻，马萨诸塞州的一个公民想出一个办法，通过报纸向关税反对者提议，请他们派代表来费城共同商讨恢复自由贸易的最佳方案。凭借媒体的力量，没几天这个提议便从缅因传到新奥尔良。对此，关税反对者反响热烈，从各地迅速集合起来并选出代表。这些代表都是知名人士，有些还是赫赫有名的大人物。后来为解决这个问题而诉诸武力的南卡罗来纳州，仅它一个州就派去63名代表。1831年10月1日，一个根据美国人习惯称为全国人民代表大会的会议在费城召开，与会成员超过200人。他们公开辩论，而且这个大会自开幕之日起就具有立法性质。会上对国会的职权范围、自由贸易理论以及关税的不同条款逐一进行讨论。在经过十天的商议并发表一封至美国人民的信

It must be acknowledged that the unrestrained liberty of political association has not hitherto produced, in the United States, those fatal consequences which might perhaps be expected from it elsewhere. The right of association was imported from England, and it has always existed in America; so that the exercise of this privilege is now amalgamated with the manners and customs of the people. At the present time the liberty of association is become a necessary guarantee against the tyranny of the majority. In the United States, as soon as a party is become preponderant, all public authority passes under its control; its private supporters occupy all the places, and have all the force of the administration at their disposal. As the most distinguished partisans of the other side of the question are unable to surmount the obstacles which exclude them from power, they require some means of establishing themselves upon their own basis, and of opposing the moral authority of the minority to the physical power which domineers over it. Thus a dangerous expedient is used to obviate a still more formidable danger.

The omnipotence of the majority appears to me to present such extreme perils to the American Republics that the dangerous measure which is used to repress it seems to be more advantageous than prejudicial. And here I am about to advance a proposition which may remind the reader of what I said before in speaking of municipal freedom: There are no countries in which associations are more needed, to prevent the despotism of faction or the arbitrary power of a prince, than those which are democratically constituted. In aristocratic nations the body of the nobles and the more opulent part of the community are in themselves natural associations, which act as checks upon the abuses of power. In countries in which these associations do not exist, if private individuals are unable to create an artificial and a temporary substitute for them, I can imagine no permanent protection against the most galling tyranny; and a great people may be oppressed by a small faction, or by a single individual, with impunity.

The meeting of a great political Convention (for there are Conventions of all kinds), which may frequently become a necessary measure, is always a serious occurrence, even in America, and one which is never looked forward to, by the judicious friends of the country, without alarm. This was

后，大会落下帷幕。在这封信中，写道：

Ⅰ 国会无权制定关税，现行关税违宪。

Ⅱ 禁止自由贸易不符合任何国家的利益，特别是美国。

必须承认，迄今为止无限制的政治结社自由在美国并没有产生有可能在其他地方出现的致命后果。美国的结社权从英格兰引进，并一直留存下来，所以现在，行使结社权已成为美国人的风尚和习惯。如今，结社自由已经成为与多数暴政对抗的必要保障。在美国，一旦一个政党占据统治地位，所有大权都落入其手，于是其党徒会把持所有职位，掌握所有行政力量。反对党最德高望重的人物也无法逾越阻碍他们取得权力的障碍，所以反对党只能在野，并用少数的道义力量对抗打压他们的强大物质力量。这是用一种危险的权宜之计去消除另一种更可怕的危险。

在我看来多数的无限权威给美国共和制度带来的危险极大，以至于用来遏制它的危险手段似乎还更好一些。这里我要提出一个想法，可能会让读者想起我在前面谈到乡镇自由时说过的内容。在我看来，没有哪类国家会比民主国家更需要结社自由来防止政党专制或一人专权。在贵族制国家，贵族阶级是防止权力滥用的天然社团。而在没有这样阶层存在的国家，如果人们无法随时创立类似的团体，在我看来没有可以保护自己免于暴政的屏障。所以，在这样的国家，不是一小撮人压迫大多数人，就是一个人独裁统治。

往往能够成为必要手段的政治大会（有各种人参加），始终都是重大事件，而且即使是一个国家头脑最精明的人们也从不对此期盼，即使在美国也是如此。这一点在1831年

very perceptible in the Convention of 1831, at which the exertions of all the most distinguished members of the Assembly tended to moderate its language, and to restrain the subjects which it treated within certain limits. It is probable, in fact, that the Convention of 1831 exercised a very great influence upon the minds of the malcontents, and prepared them for the open revolt against the commercial laws of the Union which took place in 1832.

It cannot be denied that the unrestrained liberty of association for political purposes is the privilege which a people is longest in learning how to exercise. If it does not throw the nation into anarchy, it perpetually augments the chances of that calamity. On one point, however, this perilous liberty offers a security against dangers of another kind; in countries where associations are free, secret societies are unknown. In America there are numerous factions, but no conspiracies.

Different ways in which the right of association is understood in Europe and in the United States—Different use which is made of it

The most natural privilege of man, next to the right of acting for himself, is that of combining his exertions with those of his fellow-creatures, and of acting in common with them. I am therefore led to conclude that the right of association is almost as inalienable as the right of personal liberty. No legislator can attack it without impairing the very foundations of society. Nevertheless, if the liberty of association is a fruitful source of advantages and prosperity to some nations, it may be perverted or carried to excess by others, and the element of life may be changed into an element of destruction. A comparison of the different methods which associations pursue in those countries in which they are managed with discretion, as well as in those where liberty degenerates into license, may perhaps be thought useful both to governments and to parties.

The greater part of Europeans look upon an association as a weapon which is to be hastily fashioned, and immediately tried in the conflict. A society is formed for discussion, but the idea of impending action prevails in the minds of those who constitute it: it is, in fact, an army; and the time given to parley serves to reckon up the strength and to animate the courage of the host, after which

的大会期间表现得最为明显。参加会议的那些声名显赫的大人物，发言时尽量保持语言温和，并将发言内容限定在规定的范围。实际上，1831年的大会对那些不要现状的人影响相当大，并促使他们在1832年对商业法发起公然反抗。

不可否认，人们需要很长时间才能知道如何行使带有政治目的结社自由。如果说它没有让人民陷入无政府状态，至少可以说它时刻让人民处于这种危机状态的可能性之中。然而，这种危险的自由却在一点上给了另一种危险以安全保障。在结社自由的国家，没有秘密社团。在美国，派别甚多，却没有阴谋造反。

欧洲和美国对结社权的不同理解——由此而产生的对结社权的不同使用

仅次于人类自由活动权的最天然的权利是人们把自己的力量和自己同志的力量联合起来共同行动的自由。所以，我的结论是结社权几乎与个人自由权一样不可剥夺。只要立法者对其发起攻击，必会动摇社会的根基。然而，如果结社自由是某些国家繁荣进步之源，那么它也会被另一些国家歪曲和滥用，这样它的积极因素就会变成破坏因素。对比一下正确理解自由的国家和滥用自由的国家各自社团所采用的不同方法，对政府和政党都有好处。

大多数欧洲人将结社看成匆忙成立并要马上用于斗争的武器。社团的成立为的是讨论，但是匆忙的行动冲昏了社团创办人的头脑。实际上，社团就成了一支军队。花时间商议就是要积聚力量鼓舞士气，然后让他们冲向敌人。在他们的眼中，合法的手段纵然可以

they direct their march against the enemy. Resources which lie within the bounds of the law may suggest themselves to the persons who compose it as means, but never as the only means, of success.

Such, however, is not the manner in which the right of association is understood in the United States. In America the citizens who form the minority associate, in order, in the first place, to show their numerical strength, and so to diminish the moral authority of the majority; and, in the second place, to stimulate competition, and to discover those arguments which are most fitted to act upon the majority; for they always entertain hopes of drawing over their opponents to their own side, and of afterwards disposing of the supreme power in their name. Political associations in the United States are therefore peaceable in their intentions, and strictly legal in the means which they employ; and they assert with perfect truth that they only aim at success by lawful expedients.

The difference which exists between the Americans and ourselves depends on several causes. In Europe there are numerous parties so diametrically opposed to the majority that they can never hope to acquire its support, and at the same time they think that they are sufficiently strong in themselves to struggle and to defend their cause. When a party of this kind forms an association, its object is, not to conquer, but to fight. In America the individuals who hold opinions very much opposed to those of the majority are no sort of impediment to its power, and all other parties hope to win it over to their own principles in the end. The exercise of the right of association becomes dangerous in proportion to the impossibility which excludes great parties from acquiring the majority. In a country like the United States, in which the differences of opinion are mere differences of hue, the right of association may remain unrestrained without evil consequences. The inexperience of many of the European nations in the enjoyment of liberty leads them only to look upon the liberty of association as a right of attacking the Government. The first notion which presents itself to a party, as well as to an individual, when it has acquired a consciousness of its own strength, is that of violence: the notion of persuasion arises at a later period and is only derived from experience. The English, who are divided into parties which differ most essentially from each other, rarely abuse the right of association, because they have long been accustomed to exercise it. In France the passion for war is

取得成功，但绝非走向成功的唯一之路。

但是，这并不是美国人所理解的结社权。在美国，公民之所以结成少数社团，其目的，首先是要显示他们的力量并从而削弱多数的道义权威。其次是要鼓励竞争从而发现最能打动多数的论点。因为他们一直希望能把敌人拉到自己一边，之后以多数名义行使无上的权力。因此，在美国政治结社的宗旨是和平，并严格采用合法方式。他们诚实地宣称要依靠法律手段获胜。

美国人之所以和我们存在不同，有下列一些原因。在欧洲，许多政党对多数的反对极度激烈，以至于他们永远不能指望得到多数的支持，而且同时，他们也自认为力量足够强大能够为自己的事业斗争并捍卫它。当这种政党成立社团的时候，其目的不是征服而是战斗。在美国，与多数意见大相径庭的派别绝对不会成为多数权力的障碍，因为其他所有的党派都想要拉拢多数。所以，大党越是不可能成为多数，结社权的行使就越没有危险。在一个像美国这样的国家，观点的不同不过是程度的差异，所以结社权可以自由存在下去而且也不会产生严重的后果。许多欧洲国家因为在行使结社权上没有经验，导致他们将结社自由视为攻击政府的权利。无论是对一个个人还是对一个政党，当他意识到自己的力量，第一反应就是要靠蛮力取胜，而说服他人的念头只有在获得经验之后才会出现。因彼此意见分歧而分成不同党派的英国人，很少滥用结社权，因为他们对结社权的行使经验丰富。而在法国，战争的热情如此高涨以至于凡是有关国家安危的事情人们都会疯狂f 参与其中，以至于人们认为只有用生命来捍卫它才是无上的光荣。

so intense that there is no undertaking so mad, or so injurious to the welfare of the State, that a man does not consider himself honored in defending it, at the risk of his life.

But perhaps the most powerful of the causes which tend to mitigate the excesses of political association in the United States is Universal Suffrage. In countries in which universal suffrage exists the majority is never doubtful, because neither party can pretend to represent that portion of the community which has not voted. The associations which are formed are aware, as well as the nation at large, that they do not represent the majority: this is, indeed, a condition inseparable from their existence; for if they did represent the preponderating power, they would change the law instead of soliciting its reform. The consequence of this is that the moral influence of the Government which they attack is very much increased, and their own power is very much enfeebled.

In Europe there are few associations which do not affect to represent the majority, or which do not believe that they represent it. This conviction or this pretension tends to augment their force amazingly, and contributes no less to legalize their measures. Violence may seem to be excusable in defence of the cause of oppressed right. Thus it is, in the vast labyrinth of human laws, that extreme liberty sometimes corrects the abuses of license, and that extreme democracy obviates the dangers of democratic government. In Europe, associations consider themselves, in some degree, as the legislative and executive councils of the people, which is unable to speak for itself. In America, where they only represent a minority of the nation, they argue and they petition.

The means which the associations of Europe employ are in accordance with the end which they propose to obtain. As the principal aim of these bodies is to act, and not to debate, to fight rather than to persuade, they are naturally led to adopt a form of organization which differs from the ordinary customs of civil bodies, and which assumes the habits and the maxims of military life. They centralize the direction of their resources as much as possible, and they intrust the power of the whole party to a very small number of leaders.

The members of these associations respond to a watchword, like soldiers on duty; they profess the doctrine of passive obedience; say rather, that in uniting together they at once abjure the exercise of

但是，在美国让过度政治结社缓和下来的最有力的因素也许就是普选权。在实行普选的国家里，多数不会受到质疑，因为没有哪个政党能够假冒没给他们投票的那部分人的代表。因此，每个社团知道，而且人民大众也知道，那样的党不代表多数。这正是它们存在的本身所决定的。因为如果它们真的代表多数，就可以改变法律而无须恳求进行改革。其结果就是受到它们攻击的政府的道义力量会得到大大加强，而它们自己的力量则会大大削弱。

在欧洲，几乎没有哪个社团不自认或是相信自己就是多数的代表。这种信念或是自负往往会让它们的力量变得惊人的强大，从而使它们的手段合法化。为了捍卫受压迫的权利，诉诸暴力似乎情有可原。因此，在人类错综复杂浩瀚的行动准则中，有时候极度自由反而能纠正自由的滥用，而极端的民主则可以规避民主政府的危险。在欧洲，社团在某种程度上将自己视为国家的立法和行政机构，只不过它不能发表意见。而在美国，社团只代表国家中的少数，他们需要争辩和恳求。

欧洲社团所采用的方式和它们要取得的目的是一致的。因为这些团体的主要目的就是行动而不是空谈，是战斗而不是劝说，所以它们自然会采用一种不同于普通民间团体习惯的组织形式，让其具有军事习惯和准则。它们将可以动用的资源尽可能的集中起来，并将政党所有的权力交到为数不多的几名政党领导手中。

这些社团的成员好像服役的士兵一样按命令行事。与其说他们信奉被动服从的理论，不如说他们一团结起来就立即放弃自己的判断力和自由意志。所以，社团内部的专制统治

their own judgment and free will; and the tyrannical control which these societies exercise is often far more insupportable than the authority possessed over society by the Government which they attack. Their moral force is much diminished by these excesses, and they lose the powerful interest which is always excited by a struggle between oppressors and the oppressed. The man who in given cases consents to obey his fellows with servility, and who submits his activity and even his opinions to their control, can have no claim to rank as a free citizen.

The Americans have also established certain forms of government which are applied to their associations, but these are invariably borrowed from the forms of the civil administration. The independence of each individual is formally recognized; the tendency of the members of the association points, as it does in the body of the community, towards the same end, but they are not obliged to follow the same track. No one abjures the exercise of his reason and his free will; but every one exerts that reason and that will for the benefit of a common undertaking.

往往比他们所攻击的政府对社会所实行的专制更让人难以忍受。这样的做法就大大削弱了它们的道义力量，也就失去了被压迫者反对压迫者的斗争所能得到的权力利益。满足于在特定场合卑躬屈膝听命于其几个同伙的人，并将其活动乃至思想纳于他们控制之下的人，又怎会称得上是自由公民呢？

美国人也在其社团内部成立某种形式的政府组织，而且都不约而同地借用了民间管理的形式。在社团中，个人的独立得到正式认可，就好像在社会里一样，社团里的成员们朝着同一目标前进，但并不一定要循着同样的轨迹。没有人会放弃自己的理性和自由意志，而且每个人都会运用自己的理性和意志成就共同事业的利益。

Chapter XIII: Government Of The Democracy In America—Part I

I am well aware of the difficulties which attend this part of my subject, but although every expression which I am about to make use of may clash, upon some one point, with the feelings of the different parties which divide my country, I shall speak my opinion with the most perfect openness.

In Europe we are at a loss how to judge the true character and the more permanent propensities of democracy, because in Europe two conflicting principles exist, and we do not know what to attribute to the principles themselves, and what to refer to the passions which they bring into collision. Such, however, is not the case in America; there the people reigns without any obstacle, and it has no perils to dread and no injuries to avenge. In America, democracy is swayed by its own free propensities; its course is natural and its activity is unrestrained; the United States consequently afford the most favorable opportunity of studying its real character. And to no people can this inquiry be more vitally interesting than to the French nation, which is blindly driven onwards by a daily and irresistible impulse towards a state of things which may prove either despotic or republican, but which will assuredly be democratic.

Universal Suffrage

I have already observed that universal suffrage has been adopted in all the States of the Union; it consequently occurs amongst different populations which occupy very different positions in the scale

第十三章　美国的民主政府

我已经充分意识在这一部分的讨论中会碰到一些困难。尽管我要说的每句话可能会在某些方面会让那些造成我国分裂的政党的感情受到冲击，但我还是会以最坦诚的方式表达我的观点。

在欧洲，我们不知道如何判断民主的本质和其不变的倾向。因为在欧洲有两种相互矛盾的原理存在，而我们不知道哪些是出自这些原理本身，哪些又来自它们冲撞所衍生的激情。而在美国，则没有这样的问题。在这里，人民的统治毫无障碍，没有需要担心的危险，也没有需要报复的伤痛。在美国，民主会随其所好自己摇摆，自然而然地行事，活动不受任何限制，所以美国掌握最有利的研究其本质的机会。然而，这项研究带给法国的好处远远多于任何一个国家，因为法国每天都在一种不可抗拒的推动力的作用下盲目前进，到底是走向专制还是走向共和？但社会必然要走向民主。

普选权

我已经注意到在美国各州都实行普选制，所以无论社会地位如何，人人享有这项权

of society. I have had opportunities of observing its effects in different localities, and amongst races of men who are nearly strangers to each other by their language, their religion, and their manner of life; in Louisiana as well as in New England, in Georgia and in Canada. I have remarked that Universal Suffrage is far from producing in America either all the good or all the evil consequences which are assigned to it in Europe, and that its effects differ very widely from those which are usually attributed to it.

Choice Of The People, And Instinctive Preferences Of The American Democracy

In the United States the most able men are rarely placed at the head of affairs—Reason of this peculiarity—The envy which prevails in the lower orders of France against the higher classes is not a French, but a purely democratic sentiment—For what reason the most distinguished men in America frequently seclude themselves from public affairs.

Many people in Europe are apt to believe without saying it, or to say without believing it, that one of the great advantages of universal suffrage is, that it entrusts the direction of public affairs to men who are worthy of the public confidence. They admit that the people is unable to govern for itself, but they aver that it is always sincerely disposed to promote the welfare of the State, and that it instinctively designates those persons who are animated by the same good wishes, and who are the most fit to wield the supreme authority. I confess that the observations I made in America by no means coincide with these opinions. On my arrival in the United States I was surprised to find so much distinguished talent among the subjects, and so little among the heads of the Government. It is a well-authenticated fact, that at the present day the most able men in the United States are very rarely placed at the head of affairs; and it must be acknowledged that such has been the result in proportion as democracy has outstepped all its former limits. The race of American statesmen has evidently dwindled most remarkably in the course of the last fifty years.

Several causes may be assigned to this phenomenon. It is impossible, notwithstanding the most

利。我有幸可以在不同的地区和语言、宗教及生活方式几乎全然不同的陌生的种族之间，以及路易斯安那和新英格兰，佐治亚和加拿大，看到普选权的实施效果。我曾经说过，普选权在美国远没有产生它在欧洲所产生的所有善和恶，而且其实施效果也与我们想象中的大不相同。

人民的选择和美国民主的本能偏好

在美国，最有能力的人很少出任公职——这种特殊现象产生的原因——法国下层阶级对上层阶级普遍存在的嫉妒心并非法国人所独有，而只是一种渴望民主的感情——出于何种原因美国的精英总是远离政界。

在欧洲，很多人尽管嘴上不说但心里相信，或是嘴上说心里却不信普选权的最大优势之一在于将公共事务委托给最受人民信任的人处理。他们认为人民无法自治，但是人民真心希望国家繁荣富强，这就本能地驱使他们推举与其有相同愿望且善于运用大权的人主持政务。我得承认我在美国的所见所闻完全不符合这些看法。一到美国我就惊讶地发现平民中名流才俊比比皆是，而政府中则寥寥无几。这已经是不争的事实，今天美国最具能力的人才很少去当官，而且必须承认，这是民主超越其原来所有界限而产生的结果。美国政治世家的减少在过去的这半个世纪表现得最为明显。

之所以会出现这样的现象有下面几个原因。尽管已经做出最大的努力，但依然无法使

strenuous exertions, to raise the intelligence of the people above a certain level. Whatever may be the facilities of acquiring information, whatever may be the profusion of easy methods and of cheap science, the human mind can never be instructed and educated without devoting a considerable space of time to those objects.

The greater or the lesser possibility of subsisting without labor is therefore the necessary boundary of intellectual improvement. This boundary is more remote in some countries and more restricted in others; but it must exist somewhere as long as the people is constrained to work in order to procure the means of physical subsistence, that is to say, as long as it retains its popular character. It is therefore quite as difficult to imagine a State in which all the citizens should be very well informed as a State in which they should all be wealthy; these two difficulties may be looked upon as correlative. It may very readily be admitted that the mass of the citizens are sincerely disposed to promote the welfare of their country; nay more, it may even be allowed that the lower classes are less apt to be swayed by considerations of personal interest than the higher orders: but it is always more or less impossible for them to discern the best means of attaining the end which they desire with sincerity. Long and patient observation, joined to a multitude of different notions, is required to form a just estimate of the character of a single individual; and can it be supposed that the vulgar have the power of succeeding in an inquiry which misleads the penetration of genius itself? The people has neither the time nor the means which are essential to the prosecution of an investigation of this kind: its conclusions are hastily formed from a superficial inspection of the more prominent features of a question. Hence it often assents to the clamor of a mountebank who knows the secret of stimulating its tastes, while its truest friends frequently fail in their exertions.

Moreover, the democracy is not only deficient in that soundness of judgment which is necessary to select men really deserving of its confidence, but it has neither the desire nor the inclination to find them out. It cannot be denied that democratic institutions have a very strong tendency to promote the feeling of envy in the human heart; not so much because they afford to every one the means of rising to the level of any of his fellow-citizens, as because those means perpetually disappoint the persons

人民的文化水平达到一定的高度。无论采用什么样的学习方法，无论怎样简化学习内容，如果不能投入大量的学习时间，人类根本无法学到知识并加以运用。

因此，不劳动而能维持生计的时间的长短成为学习知识的必要界限。在某些国家，这一界限更为充裕，而在另一些则更为有限，但是只要人们必须通过劳动来满足物质生活的需要，它就必然存在，也就是说它具有普遍性。所以，很难想象一个国家中人人都博学多闻，也很难想象一个国家中人人都家财万贯。这两种不可能是有关系的。我会乐于承认，广大公民都真心希望国家富强，而且还要承认，跟上层阶级相比，下层阶级往往更不容易为私利所动。但是他们都在某种程度的无法认清能达到他们真心希望的结果的最好手段。要想对一个人的性格做出公正的评价必须经过长时间的耐心观察以及各种分析。伟大的天才都会有失误的事情，难道普通人就有能力做得到吗？人们既没有时间也没有手段去做这样的事情。人们根据问题表面最鲜明的特点匆忙地得出结论。所以，往往是那些口若悬河知道如何取悦于民的骗子能够得到支持，而人民最忠诚的朋友则常常得不到人民的信任。

此外，民主制度的缺陷在于有时候并不能一定做出合理的判断选出值得信任的人，因为人们有时候不想也不愿这样做。不可否认，民主制度给人们内心的嫉妒一个极大的推动力，这并不只是因为民主制度给每个人提供了可以变得和别人平等的手段，而是因为这些手段不断地让那些使用它们的人失望。民主制度唤起并培养了人们永不满足的追求平等的热情。这种绝对的平等在人们紧紧握住它的时刻却从指间溜走了，用帕斯卡尔的话说就是

who employ them. Democratic institutions awaken and foster a passion for equality which they can never entirely satisfy. This complete equality eludes the grasp of the people at the very moment at which it thinks to hold it fast, and "flies," as Pascal says, "with eternal flight"; the people is excited in the pursuit of an advantage, which is more precious because it is not sufficiently remote to be unknown, or sufficiently near to be enjoyed. The lower orders are agitated by the chance of success, they are irritated by its uncertainty; and they pass from the enthusiasm of pursuit to the exhaustion of ill-success, and lastly to the acrimony of disappointment. Whatever transcends their own limits appears to be an obstacle to their desires, and there is no kind of superiority, however legitimate it may be, which is not irksome in their sight.

It has been supposed that the secret instinct which leads the lower orders to remove their superiors as much as possible from the direction of public affairs is peculiar to France. This, however, is an error; the propensity to which I allude is not inherent in any particular nation, but in democratic institutions in general; and although it may have been heightened by peculiar political circumstances, it owes its origin to a higher cause.

In the United States the people is not disposed to hate the superior classes of society; but it is not very favorably inclined towards them, and it carefully excludes them from the exercise of authority. It does not entertain any dread of distinguished talents, but it is rarely captivated by them; and it awards its approbation very sparingly to such as have risen without the popular support.

Whilst the natural propensities of democracy induce the people to reject the most distinguished citizens as its rulers, these individuals are no less apt to retire from a political career in which it is almost impossible to retain their independence, or to advance without degrading themselves. This opinion has been very candidly set forth by Chancellor Kent, who says, in speaking with great eulogiums of that part of the Constitution which empowers the Executive to nominate the judges: "It is indeed probable that the men who are best fitted to discharge the duties of this high office would have too much reserve in their manners, and too much austerity in their principles, for them to be returned by the majority at an election where universal suffrage is adopted." Such were the opinions which were printed without contradiction in America in the year 1830!

永久消失了。人们热衷于追求一种利益，而它之所以更加珍贵是因为它并非遥不可及也非唾手可得。下层阶级因有可能成功而激动不已，又会因其不确定性而惴惴不安。他们一开始追逐的热情会因为无法成功而疲惫不堪，最终则因为失望而变得刻薄。任何超出他们能力范围的东西都被他们看作阻碍愿望实现的障碍，而且在他们的眼中，不管优越性多么合乎法理都会令人生厌。

人们认为下层阶级把他们的上级尽其所能从引领公共事务的位置上拉下来的这种隐秘的本能只在法国出现。其实，这种说法是错误的。我所说的本能不是任何一个国家所特有，而是普遍存在于民主制度之中。尽管特定的政治环境会让其得到加强，但它并不创造这种本能。

在美国，人民对于高级阶层并不怀有仇恨，但也没有特别的好感，只是小心翼翼地不让他们掌权。人民不惧怕杰出的天才，也不大受他们的蛊惑，而且对于没有得到民众支持而发迹的人，他们会非常吝啬赞美之词。

民主的这种自然倾向诱使人们拒绝最杰出的公民做自己的领导人，所以这些人倾向于从政坛隐退，因为在这里他们无法保全自己或免于堕落。首席法官肯特就曾经直白地表达过这样的看法。他在对宪法中授权总统提名法官的条款大加赞赏后说："最适合担当要职的人为了不在普选中当选，的确有可能在行动上有所保留，原则上异常苛刻。"这个见解在1830年的美国发表出来，而且没有人持有异议。

I hold it to be sufficiently demonstrated that universal suffrage is by no means a guarantee of the wisdom of the popular choice, and that, whatever its advantages may be, this is not one of them.

Causes Which May Partly Correct These Tendencies Of The Democracy

Contrary effects produced on peoples as well as on individuals by great dangers—Why so many distinguished men stood at the head of affairs in America fifty years ago—Influence which the intelligence and the manners of the people exercise upon its choice—Example of New England— States of the Southwest—Influence of certain laws upon the choice of the people—Election by an elected body—Its effects upon the composition of the Senate.

When a State is threatened by serious dangers, the people frequently succeeds in selecting the citizens who are the most able to save it. It has been observed that man rarely retains his customary level in presence of very critical circumstances; he rises above or he sinks below his usual condition, and the same thing occurs in nations at large. Extreme perils sometimes quench the energy of a people instead of stimulating it; they excite without directing its passions, and instead of clearing they confuse its powers of perception. The Jews deluged the smoking ruins of their temple with the carnage of the remnant of their host. But it is more common, both in the case of nations and in that of individuals, to find extraordinary virtues arising from the very imminence of the danger. Great characters are then thrown into relief, as edifices which are concealed by the gloom of night are illuminated by the glare of a conflagration. At those dangerous times genius no longer abstains from presenting itself in the arena; and the people, alarmed by the perils of its situation, buries its envious passions in a short oblivion. Great names may then be drawn from the balloting-box.

I have already observed that the American statesmen of the present day are very inferior to those who stood at the head of affairs fifty years ago. This is as much a consequence of the circumstances as of the laws of the country. When America was struggling in the high cause of independence to throw off the yoke of another country, and when it was about to usher a new nation into the world,

我之所以要提这句话就是要充分说明普选权绝非民众做出智慧抉择的保障，而且不管它有多少优点，这条绝不在其中。

能够部分纠正民主这些倾向的因素

巨大的危险对国家和个人产生的不良效果——为什么50年前在美国有如此多的杰出人物支持政务——教育和民情对人民选择产生的影响——新英格兰的例子——西南各州——某些法令对人们选择的影响——两级选举制度——这种选举制度对参议院构成的影响。

当一个国家面临巨大危险的威胁，人民总是能够成功地选出最有能力挽救国家的人。应该看到，一个人在紧急时刻几乎无法保持常态，不是表现得更好就是更糟，而国家亦是如此。极度的危险有时候不但不能激发反而可能浇灭它的热情。这些危险会激荡起人们的热情但却不加以引导；虽然能触及人们的头脑却无法使他们清醒。犹太人就曾经在硝烟弥漫的神庙废墟上互相厮杀。但是在危急关头不管是国家还是个人都经常能表现出非凡的品格。大人物层出不穷，好像夜色中大厦，被大火的光芒照亮。在危险时刻，天才不再隐而不出，人民也迫于灾难，而暂时将嫉妒心放在一边。伟大的名字开始在选票箱里层出不穷。

我已经说过美国现今的政治家们远不及50年前引领政坛的人物，这不但有法律原因，

the spirits of its inhabitants were roused to the height which their great efforts required. In this general excitement the most distinguished men were ready to forestall the wants of the community, and the people clung to them for support, and placed them at its head. But events of this magnitude are rare, and it is from an inspection of the ordinary course of affairs that our judgment must be formed.

If passing occurrences sometimes act as checks upon the passions of democracy, the intelligence and the manners of the community exercise an influence which is not less powerful and far more permanent. This is extremely perceptible in the United States.

In New England the education and the liberties of the communities were engendered by the moral and religious principles of their founders. Where society has acquired a sufficient degree of stability to enable it to hold certain maxims and to retain fixed habits, the lower orders are accustomed to respect intellectual superiority and to submit to it without complaint, although they set at naught all those privileges which wealth and birth have introduced among mankind. The democracy in New England consequently makes a more judicious choice than it does elsewhere.

But as we descend towards the South, to those States in which the constitution of society is more modern and less strong, where instruction is less general, and where the principles of morality, of religion, and of liberty are less happily combined, we perceive that the talents and the virtues of those who are in authority become more and more rare.

Lastly, when we arrive at the new South-western States, in which the constitution of society dates but from yesterday, and presents an agglomeration of adventurers and speculators, we are amazed at the persons who are invested with public authority, and we are led to ask by what force, independent of the legislation and of the men who direct it, the State can be protected, and society be made to flourish.

There are certain laws of a democratic nature which contribute, nevertheless, to correct, in some measure, the dangerous tendencies of democracy. On entering the House of Representatives of Washington one is struck by the vulgar demeanor of that great assembly. The eye frequently does not

更是环境使然。当美国人为摆脱另一个国家的束缚，为自己崇高的独立事业而战的时候，当要将一个新生的国家引领到世界舞台的时候，人民的精神境界将会提升到他们的努力所需要的水准。在举国欢腾的时刻，杰出的人物来到台前，人民举手欢迎并将他们置于自己的监督之下。但是这种重量级的大事件毕竟罕见，所以还必须从对普通事物的观察来做出判断。

如果转瞬即逝的事情有时候会抑制民主的激情，人民的知识和风尚的影响则会更加强大更为持久。这在美国表现得极为明显。

在新英格兰，教育和自由源自殖民地创建者们的道德和宗教原则。社会需要充分的稳定才能形成特定的准则和固定的习惯。下层阶级在对因财富和门第而带给人们的一切优势不屑一顾的同时，却习惯于尊重知识优势，并毫无怨言的言听计从。所以，在新英格兰比在其他地方更能做出明智之选。

但是，随着我们不断向南方深入会看到，在那些州，社会形成的较晚也不够稳定，教育还不够普及，而且道德、宗教和自由的原则并没有很好地结合。所以，有才或是有德的人掌权的情况极为罕见。

最后，当我们来到新西南各州，这里的社会不过才刚刚建立，看到的全是冒险家和投机家。我对于社会管理的大权被几个人把控深表惊讶，我不得不问，除了立法机构和人的独立之外，这样的州靠什么力量长治久安，社会靠什么力量繁荣昌盛？

有一些法律具有民主性质，却可以通过某种方式纠正民主的危险倾向。但进入到华盛

discover a man of celebrity within its walls. Its members are almost all obscure individuals whose names present no associations to the mind: they are mostly village lawyers, men in trade, or even persons belonging to the lower classes of society. In a country in which education is very general, it is said that the representatives of the people do not always know how to write correctly.

At a few yards' distance from this spot is the door of the Senate, which contains within a small space a large proportion of the celebrated men of America. Scarcely an individual is to be perceived in it who does not recall the idea of an active and illustrious career: the Senate is composed of eloquent advocates, distinguished generals, wise magistrates, and statesmen of note, whose language would at all times do honor to the most remarkable parliamentary debates of Europe.

What then is the cause of this strange contrast, and why are the most able citizens to be found in one assembly rather than in the other? Why is the former body remarkable for its vulgarity and its poverty of talent, whilst the latter seems to enjoy a monopoly of intelligence and of sound judgment? Both of these assemblies emanate from the people; both of them are chosen by universal suffrage; and no voice has hitherto been heard to assert in America that the Senate is hostile to the interests of the people. From what cause, then, does so startling a difference arise? The only reason which appears to me adequately to account for it is, that the House of Representatives is elected by the populace directly, and that the Senate is elected by elected bodies. The whole body of the citizens names the legislature of each State, and the Federal Constitution converts these legislatures into so many electoral bodies, which return the members of the Senate. The senators are elected by an indirect application of universal suffrage; for the legislatures which name them are not aristocratic or privileged bodies which exercise the electoral franchise in their own right; but they are chosen by the totality of the citizens; they are generally elected every year, and new members may constantly be chosen who will employ their electoral rights in conformity with the wishes of the public. But this transmission of the popular authority through an assembly of chosen men operates an important change in it, by refining its discretion and improving the forms which it adopts. Men who are chosen in this manner accurately represent the majority of the nation which governs them; but they represent

顿众议院，必会对大会上人们的粗陋举止大吃一惊，环顾四周根本看不到名人的影子。这里的众议员都是些我从来没有听说过的无名之辈。他们多为村里的律师、商人，乃至某些社会下层的人士。在一个教育非常普及的国家，据说人民代表并非都能不写错别字。

离这里不远的地方就是参议院，在这个小小的地方聚集了美国大部分的名流。几乎看到的每一个人都会让你想起他们显赫的成就，他们是雄辩的大律师、杰出的将军、英明的行政官以及著名的政治家，他们的发言总是能够和欧洲各国国会卓越的辩论相媲美。

然而，两院的强烈对比因何而来，为什么才干之士齐聚在参议院而不是众议院呢？为什么众议院以粗陋和人才乏善可陈而著称，而参议院则可以独占饱学明理之士。两院都来自人民，都经普选产生，而且迄今为止在美国参议院也从未发出有违人民利益的声音。那么，是什么原因导致这样明显的差异存在呢？在我看来，最能够说明这种区别的原因是，众议院是人民直接选出，而参议院则是选举团选出。每州的立法机构经全体公民选出，而联邦宪法则将这些立法机构规定为选举团，并由它们选出参议院成员。参议员的选举采用的是间接普选制，因为选出参议员的立法机构并非是本身拥有选举权的贵族或是特权团体，而且它实际上经全体公民选出，一般每年改选一次，从而保证有选举权的新成员符合人民的意愿。但是通过选举团来传达人民的意志时，有可能因改进和完善其形式而产生某些大的变化。通过此种方式选出的参议员能够切实代表治理国家的多数，但是他们代表的是流行于国内的严肃的思想和促进更为高尚行为产生的倾向，而不是会引起国家动乱的激情和让国家名誉扫地的邪念。

the elevated thoughts which are current in the community, the propensities which prompt its nobler actions, rather than the petty passions which disturb or the vices which disgrace it.

The time may be already anticipated at which the American Republics will be obliged to introduce the plan of election by an elected body more frequently into their system of representation, or they will incur no small risk of perishing miserably amongst the shoals of democracy.

And here I have no scruple in confessing that I look upon this peculiar system of election as the only means of bringing the exercise of political power to the level of all classes of the people. Those thinkers who regard this institution as the exclusive weapon of a party, and those who fear, on the other hand, to make use of it, seem to me to fall into as great an error in the one case as in the other.

Influence Which The American Democracy Has Exercised On The Laws Relating To Elections

When elections are rare, they expose the State to a violent crisis—When they are frequent, they keep up a degree of feverish excitement—The Americans have preferred the second of these two evils—Mutability of the laws—Opinions of Hamilton and Jefferson on this subject.

When elections recur at long intervals the State is exposed to violent agitation every time they take place. Parties exert themselves to the utmost in order to gain a prize which is so rarely within their reach; and as the evil is almost irremediable for the candidates who fail, the consequences of their disappointed ambition may prove most disastrous; if, on the other hand, the legal struggle can be repeated within a short space of time, the defeated parties take patience. When elections occur frequently, their recurrence keeps society in a perpetual state of feverish excitement, and imparts a continual instability to public affairs.

Thus, on the one hand the State is exposed to the perils of a revolution, on the other to perpetual mutability; the former system threatens the very existence of the Government, the latter is an obstacle to all steady and consistent policy. The Americans have preferred the second of these evils

美国各共和州会因为在选举制中采用两级选举制而繁荣的日子已经不远，否则它们必会在民主的浅滩悲剧地搁浅。

这里我要毫不犹豫地说，这种特别的选举制是唯一能够让各阶级人民都能够行使政治权力的方式。而那些把其视为政党专用武器的人们，以及那些害怕使用它的人们，在我看来都同样铸下大错。

美国民主对选举法的影响

选举过少，会让国家处于危机之中——选举过多，会让国家持续处在狂热状态——美国人两害相权取后者——法律的不稳定性——汉密尔顿和杰斐逊对此问题的看法。

如果选举的间隔时间过长，每次选举的时候国家就会处于动荡之中。每个政党都会全力以赴抓住这个千载难逢的机会攫取好处。对于选举失利的候选人，伤痛几乎是无法治愈的，他们抱负的落空会产生最可怕的灾难。相反，如果合法的斗争可以很快实现，那么失败的政党就会耐心等待。当选举过于频繁，会让社会始终处于亢奋状态，并无法保证政务的持续稳定性。

因此，一方面国家会面临革命的危险，而另一方面国家又会处于动荡之中。前者会威胁政府的存在，后者会对政策的一致性和稳定性造成障碍。面对两难的抉择，美国人选择了后者，但是他们的选择更多来自他们的本能而不是理智，因为对变化的爱好是民主特有

to the first; but they were led to this conclusion by their instinct much more than by their reason; for a taste for variety is one of the characteristic passions of democracy. An extraordinary mutability has, by this means, been introduced into their legislation. Many of the Americans consider the instability of their laws as a necessary consequence of a system whose general results are beneficial. But no one in the United States affects to deny the fact of this instability, or to contend that it is not a great evil.

Hamilton, after having demonstrated the utility of a power which might prevent, or which might at least impede, the promulgation of bad laws, adds: "It might perhaps be said that the power of preventing bad laws includes that of preventing good ones, and may be used to the one purpose as well as to the other. But this objection will have little weight with those who can properly estimate the mischiefs of that inconstancy and mutability in the laws which form the greatest blemish in the character and genius of our governments." (Federalist, No. 73.) And again in No. 62 of the same work he observes: "The facility and excess of law-making seem to be the diseases to which our governments are most liable. . . . The mischievous effects of the mutability in the public councils arising from a rapid succession of new members would fill a volume: every new election in the States is found to change one-half of the representatives. From this change of men must proceed a change of opinions and of measures, which forfeits the respect and confidence of other nations, poisons the blessings of liberty itself, and diminishes the attachment and reverence of the people toward a political system which betrays so many marks of infirmity."

Jefferson himself, the greatest Democrat whom the democracy of America has yet produced, pointed out the same evils. "The instability of our laws," said he in a letter to Madison, "is really a very serious inconvenience. I think that we ought to have obviated it by deciding that a whole year should always be allowed to elapse between the bringing in of a bill and the final passing of it. It should afterward be discussed and put to the vote without the possibility of making any alteration in it; and if the circumstances of the case required a more speedy decision, the question should not be decided by a simple majority, but by a majority of at least two-thirds of both houses."

的激情之一。因此，美国宪法表现得出奇的多变。许多美国人认为其法律的多变性是总体上行之有效的制度的必然结果。但是在美国，也没有人会否认缺乏稳定性这一事实，或是硬说它不是缺陷。

汉密尔顿，在证明一种权力能够防止或是至少阻碍不良法律的颁布之后补充道："也许有人会说，防止不良法律颁布的权力可能同样会成为阻碍良好法律的权力，而且既可以用于这个目的，还可以用于其他目的。但是这样的反对意见并没有什么斤两，因为对于那些能够对法律的不连贯性和多变性带来的弊端做出正确评估的人而言，这些问题已经是我国政府特点和精神的最大污点。"（《联邦党人》第73篇）而且在同一部著作的第62篇中，他还评论说："立法的轻而易举和毫无节制似乎是我国政府的最大顽疾……由于多变性带来的议会成员的不断更新所产生的恶果说也说不完。在那些每次选举会改选半数代表的国家，人员的变化必然造成观点和措施的改变，会让其他国家对其失去尊重和信心，自由带来的好处也会受到损害，而且人民对这一政治制度的爱戴和敬畏也会随其表现出的诸多的弱点而减少。"

杰斐逊本人，最伟大的民主主义者也是美国民主的缔造者，也指出了同样的问题。"我国法律的不稳定性，"他在给麦迪逊的一封信中写到，"确实是一个严重的缺陷。我认为我们应该这样解决这一问题：一项法案的提出到最后通过的时间可以规定为一年。法案应经过讨论，在没有更改意见之后进行表决。如果情况特殊需要快速通过该法案，则不能简单地由多数决定，而要得到两院的至少三分之二的多数认可。"

Public Officers Under The Control Of The Democracy In America

Simple exterior of the American public officers—No official costume—All public officers are remunerated—Political consequences of this system—No public career exists in America—Result of this.

Public officers in the United States are commingled with the crowd of citizens; they have neither palaces, nor guards, nor ceremonial costumes. This simple exterior of the persons in authority is connected not only with the peculiarities of the American character, but with the fundamental principles of that society. In the estimation of the democracy a government is not a benefit, but a necessary evil. A certain degree of power must be granted to public officers, for they would be of no use without it. But the ostensible semblance of authority is by no means indispensable to the conduct of affairs, and it is needlessly offensive to the susceptibility of the public. The public officers themselves are well aware that they only enjoy the superiority over their fellow-citizens which they derive from their authority upon condition of putting themselves on a level with the whole community by their manners. A public officer in the United States is uniformly civil, accessible to all the world, attentive to all requests, and obliging in his replies. I was pleased by these characteristics of a democratic government; and I was struck by the manly independence of the citizens, who respect the office more than the officer, and who are less attached to the emblems of authority than to the man who bears them.

I am inclined to believe that the influence which costumes really exercise, in an age like that in which we live, has been a good deal exaggerated. I never perceived that a public officer in America was the less respected whilst he was in the discharge of his duties because his own merit was set off by no adventitious signs. On the other hand, it is very doubtful whether a peculiar dress contributes to the respect which public characters ought to have for their own position, at least when they are not otherwise inclined to respect it. When a magistrate (and in France such instances are not rare) indulges his trivial wit at the expense of the prisoner, or derides the predicament in which a culprit is placed, it would be well to deprive him of his robes of office, to see whether he would recall some portion of the natural dignity of mankind when he is reduced to the apparel of a private citizen.

美国民主制下的公务员

美国公务员的简朴——没有公务员制服——所有的公务员均有酬劳——这样做的政治后果——美国没有终身公职——其后果。

在美国，公职人员与公民大众没有区别，他们既没有宫殿也没有护卫更没有正式着装。统治者的简朴作风不但与美国人的特殊性格有关，而且还和社会基本原则有关。从民主的角度评价，政府并不是好事而必定是灾难。一定程度的权力必须要交给公职人员，因为没有权力这些人毫无用处。但是象征权力的制服并非工作中必不可少，而且毫无必要地触动公众敏感的神经。公职人员自己也充分意识到他们之所以有权向人民发号施令，是以举止不得高人一等为前提。美国的公职人员清一色的彬彬有礼，平易近人，问话亲切，答复和蔼。对民主政府的这些特点我特别喜欢，而且从尊重职务甚于尊重官员，重视人品甚于重视权力表象的那些官员身上我看到了男子汉的作风。

我倾向于认为制服的作用在我国被极度的夸大。在美国，我从未看到公职人员在执行公务时不受尊重，而且我也怀疑是否一套制服就能让人肃然起敬，因为他们之所以受人尊敬并不是因为制服而是因为他们的品格。当地方官员（这样的例子在法国屡见不鲜）沉溺于以犯人为牺牲品，耍弄小聪明或是讥讽他们所处的窘境时，我真想看看如果脱去他的官服，恢复一个普通公民的着装，是否他们能够享受人类应该享有天然尊重。然而，民主亦

A democracy may, however, allow a certain show of magisterial pomp, and clothe its officers in silks and gold, without seriously compromising its principles. Privileges of this kind are transitory; they belong to the place, and are distinct from the individual: but if public officers are not uniformly remunerated by the State, the public charges must be entrusted to men of opulence and independence, who constitute the basis of an aristocracy; and if the people still retains its right of election, that election can only be made from a certain class of citizens. When a democratic republic renders offices which had formerly been remunerated gratuitous, it may safely be believed that the State is advancing to monarchical institutions; and when a monarchy begins to remunerate such officers as had hitherto been unpaid, it is a sure sign that it is approaching toward a despotic or a republican form of government. The substitution of paid for unpaid functionaries is of itself, in my opinion, sufficient to constitute a serious revolution.

I look upon the entire absence of gratuitous functionaries in America as one of the most prominent signs of the absolute dominion which democracy exercises in that country. All public services, of whatsoever nature they may be, are paid; so that every one has not merely the right, but also the means of performing them. Although, in democratic States, all the citizens are qualified to occupy stations in the Government, all are not tempted to try for them. The number and the capacities of the candidates are more apt to restrict the choice of electors than the connections of the candidateship.

In nations in which the principle of election extends to every place in the State no political career can, properly speaking, be said to exist. Men are promoted as if by chance to the rank which they enjoy, and they are by no means sure of retaining it. The consequence is that in tranquil times public functions offer but few lures to ambition. In the United States the persons who engage in the perplexities of political life are individuals of very moderate pretensions. The pursuit of wealth generally diverts men of great talents and of great passions from the pursuit of power, and it very frequently happens that a man does not undertake to direct the fortune of the State until he has discovered his incompetence to conduct his own affairs. The vast number of very ordinary men who occupy public stations is quite as attributable to these causes as to the bad choice of the democracy. In the United States, I am not sure that the people would return the men of superior abilities who

允许官员穿金戴银在一定程度上炫富，但是不能破坏民主的原则。但是这种特权不过是短暂的，不属于个人，而是属于职位。如果国家没有给政府官员统一发放薪俸，公共开销必然来自这些富有和独立的个人，他们便成为贵族核心。而如果人民依然保有选举权，这样的选举权必定只能为一定阶层的公民所享有。如果一个民主共和国将官员的薪制改为无薪制，我可以肯定地说这个国家正在走向君主制。而当君主制国家开始实行公务员无薪制的时候，无疑正走向独裁和共和政体。在我看来，薪俸制代替无薪制本身就足以称得上一场真正的革命。

我将美国这种没有无薪公务员存在的情况看作国家实行民主制的最突出的标志之一。因此公共服务，不管其性质如何，都要获得报酬，为的就是不仅仅让每个人都有权利为公共服务，更有手段来保证这样的服务。尽管在民主国家，人人都有资格在政府任职，但并不是所有人都能当选。因为候选人的数量和当选条件会对选民的选择加以限制，而不是候选人的身份。在那些选举制遍及国家各个方面的国家里，严格地说政治算不上职业。人们似乎是经选举偶然就任公职，而且无法确定能够取得连任。结果，在平静时期，公职对野心没有什么诱惑力。在美国混迹于政界的人大多抱负不大，有才干和胸怀大志的人都转而投向追求财富。所以在美国，一个人发觉自己无法打理好自家事业而转向管理国家事务的情况时有发生。大量的平庸之辈占据公共职务很大程度上就是出于这些原因和民主制的不良选择。我不太确定在美国人民是否会支持想要当选的能力超群的人。但是可以肯定的是

might solicit its support, but it is certain that men of this description do not come forward.

Arbitrary Power Of Magistrates Under The Rule Of The American Democracy

For what reason the arbitrary power of Magistrates is greater in absolute monarchies and in democratic republics than it is in limited monarchies—Arbitrary power of the Magistrates in New England.

In two different kinds of government the magistrates exercise a considerable degree of arbitrary power; namely, under the absolute government of a single individual, and under that of a democracy. This identical result proceeds from causes which are nearly analogous.

In despotic States the fortune of no citizen is secure; and public officers are not more safe than private individuals. The sovereign, who has under his control the lives, the property, and sometimes the honor of the men whom he employs, does not scruple to allow them a great latitude of action, because he is convinced that they will not use it to his prejudice. In despotic States the sovereign is so attached to the exercise of his power, that he dislikes the constraint even of his own regulations; and he is well pleased that his agents should follow a somewhat fortuitous line of conduct, provided he be certain that their actions will never counteract his desires.

In democracies, as the majority has every year the right of depriving the officers whom it has appointed of their power, it has no reason to fear any abuse of their authority. As the people is always able to signify its wishes to those who conduct the Government, it prefers leaving them to make their own exertions to prescribing an invariable rule of conduct which would at once fetter their activity and the popular authority.

It may even be observed, on attentive consideration, that under the rule of a democracy the arbitrary power of the magistrate must be still greater than in despotic States. In the latter the sovereign has the power of punishing all the faults with which he becomes acquainted, but it would be vain for him to hope to become acquainted with all those which are committed. In the former the

这些人肯定不会出来参选。

美国民主统治下的行政官专权

何以行政官专权在专制君主制国家和民主共和制国家会比在君主立宪制国家更甚——新英格兰行政官的专权。

在两种不同制度的政府中，行政官享有很大程度的专权，一个是个人独裁政府，另一个则是民主政府。这种相同的结果产生的原因也几乎完全相同。

在专制国家，人民的命运没有保障，官员的命运也并不比普通个人更有保障。君主掌握着人们的生命、财富，有时候甚至是他们的荣誉。君主对人们无所顾忌，他们拥有很大程度的行动自由，因为他确信人们不会运用这种自由反对自己。在专制国家，君主热衷于行使自己的权力，甚至不喜欢受制于自己定下的制度的约束。而且，他也很愿意把臣民的出轨看成偶然，而且认为他们不会再做出违背自己意愿的举动。

在民主制国家，多数每年都有权剥夺他们曾授予权力的官员的权力，所以不用担心他们会滥用权力。因为人民有能力将自己的意愿传达给执政者，所以他们更愿意让执政者拥有更多更大的权力，而不是用一套死规定束缚自己的活动和执政者。

经过深入思考，甚至会发现，在民主制度统治下，行政官员专权比专制国家要有过之而无不及。在专制国家，君主有权对其所发现的各种犯罪进行惩罚，但是对他而言，发现

sovereign power is not only supreme, but it is universally present. The American functionaries are, in point of fact, much more independent in the sphere of action which the law traces out for them than any public officer in Europe. Very frequently the object which they are to accomplish is simply pointed out to them, and the choice of the means is left to their own discretion.

In New England, for instance, the selectmen of each township are bound to draw up the list of persons who are to serve on the jury; the only rule which is laid down to guide them in their choice is that they are to select citizens possessing the elective franchise and enjoying a fair reputation. In France the lives and liberties of the subjects would be thought to be in danger if a public officer of any kind was entrusted with so formidable a right. In New England the same magistrates are empowered to post the names of habitual drunkards in public-houses, and to prohibit the inhabitants of a town from supplying them with liquor. A censorial power of this excessive kind would be revolting to the population of the most absolute monarchies; here, however, it is submitted to without difficulty.

Nowhere has so much been left by the law to the arbitrary determination of the magistrate as in democratic republics, because this arbitrary power is unattended by any alarming consequences. It may even be asserted that the freedom of the magistrate increases as the elective franchise is extended, and as the duration of the time of office is shortened. Hence arises the great difficulty which attends the conversion of a democratic republic into a monarchy. The magistrate ceases to be elective, but he retains the rights and the habits of an elected officer, which lead directly to despotism.

It is only in limited monarchies that the law, which prescribes the sphere in which public officers are to act, superintends all their measures. The cause of this may be easily detected. In limited monarchies the power is divided between the King and the people, both of whom are interested in the stability of the magistrate. The King does not venture to place the public officers under the control of the people, lest they should be tempted to betray his interests; on the other hand, the people fears lest the magistrates should serve to oppress the liberties of the country, if they were entirely dependent upon the Crown; they cannot therefore be said to depend on either one or the other. The same cause which induces the king and the people to render public officers independent suggests the necessity

所有的犯罪行为根本不可能。然而在民主制国家，专权不仅程度高而且范围广。就实际情况看，美国的官员在其法律规定的职权范围内比欧洲任何官员享有的自由都更多。一般来说，只给他们简单规定出要达成的目标，至于采用的手段则留给他们自行决定。

例如，在新英格兰，每个乡镇的行政委员负责起草陪审团人员名单，而用来指导其选择的唯一规定就是：要从具有选举权和声誉良好的公民中选出陪审员。在法国，如果那种官员被授予如此强大的权利，人们会认为老百姓的生命和自由都会处于危险之中。在新英格兰，行政委员还有权将酗酒者的名字张贴到酒吧，并禁止乡镇的居民向其出售酒类。这种过度的查禁权即使是在最专制的国家也会激起人们的反抗，然而在这里却可以通行无阻。

没有任何一个地方的法律会像民主共和制国家一样，赋予行政官员如此大的专权，因为这宗专权没有产生可怕的后果。甚至可以说，随着选举权的广泛普及以及选举周期的缩短，行政官的自由更加增强。因此，要把一个民主共和国转变成为一个专制国家简直是难上加难。如果行政官不由人民选举，而他依旧保有民选行政官的权利和习惯，这就必将导致专制。

只有在君主立宪制国家，法律在对官员划定行动半径的同时，还会对他们行动的方式加以监督。其原因显而易见。在君主立宪制国家，权力由国王和人们分掌，双方都希望保持行政官员的稳定性。国王不敢将官员置于人民的控制，害怕他们会出卖国王的利益，而人民又唯恐行政官依附王权压制自由。所以，不能让他们依附于一方。国王和人民之所以要保证官员的独立性其原因相同，同时这也是国王和人民寻找防范官员滥用权力的保障，

of such securities as may prevent their independence from encroaching upon the authority of the former and the liberties of the latter. They consequently agree as to the necessity of restricting the functionary to a line of conduct laid down beforehand, and they are interested in confining him by certain regulations which he cannot evade.

Instability Of The Administration In The United States

In America the public acts of a community frequently leave fewer traces than the occurrences of a family—Newspapers the only historical remains—Instability of the administration prejudicial to the art of government.

The authority which public men possess in America is so brief, and they are so soon commingled with the ever-changing population of the country, that the acts of a community frequently leave fewer traces than the occurrences of a private family. The public administration is, so to speak, oral and traditionary. But little is committed to writing, and that little is wafted away forever, like the leaves of the Sibyl, by the smallest breeze.

The only historical remains in the United States are the newspapers; but if a number be wanting, the chain of time is broken, and the present is severed from the past. I am convinced that in fifty years it will be more difficult to collect authentic documents concerning the social condition of the Americans at the present day than it is to find remains of the administration of France during the Middle Ages; and if the United States were ever invaded by barbarians, it would be necessary to have recourse to the history of other nations in order to learn anything of the people which now inhabits them.

The instability of the administration has penetrated into the habits of the people: it even appears to suit the general taste, and no one cares for what occurred before his time. No methodical system is pursued; no archives are formed; and no documents are brought together when it would be very easy to do so. Where they exist, little store is set upon them; and I have amongst my papers several original public documents which were given to me in answer to some of my inquiries. In

为的是防止官员对王权和人民自由的侵犯。所以，双方一致认为要事先为官员行动划下范围，并热衷于通过无法规避的特定制度对其加以约束。

美国行政的不稳定性

在美国人们在社会活动方面留下的痕迹往往不如家庭生活方面——报纸是唯一的历史文献——行政的不稳定性对施政艺术有害。

在美国，人们拥有权力的时间非常短暂，而且不久就要回到每天不断变化的人民大众之中，所以，社会活动留下的痕迹往往不如家庭生活留下的痕迹。所以说，美国的行政管理多是通过口头和传统传承。几乎没有什么成文的规定，如果有过那么一星半点，也会像古代女巫写在棕榈叶上的预言一样，只要是一阵轻轻的微风就可以将它吹得无影无踪。

在美国唯一的历史文献就是报纸。但是如果短了一期报纸，时间链就会断开，现在和过去就会被割裂开。我确定，在美国想要找到过去50年来的有关美国社会状况的所有原始文件会比寻找法国中世纪行政管理文献还要困难。如果美国要是被蛮族入侵，要是想要了解现在居民的一些事情恐怕要依靠别的国家的史料记载。

行政的不稳定性已经渗入到人民的习惯。这似乎很合大众的口味，似乎没有人在意在他以前发生过什么。没有人研究管理方法，也没有人存档，而且也没有人收集文献，即使这做起来很简单。偶然落到人们手里，也几乎没有人会将这些文件保存下来。我手里就有

America society seems to live from hand to mouth, like an army in the field. Nevertheless, the art of administration may undoubtedly be ranked as a science, and no sciences can be improved if the discoveries and observations of successive generations are not connected together in the order in which they occur. One man, in the short space of his life remarks a fact; another conceives an idea; the former invents a means of execution, the latter reduces a truth to a fixed proposition; and mankind gathers the fruits of individual experience upon its way and gradually forms the sciences. But the persons who conduct the administration in America can seldom afford any instruction to each other; and when they assume the direction of society, they simply possess those attainments which are most widely disseminated in the community, and no experience peculiar to themselves. Democracy, carried to its furthest limits, is therefore prejudicial to the art of government; and for this reason it is better adapted to a people already versed in the conduct of an administration than to a nation which is uninitiated in public affairs.

 This remark, indeed, is not exclusively applicable to the science of administration. Although a democratic government is founded upon a very simple and natural principle, it always presupposes the existence of a high degree of culture and enlightenment in society. At the first glance it may be imagined to belong to the earliest ages of the world; but maturer observation will convince us that it could only come last in the succession of human history.

Charges Levied By The State Under The Rule Of The American Democracy

In all communities citizens divisible into three classes—Habits of each of these classes in the direction of public finances—Why public expenditure must tend to increase when the people governs—What renders the extravagance of a democracy less to be feared in America—Public expenditure under a democracy.

Before we can affirm whether a democratic form of government is economical or not, we must establish a suitable standard of comparison. The question would be one of easy solution if we were to attempt to

份原始文件，是一些行政部门为答复我的问题给我的。在美国，社会就好像是一支战斗中的军队那样生活。然而，行政管理艺术毫无疑问是一门科学，而且如果一代代的发现和观察没有汇集起来加以总结，科学就无法取得进步。在一个人短短的一生之中，有人笃行，有人立言，前者发明方法，后者创造理论；人类在前进的道路上收集这些个人的成果，渐渐形成科学。但是，在美国，行政人员很少互相学习，在指导社会工作的时候，只凭借自己了解的社会上广为流传的常识，毫无个人经验而言。在民主社会，这被发挥到极致，因而阻碍了行政艺术的发展。也正是基于这样的原因，民主更适合缺乏行政管理经验的国家，而不是那些在这方面已经很精通的国家。

实际上，这样的说法并不只适用于行政科学。尽管民主政府建立在简单自然的原则之上，但是往往要以一个高度开化文明的社会为前提。初看起来，它似乎属于原始时代，但是经过深入观察会发现它只可能出现在人类历史的最后阶段。

美国民主治下的公共开支

在任何社会，公民都可以分为三个等级——每个阶级对管理国家财务的嗜好——为什么人民主政公共开支必然增加——什么让民主的浪费在美国不那么令人忧心忡忡——民主制度下的公共开支。

在我们对民主制政府是否节俭给出确切说法之前，我们必须先设定一个比较标准。

draw a parallel between a democratic republic and an absolute monarchy. The public expenditure would be found to be more considerable under the former than under the latter; such is the case with all free States compared to those which are not so. It is certain that despotism ruins individuals by preventing them from producing wealth, much more than by depriving them of the wealth they have produced; it dries up the source of riches, whilst it usually respects acquired property. Freedom, on the contrary, engenders far more benefits than it destroys; and the nations which are favored by free institutions invariably find that their resources increase even more rapidly than their taxes.

My present object is to compare free nations to each other, and to point out the influence of democracy upon the finances of a State.

Communities, as well as organic bodies, are subject to certain fixed rules in their formation which they cannot evade. They are composed of certain elements which are common to them at all times and under all circumstances. The people may always be mentally divided into three distinct classes. The first of these classes consists of the wealthy; the second, of those who are in easy circumstances; and the third is composed of those who have little or no property, and who subsist more especially by the work which they perform for the two superior orders. The proportion of the individuals who are included in these three divisions may vary according to the condition of society, but the divisions themselves can never be obliterated.

It is evident that each of these classes will exercise an influence peculiar to its own propensities upon the administration of the finances of the State. If the first of the three exclusively possesses the legislative power, it is probable that it will not be sparing of the public funds, because the taxes which are levied on a large fortune only tend to diminish the sum of superfluous enjoyment, and are, in point of fact, but little felt. If the second class has the power of making the laws, it will certainly not be lavish of taxes, because nothing is so onerous as a large impost which is levied upon a small income. The government of the middle classes appears to me to be the most economical, though perhaps not the most enlightened, and certainly not the most generous, of free governments.

But let us now suppose that the legislative authority is vested in the lowest orders: there are two striking reasons which show that the tendency of the expenditure will be to increase, not to diminish.

如果我们把一个民主共和国和一个君主专制国家进行比较，这个问题解决起来就不难。显然，前者的公共开支要大大高于后者，在对自由国家和专制国家进行比较时，情况总是这样。可以肯定，专制制度会阻碍人们创造财富，而不是夺走他们创造的财富，它会使得财源枯竭，而又往往尊重既得财产。相反，自由国家创造的财富往往比他挥霍的要多得多，而且得益于自由制度的国家发觉它们的财源甚至比其税收增长得还要快。

现在，我要对各种自由国家进行比较，并指出民主制对一个国家财政的影响。

社会跟有机体一样，往往会服从于其构成所离不开的特定规则。社会由那些它们习以为常时刻存在的特定元素构成。人民往往被划分成截然不同的三个阶级。第一个阶级由富人组成，第二个阶级是那些生活安逸的人，第三个阶级则由那些几乎没有什么财产的人组成，他们靠给前两个阶级工作维持生计。这第三个等级的人数会随社会状况的不同而变化，但是这些等级不可能没有。

显然，每个阶级都会对国家财政管理有自己的特别要求。如果第一个阶级握有立法权，可能不大会节省国库开支，因为对大额财产征收的赋税对其来说只不过是九牛一毛，没什么大不了，而且实际情况也的确如此。如果由第二个阶级制定法律，则必不会挥霍国家税收，因为对不多的收入征收高额税金简直就是灾难。依我看中间阶级的政府最节约，尽管他们不会是最开明，而且也一定不是最慷慨的自由政府。

现在，让我们假设立法权由第三个阶级掌握。有两大重要原因会导致公共开支的增加

As the great majority of those who create the laws are possessed of no property upon which taxes can be imposed, all the money which is spent for the community appears to be spent to their advantage, at no cost of their own; and those who are possessed of some little property readily find means of regulating the taxes so that they are burdensome to the wealthy and profitable to the poor, although the rich are unable to take the same advantage when they are in possession of the Government.

In countries in which the poor should be exclusively invested with the power of making the laws no great economy of public expenditure ought to be expected: that expenditure will always be considerable; either because the taxes do not weigh upon those who levy them, or because they are levied in such a manner as not to weigh upon those classes. In other words, the government of the democracy is the only one under which the power which lays on taxes escapes the payment of them.

It may be objected (but the argument has no real weight) that the true interest of the people is indissolubly connected with that of the wealthier portion of the community, since it cannot but suffer by the severe measures to which it resorts. But is it not the true interest of kings to render their subjects happy, and the true interest of nobles to admit recruits into their order on suitable grounds? If remote advantages had power to prevail over the passions and the exigencies of the moment, no such thing as a tyrannical sovereign or an exclusive aristocracy could ever exist.

Again, it may be objected that the poor are never invested with the sole power of making the laws; but I reply, that wherever universal suffrage has been established the majority of the community unquestionably exercises the legislative authority; and if it be proved that the poor always constitute the majority, it may be added, with perfect truth, that in the countries in which they possess the elective franchise they possess the sole power of making laws. But it is certain that in all the nations of the world the greater number has always consisted of those persons who hold no property, or of those whose property is insufficient to exempt them from the necessity of working in order to procure an easy subsistence. Universal suffrage does therefore, in point of fact, invest the poor with the government of society.

The disastrous influence which popular authority may sometimes exercise upon the finances of a State was very clearly seen in some of the democratic republics of antiquity, in which the public

而不是减少。因为绝大多数的立法者没有财产可供征税，所以他们为社会花的所有钱都会对他们有利，而不会有任何损失。而那些有少量财产的人会想方设法把给他们带来负担的赋税转嫁给富人，而这只对穷人有利，尽管在富人当政的时候他们也无法从中获利。

在那些穷人独揽立法大权的国家，不要指望公共开支会有显著节省。公共开支之所以会大幅度增加，因为制定赋税的人很可能并不纳税，或者他们不让赋税落到自己身上。换句话说，民主政府是唯一能够让立法征税的人逃脱缴税的政府。

也许有人会反对（但是反对也没用）人民的真正利益和社会那部分有钱人的利益无法分割，因为人民会因自己所采用的措施而受到伤害。但国王的真正利益不也是其臣民的幸福所在吗？而且贵族的真正利益不也时时向人民开放吗？如果长远利益有力量克服目前的激情和要求，那么暴君的统治或是专制的贵族制度就永不会存在。

可能有人会反对不让穷人独揽立法大权，然而要是我说，只要是普选权存在的地方多数必定要行使立法权。如果经过证明穷人经常能构成多数，那就应该补充一句，在实行普选制的国家，穷人独揽立法大权。但是，毋庸置疑的是世界上所有国家的大多数的构成总是那些没有财产的人，或是财产不太多必须工作才能过上安逸生活的人。因此，普选权实际上就是要让穷人管理社会。

民权有时候会对一个国家的财政产生灾难性的影响，这在一些古代的民主共和国表现得非常清楚。在这些国家，为了救济贫苦，或是为人民提供娱乐设施，国库的财富消耗

treasure was exhausted in order to relieve indigent citizens, or to supply the games and theatrical amusements of the populace. It is true that the representative system was then very imperfectly known, and that, at the present time, the influence of popular passion is less felt in the conduct of public affairs; but it may be believed that the delegate will in the end conform to the principles of his constituents, and favor their propensities as much as their interests.

The extravagance of democracy is, however, less to be dreaded in proportion as the people acquires a share of property, because on the one hand the contributions of the rich are then less needed, and, on the other, it is more difficult to lay on taxes which do not affect the interests of the lower classes. On this account universal suffrage would be less dangerous in France than in England, because in the latter country the property on which taxes may be levied is vested in fewer hands. America, where the great majority of the citizens possess some fortune, is in a still more favorable position than France.

There are still further causes which may increase the sum of public expenditure in democratic countries. When the aristocracy governs, the individuals who conduct the affairs of State are exempted by their own station in society from every kind of privation; they are contented with their position; power and renown are the objects for which they strive; and, as they are placed far above the obscurer throng of citizens, they do not always distinctly perceive how the well-being of the mass of the people ought to redound to their own honor. They are not indeed callous to the sufferings of the poor, but they cannot feel those miseries as acutely as if they were themselves partakers of them. Provided that the people appear to submit to its lot, the rulers are satisfied, and they demand nothing further from the Government. An aristocracy is more intent upon the means of maintaining its influence than upon the means of improving its condition.

When, on the contrary, the people is invested with the supreme authority, the perpetual sense of their own miseries impels the rulers of society to seek for perpetual ameliorations. A thousand different objects are subjected to improvement; the most trivial details are sought out as susceptible of amendment; and those changes which are accompanied with considerable expense are more especially advocated, since the object is to render the condition of the poor more tolerable, who

一空。老实说，代议制在古代还鲜为人知，而现在，民众的热情对公共事务的影响表现得并不明显，但是应该相信代表终究会按照选民的要求行事，并同时会照顾他们的爱好和利益。

然而，随着人民变得富有，民主的浪费的可怕程度也会随之下降。因为一方面来说，人民富裕以后就不再那么需要富人的贡献，而且另一方面，增加赋税也会影响到下层阶级的自身的利益。就这一点而言，普选制在法国带来的危险会比英国的小，因为在英国，需要缴税的财产主要集中在少数人手中。而美国因为大多数的公民都有财产，所以跟法国相比处在一个更为有利的地位。

还有另外一些原因会导致民主国家公共开支的增加。当贵族统治国家的时候，主持国家事务的人会因其职位免受贫困，所以他们对自己的处境非常满意，权力和名誉就是他们的奋斗目标。而当他们高高在上的时候，根本无法意识到芸芸众生的幸福安康对自己的荣华富贵会有怎样的好处。尽管他们对穷人的痛苦并非麻木不仁，但是的确无法感同身受。只要人民能够安于现状，统治者就心满意足，而且只要能保住自己的统治地位便别无所求。所以贵族体制更关心维持现状的手段而不是改进现状的方法。

相反，当人民大权在握，因为他们有切身感受，所以会不断寻求变革。要改革的事情千千万，哪怕是最细枝末节的事情都不会放过，而这些改革必然需要大笔的花销，因为改革的目的是让那些无力自给的穷人的生活状况有所改善。

而且，在所有的民主社会总是存在一种难以名状的兴奋和一种不断要求革新的狂躁，

cannot pay for themselves.

Moreover, all democratic communities are agitated by an ill-defined excitement and by a kind of feverish impatience, that engender a multitude of innovations, almost all of which are attended with expense.

In monarchies and aristocracies the natural taste which the rulers have for power and for renown is stimulated by the promptings of ambition, and they are frequently incited by these temptations to very costly undertakings. In democracies, where the rulers labor under privations, they can only be courted by such means as improve their well-being, and these improvements cannot take place without a sacrifice of money. When a people begins to reflect upon its situation, it discovers a multitude of wants to which it had not before been subject, and to satisfy these exigencies recourse must be had to the coffers of the State. Hence it arises that the public charges increase in proportion as civilization spreads, and that imposts are augmented as knowledge pervades the community.

The last cause which frequently renders a democratic government dearer than any other is, that a democracy does not always succeed in moderating its expenditure, because it does not understand the art of being economical. As the designs which it entertains are frequently changed, and the agents of those designs are still more frequently removed, its undertakings are often ill conducted or left unfinished: in the former case the State spends sums out of all proportion to the end which it proposes to accomplish; in the second, the expense itself is unprofitable.

Tendencies Of The American Democracy As Regards The Salaries Of Public Officers

In the democracies those who establish high salaries have no chance of profiting by them—Tendency of the American democracy to increase the salaries of subordinate officers and to lower those of the more important functionaries—Reason of this—Comparative statement of the salaries of public officers in the United States and in France.

There is a powerful reason which usually induces democracies to economize upon the salaries of public officers. As the number of citizens who dispense the remuneration is extremely large in

而每一样革新都少不了花钱。

在君主专制和贵族专制的国家，统治者对权力和名誉的天然嗜好在野心家的鼓动下，不断地要做一些劳民伤财的事业。而在穷人主政的民主国家，主政的人只对改进民生的事业表现得积极，而这样的事业没有钱就办不了。当人民开始思量自身处境的时候，会发现有太多的以前没有想到的需要，而要满足这些需要，就得向国库求援。因此，随着文明的传播，公共开销会越来越高，而且随着教育的普及，赋税也会不断增加。

常常促使民主社会开支比其他社会更高的最后一个原因是，民主社会往往无法成功的削减开支，因为它没有节约之术。由于民主政府的目标经常变化，人员也不断更换，其推进的事业常常无法得到有力的贯彻或是半途而废。于前一种情形，国家花了钱，却没有得到相称的结果；于后一种情形，国家花了钱，却什么都没得到。

美国民主在公务人员薪俸方面呈现的趋势

在民主制国家，做出高薪规定的人没有机会从中获得好处——美国民主的趋势是提高低级公务人员的薪俸，降低高级公务人员的薪俸——其原因何在——美国和法国公务人员薪俸对比。

有一个强有力的原因驱使民主制度在公务人员的薪俸上力求节约。因为在民主制国家，负责规定公务人员薪俸的人很多，而能够从中牟利的人却很少。相反，在贵族专制的

democratic countries, so the number of persons who can hope to be benefited by the receipt of it is comparatively small. In aristocratic countries, on the contrary, the individuals who fix high salaries have almost always a vague hope of profiting by them. These appointments may be looked upon as a capital which they create for their own use, or at least as a resource for their children.

It must, however, be allowed that a democratic State is most parsimonious towards its principal agents. In America the secondary officers are much better paid, and the dignitaries of the administration much worse, than they are elsewhere.

These opposite effects result from the same cause; the people fixes the salaries of the public officers in both cases; and the scale of remuneration is determined by the consideration of its own wants. It is held to be fair that the servants of the public should be placed in the same easy circumstances as the public itself; but when the question turns upon the salaries of the great officers of State, this rule fails, and chance alone can guide the popular decision. The poor have no adequate conception of the wants which the higher classes of society may feel. The sum which is scanty to the rich appears enormous to the poor man whose wants do not extend beyond the necessaries of life; and in his estimation the Governor of a State, with his twelve or fifteen hundred dollars a year, is a very fortunate and enviable being. If you undertake to convince him that the representative of a great people ought to be able to maintain some show of splendor in the eyes of foreign nations, he will perhaps assent to your meaning; but when he reflects on his own humble dwelling, and on the hard-earned produce of his wearisome toil, he remembers all that he could do with a salary which you say is insufficient, and he is startled or almost frightened at the sight of such uncommon wealth. Besides, the secondary public officer is almost on a level with the people, whilst the others are raised above it. The former may therefore excite his interest, but the latter begins to arouse his envy.

This is very clearly seen in the United States, where the salaries seem to decrease as the authority of those who receive them augments

Under the rule of an aristocracy it frequently happens, on the contrary, that whilst the high officers are receiving munificent salaries, the inferior ones have not more than enough to procure

国家，能够制定高薪制度的人隐约都有希望可以从中牟利。这可以看成他们在为自己创造资本，或者至少是在为其后代准备财源。

然而，必须承认民主国家对其主要公务人员太过吝啬。在美国，下级公务人员的薪俸比其他国家要高出许多，但是高级公务人员的薪俸则远不如其他国家。

这两个相反的结果都出自同一种原因。在这两种情形下，公务人员的酬劳都是人民在对自己需要做出思量后规定的。公仆要像人民一样能够过上安逸的生活这才公平合理，但是当轮到制定高级公务人员薪俸的时候，这个规则就行不通了，而完全是随性而定。穷人对于社会上层生活的需要没有清楚的认识。在穷人看来的一大笔钱，有钱人可能觉得应付日常生活开支还捉襟见肘。按他们的估计，年收入为1,200或1,500美元的一个州长就是足以让人艳羡不已的人物。如果你试图让他相信一个伟大国家的代表应该在外国人的面前表现出一定的气派，他也许会赞同你的说法。但是当他想到自己的简陋居所和累死累活赚来的微薄收入，以及他用你口口声声说不够用的那笔工资所能做出的所有事情，必会对这笔财富感到吃惊，甚至被吓到。此外，当下级公务人员与人民处在几乎相同的水准，而另外一些人却高于这一水准时，前者也许还会激起他们的同情，而后者只能引起他们的嫉妒。

这在随着权力的增加而工资递减的美国表现得非常明显。

在贵族统治的国家，情况往往刚好相反，高官的工资待遇优厚，而小官的待遇不过刚够糊口，其原因不难从我上面提到过的类似原因中找到。如果民主制度不会认可富人应当享乐和穷人不会嫉妒富人，那么贵族制度就难以理解，或者准确地说，压根不知道穷人的

the necessaries of life. The reason of this fact is easily discoverable from causes very analogous to those to which I have just alluded. If a democracy is unable to conceive the pleasures of the rich or to witness them without envy, an aristocracy is slow to understand, or, to speak more correctly, is unacquainted with, the privations of the poor. The poor man is not (if we use the term aright) the fellow of the rich one; but he is a being of another species. An aristocracy is therefore apt to care but little for the fate of its subordinate agents; and their salaries are only raised when they refuse to perform their service for too scanty a remuneration.

It is the parsimonious conduct of democracy towards its principal officers which has countenanced a supposition of far more economical propensities than any which it really possesses. It is true that it scarcely allows the means of honorable subsistence to the individuals who conduct its affairs; but enormous sums are lavished to meet the exigencies or to facilitate the enjoyments of the people. The money raised by taxation may be better employed, but it is not saved. In general, democracy gives largely to the community, and very sparingly to those who govern it. The reverse is the case in aristocratic countries, where the money of the State is expended to the profit of the persons who are at the head of affairs.

Difficulty of Distinguishing The Causes Which Contribute To The Economy Of The American Government

We are liable to frequent errors in the research of those facts which exercise a serious influence upon the fate of mankind, since nothing is more difficult than to appreciate their real value. One people is naturally inconsistent and enthusiastic; another is sober and calculating; and these characteristics originate in their physical constitution or in remote causes with which we are unacquainted.

These are nations which are fond of parade and the bustle of festivity, and which do not regret the costly gaieties of an hour. Others, on the contrary, are attached to more retiring pleasures, and seem almost ashamed of appearing to be pleased. In some countries the highest value is set upon the beauty of public edifices; in others the productions of art are treated with indifference, and everything which is

贫苦。穷人跟富人不是同一类人，他们是另一族群。因此，贵族往往不怎么关心下级官员的命运，而且只有下级官员拒绝继续为他们服务的时候才会给其稍稍涨点工资。

尽管节俭并非民主制度的真正嗜好，但是民主制度对高级官员的吝啬表现出一种过分节俭的倾向。的确，民主制度可以让主政的官员过上体面的生活，但是为了满足人民的需求和安居乐业，它不惜耗费巨资。通过税收得到的资金可能得到善用，但却没能节约下来。一般来说，民主制度花在被统治者身上的钱很多，而花在统治者身上的钱则很少。而在贵族专制国家，情况恰恰相反，国家的收入主要用在主持政务的人身上。

难以识别促使美国政府厉行节约的原因

我们在寻找对人类命运产生重大影响的真相时常常会犯错，因为再也没有什么比鉴别这些事实真相的真正价值更困难的事情。一个民族天生热情洋溢难以捉摸，另一个民族则深思熟虑精于计算，这些特点都源自他们的身体条件或是一些我们不了解的古老原因。

有些民族喜欢游行和喧闹的庆典，不惜花费重金求得一时的欢乐。另一些民族则刚好相反，喜欢独善其身，并似乎羞于表现出心满意足。在一些国家，最美不过高屋广厦，而在另一些国家，艺术作品被完全忽视，对任何没有实效的东西都不屑一顾。最后，还有些国家爱慕名誉，另一些则追求金钱。

放下法律不谈，所有这些原因都会对各国财政产生非常强有力的影响。如果美国人绝不把钱花在节日庆祝上，这并不是因为税收的支出必须人民说了算，而是因为人民并不

unproductive is looked down upon with contempt. In some renown, in others money, is the ruling passion.

Independently of the laws, all these causes concur to exercise a very powerful influence upon the conduct of the finances of the State. If the Americans never spend the money of the people in galas, it is not only because the imposition of taxes is under the control of the people, but because the people takes no delight in public rejoicings. If they repudiate all ornament from their architecture, and set no store on any but the more practical and homely advantages, it is not only because they live under democratic institutions, but because they are a commercial nation. The habits of private life are continued in public; and we ought carefully to distinguish that economy which depends upon their institutions from that which is the natural result of their manners and customs.

Whether The Expenditure Of The United States Can Be Compared To That Of France

Two points to be established in order to estimate the extent of the public charges, viz., the national wealth and the rate of taxation—The wealth and the charges of France not accurately known—Why the wealth and charges of the Union cannot be accurately known—Researches of the author with a view to discover the amount of taxation of Pennsylvania—General symptoms which may serve to indicate the amount of the public charges in a given nation—Result of this investigation for the Union.

Many attempts have recently been made in France to compare the public expenditure of that country with the expenditure of the United States; all these attempts have, however, been unattended by success, and a few words will suffice to show that they could not have had a satisfactory result.

In order to estimate the amount of the public charges of a people two preliminaries are indispensable: it is necessary, in the first place, to know the wealth of that people; and in the second, to learn what portion of that wealth is devoted to the expenditure of the State. To show the amount of taxation without showing the resources which are destined to meet the demand, is to undertake a futile labor; for it is not the expenditure, but the relation of the expenditure to the revenue, which it is desirable to know.

The same rate of taxation which may easily be supported by a wealthy contributor will reduce a

喜欢隆重的庆典。如果美国人不喜欢建筑上的装饰，只重视实际功用，这并不仅仅是因为他们生活在民主制度下，而是因为他们是重商的民族。个人的生活习惯会被公共生活所接受，而且我们应该小心翼翼地把源自制度的节约和源自人们习惯和风尚的节约区分开。

能否将美国公共开支和法国的公共开支加以比较

要衡量公共开支的多少，先要确定两点：国家财富和税率——无法确切知晓法国的财富和支出——为什么联邦的财富和支出也无法准确知晓——作者为研究宾夕法尼亚州税收总额进行的调查——用来指示一个国家公共开支总额的总指标——对美国所做调查研究的结果。

最近，人们已经尝试对法国公共开支和美国公共开支进行多次比较，然而，这些所有的尝试无一成功，所以，我认为有必要谈一谈他们为什么无法得到满意的结果。

为了对一个国家的公共开支的总额进行评估，有两个步骤必不可少：首先，要知道这个国家有多少财富；第二，要了解这笔财富有多少用于国家开销。只考察税收总额而不对满足其需求的税收来源进行调查只会徒劳无功，因为我们想知道的并不只是支出，而是支出和收入的关系。

富人轻而易举便可承担的赋税，对穷人而言可能会让其倾家荡产。国家的财富由截然不同的几部分构成，第一是人口，第二是不动产，第三是个人财产。这三个元素中的第一

poor one to extreme misery. The wealth of nations is composed of several distinct elements, of which population is the first, real property the second, and personal property the third. The first of these three elements may be discovered without difficulty. Amongst civilized nations it is easy to obtain an accurate census of the inhabitants; but the two others cannot be determined with so much facility. It is difficult to take an exact account of all the lands in a country which are under cultivation, with their natural or their acquired value; and it is still more impossible to estimate the entire personal property which is at the disposal of a nation, and which eludes the strictest analysis by the diversity and the number of shapes under which it may occur. And, indeed, we find that the most ancient civilized nations of Europe, including even those in which the administration is most central, have not succeeded, as yet, in determining the exact condition of their wealth.

In America the attempt has never been made; for how would such an investigation be possible in a country where society has not yet settled into habits of regularity and tranquillity; where the national Government is not assisted by a multiple of agents whose exertions it can command and direct to one sole end; and where statistics are not studied, because no one is able to collect the necessary documents, or to find time to peruse them? Thus the primary elements of the calculations which have been made in France cannot be obtained in the Union; the relative wealth of the two countries is unknown; the property of the former is not accurately determined, and no means exist of computing that of the latter.

I consent, therefore, for the sake of the discussion, to abandon this necessary term of the comparison, and I confine myself to a computation of the actual amount of taxation, without investigating the relation which subsists between the taxation and the revenue. But the reader will perceive that my task has not been facilitated by the limits which I here lay down for my researches.

It cannot be doubted that the central administration of France, assisted by all the public officers who are at its disposal, might determine with exactitude the amount of the direct and indirect taxes levied upon the citizens. But this investigation, which no private individual can undertake, has not hitherto been completed by the French Government, or, at least, its results have not been made public. We are acquainted with the sum total of the charges of the State; we know the amount of the

个最易得到。在文明国家，得到准确的居民人口统计非常简单，而另外两个做起来则不那么容易。一个国家的耕地面积及其天然价值和附加值很难精确地计算出来，而且对于一个国家中所有个人的财产进行评估更是无法实现，即使能够算出种类繁杂数量庞大的财产总额，也无法做到正确的分析。而且，我们发现，欧洲最古老的文明国家，甚至是那些最为行政集权的国家，也不能精确的计算出它们国家的财富总额。

在美国，还没有人做过这样的尝试。因为美国社会还没有安定下来，也没有像我国一样可供调遣去完成同一项任务的大批下级官员，而且由于没有人能收集必要的文献，数据无法得到分析或是没时间研究，在这样的国家怎么可能进行这样的调查呢？所以，计算所需的主要资料无从得到，也就无法比较法国和美国的国家财富。而且，两个国家的财富根本无从得知，法国的财富还没有得出准确的结果，而美国的财富根本无从计算。

因此，为了便于讨论，我打算放弃比较这个字眼，不再考察税收和支出的关系，而只对税收实际总额进行计算。然而读者会看到尽管我将自己的研究范围加以限定但是任务丝毫没有减轻。

我毫不怀疑，在其手下所有官员的协助下，法国中央集权行政管理制度准确计算出公民直接和间接缴纳的赋税总额的可能性依旧微乎其微。但是这样的调查并非个人可以完成，而且迄今为止，法国政府也未完成，或者至少是结果还未向大众公布。我们虽然知道国家的支出总额，也知道各省的支出总额，但是却不知道各乡镇的支出情况。所以，这个法国的公共开支便无从知晓。

departmental expenditure; but the expenses of the communal divisions have not been computed, and the amount of the public expenses of France is consequently unknown.

If we now turn to America, we shall perceive that the difficulties are multiplied and enhanced. The Union publishes an exact return of the amount of its expenditure; the budgets of the four and twenty States furnish similar returns of their revenues; but the expenses incident to the affairs of the counties and the townships are unknown.

The authority of the Federal government cannot oblige the provincial governments to throw any light upon this point; and even if these governments were inclined to afford their simultaneous co-operation, it may be doubted whether they possess the means of procuring a satisfactory answer. Independently of the natural difficulties of the task, the political organization of the country would act as a hindrance to the success of their efforts. The county and town magistrates are not appointed by the authorities of the State, and they are not subjected to their control. It is therefore very allowable to suppose that, if the State was desirous of obtaining the returns which we require, its design would be counteracted by the neglect of those subordinate officers whom it would be obliged to employ. It is, in point of fact, useless to inquire what the Americans might do to forward this inquiry, since it is certain that they have hitherto done nothing at all. There does not exist a single individual at the present day, in America or in Europe, who can inform us what each citizen of the Union annually contributes to the public charges of the nation.

Hence we must conclude that it is no less difficult to compare the social expenditure than it is to estimate the relative wealth of France and America. I will even add that it would be dangerous to attempt this comparison; for when statistics are not based upon computations which are strictly accurate, they mislead instead of guiding aright. The mind is easily imposed upon by the false affectation of exactness, which prevails even in the misstatements of science, and it adopts with confidence errors which are dressed in the forms of mathematical truth.

We abandon, therefore, our numerical investigation, with the hope of meeting with data of another kind. In the absence of positive documents, we may form an opinion as to the proportion which

如果我们现在转回头看美国，会发现这一调查的难度会成倍增加。联邦将其总支出的确切数字公布给我，二十四个州也同样让我了解了他们的财政预算，但是县乡事务的行政开支谁又能告诉我呢？

联邦当局不能迫使各州政府给我提供这方面的资料，即使这些州政府有意配合，至于他们能否给我一个满意的答复我也表示怀疑。先不谈这项任务的天然困难，国家的政治结构就会成为他们努力成功的障碍。县和乡镇的行政官并非州当局任命，而且也不听其指挥。所以可以断定，如果州当局希望获得我们想要的资料，也有可能会碰到应当为其服务的下级官员的敷衍了事。实际上，向美国人询问能否提供这些材料很可能也徒劳无功，因为可以肯定迄今为止他们在这方面什么都没做。所以，今天无论是在美国还是在欧洲，都没有一个人能告诉我们美国每个公民每年要为社会承担的费用是多少。

因此，我们得出这样的结论，比较两个社会的开支并不比计算两国各自财富来的简单。我甚至还要说，进行这种比较是很危险的，因为如果数据并非通过精准的计算而来，往往会把人引入歧途而不是引向正途。人们的思想往往会盲从于精确的数据，甚至在科学领域也很常见，人们对于披着数学真理外衣的错误总是深信不疑。

所以，我们要放弃对数字的研究，寄希望于其他的方法。既然没有可靠的资料，如果想要了解人民承担的公共开支与其财产的比例关系，只能通过观察这个国家是否繁荣，观察人民在向国家纳税后穷人是否依然可以维持生计，以及富人的享受方式，以及两个阶级是否在对各自处境表示满意的同时，还在不断的追求进一步的改善，从而工业资本充足，

the taxation of a people bears to its real prosperity, by observing whether its external appearance is flourishing; whether, after having discharged the calls of the State, the poor man retains the means of subsistence, and the rich the means of enjoyment; and whether both classes are contented with their position, seeking, however, to ameliorate it by perpetual exertions, so that industry is never in want of capital, nor capital unemployed by industry. The observer who draws his inferences from these signs will, undoubtedly, be led to the conclusion that the American of the United States contributes a much smaller portion of his income to the State than the citizen of France. Nor, indeed, can the result be otherwise.

A portion of the French debt is the consequence of two successive invasions; and the Union has no similar calamity to fear. A nation placed upon the continent of Europe is obliged to maintain a large standing army; the isolated position of the Union enables it to have only 6,000 soldiers. The French have a fleet of 300 sail; the Americans have 52 vessels. How, then, can the inhabitants of the Union be called upon to contribute as largely as the inhabitants of France? No parallel can be drawn between the finances of two countries so differently situated.

It is by examining what actually takes place in the Union, and not by comparing the Union with France, that we may discover whether the American Government is really economical. On casting my eyes over the different republics which form the confederation, I perceive that their Governments lack perseverance in their undertakings, and that they exercise no steady control over the men whom they employ. Whence I naturally infer that they must often spend the money of the people to no purpose, or consume more of it than is really necessary to their undertakings. Great efforts are made, in accordance with the democratic origin of society, to satisfy the exigencies of the lower orders, to open the career of power to their endeavors, and to diffuse knowledge and comfort amongst them. The poor are maintained, immense sums are annually devoted to public instruction, all services whatsoever are remunerated, and the most subordinate agents are liberally paid. If this kind of government appears to me to be useful and rational, I am nevertheless constrained to admit that it is expensive.

Wherever the poor direct public affairs and dispose of the national resources, it appears certain that, as they profit by the expenditure of the State, they are apt to augment that expenditure.

也不会有闲置资本。从这些迹象中，观察者必然推出这样的结论，美国公民的收入中，上交给国家的那一小部分远远低于法国公民收入所缴纳的那一部分。而且结果确实如此。

法国的部分债务是连续两次受侵略的结果，而美国则没有类似的担忧。位于欧洲大陆的国家必然要维持强大的军力，而美国位于与世隔绝之地，让它只需要6,000士兵就足矣。法国人有300艘军舰，但美国人只有52艘。美国居民怎么可能像法国居民的负担那样大呢！可见，两国的财政状况差异如此巨大，根本没有可比性。

通过对美国实际情况的考察，而不是法国和美国的对比，我们发现美国政府真的很节俭。在对联邦各州进行观察后，我注意到他们的政府做事情缺乏连贯性，而且对雇佣的人员缺乏定期的监督。所以我自然得出这样的结论，他们一定经常浪费纳税人的钱，要不就是在某些事业上花的钱远超其必需的支出。为了体现社会的民主性，政府付出大量的努力满足下层阶级的需要，为他们敞开监督政府的大门，并向他们普及知识和幸福。穷人衣食无忧，而且政府每年还会斥巨资兴建教育机构，给所有的付出付酬劳，而且哪怕是最下级的官员也会有很好的待遇。尽管我认为这样的治国方式合情合理，但也不得不承认它的开销巨大。

无论在什么地方，只要穷人主政掌握国家财源，国家开支必然增长，因为他们能够从国家支出中获得好处。

所以，在没有准确的统计数字，也不想进行没有把握的对比的情况下，我得到的结论是，美国的民主政府并非人们常常说的那样是一个吝啬的政府。而且我也会毫不犹豫地预言，如果美国人民一旦陷入巨大的困境，其赋税必然快速提高到与欧洲大部分贵族专制和

I conclude, therefore, without having recourse to inaccurate computations, and without hazarding a comparison which might prove incorrect, that the democratic government of the Americans is not a cheap government, as is sometimes asserted; and I have no hesitation in predicting that, if the people of the United States is ever involved in serious difficulties, its taxation will speedily be increased to the rate of that which prevails in the greater part of the aristocracies and the monarchies of Europe.

Corruption And Vices Of The Rulers In A Democracy, And Consequent Effects Upon Public Morality

In aristocracies rulers sometimes endeavor to corrupt the people—In democracies rulers frequently show themselves to be corrupt—In the former their vices are directly prejudicial to the morality of the people—In the latter their indirect influence is still more pernicious.

A distinction must be made, when the aristocratic and the democratic principles mutually inveigh against each other, as tending to facilitate corruption. In aristocratic governments the individuals who are placed at the head of affairs are rich men, who are solely desirous of power. In democracies statesmen are poor, and they have their fortunes to make. The consequence is that in aristocratic States the rulers are rarely accessible to corruption, and have very little craving for money; whilst the reverse is the case in democratic nations.

But in aristocracies, as those who are desirous of arriving at the head of affairs are possessed of considerable wealth, and as the number of persons by whose assistance they may rise is comparatively small, the government is, if I may use the expression, put up to a sort of auction. In democracies, on the contrary, those who are covetous of power are very seldom wealthy, and the number of citizens who confer that power is extremely great. Perhaps in democracies the number of men who might be bought is by no means smaller, but buyers are rarely to be met with; and, besides, it would be necessary to buy so many persons at once that the attempt is rendered nugatory.

Many of the men who have been in the administration in France during the last forty years have

君主制国家相同的水平。

民主制国家统治者的贪污腐化及其对公共道德的影响

在贵族制国家，统治者有时试图腐化——在民主制国家，统治者往往自行腐化——前者的恶行会直接影响人民的道德——后者对人民道德的影响虽然是间接的，但是影响更糟。

当贵族制度和民主制度互相攻击对方易受腐化的时候，必须要进行分辨。在贵族制政府，主政的个人是富人，他们贪图的是权力。在民主制政府，政客们都是穷人，他们渴望财富。结果，贵族制国家的统治者很少贪污，而且对钱也没什么欲望，然而在民主制国家情况恰恰相反。

但是，在贵族制国家，贪恋权力的人都很富有，而且因为职位的数量相对很少，可以说政府是待价而沽的政府。相反，在民主制国家，渴望主政的人几乎没有富人，而且竞争当权的人为数极多。所以，在民主制国家，卖家的数量可能不会很少，但却很难碰到买家，更何况一次还要收买很多人才能达到目的。

过去的四十年来，在法国主政的人不断受到指控，说他们为了自己发财不惜以国家和盟国的利益为代价，而旧君主制下的官员则很少受到这样的斥责。但实际上，在法国几乎没有贿选的情况，而这种丑行在英国则司空见惯。在美国，我也从没听说过有人被指控花钱贿选，但我常常听说公职人员的廉洁遭到质疑，而且我还听说，他们通常是靠着阴谋诡

been accused of making their fortunes at the expense of the State or of its allies; a reproach which was rarely addressed to the public characters of the ancient monarchy. But in France the practice of bribing electors is almost unknown, whilst it is notoriously and publicly carried on in England. In the United States I never heard a man accused of spending his wealth in corrupting the populace; but I have often heard the probity of public officers questioned; still more frequently have I heard their success attributed to low intrigues and immoral practices.

If, then, the men who conduct the government of an aristocracy sometimes endeavor to corrupt the people, the heads of a democracy are themselves corrupt. In the former case the morality of the people is directly assailed; in the latter an indirect influence is exercised upon the people which is still more to be dreaded.

As the rulers of democratic nations are almost always exposed to the suspicion of dishonorable conduct, they in some measure lend the authority of the Government to the base practices of which they are accused. They thus afford an example which must prove discouraging to the struggles of virtuous independence, and must foster the secret calculations of a vicious ambition. If it be asserted that evil passions are displayed in all ranks of society, that they ascend the throne by hereditary right, and that despicable characters are to be met with at the head of aristocratic nations as well as in the sphere of a democracy, this objection has but little weight in my estimation. The corruption of men who have casually risen to power has a coarse and vulgar infection in it which renders it contagious to the multitude. On the contrary, there is a kind of aristocratic refinement and an air of grandeur in the depravity of the great, which frequently prevent it from spreading abroad.

The people can never penetrate into the perplexing labyrinth of court intrigue, and it will always have difficulty in detecting the turpitude which lurks under elegant manners, refined tastes, and graceful language. But to pillage the public purse, and to vend the favors of the State, are arts which the meanest villain may comprehend, and hope to practice in his turn.

In reality it is far less prejudicial to witness the immorality of the great than to witness that immorality which leads to greatness. In a democracy private citizens see a man of their own rank

计和不道德的手段才获得成功。

那么，如果说贵族制下的主政者有时试图腐化，那么民主制下的领导则是自行腐化。对于前一种情况，人民的道德会受到直接冲击，而后一种情况，人民受到的间接影响更加可怕。

因为民主国家的统治者几乎一直受到行为不端的怀疑，所以他们会在一定程度上利用政府的权威保护自己受到指控的卑劣行径。因此，他们就成为与恶进行斗争的善的不良示范，必然会让邪恶的野心悄然滋生。如果有人声称，邪恶之心社会各个阶层人所共有，王位的登顶靠的是世袭的权利，而且不论是在贵族制国家还是民主制国家都会有猥琐之人成为国家首脑。在我看来这样的辩解根本没什么说服力。因为偶然间掌权之人的腐化行为表现出的粗陋下流会传染给大众，然而，大人物的堕落生活所带有的贵族般的优雅和高贵的气派，却往往能使之鲜为人知。

人们永远无法了解宫廷内部的阴谋诡计，也总是难以察觉隐藏在高雅仪态、高尚品位和优雅谈吐之下的奸佞卑鄙。但是对于盗窃国库和出卖国家利益的行径，哪怕是最差劲的恶棍也能看得明白，而且还想要跃跃欲试。

在现实中，看到不道德成就大人物远远比看到大人物不道德来得更为可怕。在民主制度下，一些普通公民看到在他们自己当中，有人几年间就从一文不名的小人物一跃成为有权有势的大人物，这必定会让他们吃惊嫉妒，而且他们必然会追问昨天还与自己平起平坐的人今天怎么就成了统治者。如果将他的平步青云归结为其才德，实在让人感到不快，因

in life, who rises from that obscure position, and who becomes possessed of riches and of power in a few years; the spectacle excites their surprise and their envy, and they are led to inquire how the person who was yesterday their equal is to-day their ruler. To attribute his rise to his talents or his virtues is unpleasant; for it is tacitly to acknowledge that they are themselves less virtuous and less talented than he was. They are therefore led (and not unfrequently their conjecture is a correct one) to impute his success mainly to some one of his defects; and an odious mixture is thus formed of the ideas of turpitude and power, unworthiness and success, utility and dishonor.

Efforts Of Which A Democracy Is Capable

The Union has only had one struggle hitherto for its existence—Enthusiasm at the commencement of the war—Indifference towards its close—Difficulty of establishing military conscription or impressment of seamen in America—Why a democratic people is less capable of sustained effort than another.

I here warn the reader that I speak of a government which implicitly follows the real desires of a people, and not of a government which simply commands in its name. Nothing is so irresistible as a tyrannical power commanding in the name of the people, because, whilst it exercises that moral influence which belongs to the decision of the majority, it acts at the same time with the promptitude and the tenacity of a single man.

It is difficult to say what degree of exertion a democratic government may be capable of making a crisis in the history of the nation. But no great democratic republic has hitherto existed in the world. To style the oligarchy which ruled over France in 1793 by that name would be to offer an insult to the republican form of government. The United States afford the first example of the kind.

The American Union has now subsisted for half a century, in the course of which time its existence has only once been attacked, namely, during the War of Independence. At the commencement of that long war, various occurrences took place which betokened an extraordinary zeal for the service of the country. But as the contest was prolonged, symptoms of private egotism began to show themselves.

为这就等于承认自己的才德不如别人。因此，他们就将其成功的主要原因归结为他的某个卑劣之处（而且他们的猜想往往是对的）。所以，在卑鄙和权力，下贱和成功以及丢脸和实惠之间形成令人作呕的概念混乱。

民主能够做出的努力

迄今为止联邦为其生存只做过一次斗争——战争开始的热情——战争尾声时的漠然——在美国，建立征兵制或海员强迫服役制的困难——为什么民主国家无法像其他国家那样做出同等程度的不懈努力。

这里我要提醒一下读者，我所说的政府是真正遵从民愿的政府，而不是仅仅打着人民旗号的政府。打着人民的旗号实行专制的政府最无法抗拒，因为它在运用本属于多数的道德力量的同时，迅速而坚定地执行个人的意志。

很难说清，一个民主政府在国家危机时刻能够做出多大程度的努力。至今世界上尚未出现伟大的民主共和国。如果将1793年统治法国的寡头政府称为共和国，简直就是对共和政体的侮辱。美国称得上是共和制的第一示范。

时至今日，美联邦已有半个世纪，在此期间，它的存在只经历过一次危机，也就是在独立战争时期。在那场漫长的战争之初，人们报效祖国的热忱实属罕见。但是随着战争的旷日持久，自私自利开始在人们身上表现出来。人们不再向国库提供金钱，征兵变得越

No money was poured into the public treasury; few recruits could be raised to join the army; the people wished to acquire independence, but was very ill-disposed to undergo the privations by which alone it could be obtained. "Tax laws," says Hamilton in the "Federalist" (No. 12), "have in vain been multiplied; new methods to enforce the collection have in vain been tried; the public expectation has been uniformly disappointed and the treasuries of the States have remained empty. The popular system of administration inherent in the nature of popular government, coinciding with the real scarcity of money incident to a languid and mutilated state of trade, has hitherto defeated every experiment for extensive collections, and has at length taught the different legislatures the folly of attempting them."

The United States have not had any serious war to carry on ever since that period. In order, therefore, to appreciate the sacrifices which democratic nations may impose upon themselves, we must wait until the American people is obliged to put half its entire income at the disposal of the Government, as was done by the English; or until it sends forth a twentieth part of its population to the field of battle, as was done by France.

In America the use of conscription is unknown, and men are induced to enlist by bounties. The notions and habits of the people of the United States are so opposed to compulsory enlistment that I do not imagine it can ever be sanctioned by the laws. What is termed the conscription in France is assuredly the heaviest tax upon the population of that country; yet how could a great continental war be carried on without it? The Americans have not adopted the British impressment of seamen, and they have nothing which corresponds to the French system of maritime conscription; the navy, as well as the merchant service, is supplied by voluntary service. But it is not easy to conceive how a people can sustain a great maritime war without having recourse to one or the other of these two systems. Indeed, the Union, which has fought with some honor upon the seas, has never possessed a very numerous fleet, and the equipment of the small number of American vessels has always been excessively expensive.

I have heard American statesmen confess that the Union will have great difficulty in maintaining its rank on the seas without adopting the system of impressment or of maritime conscription; but the

来越难，尽管人们依旧希望获得独立，但是面对取得独立的艰辛却裹足不前。汉密尔顿在《联邦党人文集》（第12篇）中写道："新增的税目是徒劳的，试行的新的收税办法是徒劳的，公众的期待一律化为失望，国库也依然空空如也。迄今为止，民主制政府固有的行政管理体制，在遭遇国库资金奇缺以及由此导致的贸易疲软的状况时，并未能实现扩大税收，终于各州立法机构认识到他们做法的愚蠢。"

从那时之后，美国再也没有经历需要坚持到底的大战。因此，如果想要知道哪些牺牲是民主制度能够做出的，我们别无他法只能拭目以待，直到美国人像英国人那样被迫将自己一半的收入上交政府支配的时候，或是等到像法国人那样把其人口的二十分之一送上战场的时候。

在美国，人们不认可征兵制，丰厚的酬劳才能诱惑他们应征入伍。强制征兵跟美国人的观念和习惯相悖，所以不难想象这样的法律必然无法得到通过。在法国实行的所谓征兵制无疑是压在法国人身上最沉重的负担。但是，如果没有征兵制又怎能维持一场大战呢？当然，美国人也不会采用英国人强制海员服役的办法，而且他们也没有法国那样的海军征兵制，海军和商船的海员一样，都是自愿应征招募。但是，很难弄明白，不采用上述征兵制中的任何一种怎么能够支持一场海上大战。实际上，曾经在海上有过几次光荣战斗的合众国并没有一支庞大的舰队，而且为了装备其为数不多的舰船还往往花费不菲。

我曾经听说，美国政客坦言不实行海员强制服役制和海军征兵制美联邦很难维持其在海上的地位，但是，要诱使行使国家主权的人认可征兵制或是任何一种带有强制性的制度

difficulty is to induce the people, which exercises the supreme authority, to submit to impressment or any compulsory system.

It is incontestable that in times of danger a free people displays far more energy than one which is not so. But I incline to believe that this is more especially the case in those free nations in which the democratic element preponderates. Democracy appears to me to be much better adapted for the peaceful conduct of society, or for an occasional effort of remarkable vigor, than for the hardy and prolonged endurance of the storms which beset the political existence of nations. The reason is very evident; it is enthusiasm which prompts men to expose themselves to dangers and privations, but they will not support them long without reflection. There is more calculation, even in the impulses of bravery, than is generally attributed to them; and although the first efforts are suggested by passion, perseverance is maintained by a distinct regard of the purpose in view. A portion of what we value is exposed, in order to save the remainder.

But it is this distinct perception of the future, founded upon a sound judgment and an enlightened experience, which is most frequently wanting in democracies. The populace is more apt to feel than to reason; and if its present sufferings are great, it is to be feared that the still greater sufferings attendant upon defeat will be forgotten.

Another cause tends to render the efforts of a democratic government less persevering than those of an aristocracy. Not only are the lower classes less awakened than the higher orders to the good or evil chances of the future, but they are liable to suffer far more acutely from present privations. The noble exposes his life, indeed, but the chance of glory is equal to the chance of harm. If he sacrifices a large portion of his income to the State, he deprives himself for a time of the pleasures of affluence; but to the poor man death is embellished by no pomp or renown, and the imposts which are irksome to the rich are fatal to him.

This relative impotence of democratic republics is, perhaps, the greatest obstacle to the foundation of a republic of this kind in Europe. In order that such a State should subsist in one country of the Old World, it would be necessary that similar institutions should be introduced into all the other nations.

都很困难。

不可否认，在危机时刻，自由国家所迸发出的能量远超非自由国家。而我更趋向于认为，那些民主成分占有优势的自由国家，情况尤其如此。在我看来，民主制度更适合用来治理和平的社会，或是偶尔用来激发社会的活力，而不适合用来长期抵制威胁国家存亡的政治风暴的冲击。原因显而易见，热情虽然能够让人们不畏艰险贫困，但是深思熟虑才能让他们与之长期战斗。甚至是冲动之下的勇敢往往也并不缺少计算，尽管最初的努力是出自热情，但是毅力则需要有明确的目标才能维持下去。人们用一部分珍贵的东西去冒险，为的就是能够拯救剩下的部分。

但是，民主国家最需要的是，建立在可靠判断和开明经验之上的对未来的清晰认识。人们行事往往更容易受到感性的驱使而不是理性。所以，目前的痛苦虽大，但是并不可怕，可怕的是将失败带来的更大痛苦抛到脑后。

让民主政府的努力来的不如贵族政府坚定的另一个原因是，对于未来的祸福下层阶级不仅不如上层阶级看得清楚，而且对于目前的痛苦他们的感受也更为深刻。的确，贵族将他们的生命置于危险境地，但是获得荣耀的机会与受到伤害的机会均等。如果他将自己大部分的收入奉献给国家，所失去的不过是一段时间的享乐。但是对于穷人而言，死得光荣并没有诱惑力，而令富人也感到深恶痛绝的苛捐杂税对他们才是致命的。

民主共和国的相对弱势也许是这种制度在欧洲无法确立的最大障碍。为了能让民主共和制在旧世界里一个国家中存在下去，就必须在其他所有国家引入这种类似的制度。

I am of opinion that a democratic government tends in the end to increase the real strength of society; but it can never combine, upon a single point and at a given time, so much power as an aristocracy or a monarchy. If a democratic country remained during a whole century subject to a republican government, it would probably at the end of that period be more populous and more prosperous than the neighboring despotic States. But it would have incurred the risk of being conquered much oftener than they would in that lapse of years.

Self-Control Of The American Democracy

The American people acquiesces slowly, or frequently does not acquiesce, in what is beneficial to its interests—The faults of the American democracy are for the most part reparable.

The difficulty which a democracy has in conquering the passions and in subduing the exigencies of the moment, with a view to the future, is conspicuous in the most trivial occurrences of the United States. The people, which is surrounded by flatterers, has great difficulty in surmounting its inclinations, and whenever it is solicited to undergo a privation or any kind of inconvenience, even to attain an end which is sanctioned by its own rational conviction, it almost always refuses to comply at first. The deference of the Americans to the laws has been very justly applauded; but it must be added that in America the legislation is made by the people and for the people. Consequently, in the United States the law favors those classes which are most interested in evading it elsewhere. It may therefore be supposed that an offensive law, which should not be acknowledged to be one of immediate utility, would either not be enacted or would not be obeyed.

In America there is no law against fraudulent bankruptcies; not because they are few, but because there are a great number of bankruptcies. The dread of being prosecuted as a bankrupt acts with more intensity upon the mind of the majority of the people than the fear of being involved in losses or ruin by the failure of other parties, and a sort of guilty tolerance is extended by the public conscience to an offence which everyone condemns in his individual capacity. In the new States of the Southwest

我认为，一个民主政府最终必能让社会实力得到加强，但是永远也不能像贵族制或是君主制国家那样将如此多的力量集中于某一点或是某一刻。如果在一个民主国家的共和政府能够延续一个世纪，那么它一定能够比周围的专制国家更加繁荣富强。但是在这段时间里，它始终处于被这些专制国家不断征服的险境之中。

美国民主的自制力

美国人经过漫长的时间才默许对他们有利的东西，有时还曾拒绝接受——美国民主的大部分失误可以弥补。

为了未来的利益，民主克服暂时的激情和抑制此刻的需求遇到的困难在最微不足道的事情上表现出来。常常受到阿谀奉承的人很难自制，而且无论何时当有人向他们请求帮助和救济时，即使他认为其目的合理，在一开始也往往会拒绝。对于美国人对法律的尊重，人们赞许有加，但需要说明的是，在美国，法律是由人民为人民制定的。因此，美国的法律对那些在哪里都想逃避法律的人有利。所以，可以想到，一项于大多数人看来没有实际好处的令人生厌的法律，不是无法获得通过就是通过了也没人遵守。

在美国，没有惩治虚报破产的法律，这并不是因为美国的破产者少，而是刚好相反，因为破产的人太多。所以，大多数美国人对因破产而受到指控的恐惧，更甚于对别人的破产给自己带来的损失，而且在公众的意识中对私人告发的犯罪有一种错误的包容心理。在

the citizens generally take justice into their own hands, and murders are of very frequent occurrence. This arises from the rude manners and the ignorance of the inhabitants of those deserts, who do not perceive the utility of investing the law with adequate force, and who prefer duels to prosecutions.

Someone observed to me one day, in Philadelphia, that almost all crimes in America are caused by the abuse of intoxicating liquors, which the lower classes can procure in great abundance, from their excessive cheapness. "How comes it," said I, "that you do not put a duty upon brandy?" "Our legislators," rejoined my informant, "have frequently thought of this expedient; but the task of putting it in operation is a difficult one; a revolt might be apprehended, and the members who should vote for a law of this kind would be sure of losing their seats." "Whence I am to infer," replied I, "that the drinking population constitutes the majority in your country, and that temperance is somewhat unpopular."

When these things are pointed out to the American statesmen, they content themselves with assuring you that time will operate the necessary change, and that the experience of evil will teach the people its true interests. This is frequently true, although a democracy is more liable to error than a monarch or a body of nobles; the chances of its regaining the right path when once it has acknowledged its mistake, are greater also; because it is rarely embarrassed by internal interests, which conflict with those of the majority, and resist the authority of reason. But a democracy can only obtain truth as the result of experience, and many nations may forfeit their existence whilst they are awaiting the consequences of their errors.

The great privilege of the Americans does not simply consist in their being more enlightened than other nations, but in their being able to repair the faults they may commit. To which it must be added, that a democracy cannot derive substantial benefit from past experience, unless it be arrived at a certain pitch of knowledge and civilization. There are tribes and peoples whose education has been so vicious, and whose character presents so strange a mixture of passion, of ignorance, and of erroneous notions upon all subjects, that they are unable to discern the causes of their own wretchedness, and they fall a sacrifice to ills with which they are unacquainted.

I have crossed vast tracts of country that were formerly inhabited by powerful Indian nations

美国西南新成立的州里，公民自己掌握司法权，而且谋杀事件时有发生。这种现象产生的原因在于，生活在这片蛮荒之地上的居民粗野无知，不懂得运用法律的力量，所以他们宁可选择决斗。

一天，在费城有人跟我说，美国几乎所有的犯罪都是因为酗酒，因为酒很便宜所以下层人民可以开怀畅饮。于是我问："向烧酒征税如何？"他回答道："我们的立法者倒是总有这样的想法，但是阻力重重，因为害怕人民的反对，而且对此类法律投赞成票的议员，肯定无法再次当选。"我接着说："由此可见，在你们的国家饮酒的人是大多数，而禁酒就不得人心了。"

当跟美国的政客们谈及这些事情的时候，他们只会告诉你时间会改变一切，痛苦的经历会告诉人们他们真正利益的所在。事实的确如此。尽管民主制度往往会比君主或是贵族制度有更多的失误，但是一旦认识到错误，重回正轨的机会也要多得多，因为民主制度的内在利益与多数没有冲突，跟理性也没有抵触。但是，民主制度只能从经验中获得真理，而许多国家还没等到它们失误的后果就已经不复存在。

美国人的优势不仅在于他们比其他国家更加文明开化，而且在于他们能够纠正自己犯下的错误。需要补充的是，除非一个国家的知识和文明到达一定的高度，否则无法从过往的经验中大量获益。有一些部落和国家教育情况很糟糕，人民性格完全是激情、无知和对所有事情错误看法的大杂烩，所以他们看不到自身不幸的根源，成为自己认识不到的灾难的牺牲品。

which are now extinct; I have myself passed some time in the midst of mutilated tribes, which witness the daily decline of their numerical strength and of the glory of their independence; and I have heard these Indians themselves anticipate the impending doom of their race. Every European can perceive means which would rescue these unfortunate beings from inevitable destruction. They alone are insensible to the expedient; they feel the woe which year after year heaps upon their heads, but they will perish to a man without accepting the remedy. It would be necessary to employ force to induce them to submit to the protection and the constraint of civilization.

The incessant revolutions which have convulsed the South American provinces for the last quarter of a century have frequently been adverted to with astonishment, and expectations have been expressed that those nations would speedily return to their natural state. But can it be affirmed that the turmoil of revolution is not actually the most natural state of the South American Spaniards at the present time? In that country society is plunged into difficulties from which all its efforts are insufficient to rescue it. The inhabitants of that fair portion of the Western Hemisphere seem obstinately bent on pursuing the work of inward havoc. If they fall into a momentary repose from the effects of exhaustion, that repose prepares them for a fresh state of frenzy. When I consider their condition, which alternates between misery and crime, I should be inclined to believe that despotism itself would be a benefit to them, if it were possible that the words despotism and benefit could ever be united in my mind.

Conduct Of Foreign Affairs By The American Democracy

Direction given to the foreign policy of the United States by Washington and Jefferson—Almost all the defects inherent in democratic institutions are brought to light in the conduct of foreign affairs—Their advantages are less perceptible.

We have seen that the Federal Constitution entrusts the permanent direction of the external interests of the nation to the President and the Senate, which tends in some degree to detach the

我曾途经一些广袤地区，那里原先由强大的印第安部族统治而今却已见不到他们的踪影；我也曾在一些印第安部落流连，它们目睹自己人口的衰败和独立荣耀的丧失；而且我还曾听说印第安人自己也预言自己种族的灭亡为时不远。每个欧洲人都认为到要采取一些措施挽救这些不幸之人注定的灭亡。但是他们自己却无所作为。他们感到灾难一年年向他们逼近，但是即使毁灭到只剩一人，他们也不愿接受救助。所以，将来有必要采取武力迫使他们接受保护和文明的约束。

过去25年来，南美各国革命接连不断让人感到吃惊，人们期待着这些国家能够迅速恢复到自然状态。但是谁又能肯定革命的骚动就不是现在南美西班牙人的最自然状态呢？在那里，社会陷入深渊之中，凭借其自身的力量无法走出来。那些居住在西半球美丽土地上的人民似乎一心专注于内部的混乱。如果他们因疲不堪而暂时休战，而休战过后他们又会陷入新的疯狂。当我想到他们不是受苦就是作孽的情景，更愿意相信专制对他们是一种福泽，而这是专制和福泽能够在我头脑中统一起来的唯一可能。

美国民主处理对外事务的做法

华盛顿和杰斐逊对美国外交政策的指导——在对外事务上，民主制度的所有固有缺陷表露无遗——其优点难以为人察觉。

我们已经看到，联邦宪法把外交事务的指导权交给了总统和参议院，这在一定程度

general foreign policy of the Union from the control of the people. It cannot therefore be asserted with truth that the external affairs of State are conducted by the democracy.

The policy of America owes its rise to Washington, and after him to Jefferson, who established those principles which it observes at the present day. Washington said in the admirable letter which he addressed to his fellow-citizens, and which may be looked upon as his political bequest to the country: "The great rule of conduct for us in regard to foreign nations is, in extending our commercial relations, to have with them as little political connection as possible. So far as we have already formed engagements, let them be fulfilled with perfect good faith. Here let us stop. Europe has a set of primary interests which to us have none, or a very remote relation. Hence, she must be engaged in frequent controversies, the causes of which are essentially foreign to our concerns. Hence, therefore, it must be unwise in us to implicate ourselves, by artificial ties, in the ordinary vicissitudes of her politics, or the ordinary combinations and collisions of her friendships or enmities. Our detached and distant situation invites and enables us to pursue a different course. If we remain one people, under an efficient government, the period is not far off when we may defy material injury from external annoyance; when we may take such an attitude as will cause the neutrality we may at any time resolve upon to be scrupulously respected; when belligerent nations, under the impossibility of making acquisitions upon us, will not lightly hazard the giving us provocation; when we may choose peace or war, as our interest, guided by justice, shall counsel. Why forego the advantages of so peculiar a situation? Why quit our own to stand upon foreign ground? Why, by interweaving our destiny with that of any part of Europe, entangle our peace and prosperity in the toils of European ambition, rivalship, interest, humor, or caprice? It is our true policy to steer clear of permanent alliances with any portion of the foreign world; so far, I mean, as we are now at liberty to do it; for let me not be understood as capable of patronizing infidelity to existing engagements. I hold the maxim no less applicable to public than to private affairs, that honesty is always the best policy. I repeat it; therefore, let those engagements be observed in their genuine sense; but in my opinion it is unnecessary, and would be unwise, to extend them. Taking care always to keep ourselves, by suitable

上使得联邦总的对外政策能够脱离人民的控制。因此说美国的外交事务采用的并不是民主制。

美国对外政策首先要得益于华盛顿，其次是杰斐逊，他们制定的那些政策一直沿用至今。华盛顿的一封值得赞美的信，也可以看作他留给这个国家的政治遗训，信中他对同胞这样说道："在外交方面，我国首要的行事原则是，扩大对外的贸易往来，同时尽可能减少与他国发生政治联系。就已经缔结的条约，必须忠实履行。但是，我们会停在此处。欧洲有一套基本利益，这与我们无关或者说关联甚少。因此，他们必然不断卷入纷争，究其原因与我们毫不相干。所以，通过人为的纽带，卷入欧洲日常的政治变迁，或是欧洲各国间时而友好时而敌对的分分合合，对我们而言是非常不明智的。我国独处一方，远离他国的地理位置允许并促使我们奉行一条不同的路线。如果我们能够在一个高效政府的领导下团结一致，那么不久的将来我们将无惧外来干扰给我们造成的物质伤害。我们就可以采取一种姿态，使我们在任何时候想要保持中立时，能够得到他国的严正尊重；好战之国不能从我们这里得到好处时，也不敢轻易向我们挑战；我们可以在正义的指引下，依据我国的利益，或战或和。为什么要放弃这样得天独厚的地理优势？为什么要离开自己的故土站到外国的土地？为什么，要让我们的命运和欧洲某一部分的命运交织在一起，让我国的和平与繁荣跟欧洲人的野心、敌对、利益、肆意妄为和反复无常纠缠起来？我们真正的政策是不与世界上任何国家永久结盟。我的意思是说，我们要像现在一样不受约束自由行动，但不要理解成为可以不遵守现有的条约。无论于公还是于私，我始终坚信诚实是最好的策

establishments, in a respectable defensive posture, we may safely trust to temporary alliances for extraordinary emergencies." In a previous part of the same letter Washington makes the following admirable and just remark: "The nation which indulges towards another an habitual hatred or an habitual fondness is in some degree a slave. It is a slave to its animosity or to its affection, either of which is sufficient to lead it astray from its duty and its interest."

The political conduct of Washington was always guided by these maxims. He succeeded in maintaining his country in a state of peace whilst all the other nations of the globe were at war; and he laid it down as a fundamental doctrine, that the true interest of the Americans consisted in a perfect neutrality with regard to the internal dissensions of the European Powers.

Jefferson went still further, and he introduced a maxim into the policy of the Union, which affirms that "the Americans ought never to solicit any privileges from foreign nations, in order not to be obliged to grant similar privileges themselves."

These two principles, which were so plain and so just as to be adapted to the capacity of the populace, have greatly simplified the foreign policy of the United States. As the Union takes no part in the affairs of Europe, it has, properly speaking, no foreign interests to discuss, since it has at present no powerful neighbors on the American continent. The country is as much removed from the passions of the Old World by its position as by the line of policy which it has chosen, and it is neither called upon to repudiate nor to espouse the conflicting interests of Europe; whilst the dissensions of the New World are still concealed within the bosom of the future.

The Union is free from all pre-existing obligations, and it is consequently enabled to profit by the experience of the old nations of Europe, without being obliged, as they are, to make the best of the past, and to adapt it to their present circumstances; or to accept that immense inheritance which they derive from their forefathers—an inheritance of glory mingled with calamities, and of alliances conflicting with national antipathies. The foreign policy of the United States is reduced by its very nature to await the chances of the future history of the nation, and for the present it consists more in abstaining from interference than in exerting its activity.

略。因此，我要再次重复，我们要谨遵条约的本意，因为在我看来，对于原有条约的任何延伸都是不必要也是不明智的。通过采取适当的措施，要小心谨慎地让我们自己始终处于受人尊重的防御姿态，从而当出现意外的危险之时，也可以确保利用暂时的同盟。"在信中这段话之前，华盛顿还说过一句至理名言："沉溺于对另一国家习惯性的憎恨和喜爱的一个国家，在某种程度上说就是一个奴隶，即自己爱憎的奴隶，无论还是爱还是憎都足以使自己偏离自身的责任和利益而误入歧途。"

华盛顿的政治活动始终奉行这些箴言。当世界所有其他国家处于战乱之中的时候，他成功地让自己的国家保持和平状态。他认为美国人的真正利益在于能够对欧洲大国间的内部纷争保持中立，并将此视为自己的基本信条。

杰斐逊走得更远，他对美国对外事务上信奉的箴言是："美国不向他国要求特权，以免自己被迫出让相同的特权。"

这两条原则如此直白公正，易于理解，大大简化了美国的对外政策。因为美国不参与欧洲事务，严格来说，没有什么国外利益好谈，因为目前在美洲大陆还没有与之抗衡的强邻。因为美国所处的地理位置和奉行的政策，旧世界的那种激情丝毫没有感染到这个国家；而且也没有人要求它对欧洲的利益冲突表示反对或是支持，新世界的纷争还隐藏在未来之中。

联邦政府不受旧条约的约束，因而能够从欧洲旧国家的经验中汲取好处，而且不必像他们那样不得不利用过去并使之适应现在；或是被迫接受祖先留下的巨大遗产，而这些遗

It is therefore very difficult to ascertain, at present, what degree of sagacity the American democracy will display in the conduct of the foreign policy of the country; and upon this point its adversaries, as well as its advocates, must suspend their judgment. As for myself I have no hesitation in avowing my conviction, that it is most especially in the conduct of foreign relations that democratic governments appear to me to be decidedly inferior to governments carried on upon different principles. Experience, instruction, and habit may almost always succeed in creating a species of practical discretion in democracies, and that science of the daily occurrences of life which is called good sense. Good sense may suffice to direct the ordinary course of society; and amongst a people whose education has been provided for, the advantages of democratic liberty in the internal affairs of the country may more than compensate for the evils inherent in a democratic government. But such is not always the case in the mutual relations of foreign nations.

Foreign politics demand scarcely any of those qualities which a democracy possesses; and they require, on the contrary, the perfect use of almost all those faculties in which it is deficient. Democracy is favorable to the increase of the internal resources of the State; it tends to diffuse a moderate independence; it promotes the growth of public spirit, and fortifies the respect which is entertained for law in all classes of society; and these are advantages which only exercise an indirect influence over the relations which one people bears to another. But a democracy is unable to regulate the details of an important undertaking, to persevere in a design, and to work out its execution in the presence of serious obstacles. It cannot combine its measures with secrecy, and it will not await their consequences with patience. These are qualities which more especially belong to an individual or to an aristocracy; and they are precisely the means by which an individual people attains to a predominant position.

If, on the contrary, we observe the natural defects of aristocracy, we shall find that their influence is comparatively innoxious in the direction of the external affairs of a State. The capital fault of which aristocratic bodies may be accused is that they are more apt to contrive their own advantage than that of the mass of the people. In foreign politics it is rare for the interest of the aristocracy to be in any way distinct from that of the people.

产之中，既有荣耀也有灾难，以及国家间的友好和憎恨。美国的外交政策溯其本质就是观望政策，就目前而言，其政策就是有所不为，而不是有所作为。

所以，目前很难确定，美国的民主在对外政策上会显示出多大程度的远见卓识。就这一点，无论是敌是友都无法做出判断。至于我，则会毫不犹豫地公开承认，民主政府特别就其外交行事政策而言，绝对不如奉行不同原则的其他政府。经验、教育和习惯往往总是可以成功地为民主制度创建各种实用的知识，以及称之为常识的日常生活小事的学问。常识也许足以指导社会的日常进程，而对于一个教育完备的国家，民主的自由在处理国内事务上的优势能够很大程度上弥补民主政府固有的缺陷。但是，在处理对外关系问题上，则往往并非如此。

外交政策对民主本身所具备的素质似乎并不需要，相反，所需要充分运用的恰恰是民主所不具备的那些素质。民主有利于国家内部资源的增加，让人民过的舒适，促进公益精神，并巩固社会各阶级对法律的尊重，而这些只能对一个国家的对外关系起到间接作用。但是，民主无法对重大事业细节进行规范，只能做出规划，并克服障碍监督实行。民主无法采取秘密措施，更无法耐心等着这些措施的结果。这些个人或贵族所特有的素质，在一个国家经过长期的治理之后也能够获得。

相反，如果你考察一下贵族制的天然缺陷，会发现它们对国家的对外事务几乎没有明显的影响。贵族政体应受指责的首要问题是，它们往往是为自己谋利而不是人民大众。然而，在外交政策上，贵族的利益与人民大众的利益则罕有不同。

The propensity which democracies have to obey the impulse of passion rather than the suggestions of prudence, and to abandon a mature design for the gratification of a momentary caprice, was very clearly seen in America on the breaking out of the French Revolution. It was then as evident to the simplest capacity as it is at the present time that the interest of the Americans forbade them to take any part in the contest which was about to deluge Europe with blood, but which could by no means injure the welfare of their own country. Nevertheless the sympathies of the people declared themselves with so much violence in behalf of France that nothing but the inflexible character of Washington, and the immense popularity which he enjoyed, could have prevented the Americans from declaring war against England. And even then, the exertions which the austere reason of that great man made to repress the generous but imprudent passions of his fellow-citizens, very nearly deprived him of the sole recompense which he had ever claimed—that of his country's love. The majority then reprobated the line of policy which he adopted, and which has since been unanimously approved by the nation. If the Constitution and the favor of the public had not entrusted the direction of the foreign affairs of the country to Washington, it is certain that the American nation would at that time have taken the very measures which it now condemns.

Almost all the nations which have ever exercised a powerful influence upon the destinies of the world by conceiving, following up, and executing vast designs—from the Romans to the English—have been governed by aristocratic institutions. Nor will this be a subject of wonder when we recollect that nothing in the world has so absolute a fixity of purpose as an aristocracy. The mass of the people may be led astray by ignorance or passion; the mind of a king may be biased, and his perseverance in his designs may be shaken—besides which a king is not immortal—but an aristocratic body is too numerous to be led astray by the blandishments of intrigue, and yet not numerous enough to yield readily to the intoxicating influence of unreflecting passion: it has the energy of a firm and enlightened individual, added to the power which it derives from perpetuity.

在法国大革命爆发的时候，民主服从感性的激情而不是理性的审慎以及为满足一时之悦而放弃成熟计划的倾向，在美国表现得非常明显。当时和现在一样，在美国的精明之人看来，美国人的利益迫使他们不介入血洗欧洲的争端，从而使自己国家的利益免受损害。然而，人民对法国的同情如此强烈，如果不是华盛顿的坚持不懈以及人民对他的爱戴，美国必将会对英国宣战。当时，这位伟人用自己缜密的理性去抑制同胞们慷慨而轻率的热情，这几乎让自己失去国家对他的热爱。甚至有很多人声讨他所采取的对外政策，但是现在人民都对其政策一致赞成。如果宪法和人民没有将处理国家对外事务的权力交给华盛顿，美国人当时肯定会采取那些在今天会受到谴责的措施。

从罗马人到英国人，几乎对世界命运产生强大影响的，曾拟定、遵循和执行伟大计划的所有国家都采用贵族统治。当我们想到世界上贵族制度的目标最是坚定，便不会对这样的显现表示讶异。人民大众也许会被无知和激情所迷惑，但是国王也会因为意志不坚在执行计划的时候犹豫不决，而且国王也无法永生，但是一个贵族政体却可以因为人多而免于误入歧途，免受激情的左右。它就像一个永生的意志坚定且开明的个人。

Chapter XIV: Advantages American Society Derive From Democracy

What The Real Advantages Are Which American Society Derives From The Government Of The Democracy

Before I enter upon the subject of the present chapter I am induced to remind the reader of what I have more than once adverted to in the course of this book. The political institutions of the United States appear to me to be one of the forms of government which a democracy may adopt; but I do not regard the American Constitution as the best, or as the only one, which a democratic people may establish. In showing the advantages which the Americans derive from the government of democracy, I am therefore very far from meaning, or from believing, that similar advantages can only be obtained from the same laws.

General Tendency Of The Laws Under The Rule Of The American Democracy, And Habits Of Those Who Apply Them

Defects of a democratic government easy to be discovered—Its advantages only to be discerned by long observation—Democracy in America often inexpert, but the general tendency of the laws advantageous—In the American democracy public officers have no permanent interests distinct from those of the majority—Result of this state of things.

第十四章 民主制带给美国社会的好处

美国社会从民主政府中得到的真正好处

在我进入这一章节之前，我想要提醒读者我曾不止一次在本书中谈到的观点。在我看来，美国的政治体制只是民主国家所能采用的形式之一，而且我也不认为它是民主国家所能采用的最好或是唯一的一种形式。因此，通过呈现美国人从民主政府中获得的好处，我绝不断言也不认为只有采用同样的法律才能取得类似的利益。

美国民主制度下法制的总趋势以及人们的应用习惯

民主政府的问题容易发觉——其好处只有通过长期观察才能发现——美国的民主不成熟，但法制的总趋势向善——在美国民主共和制度下，公务员与多数的长远利益并无不同——由此产生的结果。

民主政府的缺陷和弱点很容易被发现，并得到一些明显的事实的印证，但是它的积极

The defects and the weaknesses of a democratic government may very readily be discovered; they are demonstrated by the most flagrant instances, whilst its beneficial influence is less perceptibly exercised. A single glance suffices to detect its evil consequences, but its good qualities can only be discerned by long observation. The laws of the American democracy are frequently defective or incomplete; they sometimes attack vested rights, or give a sanction to others which are dangerous to the community; but even if they were good, the frequent changes which they undergo would be an evil. How comes it, then, that the American republics prosper and maintain their position?

In the consideration of laws a distinction must be carefully observed between the end at which they aim and the means by which they are directed to that end, between their absolute and their relative excellence. If it be the intention of the legislator to favor the interests of the minority at the expense of the majority, and if the measures he takes are so combined as to accomplish the object he has in view with the least possible expense of time and exertion, the law may be well drawn up, although its purpose be bad; and the more efficacious it is, the greater is the mischief which it causes.

Democratic laws generally tend to promote the welfare of the greatest possible number; for they emanate from the majority of the citizens, who are subject to error, but who cannot have an interest opposed to their own advantage. The laws of an aristocracy tend, on the contrary, to concentrate wealth and power in the hands of the minority, because an aristocracy, by its very nature, constitutes a minority. It may therefore be asserted, as a general proposition, that the purpose of a democracy in the conduct of its legislation is useful to a greater number of citizens than that of an aristocracy. This is, however, the sum total of its advantages.

Aristocracies are infinitely more expert in the science of legislation than democracies ever can be. They are possessed of a self-control which protects them from the errors of temporary excitement, and they form lasting designs which they mature with the assistance of favorable opportunities. Aristocratic government proceeds with the dexterity of art; it understands how to make the collective force of all its laws converge at the same time to a given point. Such is not the case with democracies, whose laws are almost always ineffective or inopportune. The means of democracy are

影响则悄然进行。民主政府的缺点一看便知，但是其优点只有通过长期观察才能发现。美国的民主法治往往存有缺陷不够完善，有时候会侵犯既得利益，或是由此对侵权的危险行为表示认可。即使美国的法律都很好，但是不断地变化也会成为一个缺点。那么，美国共和国的繁荣和长存又何以维持呢？

谈到法律，必须要对法律所要达到的目的和其为达目的所运用的手段进行认真区分，以及对法律的绝对善与相对善进行认真区分。如果立法者的目的是牺牲多数的利益以保全少数的利益，而且如果为达目的他采用了最省事省力的手段，法律也许可以制定的很好但是其目的不良，而且其效力越大，造成的伤害也越大。

一般来说，民主的法制趋向于照顾绝大多数人的利益，因为它源自多数公民，尽管他们有可能犯错，但是绝不会忤逆自己的利益。相反，贵族的法制趋向于将财富和权力集中到少数人手中，因为贵族，就其本质而言，是由少数构成。因此，总的来说可以断言，民主法制的立法目的比贵族立法的目的更有利于大多数公民。然而，民主立法的好处也就止于此。

贵族制度对立法学的精通远非民主制度可比。贵族的自控能力可以避免因一时冲动而犯下错误，而且他们有长远的计划并能够利用成熟的时机加以实现。贵族政府讲究治国之术，懂得如何将所有法律的力量集合起来汇与一点。而民主政府则不精于此道，其法律也往往不是不够完善就是不合时宜。因此，民主制度的手段不如贵族制度完备，而且采用的手段也往往不够明智，甚至常常跟自己的事业背道而驰，但是它的目的更有利于人民。

therefore more imperfect than those of aristocracy, and the measures which it unwittingly adopts are frequently opposed to its own cause; but the object it has in view is more useful.

Let us now imagine a community so organized by nature, or by its constitution, that it can support the transitory action of bad laws, and that it can await, without destruction, the general tendency of the legislation: we shall then be able to conceive that a democratic government, notwithstanding its defects, will be most fitted to conduce to the prosperity of this community. This is precisely what has occurred in the United States; and I repeat, what I have before remarked, that the great advantage of the Americans consists in their being able to commit faults which they may afterward repair.

An analogous observation may be made respecting public officers. It is easy to perceive that the American democracy frequently errs in the choice of the individuals to whom it entrusts the power of the administration; but it is more difficult to say why the State prospers under their rule. In the first place it is to be remarked, that if in a democratic State the governors have less honesty and less capacity than elsewhere, the governed, on the other hand, are more enlightened and more attentive to their interests. As the people in democracies is more incessantly vigilant in its affairs and more jealous of its rights, it prevents its representatives from abandoning that general line of conduct which its own interest prescribes. In the second place, it must be remembered that if the democratic magistrate is more apt to misuse his power, he possesses it for a shorter period of time. But there is yet another reason which is still more general and conclusive. It is no doubt of importance to the welfare of nations that they should be governed by men of talents and virtue; but it is perhaps still more important that the interests of those men should not differ from the interests of the community at large; for, if such were the case, virtues of a high order might become useless, and talents might be turned to a bad account. I say that it is important that the interests of the persons in authority should not conflict with or oppose the interests of the community at large; but I do not insist upon their having the same interests as the whole population, because I am not aware that such a state of things ever existed in any country.

No political form has hitherto been discovered which is equally favorable to the prosperity and the

现在让我们想象有这样一个社会，其本质和体制能够允许不良法律暂时通行，而且能够等到立法总趋势的结果而不致毁灭。那么，我们应该能够想象，这个民主政府尽管有其缺陷，但是却是最有利于这个社会繁荣昌盛的政府。这就是在美国已经实实在在发生的事情，而且，我还要重复强调我以前说过的话，美国人的最大优势在于他们能够自行修正前面犯下的错误。

在公务员的甄选上也能够看到类似的情况。美国的民主在对行政管理大权委托人的选择上错误不断，但更难说清的是为什么在这种错误连连的情形下美国依旧能够繁荣昌盛。首先要说的是，如果一个民主政府的统治者不如其他地方的诚实能干，其被统治者往往更加精明，更加关注自身的利益。因为在民主制度下，人民时刻予以自己的事务更多关注，并予以自己的权利更多的重视，从而避免选出的代表偏离人民规划出的总路线。第二，还要注意，如果民主国家的行政官员想要滥用权力，那么他的任期就长不了。但是，还有一个更普遍更有说服力的理由。毫无疑问，统治者的才德对于国家富强的重要性不言而喻，但是更重要的也许是统治者和被统治者之间总体上没有相悖的利益。因为，如果存在利益冲突，高尚的德行也毫无用处，才干则会被用来做坏事。所以，我认为当权者的利益与大众的利益不存在冲突或矛盾是非常重要的。但是，我并不坚持他们的利益要跟全体大众利益完全一致，因为这种事从未在任何一个国家出现过。

迄今为止，尚未发现有任何政体能够同样有利于社会各阶级的繁荣和发展。各阶级就好像一个国家中的不同小国，经验告诉我们将其他阶级的命运完全交给任何一个阶级掌

development of all the classes into which society is divided. These classes continue to form, as it were, a certain number of distinct nations in the same nation; and experience has shown that it is no less dangerous to place the fate of these classes exclusively in the hands of any one of them than it is to make one people the arbiter of the destiny of another. When the rich alone govern, the interest of the poor is always endangered; and when the poor make the laws, that of the rich incurs very serious risks. The advantage of democracy does not consist, therefore, as has sometimes been asserted, in favoring the prosperity of all, but simply in contributing to the well-being of the greatest possible number.

The men who are entrusted with the direction of public affairs in the United States are frequently inferior, both in point of capacity and of morality, to those whom aristocratic institutions would raise to power. But their interest is identified and confounded with that of the majority of their fellow-citizens. They may frequently be faithless and frequently mistaken, but they will never systematically adopt a line of conduct opposed to the will of the majority; and it is impossible that they should give a dangerous or an exclusive tendency to the government.

The mal-administration of a democratic magistrate is a mere isolated fact, which only occurs during the short period for which he is elected. Corruption and incapacity do not act as common interests, which may connect men permanently with one another. A corrupt or an incapable magistrate will not concert his measures with another magistrate, simply because that individual is as corrupt and as incapable as himself; and these two men will never unite their endeavors to promote the corruption and inaptitude of their remote posterity. The ambition and the manoeuvres of the one will serve, on the contrary, to unmask the other. The vices of a magistrate, in democratic states, are usually peculiar to his own person.

But under aristocratic governments public men are swayed by the interest of their order, which, if it is sometimes confounded with the interests of the majority, is very frequently distinct from them. This interest is the common and lasting bond which unites them together; it induces them to coalesce, and to combine their efforts in order to attain an end which does not always ensure the greatest happiness of the greatest number; and it serves not only to connect the persons in authority, but to

管，其危险性不亚于将其他民族的命运交给一个民族掌控。当有钱人单独主政的时候，穷人的利益就会受到损害，而当穷人制定法律的时候，富人的利益也岌岌可危。因此，民主制的优势，并非人们所声称的那样能够促进所有阶级的共同繁荣，而不过是有利于最大多数的利益。

在美国，那些负责国家事务的人们，无论从能力还是道德上，都不及贵族国家的执政者。但是他们的利益和国家大多数同胞相同并一致。因此，他们也许常常会不忠于职守或不断出错，但却永远不会有系统有计划的采取有悖于多数意志的方针政策，也不可能让政府具有危险的或是独断专行的倾向。

民主制度下行政长官的不良政绩不过是个别现象，只会在其有限的任期内发生。腐化和无能绝不可能成为将人们永久联系起来的共同利益。一个腐化无能的执政官不能指望另一个执政官员因为跟他同样腐化无能而和他同心协力，而且也不可能团结起来让腐化和无能在他们之后绵延后嗣。相反，一个行政官员的野心和花招，会促使他去揭露另一个行政官。在民主国家，行政官员的劣行只属于其个人。

但是在贵族制政府，公职人员会受其阶级利益的左右，尽管有时候会跟多数的利益相一致，但是通常而言，会与多数的利益相反。阶级利益是将官员们联合起来的共同而持久的纽带，会促使他们联合起来，共同努力实现并不能使绝大多数人幸福的目标，而且它不但能让当权者勾结起来，而且还能将一大部分的被统治者团结起来，因为公民中有相当一部分贵族并没有官职。因此，贵族制的行政官员既得到社会一部分人的坚定支持，又得到

unite them to a considerable portion of the community, since a numerous body of citizens belongs to the aristocracy, without being invested with official functions. The aristocratic magistrate is therefore constantly supported by a portion of the community, as well as by the Government of which he is a member.

The common purpose which connects the interest of the magistrates in aristocracies with that of a portion of their contemporaries identifies it with that of future generations; their influence belongs to the future as much as to the present. The aristocratic magistrate is urged at the same time toward the same point by the passions of the community, by his own, and I may almost add by those of his posterity. Is it, then, wonderful that he does not resist such repeated impulses? And indeed aristocracies are often carried away by the spirit of their order without being corrupted by it; and they unconsciously fashion society to their own ends, and prepare it for their own descendants.

The English aristocracy is perhaps the most liberal which ever existed, and no body of men has ever, uninterruptedly, furnished so many honorable and enlightened individuals to the government of a country. It cannot, however, escape observation that in the legislation of England the good of the poor has been sacrificed to the advantage of the rich, and the rights of the majority to the privileges of the few. The consequence is, that England, at the present day, combines the extremes of fortune in the bosom of her society, and her perils and calamities are almost equal to her power and her renown.

In the United States, where the public officers have no interests to promote connected with their caste, the general and constant influence of the Government is beneficial, although the individuals who conduct it are frequently unskilful and sometimes contemptible. There is indeed a secret tendency in democratic institutions to render the exertions of the citizens subservient to the prosperity of the community, notwithstanding their private vices and mistakes; whilst in aristocratic institutions there is a secret propensity which, notwithstanding the talents and the virtues of those who conduct the government, leads them to contribute to the evils which oppress their fellow-creatures. In aristocratic governments public men may frequently do injuries which they do not intend, and in democratic states they produce advantages which they never thought of.

政府的坚定支持。

将行政官员的利益和一部分与其同时代人的共同利益联系起来，进而与他们子孙的利益统一起来，从而保证他们的影响力能够从现在持续到未来，这就是贵族政体的共同目的。贵族政体的行政官员在被社会的激情和自己的激情乃至子孙后代激情的驱使下，奔向同一目标。那么，他抵不住这些不断的刺激难道是很奇怪吗？所以，贵族总是会在其阶级精神的指引下行动而不会被其腐化，而且他们还会无意识地让社会随他们的目的而变化，并为将这个社会传给他们自己的子孙后代做准备。

没有哪个国家的政体能够像英国的贵族政体那样自由，并源源不断给国家政府输送如此众多高尚且开明的人士。然而，英国立法常常会因为富人利益而牺牲穷人利益，从而让大多数人的权利为少数人所专有，这样的事实也无法逃过人们的眼睛。如今我们看到的结果就是英国社会集极富和极穷于一身，它的危机和灾难与它的力量和荣耀几乎相等。

在美国，公职人员没有促使他们与其所在阶级联系起来的利益，所以，尽管执政者往往无能且卑鄙，但是政府总体上是对人民一直有利的。在民主体制下，确实存在一种潜在的趋势，尽管存在个人的恶行和错误，但是公民的努力能够促使社会走向繁荣。然而，在贵族体制下，也有一种潜在的倾向，尽管治理国家的都是些才德之士，但是他们却给同胞带来痛苦。在贵族政府中，公职人员造成的伤害也许出自无心之举，然而，在民主国家中，公职人员所做的好事也并不一定是故意而为之。

Public Spirit In The United States

Patriotism of instinct—Patriotism of reflection—Their different characteristics—Nations ought to strive to acquire the second when the first has disappeared—Efforts of the Americans to it—Interest of the individual intimately connected with that of the country.

There is one sort of patriotic attachment which principally arises from that instinctive, disinterested, and undefinable feeling which connects the affections of man with his birthplace. This natural fondness is united to a taste for ancient customs, and to a reverence for ancestral traditions of the past; those who cherish it love their country as they love the mansions of their fathers. They enjoy the tranquillity which it affords them; they cling to the peaceful habits which they have contracted within its bosom; they are attached to the reminiscences which it awakens, and they are even pleased by the state of obedience in which they are placed. This patriotism is sometimes stimulated by religious enthusiasm, and then it is capable of making the most prodigious efforts. It is in itself a kind of religion; it does not reason, but it acts from the impulse of faith and of sentiment. By some nations the monarch has been regarded as a personification of the country; and the fervor of patriotism being converted into the fervor of loyalty, they took a sympathetic pride in his conquests, and gloried in his power. At one time, under the ancient monarchy, the French felt a sort of satisfaction in the sense of their dependence upon the arbitrary pleasure of their king, and they were wont to say with pride, "We are the subjects of the most powerful king in the world."

But, like all instinctive passions, this kind of patriotism is more apt to prompt transient exertion than to supply the motives of continuous endeavor. It may save the State in critical circumstances, but it will not unfrequently allow the nation to decline in the midst of peace. Whilst the manners of a people are simple and its faith unshaken, whilst society is steadily based upon traditional institutions whose legitimacy has never been contested, this instinctive patriotism is wont to endure.

But there is another species of attachment to a country which is more rational than the one we have been describing. It is perhaps less generous and less ardent, but it is more fruitful and more

美国的公共精神

本能的爱国主义——理性的爱国主义——两者的不同特点——在前者消失后，各国应努力培养后者——美国人为此做出的努力——个人利益与国家利益的紧密联系。

有一种爱国情怀是本能的、无私的、难以名状的，将人们和生养他的那片土地联系起来。这种与生俱来的喜爱掺杂着对古老习惯的爱好，以及对祖先的尊敬和对过去的留恋。怀有这份爱国情怀的人对国家的热爱就像对祖辈传下来的老宅的热爱一样。他们享受祖国带给自己的宁静，遵从在祖国养成的习惯，喜欢浮现在脑海的记忆，甚至乐于在祖国做个顺民。这种热情有时候会在宗教激情的刺激下，能够做出非凡的成就。爱国心本身就是一种宗教信仰，缺乏理性，只追随信仰和情感行事。在有些国家，君主被当成国家的象征，狂热的爱国主义激情转化为忠君的热情，为君主的胜利而自豪，为君主的强大而骄傲。在旧君主统治时期的法国，人民曾一度感到依附于国王的专制统治令他们心满意足，他们甚至会骄傲地说："我们是世界上最强大的国王的子民。"

但是，像所有本能的热情一样，凭着这种爱国精神虽然能逞一时之勇，但是却无法长久持续下去。它也许能够拯救国家于水火，但是也往往会令国家在安定中衰亡。当一个民族的生活习惯简朴，宗教信仰坚定的时候，当社会赖以存在的旧秩序的合法性尚未遭到质疑的时候，这种自发的爱国主义将会一直持续下去。

但是，还有另一种爱国热情，比我们刚刚说的那种爱国热情更加的理智。它也许没那

lasting; it is coeval with the spread of knowledge, it is nurtured by the laws, it grows by the exercise of civil rights, and, in the end, it is confounded with the personal interest of the citizen. A man comprehends the influence which the prosperity of his country has upon his own welfare; he is aware that the laws authorize him to contribute his assistance to that prosperity, and he labors to promote it as a portion of his interest in the first place, and as a portion of his right in the second.

But epochs sometimes occur, in the course of the existence of a nation, at which the ancient customs of a people are changed, public morality destroyed, religious belief disturbed, and the spell of tradition broken, whilst the diffusion of knowledge is yet imperfect, and the civil rights of the community are ill secured, or confined within very narrow limits. The country then assumes a dim and dubious shape in the eyes of the citizens; they no longer behold it in the soil which they inhabit, for that soil is to them a dull inanimate clod; nor in the usages of their forefathers, which they have been taught to look upon as a debasing yoke; nor in religion, for of that they doubt; nor in the laws, which do not originate in their own authority; nor in the legislator, whom they fear and despise. The country is lost to their senses, they can neither discover it under its own nor under borrowed features, and they entrench themselves within the dull precincts of a narrow egotism. They are emancipated from prejudice without having acknowledged the empire of reason; they are neither animated by the instinctive patriotism of monarchical subjects nor by the thinking patriotism of republican citizens; but they have stopped halfway between the two, in the midst of confusion and of distress.

In this predicament, to retreat is impossible; for a people cannot restore the vivacity of its earlier times, any more than a man can return to the innocence and the bloom of childhood; such things may be regretted, but they cannot be renewed. The only thing, then, which remains to be done is to proceed, and to accelerate the union of private with public interests, since the period of disinterested patriotism is gone by forever.

I am certainly very far from averring that, in order to obtain this result, the exercise of political rights should be immediately granted to all the members of the community. But I maintain that the most powerful, and perhaps the only, means of interesting men in the welfare of their country which

么豪爽和热烈，但却更加坚定和持久。它随着知识的传播而流传，在法律的孕育下成长，随着公民权利的行使而长大，最终跟个人的私利密不可分。一个人明白国家的兴衰对其个人福祉的影响。他意识到法律要求自己为国家的繁荣做出贡献，而自己努力促进国家的繁荣首先对自己有利，其次也是自己的权利之一。

但是，在一个国家存在的过程中，有时会出现这样的时期：在旧的习惯发生改变，公共道德遭到破坏，宗教信仰受到动摇，传统的荣耀已被打破的同时，知识的传播尚待普及，社会的公民权尚待保障或受到严格限制。此时，在人们的眼中，国家的样子变得模糊不清，他们不再将国家跟自己居住的土地联系起来，因为土地已经变成一片不毛之地；他们也不再用祖辈相传的方式去看待自己的国家，因为这已经成为他们的羁绊；也不再从宗教去看国家，因为他们已对宗教存疑；也不再从法律去看国家，因为法律并非出自他们之手；也不再从立法机关去看国家，因为他们对它既害怕又鄙视。国家对他们不再有意义，最终将自己局限在狭隘的个人主义之中。他们虽然被从偏见中释放出来，但却不承认理性的王国；他们既没有君主国臣民的那种本能的爱国主义，也没有共和国公民的那种理性的爱国主义，他们停在了两者之间，混沌苦恼不知何去何从。

在这种窘境中，退后已无可能，因为人民已经无法恢复原来的活力，就好像一个人无法回到懵懂无知的孩提时代。这样的事情也许让人感到遗憾，但是谁也不能让青葱的岁月复返。那么，剩下的唯一能够继续下去的事情就是加速公共利益和个人利益的统一，因为无私的爱国主义已经一去不复返。

we still possess is to make them partakers in the Government. At the present time civic zeal seems to me to be inseparable from the exercise of political rights; and I hold that the number of citizens will be found to augment or to decrease in Europe in proportion as those rights are extended.

In the United States the inhabitants were thrown but as yesterday upon the soil which they now occupy, and they brought neither customs nor traditions with them there; they meet each other for the first time with no previous acquaintance; in short, the instinctive love of their country can scarcely exist in their minds; but everyone takes as zealous an interest in the affairs of his township, his county, and of the whole State, as if they were his own, because everyone, in his sphere, takes an active part in the government of society.

The lower orders in the United States are alive to the perception of the influence exercised by the general prosperity upon their own welfare; and simple as this observation is, it is one which is but too rarely made by the people. But in America the people regards this prosperity as the result of its own exertions; the citizen looks upon the fortune of the public as his private interest, and he co-operates in its success, not so much from a sense of pride or of duty, as from what I shall venture to term cupidity.

It is unnecessary to study the institutions and the history of the Americans in order to discover the truth of this remark, for their manners render it sufficiently evident. As the American participates in all that is done in his country, he thinks himself obliged to defend whatever may be censured; for it is not only his country which is attacked upon these occasions, but it is himself. The consequence is, that his national pride resorts to a thousand artifices, and to all the petty tricks of individual vanity.

Nothing is more embarrassing in the ordinary intercourse of life than this irritable patriotism of the Americans. A stranger may be very well inclined to praise many of the institutions of their country, but he begs permission to blame some of the peculiarities which he observes—a permission which is, however, inexorably refused. America is therefore a free country, in which, lest anybody should be hurt by your remarks, you are not allowed to speak freely of private individuals, or of the State, of the citizens or of the authorities, of public or of private undertakings, or, in short, of anything at all,

我绝不敢断言，为了获得这一结果，应该立即将政治权利交付社会全体成员行使。但是我坚持认为，最有力的可能也是唯一一种让人民关心国家利益的手段就是让他们参与政府的管理。如今，在我看来，人民的热情似乎和政治权利的行使密不可分，而且，我相信，在欧洲，公民的数量将与这些权利的增加和减少成正比。

在美国，居民是昨天才被丢弃到这片他们如今居住的土地，他们并未带来故土的习惯和传统，他们彼此初次相识。简而言之，在他们的脑海里并没有对祖国那种自发的热爱，但是，每个人对本乡、本县、本州事务的热情不亚于自己的事务。因为，每个人都在自己的领域积极参与了社会管理。

在美国，人民知道国家的普遍繁荣对自身福祉的影响。这个观点虽然看似简单，却罕为人民所认知。但是，在美国人民认为祖国的繁荣是自己的功劳，公民将公共财富视为私人财富，并愿意为国家的富强而努力，但他们这样做并不仅出于自豪感和责任感，而且还出于恕我直言贪婪之心。

要证明这个说法的真实性无须研究美国人的制度和历史，因为他们的行事方式已经足以证明。因为美国人参与所有的国家事务，所以认为必须要捍卫受到指责的所有事情；因为受到攻击的不仅仅是他们的国家，而且也包括他们自己。因此，在维护国家荣誉的时候，他们会使出各种手段，甚至会出于个人的虚荣心耍各种小聪明。

在日常的交往中，没有什么比美国人这种敏感的爱国主义更让人尴尬的了。一个外国人往往会对美国的许多事情大加赞赏，但是如果他要问能否对他所看到的某些问题提出批

except it be of the climate and the soil; and even then Americans will be found ready to defend either the one or the other, as if they had been contrived by the inhabitants of the country.

In our times option must be made between the patriotism of all and the government of a few; for the force and activity which the first confers are irreconcilable with the guarantees of tranquillity which the second furnishes.

Notion Of Rights In The United States

No great people without a notion of rights—How the notion of rights can be given to people—Respect of rights in the United States—Whence it arises.

After the idea of virtue, I know no higher principle than that of right; or, to speak more accurately, these two ideas are commingled in one. The idea of right is simply that of virtue introduced into the political world. It is the idea of right which enabled men to define anarchy and tyranny; and which taught them to remain independent without arrogance, as well as to obey without servility. The man who submits to violence is debased by his compliance; but when he obeys the mandate of one who possesses that right of authority which he acknowledges in a fellow-creature, he rises in some measure above the person who delivers the command. There are no great men without virtue, and there are no great nations—it may almost be added that there would be no society—without the notion of rights; for what is the condition of a mass of rational and intelligent beings who are only united together by the bond of force?

I am persuaded that the only means which we possess at the present time of inculcating the notion of rights, and of rendering it, as it were, palpable to the senses, is to invest all the members of the community with the peaceful exercise of certain rights: this is very clearly seen in children, who are men without the strength and the experience of manhood. When a child begins to move in the midst of the objects which surround him, he is instinctively led to turn everything which he can lay his hands upon to his own purposes; he has no notion of the property of others; but as he gradually learns

评的时候，一定会遭到拒绝。因为，美国虽然是一个自由国家，但是为了避免使任何人感到不快，你不能随意议论别人的私事或国家大事，不能随意议论被统治者和统治者，也不能随便议论公私事业。总而言之，除了气候和土地外，什么都不行。即使是在谈论气候和土地的时候，美国人也会随时为它们辩护，似乎这些也是他们造出来的。

在我们这个时代，必须要在全体人的爱国主义和少数人的政府之间做出选择，因为前者赋予的社会力量和积极性与后者提供的社会安宁的保障无法协调起来。

美国的权利观念

没有一个伟大的民族没有权利观念——如何将权利观念传达给人民——在美国人们对权利的尊重——这种尊重从何而来。

除了道德观念之外，我认为没有能够凌驾于权利观念之上的原则，或者更准确地说，这两种观念浑然一体。权利观念无非是道德观念在政治领域的应用。权利观念能够让人们明确什么是无政府状态什么是暴政，教会他们自立而不自大，服从而不屈从。屈服于暴力的人会因自己的顺从而自卑，但是当他服从有权发号施令的跟他同样的人时，他又似乎多多少少高于下命令的人。没有一个伟大的人物没有德行，没有一个伟大的民族没有权利观念。因为一个理性智慧的群体怎么能仅靠强制力结合起来呢？

我要说，现在这个时代，我们所拥有的向人民灌输权利观念并使之能够有意识行使权

the value of things, and begins to perceive that he may in his turn be deprived of his possessions, he becomes more circumspect, and he observes those rights in others which he wishes to have respected in himself. The principle which the child derives from the possession of his toys is taught to the man by the objects which he may call his own. In America those complaints against property in general which are so frequent in Europe are never heard, because in America there are no paupers; and as everyone has property of his own to defend, everyone recognizes the principle upon which he holds it.

The same thing occurs in the political world. In America the lowest classes have conceived a very high notion of political rights, because they exercise those rights; and they refrain from attacking those of other people, in order to ensure their own from attack. Whilst in Europe the same classes sometimes recalcitrate even against the supreme power, the American submits without a murmur to the authority of the pettiest magistrate.

This truth is exemplified by the most trivial details of national peculiarities. In France very few pleasures are exclusively reserved for the higher classes; the poor are admitted wherever the rich are received, and they consequently behave with propriety, and respect whatever contributes to the enjoyments in which they themselves participate. In England, where wealth has a monopoly of amusement as well as of power, complaints are made that whenever the poor happen to steal into the enclosures which are reserved for the pleasures of the rich, they commit acts of wanton mischief: can this be wondered at, since care has been taken that they should have nothing to lose?

The government of democracy brings the notion of political rights to the level of the humblest citizens, just as the dissemination of wealth brings the notion of property within the reach of all the members of the community; and I confess that, to my mind, this is one of its greatest advantages. I do not assert that it is easy to teach men to exercise political rights; but I maintain that, when it is possible, the effects which result from it are highly important; and I add that, if there ever was a time at which such an attempt ought to be made, that time is our own. It is clear that the influence of religious belief is shaken, and that the notion of divine rights is declining; it is evident that public morality is vitiated, and the notion of moral rights is also disappearing: these are general symptoms

利的唯一方法就是，让社会全体成员都能够和平的行使一定的权利。这在那些没有力量和经验的儿童身上体现的特别明显。当一个孩子开始移动自己的身体，他会本能地去抓周边能够摸得到的东西，他没有物品归属的财产观念，但是，随着成长，他渐渐明白物品的价值，开始意识到别人会从他手里抢走他的东西的时候，就会变得更加谨慎，并通过尊重别人的权利，以期自己的权利获得同样的尊重。儿童希望获得玩具的心理后来发展成为成年人希望获得财物的心理。在美国，听不到在欧洲普遍存在的对没有财产的抱怨，因为这里没有穷人，每个人都有需要捍卫的自己的财产，每个人都认可财产权。

政界的事情亦是如此。在美国，各阶级都有很高的政治权利意识，因为他们行使这些权利，而且为了确保自己的权利不受攻击，他们不会去攻击别人的权利。然而，在欧洲，拥有政治权利的人连国家主权都不放在眼里，而美国人则会毫无怨言地服从芝麻大的小官。

这个真理还表现在人民生活最微不足道的细枝末节上。在法国，几乎没有什么享乐是专为上层阶级而设，富人能去的地方穷人也能去。因此，他们举止得体并尊重他们参与的一切享乐。而在英国，财富垄断了所有的享乐和权力，所以人们常常抱怨穷人遛进富人独享的娱乐场所肆意胡闹。这有什么好吃惊的？因为他们知道自己不会有任何损失。

民主政府将政治权利的观念深入到最底层的公民之中，就好像财产的分配让社会全体成员都具有财产观念一样。我要承认，这是民主政府的最大优点之一。我并不是说，教会人们行使政治权利是一件简单的事情，但是我认为如果可以办得到，其产生的效果将会非常巨大。而且我还要说，如果哪个时代可以做这样的尝试，那就是我们这个时代。显然，

of the substitution of argument for faith, and of calculation for the impulses of sentiment. If, in the midst of this general disruption, you do not succeed in connecting the notion of rights with that of personal interest, which is the only immutable point in the human heart, what means will you have of governing the world except by fear? When I am told that, since the laws are weak and the populace is wild, since passions are excited and the authority of virtue is paralyzed, no measures must be taken to increase the rights of the democracy, I reply, that it is for these very reasons that some measures of the kind must be taken; and I am persuaded that governments are still more interested in taking them than society at large, because governments are liable to be destroyed and society cannot perish.

I am not, however, inclined to exaggerate the example which America furnishes. In those States the people are invested with political rights at a time when they could scarcely be abused, for the citizens were few in number and simple in their manners. As they have increased, the Americans have not augmented the power of the democracy, but they have, if I may use the expression, extended its dominions. It cannot be doubted that the moment at which political rights are granted to a people that had before been without them is a very critical, though it be a necessary one. A child may kill before he is aware of the value of life; and he may deprive another person of his property before he is aware that his own may be taken away from him. The lower orders, when first they are invested with political rights, stand, in relation to those rights, in the same position as the child does to the whole of nature, and the celebrated adage may then be applied to them, Homo puer robustus. This truth may even be perceived in America. The States in which the citizens have enjoyed their rights longest are those in which they make the best use of them.

It cannot be repeated too often that nothing is more fertile in prodigies than the art of being free; but there is nothing more arduous than the apprenticeship of liberty. Such is not the case with despotic institutions: despotism often promises to make amends for a thousand previous ills; it supports the right, it protects the oppressed, and it maintains public order. The nation is lulled by the temporary prosperity which accrues to it, until it is roused to a sense of its own misery. Liberty, on

宗教信仰的影响力已被撼动，王权神授的观念日渐衰微，公共道德已然败坏，道德权利的观念逐渐消失，诡辩代替了信仰，算计代替了情感。在这样普遍的动荡之中，如果不能成功地将植根在人们心中的个人利益和权利观念结合起来，又怎会有什么方法让你安心治理国家呢？当有人对我说因为法律乏力而人民躁动，热情激荡而德行全无，所以不应该扩大民主权利的时候，我的回答是，正是基于这些原因，必须要扩大民主权利。而且，我确信对扩大民主权利政府要比社会更有兴趣，因为政府有可能被推翻，而社会永不会毁灭。

然而，我并非想要夸大美国给出的范例。在美国，当人口不多，民风朴素且人们尚不会滥用权利的时候，就已经拥有政治权利。随着人口数量的增加，美国人的民主权利并未得到壮大，而是民主范围得到扩大。毋庸置疑，对于从未拥有过政治权力的人民而言，赋予他们政治权力的时刻很关键，而且也很必要。一个孩子会在不了解生命的价值之前杀人，也会在没有意识到自己的财产会被别人剥夺之前剥夺他人的财产。成年人当他们第一次获得政治权利时，权利于他们就好像那些孩子所呈现的自然状态一样，这也正是他们适用"homo puer robustus（年富力强）"这句名言的时候。在美国也可以看到同样地事实。在公民最先享有政治权利的那些州，人民也最善于运用这些权利。

所以一再重复这样的观点并不过分，自由的技巧能创造最丰硕的成果，而其学习的过程也最为艰苦。然而，在专制体制下事情往往不是这个样子。专制主义往往承诺对以往的种种错误做出修正，要支持正当权利，保护受压迫者并维护公共秩序。人民会被其制造出的暂时繁荣所麻痹，醒来后才会感到痛苦。相反，自由通常在动荡中确立，在内乱中完

the contrary, is generally established in the midst of agitation, it is perfected by civil discord, and its benefits cannot be appreciated until it is already old.

Respect For The Law In The United States

Respect of the Americans for the law—Parental affection which they entertain for it—Personal interest of everyone to increase the authority of the law.

It is not always feasible to consult the whole people, either directly or indirectly, in the formation of the law; but it cannot be denied that, when such a measure is possible the authority of the law is very much augmented. This popular origin, which impairs the excellence and the wisdom of legislation, contributes prodigiously to increase its power. There is an amazing strength in the expression of the determination of a whole people, and when it declares itself the imagination of those who are most inclined to contest it is overawed by its authority. The truth of this fact is very well known by parties, and they consequently strive to make out a majority whenever they can. If they have not the greater number of voters on their side, they assert that the true majority abstained from voting; and if they are foiled even there, they have recourse to the body of those persons who had no votes to give.

In the United States, except slaves, servants, and paupers in the receipt of relief from the townships, there is no class of persons who do not exercise the elective franchise, and who do not indirectly contribute to make the laws. Those who design to attack the laws must consequently either modify the opinion of the nation or trample upon its decision.

A second reason, which is still more weighty, may be further adduced; in the United States everyone is personally interested in enforcing the obedience of the whole community to the law; for as the minority may shortly rally the majority to its principles, it is interested in professing that respect for the decrees of the legislator which it may soon have occasion to claim for its own. However irksome an enactment may be, the citizen of the United States complies with it, not only

善，而其优点只能在其成熟后才能被认识到。

美国对法律的尊重

美国人对法律的尊重——美国人爱法律如爱父母——个人利益随着法律力量的增强而增加。

号召人民制定法律，不管是间接还是直接，并不总能奏效。但是也不能否认，通过这样方式制定的法律，其权威性能够得到极大的加强。法律的这种平民出身，虽然对其卓越和智慧有损，但是对其力量则有巨大的强化。全民意志的表达存在一种无比强大的力量，它会用自己的权威震慑住那些想要反对它的人们。各党派深知这种情况的真实性，所以只要有可能，他们会尽其所能争取多数。如果他们未能在投票者中获得多数，他们会声称，投弃权票的人才是多数；而如果他们依旧没有得偿所愿的时候，他们又会到未投票的人当中寻求多数。

在美国，除了奴隶、仆人和依靠国家救济的穷人以外，各阶级都享有选举权，并间接影响法律的制定。所以那些想要攻击法律的人，只能设法改变国民的观念，或者践踏人民的意志。

要进一步说明的另外一个更有分量的原因是，在美国，每个人对全社会对法律的服从都非常关心，因为，不久之后少数也可能会跟多数为伍，而那些原本宣称服从立法者意志

because it is the work of the majority, but because it originates in his own authority, and he regards it as a contract to which he is himself a party.

In the United States, then, that numerous and turbulent multitude does not exist which always looks upon the law as its natural enemy, and accordingly surveys it with fear and with fear and with distrust. It is impossible, on the other hand, not to perceive that all classes display the utmost reliance upon the legislation of their country, and that they are attached to it by a kind of parental affection.

I am wrong, however, in saying all classes; for as in America the European scale of authority is inverted, the wealthy are there placed in a position analogous to that of the poor in the Old World, and it is the opulent classes which frequently look upon the law with suspicion. I have already observed that the advantage of democracy is not, as has been sometimes asserted, that it protects the interests of the whole community, but simply that it protects those of the majority. In the United States, where the poor rule, the rich have always some reason to dread the abuses of their power. This natural anxiety of the rich may produce a sullen dissatisfaction, but society is not disturbed by it; for the same reason which induces the rich to withhold their confidence in the legislative authority makes them obey its mandates; their wealth, which prevents them from making the law, prevents them from withstanding it. Amongst civilized nations revolts are rarely excited, except by such persons as have nothing to lose by them; and if the laws of a democracy are not always worthy of respect, at least they always obtain it; for those who usually infringe the laws have no excuse for not complying with the enactments they have themselves made, and by which they are themselves benefited, whilst the citizens whose interests might be promoted by the infraction of them are induced, by their character and their stations, to submit to the decisions of the legislature, whatever they may be. Besides which, the people in America obeys the law not only because it emanates from the popular authority, but because that authority may modify it in any points which may prove vexatory; a law is observed because it is a self-imposed evil in the first place, and an evil of transient duration in the second.

的人也许会要求别人服从他的意志。然而，无论一条法律多么让人讨厌，美国公民都会表示服从，这并不仅仅因为它是多数人的作品，而是因为它也是自己的作品，并将其视作自己参与订立的契约。

所以，在美国，没有大批的不安分的群众会将法律视为其天然的敌人，对其法律表示害怕和怀疑。相反，你无法不注意到所有的阶级都对法律表示出极大的信任，他们爱法律如爱父母。

也许我不应该说所有阶级，因为在美国人们把欧洲的权力阶梯倒置过来，富人所处的地位跟旧世界里的穷人一样，所以对法律不断产生怀疑的正是富人阶级。我已经说过，民主制度的优点，并不像人们有时断言的那样，在于它能保护所有人的利益，而仅在于它能够保护多数的利益。在美国，穷人统治国家，富人自然有理由害怕他们会滥用权力。富人这种自然而然的忧虑会让他们闷闷不乐，但是社会并不会因此而动荡，因为让他们无法信任立法者的那个理由也同样让他们不得不服从。他们的财富让他们无法制定法律，也无法抗拒法律。在文明国家，只有那些一无所失的人才会造反，而且即便是民主的法律并不总值得尊重，但至少总能得到尊重。因为那些常常违反法律的人没有理由不遵守自己制定的并能从中获益的法律，而那些通过违法能够获益的人们也会摄于自己的人格和地位服从任何立法的规定。除此之外，美国人之所以服从法律不仅仅因为其源自人民，而是因为当证明法律有害时他们有权对其进行修正。因为在人们看来，法律首先是自行加诸的灾难，其次是可以解约的短期灾难。

Activity Which Pervades All The Branches Of The Body Politic In The United States; Influence Which It Exercises Upon Society

More difficult to conceive the political activity which pervades the United States than the freedom and equality which reign there—The great activity which perpetually agitates the legislative bodies is only an episode to the general activity—Difficult for an American to confine himself to his own business—Political agitation extends to all social intercourse—Commercial activity of the Americans partly attributable to this cause—Indirect advantages which society derives from a democratic government.

On passing from a country in which free institutions are established to one where they do not exist, the traveller is struck by the change; in the former all is bustle and activity, in the latter everything is calm and motionless. In the one, amelioration and progress are the general topics of inquiry; in the other, it seems as if the community only aspired to repose in the enjoyment of the advantages which it has acquired. Nevertheless, the country which exerts itself so strenuously to promote its welfare is generally more wealthy and more prosperous than that which appears to be so contented with its lot; and when we compare them together, we can scarcely conceive how so many new wants are daily felt in the former, whilst so few seem to occur in the latter.

If this remark is applicable to those free countries in which monarchical and aristocratic institutions subsist, it is still more striking with regard to democratic republics. In these States it is not only a portion of the people which is busied with the amelioration of its social condition, but the whole community is engaged in the task; and it is not the exigencies and the convenience of a single class for which a provision is to be made, but the exigencies and the convenience of all ranks of life.

It is not impossible to conceive the surpassing liberty which the Americans enjoy; some idea may likewise be formed of the extreme equality which subsists amongst them, but the political activity which pervades the United States must be seen in order to be understood. No sooner do you set foot upon the American soil than you are stunned by a kind of tumult; a confused clamor is heard on

美国各党派在政界的活动及其对社会的影响

叙述流行于美国的政治活动比叙述盛行于美国的自由和平等要更困难——立法机构不断煽动起来的重大活动，不过是遍及全国的政治活动的插曲——很难看到美国人只专注于个人私事——政治风潮延展到所有社会交往——这是美国人商业活动的部分原因——社会从民主政府获得的间接好处。

如果你从一个自由国家而来，在途经一个非自由国家的时候，必定会惊异于其间的变化。前一个国家看起来熙熙攘攘，人们忙于各种活动；在后一个国家则看起来平静异常，人们默然无动于衷。在一个国家，改革和进步是人们普遍的话题，在另一个，整个社会似乎只想坐享已然取得的成就。然而，不断奋发向上促进国家繁荣的国家往往比那些安于现状的国家更加繁荣昌盛。然而，当我们将两者进行比较的时候，我们难以想象为什么前者每天都觉得需要创新，而后者几乎完全没有这种需要。

如果这种说法适用于那些依旧保持君主政体或是贵族制度的自由国家，那么就更适合民主共和国。在这些国家中，忙于改善社会状况的不仅仅是一部分人，而是所有社会成员都全情投入；生活的必需品和舒适也不仅仅为某个阶级所独享，而是面向社会所有阶层。

想象美国人所享有的非凡自由并非一无可能，同样地，人们对美国人的极端平等也可以形成初步的概念，但是盛行于美国的政治活动只有亲眼看见才能有所理解。一踏上美国的土地，你一定会惊讶于这里的喧闹，嘈杂之声四起，要求立即满足其社会需求的声音此

every side; and a thousand simultaneous voices demand the immediate satisfaction of their social wants. Everything is in motion around you; here, the people of one quarter of a town are met to decide upon the building of a church; there, the election of a representative is going on; a little further the delegates of a district are posting to the town in order to consult upon some local improvements; or in another place the laborers of a village quit their ploughs to deliberate upon the project of a road or a public school. Meetings are called for the sole purpose of declaring their disapprobation of the line of conduct pursued by the Government; whilst in other assemblies the citizens salute the authorities of the day as the fathers of their country. Societies are formed which regard drunkenness as the principal cause of the evils under which the State labors, and which solemnly bind themselves to give a constant example of temperance.

The great political agitation of the American legislative bodies, which is the only kind of excitement that attracts the attention of foreign countries, is a mere episode or a sort of continuation of that universal movement which originates in the lowest classes of the people and extends successively to all the ranks of society. It is impossible to spend more efforts in the pursuit of enjoyment.

The cares of political life engross a most prominent place in the occupation of a citizen in the United States, and almost the only pleasure of which an American has any idea is to take a part in the Government, and to discuss the part he has taken. This feeling pervades the most trifling habits of life; even the women frequently attend public meetings and listen to political harangues as a recreation after their household labors. Debating clubs are to a certain extent a substitute for theatrical entertainments: an American cannot converse, but he can discuss; and when he attempts to talk he falls into a dissertation. He speaks to you as if he was addressing a meeting; and if he should chance to warm in the course of the discussion, he will infallibly say, "Gentlemen," to the person with whom he is conversing.

In some countries the inhabitants display a certain repugnance to avail themselves of the political privileges with which the law invests them; it would seem that they set too high a value upon their time to spend it on the interests of the community; and they prefer to withdraw within the exact

起彼伏。周边的一切都蠢蠢欲动：在这里，镇里一些人在开会商议教堂的兴建；在那里，另一些人忙于选举一名议员；再远一点，还有一个选区的代表们正匆忙赶往某个乡镇商谈地方改革事务；在另一个地方，村里人放下田里的工作，专程来参与乡里道路和学校修建事宜的讨论。有时候人们聚集一处目的就是要表达对政府施政的不满，有时候则是为宣布某一政府官员为本地之父。在美国还有一些团体视酗酒为国家万恶之首，并庄严地宣称要以身作则。

美国立法机构不断进行的重大政治活动，是能够引起外国注意的兴奋点。这些活动，不过是始于底层人民继而扩展到社会各阶层的全国运动的一个插曲或是一种延续而已。为了追求幸福，再没有比这更吃力的了。

在美国公民的心中，对政治生活的关心占有极为重要的地位，而且参与政府管理及讨论几乎已经成为他们的唯一乐趣。这种情绪体现在美国人生活的最微小的细节，甚至女人们都经常参加政治集会并在干完家务活后将倾听政治演讲当成一种消遣。辩论俱乐部在一定程度上取代了娱乐场所。美国人不善交谈，但却善辩，而且往往说着说着就变成长篇大论。他跟你说话的时候就好像在大会上发言，而当他谈得兴高采烈的时候，还会跟对话者说上一句：先生们。

在一些国家，居民们总是会对法律赋予他们的政治权利表示抵触，似乎对他们而言，将时间花在公共利益上简直是浪费时间，所以他们更愿意退回到完全以自我为中心的圈子

limits of a wholesome egotism, marked out by four sunk fences and a quickset hedge. But if an American were condemned to confine his activity to his own affairs, he would be robbed of one half of his existence; he would feel an immense void in the life which he is accustomed to lead, and his wretchedness would be unbearable. I am persuaded that, if ever a despotic government is established in America, it will find it more difficult to surmount the habits which free institutions have engendered than to conquer the attachment of the citizens to freedom.

This ceaseless agitation which democratic government has introduced into the political world influences all social intercourse. I am not sure that upon the whole this is not the greatest advantage of democracy. And I am much less inclined to applaud it for what it does than for what it causes to be done. It is incontestable that the people frequently conducts public business very ill; but it is impossible that the lower orders should take a part in public business without extending the circle of their ideas, and without quitting the ordinary routine of their mental acquirements. The humblest individual who is called upon to co-operate in the government of society acquires a certain degree of self-respect; and as he possesses authority, he can command the services of minds much more enlightened than his own. He is canvassed by a multitude of applicants, who seek to deceive him in a thousand different ways, but who instruct him by their deceit. He takes a part in political undertakings which did not originate in his own conception, but which give him a taste for undertakings of the kind. New ameliorations are daily pointed out in the property which he holds in common with others, and this gives him the desire of improving that property which is more peculiarly his own. He is perhaps neither happier nor better than those who came before him, but he is better informed and more active. I have no doubt that the democratic institutions of the United States, joined to the physical constitution of the country, are the cause (not the direct, as is so often asserted, but the indirect cause) of the prodigious commercial activity of the inhabitants. It is not engendered by the laws, but the people learns how to promote it by the experience derived from legislation.

When the opponents of democracy assert that a single individual performs the duties which he undertakes much better than the government of the community, it appears to me that they are perfectly right. The government of an individual, supposing an equality of instruction on either side,

之内，在四周修起矮墙竖起树篱与世隔绝。但是如果将一个美国人活动限制在自己的事务上，就如同夺走他半条命。他会觉得生活了无生趣，痛苦得难以忍受。

民主政府这种无休止躁动的影响已经从政界扩展到社会交往的方方面面。我不知道这是不是民主政府的最大优势所在，但我希望民主政府的未来比现在要更好。但是不争的事实是，人们不断地插手公共事务往往把事情弄得一团糟。但是，如果下层人民不提高思想境界，不摒弃陈规旧习，他们就不可能参与公共事务。参与社会管理的最卑微的人，要有一定程度的自重，而当他掌握权力后，可以让比他智慧的人为其服务。人们纷纷拉拢他，并使出各种花招妄图欺骗他，他自己也从中获得教训。他参与到并非出自其本意的一些政治事业，但是却让自己喜欢上了这类活动。人们每天都在向他提出促进公共财富的新建议，这让他产生增进自己私人财产的愿望。他也许并不比其前任更幸福更优秀，但却更加有见识更加活跃。我丝毫不怀疑美国的民主制度及其国家物质条件是美国巨大商业活动的动因（但并非人们所说的直接动因而是间接动因）。商业活动并非因法律而起，但是人们通过立法经验学会如何促进它。

当民主制度的反对者宣称由一个人履行其承担的职责会比让众人管理政府要好得多时，我会觉得他们说得很在理。如果在双方实力均等的条件下，一个人主持的政府比众人主持的政府更一致，更坚定也能够更好地甄选官员。如果有人对我所说提出异议，他们不是一定没有见过民主政府，就是一定以偏概全。甚至当地方情况和民意允许民主制度存

is more consistent, more persevering, and more accurate than that of a multitude, and it is much better qualified judiciously to discriminate the characters of the men it employs. If any deny what I advance, they have certainly never seen a democratic government, or have formed their opinion upon very partial evidence. It is true that even when local circumstances and the disposition of the people allow democratic institutions to subsist, they never display a regular and methodical system of government. Democratic liberty is far from accomplishing all the projects it undertakes, with the skill of an adroit despotism. It frequently abandons them before they have borne their fruits, or risks them when the consequences may prove dangerous; but in the end it produces more than any absolute government, and if it do fewer things well, it does a greater number of things. Under its sway the transactions of the public administration are not nearly so important as what is done by private exertion. Democracy does not confer the most skilful kind of government upon the people, but it produces that which the most skilful governments are frequently unable to awaken, namely, an all-pervading and restless activity, a superabundant force, and an energy which is inseparable from it, and which may, under favorable circumstances, beget the most amazing benefits. These are the true advantages of democracy.

In the present age, when the destinies of Christendom seem to be in suspense, some hasten to assail democracy as its foe whilst it is yet in its early growth; and others are ready with their vows of adoration for this new deity which is springing forth from chaos: but both parties are very imperfectly acquainted with the object of their hatred or of their desires; they strike in the dark, and distribute their blows by mere chance.

We must first understand what the purport of society and the aim of government is held to be. If it be your intention to confer a certain elevation upon the human mind, and to teach it to regard the things of this world with generous feelings, to inspire men with a scorn of mere temporal advantage, to give birth to living convictions, and to keep alive the spirit of honorable devotedness; if you hold it to be a good thing to refine the habits, to embellish the manners, to cultivate the arts of a nation, and to promote the love of poetry, of beauty, of renown; if you would constitute a people not

在，民主制度也无法马上提出一套规范的系统化的政府管理制度，这也是实情。民主自由远不能像高明的专制制度那样，实现它要实现的所有事业。它不断地在事业行将取得硕果之时半途而废，或是拿着事业去犯险。但是最终它会取得比任何专制政府更加丰硕的成果，尽管它做好的事情不多，但是它的确办了很多事情。在民主制度下，私人的努力比公共管理来得更加重要。民主制度并不总能给人民最精明的政府，但却能创造出最精明的政府也难以创造的东西，也就是，普遍而持久的积极性，充沛的活力，以及与其密不可分并在任何不利条件下依旧能够产生惊人奇迹的精力。这些才是民主制度的真正优势。

在基督教世界悬而未决的今天，一些人匆忙地将尚在成长之中的民主制视为敌人，而另一些人则已经宣誓崇拜这个源自混沌的新神，但是双方对其憎恨或崇拜的对象都并没有完全地了解，他们在黑暗中互相厮打，只是偶尔能够击中对方。

我们必须首先明白人们要社会和政府做些什么。如果你的目的是要将人类的思想境界提到一定的高度，教会他们用慷慨的胸怀面对世界，鼓励人们对暂时的好处不屑一顾，创造出活生生的信念，保持住令人敬佩的奉献精神；如果你是要使风尚高雅，举止文明并培养一个民族的艺术性，以及对诗歌、美和荣誉的热爱；如果你要建立一个对其他国家动用武力的国家，或是不顾成败创办那些名垂青史的伟大事业。如果你认为这些就是社会的主要目的，那就不要选择民主政府，因为它无法助你实现你的目的。

但是，如果你认为将人们的道德和智力活动用于满足物质生活需要和创造生活必需品是有益的，如果你认为理性的判断会比天才来的更有利，如果你的目的不是激发英雄主

unfitted to act with power upon all other nations, nor unprepared for those high enterprises which, whatever be the result of its efforts, will leave a name forever famous in time—if you believe such to be the principal object of society, you must avoid the government of democracy, which would be a very uncertain guide to the end you have in view.

But if you hold it to be expedient to divert the moral and intellectual activity of man to the production of comfort, and to the acquirement of the necessaries of life; if a clear understanding be more profitable to man than genius; if your object be not to stimulate the virtues of heroism, but to create habits of peace; if you had rather witness vices than crimes and are content to meet with fewer noble deeds, provided offences be diminished in the same proportion; if, instead of living in the midst of a brilliant state of society, you are contented to have prosperity around you; if, in short, you are of opinion that the principal object of a Government is not to confer the greatest possible share of power and of glory upon the body of the nation, but to ensure the greatest degree of enjoyment and the least degree of misery to each of the individuals who compose it—if such be your desires, you can have no surer means of satisfying them than by equalizing the conditions of men, and establishing democratic institutions.

But if the time be passed at which such a choice was possible, and if some superhuman power impel us towards one or the other of these two governments without consulting our wishes, let us at least endeavor to make the best of that which is allotted to us; and let us so inquire into its good and its evil propensities as to be able to foster the former and repress the latter to the utmost.

义的美德，而是建立和平的习惯；如果你宁愿看到恶习而不是罪责，并满足于只要能够减少犯罪，少一些高尚行为也无所谓；如果你满足于生活在一个繁荣，而不是一个堂皇的社会；简而言之，如果你秉持的观点是政府的主要目标并不是让国家拥有尽可能大的力量和荣耀，而是要确保国民拥有最大程度的福祉以及最少的苦难，如果这是你的愿望，保证人们身份平等并组建民主政府就是你达成目标的不二选择。

但是，如果进行选择的时机已过，并且有一个超凡力量不经我们的同意就将我们推向两者之一，那至少要充分利用摊派给我们的这个政府的所有好处，并在探明其善的本性和恶的倾向后，倾尽全力促进前者抑制后者。

Chapter XV: Unlimited Power Of Majority, And Its Consequences

Chapter Summary

Natural strength of the majority in democracies—Most of the American Constitutions have increased this strength by artificial means—How this has been done—Pledged delegates—Moral power of the majority—Opinion as to its infallibility—Respect for its rights, how augmented in the United States.

Unlimited Power Of The Majority In The United States, And Its Consequences

The very essence of democratic government consists in the absolute sovereignty of the majority; for there is nothing in democratic States which is capable of resisting it. Most of the American Constitutions have sought to increase this natural strength of the majority by artificial means.

The legislature is, of all political institutions, the one which is most easily swayed by the wishes of the majority. The Americans determined that the members of the legislature should be elected by the people immediately, and for a very brief term, in order to subject them, not only to the general convictions, but even to the daily passion, of their constituents. The members of both houses are taken from the same class in society, and are nominated in the same manner; so that the modifications of the legislative bodies are almost as rapid and quite as irresistible as those of a single assembly. It is to a legislature thus constituted that almost all the authority of the government has been entrusted.

第十五章　多数的无限力量及其后果

本章提要

多数在民主制中的天然力量——美国大部分州的宪法人为地加强了这种力量——如何加强的——强制性委托——多数的道义力量——多数无错论——尊重多数的权利——这种尊重在美国的推广。

在美国多数的无限力量及其后果

民主政府的本质在于多数的绝对统治，因为在民主国家，谁也无法与多数对抗。美国大多数州的宪法人为地加强了多数的这种天然力量。

在所有的政治机构中，立法机构最容易为多数的意愿所左右。美国人规定立法机构的成员应该由人民直接选出，并且任期较短，为的是让他们不仅要服从选民的普遍的信念，甚至还要服从选民的临时起意。美国两院的议员都源自社会同一阶层，并采用同样的提名方式，因此，由两院组成的立法机构能像单一的立法机构一样做出迅速且不可抗拒的行动。以此种方式建立起来的立法机构几乎将政府所有的权力都握在手中。

But whilst the law increased the strength of those authorities which of themselves were strong, it enfeebled more and more those which were naturally weak. It deprived the representatives of the executive of all stability and independence, and by subjecting them completely to the caprices of the legislature, it robbed them of the slender influence which the nature of a democratic government might have allowed them to retain. In several States the judicial power was also submitted to the elective discretion of the majority, and in all of them its existence was made to depend on the pleasure of the legislative authority, since the representatives were empowered annually to regulate the stipend of the judges.

Custom, however, has done even more than law. A proceeding which will in the end set all the guarantees of representative government at naught is becoming more and more general in the United States; it frequently happens that the electors, who choose a delegate, point out a certain line of conduct to him, and impose upon him a certain number of positive obligations which he is pledged to fulfil. With the exception of the tumult, this comes to the same thing as if the majority of the populace held its deliberations in the market-place.

Several other circumstances concur in rendering the power of the majority in America not only preponderant, but irresistible. The moral authority of the majority is partly based upon the notion that there is more intelligence and more wisdom in a great number of men collected together than in a single individual, and that the quantity of legislators is more important than their quality. The theory of equality is in fact applied to the intellect of man: and human pride is thus assailed in its last retreat by a doctrine which the minority hesitate to admit, and in which they very slowly concur. Like all other powers, and perhaps more than all other powers, the authority of the many requires the sanction of time; at first it enforces obedience by constraint, but its laws are not respected until they have long been maintained.

The right of governing society, which the majority supposes itself to derive from its superior intelligence, was introduced into the United States by the first settlers, and this idea, which would be sufficient of itself to create a free nation, has now been amalgamated with the manners of the people

但是法律在加强那些自身已经很强大的权力当局的力量的同时，也使得原本就弱小的权力当局愈发虚弱。它剥夺了行政权代表的稳定性和独立性，迫使他们完全服从立法机构的肆意妄为，并掠走民主政府本性允许行政权代表所保有的些许权力。在一些州，司法权也变为由多数裁定，而且在所有的州，司法人员的命运也完全仰仗立法机构，因为立法机构每年将规定法官薪俸的权力也交给其代表。

习惯法比成文法作用更大。在美国，一种不把代议制政府的保障推翻誓不罢休的习惯日益盛行。选民在选举一名议员时，不但会为其拟定一套行动纲领还会摊派给他一定数量的务必履行的义务，这样的事情在选举中时有发生。这样的多数表决，就如同市场上的讨价还价。

在一些其他的情况的共同作用下，在美国多数的力量不仅占据绝对优势，而且不可抗拒。多数的道义权威，部分源自这样一种思想：众人集合的智慧和才智比一个人要强大，而且立法者的数量比其质量要重要。这实际上是将平等的理论应用于人的才智。这个反对人类的骄傲，并对其穷追猛打的理论不容易被少数接受，但渐渐地他们便不以为意。像所有的权力一样，多数的权威需要一定的时间来实现，也许这段时间来得比所有其他权力都长。起初，多数的权力需要强制力才能得以维护，而其法律只有经过长期的坚持才能得到尊重。

多数自认拥有社会管理权的思想源自来到美国的最初的移民，而且仅凭这一思想就足以创立一个自由国家，现在它已经风行全社会并渗透到日常生活的所有细节。

在旧君主制统治时期，法国人信奉的信条是：国王不会犯错，即使国王犯了错，也应

and the minor incidents of social intercourse.

The French, under the old monarchy, held it for a maxim (which is still a fundamental principle of the English Constitution) that the King could do no wrong; and if he did do wrong, the blame was imputed to his advisers. This notion was highly favorable to habits of obedience, and it enabled the subject to complain of the law without ceasing to love and honor the lawgiver. The Americans entertain the same opinion with respect to the majority.

The moral power of the majority is founded upon yet another principle, which is, that the interests of the many are to be preferred to those of the few. It will readily be perceived that the respect here professed for the rights of the majority must naturally increase or diminish according to the state of parties. When a nation is divided into several irreconcilable factions, the privilege of the majority is often overlooked, because it is intolerable to comply with its demands.

If there existed in America a class of citizens whom the legislating majority sought to deprive of exclusive privileges which they had possessed for ages, and to bring down from an elevated station to the level of the ranks of the multitude, it is probable that the minority would be less ready to comply with its laws. But as the United States were colonized by men holding equal rank amongst themselves, there is as yet no natural or permanent source of dissension between the interests of its different inhabitants.

There are certain communities in which the persons who constitute the minority can never hope to draw over the majority to their side, because they must then give up the very point which is at issue between them. Thus, an aristocracy can never become a majority whilst it retains its exclusive privileges, and it cannot cede its privileges without ceasing to be an aristocracy.

In the United States political questions cannot be taken up in so general and absolute a manner, and all parties are willing to recognize the right of the majority, because they all hope to turn those rights to their own advantage at some future time. The majority therefore in that country exercises a prodigious actual authority, and a moral influence which is scarcely less preponderant; no obstacles exist which can impede or so much as retard its progress, or which can induce it to heed the

归咎于国王的顾问们。（这仍然是英国宪法的一条基本原则）这种思想特别有利于统治，它能让臣民对法律怨声载道的同时依旧热爱尊重法律的制定者。美国人对于多数也秉持相同的观点。

多数的道义力量还基于另一个原则：多数的利益应优先于少数的利益。因此，不难发现，对于多数权利的尊重必然会随党派情况而自然的增减。当一个国家分裂成几个不可调和的利益集团，多数的特权往往会被忽略，因为多数的特权让他们难以忍受。

如果在美国存在一个阶层，作为立法者的多数想要剥夺他们长期独享的特权，并要把他们从高高在上的地位上拉下来跟多数平起平坐，那么少数很可能并不打算遵守多数制定的法律。但是，美国是由一些彼此平等的人们建立起来的，而且在不同居民的利益上不存在天然或是永久的纷争。

在有些国家，少数永远也不要指望能把多数拉拢到他们自己一边，因为他们必须要放弃与多数斗争这个目的本身。因此，保留特权的贵族永远成不了多数，而如果放弃贵族特权，贵族制度也就不复存在。

在美国，政治问题不能以如此笼统绝对的方式提出，而且所有的党派都愿意认可多数的权利，因为他们都希望有朝一日多数的权利能为自己所用。因此，在美国多数不但拥有强大的实权而且道义力量也异常强大，没有任何障碍能够阻止或是妨碍它，甚至没有什么障碍能够让它稍作停顿倾听一下反对者的呼声，而是从他们身上直接踏过去。这样的状态不仅对自身是致命的，而且对未来也是危险的。

complaints of those whom it crushes upon its path. This state of things is fatal in itself and dangerous for the future.

How The Unlimited Power Of The Majority Increases In America The Instability Of Legislation And Administration Inherent In Democracy

The Americans increase the mutability of the laws which is inherent in democracy by changing the legislature every year, and by investing it with unbounded authority—The same effect is produced upon the administration—In America social amelioration is conducted more energetically but less perseveringly than in Europe.

I have already spoken of the natural defects of democratic institutions, and they all of them increase at the exact ratio of the power of the majority. To begin with the most evident of them all; the mutability of the laws is an evil inherent in democratic government, because it is natural to democracies to raise men to power in very rapid succession. But this evil is more or less sensible in proportion to the authority and the means of action which the legislature possesses.

In America the authority exercised by the legislative bodies is supreme; nothing prevents them from accomplishing their wishes with celerity, and with irresistible power, whilst they are supplied by new representatives every year. That is to say, the circumstances which contribute most powerfully to democratic instability, and which admit of the free application of caprice to every object in the State, are here in full operation. In conformity with this principle, America is, at the present day, the country in the world where laws last the shortest time. Almost all the American constitutions have been amended within the course of thirty years: there is therefore not a single American State which has not modified the principles of its legislation in that lapse of time. As for the laws themselves, a single glance upon the archives of the different States of the Union suffices to convince one that in America the activity of the legislator never slackens. Not that the American democracy is naturally less stable than any other, but that it is allowed to follow its capricious propensities in the formation

多数的无限权威在美国如何增加民主固有的立法和行政的不稳定性

通过每年对立法机构进行改选以及赋予立法者无限权力，美国人增加了民主固有的立法的不稳定性——在行政方面产生同样的效果——在美国，社会改良进行得比欧洲更为热烈但却不及欧洲持久。

我已经谈到过民主制度的天然缺陷，而且所有这些缺陷都会随着多数力量的增强而扩大。首先来谈一谈所有缺陷中最显著的一个。法制的不稳定性是民主政府的天然弊端，因为不断改换新人执政是民主制度的天然属性。但是这个缺陷会随立法者所拥有的权限和行动手段的增减而增减。

在美国，立法机构的权威至高无上，它可以迅速不受阻碍地实现自己的意愿，而且每年还要进行新议员的增补。这就是说，助推民主不稳定性以及迫使政府接受议员的反复无常的所有因素，都在起作用。基于这样的原则，今天美国成为世界上法律寿命最短的国家。30年来，美国各州的宪法几乎都有过修正，因此，在此期间美国没有一个州没有对立法原则做出修改。至于法律本身，只要到美国各州的档案馆看一看就足以确定美国的立法者的活跃程度从未减退。这并不是说美国的民主制与生俱来就比其他国家缺少稳定性，而是说它允许其与生俱来的反复无常的倾向进入到立法工作。

在美国，多数的无限力量以及其雷厉风行的决策方式，不仅影响了法律的稳定性，而且对法律的执行和国家行政管理活动产生了同样的影响。因为多数是唯一要巴结的权威，

of the laws.

The omnipotence of the majority, and the rapid as well as absolute manner in which its decisions are executed in the United States, has not only the effect of rendering the law unstable, but it exercises the same influence upon the execution of the law and the conduct of the public administration. As the majority is the only power which it is important to court, all its projects are taken up with the greatest ardor, but no sooner is its attention distracted than all this ardor ceases; whilst in the free States of Europe the administration is at once independent and secure, so that the projects of the legislature are put into execution, although its immediate attention may be directed to other objects.

In America certain ameliorations are undertaken with much more zeal and activity than elsewhere; in Europe the same ends are promoted by much less social effort, more continuously applied.

Some years ago several pious individuals undertook to ameliorate the condition of the prisons. The public was excited by the statements which they put forward, and the regeneration of criminals became a very popular undertaking. New prisons were built, and for the first time the idea of reforming as well as of punishing the delinquent formed a part of prison discipline. But this happy alteration, in which the public had taken so hearty an interest, and which the exertions of the citizens had irresistibly accelerated, could not be completed in a moment. Whilst the new penitentiaries were being erected (and it was the pleasure of the majority that they should be terminated with all possible celerity), the old prisons existed, which still contained a great number of offenders. These jails became more unwholesome and more corrupt in proportion as the new establishments were beautified and improved, forming a contrast which may readily be understood. The majority was so eagerly employed in founding the new prisons that those which already existed were forgotten; and as the general attention was diverted to a novel object, the care which had hitherto been bestowed upon the others ceased. The salutary regulations of discipline were first relaxed, and afterwards broken; so that in the immediate neighborhood of a prison which bore witness to the mild and enlightened spirit of our time, dungeons might be met with which reminded the visitor of the barbarity of the Middle Ages.

其提出的所有建议都受到人们的追捧，但是一旦多数的注意力发生转移，人们的热情也随之戛然而止。然而，在欧洲的自由国家，行政权拥有独立性并受到保护，为的就是当立法机构将注意力转移到别处后，行政机构依旧能够执行立法机构原来的决定。

在美国，人们对改良的热情和积极性比其他任何地方都要高，但是在欧洲，人们为改良所做的努力并不大，但却很持久。

多年以前，一些虔诚的信徒致力于推进监狱条件的改善。公众被他们的宣传所感动，帮助犯人重获新生也成为非常流行的事业。新的监狱兴建起来，而且改造犯人和惩罚罪犯的观点第一次同时列入监狱纪律。但是这种公众热心参与并积极推进的喜人变化，并未能一蹴而就。当新的感化院正在兴建的时候（而多数也乐见其能够迅速完成），旧监狱依旧存在，仍然关押着大批犯人。随着新的感化院的日臻完善和健全，与其形成鲜明对比的这些旧监狱显得越发有害和腐败。多数热情高涨地兴建新监狱以至于完全忘记了旧监狱的存在。而且因为人们都把注意力转移到新事物上，对旧监狱的关注自然就停止了。一些行之有效的管教制度首先松懈下来，之后便遭到破坏。因此，在足以表现当今温良开明的时代精神的监狱中，地牢的存在会让参观者想起中世纪的野蛮。

多数的暴政

人民主权原则应该如何理解——混合政府设想的不可能性——最高主权必然有其所在——必须采取预防措施来控制最高主权的行动——美国曾经未采取任何预防措施——由

Tyranny Of The Majority

How the principle of the sovereignty of the people is to be understood—Impossibility of conceiving a mixed government—The sovereign power must centre somewhere—Precautions to be taken to control its action—These precautions have not been taken in the United States—Consequences.

I hold it to be an impious and an execrable maxim that, politically speaking, a people has a right to do whatsoever it pleases, and yet I have asserted that all authority originates in the will of the majority. Am I then, in contradiction with myself?

A general law—which bears the name of Justice—has been made and sanctioned, not only by a majority of this or that people, but by a majority of mankind. The rights of every people are consequently confined within the limits of what is just. A nation may be considered in the light of a jury which is empowered to represent society at large, and to apply the great and general law of justice. Ought such a jury, which represents society, to have more power than the society in which the laws it applies originate?

When I refuse to obey an unjust law, I do not contest the right which the majority has of commanding, but I simply appeal from the sovereignty of the people to the sovereignty of mankind. It has been asserted that a people can never entirely outstep the boundaries of justice and of reason in those affairs which are more peculiarly its own, and that consequently, full power may fearlessly be given to the majority by which it is represented. But this language is that of a slave.

A majority taken collectively may be regarded as a being whose opinions, and most frequently whose interests, are opposed to those of another being, which is styled a minority. If it be admitted that a man, possessing absolute power, may misuse that power by wronging his adversaries, why should a majority not be liable to the same reproach? Men are not apt to change their characters by agglomeration; nor does their patience in the presence of obstacles increase with the consciousness of their strength. And for these reasons I can never willingly invest any number of my fellow-creatures with that unlimited authority which I should refuse to any one of them.

此产生的后果。

我一直认为，人民的多数在政治方面有权随心所欲，这样的信条渎神且令人讨厌。我也说过多数的意志是一切权力之源。那么，我难道不是自相矛盾吗？

一项通行的拥有正义之名的法律，不仅在一个国家中由人民的多数制定并认可，而且还会得到全人类多数的认可。因此，每个国家的权利得到公正的限定。一个国家就像一个大陪审团，被授权代表整个社会并维护公正。代表社会的这样的一个大陪审团难道不应该比它在其中实施法律的社会拥有更大的力量吗？

当我拒绝服从不公正的法律，并不意味着我反对多数的支配权，而仅仅是从要求人民主权转变成要求人类主权。有人曾经宣称，在与自身相关的事务上，人民绝不应逾越公正和理性的界限，而是要无畏地将所有权力都授予代表自己的多数，但这是奴隶的语言。

基于观念以及更多的是利益因素而团结起来的像一个人的多数跟少数团结而成的另一个人进行对抗。如果人们承认拥有绝对权力的一个人会滥用其权力残害对手，那么为什么团结起来的多数不可能犯同样的错误呢？团结并不会让人们的性格发生变化，在面临困难时，其耐性也不会随其力量的强大而强大。正是基于这些原因，我绝不会将这种无限的权力交给任何一个同胞掌握，也绝不会将其赋予几个同胞。

我不认为，为了维护自由，可以把几个原则混合到一个政府，因为它们会互相抵触。在我看来，所谓的混合政府不过是异想天开。准确地说，从来就没有过混合政府，因为在

I do not think that it is possible to combine several principles in the same government, so as at the same time to maintain freedom, and really to oppose them to one another. The form of government which is usually termed mixed has always appeared to me to be a mere chimera. Accurately speaking there is no such thing as a mixed government (with the meaning usually given to that word), because in all communities some one principle of action may be discovered which preponderates over the others. England in the last century, which has been more especially cited as an example of this form of Government, was in point of fact an essentially aristocratic State, although it comprised very powerful elements of democracy; for the laws and customs of the country were such that the aristocracy could not but preponderate in the end, and subject the direction of public affairs to its own will. The error arose from too much attention being paid to the actual struggle which was going on between the nobles and the people, without considering the probable issue of the contest, which was in reality the important point. When a community really has a mixed government, that is to say, when it is equally divided between two adverse principles, it must either pass through a revolution or fall into complete dissolution.

I am therefore of opinion that some one social power must always be made to predominate over the others; but I think that liberty is endangered when this power is checked by no obstacles which may retard its course, and force it to moderate its own vehemence.

Unlimited power is in itself a bad and dangerous thing; human beings are not competent to exercise it with discretion, and God alone can be omnipotent, because His wisdom and His justice are always equal to His power. But no power upon earth is so worthy of honor for itself, or of reverential obedience to the rights which it represents, that I would consent to admit its uncontrolled and all-predominant authority. When I see that the right and the means of absolute command are conferred on a people or upon a king, upon an aristocracy or a democracy, a monarchy or a republic, I recognize the germ of tyranny, and I journey onward to a land of more hopeful institutions.

In my opinion the main evil of the present democratic institutions of the United States does not arise, as is often asserted in Europe, from their weakness, but from their overpowering strength;

任何社会中必然会有一个具有压倒性优势的行动原则。人们常常引用18世纪的英国政府作为这种政府的例子，尽管它有很多非常重要的民主因素，但究其本质依旧是一个贵族国家。因为国家的法律和习俗终究是贵族占据主导，并按照其意志指导公共事务。之所以会有这样的引证错误，是因为人们只注意到贵族和人民之间斗争本身，而没有考虑斗争的结果，但这才是重点之所在。如果一个社会真正建立一个混合政府，也就是说，两种对立原则并行的时候，一定会导致爆发革命或是土崩瓦解。

因此，我的观点是，某一种社会权力必然会凌驾于其他权力之上。但是我认为，当没有任何障碍可以对这个权力进行抑制、阻碍并延缓其前进的时候，自由会变得岌岌可危。

无限权力就其本质而言是坏的危险的东西。人类不具备行使无限权力的能力，而上帝之所以能驾驭这种权力，是因为他拥有与其权力相匹配的智慧和公正。但是人世间没有一个权威因其本身而值得敬仰或是因其拥有的权力而值得尊敬，并让我乐于认可其不受约束，号令天下。在我看来，无论是将绝对命令的权力和手段交付给人民或是国王，贵族政府或是民主政府，君主制或是共和制，都埋下了暴政的祸根，而我则会离开这里前往更有希望的体制存在的地方。

我认为，当今美国的民主制度的真正危机并非像欧洲人常说的那样来自其弱点，而是来自其绝对力量。对于美国推行的极端民主我并不感忧虑，而令我深感忧虑的是其缺少对抗暴政的措施。

在美国，当一个个人或是一个党派受到不公正待遇的时候，他或它能向谁诉苦呢？向

and I am not so much alarmed at the excessive liberty which reigns in that country as at the very inadequate securities which exist against tyranny.

When an individual or a party is wronged in the United States, to whom can he apply for redress? If to public opinion, public opinion constitutes the majority; if to the legislature, it represents the majority, and implicitly obeys its injunctions; if to the executive power, it is appointed by the majority, and remains a passive tool in its hands; the public troops consist of the majority under arms; the jury is the majority invested with the right of hearing judicial cases; and in certain States even the judges are elected by the majority. However iniquitous or absurd the evil of which you complain may be, you must submit to it as well as you can.

If, on the other hand, a legislative power could be so constituted as to represent the majority without necessarily being the slave of its passions; an executive, so as to retain a certain degree of uncontrolled authority; and a judiciary, so as to remain independent of the two other powers; a government would be formed which would still be democratic without incurring any risk of tyrannical abuse.

I do not say that tyrannical abuses frequently occur in America at the present day, but I maintain that no sure barrier is established against them, and that the causes which mitigate the government are to be found in the circumstances and the manners of the country more than in its laws.

Effects Of The Unlimited Power Of The Majority Upon The Arbitrary Authority Of The American Public Officers

Liberty left by the American laws to public officers within a certain sphere—Their power.

A distinction must be drawn between tyranny and arbitrary power. Tyranny may be exercised by means of the law, and in that case it is not arbitrary; arbitrary power may be exercised for the good of the community at large, in which case it is not tyrannical. Tyranny usually employs arbitrary means, but, if necessary, it can rule without them.

社会舆论？社会舆论源自多数；向立法机构？立法机构代表多数，并谨遵多数懿旨；向行政当局？行政当局由多数委任，而且是多数百依百顺的工具；向警察机关？警察不过是多数掌控的军队；向陪审团？但陪审团就是拥有裁判权的多数，而且在有些州法官也由多数选出。所以，无论你要控诉的事情多不公正多荒唐，你都只能俯首听命。

相反，如果立法权能够组织成既能代表多数又不会为其激情所左右，使行政权有一定程度的自主性，司法当局又能独立于立法权和行政权，这样就能建立起一个不存在暴政威胁的民主政府。

我并不是说，在今天的美国暴政一再出现，而是要强调美国没有预防暴政的措施，而要发现美国政府之所以能够不那么暴戾的原因，与其在其法律中寻找，不如去其地理位置和民情中寻找。

多数的无限权力对美国公务人员专断权的影响

美国法律允许公务人员在一定范围内享有自由——公务人员的权力。

暴政和专断权必须要明确两者的不同。暴政通过法律的手段实施，而专断权则不然。专断权往往是为被统治者的整体利益而行使，绝非暴政。暴政通常也会利用专断权，但是必要时可以弃之不用。

在美国，多数的无限权力不但有利于立法机构的专制，而且也有利于行政官员行使

In the United States the unbounded power of the majority, which is favorable to the legal despotism of the legislature, is likewise favorable to the arbitrary authority of the magistrate. The majority has an entire control over the law when it is made and when it is executed; and as it possesses an equal authority over those who are in power and the community at large, it considers public officers as its passive agents, and readily confides the task of serving its designs to their vigilance. The details of their office and the privileges which they are to enjoy are rarely defined beforehand; but the majority treats them as a master does his servants when they are always at work in his sight, and he has the power of directing or reprimanding them at every instant.

In general the American functionaries are far more independent than the French civil officers within the sphere which is prescribed to them. Sometimes, even, they are allowed by the popular authority to exceed those bounds; and as they are protected by the opinion, and backed by the co-operation, of the majority, they venture upon such manifestations of their power as astonish a European. By this means habits are formed in the heart of a free country which may some day prove fatal to its liberties.

Power Exercised By The Majority In America Upon Opinion

In America, when the majority has once irrevocably decided a question, all discussion ceases— Reason of this—Moral power exercised by the majority upon opinion—Democratic republics have deprived despotism of its physical instruments—Their despotism sways the minds of men.

It is in the examination of the display of public opinion in the United States that we clearly perceive how far the power of the majority surpasses all the powers with which we are acquainted in Europe. Intellectual principles exercise an influence which is so invisible, and often so inappreciable, that they baffle the toils of oppression. At the present time the most absolute monarchs in Europe are unable to prevent certain notions, which are opposed to their authority, from circulating in secret throughout their dominions, and even in their courts. Such is not the case in America; as long as

专断权。多数对法律的制定和施行拥有绝对控制权，并对治人者和被治者有同样的绝对权威，它视公务人员为任其摆布的下属，放心地将自己的计划交托给他们去执行，而对他们工作的细节和享有的特权却很少提前进行规定。多数对待他们就好像主人对待仆人，会对他们的一举一动进行监督，并有权随时对他们指导和修正。

总体而言，与法国公务人员相比，美国公务人员在其职权范围内享有更大的独立性。他们有时候甚至被允许一些越界的举动。有了舆论的保护和多数的支持，他们运用自己的权力敢做出一些让习惯专断权的欧洲人都大吃一惊的事情。这就意味着一些习惯在自由国度形成，而有一天终将给其自由带来致命的危险。

多数在美国对思想的影响

在美国，多数一旦对一个问题做出不可改变的决定，这个问题便无须讨论——其原因何在——多数对思想和道义影响——民主共和制不依赖物质力量进行专制——他们通过左右人们的思想进行专制。

通过对美国公共舆论的考察，我们可以清楚地看到多数的影响力大大超越我们所了解的欧洲一切权威的力量。思想的影响力看不到摸不着，会让暴政的压迫变得徒劳无益。今天欧洲最专制的君主也不能阻止敌视其权威的思想在其领土乃至宫廷悄然传播。然而在美国就不存在这种现象，只要多数尚未做出决定，讨论就会持续下去；可一旦多数做出不可

the majority is still undecided, discussion is carried on; but as soon as its decision is irrevocably pronounced, a submissive silence is observed, and the friends, as well as the opponents, of the measure unite in assenting to its propriety. The reason of this is perfectly clear: no monarch is so absolute as to combine all the powers of society in his own hands, and to conquer all opposition with the energy of a majority which is invested with the right of making and of executing the laws.

The authority of a king is purely physical, and it controls the actions of the subject without subduing his private will; but the majority possesses a power which is physical and moral at the same time; it acts upon the will as well as upon the actions of men, and it represses not only all contest, but all controversy. I know no country in which there is so little true independence of mind and freedom of discussion as in America. In any constitutional state in Europe every sort of religious and political theory may be advocated and propagated abroad; for there is no country in Europe so subdued by any single authority as not to contain citizens who are ready to protect the man who raises his voice in the cause of truth from the consequences of his hardihood. If he is unfortunate enough to live under an absolute government, the people is upon his side; if he inhabits a free country, he may find a shelter behind the authority of the throne, if he require one. The aristocratic part of society supports him in some countries, and the democracy in others. But in a nation where democratic institutions exist, organized like those of the United States, there is but one sole authority, one single element of strength and of success, with nothing beyond it.

In America the majority raises very formidable barriers to the liberty of opinion: within these barriers an author may write whatever he pleases, but he will repent it if he ever step beyond them. Not that he is exposed to the terrors of an auto-da-fe, but he is tormented by the slights and persecutions of daily obloquy. His political career is closed forever, since he has offended the only authority which is able to promote his success. Every sort of compensation, even that of celebrity, is refused to him. Before he published his opinions he imagined that he held them in common with many others; but no sooner has he declared them openly than he is loudly censured by his overbearing opponents, whilst those who think without having the courage to speak, like him,

更改的决断，接下来就会变得寂静无声，无论是朋友还是对手，都会团结一致表示坚决拥护。其原因显而易见，没有一个君主能够像既拥有立法权又拥有执法权的多数那样，可以专制到将社会所有力量都握在手中，并征服所有反对派。

国王拥有的只是物质力量，它虽可以影响臣民的行动却不能征服他们的意志。但是多数则同时掌控物质力量和精神力量，所以既能控制人民的行动也能控制人民的思想，而且不但能压制反抗，还能平抑所有争议。据我所知，世界上没有哪个国家真正的思想独立和讨论自由像美国那样少。在欧洲许多君主立宪制国家，各种宗教和政治理论都可以自由宣传，并向国外传播，因为在欧洲没有一个国家的权威能够独断专行到容不下敢说真话的公民。如果他很不幸生活在专制政府的统治下，而人民会站在他的一边；而如果他居住在自由国家，在必要时他可以得到王权的庇护。在一些国家他会得到贵族的支持，而在另一些国家则会得到民主的支持。然而在一个民主制组织的像美国的国家中，只有一个权威存在，一个力量和成功的源泉，除此之外再无其他。

在美国，多数成为舆论自由不可逾越的高墙。在高墙的范围内，作家可以随意创作，而如果他敢越雷池一步，必定要倒大霉。这并不是说他要面临异教徒火刑的威胁，而是要面对终日遭人唾弃谩骂的折磨。他的政治生涯也就此结束，因为他冒犯了唯一能够助其成功的权威。人们什么也不给他，哪怕是个空名也不给。在他公开发表自己的观点之前，本以为会有很多志同道合之士，但是他一开口，反对者的责难铺天盖地而来，纵使有人跟他想法相同，也不敢开口，默默弃他而去。最终他屈服了，不堪重负，默不作声，似乎在为

abandon him in silence. He yields at length, oppressed by the daily efforts he has been making, and he subsides into silence, as if he was tormented by remorse for having spoken the truth.

Fetters and headsmen were the coarse instruments which tyranny formerly employed; but the civilization of our age has refined the arts of despotism which seemed, however, to have been sufficiently perfected before. The excesses of monarchical power had devised a variety of physical means of oppression: the democratic republics of the present day have rendered it as entirely an affair of the mind as that will which it is intended to coerce. Under the absolute sway of an individual despot the body was attacked in order to subdue the soul, and the soul escaped the blows which were directed against it and rose superior to the attempt; but such is not the course adopted by tyranny in democratic republics; there the body is left free, and the soul is enslaved. The sovereign can no longer say, "You shall think as I do on pain of death;" but he says, "You are free to think differently from me, and to retain your life, your property, and all that you possess; but if such be your determination, you are henceforth an alien among your people. You may retain your civil rights, but they will be useless to you, for you will never be chosen by your fellow-citizens if you solicit their suffrages, and they will affect to scorn you if you solicit their esteem. You will remain among men, but you will be deprived of the rights of mankind. Your fellow-creatures will shun you like an impure being, and those who are most persuaded of your innocence will abandon you too, lest they should be shunned in their turn. Go in peace! I have given you your life, but it is an existence in comparably worse than death."

Monarchical institutions have thrown an odium upon despotism; let us beware lest democratic republics should restore oppression, and should render it less odious and less degrading in the eyes of the many, by making it still more onerous to the few.

Works have been published in the proudest nations of the Old World expressly intended to censure the vices and deride the follies of the times; Labruyere inhabited the palace of Louis XIV when he composed his chapter upon the Great, and Moliere criticised the courtiers in the very pieces which were acted before the Court. But the ruling power in the United States is not to be made game of;

说了真话而懊悔不已。

枷锁和刽子手是暴政旧时使用的野蛮工具，而在我们这个文明时代，原本已自认为足够完美的专制技艺似乎也得到了完善。昔日的君主专制通过一系列物质力量的手段进行镇压，而如今的民主共和国则完全靠精神力量进行镇压，甚至连意志也要一并征服。在暴君一人的专制统治下，靠折磨人的身体屈其灵魂，而躲过专制拳头的灵魂，却得到了升华，但民主共和国的暴政并不用这一套：在那里，人的身体是自由的，而灵魂却被奴役。现在，国家的统治者不会再说："你的想法应该跟我保持一致，否则死路一条。"，而会说："你是自由的，可以跟我的想法不一致，而且你的生活、财产以及一切依旧归你所有，但是如果你下定决心，那么从今以后你不再是人民中的一员。你依然有公民权利，但是它们于你会毫无用处。因为即使你乞求同胞为你投票，他们也不会这样做；而如果你妄想得到他们的尊重，他们也只会假装表示尊重。你依然留在人们之中，但却已被剥夺做人的权利。你的同胞躲避你就像躲避瘟疫，那些最笃信你清白的人也会离你而去，唯恐人们会对他们也避之不及。平静得活下去吧，我会将你的生活还给你，即使这样的生活让你觉得生不如死。"

君主专制制度已经让专制为人所不齿；我们必须小心防止民主共和制让专制死灰复燃，还要防止它通过让少数不堪重负而在多数人的眼中显得不那么可憎不那么可耻。

在旧世界中一些国家最辉煌的时候，依然会有人发表旨在针砭时弊讥讽时代的作品。拉布吕耶尔曾在路易十四的宫中完成其巨著中《论伟大》一章（拉布吕耶尔的巨著为《品

the smallest reproach irritates its sensibility, and the slightest joke which has any foundation in truth renders it indignant; from the style of its language to the more solid virtues of its character, everything must be made the subject of encomium. No writer, whatever be his eminence, can escape from this tribute of adulation to his fellow-citizens. The majority lives in the perpetual practice of self-applause, and there are certain truths which the Americans can only learn from strangers or from experience.

If great writers have not at present existed in America, the reason is very simply given in these facts; there can be no literary genius without freedom of opinion, and freedom of opinion does not exist in America. The Inquisition has never been able to prevent a vast number of anti-religious books from circulating in Spain. The empire of the majority succeeds much better in the United States, since it actually removes the wish of publishing them. Unbelievers are to be met with in America, but, to say the truth, there is no public organ of infidelity. Attempts have been made by some governments to protect the morality of nations by prohibiting licentious books. In the United States no one is punished for this sort of works, but no one is induced to write them; not because all the citizens are immaculate in their manners, but because the majority of the community is decent and orderly.

In these cases the advantages derived from the exercise of this power are unquestionable, and I am simply discussing the nature of the power itself. This irresistible authority is a constant fact, and its judicious exercise is an accidental occurrence.

Effects Of The Tyranny Of The Majority Upon The National Character Of The Americans

Effects of the tyranny of the majority more sensibly felt hitherto in the manners than in the conduct of society—They check the development of leading characters—Democratic republics organized like the United States bring the practice of courting favor within the reach of the many—Proofs of this spirit in the United States—Why there is more patriotism in the people than in those who govern in its name.

格论》），莫里哀也曾在宫廷演出讽刺朝臣的戏剧。但是美国的统治阶级却不容嘲弄。最轻微的谴责也会让他们大发雷霆，最无关痛痒的真实笑话也会让他们义愤填膺。从说话方式到品格德行，一切都应得到赞美。无论多么著名的作家，也无可避免地要对同胞溜须拍马。多数永远生活在一片自己喝彩的声音之中，而真相，美国人只能从外国人那里听说，或是从经验中察觉。

美国之所以到现在还没有出现过伟大的作家，其原因就出在这里。没有言论自由就出不了文学天才，而在美国恰恰没有言论自由。宗教裁判所终究没能阻挡大量反宗教书籍在西班牙的流传。而在美国，多数的所作所为显然要技高一筹，他们打消了人们想要出版这种书籍的念头。在美国虽然有不信教的人，但是老实说，他们并没有散播无神论的渠道。有些政府曾经尝试采用查禁淫秽书籍的办法维护社会风气。在美国，虽然没有人曾经因此而受过惩罚，但是并没有人想要写这种书。这并不是因为所有的美国公民行事都纯洁高尚，而是因为社会的多数都表现得有礼有节。

在这些方面，行使权力的好处毋庸置疑，而我要谈的是权力的本质。这种不可抗拒的权威一直存在，而且其正确的行使不过是偶然为之。

多数的暴政对美国国民性的影响

迄今为止，多数暴政对民风民情的影响大于对社会行为的影响——这些影响妨碍了大人物的成长——如美国这般组织的民主共和制，使人容易产生巴结大多数的想法——这种

The tendencies which I have just alluded to are as yet very slightly perceptible in political society, but they already begin to exercise an unfavorable influence upon the national character of the Americans. I am inclined to attribute the singular paucity of distinguished political characters to the ever-increasing activity of the despotism of the majority in the United States. When the American Revolution broke out they arose in great numbers, for public opinion then served, not to tyrannize over, but to direct the exertions of individuals. Those celebrated men took a full part in the general agitation of mind common at that period, and they attained a high degree of personal fame, which was reflected back upon the nation, but which was by no means borrowed from it.

In absolute governments the great nobles who are nearest to the throne flatter the passions of the sovereign, and voluntarily truckle to his caprices. But the mass of the nation does not degrade itself by servitude: it often submits from weakness, from habit, or from ignorance, and sometimes from loyalty. Some nations have been known to sacrifice their own desires to those of the sovereign with pleasure and with pride, thus exhibiting a sort of independence in the very act of submission. These peoples are miserable, but they are not degraded. There is a great difference between doing what one does not approve and feigning to approve what one does; the one is the necessary case of a weak person, the other befits the temper of a lackey.

In free countries, where everyone is more or less called upon to give his opinion in the affairs of state; in democratic republics, where public life is incessantly commingled with domestic affairs, where the sovereign authority is accessible on every side, and where its attention can almost always be attracted by vociferation, more persons are to be met with who speculate upon its foibles and live at the cost of its passions than in absolute monarchies. Not because men are naturally worse in these States than elsewhere, but the temptation is stronger, and of easier access at the same time. The result is a far more extensive debasement of the characters of citizens.

Democratic republics extend the practice of currying favor with the many, and they introduce it into a greater number of classes at once: this is one of the most serious reproaches that can be addressed to them. In democratic States organized on the principles of the American republics, this is

思想在美国的表现——人民的爱国主义热情为什么比那些以人民名义进行统治的人的爱国主义热情要高涨。

我刚刚指出的这种趋势在政界表现得并不显眼，但是他们已经对美国的国民性产生了负面的影响。我认为，美国杰出的政治家之所以屈指可数，其原因就是多数专制的日益加强。当美国革命爆发的时候，杰出的政治人才大量涌现，他们的观点并非进行专制统治，而是为了指引人们的行动。那时，这些著名人物普遍参与人民群众的精神活动，并赢得很高的声望，进而辐射到全国，但却从未借助全国的力量提高自己的声望。

在专制政府中，最接近王权的显贵热衷于对统治者奉承谄媚，并对其肆意妄为阿谀奉迎。但是，全国人民大众并不打算奴颜婢膝：他们之所以服从往往是因为自身的软弱、习惯或是无知，甚至有时是愚忠。在一些国家，人们牺牲自己的愿望来满足统治者的享乐和骄傲，因此其服从中仍显示出一种独立性。这些人虽然可怜但不堕落。做自己不赞同的事情和做自己假装赞同的事情有很大的区别。前者是出于人的软弱无能，后者则是出于人的奴性。

在自由国家，每个人都可以或多或少的对国家事务发表看法。在民主共和国家，公共生活不断有私人生活掺杂其中，各方都能插手主权，而人民的意见也总是能够得到它的重视。因此，与君主专制国家比起来，在这些国家中会看到更多利用主权弱点和讨好主权而生活的人。这并不是因为这里的人们天生就比别的国家坏，而是因为这里有更多的诱惑，

more especially the case, where the authority of the majority is so absolute and so irresistible that a man must give up his rights as a citizen, and almost abjure his quality as a human being, if te intends to stray from the track which it lays down.

In that immense crowd which throngs the avenues to power in the United States I found very few men who displayed any of that manly candor and that masculine independence of opinion which frequently distinguished the Americans in former times, and which constitutes the leading feature in distinguished characters, wheresoever they may be found. It seems, at first sight, as if all the minds of the Americans were formed upon one model, so accurately do they correspond in their manner of judging. A stranger does, indeed, sometimes meet with Americans who dissent from these rigorous formularies; with men who deplore the defects of the laws, the mutability and the ignorance of democracy; who even go so far as to observe the evil tendencies which impair the national character, and to point out such remedies as it might be possible to apply; but no one is there to hear these things besides yourself, and you, to whom these secret reflections are confided, are a stranger and a bird of passage. They are very ready to communicate truths which are useless to you, but they continue to hold a different language in public.

If ever these lines are read in America, I am well assured of two things: in the first place, that all who peruse them will raise their voices to condemn me; and in the second place, that very many of them will acquit me at the bottom of their conscience.

I have heard of patriotism in the United States, and it is a virtue which may be found among the people, but never among the leaders of the people. This may be explained by analogy; despotism debases the oppressed much more than the oppressor: in absolute monarchies the king has often great virtues, but the courtiers are invariably servile. It is true that the American courtiers do not say "Sire," or "Your Majesty"—a distinction without a difference. They are forever talking of the natural intelligence of the populace they serve; they do not debate the question as to which of the virtues of their master is pre-eminently worthy of admiration, for they assure him that he possesses all the virtues under heaven without having acquired them, or without caring to acquire them; they do not

并驱使人们同时向往它们。所以，国民性的堕落大范围的存在。

在民主共和国，巴结多数的行为不断蔓延，并立刻渗透到各个阶级。这是人们对民主共和的主要诟病之一。基于美国共和理念建立起的民主国家尤其如此。在这样的国家中，多数的权威如此的绝对不可抗拒以至于如果一个人想要脱离多数的轨道，必须放弃作为公民的权利，乃至作为人的基本素质。

在美国，涌向通往权力大道的一大群人中，我发现几乎没有人具有以往杰出的美国人总能随时随地表现出的豪气和刚正，而这也恰恰是伟人所应具有的主要品质。初看起来，美国人的思想都是一个模式，他们的评判方式都丝毫不差。外国人有时候在美国的确会遇到一些离经叛道的人，以及一些声讨法律弊端和民主多变无知的人；他们甚至有远见卓识能够注意到这些不良的趋势会对国民性造成影响，并指出可能的相应对策；然而你作为他们唯一的听众以及吐露心声的人，却是一个外国人，一个过客。他们之所以愿意坦诚相告，是因为这些对你没有意义，而在公共场合他们会有另一套说辞。

如果美国人读到这些话，我想肯定会出现两种情况：第一，读过这段话的人们必会对我高声谴责；第二，其中大多数人的良心会恕我无罪。

在美国，我听到人们谈论爱国主义，而且也能在人民身上看到它，但却从未在领导人身上看到爱国主义的表现。我们可以用类推的方式对此加以解释。专制主义对被统治者的损害远大于统治者：在君主专制国家，国王往往品德高尚，但是朝臣多为奴颜婢膝之辈。的确美国的官员并不会将"大人"或"陛下"挂在嘴边，但他们跟君主国的朝臣并没有什

give him their daughters and their wives to be raised at his pleasure to the rank of his concubines, but, by sacrificing their opinions, they prostitute themselves. Moralists and philosophers in America are not obliged to conceal their opinions under the veil of allegory; but, before they venture upon a harsh truth, they say, "We are aware that the people which we are addressing is too superior to all the weaknesses of human nature to lose the command of its temper for an instant; and we should not hold this language if we were not speaking to men whom their virtues and their intelligence render more worthy of freedom than all the rest of the world." It would have been impossible for the sycophants of Louis XIV to flatter more dexterously. For my part, I am persuaded that in all governments, whatever their nature may be, servility will cower to force, and adulation will cling to power. The only means of preventing men from degrading themselves is to invest no one with that unlimited authority which is the surest method of debasing them.

The Greatest Dangers Of The American Republics Proceed From The Unlimited Power Of The Majority

Democratic republics liable to perish from a misuse of their power, and not by impotence—The Governments of the American republics are more centralized and more energetic than those of the monarchies of Europe—Dangers resulting from this—Opinions of Hamilton and Jefferson upon this point.

Governments usually fall a sacrifice to impotence or to tyranny. In the former case their power escapes from them; it is wrested from their grasp in the latter. Many observers, who have witnessed the anarchy of democratic States, have imagined that the government of those States was naturally weak and impotent. The truth is, that when once hostilities are begun between parties, the government loses its control over society. But I do not think that a democratic power is naturally without force or without resources: say, rather, that it is almost always by the abuse of its force and the misemployment of its resources that a democratic government fails. Anarchy is almost always

么区别。他们盛赞人民大众天生智慧，哪些是他们主子的美德也不是他们要争论的问题，因为他们确信人民大众具备普天之下所有的美德，哪怕现在还没有或不想有，但将来一定会有。他们不会让自己的妻女侍奉主人，但是他们牺牲自己的观点出卖了自己。美国的道德学家和哲学家们虽然不必将自己的观点隐藏在寓言之中，但是，在他们胆敢抛出残酷的真相前，会说："我们知道，听我们讲话的人民品德超群，丝毫没有会令其失去发号施令权力的那些人性的弱点。而且，如果听我们讲话的人不是品德和学识优秀得让他比世界上其他人都值得拥有自由，我们也就不会说这些话了。"这样的谄媚绝非在路易十四面前阿谀之人能比。在我看来，可以肯定的是，无论政府的性质如何，奴颜婢膝之人必趋炎，阿谀奉承之人必附势。然而，能够防止人们自行堕落的唯一方式就是不要将无限权威赋予任何人，这是避免他们堕落的最好办法。

美国共和制的最大危险来自多数的无限权威

民主共和制会亡于政府权力的滥用，而不是政府的无能——美国民主共和政府比那些欧洲君主国更加集权，更加强大——由此而生的危险——汉密尔顿和杰斐逊对此的看法。

政府常常成为无能和暴政的牺牲品。于前者权力会从他们手中溜走，而于后者，权力会从他们的手中被夺走。许多见证民主国家的无政府状态的人会想当然的认为这些国家的政府天生软弱无力。然而，事实上，国家的政党之间一旦开始出现敌对，政府就失去对社

produced by its tyranny or its mistakes, but not by its want of strength.

It is important not to confound stability with force, or the greatness of a thing with its duration. In democratic republics, the power which directs society is not stable; for it often changes hands and assumes a new direction. But whichever way it turns, its force is almost irresistible. The Governments of the American republics appear to me to be as much centralized as those of the absolute monarchies of Europe, and more energetic than they are. I do not, therefore, imagine that they will perish from weakness.

If ever the free institutions of America are destroyed, that event may be attributed to the unlimited authority of the majority, which may at some future time urge the minorities to desperation, and oblige them to have recourse to physical force. Anarchy will then be the result, but it will have been brought about by despotism.

Mr. Hamilton expresses the same opinion in the "Federalist," No. 51. "It is of great importance in a republic not only to guard the society against the oppression of its rulers, but to guard one part of the society against the injustice of the other part. Justice is the end of government. It is the end of civil society. It ever has been, and ever will be, pursued until it be obtained, or until liberty be lost in the pursuit. In a society, under the forms of which the stronger faction can readily unite and oppress the weaker, anarchy may as truly be said to reign as in a state of nature, where the weaker individual is not secured against the violence of the stronger: and as in the latter state even the stronger individuals are prompted by the uncertainty of their condition to submit to a government which may protect the weak as well as themselves, so in the former state will the more powerful factions be gradually induced by a like motive to wish for a government which will protect all parties, the weaker as well as the more powerful. It can be little doubted that, if the State of Rhode Island was separated from the Confederacy and left to itself, the insecurity of right under the popular form of government within such narrow limits would be displayed by such reiterated oppressions of the factious majorities, that some power altogether independent of the people would soon be called for by the voice of the very factions whose misrule had proved the necessity of it."

会的控制。但是，我并不认为民主政府天生缺少人力和物力，也许这样说更合适，民主政府之所以垮台，常常总是因为滥用人力和物力。无政府状态往往是暴政和其错误的产物，但绝不是因为政府对权力的渴望。

不要把稳定和力量，以及事情的伟大性和持久性混为一谈，这非常重要。在民主共和国家，指导社会的权力并不稳定，因为权力不断易手，方向也随之改变。但是无论它如何易手，其力量几乎是不可抗拒的。在我看来美国的共和政府比欧洲那些君主专制国家的政府更加集权，而且更加强大。因此，我无法想象它会因软弱无力而灭亡。

如果美国的自由制度一旦遭到破坏，必定是多数无限权威使然，因为多数的无限权威将来必会让少数忍无可忍，并使他们被迫诉诸武力，无政府状态必然出现，但是专制也可能导致这种情况的出现。

汉密尔顿先生在《联邦党人》第51篇中表达过相同的看法，他说："对于共和制而言，重要的不仅是要捍卫社会免受统治者的压迫，还要保卫一部分人免受另一部分人的不公正对待。这是公民社会的目标所在，而且曾经是并永远是人们追求的目标，直至有一天得偿所愿，或是在追求的过程中因失去自由而终止。在一个社会，更强大的一部分能够随时团结起来压迫弱小，便可断言社会将自然而然陷入无政府状态，弱者会失去抵御强者暴力的一切保障。而且在这种情况下，甚至强者也会对不稳定的现状产生不满，并愿意服从一个既能保护弱者也能保护自己的政府。出于同样的动机，拥有更强力量的那部分也希望能够组建一个可以保护所有派系的政府。不用怀疑，如果罗得岛州脱离联邦并独立，以人

Jefferson has also thus expressed himself in a letter to Madison: "The executive power in our Government is not the only, perhaps not even the principal, object of my solicitude. The tyranny of the Legislature is really the danger most to be feared, and will continue to be so for many years to come. The tyranny of the executive power will come in its turn, but at a more distant period." I am glad to cite the opinion of Jefferson upon this subject rather than that of another, because I consider him to be the most powerful advocate democracy has ever sent forth.

民名义在有限范围内统治的权利的不稳定性，必然会通过多数不断的暴政表现出来，而需要暴政的多数不久就会迫不及待地呼吁要求获得不受人民控制的权力。"

　　杰斐逊在给麦迪逊的一封信中，这样说："我国政府的行政权力，并非我所担心的唯一问题，或者说主要问题。立法机构的暴政才是最可怕的危险所在，而且今后很长一段时间都是如此。行政权力的暴政虽然也会出现，但这是很久以后才会出现的事。"针对这个问题，我更乐于引用杰斐逊的话，而不是其他人，因为我认为他是有史以来最坚定的民主倡导者。

Chapter XVI: Causes Mitigating Tyranny In The United States

Chapter Summary

The national majority does not pretend to conduct all business—Is obliged to employ the town and county magistrates to execute its supreme decisions.

I have already pointed out the distinction which is to be made between a centralized government and a centralized administration. The former exists in America, but the latter is nearly unknown there. If the directing power of the American communities had both these instruments of government at its disposal, and united the habit of executing its own commands to the right of commanding; if, after having established the general principles of government, it descended to the details of public business; and if, having regulated the great interests of the country, it could penetrate into the privacy of individual interests, freedom would soon be banished from the New World.

But in the United States the majority, which so frequently displays the tastes and the propensies of a despot, is still destitute of the more perfect instruments of tyranny. In the American republics the activity of the central Government has never as yet been extended beyond a limited number of objects sufficiently prominent to call forth its attention. The secondary affairs of society have never been regulated by its authority, and nothing has hitherto betrayed its desire of interfering in them.

第十六章 美国如何削弱多数的暴政

行政集权的缺位

国家的多数并没有包办一切的想法——多数必须借助镇县的行政委员执行其最高决策。

对于政府集权和行政集权的区别，我已经在前面做过说明。在美国，只存在政府集权，而没有行政集权。如果领导美国社会的力量将这两种集权都握在手中，并将发号施令的权利和执行命令的习惯结合起来；如果在国家管理的一般原则确立后，它还要去屈尊降驾的管理公共事务的细枝末节；如果在对国家的重大利益做出规定之后，它还要去过问个人利益，那么不久自由就会在新大陆消失。

但是，在美国，尽管多数不断表现出暴君的嗜好和脾气，但却依旧苦于没有施行暴政的更完美手段。在美国各州，中央政府的活动仅限于能够充分引起它注意的一些有限的事务，社会的次要事务并不归它管理，而且迄今为止它也并没有要插手的想法。多数虽然变得越来越专制，但是并未给中央政府增加特权，而始终将那些大权把持在自己手中，而

The majority is become more and more absolute, but it has not increased the prerogatives of the central government; those great prerogatives have been confined to a certain sphere; and although the despotism of the majority may be galling upon one point, it cannot be said to extend to all. However the predominant party in the nation may be carried away by its passions, however ardent it may be in the pursuit of its projects, it cannot oblige all the citizens to comply with its desires in the same manner and at the same time throughout the country. When the central Government which represents that majority has issued a decree, it must entrust the execution of its will to agents, over whom it frequently has no control, and whom it cannot perpetually direct. The townships, municipal bodies, and counties may therefore be looked upon as concealed break-waters, which check or part the tide of popular excitement. If an oppressive law were passed, the liberties of the people would still be protected by the means by which that law would be put in execution: the majority cannot descend to the details and (as I will venture to style them) the puerilities of administrative tyranny. Nor does the people entertain that full consciousness of its authority which would prompt it to interfere in these matters; it knows the extent of its natural powers, but it is unacquainted with the increased resources which the art of government might furnish.

This point deserves attention, for if a democratic republic similar to that of the United States were ever founded in a country where the power of a single individual had previously subsisted, and the effects of a centralized administration had sunk deep into the habits and the laws of the people, I do not hesitate to assert, that in that country a more insufferable despotism would prevail than any which now exists in the monarchical States of Europe, or indeed than any which could be found on this side of the confines of Asia.

The Profession Of The Law In The United States Serves To Counterpoise The Democracy

Utility of discriminating the natural propensities of the members of the legal profession—These men called upon to act a prominent part in future society—In what manner the peculiar pursuits of lawyers give an aristocratic turn to their ideas—Accidental causes which may check this tendency—

且尽管多数的专制在某一点上得到大大强化，但并未扩展到面上。然而，在追求事业的过程中，无论在国家中占据支配地位的多数多么的激情澎湃，多么的热情高涨，也无法用同样的方法同时迫使全国上下所有公民服从它的意愿。当中央政府代表的多数颁布一项法令时，必须责成官员代为执行，而这些官员并不总是归其管辖，也无法对他们进行时刻指导。因此，乡镇、县的行政机构看起来就像一座座暗礁，不但会影响人民意志的推进速度，还会令其方向发生变化。如果一项压迫性法律得到批准，人民的自由依然可以在法律实施的过程中得到庇护：多数不负责细枝末节，甚至我敢说管不了行政当局的敷衍塞责。而且，因为多数对自己的权力尚未有充分的认识，所以自己并不认为能够插手这些事情。多数了解自己的天然力量，但是并不知道壮大其力量的技巧。

这一点值得注意，因为如果类似于美国的民主共和国制在一个国家建立起来，而这个国家曾经在一个人的专制统治之下，行政集权已深入人心并成为法律，那么我会毫不犹豫地断言，在这个国家，专制令人难以忍受的程度会超过现在欧洲任何君主专制国家，或者说，只有到亚洲，才能找到与之媲美的一些事实。

美国的法律家成为平衡民主的力量

探讨法学家天性偏好的用处——法学家在未来社会作用突出——法学家从事的工作何以让其思想具有贵族气质——可以抑制这种倾向的偶然原因——贵族发现自己易与法学家联合起来——法学家为暴君所用的可能性——法学家与民主的天然要素结合起来形成其唯

Ease with which the aristocracy coalesces with legal men—Use of lawyers to a despot—The profession of the law constitutes the only aristocratic element with which the natural elements of democracy will combine—Peculiar causes which tend to give an aristocratic turn of mind to the English and American lawyers—The aristocracy of America is on the bench and at the bar—Influence of lawyers upon American society—Their peculiar magisterial habits affect the legislature, the administration, and even the people.

In visiting the Americans and in studying their laws we perceive that the authority they have entrusted to members of the legal profession, and the influence which these individuals exercise in the Government, is the most powerful existing security against the excesses of democracy. This effect seems to me to result from a general cause which it is useful to investigate, since it may produce analogous consequences elsewhere.

The members of the legal profession have taken an important part in all the vicissitudes of political society in Europe during the last five hundred years. At one time they have been the instruments of those who were invested with political authority, and at another they have succeeded in converting political authorities into their instrument. In the Middle Ages they afforded a powerful support to the Crown, and since that period they have exerted themselves to the utmost to limit the royal prerogative. In England they have contracted a close alliance with the aristocracy; in France they have proved to be the most dangerous enemies of that class. It is my object to inquire whether, under all these circumstances, the members of the legal profession have been swayed by sudden and momentary impulses; or whether they have been impelled by principles which are inherent in their pursuits, and which will always recur in history. I am incited to this investigation by reflecting that this particular class of men will most likely play a prominent part in that order of things to which the events of our time are giving birth.

Men who have more especially devoted themselves to legal pursuits derive from those occupations certain habits of order, a taste for formalities, and a kind of instinctive regard for the

一的贵族因素——使英国和美国法律家思想易产生贵族化倾向的特定原因——美国的贵族是律师和法官——法学家对美国社会的影响——他们特有的行政官员的习惯对立法机构、行政机构乃至人民产生影响。

造访美国并研习其法律后，我意识到美国人赋予法学家的权威，以及这些个人对政府施以的影响，是美国防止民主偏离正轨的最强有力的保障。在我看来，其影响来自一个值得深入研究的一般原因，因为它会在别处制造出类似的结果。

在过去的500年来，法学家在欧洲政治社会的变迁中扮演了非常重要的角色。他们有时沦为政权的工具，有时又能成功地将政权转化为自己手中的工具。在中世纪，他们是王权强有力的支持者，而且自那之后，他们开始竭尽全力限制王权。在英国，他们跟贵族结成紧密联盟；在法国，他们则成为贵族最危险的敌人。然而，我的目的就是要弄清，在所有这些情况下，法学家们是否为偶然暂时的冲动所左右，又是否为其一再出现的天性所驱使。我之所以要对此进行研究是因为这些法学家们极有可能在行将建立的民主社会中扮演至关重要的角色。

从事法律工作的人们，在工作中养成按部就班的习惯，讲究规范的爱好，并对思想的有规律的联系有一种本能的嗜好，而这自然而然让他们特别反对多数的革命精神和轻率的激情。

法学家们通过学习获得的专门的知识让他们在社会中占有一席之地，并成为知识界的

regular connection of ideas, which naturally render them very hostile to the revolutionary spirit and the unreflecting passions of the multitude.

The special information which lawyers derive from their studies ensures them a separate station in society, and they constitute a sort of privileged body in the scale of intelligence. This notion of their superiority perpetually recurs to them in the practice of their profession: they are the masters of a science which is necessary, but which is not very generally known; they serve as arbiters between the citizens; and the habit of directing the blind passions of parties in litigation to their purpose inspires them with a certain contempt for the judgment of the multitude. To this it may be added that they naturally constitute a body, not by any previous understanding, or by an agreement which directs them to a common end; but the analogy of their studies and the uniformity of their proceedings connect their minds together, as much as a common interest could combine their endeavors.

A portion of the tastes and of the habits of the aristocracy may consequently be discovered in the characters of men in the profession of the law. They participate in the same instinctive love of order and of formalities; and they entertain the same repugnance to the actions of the multitude, and the same secret contempt of the government of the people. I do not mean to say that the natural propensities of lawyers are sufficiently strong to sway them irresistibly; for they, like most other men, are governed by their private interests and the advantages of the moment.

In a state of society in which the members of the legal profession are prevented from holding that rank in the political world which they enjoy in private life, we may rest assured that they will be the foremost agents of revolution. But it must then be inquired whether the cause which induces them to innovate and to destroy is accidental, or whether it belongs to some lasting purpose which they entertain. It is true that lawyers mainly contributed to the overthrow of the French monarchy in 1789; but it remains to be seen whether they acted thus because they had studied the laws, or because they were prohibited from co-operating in the work of legislation.

Five hundred years ago the English nobles headed the people, and spoke in its name; at the present time the aristocracy supports the throne, and defends the royal prerogative. But aristocracy

特权阶层。他们在从业的过程中时时觉得自己优越：他们是一门并不广为人知但却必不可少的科学的大师，是公民间的仲裁者，而将诉讼人的盲目激情引上正轨的习惯又让他们在一定程度上蔑视人民的判断。除此之外，他们自发的形成一个团体，但却并不是因为彼此的互相理解或是齐心协力奔向共同的目标，而是因为其专业的相同和方法的一致将他们的思想联系起来，就好像共同利益能够将他们联合起来一样。

结果，在法学家身上会看到一些贵族的爱好和习惯。跟贵族一样，他们天生热爱秩序和规范，并同样反感多数的行动，而且同样怀有对人民政府的蔑视。我并不是说法学家的天性对他们的影响牢不可破，因为他们像大多数其他人一样，也会受个人利益以及眼前利益的支配。

如果有一种社会，法律从业者们在政界不能享有他们在民间同样的地位，我会放心大胆地保证他们必将成为革命的急先锋。但是还需要探究一下诱使他们破坏并革新的原因是出于偶然呢？还是属于其固有本性。法律人士对1789年法国王权覆灭的功劳首屈一指，但是他们之所以这样做到底是出于对法律的研究还是因为未能参与法律的制定仍然还是一个未知数。

500年前，英国的贵族领导人民并代表人民说话，而如今，贵族支持王权，并捍卫皇室特权。尽管如此，贵族依然有其特有的天性和喜好。我们必须注意不要将团体中的个别成员视为团体本身。在所有自由政府中，无论其形式如何，法律人士总是居于各派之首。而且这也同样适用于贵族政体，因为世界上几乎所有的民主运动都是在贵族的指导下发动的。

has, notwithstanding this, its peculiar instincts and propensities. We must be careful not to confound isolated members of a body with the body itself. In all free governments, of whatsoever form they may be, members of the legal profession will be found at the head of all parties. The same remark is also applicable to the aristocracy; for almost all the democratic convulsions which have agitated the world have been directed by nobles.

A privileged body can never satisfy the ambition of all its members; it has always more talents and more passions to content and to employ than it can find places; so that a considerable number of individuals are usually to be met with who are inclined to attack those very privileges which they find it impossible to turn to their own account.

I do not, then, assert that all the members of the legal profession are at all times the friends of order and the opponents of innovation, but merely that most of them usually are so. In a community in which lawyers are allowed to occupy, without opposition, that high station which naturally belongs to them, their general spirit will be eminently conservative and anti-democratic. When an aristocracy excludes the leaders of that profession from its ranks, it excites enemies which are the more formidable to its security as they are independent of the nobility by their industrious pursuits; and they feel themselves to be its equal in point of intelligence, although they enjoy less opulence and less power. But whenever an aristocracy consents to impart some of its privileges to these same individuals, the two classes coalesce very readily, and assume, as it were, the consistency of a single order of family interests.

I am, in like manner, inclined to believe that a monarch will always be able to convert legal practitioners into the most serviceable instruments of his authority. There is a far greater affinity between this class of individuals and the executive power than there is between them and the people; just as there is a greater natural affinity between the nobles and the monarch than between the nobles and the people, although the higher orders of society have occasionally resisted the prerogative of the Crown in concert with the lower classes.

Lawyers are attached to public order beyond every other consideration, and the best security

一个特权团体永远也不可能满足其所有成员的各种野心，其成员总是有更多的才智和热情无处挥发，所以很多个人往往因为无法享有应有的特权而对其发起攻击。

我并不是断言，所有法律人士在任何时候都是秩序的朋友和变革的敌人，但是他们大多数情况下往往如此。在一个社会中，法律人士占据高位而无人反对，他们会普遍具有保守和反民主的精神。当贵族政体将法学家们排除在领导层之外的时候，他们会成为威胁其安危的最可怕的敌人，尽管他们在财力物力上不及贵族，但是他们在活动上独立与贵于，并在智力上与其相当。但是无论何时只要贵族政体同意赋予他们部分特权，这两个阶级就能随时联合起来，甚至可以说，能够成为一家人。

我也趋向于认为，国王往往能够轻而易举地将法学家们转化为自身政权最得力的工具。这一阶层和行政权之间的亲密度大大超越他们与人民之间的亲密度，就好像贵族和国王之间比贵族与人民之间更亲密一样，尽管社会上层阶级和下层阶级联手抵制王权的事情时不时也会上演。法学家们对公共秩序的热爱胜于一切，而公共秩序最好的保障是权威。但是不要忘记，尽管在他们眼中自由诚可贵，但是法治价更高。他们对专权的畏惧大于暴政，而且如果立法机构通过立法剥夺人们的自由，他们不会对此有什么不满。

因此，我确信，面对民主制度的不断侵入，如果一个君主在其土地上试图努力打破司法权并削弱法学家们的影响力，必将铸下大错。他会失去权威，变得徒有其表。他要够聪明会将法律人士引入政府，而如果政府的专制带有暴力的标志，在他们手里，专制会披上公正和法治的外衣。

of public order is authority. It must not be forgotten that, if they prize the free institutions of their country much, they nevertheless value the legality of those institutions far more: they are less afraid of tyranny than of arbitrary power; and provided that the legislature take upon itself to deprive men of their independence, they are not dissatisfied.

I am therefore convinced that the prince who, in presence of an encroaching democracy, should endeavor to impair the judicial authority in his dominions, and to diminish the political influence of lawyers, would commit a great mistake. He would let slip the substance of authority to grasp at the shadow. He would act more wisely in introducing men connected with the law into the government; and if he entrusted them with the conduct of a despotic power, bearing some marks of violence, that power would most likely assume the external features of justice and of legality in their hands.

The government of democracy is favorable to the political power of lawyers; for when the wealthy, the noble, and the prince are excluded from the government, they are sure to occupy the highest stations, in their own right, as it were, since they are the only men of information and sagacity, beyond the sphere of the people, who can be the object of the popular choice. If, then, they are led by their tastes to combine with the aristocracy and to support the Crown, they are naturally brought into contact with the people by their interests. They like the government of democracy, without participating in its propensities and without imitating its weaknesses; whence they derive a twofold authority, from it and over it. The people in democratic states does not mistrust the members of the legal profession, because it is well known that they are interested in serving the popular cause; and it listens to them without irritation, because it does not attribute to them any sinister designs. The object of lawyers is not, indeed, to overthrow the institutions of democracy, but they constantly endeavor to give it an impulse which diverts it from its real tendency, by means which are foreign to its nature. Lawyers belong to the people by birth and interest, to the aristocracy by habit and by taste, and they may be looked upon as the natural bond and connecting link of the two great classes of society.

The profession of the law is the only aristocratic element which can be amalgamated without violence with the natural elements of democracy, and which can be advantageously and permanently combined with them. I am not unacquainted with the defects which are inherent in the character of

民主政府有助于加强法学家们政治权力，因为当把富人、贵族和君主排除在政府之外，他们必将占据最高的地位，因为他们是人民所能找到的最有知识和能力的人。法学家们一方面因其爱好而与贵族为伍支持王权，另一方面他们与人民有着天然的共同利益。因此，法学家们喜欢民主政府，而又没有民主的偏好和弱点，所以能够通过民主并超越民主变得加倍强大。在民主国家，人民信任法律人士，因为众所周知服务于人民事业是其利益之所在；而且人民也不会被法学家们的话激怒，因为人民认为法学家们不会出什么坏主意。实际上，法学家们的目的并不是要推翻民主制度，而是运用非民主的手段，不断努力刺激它偏离民主的原有轨道。法学家们从出身和利益上属于人民，从习惯和爱好上属于贵族，所以他们可以成为联系社会两大阶级的天然纽带。

法律行业是能与民主的自然因素，和平且有益并永久结合在一起的唯一贵族因素。对于法学家们的固有缺陷我并不了解，但是如果没有法学家精神和民主原则的结合，我对民主制度能否长期存在表示质疑；而且，我不相信，如果法律人士对公共事务的影响力并未随人民权力的增强而增强，一个共和国能够维持到我们现在这个时代。

法学家身上普遍体现的贵族特征，在美国和英国表现得比其他国家都要更为明显。这并不仅仅是因为英美法学家们对立法工作的研究，还在于立法自身的性质，以及这些法学家们在两个国家中所占据的地位。英国人和美国人都保留了比附先例的立法原则，也就是说，他们会继续遵循祖先的法学观点和法律裁定来确立他们的法学观点和法庭裁决。在一

that body of men; but without this admixture of lawyer-like sobriety with the democratic principle, I question whether democratic institutions could long be maintained, and I cannot believe that a republic could subsist at the present time if the influence of lawyers in public business did not increase in proportion to the power of the people.

This aristocratic character, which I hold to be common to the legal profession, is much more distinctly marked in the United States and in England than in any other country. This proceeds not only from the legal studies of the English and American lawyers, but from the nature of the legislation, and the position which those persons occupy in the two countries. The English and the Americans have retained the law of precedents; that is to say, they continue to found their legal opinions and the decisions of their courts upon the opinions and the decisions of their forefathers. In the mind of an English or American lawyer a taste and a reverence for what is old is almost always united to a love of regular and lawful proceedings.

This predisposition has another effect upon the character of the legal profession and upon the general course of society. The English and American lawyers investigate what has been done; the French advocate inquires what should have been done; the former produce precedents, the latter reasons. A French observer is surprised to hear how often an English dr an American lawyer quotes the opinions of others, and how little he alludes to his own; whilst the reverse occurs in France. There the most trifling litigation is never conducted without the introduction of an entire system of ideas peculiar to the counsel employed; and the fundamental principles of law are discussed in order to obtain a perch of land by the decision of the court. This abnegation of his own opinion, and this implicit deference to the opinion of his forefathers, which are common to the English and American lawyer, this subjection of thought which he is obliged to profess, necessarily give him more timid habits and more sluggish inclinations in England and America than in France.

The French codes are often difficult of comprehension, but they can be read by every one; nothing, on the other hand, can be more impenetrable to the uninitiated than a legislation founded upon precedents. The indispensable want of legal assistance which is felt in England and in the United States, and the high opinion which is generally entertained of the ability of the legal profession,

个英国或美国法律人士心中，总是会把对古老东西的偏爱和礼遇与对正规合法程序的热爱结合起来。

这种倾向对法学家的精神和社会动向产生另一种影响。英国和美国的法律人士会对已经发生的事情进行调查，而法国人则更愿意追问为什么会出现这样的事，前者给出过程，后者给出原因。法国人在听到英国或美国律师不断引用他人观点并极少发表自己见解的时候，会感到非常惊讶。因为在法国事情刚好相反。在这里，哪怕是最小的案件，法国的律师也不会忘记引用自己所持的成套法学思想，并对这些法律的基本原则进行讨论以便于能够让法庭对其裁定做出让步。英国和美国的法律人士普遍放弃个人观点，并盲目遵从祖先的思想，这种盲从的思想必然会让他们养成畏首畏尾的习惯，而且怠惰的倾向也会比在法国更甚。

法国的法典往往难以理解，但是人人都可以研读。而从另一方面来说，没有什么比以先例为基础的立法会更让普通人摸不着头脑。在英国和美国法学家们对先例的这种尊重，以及他们所普遍所持的观点，让他们日益脱离群众成为一个独立的阶级。法国的法学家们普遍不过是熟知国家法条的学者，但是英国和美国的法学家们则跟埃及的祭司很相像，因为同祭司们一样，他们是一门玄秘学科的唯一解释者。

在英国和美国法律人士所处的地位，对他们的习惯和思想产生的影响不可谓不大。英国的贵族，小心翼翼地将所有与其性质类似的东西都拉拢到自己身边，所以很重视法律

tend to separate it more and more from the people, and to place it in a distinct class. The French lawyer is simply a man extensively acquainted with the statutes of his country; but the English or American lawyer resembles the hierophants of Egypt, for, like them, he is the sole interpreter of an occult science.

The station which lawyers occupy in England and America exercises no less an influence upon their habits and their opinions. The English aristocracy, which has taken care to attract to its sphere whatever is at all analogous to itself, has conferred a high degree of importance and of authority upon the members of the legal profession. In English society lawyers do not occupy the first rank, but they are contented with the station assigned to them; they constitute, as it were, the younger branch of the English aristocracy, and they are attached to their elder brothers, although they do not enjoy all their privileges. The English lawyers consequently mingle the taste and the ideas of the aristocratic circles in which they move with the aristocratic interests of their profession.

And indeed the lawyer-like character which I am endeavoring to depict is most distinctly to be met with in England: there laws are esteemed not so much because they are good as because they are old; and if it be necessary to modify them in any respect, or to adapt them the changes which time operates in society, recourse is had to the most inconceivable contrivances in order to uphold the traditionary fabric, and to maintain that nothing has been done which does not square with the intentions and complete the labors of former generations. The very individuals who conduct these changes disclaim all intention of innovation, and they had rather resort to absurd expedients than plead guilty to so great a crime. This spirit appertains more especially to the English lawyers; they seem indifferent to the real meaning of what they treat, and they direct all their attention to the letter, seeming inclined to infringe the rules of common sense and of humanity rather than to swerve one title from the law. The English legislation may be compared to the stock of an old tree, upon which lawyers have engrafted the most various shoots, with the hope that, although their fruits may differ, their foliage at least will be confounded with the venerable trunk which supports them all.

In America there are no nobles or men of letters, and the people is apt to mistrust the wealthy; lawyers consequently form the highest political class, and the most cultivated circle of society. They have therefore nothing to gain by innovation, which adds a conservative interest to their natural

界人士，并赋予他们很大的权力。在英国社会中，法学家们虽不属于最高阶层，但也满足于自己所处的地位。他们是英国贵族中的新军，热爱自己的老大哥，尽管不能享受与老大哥们同样的特权。因此，英国的法律人士将所处的贵族圈子的爱好和思想与其职业的贵族利益结合起来。

确实，我努力想要描述的这种法学家的形象，在英国表现得最为突出。在这里，法学家们之所以尊重法律并不是因为法律良好而是因为它们古老，而且如果有必要对法律的某一方面进行修订以适应社会适时的变化，他们也会想方设法做到万变不离其宗，保证不做任何忤逆祖先意图和破坏祖先成果的事情。那些要对法律进行修改的人们拒绝任何革新的意图，他们宁愿采用荒谬的权宜之计，也不愿承担冒犯先人的大罪。这种思想在英国法学家身上表现得特别明显。他们似乎对事物的本质漠不关心，将全部的注意力都集中到字眼上，似乎宁可违背常识和人性也不愿变动法条的一字一句。英国的立法可以比作古树的树干，法学家们要在树干上嫁接各式各样的枝条，并期待能够结出不同的果实，或至少希望繁茂的枝叶能够簇拥着支持它们的树干。

在美国，既没有贵族也没有文人雅士，人们总是不能信任富人，所以，法律人士称为最高的政治阶层，最有知识的社会圈子。因此，他们没有锐意革新而是让自己热爱秩序的天性增添了保守的趣味。如果有人问我美国的贵族在哪里，我会毫不犹豫地回答，他们并不是富人，因为没有共同的纽带将他们联系起来，美国的贵族是那些从事司法工作坐在法

taste for public order. If I were asked where I place the American aristocracy, I should reply without hesitation that it is not composed of the rich, who are united together by no common tie, but that it occupies the judicial bench and the bar.

The more we reflect upon all that occurs in the United States the more shall we be persuaded that the lawyers as a body form the most powerful, if not the only, counterpoise to the democratic element. In that country we perceive how eminently the legal profession is qualified by its powers, and even by its defects, to neutralize the vices which are inherent in popular government. When the American people is intoxicated by passion, or carried away by the impetuosity of its ideas, it is checked and stopped by the almost invisible influence of its legal counsellors, who secretly oppose their aristocratic propensities to its democratic instincts, their superstitious attachment to what is antique to its love of novelty, their narrow views to its immense designs, and their habitual procrastination to its ardent impatience.

The courts of justice are the most visible organs by which the legal profession is enabled to control the democracy. The judge is a lawyer, who, independently of the taste for regularity and order which he has contracted in the study of legislation, derives an additional love of stability from his own inalienable functions. His legal attainments have already raised him to a distinguished rank amongst his fellow-citizens; his political power completes the distinction of his station, and gives him the inclinations natural to privileged classes.

Armed with the power of declaring the laws to be unconstitutional, the American magistrate perpetually interferes in political affairs. He cannot force the people to make laws, but at least he can oblige it not to disobey its own enactments; or to act inconsistently with its own principles. I am aware that a secret tendency to diminish the judicial power exists in the United States, and by most of the constitutions of the several States the Government can, upon the demand of the two houses of the legislature, remove the judges from their station. By some other constitutions the members of the tribunals are elected, and they are even subjected to frequent re-elections. I venture to predict that these innovations will sooner or later be attended with fatal consequences, and that it will be found out at some future period that the attack which is made upon the judicial power has affected the democratic republic itself.

官席上的人们。

　　我们对美国所发生的一切越是深思，越是笃定即使不是唯一，法律界也必然是民主最强有力的平衡力量。在这个国家，我们可以清楚地看到法律行业如何凭借其力量乃至其不足中和了人民政府普遍存在的固有弊端。当美国人民热情高涨，或是被冲动冲昏头脑的时候，法学家们会运用无形的影响力让他们冷静并安定下来。法学家们悄然的用他们贵族的本性对抗民主的本能，用他们对古老事物的迷恋对抗民主对新生事物的热爱，用他们谨慎的观点对抗民主的好大喜功，用他们习惯的沉稳对抗民主的急躁。

　　法院是法学家们可以掌控民主的最醒目的机构。法官就是法学家，他们除了爱好在研究立法时所获悉的秩序和规则外，还特别钟情于安宁，而这恰恰源自其职业的终身性。他们的法律知识已经让他们从同胞中脱颖而出，其政治权力让他们高人一等的地位得到巩固，并让他们养成特权阶级的天然秉性。

　　拥有宣布法律违宪的权力作为武器，美国的司法官员能够一直插手政治事务。他们虽不能强制人民制定法律，但是至少能够迫使人民遵守自己制定的法律，或是要求他们言行一致。我注意到在美国存在一个潜在的削弱司法权的趋势，通过一些州的宪法，州政府可以在两院的要求下撤换法官。而另一些州的宪法规定，法庭成员经选举产生，并允许多次连选连任。我大胆地揣测这些革新迟早会产生致命的结果，而且在未来的某个时候，它们对司法权的打击还会波及民主共和制度本身。

It must not, however, be supposed that the legal spirit of which I have been speaking has been confined, in the United States, to the courts of justice; it extends far beyond them. As the lawyers constitute the only enlightened class which the people does not mistrust, they are naturally called upon to occupy most of the public stations. They fill the legislative assemblies, and they conduct the administration; they consequently exercise a powerful influence upon the formation of the law, and upon its execution. The lawyers are, however, obliged to yield to the current of public opinion, which is too strong for them to resist it, but it is easy to find indications of what their conduct would be if they were free to act as they chose. The Americans, who have made such copious innovations in their political legislation, have introduced very sparing alterations in their civil laws, and that with great difficulty, although those laws are frequently repugnant to their social condition. The reason of this is, that in matters of civil law the majority is obliged to defer to the authority of the legal profession, and that the American lawyers are disinclined to innovate when they are left to their own choice.

It is curious for a Frenchman, accustomed to a very different state of things, to hear the perpetual complaints which are made in the United States against the stationary propensities of legal men, and their prejudices in favor of existing institutions.

The influence of the legal habits which are common in America extends beyond the limits I have just pointed out. Scarcely any question arises in the United States which does not become, sooner or later, a subject of judicial debate; hence all parties are obliged to borrow the ideas, and even the language, usual in judicial proceedings in their daily controversies. As most public men are, or have been, legal practitioners, they introduce the customs and technicalities of their profession into the affairs of the country. The jury extends this habitude to all classes. The language of the law thus becomes, in some measure, a vulgar tongue; the spirit of the law, which is produced in the schools and courts of justice, gradually penetrates beyond their walls into the bosom of society, where it descends to the lowest classes, so that the whole people contracts the habits and the tastes of the magistrate. The lawyers of the United States form a party which is but little feared and scarcely perceived, which has no badge peculiar to itself, which adapts itself with great flexibility to the

然而，千万不要以为，在美国我一直在说的立法精神被限定在法院的范围之内，实际上它早已远远波及法院之外。因为法学家们是人民信任的唯一知识阶层，公职自然大多数的被他们所占据。他们把持立法机构，主持行政工作，因此，对法律的制定和执行具有重大影响。然而，法学家们也必须顺应他们无法抵制的公众舆论的潮流，而且如果他们打算自行其是，这样的苗头也能被及早察觉到。对政治法律进行众多革新的美国人，在民法的修订上显得非常保守，而且即使如此有限的改革也大费周章，尽管这些法律已与美国社会的现状冲突不断。究其原因，在民法方面，多数往往将其委托给法学家们处理，而当美国的法学家们能够自行做主的时候，他们往往不愿进行革新。

已经习惯了一种完全不同状况的法国人，在美国听到人们不断抱怨法学家的惰性和乐于维持现状时，会感到大吃一惊。

普遍存在于美国的立法习惯的影响已经超出了我刚刚指出的范围。在美国出现的任何问题几乎迟早都要成为司法问题，所以所有的党派在其日常辩论中，都要借用司法概念乃至司法语言。当大多数的公职人员是或曾是法律人士的时候，他们会将其职业习惯和技艺运用到国家事务中。陪审制度将这种习惯扩展到所有阶级。因此，法律的语言在某种程度上已经成为百姓的语言。来自学校和法院的法律精神渐渐越过它们的围墙蔓延到社会，深入到社会最底层，以至于全体人民都沾染上司法官员的习惯和喜好。美国的法学家们形成一个不足为惧且难以察觉的派别，它没有自己的旗帜，会随时代的变革发生改变，并顺应一切社会运动，但是这个派别蔓延到全社会，深入到社会各个阶层，悄然影响国家，并最

exigencies of the time, and accommodates itself to all the movements of the social body; but this party extends over the whole community, and it penetrates into all classes of society; it acts upon the country imperceptibly, but it finally fashions it to suit its purposes.

Trial By Jury In The United States Considered As A Political Institution

Trial by jury, which is one of the instruments of the sovereignty of the people, deserves to be compared with the other laws which establish that sovereignty—Composition of the jury in the United States—Effect of trial by jury upon the national character—It educates the people—It tends to establish the authority of the magistrates and to extend a knowledge of law among the people.

Since I have been led by my subject to recur to the administration of justice in the United States, I will not pass over this point without adverting to the institution of the jury. Trial by jury may be considered in two separate points of view, as a judicial and as a political institution. If it entered into my present purpose to inquire how far trial by jury (more especially in civil cases) contributes to insure the best administration of justice, I admit that its utility might be contested. As the jury was first introduced at a time when society was in an uncivilized state, and when courts of justice were merely called upon to decide on the evidence of facts, it is not an easy task to adapt it to the wants of a highly civilized community when the mutual relations of men are multiplied to a surprising extent, and have assumed the enlightened and intellectual character of the age.

My present object is to consider the jury as a political institution, and any other course would divert me from my subject. Of trial by jury, considered as a judicial institution, I shall here say but very few words. When the English adopted trial by jury they were a semi-barbarous people; they are become, in course of time, one of the most enlightened nations of the earth; and their attachment to this institution seems to have increased with their increasing cultivation. They soon spread beyond their insular boundaries to every corner of the habitable globe; some have formed colonies, others independent states; the mother-country has maintained its monarchical constitution; many of its

终将社会塑造成自己想要的样子。

在美国陪审团被视为政治机构

陪审团，是人民主权的工具之一，必须与确立这一主权的其他法律协调一致——美国陪审团的构成——陪审团制对国民性的影响——陪审团制对人民的教育作用——陪审团制确立司法官员的权威并使法律知识在人民中得到普及。

因为我的主题不断将我引到美国的司法制度，因此我不能对陪审团制避而不谈。陪审团制度具有双重性，既是司法机构又是政治机构。如果要探讨陪审团制能够多大程度有利于司法行政管理（特别是民事案件），我承认陪审团的功用也许会受到质疑。因为陪审团制最初出现在社会不发达时期，那时法院只需按照实事证据审理案件，然而陪审团制要想适应一个高度文明社会的需要并不是件容易事。因为在高度文明的社会，人与人之间的相互关系复杂得惊人，并具有需要文明和智慧才能加以判定的性质。

目前，我的目的就是从政治方面对陪审团制度进行考察，其他任何路径都会让我离题。但是，这里我还是会从司法方面简单地谈一谈陪审团制度。当英国人采用陪审团制度的时候还是一个半野蛮民族，随着时间的流逝，他们成为地球上最文明的国家之一，然而随着自身文明程度的提高，他们好像越发热爱这样的制度。不久，他们走出国门向世界各地发展，甚至在有些地方建立了殖民地，在另一些地方建立了独立的国家。然而母国依旧保

offspring have founded powerful republics; but wherever the English have been they have boasted of the privilege of trial by jury. They have established it, or hastened to re-establish it, in all their settlements. A judicial institution which obtains the suffrages of a great people for so long a series of ages, which is zealously renewed at every epoch of civilization, in all the climates of the earth and under every form of human government, cannot be contrary to the spirit of justice.

I turn, however, from this part of the subject. To look upon the jury as a mere judicial institution is to confine our attention to a very narrow view of it; for however great its influence may be upon the decisions of the law courts, that influence is very subordinate to the powerful effects which it produces on the destinies of the community at large. The jury is above all a political institution, and it must be regarded in this light in order to be duly appreciated.

By the jury I mean a certain number of citizens chosen indiscriminately, and invested with a temporary right of judging. Trial by jury, as applied to the repression of crime, appears to me to introduce an eminently republican element into the government upon the following grounds:—

The institution of the jury may be aristocratic or democratic, according to the class of society from which the jurors are selected; but it always preserves its republican character, inasmuch as it places the real direction of society in the hands of the governed, or of a portion of the governed, instead of leaving it under the authority of the Government. Force is never more than a transient element of success; and after force comes the notion of right. A government which should only be able to crush its enemies upon a field of battle would very soon be destroyed. The true sanction of political laws is to be found in penal legislation, and if that sanction be wanting the law will sooner or later lose its cogency. He who punishes infractions of the law is therefore the real master of society. Now the institution of the jury raises the people itself, or at least a class of citizens, to the bench of judicial authority. The institution of the jury consequently invests the people, or that class of citizens, with the direction of society.

In England the jury is returned from the aristocratic portion of the nation; the aristocracy makes the laws, applies the laws, and punishes all infractions of the laws; everything is established upon a

留了原有的君主立宪政体，而其他的子国则成立了强有力的共和国。但是，无论英国人走到哪里，他们都不忘记吹嘘陪审团制度的好处。在所有定居点，他们不是已经确立陪审团制度，就是忙于这项制度重建。这个民族所提倡的这一司法制度被保留下来，并随着每个文明时代不断更新，无论在地球上什么样的环境什么样的政府，从未受到司法界的反对。

然而，我要谈的不是这个问题。仅将陪审团制度视为司法制度是一种非常狭隘的观点，因为无论其对庭审结果产生如何巨大的影响，其程度绝不及对诉讼当事人命运产生的影响。因此，陪审团制度首先是一种政治制度，而且应始终从这个角度对陪审团制度进行评判。

我所说的陪审团制指的是随机选出的一定数量的公民，并赋予他们暂时参加审判的权利。用于惩治犯罪的陪审团制度在我看来是将完美的共和成分引入政府，其理由如下：

根据陪审团成员所属的社会阶层，陪审团制度既可以具有贵族性质也可以具有民主性质；但是，只要它不将这项工作的实际领导权交给统治者或是交给部分统治者的手中，它会一直具备共和特征。强迫不过是短暂的成功要素，而强制过后人们会产生权利观念。一个只会在战场上将敌人置之死地的政府会很快瓦解。真正的政治法律的制裁应该建立在刑法的基础之上，没有惩治，法律迟早会失去其强制力量。因此，对侵犯法律行为进行惩治的人才是社会真正的主人。实行陪审团制就是将人民，至少是部分公民提高到法官的地位。所以，陪审团制度将社会的领导权交到人民或是部分人民手中。

在英国，陪审团成员来自国家的贵族。贵族不但制定法律，而且执行法律并对所有违

consistent footing, and England may with truth be said to constitute an aristocratic republic. In the United States the same system is applied to the whole people. Every American citizen is qualified to be an elector, a juror, and is eligible to office. The system of the jury, as it is understood in America, appears to me to be as direct and as extreme a consequence of the sovereignty of the people as universal suffrage. These institutions are two instruments of equal power, which contribute to the supremacy of the majority. All the sovereigns who have chosen to govern by their own authority, and to direct society instead of obeying its directions, have destroyed or enfeebled the institution of the jury. The monarchs of the House of Tudor sent to prison jurors who refused to convict, and Napoleon caused them to be returned by his agents.

However clear most of these truths may seem to be, they do not command universal assent, and in France, at least, the institution of trial by jury is still very imperfectly understood. If the question arises as to the proper qualification of jurors, it is confined to a discussion of the intelligence and knowledge of the citizens who may be returned, as if the jury was merely a judicial institution. This appears to me to be the least part of the subject. The jury is pre-eminently a political institution; it must be regarded as one form of the sovereignty of the people; when that sovereignty is repudiated, it must be rejected, or it must be adapted to the laws by which that sovereignty is established. The jury is that portion of the nation to which the execution of the laws is entrusted, as the Houses of Parliament constitute that part of the nation which makes the laws; and in order that society may be governed with consistency and uniformity, the list of citizens qualified to serve on juries must increase and diminish with the list of electors. This I hold to be the point of view most worthy of the attention of the legislator, and all that remains is merely accessory.

I am so entirely convinced that the jury is pre-eminently a political institution that I still consider it in this light when it is applied in civil causes. Laws are always unstable unless they are founded upon the manners of a nation; manners are the only durable and resisting power in a people. When the jury is reserved for criminal offences, the people only witnesses its occasional action in certain particular cases; the ordinary course of life goes on without its interference, and it is considered as an

法行为进行惩处，一切都要由贵族决定，英国可以称得上是一个真正的贵族共和国。在美国，同样的制度却可以为全体人民享有。每个美国公民都有选举权，有资格成为选举人和陪审员。在我看来，依照美国人的理解，陪审团制度跟普选权一样，是人民主权学说的直接及极端结果。陪审团制度和普选权是多数的两个同样有力的统治工具。所有那些选择用自己的力量进行统治并领导社会而不服从社会领导的统治者们，都曾对陪审团制度进行破坏或削弱。都铎王朝曾将拒绝做有罪判定的陪审团送进监狱，而拿破仑曾让自己的亲信挑选陪审员。

无论这些真相多么的显而易见，都无法得到所有人的认同，至少在法国，人们对陪审团制度依然不十分理解。如果要探讨陪审员的资格，只需将陪审制度当作一种司法制度讨论一下陪审员应具有的能力和知识就可以了。我觉得这部分最无关紧要。陪审制度首先是一种政治制度，应被视为人民主权的形式之一，当人民主权被推翻，陪审制度必然遭到抛弃，然而当人民主权得以确立的时候，它也必须进行调整以保持与该主权法律的一致性。就好像议会是国家的立法机关一样，陪审团是国家负责执行法律的机构，为了让社会得到稳定统一的管理，陪审团的名单应该随选民名单的扩大而扩大，缩小而缩小。我认为这一点特别值得立法者注意，至于其他都是次要的。

将陪审制度应用于民事诉讼时，我依然认为它首先是一项政治制度，对此我深信不疑。不以民情为基础的法律往往不稳定，民情是一个民族唯一持久稳定的力量。当陪审制度为刑事案件专用时，人民只会在特定案件中看到它发挥作用，人们的日常生活不会受到

instrument, but not as the only instrument, of obtaining justice. This is true a fortiori when the jury is only applied to certain criminal causes.

When, on the contrary, the influence of the jury is extended to civil causes, its application is constantly palpable; it affects all the interests of the community; everyone co-operates in its work: it thus penetrates into all the usages of life, it fashions the human mind to its peculiar forms, and is gradually associated with the idea of justice itself.

The institution of the jury, if confined to criminal causes, is always in danger, but when once it is introduced into civil proceedings it defies the aggressions of time and of man. If it had been as easy to remove the jury from the manners as from the laws of England, it would have perished under Henry VIII, and Elizabeth, and the civil jury did in reality, at that period, save the liberties of the country. In whatever manner the jury be applied, it cannot fail to exercise a powerful influence upon the national character; but this influence is prodigiously increased when it is introduced into civil causes. The jury, and more especially the jury in civil cases, serves to communicate the spirit of the judges to the minds of all the citizens; and this spirit, with the habits which attend it, is the soundest preparation for free institutions. It imbues all classes with a respect for the thing judged, and with the notion of right. If these two elements be removed, the love of independence is reduced to a mere destructive passion. It teaches men to practice equity, every man learns to judge his neighbor as he would himself be judged; and this is especially true of the jury in civil causes, for, whilst the number of persons who have reason to apprehend a criminal prosecution is small, every one is liable to have a civil action brought against him. The jury teaches every man not to recoil before the responsibility of his own actions, and impresses him with that manly confidence without which political virtue cannot exist. It invests each citizen with a kind of magistracy, it makes them all feel the duties which they are bound to discharge towards society, and the part which they take in the Government. By obliging men to turn their attention to affairs which are not exclusively their own, it rubs off that individual egotism which is the rust of society.

The jury contributes most powerfully to form the judgement and to increase the natural

它的影响，而它也只会被视为获得公正的一种手段而不是唯一的手段。当陪审团仅用于刑事案件时，尤其如此。

然而，当陪审制度的影响力延伸到民事案件的时候，人们会不断感受到它的作用，会影响每个人的利益，每个人都想得到它的帮助，因此会深入到生活的习惯，并按照它的想法塑造人们的思想，并渐渐将它和公正等同起来。

如果只将陪审制度用在刑事案件上，它会一直处于困境；但是一旦被引入到民事诉讼，它能够顶住时间和人们反抗的考验。如果在英国陪审制度能够像从法律中剔除一样被轻而易举地从民情中剔除出去，它早就会在亨利八世、伊丽莎白时代消亡了。因此，挽救英国自由的正是民事陪审制度。无论如何应用陪审团制度，它都会对国民性产生重大影响，然而将其引入民事案件后，其影响力会惊人地增加。陪审制度特别是民事陪审制度有助于将法官精神灌输到全体公民头脑，而这种精神以及由其而生的习惯是为自由制度所做的最佳准备。陪审制度向所有阶级灌输要尊重判决的思想，以及权利观念。如果没有这两者，人们对自由的热爱不过是一种破坏性的激情。陪审制度教导人们要公平行事，每个人在陪审他人的时候也会意识到别人也会陪审自己，而且在民事案件上，尤其如此。因为，尽管受到刑事诉讼指控的人数非常少，但是每个人都可能惹上民事诉讼。陪审制度教导每个人不要退缩，要勇于为自己的行为负责，并要有男子汉的气魄，没有这种气魄政治节操就无从谈起。它赋予每个公民一种管理职责，让他们时刻觉得对社会负有责任，是政府中的一分子。通过迫使人们将注意力转移到与己无关的事务，它将个人主义的社会尘垢剥离

intelligence of a people, and this is, in my opinion, its greatest advantage. It may be regarded as a gratuitous public school ever open, in which every juror learns to exercise his rights, enters into daily communication with the most learned and enlightened members of the upper classes, and becomes practically acquainted with the laws of his country, which are brought within the reach of his capacity by the efforts of the bar, the advice of the judge, and even by the passions of the parties. I think that the practical intelligence and political good sense of the Americans are mainly attributable to the long use which they have made of the jury in civil causes. I do not know whether the jury is useful to those who are in litigation; but I am certain it is highly beneficial to those who decide the litigation; and I look upon it as one of the most efficacious means for the education of the people which society can employ.

What I have hitherto said applies to all nations, but the remark I am now about to make is peculiar to the Americans and to democratic peoples. I have already observed that in democracies the members of the legal profession and the magistrates constitute the only aristocratic body which can check the irregularities of the people. This aristocracy is invested with no physical power, but it exercises its conservative influence upon the minds of men, and the most abundant source of its authority is the institution of the civil jury. In criminal causes, when society is armed against a single individual, the jury is apt to look upon the judge as the passive instrument of social power, and to mistrust his advice. Moreover, criminal causes are entirely founded upon the evidence of facts which common sense can readily appreciate; upon this ground the judge and the jury are equal. Such, however, is not the case in civil causes; then the judge appears as a disinterested arbiter between the conflicting passions of the parties. The jurors look up to him with confidence and listen to him with respect, for in this instance their intelligence is completely under the control of his learning. It is the judge who sums up the various arguments with which their memory has been wearied out, and who guides them through the devious course of the proceedings; he points their attention to the exact question of fact which they are called upon to solve, and he puts the answer to the question of law into their mouths. His influence upon their verdict is almost unlimited.

出去。

陪审制度最大的贡献就在于让人们形成判断力并提高人们的知识。在我看来，这正是它的最大优势。陪审团可以被看成是一个常设的免费学校，在这里，每个陪审员学习行使自己的权利，与社会上层最博学开明的人士进行日常交流，并在法官指点和律师的帮助，甚至各党派的问责下，精通本国的法律。我认为，美国人实践知识和政治常识主要来自民事陪审制度的长期应用。我不知道陪审制度是否有利于诉讼当事人，但我可以肯定会对参与审判的人大有裨益。所以，我将陪审制度视为社会可以用来教育人民的最行之有效的手段之一。

到现在为止，我所说的是就所有国家而言，但是现在我要说的则是针对美国及其一般民主国家。我已经注意到，在民主国家，法学家以及司法人士构成唯一可以抑制人民违法犯罪的贵族团体。这个贵族阶层并不具备任何物质力量，但却可以对人们的思想施以保守的影响，而且其权威最根本的来源就是民事陪审制度。刑事案件是社会与个人的斗争，陪审团往往会把法官看成受社会力量摆布的工具，对其意见持怀疑态度。而且，刑事案件完全以常识普遍理解的事实证据为基础，而在这一点上，法官和陪审团没有什么不同。然而，在民事案件上却不是这么回事。因为在民事案件中，法官是冲突双方的中立的仲裁人；陪审团对法官充满信心，并对其裁决表示尊重，因为在这方面，法官的学识远远在陪审员之上。在陪审团面前总结他们已记不清楚的各种法律论据的是法官，引导他们完成曲折诉讼程序的也是法官；法官将陪审团的注意力引向他们要处理的事实问题，并告诉他们

If I am called upon to explain why I am but little moved by the arguments derived from the ignorance of jurors in civil causes, I reply, that in these proceedings, whenever the question to be solved is not a mere question of fact, the jury has only the semblance of a judicial body. The jury sanctions the decision of the judge, they by the authority of society which they represent, and he by that of reason and of law.

In England and in America the judges exercise an influence upon criminal trials which the French judges have never possessed. The reason of this difference may easily be discovered; the English and American magistrates establish their authority in civil causes, and only transfer it afterwards to tribunals of another kind, where that authority was not acquired. In some cases (and they are frequently the most important ones) the American judges have the right of deciding causes alone. Upon these occasions they are accidentally placed in the position which the French judges habitually occupy, but they are invested with far more power than the latter; they are still surrounded by the reminiscence of the jury, and their judgment has almost as much authority as the voice of the community at large, represented by that institution. Their influence extends beyond the limits of the courts; in the recreations of private life as well as in the turmoil of public business, abroad and in the legislative assemblies, the American judge is constantly surrounded by men who are accustomed to regard his intelligence as superior to their own, and after having exercised his power in the decision of causes, he continues to influence the habits of thought and the characters of the individuals who took a part in his judgment.

The jury, then, which seems to restrict the rights of magistracy, does in reality consolidate its power, and in no country are the judges so powerful as there, where the people partakes their privileges. It is more especially by means of the jury in civil causes that the American magistrates imbue all classes of society with the spirit of their profession. Thus the jury, which is the most energetic means of making the people rule, is also the most efficacious means of teaching it to rule well.

应该如何回答法律问题。法官对于陪审团判决的影响简直难以估量。

如果有人要我说明为什么我对陪审员未能在民事案件中引用法律论据无动于衷，我的回答是在民事诉讼中，凡是不涉及事实的问题，陪审团不过是徒有其表。陪审团宣布法官的裁决，前者代表的是社会权威，后者代表的是理性和法律的权威。

法国法官从未拥有过英国和美国法官对刑事案件的那种影响力。这种不同产生的原因不难发现，英国和美国的司法人士通过民事诉讼确立自己的权威，然后将这种权威原封不动地搬到一个他们本不具权威的另一法庭。在有些案件中（而且往往是重要案件），美国法官有权独自进行裁决。在这些情形下，他们的地位时不时地会和法国法官通常的地位相同，但是他们握有的力量则远远超出后者，在他们的身边陪审团依然存在，他们的判断与代表社会呼声的陪审团的声音几乎同样权威。他们的影响力超越了法庭；无论是在私人娱乐还是在政治活动中，在司法机构之内还是之外，美国法官身边总是围绕着一群习惯于认为法官的智慧比自己高出一筹的人，而且法官行使权力完成对案件的判决之后，会对其审理案件中参与的各方的思维习惯和性格产生持续的影响。

因此，陪审团制度表面上似乎是对司法权的限制，但实际则是对司法权的巩固，而且世界上没有任何一个国家的法官，能像人民分享法官权力的国家中的法官一样，拥有那么强大的力量。美国的司法人员之所以能够将法律精神灌输到社会各阶层更多的是依靠陪审制度在民事案件中的应用。因此，陪审制度作为实行人民统治最有力的手段，也是教会人民如何统治的最有效的手段。

Chapter XVII: Principal Causes Maintaining The Democratic Republic

Principal Causes Which Tend To Maintain The Democratic Republic In The United States

A democratic republic subsists in the United States, and the principal object of this book has been to account for the fact of its existence. Several of the causes which contribute to maintain the institutions of America have been involuntarily passed by or only hinted at as I was borne along by my subject. Others I have been unable to discuss, and those on which I have dwelt most are, as it were, buried in the details of the former parts of this work. I think, therefore, that before I proceed to speak of the future, I cannot do better than collect within a small compass the reasons which best explain the present. In this retrospective chapter I shall be succinct, for I shall take care to remind the reader very summarily of what he already knows; and I shall only select the most prominent of those facts which I have not yet pointed out.

All the causes which contribute to the maintenance of the democratic republic in the United States are reducible to three heads:—

I. The peculiar and accidental situation in which Providence has placed the Americans.

II. The laws.

III. The manners and customs of the people.

第十七章　　民主共和制度得以维持的主要原因

在美国有助于维护民主共和制度的主要原因

美国实行的是民主共和制，而本书的主要目的就是解释这一现象的原因。在这些原因中，有几个因为我要保证叙述的连续性被迫略过，或只稍作提示。因此，有一些原因我还未能谈及，还有一些已被淹没在我对前面细节的叙述之中。我认为，在继续对美国的未来进行评说之前，我应该集中谈一下能够说明美国现状的所有原因。在本章中，我会向读者简明扼要地回顾前面已经总结过的内容，并在尚未提及的内容中选择最重要的加以叙述。

在美国，有利于维护民主共和制度的所有原因可以归为以下三项：

1. 上帝为美国人安排的独特的、幸运的地理位置。

2. 法律。

3. 生活习惯和民情。

Accidental Or Providential Causes Which Contribute To The Maintenance Of The Democratic Republic In The United States

The Union has no neighbors—No metropolis—The Americans have had the chances of birth in their favor—America an empty country—How this circumstance contributes powerfully to the maintenance of the democratic republic in America—How the American wilds are peopled—Avidity of the Anglo-Americans in taking possession of the solitudes of the New World—Influence of physical prosperity upon the political opinions of the Americans.

A thousand circumstances, independent of the will of man, concur to facilitate the maintenance of a democratic republic in the United States. Some of these peculiarities are known, the others may easily be pointed out; but I shall confine myself to the most prominent amongst them.

The Americans have no neighbors, and consequently they have no great wars, or financial crises, or inroads, or conquest to dread; they require neither great taxes, nor great armies, nor great generals; and they have nothing to fear from a scourge which is more formidable to republics than all these evils combined, namely, military glory. It is impossible to deny the inconceivable influence which military glory exercises upon the spirit of a nation. General Jackson, whom the Americans have twice elected to the head of their Government, is a man of a violent temper and mediocre talents; no one circumstance in the whole course of his career ever proved that he is qualified to govern a free people, and indeed the majority of the enlightened classes of the Union has always been opposed to him. But he was raised to the Presidency, and has been maintained in that lofty station, solely by the recollection of a victory which he gained twenty years ago under the walls of New Orleans, a victory which was, however, a very ordinary achievement, and which could only be remembered in a country where battles are rare. Now the people which is thus carried away by the illusions of glory is unquestionably the most cold and calculating, the most unmilitary (if I may use the expression), and the most prosaic of all the peoples of the earth.

America has no great capital city, whose influence is directly or indirectly felt over the whole extent

有助于美国维护民主共和制度的偶然或天赐原因

联邦没有强邻——没有大都市——美国人生而有幸——美国地广人稀——环境因素何以大大利于美国民主共和制度的维护——美国的荒野是如何开发的——英裔美国人占据新大陆荒野的贪欲——物质繁荣对美国人政治观念的影响。

许许多多不以人们意志为转移的环境因素共同促成美国民主共和制度的存在。其中的一些众所周知，另一些也很容易说明，而我只想说一说其中最主要的那些。

美国人没有强邻，自然不必害怕战争、金融危机、入侵或被人征服。他们既不需要巨额的税收，也不需要庞大的军队和伟大的将军，而且完全不用担心军事的荣耀带来的灾祸，而这对共和制的伤害比所有那些不幸加起来都要大。不能否认军事的荣耀对一个国家精神的非同一般的影响。曾两次被人民选为美国首脑的杰克逊将军，脾气暴躁资质平平，在其整个任期中没有任何一件事情能够证明他有资格统治一个自由的民族，而且联邦知识阶层的绝大多数人都反对他。但是他却当选成为美国总统，并轻松获得连任，靠的就是二十年前他曾在新奥尔良城打过的一次胜仗，尽管这次胜利并无可圈可点之处，但是在罕有战事的美国却始终为人民所记忆。因为被荣耀的假象蒙住眼睛的民族必定是地球上最冷血，最斤斤计较，最不懂军事的，以及最平庸的民族。

美国没有能够直接或间接影响全国的巨大首都，而我认为这是美国共和制度得以维持的主要原因之一。在城市中，无法阻止人们集会，引发情绪共鸣突发过激行动。城市可以

of the country, which I hold to be one of the first causes of the maintenance of republican institutions in the United States. In cities men cannot be prevented from concerting together, and from awakening a mutual excitement which prompts sudden and passionate resolutions. Cities may be looked upon as large assemblies, of which all the inhabitants are members; their populace exercises a prodigious influence upon the magistrates, and frequently executes its own wishes without their intervention.

To subject the provinces to the metropolis is therefore not only to place the destiny of the empire in the hands of a portion of the community, which may be reprobated as unjust, but to place it in the hands of a populace acting under its own impulses, which must be avoided as dangerous. The preponderance of capital cities is therefore a serious blow upon the representative system, and it exposes modern republics to the same defect as the republics of antiquity, which all perished from not having been acquainted with that form of government.

It would be easy for me to adduce a great number of secondary causes which have contributed to establish, and which concur to maintain, the democratic republic of the United States. But I discern two principal circumstances amongst these favorable elements, which I hasten to point out. I have already observed that the origin of the American settlements may be looked upon as the first and most efficacious cause to which the present prosperity of the United States may be attributed. The Americans had the chances of birth in their favor, and their forefathers imported that equality of conditions into the country whence the democratic republic has very naturally taken its rise. Nor was this all they did; for besides this republican condition of society, the early settler bequeathed to their descendants those customs, manners, and opinions which contribute most to the success of a republican form of government. When I reflect upon the consequences of this primary circumstance, methinks I see the destiny of America embodied in the first Puritan who landed on those shores, just as the human race was represented by the first man.

The chief circumstance which has favored the establishment and the maintenance of a democratic republic in the United States is the nature of the territory which the American inhabit. Their ancestors gave them the love of equality and of freedom, but God himself gave them the means of remaining

被看成是一个人民大会，所有居民都是大会成员，城市居民对其司法人员和行政官员影响巨大，并总是不经官员的同意自行其是。

因此，让地方服从首都不仅不公平的将整个国家的命运交给了一部分人，而且还冒险将其交到了一部分自行其是的人手中。所以，首都的优势对代议制绝对是严重的打击，也让现代共和国出现古代共和国同样的弊端，而古代的共和国正是因为未能认识到这一点才全部灭亡。

对我来说，罗列一些有助于美国共和制确立及维护的次要原因易如反掌。但是，我注意到在众多的有利因素中有两个环境因素极为重要，我急于要说一说。我已经说过，美国人的起源对美国当前的繁荣有着最重要最有力的贡献。美国人的幸运与生俱来，他们祖先将身份平等带到这个国家，因此民主共和制自然应运而生。而且这并不是全部的所在，因为除了民主共和的社会状况外，最初的居民还将最有利于共和制度成功的民情、风俗和观念留给自己的子孙后代。在我对这个重要事实产生的后果反复思量的时候，我想我从登上这片大陆的第一个新教徒身上看到了美国的命运，就像从人类的第一个人身上看到整个人类的命运一样。

有利于美国民主共和制度建立和维持的首当其冲的因素就是美国得天独厚的地理位置。他们的祖先留给他们对平等自由的热爱，但赋予他们保持平等自由的手段，并将其安置在这片广阔无垠的大地上的是上帝本人。社会的普遍繁荣有利于一切政府的稳定性，对民主政府尤其如此，因为民主政府的稳定依赖于多数的情绪，而且特别是那部分最贫困阶

equal and free, by placing them upon a boundless continent, which is open to their exertions. General prosperity is favorable to the stability of all governments, but more particularly of a democratic constitution, which depends upon the dispositions of the majority, and more particularly of that portion of the community which is most exposed to feel the pressure of want. When the people rules, it must be rendered happy, or it will overturn the State, and misery is apt to stimulate it to those excesses to which ambition rouses kings. The physical causes, independent of the laws, which contribute to promote general prosperity, are more numerous in America than they have ever been in any other country in the world, at any other period of history. In the United States not only is legislation democratic, but nature herself favors the cause of the people.

In what part of human tradition can be found anything at all similar to that which is occurring under our eyes in North America? The celebrated communities of antiquity were all founded in the midst of hostile nations, which they were obliged to subjugate before they could flourish in their place. Even the moderns have found, in some parts of South America, vast regions inhabited by a people of inferior civilization, but which occupied and cultivated the soil. To found their new states it was necessary to extirpate or to subdue a numerous population, until civilization has been made to blush for their success. But North America was only inhabited by wandering tribes, who took no thought of the natural riches of the soil, and that vast country was still, properly speaking, an empty continent, a desert land awaiting its inhabitants.

Everything is extraordinary in America, the social condition of the inhabitants, as well as the laws; but the soil upon which these institutions are founded is more extraordinary than all the rest. When man was first placed upon the earth by the Creator, the earth was inexhaustible in its youth, but man was weak and ignorant; and when he had learned to explore the treasures which it contained, hosts of his fellow creatures covered its surface, and he was obliged to earn an asylum for repose and for freedom by the sword. At that same period North America was discovered, as if it had been kept in reserve by the Deity, and had just risen from beneath the waters of the deluge.

That continent still presents, as it did in the primeval time, rivers which rise from never-failing

层的情绪。当人民进行统治的时候，只要没有人颠覆国家，人民必感幸福，只有怀有野心想要称王的人，才会希望国家动荡不安。除法律以外，在美国拥有的有利于促进共同繁荣的物质原因比世界上任何国家以及历史上任何时代都要多。在美国，不仅立法是民主的，而且大自然本身也在助人民一臂之力。

人类历史上何时出现过与眼前北美所发生的一切相似的情况？古代名声显赫的国家都处在敌对国家的虎视眈眈之中，必须征服这些国家才能成就自己的繁荣。甚至在南美的某些地区，现在人们依然还能看到大片的土地被半开化的民族占据耕作。因此现代人为了能够建立自己的国家，必须铲除或征服这些土著人口，直到他们取得的成功让文明感到汗颜。但是在北美只有一些游牧部落，从未想过利用土地天然的丰富养分，因此，可以说，这片广袤的土地依旧没有人烟，是一片等待主人的荒野。

在美国，无论是社会情况还是法律都与众不同，但是最不同寻常的就是这些与众不同所赖以存在的土地。当造物主将大地赐给人类的时候，地球年富力强，资源取之不尽用之不竭，而人类则弱小无知；而当人类学会如何开发大地蕴含的宝藏的时候，人类的踪影已遍布大地，必须通过厮杀才能获得自由喘息的一席之地。就在此时，北美被发现了，似乎上帝一直将其隐藏起来，现在才从洪水之中浮现出来。

这片大陆呈现的依旧是其原始的模样，一条条永不枯竭的河流，一块块葱郁湿润的荒野，一片片未曾被犁过的土地。它就这样呈现在世人面前，但是此时的人类已非从前孤立的野蛮人，他们是深谙大自然奥秘、团结一致、拥有五千年阅历的人。在我写这本书的时

sources, green and moist solitudes, and fields which the ploughshare of the husbandman has never turned. In this state it is offered to man, not in the barbarous and isolated condition of the early ages, but to a being who is already in possession of the most potent secrets of the natural world, who is united to his fellow-men, and instructed by the experience of fifty centuries. At this very time thirteen millions of civilized Europeans are peaceably spreading over those fertile plains, with whose resources and whose extent they are not yet themselves accurately acquainted. Three or four thousand soldiers drive the wandering races of the aborigines before them; these are followed by the pioneers, who pierce the woods, scare off the beasts of prey, explore the courses of the inland streams, and make ready the triumphal procession of civilization across the waste.

The favorable influence of the temporal prosperity of America upon the institutions of that country has been so often described by others, and adverted to by myself, that I shall not enlarge upon it beyond the addition of a few facts. An erroneous notion is generally entertained that the deserts of America are peopled by European emigrants, who annually disembark upon the coasts of the New World, whilst the American population increases and multiplies upon the soil which its forefathers tilled. The European settler, however, usually arrives in the United States without friends, and sometimes without resources; in order to subsist he is obliged to work for hire, and he rarely proceeds beyond that belt of industrious population which adjoins the ocean. The desert cannot be explored without capital or credit; and the body must be accustomed to the rigors of a new climate before it can be exposed to the chances of forest life. It is the Americans themselves who daily quit the spots which gave them birth to acquire extensive domains in a remote country. Thus the European leaves his cottage for the trans-Atlantic shores; and the American, who is born on that very coast, plunges in his turn into the wilds of Central America. This double emigration is incessant; it begins in the remotest parts of Europe, it crosses the Atlantic Ocean, and it advances over the solitudes of the New World. Millions of men are marching at once towards the same horizon; their language, their religion, their manners differ, their object is the same. The gifts of fortune are promised in the West, and to the West they bend their course.

候，1300万文明的欧洲人和平地生活在这这片富饶的土地，尽管他们还并不确切地知道这片土地的资源何等的富饶，幅员何等的辽阔。在他们前面，有三四千士兵在驱赶居无定所的土著人，随之而来的是一批批拓殖者，他们披荆斩棘，驱走豺狼虎豹，开辟内河航道，为文明成功占据这片荒芜之地做着充分的准备。

美国目前的繁荣对这个国家制度的积极影响人们已经说过多次，至于我自己，并不想再对此多加赘述，但还想补充一些事实。一个普遍存在的错误看法是居住在美国荒野的是年复一年登陆到这片新世界的欧洲移民，而美国人依旧在他们祖先耕作的土地上繁衍。然而，初来乍到的欧洲人通常既无亲友投靠，又无财产傍身，为了活下去他必须找份工作，所以很少有人离开大洋沿岸的工业带前往内陆。没有资本和贷款，荒野根本就无法开发，此外，在前往森林地带生活之前，还必须学会适应那里的气候。放弃自己的出生之地到遥远荒野开拓的正是美国人自己。因为欧洲人离开自己的茅草屋，漂洋过海来到美国，而美国人则离开自己出生的那片海岸涌入美国中部的荒野之地。这种双重移民持续不断，始自遥远的欧洲，跨越大西洋，朝着新世界的腹地前进。数以百万计的人们同时朝着地平线的同一方向行进。尽管他们的语言、宗教和风俗都不相同，但是他们的目标相同。有人说去西部可以发财致富，于是人们便匆忙奔向那里。

也许除了导致罗马帝国崩溃的那次大迁徙以外，再没有什么能够跟这场持续不断的人类迁徙相提并论。因为那时像现在一样，一代代的人们朝着同一个方向前进，闹哄哄地聚在同一地点；但是如今上帝的安排已然发生改变。那时，等待着每个新来之人的是毁灭和

No event can be compared with this continuous removal of the human race, except perhaps those irruptions which preceded the fall of the Roman Empire. Then, as well as now, generations of men were impelled forwards in the same direction to meet and struggle on the same spot; but the designs of Providence were not the same; then, every newcomer was the harbinger of destruction and of death; now, every adventurer brings with him the elements of prosperity and of life. The future still conceals from us the ulterior consequences of this emigration of the Americans towards the West; but we can readily apprehend its more immediate results. As a portion of the inhabitants annually leave the States in which they were born, the population of these States increases very slowly, although they have long been established: thus in Connecticut, which only contains fifty-nine inhabitants to the square mile, the population has not increased by more than one-quarter in forty years, whilst that of England has been augmented by one-third in the lapse of the same period. The European emigrant always lands, therefore, in a country which is but half full, and where hands are in request: he becomes a workman in easy circumstances; his son goes to seek his fortune in unpeopled regions, and he becomes a rich landowner. The former amasses the capital which the latter invests, and the stranger as well as the native is unacquainted with want.

The laws of the United States are extremely favorable to the division of property; but a cause which is more powerful than the laws prevents property from being divided to excess. This is very perceptible in the States which are beginning to be thickly peopled; Massachusetts is the most populous part of the Union, but it contains only eighty inhabitants to the square mile, which is must less than in France, where 162 are reckoned to the same extent of country. But in Massachusetts estates are very rarely divided; the eldest son takes the land, and the others go to seek their fortune in the desert. The law has abolished the rights of primogeniture, but circumstances have concurred to re-establish it under a form of which none can complain, and by which no just rights are impaired.

A single fact will suffice to show the prodigious number of individuals who leave New England, in this manner, to settle themselves in the wilds. We were assured in 1830 that thirty-six of the members of Congress were born in the little State of Connecticut. The population of Connecticut, which

死亡，而如今的冒险家们带来的是繁荣和生命之种。美国人向西部的移民潜在的后果依旧不明朗，但是直接结果已经显而易见。随着一部分居住者每年不断地从自己的出生之地出走，尽管这些州已由来已久，但人口的增长非常缓慢。比如康涅狄格州，每平方英里的居民只有59人，而且40年来，这个州的人口只增长了1/4，而在同一时期，英国的人口却已增加了1/3。因此欧洲的移民不断来到这个人口不多而且劳动力短缺的国家，在这里他成为过着舒适生活的工人，而他们的子孙则前往地广人稀的地方寻找发财的机会，随后变成地主。前者为后者积累下投资的资本，无论是外来的移民还是出生在此处的人都不贫穷。

美国的法律非常有利于财产的分配，但是有一个比法律更为强大的因素可以防止财产被过度分配。在那些人口正在开始变稠密的州，这种现象特别明显。马萨诸塞州曾是美国最早被开发的地区，每平方英里的居民只有80人，这比法国每平方英里162人的人口密度要小得多。但是在马萨诸州很少出现土地的过度分割，因为在这里由长子继承土地，而其他的子女要到美国的荒野寻求发财的机会。

一个事实足以证明有大量的人以此种方式离开新英格兰前往荒野安家立业。1830年，国会中有36人出生在康涅狄格这样的小州。而康涅狄格州的人口只占美国人口的1/43，而出自这个州的议员却占国会议员总量的1/8。然而，真正由康涅狄格州选送的国会议员只有5名，其余31人均代表新建的西部各州。如果这31人都没有离开康涅狄格州，他们很可能成不了现在富裕的地主，而依旧是卑微的劳动者，依旧默默无闻地生活，根本无法跻身政界，更不用说当上举足轻重的立法人员，他们甚至有可能成为桀骜难驯的公民。

constitutes only one forty-third part of that of the United States, thus furnished one-eighth of the whole body of representatives. The States of Connecticut, however, only sends five delegates to Congress; and the thirty-one others sit for the new Western States. If these thirty-one individuals had remained in Connecticut, it is probable that instead of becoming rich landowners they would have remained humble laborers, that they would have lived in obscurity without being able to rise into public life, and that, far from becoming useful members of the legislature, they might have been unruly citizens.

These reflections do not escape the observation of the Americans any more than of ourselves. "It cannot be doubted," says Chancellor Kent in his "Treatise on American Law," "that the division of landed estates must produce great evils when it is carried to such excess as that each parcel of land is insufficient to support a family; but these disadvantages have never been felt in the United States, and many generations must elapse before they can be felt. The extent of our inhabited territory, the abundance of adjacent land, and the continual stream of emigration flowing from the shores of the Atlantic towards the interior of the country, suffice as yet, and will long suffice, to prevent the parcelling out of estates."

It is difficult to describe the rapacity with which the American rushes forward to secure the immense booty which fortune proffers to him. In the pursuit he fearlessly braves the arrow of the Indian and the distempers of the forest; he is unimpressed by the silence of the woods; the approach of beasts of prey does not disturb him; for he is goaded onwards by a passion more intense than the love of life. Before him lies a boundless continent, and he urges onwards as if time pressed, and he was afraid of finding no room for his exertions. I have spoken of the emigration from the older States, but how shall I describe that which takes place from the more recent ones? Fifty years have scarcely elapsed since that of Ohio was founded; the greater part of its inhabitants were not born within its confines; its capital has only been built thirty years, and its territory is still covered by an immense extent of uncultivated fields; nevertheless the population of Ohio is already proceeding westward, and most of the settlers who descend to the fertile savannahs of Illinois are citizens of Ohio. These men left their first country to improve their condition; they quit their resting-place to ameliorate it

与我们一样，美国人也有同样的认识。肯特大法官在《美国宪法释义》中说过："毋庸置疑，土地的过度分割必然会产生可怕的灾难，因为那小小的一块土地不足以养活一个家庭，但是这些不良后果并没有在美国出现，而且要在很多代人之后才会出现。我国土地辽阔，待开发的地区很多，来自大西洋沿岸的移民源源不断地向内陆迁徙，足以并将在很长一段时间内足够防止土地的过度分割。"

很难形容美国人冲向西部攫取命运赋予他们的巨大利益的贪婪。为了追求，他们无所畏惧，不畏印第安人的弓箭，无惧荒野的疫症，不怕林中的寂静，野兽的攻击也不为所动，因为有一股比对生命的热爱还要强烈的激情刺激他们不断向前。在他们的面前是一片无垠的大陆，可是他们却感到时间紧迫，生怕找不到可以开发的土地，因此不断向前。对于一些旧州居民的迁移我已经说过，但是我要如何描述这些新州中居民的迁徙呢？在50年前俄亥俄州成立还不到50年，绝大部分的居民都不出生在此，首府的成立也还不到30年，大片的土地尚未开发，然而俄亥俄州的人口已经开始向西迁徙，其中大多数人来到土地肥沃的伊利诺伊州的大草原定居。为了追求幸福这些人离开自己的第一故乡，然而为了过得更加幸福他们又离开自己的第二故乡，任何地方都有幸福在等待着他们，但是并不是每个人都能得到这份幸运。随着他们得到的越来越多，渴望富裕的这份激情变得越来越狂热难耐。他们先是挣断与出生之地的纽带，然而一路上却未能与新的地方重新建立这种联系。最初，迁移是他们谋生的必要的手段，而不久便成为一种不但能得到物质满足而且能得到情感满足的投机游戏。

still more; fortune awaits them everywhere, but happiness they cannot attain. The desire of prosperity is become an ardent and restless passion in their minds which grows by what it gains. They early broke the ties which bound them to their natal earth, and they have contracted no fresh ones on their way. Emigration was at first necessary to them as a means of subsistence; and it soon becomes a sort of game of chance, which they pursue for the emotions it excites as much as for the gain it procures.

Sometimes the progress of man is so rapid that the desert reappears behind him. The woods stoop to give him a passage, and spring up again when he has passed. It is not uncommon in crossing the new States of the West to meet with deserted dwellings in the midst of the wilds; the traveller frequently discovers the vestiges of a log house in the most solitary retreats, which bear witness to the power, and no less to the inconstancy of man. In these abandoned fields, and over these ruins of a day, the primeval forest soon scatters a fresh vegetation, the beasts resume the haunts which were once their own, and Nature covers the traces of man's path with branches and with flowers, which obliterate his evanescent track.

I remember that, in crossing one of the woodland districts which still cover the State of New York, I reached the shores of a lake embosomed in forests coeval with the world. A small island, covered with woods whose thick foliage concealed its banks, rose from the centre of the waters. Upon the shores of the lake no object attested the presence of man except a column of smoke which might be seen on the horizon rising from the tops of the trees to the clouds, and seeming to hang from heaven rather than to be mounting to the sky. An Indian shallop was hauled up on the sand, which tempted me to visit the islet that had first attracted my attention, and in a few minutes I set foot upon its banks. The whole island formed one of those delicious solitudes of the New World which almost lead civilized man to regret the haunts of the savage. A luxuriant vegetation bore witness to the incomparable fruitfulness of the soil. The deep silence which is common to the wilds of North America was only broken by the hoarse cooing of the wood-pigeon, and the tapping of the woodpecker upon the bark of trees. I was far from supposing that this spot had ever been inhabited, so completely did Nature seem to be left to her own caprices; but when I reached the centre of the

有时候，人们前进的速度太快，以至于荒野很快又在他们身后出现。林木刚刚才向他们屈服为其开辟一条道路，然而在他们走过之后，草木又很快繁茂起来。在途经西部的一些新州的时候，你总能在荒野中看到一些废弃的房舍，行者们在荒野深处不断发现的那些木屋的断壁残垣，既见证了人类的力量，又证明了人类的无常。在那些被遗弃的田野和那些才出现不久的废墟之上，原先的森林又冒出新芽，从前出没于此的野兽再次现身，大自然用绿草和鲜花将人类的足迹掩盖。

在经过一个纽约州的林地时，我记得到过一个环抱在森林之中的湖泊。在这片水中央，有一座小小的孤岛，岛上茂密的植被将整个小岛包裹起来。在湖岸上没有任何东西能证明有人住在这里，所能看到的不过是天边的一缕炊烟从树梢袅袅升起，飘向云端，似乎它并非从地上升起，而是从天而降一般。一叶印第安人的扁舟泊在滩岸上，引起了我的注意并勾起我想要上岛的冲动，几分钟之后我便登上了这座小岛。整个小岛笼罩着新世界那种惬意的幽静，几乎让文明人都要羡慕野蛮人的生活了。繁茂的植被证明这片土地的肥沃。就像北美的荒野一样，除了偶尔会有野鸽的咕咕声和啄木鸟啄木的声音打破这片沉寂外，四周静谧一片。我根本不认为这里曾经有人居住过，因为大自然依旧保留着它原始的样子。但是当我来到岛中央，我认为我看到的是一些人类活动的痕迹。接着，我小心地查看四周的一些东西，并立即确信曾经有一个欧洲人栖身在这里。但是他曾劳作过的地方发生了多大的变化呀！当初他匆忙伐倒用来搭建栖身之所的树木已长出了新芽，原来的篱笆已长成密实的树墙，他的小屋也破败得只剩一片阴凉。在这一片灌木丛中能够看见几块被

isle I thought that I discovered some traces of man. I then proceeded to examine the surrounding objects with care, and I soon perceived that a European had undoubtedly been led to seek a refuge in this retreat. Yet what changes had taken place in the scene of his labors! The logs which he had hastily hewn to build himself a shed had sprouted afresh; the very props were intertwined with living verdure, and his cabin was transformed into a bower. In the midst of these shrubs a few stones were to be seen, blackened with fire and sprinkled with thin ashes; here the hearth had no doubt been, and the chimney in falling had covered it with rubbish. I stood for some time in silent admiration of the exuberance of Nature and the littleness of man: and when I was obliged to leave that enchanting solitude, I exclaimed with melancholy, "Are ruins, then, already here?"

In Europe we are wont to look upon a restless disposition, an unbounded desire of riches, and an excessive love of independence, as propensities very formidable to society. Yet these are the very elements which ensure a long and peaceful duration to the republics of America. Without these unquiet passions the population would collect in certain spots, and would soon be subject to wants like those of the Old World, which it is difficult to satisfy; for such is the present good fortune of the New World, that the vices of its inhabitants are scarcely less favorable to society than their virtues. These circumstances exercise a great influence on the estimation in which human actions are held in the two hemispheres. The Americans frequently term what we should call cupidity a laudable industry; and they blame as faint-heartedness what we consider to be the virtue of moderate desires.

In France, simple tastes, orderly manners, domestic affections, and the attachments which men feel to the place of their birth, are looked upon as great guarantees of the tranquillity and happiness of the State. But in America nothing seems to be more prejudicial to society than these virtues. The French Canadians, who have faithfully preserved the traditions of their pristine manners, are already embarrassed for room upon their small territory; and this little community, which has so recently begun to exist, will shortly be a prey to the calamities incident to old nations. In Canada, the most enlightened, patriotic, and humane inhabitants make extraordinary efforts to render the people

火烧黑的石头，周围还散落着一些灰烬。毫无疑问，这里就是当时的炉灶，烟囱已经倒塌，落下的石块就掉在这里。我默默地在这里站了一会，慨叹大自然的活力和人类的渺小，而当我不得不离开这让人迷恋的地方时，不由得又一次忧伤地感叹："怎么这么快就成了一片废墟呢？"

在欧洲，我们习惯于把人不安分的性情、对财富不尽的贪欲以及对自由的过度热衷看作是社会的巨大威胁，但这些正是美国共和制得以和平长存的非常重要的因素。缺少了这些不安分的激情，人们就会聚集到特定的地方，不久之后就会像欧洲那样体会到难以满足的匮乏。新世界之所以幸运正是因为这里人们的恶习跟他们的品德一样有利于社会。这些对于评价东西半球人们的活动有非常重大的意义。美国人总是把我们口中的贪婪说成值得褒赞的勤奋，而把我们眼里的清心寡欲看成胆小怕事。

在法国，简单的趣味，规矩的举止，亲情的观念，以及对故土的热爱被视为国家安定幸福的保障。但是，在美国，没有什么比这些美德更加有碍社会的发展。依旧固守着质朴古老习俗的法裔加拿大人已经感觉到他们生活地方的狭小带来的尴尬，而这个最近才刚出现的社区不久也将成为他们与古老民族伴生而来的灾难的牺牲品。在加拿大，最开明、最爱国和最具人道主义精神的人不遗余力地让人们不要安于现状。在这里人们盛赞财富的诱惑力，就好像在旧世界里人们盛赞安贫乐道的魅力一样热情洋溢，并不断煽动起人们的激情，而不是像在其他地方那样要让人们平静下来。如果倾听他们的声音，我们会发现，他们赞扬的不是坚守故土安贫乐道，而是远走他乡发财致富，离开祖辈相传的家园。总而言

dissatisfied with those simple enjoyments which still content it. There, the seductions of wealth are vaunted with as much zeal as the charms of an honest but limited income in the Old World, and more exertions are made to excite the passions of the citizens there than to calm them elsewhere. If we listen to their eulogies, we shall hear that nothing is more praiseworthy than to exchange the pure and homely pleasures which even the poor man tastes in his own country for the dull delights of prosperity under a foreign sky; to leave the patrimonial hearth and the turf beneath which his forefathers sleep; in short, to abandon the living and the dead in quest of fortune.

At the present time America presents a field for human effort far more extensive than any sum of labor which can be applied to work it. In America too much knowledge cannot be diffused; for all knowledge, whilst it may serve him who possesses it, turns also to the advantage of those who are without it. New wants are not to be feared, since they can be satisfied without difficulty; the growth of human passions need not be dreaded, since all passions may find an easy and a legitimate object; nor can men be put in possession of too much freedom, since they are scarcely ever tempted to misuse their liberties.

The American republics of the present day are like companies of adventurers formed to explore in common the waste lands of the New World, and busied in a flourishing trade. The passions which agitate the Americans most deeply are not their political but their commercial passions; or, to speak more correctly, they introduce the habits they contract in business into their political life. They love order, without which affairs do not prosper; and they set an especial value upon a regular conduct, which is the foundation of a solid business; they prefer the good sense which amasses large fortunes to that enterprising spirit which frequently dissipates them; general ideas alarm their minds, which are accustomed to positive calculations, and they hold practice in more honor than theory.

It is in America that one learns to understand the influence which physical prosperity exercises over political actions, and even over opinions which ought to acknowledge no sway but that of reason; and it is more especially amongst strangers that this truth is perceptible. Most of the European emigrants to the New World carry with them that wild love of independence and of change which our calamities are so apt to engender. I sometimes met with Europeans in the United States

之，为了追求财富不惜抛却活着的人和死去的人。

如今，美国给人们提供了无尽的土地，只要肯努力，土地任你开垦。在美国，知识并没有多大用武之地，因为知识既可以服务于有知识的人自己，也可以服务于那些没有知识的人。在这里新的需求并不可怕，因为它们很容易得到满足；人们日益高涨的热情也不可怕，因为所有的热情都能轻而易举地找到合法的发泄对象；当然也不用担心赋予人们的自由过多，因为他们从没想让人滥用自由。

今天美国的共和社会更像一些生意兴隆的公司，而这些公司则是一些冒险家为了共同开发新世界荒地而成立起来的。最能令美国人迸发的并不是政治热情而是商业热情，或者更准确地说，他们将商人的习惯带到政界。他们热爱秩序，没有秩序事业就无法繁荣；他们特别循规蹈矩，因为这是他们生意的根本。他们宁可靠良好的意识慢慢累积财富，而不愿凭冒险精神去发大财。循规蹈矩的思想让他们习惯于本分做事的头脑保持警惕，他们更重视实践而不是理论。

只有在美国，一个人才能明白物质财富对政治活动的影响，乃至对本不应受其左右的舆论产生影响的原因。而对于外国人来说，这点特别值得注意。大多数新世界的欧洲移民怀抱着对自由的向往和对摆脱窘迫的渴望来到这里。在美国我经常可以看到一些欧洲人是因为政治见解才不得已离乡背井。他们的言谈让我大吃一惊，其中有一个人让我最为吃惊。在我经过宾夕法尼亚州一个偏远地方的时候，天色已晚，不得不找个地方投宿，于是

who had been obliged to leave their own country on account of their political opinions. They all astonished me by the language they held, but one of them surprised me more than all the rest. As I was crossing one of the most remote districts of Pennsylvania I was benighted, and obliged to beg for hospitality at the gate of a wealthy planter, who was a Frenchman by birth. He bade me sit down beside his fire, and we began to talk with that freedom which befits persons who meet in the backwoods, two thousand leagues from their native country. I was aware that my host had been a great leveller and an ardent demagogue forty years ago, and that his name was not unknown to fame. I was, therefore, not a little surprised to hear him discuss the rights of property as an economist or a landowner might have done: he spoke of the necessary gradations which fortune establishes among men, of obedience to established laws, of the influence of good morals in commonwealths, and of the support which religious opinions give to order and to freedom; he even went to far as to quote an evangelical authority in corroboration of one of his political tenets.

I listened, and marvelled at the feebleness of human reason. A proposition is true or false, but no art can prove it to be one or the other, in the midst of the uncertainties of science and the conflicting lessons of experience, until a new incident disperses the clouds of doubt; I was poor, I become rich, and I am not to expect that prosperity will act upon my conduct, and leave my judgment free; my opinions change with my fortune, and the happy circumstances which I turn to my advantage furnish me with that decisive argument which was before wanting. The influence of prosperity acts still more freely upon the American than upon strangers. The American has always seen the connection of public order and public prosperity, intimately united as they are, go on before his eyes; he does not conceive that one can subsist without the other; he has therefore nothing to forget; nor has he, like so many Europeans, to unlearn the lessons of his early education.

Influence Of The Laws Upon The Maintenance Of The Democratic Republic In The United States

Three principal causes of the maintenance of the democratic republic—Federal Constitutions—Municipal institutions—Judicial power.

我敲开了一个富有的种植园主的大门。种植园的主人出生在法国。他请我到壁炉边坐下，在远离故土两千英里之外的森林中偶遇的两个人自由地畅谈起来。后来，我了解到这里的主人40年前曾经是一个伟大的平等主义者，鼓动人心的激进政客，而且还挺有名气。因此，听着他像经济学家那样大谈土地所有权的时候让我惊讶不已。他谈到财富必然会使人们出现等级差别，谈到要服从已制定的法律，谈到良好的道德风尚对共和制的影响，谈到宗教对秩序和自由的支持。他甚至还引用耶稣基督的权威来支持他的政治见解。

我一边倾听，一边感叹人类理性的脆弱。在学说的变化无常和经验教训的不同中怎能证明一个学说的对与错？直到后来他的一席话才驱散我心中的疑云：我原来很穷，而现在很富有，我没料到财富会影响到我的行动，能让我自由做出判断，我的观点随我财富的变化而变化，在有利于我的环境中，我才找到我以前一直想要找的决定性论据。富裕对美国人的影响比对外国人更加广泛。美国人一直以来认为公共秩序和社会繁荣密不可分，在他们眼中，这两者谁也离不开谁。因此，他们不会像欧洲人那样，把小学时学到的东西都忘掉。

法律对维护美国民主共和制度的影响

维护民主共和制度的三大因素——联邦体制、乡镇制度、司法权。

本书的主要目的就是要让读者了解美国的法制。如果这个目的已经达成，读者就已经

The principal aim of this book has been to make known the laws of the United States; if this purpose has been accomplished, the reader is already enabled to judge for himself which are the laws that really tend to maintain the democratic republic, and which endanger its existence. If I have not succeeded in explaining this in the whole course of my work, I cannot hope to do so within the limits of a single chapter. It is not my intention to retrace the path I have already pursued, and a very few lines will suffice to recapitulate what I have previously explained.

Three circumstances seem to me to contribute most powerfully to the maintenance of the democratic republic in the United States.

The first is that Federal form of Government which the Americans have adopted, and which enables the Union to combine the power of a great empire with the security of a small State.

The second consists in those municipal institutions which limit the despotism of the majority, and at the same time impart a taste for freedom and a knowledge of the art of being free to the people.

The third is to be met with in the constitution of the judicial power. I have shown in what manner the courts of justice serve to repress the excesses of democracy, and how they check and direct the impulses of the majority without stopping its activity.

Influence Of Manners Upon The Maintenance Of The Democratic Republic In The United States

I have previously remarked that the manners of the people may be considered as one of the general causes to which the maintenance of a democratic republic in the United States is attributable. I here used the word manners with the meaning which the ancients attached to the word mores, for I apply it not only to manners in their proper sense of what constitutes the character of social intercourse, but I extend it to the various notions and opinions current among men, and to the mass of those ideas which constitute their character of mind. I comprise, therefore, under this term the whole moral and intellectual condition of a people. My intention is not to draw a picture of American manners, but simply to point out such features of them as are favorable to the maintenance of political institutions.

能够自行判断哪些法律真正有利于民主共和制，而哪些法律威胁到民主共和制的存在。如果书中已述的所有内容都未能做到这一点，那么在这一章中我就更难以达到这一目标。我并无意追溯曾经走过的路，而这寥寥几行便足以对我前面讲过的内容进行一下总结。

在我看来，有三个情况最有利于美国民主共和制度的维护。

第一是美国政府采用的联邦形式，能够使美联邦集大国的力量和小国的安定于一身。

第二是乡镇制度，在限制多数专制的同时赋予人们对自由的热爱并掌握行使自由的艺术。

第三是司法权的组织结构。我已经说明法院采用何种方式限制过度的民主，以及如何在不禁止多数活动的情况下对其活动进行监督指导。

民情对维护美国民主共和制度的影响

前面我已经说过，民情应当被视为美国民主共和制度得以维护的重大因素之一。我这里所用的民情一词其含义与这个词的古义相同，它不仅指社会交往中通常所具有的意义，还包括人们普遍具有的各种观念和见解，以及形成人们观念的众多思想。因此，我把这个词理解成一个民族总体的道德和精神面貌。我的目的不是描摹一幅美国民情的画卷，而不过是要指出美国民情中有利于维护其政治制度的一些特征。

作为一种政治制度的宗教，如何有力地帮助美国人维护民主共和制度

Religion Considered As A Political Institution, Which Powerfully Contributes To The Maintenance Of The Democratic Republic Amongst The Americans

North America peopled by men who professed a democratic and republican Christianity—Arrival of the Catholics—For what reason the Catholics form the most democratic and the most republican class at the present time.

Every religion is to be found in juxtaposition to a political opinion which is connected with it by affinity. If the human mind be left to follow its own bent, it will regulate the temporal and spiritual institutions of society upon one uniform principle; and man will endeavor, if I may use the expression, to harmonize the state in which he lives upon earth with the state which he believes to await him in heaven. The greatest part of British America was peopled by men who, after having shaken off the authority of the Pope, acknowledged no other religious supremacy; they brought with them into the New World a form of Christianity which I cannot better describe than by styling it a democratic and republican religion. This sect contributed powerfully to the establishment of a democracy and a republic, and from the earliest settlement of the emigrants politics and religion contracted an alliance which has never been dissolved.

About fifty years ago Ireland began to pour a Catholic population into the United States; on the other hand, the Catholics of America made proselytes, and at the present moment more than a million of Christians professing the truths of the Church of Rome are to be met with in the Union. The Catholics are faithful to the observances of their religion; they are fervent and zealous in the support and belief of their doctrines. Nevertheless they constitute the most republican and the most democratic class of citizens which exists in the United States; and although this fact may surprise the observer at first, the causes by which it is occasioned may easily be discovered upon reflection.

I think that the Catholic religion has erroneously been looked upon as the natural enemy of democracy. Amongst the various sects of Christians, Catholicism seems to me, on the contrary, to be one of those which are most favorable to the equality of conditions. In the Catholic Church, the

住在北美的是信仰民主和共和制度的基督徒——天主教徒的到来——是什么原因让天主教徒成为今天最民主最共和的阶级。

每种宗教身边都有一种与之契合的政治见解。如果任由人类的理性随其所好，它必然会用统一的原则管理社会和天国，而且如果我可以这么说的话，人必然会努力让尘世和他所信仰的天国和谐起来。绝大多数英裔美国人的聚居地居住的都是些反对教皇权威和宗教至高无上的人。他们将一种新型的基督教带到新大陆，我觉得除了称之为民主共和的基督教外再没有更适合的称呼。这个教派有力地推动了民主共和制度的建立，并形成最早的移民点，在这里，政治和宗教一开始就结为联盟，而且自此之后从未间断。

大约50年前，爱尔兰的天主教徒开始大量涌入美国，而且随着他们的到来，美国的天主教徒逐渐增长。如今在美国，信奉罗马教会真理的基督教徒已达100多万。天主教徒忠诚地遵从其宗教仪式，狂热虔诚地信奉他们的教义。然而，他们形成了美国公民中最民主最共和的阶级，尽管这样的事实可能会让人最初大吃一惊，但是稍加思考，这种情况产生的原因便不难发现。

我认为将天主教视为民主与生俱来的大敌是大错特错的，相反，在基督教众多教派之中，依我之见，天主教是最有利于身份平等的教派。天主教教会只由两部分构成：神职人员和教徒。只有神职人员地位高于其他教众，在其之下所有教众皆平等。

从天主教教义来看，它信奉众人资质皆平等，它要求智者和蠢材、天才和庸者同样遵

religious community is composed of only two elements, the priest and the people. The priest alone rises above the rank of his flock, and all below him are equal.

On doctrinal points the Catholic faith places all human capacities upon the same level; it subjects the wise and ignorant, the man of genius and the vulgar crowd, to the details of the same creed; it imposes the same observances upon the rich and needy, it inflicts the same austerities upon the strong and the weak, it listens to no compromise with mortal man, but, reducing all the human race to the same standard, it confounds all the distinctions of society at the foot of the same altar, even as they are confounded in the sight of God. If Catholicism predisposes the faithful to obedience, it certainly does not prepare them for inequality; but the contrary may be said of Protestantism, which generally tends to make men independent, more than to render them equal.

Catholicism is like an absolute monarchy; if the sovereign be removed, all the other classes of society are more equal than they are in republics. It has not unfrequently occurred that the Catholic priest has left the service of the altar to mix with the governing powers of society, and to take his place amongst the civil gradations of men. This religious influence has sometimes been used to secure the interests of that political state of things to which he belonged. At other times Catholics have taken the side of aristocracy from a spirit of religion.

But no sooner is the priesthood entirely separated from the government, as is the case in the United States, than is found that no class of men are more naturally disposed than the Catholics to transfuse the doctrine of the equality of conditions into the political world. If, then, the Catholic citizens of the United States are not forcibly led by the nature of their tenets to adopt democratic and republican principles, at least they are not necessarily opposed to them; and their social position, as well as their limited number, obliges them to adopt these opinions. Most of the Catholics are poor, and they have no chance of taking a part in the government unless it be open to all the citizens. They constitute a minority, and all rights must be respected in order to insure to them the free exercise of their own privileges. These two causes induce them, unconsciously, to adopt political doctrines, which they would perhaps support with less zeal if they were rich and preponderant.

守教义的所有细节；它要求富人和穷人履行同样的宗教仪式；它要求强者和弱者进行同样的苦修；它不与人妥协，而且对待所有人一视同仁；它要求社会各阶层都匍匐在神坛下一起做弥撒，就好像将他们都带到神的面前一样。虽然天主教要求信徒服从，但是这并不是允许不平等，而新教则刚好相反，一般来说它让人们趋于自由而不是平等。

天主教就像一个专制的君主国，如果将君主放在一边，社会各阶层要比在共和国更加平等。天主教神职人员辞去神职混迹于社会公职并沦为社会某一阶层的情况时常发生。有时候，他们还会利用这种宗教影响确保自己参与的事务的政治利益；还有些时候，天主教往往会出于其宗教精神而拥护贵族统治。

但是，一旦神职人员就像在美国那样脱离政府，人们就会发现再也没有任何阶层的人会像天主教信徒那样将身份平等的信条引入政界。因此，即使美国的天主教徒并非因其教义的天然属性而被迫接受民主和共和原则，但至少他们必不会反对这些原则，而且天主教徒的社会地位以及其有限的人数也必然让他们支持这样的观点。大多数的天主教徒是穷人，除非允许全体公民参政，否则他们根本没有机会。他们本身是少数，所以为了保证他们自己能够自由地行使权利必须尊重一切权利。这两个原因诱使他们不知不觉地采纳了那些如果他们有钱有势就不那么热衷的政治学说。

美国的天主教神职人员不但从没试图反对这种政治倾向，反而努力证明其合理性。在美国，教士将所有知识分为两类：一类是毫不犹豫表示认同的宗教教义；另一类是让人类自由探索的政治真理。因此，美国的天主教徒不但是最忠诚的信徒而且是最狂热的公民。

The Catholic clergy of the United States has never attempted to oppose this political tendency, but it seeks rather to justify its results. The priests in America have divided the intellectual world into two parts: in the one they place the doctrines of revealed religion, which command their assent; in the other they leave those truths which they believe to have been freely left open to the researches of political inquiry. Thus the Catholics of the United States are at the same time the most faithful believers and the most zealous citizens.

It may be asserted that in the United States no religious doctrine displays the slightest hostility to democratic and republican institutions. The clergy of all the different sects hold the same language, their opinions are consonant to the laws, and the human intellect flows onwards in one sole current.

I happened to be staying in one of the largest towns in the Union, when I was invited to attend a public meeting which had been called for the purpose of assisting the Poles, and of sending them supplies of arms and money. I found two or three thousand persons collected in a vast hall which had been prepared to receive them. In a short time a priest in his ecclesiastical robes advanced to the front of the hustings: the spectators rose, and stood uncovered, whilst he spoke in the following terms:—

"Almighty God! the God of Armies! Thou who didst strengthen the hearts and guide the arms of our fathers when they were fighting for the sacred rights of national independence; Thou who didst make them triumph over a hateful oppression, and hast granted to our people the benefits of liberty and peace; Turn, O Lord, a favorable eye upon the other hemisphere; pitifully look down upon that heroic nation which is even now struggling as we did in the former time, and for the same rights which we defended with our blood. Thou, who didst create Man in the likeness of the same image, let not tyranny mar Thy work, and establish inequality upon the earth. Almighty God! do Thou watch over the destiny of the Poles, and render them worthy to be free. May Thy wisdom direct their councils, and may Thy strength sustain their arms! Shed forth Thy terror over their enemies, scatter the powers which take counsel against them; and vouchsafe that the injustice which the world has witnessed for fifty years, be not consummated in our time. O Lord, who holdest alike the hearts of nations and of men in Thy powerful hand; raise up allies to the sacred cause of right; arouse

可以说，在美国任何宗教信条对民主共和制度不存有丝毫的敌意。不同教派的教士使用同一种语言，他们的观点与法律保持一致，人们思想潮流的方向也一致。

我有幸在美国大城市待过一阵子，曾被邀请参加一个声援波兰人的集会，向他们提供武器和金钱。我看到两三千人会聚在一个为集会准备的大厅，不一会儿一个身着教袍的教士来到讲坛前，在场的人全部起立脱帽，聆听他的讲话：

"万能的主！万军之神！当我们的祖先为民族神圣的自由战斗之时，您坚定了他们的决心指引了他们的行动。您让他们战胜可恶的压迫者们，赐予人民自由与和平。啊！主啊，请将您慈悲的目光投向另一半球，垂怜一下现在依旧像我们曾经那样战斗的英勇民族，他们正在用鲜血捍卫我们曾捍卫的权利。主啊，您创造了人类，赋予他们相同的样貌，请不要让暴政践踏您的杰作，在人世间建立起不平。万能的主！您是否正在注视波兰人的命运，请让他们获得自由。请您用智慧指引他们，用力量支持他们；让他们的敌人感到恐惧，并分裂妄图瓜分他们的列强，不要让50年来人们目睹的不义之举在我们这个时代继续下去。啊，主啊！您强大的手，犹如掌握世人的心一样，也掌握着各民族的心。愿您唤起同盟者投身这神圣的事业，把法兰西民族从统治者使其所处的麻木状态中唤醒，再次冲向前为世界自由而战。

"主啊，请不要将您的脸从我们这里转向别处，因为我们会永远是世间最虔诚最自由的民族。万能的主，愿您能聆听我们今天的祈祷。拯救波兰人民，以您爱子的名义，即为拯救全人类死于十字架上的我主耶稣基督的名义向您乞求。阿门！"

the French nation from the apathy in which its rulers retain it, that it go forth again to fight for the liberties of the world.

"Lord, turn not Thou Thy face from us, and grant that we may always be the most religious as well as the freest people of the earth. Almighty God, hear our supplications this day. Save the Poles, we beseech Thee, in the name of Thy well-beloved Son, our Lord Jesus Christ, who died upon the cross for the salvation of men. Amen."

The whole meeting responded "Amen!" with devotion.

Indirect Influence Of Religious Opinions Upon Political Society In The United States

Christian morality common to all sects—Influence of religion upon the manners of the Americans—Respect for the marriage tie—In what manner religion confines the imagination of the Americans within certain limits, and checks the passion of innovation—Opinion of the Americans on the political utility of religion—Their exertions to extend and secure its predominance.

I have just shown what the direct influence of religion upon politics is in the United States, but its indirect influence appears to me to be still more considerable, and it never instructs the Americans more fully in the art of being free than when it says nothing of freedom.

The sects which exist in the United States are innumerable. They all differ in respect to the worship which is due from man to his Creator, but they all agree in respect to the duties which are due from man to man. Each sect adores the Deity in its own peculiar manner, but all the sects preach the same moral law in the name of God. If it be of the highest importance to man, as an individual, that his religion should be true, the case of society is not the same. Society has no future life to hope for or to fear; and provided the citizens profess a religion, the peculiar tenets of that religion are of very little importance to its interests. Moreover, almost all the sects of the United States are comprised within the great unity of Christianity, and Christian morality is everywhere the same.

It may be believed without unfairness that a certain number of Americans pursue a peculiar form

全场虔诚齐呼"阿门！"。

宗教信仰对美国政治社会的间接影响

各教派共通的基督教道德——宗教对美国民情的影响——对婚姻关系的尊重——宗教运用何种方式将美国人的想象力限定在一定的范围，并抑制美国人创新的热情——美国人对宗教政治功用的看法——美国人为扩大和保证宗教权威所做的努力。

我刚刚已经阐述过宗教对美国政治的直接影响，但在我看来，宗教的间接影响力更加强大。尽管它并没有大谈自由，但却对美国人如何掌握行使自由的技巧给予最充分的教导。

美国现有的教派数不胜数。各教派信仰的从人到创世主各不相同，但是它们在人与人的义务上表现得非常一致。每个教派都用自己的方式对神灵顶礼膜拜，但是所有的教派都以上帝的名义宣扬同样的道德准则。宗教对于个人来说可能极为重要，但是对于整个社会而言则并非如此。社会对来世既没有希冀也没有恐惧，而且对于社会来说，最重要的不是全体公民信奉什么教派，而是全体公民信奉宗教。此外，美国几乎所有的教派都团结在基督教的周围，而且基督教的道德各处都一样。

可以公平地说，有一定数量的美国人追求的是一种礼拜的形式，更多的是出于习惯，而不是信仰。在美国，主权者必须信奉宗教，因此佯装信教的现象一定非常普遍，但是世界上没有任何一个国家能够像美国一样，能够让基督教对人类灵魂产生如此巨大的影响，

of worship, from habit more than from conviction. In the United States the sovereign authority is religious, and consequently hypocrisy must be common; but there is no country in the whole world in which the Christian religion retains a greater influence over the souls of men than in America; and there can be no greater proof of its utility, and of its conformity to human nature, than that its influence is most powerfully felt over the most enlightened and free nation of the earth.

I have remarked that the members of the American clergy in general, without even excepting those who do not admit religious liberty, are all in favor of civil freedom; but they do not support any particular political system. They keep aloof from parties and from public affairs. In the United States religion exercises but little influence upon the laws and upon the details of public opinion, but it directs the manners of the community, and by regulating domestic life it regulates the State.

I do not question that the great austerity of manners which is observable in the United States, arises, in the first instance, from religious faith. Religion is often unable to restrain man from the numberless temptations of fortune; nor can it check that passion for gain which every incident of his life contributes to arouse, but its influence over the mind of woman is supreme, and women are the protectors of morals. There is certainly no country in the world where the tie of marriage is so much respected as in America, or where conjugal happiness is more highly or worthily appreciated. In Europe almost all the disturbances of society arise from the irregularities of domestic life. To despise the natural bonds and legitimate pleasures of home, is to contract a taste for excesses, a restlessness of heart, and the evil of fluctuating desires. Agitated by the tumultuous passions which frequently disturb his dwelling, the European is galled by the obedience which the legislative powers of the State exact. But when the American retires from the turmoil of public life to the bosom of his family, he finds in it the image of order and of peace. There his pleasures are simple and natural, his joys are innocent and calm; and as he finds that an orderly life is the surest path to happiness, he accustoms himself without difficulty to moderate his opinions as well as his tastes. Whilst the European endeavors to forget his domestic troubles by agitating society, the American derives from his own home that love of order which he afterwards carries with him into public affairs.

而且再没有什么能更好地证明它更有利于人、更符合人性，因为这个国家在宗教的强大影响下，已成为世界上最文明自由的国家。

我已经说过，美国的神职人员普遍支持公民自由，即使那些反对宗教自由的人也不例外，但是他们并不支持任何特定的政治派系。他们不与各党派亲近，不参与政治事务，但对人们的行事方式施以影响，进而通过规范家庭生活对国家进行规范。

我并不置疑美国行事方式上表现出的严肃性首先来自宗教信仰。宗教通常无法阻挡命运对人们设下的种种诱惑，也无法抑制人们想要发财致富的热情，但是它对女人思想的控制则是绝对的，而女人正是道德的捍卫者。美国是世界上最尊重婚姻关系的国家，而且婚姻幸福也受到特别重视。在欧洲，社会的混乱几乎都因为家庭生活的问题。忽视家庭的天然结合及合法乐趣是喜欢毫无节制，心性不定，朝三暮四的表现。在这些导致家庭不安的情绪影响下，欧洲人难以服从国家的立法权。但是当美国人从公共生活的混乱回归家庭的怀抱，会感到安宁和平静。在这里，他的快乐朴素而自然，他的喜悦纯真且宁静，而且当他发现有秩序的生活能确保自己获得幸福时，便能轻而易举地调整自己的观念和爱好。欧洲人通过将社会搅得不得安宁，来努力忘记家庭生活的问题，而美国人则将通过从家庭生活中获得的对秩序的热爱带到公共事务之中。

在美国，宗教的影响并不仅限于行为风尚，而且还延伸到人们的智力。在英裔美国人中，有一些人信奉基督教的教义是出于对这些教义的虔诚信仰，而有些人尽管也信奉基督教教义，但却是因为怕别人说他们没有信仰。因此基督教在得到一致认可后，毫无阻碍地

In the United States the influence of religion is not confined to the manners, but it extends to the intelligence of the people. Amongst the Anglo-Americans, there are some who profess the doctrines of Christianity from a sincere belief in them, and others who do the same because they are afraid to be suspected of unbelief. Christianity, therefore, reigns without any obstacle, by universal consent; the consequence is, as I have before observed, that every principle of the moral world is fixed and determinate, although the political world is abandoned to the debates and the experiments of men. Thus the human mind is never left to wander across a boundless field; and, whatever may be its pretensions, it is checked from time to time by barriers which it cannot surmount. Before it can perpetrate innovation, certain primal and immutable principles are laid down, and the boldest conceptions of human device are subjected to certain forms which retard and stop their completion.

The imagination of the Americans, even in its greatest flights, is circumspect and undecided; its impulses are checked, and its works unfinished. These habits of restraint recur in political society, and are singularly favorable both to the tranquillity of the people and to the durability of the institutions it has established. Nature and circumstances concurred to make the inhabitants of the United States bold men, as is sufficiently attested by the enterprising spirit with which they seek for fortune. If the mind of the Americans were free from all trammels, they would very shortly become the most daring innovators and the most implacable disputants in the world. But the revolutionists of America are obliged to profess an ostensible respect for Christian morality and equity, which does not easily permit them to violate the laws that oppose their designs; nor would they find it easy to surmount the scruples of their partisans, even if they were able to get over their own. Hitherto no one in the United States has dared to advance the maxim, that everything is permissible with a view to the interests of society; an impious adage which seems to have been invented in an age of freedom to shelter all the tyrants of future ages. Thus whilst the law permits the Americans to do what they please, religion prevents them from conceiving, and forbids them to commit, what is rash or unjust.

Religion in America takes no direct part in the government of society, but it must nevertheless be regarded as the foremost of the political institutions of that country; for if it does not impart a taste

取得支配地位，结果正如我前面说的，道德方面的准则固定并决定下来，尽管政治方面还有待人们的讨论和研究。因此，在基督教面前人的思想从来不能毫无限制地自由活动，而且无论它多么自负，都会时不时地在其无法逾越的障碍面前止步。在人们想要施行革新之前，必须要预先规定好一些重要的原则，哪怕是最大胆的人类构想也要服从某些会对其产生阻碍和延迟的特定形式。

美国人的想象力，哪怕驰骋在最高空，也会小心谨慎犹豫不决；它的冲动受到束缚，它的目标难以达成。这些谨小慎微的习惯在政界一再出现，既利于国家的宁静又利于现有制度的长治久安。自然和环境共同作用将美国的居民塑造成为大胆的人，为了追求财富他们所表现出的进取精神就是最充分的证明。如果美国人的思想摆脱了所有的束缚，用不了多久他们就会成为世界上最胆大的革新者和最难对付的辩论者。但是，美国的革命家们必须要对基督教道德及公正显示出表面的尊重，这就使得他们不能随意违背忤逆自己意图的法律，即使他们能过自己这一关，也难以逾越同党人的责难。迄今为止，在美国没有人胆敢提出这样的信条：凡事要服从社会的利益。这样大不敬的箴言曾经在某个自由时代为了庇护其未来所有的暴政提出过。因此，当法律允许美国人按自己的意愿行事的时候，宗教阻止他们想入非非，禁止他们做出鲁莽不正义的举动。

在美国宗教没有直接参与社会管理，但却被视为这个国家政治体制中最重要的一环，因为尽管它没有向美国人鼓吹热爱自由，却让美国人能够将自由运用得得心应手。的确，美国的居民正是运用同样的观点看待宗教信仰。我不知道是否所有的美国人都笃信宗教，

for freedom, it facilitates the use of free institutions. Indeed, it is in this same point of view that the inhabitants of the United States themselves look upon religious belief. I do not know whether all the Americans have a sincere faith in their religion, for who can search the human heart? but I am certain that they hold it to be indispensable to the maintenance of republican institutions. This opinion is not peculiar to a class of citizens or to a party, but it belongs to the whole nation, and to every rank of society.

In the United States, if a political character attacks a sect, this may not prevent even the partisans of that very sect from supporting him; but if he attacks all the sects together, everyone abandons him, and he remains alone.

Whilst I was in America, a witness, who happened to be called at the assizes of the county of Chester (State of New York), declared that he did not believe in the existence of God, or in the immortality of the soul. The judge refused to admit his evidence, on the ground that the witness had destroyed beforehand all the confidence of the Court in what he was about to say. The newspapers related the fact without any further comment.

The Americans combine the notions of Christianity and of liberty so intimately in their minds, that it is impossible to make them conceive the one without the other; and with them this conviction does not spring from that barren traditionary faith which seems to vegetate in the soul rather than to live.

I have known of societies formed by the Americans to send out ministers of the Gospel into the new Western States to found schools and churches there, lest religion should be suffered to die away in those remote settlements, and the rising States be less fitted to enjoy free institutions than the people from which they emanated. I met with wealthy New Englanders who abandoned the country in which they were born in order to lay the foundations of Christianity and of freedom on the banks of the Missouri, or in the prairies of Illinois. Thus religious zeal is perpetually stimulated in the United States by the duties of patriotism. These men do not act from an exclusive consideration of the promises of a future life; eternity is only one motive of their devotion to the cause; and if you converse with these missionaries of Christian civilization, you will be surprised to find how much

因为没人能够看穿人的内心，不是吗？但是我很确定他们都笃信维护共和政体。这样的观点并非某一特定阶层或是党派所独有，而是整个国家各个社会阶层所共有。

在美国，如果一个政治人物攻击一个教派，甚至可能并不会妨碍这个教派的信徒对他的支持，但是如果他攻击所有的教派，那么所有人都会将其抛弃，最后落得孤家寡人。

我在美国期间，刚好有一个证人被传唤到切斯特县（隶属纽约州）法庭作证，他在法庭上宣称自己不相信上帝的存在，以及灵魂的不灭。所以法官拒绝他出庭作证，理由是证人在法庭允许其作证前已经摧毁了法庭对其证言的信任。报纸刊登了这条消息但是没有做出任何评论。

在美国人的心中基督教和自由已经密不可分，以至于根本不可能让他们只想一个而不想到另一个，而且美国人的这种信念并不是源自深植于灵魂深处行将覆灭的空洞的传统信仰。

我曾了解到美国人向西部新建的各州派遣神职人员，并在那里兴建学校和教堂，以防宗教在这些偏远地区销声匿迹，害怕迁移至此的人们在这里无法得享自由。我曾碰到一些富有的新英格兰居民，他们背井离乡为的就是在密苏里河两岸和伊利诺伊大草原给基督教和自由奠定基础。所以，在爱国主义责任感的作用下，宗教的热情在美国不断高涨。这些人这么做并不只是为了来世，永生只是他们奉献的动力之一，如果你跟这些基督教文明的传道者攀谈，便会惊讶地发现他们对今生的好处多么津津乐道，而且也会惊讶于教士在与你攀谈的时候会显露出政客的面目。他们会跟你说："美国所有的共和州都相互依赖，如果西部的共和州陷入混乱或是落入暴君之手，在大西洋沿岸蒸蒸日上的共和制度将会遭到

value they set upon the goods of this world, and that you meet with a politician where you expected to find a priest. They will tell you that "all the American republics are collectively involved with each other; if the republics of the West were to fall into anarchy, or to be mastered by a despot, the republican institutions which now flourish upon the shores of the Atlantic Ocean would be in great peril. It is, therefore, our interest that the new States should be religious, in order to maintain our liberties."

Such are the opinions of the Americans, and if any hold that the religious spirit which I admire is the very thing most amiss in America, and that the only element wanting to the freedom and happiness of the human race is to believe in some blind cosmogony, or to assert with Cabanis the secretion of thought by the brain, I can only reply that those who hold this language have never been in America, and that they have never seen a religious or a free nation. When they return from their expedition, we shall hear what they have to say.

There are persons in France who look upon republican institutions as a temporary means of power, of wealth, and distinction; men who are the condottieri of liberty, and who fight for their own advantage, whatever be the colors they wear: it is not to these that I address myself. But there are others who look forward to the republican form of government as a tranquil and lasting state, towards which modern society is daily impelled by the ideas and manners of the time, and who sincerely desire to prepare men to be free. When these men attack religious opinions, they obey the dictates of their passions to the prejudice of their interests. Despotism may govern without faith, but liberty cannot. Religion is much more necessary in the republic which they set forth in glowing colors than in the monarchy which they attack; and it is more needed in democratic republics than in any others. How is it possible that society should escape destruction if the moral tie be not strengthened in proportion as the political tie is relaxed? and what can be done with a people which is its own master, if it be not submissive to the Divinity?

Principal Causes Which Render Religion Powerful In America
Care taken by the Americans to separate the Church from the State—The laws, public opinion,

灭顶之灾。因此，为了维护自由，我们希望新建各州也要笃信宗教。"

这就是美国人的观念。如果有任何人认为我所称道的这种宗教精神是大错特错的，以及人类对自由幸福的渴望不过是对某种盲目的宇宙进化论的信仰，或者是同卡巴尼斯一样主张思想不过是大脑的分泌物，我的回答只能是，这样说的人一定没有来过美国，也从没见过信奉宗教和享有自由的民族。我们要听一听他们从美国探险归来之后会说些什么。

在法国，有些人将共和制度视为享有权力、财富和享乐的一种暂时手段，这些人是自由雇佣军，为自己的利益而战，不管他们披着哪种颜色的战袍，而这些人并不是我想谈的。而另一些人他们期望共和制度能让国家长治久安，是现代社会每天在理想和民情驱使下要达成的目标，并真诚地希望把人塑造成为自由的人。当这些人攻击宗教的时候，他们遵从的是自己的热情，而不是自己的利益。专制统治可以没有宗教信仰，但是自由不行。跟他们所攻击的君主专制相比，在他们津津乐道的共和制度下，宗教更加不可或缺。在政治纽带松弛且道德纽带没有得到加强的时候，社会怎可能逃脱崩溃的命运？而一个自己当家做主的民族，如果不信奉上帝又会有什么样的举动呢？

宗教在美国强有力的主要原因
美国人小心翼翼地将政教分离——法律、舆论以及神职人员本身都为达成这一目标而共同努力——在美国宗教之所以能够对人的精神产生影响应归功于这一原因——为什么——什么是人们当今在宗教方面的自然状态——在某些国家，阻碍人们达到这种状况的

and even the exertions of the clergy concur to promote this end—Influence of religion upon the mind in the United States attributable to this cause—Reason of this—What is the natural state of men with regard to religion at the present time—What are the peculiar and incidental causes which prevent men, in certain countries, from arriving at this state.

The philosophers of the eighteenth century explained the gradual decay of religious faith in a very simple manner. Religious zeal, said they, must necessarily fail, the more generally liberty is established and knowledge diffused. Unfortunately, facts are by no means in accordance with their theory. There are certain populations in Europe whose unbelief is only equalled by their ignorance and their debasement, whilst in America one of the freest and most enlightened nations in the world fulfils all the outward duties of religious fervor.

Upon my arrival in the United States, the religious aspect of the country was the first thing that struck my attention; and the longer I stayed there the more did I perceive the great political consequences resulting from this state of things, to which I was unaccustomed. In France I had almost always seen the spirit of religion and the spirit of freedom pursuing courses diametrically opposed to each other; but in America I found that they were intimately united, and that they reigned in common over the same country. My desire to discover the causes of this phenomenon increased from day to day. In order to satisfy it I questioned the members of all the different sects; and I more especially sought the society of the clergy, who are the depositaries of the different persuasions, and who are more especially interested in their duration. As a member of the Roman Catholic Church I was more particularly brought into contact with several of its priests, with whom I became intimately acquainted. To each of these men I expressed my astonishment and I explained my doubts; I found that they differed upon matters of detail alone; and that they mainly attributed the peaceful dominion of religion in their country to the separation of Church and State. I do not hesitate to affirm that during my stay in America I did not meet with a single individual, of the clergy or of the laity, who was not of the same opinion upon this point.

特殊和偶然原因。

18世纪的哲学家曾用非常简单的方式解释宗教信仰的逐渐衰败。他们说，宗教的热情必然会随着自由的普遍确立和知识的传播不断衰退，但不幸的是，事实跟他们的理论并不一致。在欧洲，有些人不信奉宗教只是出于他们的无知和愚蠢，而在美国这个世界上最自由最文明的国家，人们拿出极大的热情履行宗教赋予的义务。

我一到美国，宗教在这个国家的作用最先引起了我的注意，而且我在这里待的时间越长，越感到我所不熟悉的这种状况对政治的巨大影响。在法国，我看到宗教精神和自由精神所追求的东西总是背道而驰；但是在美国我发现它们紧密地结合在一起，共同统治同一个国家。想要发现其中奥妙的愿望与日俱增。为了能够弄个明白，我访遍各教派信徒，更特别寻访了不同教派和终身献身于宗教事业的教士团体。作为罗马天主教的信徒，我特别愿意跟天主教的神职人员接触，并跟他们熟络起来。我对他们每个人都讲到我的惊讶，也说明我的疑惑，结果我发现他们只是在细枝末节上有所不同而已，而总体而言，他们都将宗教在美国的和平统治归功于政教分离。我可以毫不犹疑地说，在美国逗留的这段时间，我从没碰到过任何一个人，不管是神职人员还是俗人，在这个问题上持不同意见。

这让我比以往更加关注美国神职人员在政界的地位。我惊讶地发现没有任何一个神职人员担任公职，行政机构里看不到神职人员的影子，而且在立法机构也看不到他们的代

This led me to examine more attentively than I had hitherto done, the station which the American clergy occupy in political society. I learned with surprise that they filled no public appointments; not one of them is to be met with in the administration, and they are not even represented in the legislative assemblies. In several States the law excludes them from political life, public opinion in all. And when I came to inquire into the prevailing spirit of the clergy I found that most of its members seemed to retire of their own accord from the exercise of power, and that they made it the pride of their profession to abstain from politics.

I heard them inveigh against ambition and deceit, under whatever political opinions these vices might chance to lurk; but I learned from their discourses that men are not guilty in the eye of God for any opinions concerning political government which they may profess with sincerity, any more than they are for their mistakes in building a house or in driving a furrow. I perceived that these ministers of the gospel eschewed all parties with the anxiety attendant upon personal interest. These facts convinced me that what I had been told was true; and it then became my object to investigate their causes, and to inquire how it happened that the real authority of religion was increased by a state of things which diminished its apparent force: these causes did not long escape my researches.

The short space of threescore years can never content the imagination of man; nor can the imperfect joys of this world satisfy his heart. Man alone, of all created beings, displays a natural contempt of existence, and yet a boundless desire to exist; he scorns life, but he dreads annihilation. These different feelings incessantly urge his soul to the contemplation of a future state, and religion directs his musings thither. Religion, then, is simply another form of hope; and it is no less natural to the human heart than hope itself. Men cannot abandon their religious faith without a kind of aberration of intellect, and a sort of violent distortion of their true natures; but they are invincibly brought back to more pious sentiments; for unbelief is an accident, and faith is the only permanent state of mankind. If we only consider religious institutions in a purely human point of view, they may be said to derive an inexhaustible element of strength from man himself, since they belong to one of

表。在一些州，法律将神职人员排除在政坛之外，而且舆论也都持相同的观点。而且当问及神职人员对此的普遍看法时，我发现大多数的神职人员似乎自发地不愿从政，并将远离政治视作其职业的荣誉。

我听到他们痛斥野心和谎言，不管它们以何种政治观点做掩护。但我也从他们的言谈中了解到在上帝的眼中，只要人们对政治管理的看法出自真心都不会获罪，而且也不会比盖错一座房或耕错一块地的罪过更大。我注意到，他们避开所有的党派，唯恐损害到自己的利益。这些事实让我笃信他们说的都是实话，因此我打算探究事实的成因，并追问宗教的表面力量被削弱后其真正影响力何以变得更强大。经过我的研究，个中的原因不久定能浮出水面。

短短60年的光阴，不足以充分发挥人的想象力，而不完美的现世生活也不足以让他们感到满足。在所有的生物中只有人表现出对其本身存在的与生俱来的不满，并总是希望人生无可限量。他轻视生命，却又害怕死亡。这些不同的情感不断驱使人的灵魂期待来生，而宗教恰好可以将人引向来世。因此，宗教便成为希望的另外一种表现形式，并同希望一样自然而然深入人心。如果不是神智错乱，或是某种对人之本性的暴力扭曲，人不会放弃宗教信仰，但是有一种不可战胜的力量会让人更为虔诚地信奉宗教。因为没有信仰只是偶然，有信仰才是人类的常态。如果我们仅从人的角度考察宗教组织，可以说它们是人永不枯竭的力量元素，因为它们是人性的主要构成因素之一。

我知道，在某些时代，宗教除得益于本身固有的影响之外，还能得到人为制定的法律

the constituent principles of human nature.

I am aware that at certain times religion may strengthen this influence, which originates in itself, by the artificial power of the laws, and by the support of those temporal institutions which direct society. Religions, intimately united to the governments of the earth, have been known to exercise a sovereign authority derived from the twofold source of terror and of faith; but when a religion contracts an alliance of this nature, I do not hesitate to affirm that it commits the same error as a man who should sacrifice his future to his present welfare; and in obtaining a power to which it has no claim, it risks that authority which is rightfully its own. When a religion founds its empire upon the desire of immortality which lives in every human heart, it may aspire to universal dominion; but when it connects itself with a government, it must necessarily adopt maxims which are only applicable to certain nations. Thus, in forming an alliance with a political power, religion augments its authority over a few, and forfeits the hope of reigning over all.

As long as a religion rests upon those sentiments which are the consolation of all affliction, it may attract the affections of mankind. But if it be mixed up with the bitter passions of the world, it may be constrained to defend allies whom its interests, and not the principle of love, have given to it; or to repel as antagonists men who are still attached to its own spirit, however opposed they may be to the powers to which it is allied. The Church cannot share the temporal power of the State without being the object of a portion of that animosity which the latter excites.

The political powers which seem to be most firmly established have frequently no better guarantee for their duration than the opinions of a generation, the interests of the time, or the life of an individual. A law may modify the social condition which seems to be most fixed and determinate; and with the social condition everything else must change. The powers of society are more or less fugitive, like the years which we spend upon the earth; they succeed each other with rapidity, like the fleeting cares of life; and no government has ever yet been founded upon an invariable disposition of the human heart, or upon an imperishable interest.

As long as a religion is sustained by those feelings, propensities, and passions which are found

的帮助，以及指导社会的那些当时政府的支持。宗教和人世的政府紧密结合起来，用恐怖和信仰进行专制统治。但是当宗教和人世的政府建立起这样的同盟后，我敢断定它会像一个人一样犯下同样错误，为了眼前的利益会不惜牺牲未来，为了获取本不属于它的权力而放弃自己的正当权力。当一个宗教把它的帝国建立在人人向往的永生的愿望之上的时候，便可以期待普世统治；但是，当它把自己跟一个政府拴在一起，必然只能采用适应某些人的准则。因此，跟政治力量结盟，其权力会有所增加，同时会丧失普世统治的可能。

只要宗教以慰藉人类痛苦的感情为基础，就能得到全人类的爱戴。但是如果它跟人世间痛苦的感情搅到一起，就只能被迫帮助那些不是要求爱而是要求利益的盟友，或是将那些依旧热爱它但却反对其盟友的人斥为敌人。因此，教会只要不分享国家的现世权力，就不会成为统治者煽动起来的仇恨的目标。

看起来建立得非常稳固的政治权力往往无法保证会比一代人的观点更持久，比一个时代的利益更长远，乃至比一个人的生命更长久。一条法律常常能够让似乎最牢不可破、最确定无疑的社会状况发生改变，而且随着社会状况的变化所有一切都必定会发生改变。社会的力量总是变化无常，就好像人生在世一样，而且迄今为止从未有一个政府能够自始至终得到人们发自内心的拥护，或是依靠一种永不消失的利益。一种宗教只要得到那些在不同历史时期不断以同样形式出现的情感、偏好以及激情的支持，就能跟时间抗衡长期兴盛，或者至少不会被另一种宗教所摧毁。但是当宗教依附于尘世利益时，便几乎会像世间任何一种权力一样虚弱不堪。唯有宗教有希望不朽，但是如果它跟那些转瞬即逝的权力结

to occur under the same forms, at all the different periods of history, it may defy the efforts of time; or at least it can only be destroyed by another religion. But when religion clings to the interests of the world, it becomes almost as fragile a thing as the powers of earth. It is the only one of them all which can hope for immortality; but if it be connected with their ephemeral authority, it shares their fortunes, and may fall with those transient passions which supported them for a day. The alliance which religion contracts with political powers must needs be onerous to itself; since it does not require their assistance to live, and by giving them its assistance to live, and by giving them its assistance it may be exposed to decay.

The danger which I have just pointed out always exists, but it is not always equally visible. In some ages governments seem to be imperishable; in others, the existence of society appears to be more precarious than the life of man. Some constitutions plunge the citizens into a lethargic somnolence, and others rouse them to feverish excitement. When governments appear to be so strong, and laws so stable, men do not perceive the dangers which may accrue from a union of Church and State. When governments display so much weakness, and laws so much inconstancy, the danger is self-evident, but it is no longer possible to avoid it; to be effectual, measures must be taken to discover its approach.

In proportion as a nation assumes a democratic condition of society, and as communities display democratic propensities, it becomes more and more dangerous to connect religion with political institutions; for the time is coming when authority will be bandied from hand to hand, when political theories will succeed each other, and when men, laws, and constitutions will disappear, or be modified from day to day, and this, not for a season only, but unceasingly. Agitation and mutability are inherent in the nature of democratic republics, just as stagnation and inertness are the law of absolute monarchies.

If the Americans, who change the head of the Government once in four years, who elect new legislators every two years, and renew the provincial officers every twelvemonth; if the Americans, who have abandoned the political world to the attempts of innovators, had not placed religion

盟，分享他们的财富，而同时也会随着曾支持他们的热情的消失而消失。宗教和政治力量的结盟必定会令自己背上沉重的负担，因为宗教不需要依靠他们的力量而存在，或是通过帮助他们而存在，而且给予政治力量以帮助还会给自己招来灭顶之灾。

我所指出的危险在任何时代都存在，但并不总是显而易见。在某些时代，政府似乎会千秋万代；而在另一些时代，社会的生存似乎比人的生命还要脆弱。一些政体弄得公民昏昏欲睡毫无生气，而另一些则令公民情绪激昂。当政府看上去非常强大，法制似乎非常稳定的时候，人们难以察觉政教合体会带来的危险。而当政府显得十分虚弱，法制十分缺乏一贯性的时候，危险便有目共睹，但此时它已无法避免，为了能够采取行之有效的措施必须要提前预见危机的走向。

一个国家社会状况越是民主，社会的共和倾向越是明显，政教结合的危险性就会越大，因为在此期间，政权不断易手更迭，政治理论层出不穷，而且人事、法律和制度不是不复存在，就是一天一变，而且这并不会是短期现象，而会长期如此。躁动和不安是民主共和的本性，就好像停滞和怠惰是君主专制的法则一样。

美国人每4年改选一次政府首脑，每2年改选一次新的立法者，且每12个月改选一次地方官员。美国人将政界留给野心勃勃的改革者，而不给宗教插手的余地，那么，在跌宕起伏的舆论之中宗教要在何处立足？在党派斗争中它又能从哪里获得应有的尊重？在周围一切都处于毁灭状态之中时它又能否永垂不朽？美国的神职人员首先认识到这一事实，并依据这一事实采取了相应的行动。他们明白如果想要谋求政治权力，就必须放弃他们的宗教

beyond their reach, where could it abide in the ebb and flow of human opinions? where would that respect which belongs to it be paid, amidst the struggles of faction? and what would become of its immortality, in the midst of perpetual decay? The American clergy were the first to perceive this truth, and to act in conformity with it. They saw that they must renounce their religious influence, if they were to strive for political power; and they chose to give up the support of the State, rather than to share its vicissitudes.

In America, religion is perhaps less powerful than it has been at certain periods in the history of certain peoples; but its influence is more lasting. It restricts itself to its own resources, but of those none can deprive it: its circle is limited to certain principles, but those principles are entirely its own, and under its undisputed control.

On every side in Europe we hear voices complaining of the absence of religious faith, and inquiring the means of restoring to religion some remnant of its pristine authority. It seems to me that we must first attentively consider what ought to be the natural state of men with regard to religion at the present time; and when we know what we have to hope and to fear, we may discern the end to which our efforts ought to be directed.

The two great dangers which threaten the existence of religions are schism and indifference. In ages of fervent devotion, men sometimes abandon their religion, but they only shake it off in order to adopt another. Their faith changes the objects to which it is directed, but it suffers no decline. The old religion then excites enthusiastic attachment or bitter enmity in either party; some leave it with anger, others cling to it with increased devotedness, and although persuasions differ, irreligion is unknown. Such, however, is not the case when a religious belief is secretly undermined by doctrines which may be termed negative, since they deny the truth of one religion without affirming that of any other. Progidious revolutions then take place in the human mind, without the apparent co-operation of the passions of man, and almost without his knowledge. Men lose the objects of their fondest hopes, as if through forgetfulness. They are carried away by an imperceptible current which they have not the courage to stem, but which they follow with regret, since it bears them from a faith they love, to a

影响力；最终他们选择放弃对政权的支持，分享国家的兴衰变迁。

在美国，宗教也许不如它曾经在某些时期某些国家那样强大，但是它的影响力更加长久。它只依靠自己的资源，而这些任什么人也无法剥夺。它的活动领域虽然受限于特定的原则，但这些原则完全隶属于它，并由它掌控。

在欧洲各地，缺乏宗教信仰的抱怨不绝于耳，人们呼吁设法恢复宗教原有的某些权威。在我看来，应当首先认真思索在我们这个时代人们在宗教上的自然状态应该是什么样子；当我们了解我们所希望所害怕的是什么，我们也许就可以领悟到应该朝哪个方向努力。

威胁宗教生存的两个巨大危险是教派的分裂和人们对宗教的漠不关心。在宗教的狂热时代，人们有时候会放弃他们的宗教信仰，但是他们之所以这样做为的就是信奉另一种宗教。他们信仰的目标发生了变化，但是宗教并未因此而削弱。然而旧的宗教不是激起人们的狂热的爱戴就是得到人们的痛恨。一些人愤怒地离它而去，另一些则更加虔诚地笃信它。所以尽管信念有所不同，但是并不是没有宗教信仰。然而，当一个宗教信仰遭到称之为否定的学说的暗中破坏的时候，就不再是这么回事了，因为他们在否定一种宗教的真实性时并没有对另一种宗教的真实性表示肯定。这样，人们思想中的巨大革命便在没有激情的协助之下，乃至毫无察觉地发生了。人好像忘记什么似的，失去了他们最喜爱的希望这个目标。人们被冷漠无情的潮流卷走，他们没有反抗的勇气，只有满腹遗憾地追随，因此，他们放弃心爱的信仰追随将他们推向深渊的怀疑。

scepticism that plunges them into despair.

In ages which answer to this description, men desert their religious opinions from lukewarmness rather than from dislike; they do not reject them, but the sentiments by which they were once fostered disappear. But if the unbeliever does not admit religion to be true, he still considers it useful. Regarding religious institutions in a human point of view, he acknowledges their influence upon manners and legislation. He admits that they may serve to make men live in peace with one another, and to prepare them gently for the hour of death. He regrets the faith which he has lost; and as he is deprived of a treasure which he has learned to estimate at its full value, he scruples to take it from those who still possess it.

On the other hand, those who continue to believe are not afraid openly to avow their faith. They look upon those who do not share their persuasion as more worthy of pity than of opposition; and they are aware that to acquire the esteem of the unbelieving, they are not obliged to follow their example. They are hostile to no one in the world; and as they do not consider the society in which they live as an arena in which religion is bound to face its thousand deadly foes, they love their contemporaries, whilst they condemn their weaknesses and lament their errors.

As those who do not believe, conceal their incredulity; and as those who believe, display their faith, public opinion pronounces itself in favor of religion: love, support, and honor are bestowed upon it, and it is only by searching the human soul that we can detect the wounds which it has received. The mass of mankind, who are never without the feeling of religion, do not perceive anything at variance with the established faith. The instinctive desire of a future life brings the crowd about the altar, and opens the hearts of men to the precepts and consolations of religion.

But this picture is not applicable to us: for there are men amongst us who have ceased to believe in Christianity, without adopting any other religion; others who are in the perplexities of doubt, and who already affect not to believe; and others, again, who are afraid to avow that Christian faith which they still cherish in secret.

Amidst these lukewarm partisans and ardent antagonists a small number of believers exist, who

在我所描述的那样的时代，人们之所以抛弃他们的宗教观念是出于冷漠而不是厌恶。他们并没有抛弃信仰，而是他们曾经怀有的情感消失了。但是尽管不信教的人不承认宗教的真实性，但是他们依然认可宗教是有用的。他们从人类的角度看宗教机构，认可宗教对人们行为方式和法制的影响。他们承认宗教有助于人与人的和平相处，能够让人安然面对死亡。他们为失去信仰扼腕叹息，就好像是一笔深知其价值的财富被夺走后在思量着是否要将它再夺回来。

然而，那些继续信教的人则不怕公开承认他们的信仰。在他们的眼中，那些与他们信念不同的人并不是他们的敌人而是值得同情的人，而且他们意识到要获得不信教人的尊重，并不一定要效仿他们的做法。他们不憎恨世上的任何人，也没有把他们生活的社会看成是宗教跟无数死敌决斗的竞技场，他们爱他们同时代的人，同时也谴责他们的软弱无力，为他们的过错长叹不已。

因为那些不信教的人将他们的怀疑隐藏起来，而那些信教的人则公开表示信教，所以舆论对宗教有利，也就是可以引导人们热爱、支持和赞颂宗教，通过触及人灵魂的深处找到它所受的创伤。那些永不放弃宗教信仰的民众，没有什么能使这种情感背弃已建立起的信仰。对来生本能的希冀将人们引到圣坛前，敞开心扉接受宗教的告解和慰藉。

但是这样的描述并不适合我们，因为在法国，有些人已经不再信仰基督教，也没有改信其他的宗教；还有一些人还在疑惑中徘徊，有些已经不再信教；更有一些人虽不敢公开宣称，但依旧偷偷信教。

are ready to brave all obstacles and to scorn all dangers in defence of their faith. They have done violence to human weakness, in order to rise superior to public opinion. Excited by the effort they have made, they scarcely knew where to stop; and as they know that the first use which the French made of independence was to attack religion, they look upon their contemporaries with dread, and they recoil in alarm from the liberty which their fellow-citizens are seeking to obtain. As unbelief appears to them to be a novelty, they comprise all that is new in one indiscriminate animosity. They are at war with their age and country, and they look upon every opinion which is put forth there as the necessary enemy of the faith.

Such is not the natural state of men with regard to religion at the present day; and some extraordinary or incidental cause must be at work in France to prevent the human mind from following its original propensities and to drive it beyond the limits at which it ought naturally to stop. I am intimately convinced that this extraordinary and incidental cause is the close connection of politics and religion. The unbelievers of Europe attack the Christians as their political opponents, rather than as their religious adversaries; they hate the Christian religion as the opinion of a party, much more than as an error of belief; and they reject the clergy less because they are the representatives of the Divinity than because they are the allies of authority.

In Europe, Christianity has been intimately united to the powers of the earth. Those powers are now in decay, and it is, as it were, buried under their ruins. The living body of religion has been bound down to the dead corpse of superannuated polity: cut but the bonds which restrain it, and that which is alive will rise once more. I know not what could restore the Christian Church of Europe to the energy of its earlier days; that power belongs to God alone; but it may be the effect of human policy to leave the faith in the full exercise of the strength which it still retains.

How The Instruction, The Habits, And The Practical Experience Of The Americans Promote The Success Of Their Democratic Institutions

What is to be understood by the instruction of the American people—The human mind more

在这些冷漠的教友和热烈的反对者中，还有很少的信徒存在。为了捍卫自己的信仰，他们已准备好克服一切障碍，对所有危险不屑一顾。为了不为舆论所左右，他们粗暴地攻击人类的弱点。他们在这种激情的鼓舞下忘乎所以，不知该在何处止步，而且因为他们知道法国人民获得独立首先采用的方法就是攻击宗教，所以他们害怕同时代的人，并惊恐地排斥他们那些同胞追求的自由。在他们眼中不信教是新鲜事，而他们对所有新鲜事物不分青红皂白一律表示厌恶。他们跟自己的时代、自己的国家为敌，将人们提出的每种见解都视为信仰理所当然的敌人。

这并不是当今人在宗教方面的自然状态，在法国有某种特殊偶然的原因在起作用，阻止人的思想遵循其原有的轨迹并迫使它冲破自己应该自然停止的界限。我清楚地意识到，这个特殊偶然的原因就是政治与宗教的紧密结合。欧洲的不信教者将基督教视为他们的政治敌人来攻击，而不是他们的宗教敌人。他们对基督教的憎恨有如对一个政党观念的憎恨，而不是将其视为错误的信仰。他们之所以排斥神职人员，不是因为他们是上帝的代表，而是因为他们是政权的盟友。

在欧洲，基督教已经和世间的政权密不可分。现在这些政权已经衰落，而基督教自己也被掩埋在它们的废墟之下。宗教活生生的躯体被压在腐朽政体的尸身之下，只要将宗教与它们的纽带斩断，它必然重获新生。我不知道怎样做才能让欧洲的基督教会重获往日的活力，因为这是只有上帝才能做到的事，但同时也有赖于人依旧相信宗教所保有的全部力量。

superficially instructed in the United States than in Europe—No one completely uninstructed—Reason of this—Rapidity with which opinions are diffused even in the uncultivated States of the West—Practical experience more serviceable to the Americans than book-learning.

I have but little to add to what I have already said concerning the influence which the instruction and the habits of the Americans exercise upon the maintenance of their political institutions.

America has hitherto produced very few writers of distinction; it possesses no great historians, and not a single eminent poet. The inhabitants of that country look upon what are properly styled literary pursuits with a kind of disapprobation; and there are towns of very second-rate importance in Europe in which more literary works are annually published than in the twenty-four States of the Union put together. The spirit of the Americans is averse to general ideas; and it does not seek theoretical discoveries. Neither politics nor manufactures direct them to these occupations; and although new laws are perpetually enacted in the United States, no great writers have hitherto inquired into the general principles of their legislation. The Americans have lawyers and commentators, but no jurists; and they furnish examples rather than lessons to the world. The same observation applies to the mechanical arts. In America, the inventions of Europe are adopted with sagacity; they are perfected, and adapted with admirable skill to the wants of the country. Manufactures exist, but the science of manufacture is not cultivated; and they have good workmen, but very few inventors. Fulton was obliged to proffer his services to foreign nations for a long time before he was able to devote them to his own country.

The observer who is desirous of forming an opinion on the state of instruction amongst the Anglo-Americans must consider the same object from two different points of view. If he only singles out the learned, he will be astonished to find how rare they are; but if he counts the ignorant, the American people will appear to be the most enlightened community in the world. The whole population, as I observed in another place, is situated between these two extremes. In New England, every citizen receives the elementary notions of human knowledge; he is moreover taught the

美国人的教育、习惯和实践经验如何推动其民主制度的成功

如何理解美国人的教育——与欧洲相比，美国对人的思想教育更加肤浅——没有人完全没有接受过教育——其原因何在——即使在未开化的西部各州思想的传播速度依旧迅速——对美国人而言，实践经验比书本知识更有用。

有关美国人的教育和习惯对维护其共和制度的影响我已经说过很多，但是依然有些东西需要补充一下。

迄今为止，美国出产的著名作家寥寥无几，也没有伟大的历史学家，而且也没有杰出的诗人。这个国家的居民对名副其实的真正文学所追求的东西怀有不赞同的态度，而且欧洲一个二流城市每年出版的文学作品，也要比美国24个州合起来还要多。美国人的思想缺少一般观念，他们不追求理论的发现，而他们的政治和实业也并未朝这个方向引导他们，而且尽管美国不断制定新的法律，但是时至今日依然没有出现一位探讨一般法理的伟大学者。美国人有法律人士，有评论家，但是没有法学家；他们向世界展示的是范例而不是教训。之于技术，也会看到同样的情况。在美国，欧洲的发明得到很好的利用，他们将其完善，使之成为适应本国需求的令人赞叹的技术。美国有实业，但并未得到科学的训练；美国有好的工人，但却没有多少发明家。富尔顿在为外国服务很长一段时间之后，才能将自己的才学奉献给自己的祖国。

想要考察英裔美国人教育状况的人必须从两个不同的角度去思考这个问题。如果他只

doctrines and the evidences of his religion, the history of his country, and the leading features of its Constitution. In the States of Connecticut and Massachusetts, it is extremely rare to find a man imperfectly acquainted with all these things, and a person wholly ignorant of them is a sort of phenomenon.

When I compare the Greek and Roman republics with these American States; the manuscript libraries of the former, and their rude population, with the innumerable journals and the enlightened people of the latter; when I remember all the attempts which are made to judge the modern republics by the assistance of those of antiquity, and to infer what will happen in our time from what took place two thousand years ago, I am tempted to burn my books, in order to apply none but novel ideas to so novel a condition of society.

What I have said of New England must not, however, be applied indistinctly to the whole Union; as we advance towards the West or the South, the instruction of the people diminishes. In the States which are adjacent to the Gulf of Mexico, a certain number of individuals may be found, as in our own countries, who are devoid of the rudiments of instruction. But there is not a single district in the United States sunk in complete ignorance; and for a very simple reason: the peoples of Europe started from the darkness of a barbarous condition, to advance toward the light of civilization; their progress has been unequal; some of them have improved apace, whilst others have loitered in their course, and some have stopped, and are still sleeping upon the way.

Such has not been the case in the United States. The Anglo-Americans settled in a state of civilization, upon that territory which their descendants occupy; they had not to begin to learn, and it was sufficient for them not to forget. Now the children of these same Americans are the persons who, year by year, transport their dwellings into the wilds; and with their dwellings their acquired information and their esteem for knowledge. Education has taught them the utility of instruction, and has enabled them to transmit that instruction to their posterity. In the United States society has no infancy, but it is born in man's estate.

The Americans never use the word "peasant," because they have no idea of the peculiar class

考察学者，必定会惊异于美国学者数量的稀少，但是如果他将无知的人也算在内，美国人将会是世界上知识水平最高的国家。我在另一本书中曾经指出，全体美国人的知识水平处于最高和最低的两极之间。在新英格兰，每个人都接受初等教育，或多或少都会学到宗教的教义和论据、本国的历史以及宪法的主要特征。在康涅狄格和马萨诸塞州，对这些一无所知的人几乎没有，对这些完全不了解的人简直是奇葩。

当我将希腊和罗马共和国制度跟美国的共和国制度进行比较，用前者的手抄本馆藏和其无知的民众与后者数不胜数的报刊和知识分子进行比较，并回顾我们为了古为今用和用两千年前的经验揣测未来的所有尝试的时候，我简直想把我的书付之一炬，这样才能用从未有过的全新观点去解读如此全新的社会状况。

但是，我所说的有关新英格兰的一切并不能笼统地推及整个联邦，因为随着我们越向西向南深入，人民的教育水平也随之下降。在毗邻墨西哥湾的各州，可以看到有些人就跟在我国一样，缺乏最初级的教育。但是，在美国根本找不到一个居民全都无知的地区，其原因很简单，欧洲各国是从野蛮的蒙昧状态朝着文明之光一步步走来，他们的进步参差不齐，有些国家疾步前行，还有些国家闲庭信步，甚至有些国家在征途上停下脚步埋头大睡。

美国的情况并不是这样。本已开化的英裔美国人定居在这片土地繁衍生息，他们不需要从头学起，只要不忘记已经学过的就足够了。如今这些美国人的后代，年复一年迁居荒野，而且随着他们的到来，也带来了原有的知识和对知识的尊重。教育教会他们知识的效

which that term denotes; the ignorance of more remote ages, the simplicity of rural life, and the rusticity of the villager have not been preserved amongst them; and they are alike unacquainted with the virtues, the vices, the coarse habits, and the simple graces of an early stage of civilization. At the extreme borders of the Confederate States, upon the confines of society and of the wilderness, a population of bold adventurers have taken up their abode, who pierce the solitudes of the American woods, and seek a country there, in order to escape that poverty which awaited them in their native provinces. As soon as the pioneer arrives upon the spot which is to serve him for a retreat, he fells a few trees and builds a loghouse. Nothing can offer a more miserable aspect than these isolated dwellings. The traveller who approaches one of them towards nightfall, sees the flicker of the hearth-flame through the chinks in the walls; and at night, if the wind rises, he hears the roof of boughs shake to and fro in the midst of the great forest trees. Who would not suppose that this poor hut is the asylum of rudeness and ignorance? Yet no sort of comparison can be drawn between the pioneer and the dwelling which shelters him. Everything about him is primitive and unformed, but he is himself the result of the labor and the experience of eighteen centuries. He wears the dress, and he speaks the language of cities; he is acquainted with the past, curious of the future, and ready for argument upon the present; he is, in short, a highly civilized being, who consents, for a time, to inhabit the backwoods, and who penetrates into the wilds of the New World with the Bible, an axe, and a file of newspapers.

It is difficult to imagine the incredible rapidity with which public opinion circulates in the midst of these deserts. I do not think that so much intellectual intercourse takes place in the most enlightened and populous districts of France. It cannot be doubted that, in the United States, the instruction of the people powerfully contributes to the support of a democratic republic; and such must always be the case, I believe, where instruction which awakens the understanding is not separated from moral education which amends the heart. But I by no means exaggerate this benefit, and I am still further from thinking, as so many people do think in Europe, that men can be instantaneously made citizens by teaching them to read and write. True information is mainly derived from experience; and if the

用，让他们能够将知识传给子孙后代。美国社会从未经历过孩提时代，它一出生便已成年。

美国人从来不用"农民"这个词。因为他们不了解这个词汇所特指的阶层。古老时代的蒙昧、田园生活的单调以及乡村的粗犷在他们身上没有任何残留；而且他们似乎对文明早期的美德、恶行、陋习以及单纯的美好同样一无所知。在联邦的边远地区，在人口稠密的地区和荒野的交界地区，一些胆大的冒险家定居下来。他们深入美国人迹罕至的森林，在那里建立起家园，为的就是能够摆脱在故土等待他们的贫穷。开荒者们一到达能够安身立命的地方，便开始伐树建屋。再没有什么比这些孤零零的房子更让人感到凄惨的了。夜幕降临，朝这些房子走来的行路人，看到墙上裂缝透出点点炉火的光亮；在夜里，如果有风刮起，还能听到树枝搭建的屋顶在大森林中被吹得摇摇晃晃的声响。有谁会不认为这个破陋的小屋是粗鲁无知之辈的栖身之所？但是在拓荒者和他们的居所之间并没有这样的共同点。他周遭的一切虽原始粗陋，但他本人却是19世纪劳动和经验的体现。他穿着城里人的衣服，说着城里人的话；他熟悉过去，憧憬未来，正视现在。简而言之，他是非常文明的人，一段时间之后，开始适应森林里的生活，而他在深入新世界荒地之初随身带的只有一部圣经、一把斧头和一沓报纸。

很难想象舆论以难以置信的速度在这些荒芜之地传播。我认为，在法国最开化、人口最多的地区会有如此规模的知识传播。毋庸置疑，在美国国民教育给予民主共和制度强有力的支持，而且我相信，在启迪智慧的教育和匡正人心的道德教化相辅相成的地方，情况总是如此。但是我并没有想要将其夸大之意，也没有像许多欧洲人那样进而认为只要人学

Americans had not been gradually accustomed to govern themselves, their book-learning would not assist them much at the present day.

I have lived a great deal with the people in the United States, and I cannot express how much I admire their experience and their good sense. An American should never be allowed to speak of Europe; for he will then probably display a vast deal of presumption and very foolish pride. He will take up with those crude and vague notions which are so useful to the ignorant all over the world. But if you question him respecting his own country, the cloud which dimmed his intelligence will immediately disperse; his language will become as clear and as precise as his thoughts. He will inform you what his rights are, and by what means he exercises them; he will be able to point out the customs which obtain in the political world. You will find that he is well acquainted with the rules of the administration, and that he is familiar with the mechanism of the laws. The citizen of the United States does not acquire his practical science and his positive notions from books; the instruction he has acquired may have prepared him for receiving those ideas, but it did not furnish them. The American learns to know the laws by participating in the act of legislation; and he takes a lesson in the forms of government from governing. The great work of society is ever going on beneath his eyes, and, as it were, under his hands.

In the United States politics are the end and aim of education; in Europe its principal object is to fit men for private life. The interference of the citizens in public affairs is too rare an occurrence for it to be anticipated beforehand. Upon casting a glance over society in the two hemispheres, these differences are indicated even by its external aspect.

In Europe we frequently introduce the ideas and the habits of private life into public affairs; and as we pass at once from the domestic circle to the government of the State, we may frequently be heard to discuss the great interests of society in the same manner in which we converse with our friends. The Americans, on the other hand, transfuse the habits of public life into their manners in private; and in their country the jury is introduced into the games of schoolboys, and parliamentary forms are observed in the order of a feast.

会读书写字就马上变身成公民。真正的知识来源于经验，而且如果美国人没有渐渐习惯于自治，他们的书本知识今天也不会给他们带来多大帮助。

在美国，我同美国人生活过很长时间，我无法表达我是多么得羡慕他们丰富的经验和良好的判断力。不要让美国人谈论欧洲，因为他们很可能会表现出相当的放肆和非常愚蠢的傲慢。他们拿出的那些笼统含糊的观点只能哄住世界上的无知之辈。但是如果将话题转到自己国家，掩盖住其智慧之光的阴云便立即烟消云散，他的语言跟他的思想都同样清晰而准确。他会告诉你他的权利是什么，以及通过哪种方式行使权利；他还能指出政界中的惯例。你会发现他非常熟悉行政制度，并深谙法律机制。美国的公民并不是从书本上获得实践经验和实证思想，教育只是培养了他们接受这些思想的能力，而不是将这些直接灌输给他们。美国人通过参与立法了解法律，通过参政了解政府的组织形式。社会的主要工作每天都在他们的监督下进行，而且也同样在他们的手中完成。

在美国，政治是教育的目的和目标；在欧洲，教育的主要目标就是让人们能处理好私人生活。公民参与公共事务极少需要提前学习。只要瞥一眼这两种社会，这方面的不同便立刻呈现在眼前。

在欧洲，我们不断将私人生活的观念和习惯引入公共事务，而当我们一下子从家庭生活的圈子插手国家管理的时候，我们往往像在家里与朋友攀谈那样来讨论国家大事。然而，美国人则将公共生活的习惯带回私人生活，而且在他们的国家，陪审团已经成为学生的游戏之一，甚至还能看到代议制被用来组织宴会。

The Laws Contribute More To The Maintenance Of The Democratic Republic In The United States Than The Physical Circumstances Of The Country, And The Manners More Than The Laws

All the nations of America have a democratic state of society—Yet democratic institutions only subsist amongst the Anglo-Americans—The Spaniards of South America, equally favored by physical causes as the Anglo-Americans, unable to maintain a democratic republic—Mexico, which has adopted the Constitution of the United States, in the same predicament—The Anglo-Americans of the West less able to maintain it than those of the East—Reason of these different results.

I have remarked that the maintenance of democratic institutions in the United States is attributable to the circumstances, the laws, and the manners of that country. Most Europeans are only acquainted with the first of these three causes, and they are apt to give it a preponderating importance which it does not really possess.

It is true that the Anglo-Saxons settled in the New World in a state of social equality; the low-born and the noble were not to be found amongst them; and professional prejudices were always as entirely unknown as the prejudices of birth. Thus, as the condition of society was democratic, the empire of democracy was established without difficulty. But this circumstance is by no means peculiar to the United States; almost all the trans-Atlantic colonies were founded by men equal amongst themselves, or who became so by inhabiting them. In no one part of the New World have Europeans been able to create an aristocracy. Nevertheless, democratic institutions prosper nowhere but in the United States.

The American Union has no enemies to contend with; it stands in the wilds like an island in the ocean. But the Spaniards of South America were no less isolated by nature; yet their position has not relieved them from the charge of standing armies. They make war upon each other when they have no foreign enemies to oppose; and the Anglo-American democracy is the only one which has hitherto been able to maintain itself in peace.

法律对维护美国民主共和制的贡献比自然环境大，而民情的贡献比法律还要大

美洲的所有民族都有民主的社会状况——然而民主制度只得到英裔美国人的支持——南美的西班牙人虽与英裔美国人同样享有自然优势，但却未能维护民主共和制度——沿袭美国宪法的墨西哥遭遇同样的困境——西部的英裔美国人维护这一制度的难度比东部的英裔美国人大——出现这些不同情况的原因。

我已经说过美国民主制度的维护得益于地理环境、法律和民情。大多数欧洲人只知道这三个因素中的第一个，然后赋予其超乎实际的重大作用。

的确，定居在新世界的英裔美国人处于一种身份平等的状态，在他们之中既没有出身低下的人也没有贵族，行业偏见和出身偏见都不存在。因此，当社会处于民主状况，民主制度就毫不费力地建立起来。但是这种情况绝非美国所独有，几乎所有的跨大西洋的殖民地都是由彼此平等或是定居此处后变得平等的人们建立。新世界中没有任何一块地方能让欧洲人建立贵族政体。然而，民主制度却只在美国繁荣昌盛。

美联邦没有与之竞争的敌人，就像海上的孤岛一般矗立在荒野之中。但是，大自然同样也让西班牙人孤零零地屹立在南美，然而，他们得天独厚的地理位置并没有让他们松懈而忽视常备军的建设。在他们没有外敌抗衡的时候，互相争斗；而英裔美国人的民主是迄今为止唯一一个能够采用和平方式维系下来的民主制度。

美国的疆域给人类的活动提供无限的土地，并为工业和劳动提供永不枯竭的资源。在这里，发财致富的欲望代替了争名逐利的野心，社会的繁荣缓和了派系的争斗。但是在地

The territory of the Union presents a boundless field to human activity, and inexhaustible materials for industry and labor. The passion of wealth takes the place of ambition, and the warmth of faction is mitigated by a sense of prosperity. But in what portion of the globe shall we meet with more fertile plains, with mightier rivers, or with more unexplored and inexhaustible riches than in South America?

Nevertheless, South America has been unable to maintain democratic institutions. If the welfare of nations depended on their being placed in a remote position, with an unbounded space of habitable territory before them, the Spaniards of South America would have no reason to complain of their fate. And although they might enjoy less prosperity than the inhabitants of the United States, their lot might still be such as to excite the envy of some nations in Europe. There are, however, no nations upon the face of the earth more miserable than those of South America.

Thus, not only are physical causes inadequate to produce results analogous to those which occur in North America, but they are unable to raise the population of South America above the level of European States, where they act in a contrary direction. Physical causes do not, therefore, affect the destiny of nations so much as has been supposed.

I have met with men in New England who were on the point of leaving a country, where they might have remained in easy circumstances, to go to seek their fortune in the wilds. Not far from that district I found a French population in Canada, which was closely crowded on a narrow territory, although the same wilds were at hand; and whilst the emigrant from the United States purchased an extensive estate with the earnings of a short term of labor, the Canadian paid as much for land as he would have done in France. Nature offers the solitudes of the New World to Europeans; but they are not always acquainted with the means of turning her gifts to account. Other peoples of America have the same physical conditions of prosperity as the Anglo-Americans, but without their laws and their manners; and these peoples are wretched. The laws and manners of the Anglo-Americans are therefore that efficient cause of their greatness which is the object of my inquiry.

I am far from supposing that the American laws are preeminently good in themselves; I do not hold them to be applicable to all democratic peoples; and several of them seem to be dangerous,

球上的哪个部分我们还能找到比南美更加肥沃的平原，更加壮阔的大河，以及更有待开发和用之不竭的资源呢？

然而，南美却未能建立起民主制度。如果民族的富裕与他们偏远的位置有关，南美的西班牙人则毫无理由怨天尤人。尽管他们也许并不如美国居民幸福，但至少够让欧洲人羡慕的了。可是，地球上却再没有比南美各国更加悲惨的了。

可见，仅凭地理环境的优势非但不足以使南美出现类似北美的情形，甚至在某些方面还比不上自然环境差强人意的欧洲国家。所以，地理因素对国家命运的影响远没有人们想象的那么大。

在新英格兰我碰到一些人，他们本可以在故土安居乐业却偏要前往荒野寻求幸福。离此不远，我见到加拿大的法国移民，尽管同样的荒野近在咫尺，他们却宁愿挤在一块人满为患的狭长地带。与此同时，来自美国的移民用不长时间的劳动收入就能在这里买下大片的土地，而加拿大人却愿意用比在法国还要高的价格购买人口密集地区的土地。大自然将新世界的荒野同样赐给欧洲人，但是他们却始终没有找到利用这个礼物的要领。美洲其他国家与英裔美国人有着同样富饶的自然条件，但是却并不具备他们所有的法制和民情，而且这些国家都很贫穷。因此，英裔美国人的法制和民情是其强大的有利因素，也正是我研究的对象。

我根本不认为美国的法律本身特别出类拔萃，也不认为它适用于所有的民主国家，而且有些法律甚至在美国也很危险。然而，不可否认的是美国的立法总体来说非常适应它所

even in the United States. Nevertheless, it cannot be denied that the American legislation, taken collectively, is extremely well adapted to the genius of the people and the nature of the country which it is intended to govern. The American laws are therefore good, and to them must be attributed a large portion of the success which attends the government of democracy in America: but I do not believe them to be the principal cause of that success; and if they seem to me to have more influence upon the social happiness of the Americans than the nature of the country, on the other hand there is reason to believe that their effect is still inferior to that produced by the manners of the people.

The Federal laws undoubtedly constitute the most important part of the legislation of the United States. Mexico, which is not less fortunately situated than the Anglo-American Union, has adopted the same laws, but is unable to accustom itself to the government of democracy. Some other cause is therefore at work, independently of those physical circumstances and peculiar laws which enable the democracy to rule in the United States.

Another still more striking proof may be adduced. Almost all the inhabitants of the territory of the Union are the descendants of a common stock; they speak the same language, they worship God in the same manner, they are affected by the same physical causes, and they obey the same laws. Whence, then, do their characteristic differences arise? Why, in the Eastern States of the Union, does the republican government display vigor and regularity, and proceed with mature deliberation? Whence does it derive the wisdom and the durability which mark its acts, whilst in the Western States, on the contrary, society seems to be ruled by the powers of chance? There, public business is conducted with an irregularity and a passionate and feverish excitement, which does not announce a long or sure duration.

I am no longer comparing the Anglo-American States to foreign nations; but I am contrasting them with each other, and endeavoring to discover why they are so unlike. The arguments which are derived from the nature of the country and the difference of legislation are here all set aside. Recourse must be had to some other cause; and what other cause can there be except the manners of the people?

It is in the Eastern States that the Anglo-Americans have been longest accustomed to the government of democracy, and that they have adopted the habits and conceived the notions most favorable to its

要治理的人民的才智和国家的性质。因此说美国的法律良好，而且美国民主制度的成功很大一部分也归功于它，但是我不认为它们是美国成功的主要原因。尽管我认为它们对美国人的社会幸福影响大于自然环境，但是另一方面，我也有理由相信它们的作用不及民情大。

毋庸置疑，联邦法律是美国立法最为重要的组成部分。跟美联邦地理环境同样得天独厚的墨西哥采用了同样的法律，却未能让自己适应民主制度。因此除了地理环境和独特的法律外，还有其他的原因让民主制度统治美国发挥着作用。

当然还需要对这个原因进行更有力的证明。生活在联邦土地上的几乎所有居民都是同一种族的后裔，他们操着同样的语言，以同样的方式膜拜上帝，受同样物质条件的影响，遵守同样的法律。那么，他们的差异从何而来呢？为什么在联邦的东部，共和政府表现得生机勃勃，有条不紊，且成熟而从容？而政府行为的明智性和持久性又源自何处呢？相反，在西部各州社会的管理则显得随意。在西部，公共事业表现得混乱而且癫狂，不考虑长远的未来。

我不想再将英裔美国人和外国加以比较，而是将他们相互比较，并努力探寻他们互不相同的原因。在这里，源自国家自然环境和立法差别的论点毫无用处，只能向其他原因求助，而除了民情还能有什么呢？

正是在东部各州，英裔美国人长久以来已经习惯于民主管理制度，且将习性付诸实践并形成最有利于维护民主制度的观点。民主渐渐深入他们的习俗、观念以及社交方式，并

maintenance. Democracy has gradually penetrated into their customs, their opinions, and the forms of social intercourse; it is to be found in all the details of daily life equally as in the laws. In the Eastern States the instruction and practical education of the people have been most perfected, and religion has been most thoroughly amalgamated with liberty. Now these habits, opinions, customs, and convictions are precisely the constituent elements of that which I have denominated manners.

In the Western States, on the contrary, a portion of the same advantages is still wanting. Many of the Americans of the West were born in the woods, and they mix the ideas and the customs of savage life with the civilization of their parents. Their passions are more intense; their religious morality less authoritative; and their convictions less secure. The inhabitants exercise no sort of control over their fellow-citizens, for they are scarcely acquainted with each other. The nations of the West display, to a certain extent, the inexperience and the rude habits of a people in its infancy; for although they are composed of old elements, their assemblage is of recent date.

The manners of the Americans of the United States are, then, the real cause which renders that people the only one of the American nations that is able to support a democratic government; and it is the influence of manners which produces the different degrees of order and of prosperity that may be distinguished in the several Anglo-American democracies. Thus the effect which the geographical position of a country may have upon the duration of democratic institutions is exaggerated in Europe. Too much importance is attributed to legislation, too little to manners. These three great causes serve, no doubt, to regulate and direct the American democracy; but if they were to be classed in their proper order, I should say that the physical circumstances are less efficient than the laws, and the laws very subordinate to the manners of the people. I am convinced that the most advantageous situation and the best possible laws cannot maintain a constitution in spite of the manners of a country; whilst the latter may turn the most unfavorable positions and the worst laws to some advantage. The importance of manners is a common truth to which study and experience incessantly direct our attention. It may be regarded as a central point in the range of human observation, and the common termination of all inquiry. So seriously do I insist upon this head, that if I have hitherto failed in making the reader feel the important influence which I attribute to the practical experience,

表现在日常生活和法律的方方面面。在东部各州，人民的书本知识和实践教育都已最为完美，而宗教也最具自由主义色彩。现在，这些习惯、观念、风俗以及信念恰恰就是我所说的民情的组成成分。

与之相反，在西部各州，这些优势中仍有一部分还不存在。许多西部的美国人出生在森林地区，他们思想和生活方式的野蛮和祖辈的文明交织在一起。他们的热情更加强烈，宗教道德观念较为淡薄，信念也不够坚定。西部各州在一定程度上显示出一个民族孩提时代的缺乏经验和粗野。在这里，它们虽然由旧社会的人组成，但不过是最近才聚在一起。

因此，美国人的民情才是使之能够维护民主制度的真正原因，而且正是民情的影响才使得英裔美国人建立的各州在细节和发展程度上有所不同。因此，一个国家的地理位置对民主制度寿命的影响在欧洲被夸大了，且法制的重要性也被高估，但民情的影响却被低估。毫无疑问，这三个重要因素对美国的民主制度进行了规范和指导，但是如果要按照它们的贡献分出三六九等，我要说自然环境不及法制，而法制则远不及民情。我可以肯定，最有利的地理位置和最佳的法律，缺少了民情的支持都无法维护一个政体，而后者则可以将最不利的地理位置和最糟糕的法律转变成某种优势。民情的重要性是研究和经验不断提醒我们注意的一个普遍真理。它可以被视为人类观察的视角，以及所有研究的终点。如果迄今为止我未能让读者认识到我所述的实践经验、习惯、观念，简而言之就是美国的民情对维护其制度的重要性，我就没能达成自己写这本书的主要目的。

the habits, the opinions, in short, to the manners of the Americans, upon the maintenance of their institutions, I have failed in the principal object of my work.

Whether Laws And Manners Are Sufficient To Maintain Democratic Institutions In Other Countries Besides America

The Anglo-Americans, if transported into Europe, would be obliged to modify their laws— Distinction to be made between democratic institutions and American institutions—Democratic laws may be conceived better than, or at least different from, those which the American democracy has adopted—The example of America only proves that it is possible to regulate democracy by the assistance of manners and legislation.

I have asserted that the success of democratic institutions in the United States is more intimately connected with the laws themselves, and the manners of the people, than with the nature of the country. But does it follow that the same causes would of themselves produce the same results, if they were put into operation elsewhere; and if the country is no adequate substitute for laws and manners, can laws and manners in their turn prove a substitute for the country? It will readily be understood that the necessary elements of a reply to this question are wanting: other peoples are to be found in the New World besides the Anglo-Americans, and as these people are affected by the same physical circumstances as the latter, they may fairly be compared together. But there are no nations out of America which have adopted the same laws and manners, being destitute of the physical advantages peculiar to the Anglo-Americans. No standard of comparison therefore exists, and we can only hazard an opinion upon this subject.

It appears to me, in the first place, that a careful distinction must be made between the institutions of the United States and democratic institutions in general. When I reflect upon the state of Europe, its mighty nations, its populous cities, its formidable armies, and the complex nature of its politics, I cannot suppose that even the Anglo-Americans, if they were transported to our hemisphere, with their ideas, their religion, and their manners, could exist without considerably altering their laws.

除美国之外，在其他国家法制和民情是否足以维护民主制度

如果英裔美国人重返欧洲，将不得不对其法律进行修改——一般民主制度和美国民主制度的区别——民主法制可以设想得更好，至少不同于美国所采用的那些法制——美国的例子只能证明在民情和法制的帮助下有可能建立民主制度。

我已经说过，民主制度在美国的成功与法制和民情的关系比地理环境更为密切。但是，如果将这些相同的因素放在别处必然会产生同样的结果吗？既然自然环境无法代替法制和民情，那么法制和民情能够代替自然环境吗？不难设想，我们还缺少必要的证据对此问题做出答复，除了英裔美国人以外，在新世界还有其他的民族，他们拥有和英裔美国人同样的物质条件，所以很适合做比较。但是除了美国以外，世界上没有一个不具备美国那样自然条件的国家采用与美国相同的法制，拥有与其相同的民情。因此，并不存在可与美国相比较的对象，我只能斗胆对此谈谈自己的看法。

在我看来，必须首先要对一般民主制度和美国的民主制度进行仔细的区分。当我回想欧洲的状况——那些强大的国家，人口稠密的城市，势如破竹的军队，以及复杂的政治局势时，我不相信如果英裔美国人带着他们的思想、宗教和民情迁回欧洲，能在不对其法制进行大改变的前提下继续存在下去。但是，可以想象一个不按照美国方式建立起的民主国家，可以设想一个国家是真正建立在多数人的意愿之上，但是这个多数愿意为了国家的

But a democratic nation may be imagined, organized differently from the American people. It is not impossible to conceive a government really established upon the will of the majority; but in which the majority, repressing its natural propensity to equality, should consent, with a view to the order and the stability of the State, to invest a family or an individual with all the prerogatives of the executive. A democratic society might exist, in which the forces of the nation would be more centralized than they are in the United States; the people would exercise a less direct and less irresistible influence upon public affairs, and yet every citizen invested with certain rights would participate, within his sphere, in the conduct of the government. The observations I made amongst the Anglo-Americans induce me to believe that democratic institutions of this kind, prudently introduced into society, so as gradually to mix with the habits and to be interfused with the opinions of the people, might subsist in other countries besides America. If the laws of the United States were the only imaginable democratic laws, or the most perfect which it is possible to conceive, I should admit that the success of those institutions affords no proof of the success of democratic institutions in general, in a country less favored by natural circumstances. But as the laws of America appear to me to be defective in several respects, and as I can readily imagine others of the same general nature, the peculiar advantages of that country do not prove that democratic institutions cannot succeed in a nation less favored by circumstances, if ruled by better laws.

If human nature were different in America from what it is elsewhere; or if the social condition of the Americans engendered habits and opinions amongst them different from those which originate in the same social condition in the Old World, the American democracies would afford no means of predicting what may occur in other democracies. If the Americans displayed the same propensities as all other democratic nations, and if their legislators had relied upon the nature of the country and the favor of circumstances to restrain those propensities within due limits, the prosperity of the United States would be exclusively attributable to physical causes, and it would afford no encouragement to a people inclined to imitate their example, without sharing their natural advantages. But neither of these suppositions is borne out by facts.

In America the same passions are to be met with as in Europe; some originating in human nature,

秩序和稳定压抑自己要求平等的天性，而将所有的特权都赋予一个家族或是一个人手中。也许会存在这样一个民主社会，其国家权力比美国更集中，人民对公共事务的影响更为间接且并非不可抗拒，而且每个公民可以在其权利范围内参与国家管理。通过对英裔美国人的观察使我相信为了能够让上述这类的民主制度逐渐融入人民的习惯并深入人民的思想观念，要将其谨慎地引入一个社会，这样也许民主制度可以在美国以外的地方存在。如果美国的法制是人们可以想到的唯一的民主法制，或者是能想到的最完美的民主法制，那么我只能承认，美国法制的成功根本无法证明一般的民主法制在自然条件欠优越的国家能够取得成功。但是，在我看来美国的法制在一些方面并不尽如人意，而且也不难构思出一些其他的良好法制，那么美国的独特优势也并不能证明民主制度无法在条件稍逊但法制优越的国家取得成功。

如果美国人的天性有别于其他地方，或者美国人的社会条件造就的习惯和观念不同于旧世界同样社会条件下产生的习惯和观念，那么无法预料美国人的民主在其他国家会产生什么样的结果。如果美国人表现出与其他所有国家人民同样的趣味，而且他们的立法者能够凭借国家的自然条件和环境优势将他们的爱好约束在适当的范围内，则美国的繁荣应当首先归功于自然原因，那么对于想要模仿美国而又缺乏同样自然条件的国家也不会有什么借鉴作用。但是所有这些假设都没有经过事实证明。

在美国，人们有着和欧洲人同样的激情，其中一部分来自人性，另一部分来自社会

others in the democratic condition of society. Thus in the United States I found that restlessness of heart which is natural to men, when all ranks are nearly equal and the chances of elevation are the same to all. I found the democratic feeling of envy expressed under a thousand different forms. I remarked that the people frequently displayed, in the conduct of affairs, a consummate mixture of ignorance and presumption; and I inferred that in America, men are liable to the same failings and the same absurdities as amongst ourselves. But upon examining the state of society more attentively, I speedily discovered that the Americans had made great and successful efforts to counteract these imperfections of human nature, and to correct the natural defects of democracy. Their divers municipal laws appeared to me to be a means of restraining the ambition of the citizens within a narrow sphere, and of turning those same passions which might have worked havoc in the State, to the good of the township or the parish. The American legislators have succeeded to a certain extent in opposing the notion of rights to the feelings of envy; the permanence of the religious world to the continual shifting of politics; the experience of the people to its theoretical ignorance; and its practical knowledge of business to the impatience of its desires.

The Americans, then, have not relied upon the nature of their country to counterpoise those dangers which originate in their Constitution and in their political laws. To evils which are common to all democratic peoples they have applied remedies which none but themselves had ever thought of before; and although they were the first to make the experiment, they have succeeded in it.

The manners and laws of the Americans are not the only ones which may suit a democratic people; but the Americans have shown that it would be wrong to despair of regulating democracy by the aid of manners and of laws. If other nations should borrow this general and pregnant idea from the Americans, without however intending to imitate them in the peculiar application which they have made of it; if they should attempt to fit themselves for that social condition, which it seems to be the will of Providence to impose upon the generations of this age, and so to escape from the despotism or the anarchy which threatens them; what reason is there to suppose that their efforts would not be crowned with success? The organization and the establishment of democracy in Christendom is the

的民主制度。所以，在美国我看到当所有人的身份接近平等且人人有机会更上一层楼的时候，人心自然而然地浮躁。我看到民主嫉妒感的形式千变万化。我曾说过美国人在处理事务的时候不断表现出无知和傲慢，而且我也曾由此得出结论，在美国也像在法国一样，人们也同样有失败，同样有蠢行。但是，在对美国的社会状况进行深入考察之后，我很快发现美国人为此已经付出巨大宝贵的努力来抑制那些人性的缺陷，纠正民主的天然缺陷。美国各种地方性的法律是将公民的野心限定在一个狭小范围的手段，是将不利于国家的激情转变成对地方有利的激情的手段。美国的立法者在一定程度上已经成功地以权利观念反对嫉妒感，以宗教世界的永生对抗政治的变幻莫测，以人们的经验弥补理论的不足，以及以处事的实践知识抑制欲望的急切。

因此，美国人并不是依靠国家的天然优势抗衡其宪法和政治法律的危险。对于那些所有民主国家都存在的弊端，他们已经采用迄今为止只有他们想到的解决之策，而且尽管他们是第一个吃螃蟹的人，但是他们成功了。

美国的民情和法制并非只适合民主国家，而且美国人已经证明可以寄希望于用民情和法制来调整民主制度。如果其他国家借鉴美国人这种普遍且有益的思想，却不打算照搬美国人的独特应用方法；如果他们想尝试自我调整以适应上帝为我们这个时代的人所规定的社会状况，并以此来避免专制和无政府主义的威胁：那么我们有什么理由认为他们的努力一定会失败呢？在基督教世界，民主制度的组织和建立是这个时代最重大的政治问题。毫无疑问，美国人并没有解决这个问题，但是他们为试图解决这个问题的那些人提供了有用

great political problem of the time. The Americans, unquestionably, have not resolved this problem, but they furnish useful data to those who undertake the task.

Importance Of What Precedes With Respect To The State Of Europe

It may readily be discovered with what intention I undertook the foregoing inquiries. The question here discussed is interesting not only to the United States, but to the whole world; it concerns, not a nation, but all mankind. If those nations whose social condition is democratic could only remain free as long as they are inhabitants of the wilds, we could not but despair of the future destiny of the human race; for democracy is rapidly acquiring a more extended sway, and the wilds are gradually peopled with men. If it were true that laws and manners are insufficient to maintain democratic institutions, what refuge would remain open to the nations, except the despotism of a single individual? I am aware that there are many worthy persons at the present time who are not alarmed at this latter alternative, and who are so tired of liberty as to be glad of repose, far from those storms by which it is attended. But these individuals are ill acquainted with the haven towards which they are bound. They are so deluded by their recollections, as to judge the tendency of absolute power by what it was formerly, and not by what it might become at the present time.

If absolute power were re-established amongst the democratic nations of Europe, I am persuaded that it would assume a new form, and appear under features unknown to our forefathers. There was a time in Europe when the laws and the consent of the people had invested princes with almost unlimited authority; but they scarcely ever availed themselves of it. I do not speak of the prerogatives of the nobility, of the authority of supreme courts of justice, of corporations and their chartered rights, or of provincial privileges, which served to break the blows of the sovereign authority, and to maintain a spirit of resistance in the nation. Independently of these political institutions—which, however opposed they might be to personal liberty, served to keep alive the love of freedom in the mind of the public, and which may be esteemed to have been useful in this respect—the manners and opinions of the nation confined the royal authority within barriers which were not less powerful,

的经验。

已发生的事情对欧洲的重要性

我之所以要探讨上述问题的意图并不难发现。这里所讨论的问题不仅涉及美国，还涉及整个世界；它不仅与一个民族有关，还和整个人类有关。如果那些具备民主社会状况的国家只有身处荒野才能保持自由，那么对于人类未来的命运我们只有绝望了，因为民主正在迅速蔓延，而荒野已经渐渐人满为患。如果法律和民情不足以维护民主制度，那么除了个人专政以外，哪里还有避难所为它们敞开大门呢？我知道现在还有许多杰出的人没有被这样的可能吓倒，但是他们厌烦自由，更愿意避开自由的风暴独善其身。但是这些人对他们所驶向的避风港并不熟悉。他们对绝对专权原来的样子记忆犹新，并依此对绝对专权进行评价，而不是依据它今天可能的表现来评价它。

如果绝对专权在欧洲民主国家得以重建，我确信它会采用一种新的形式，并表现出我们的祖先从未见过的特点。在欧洲，在法律和人民的许可下，国王曾经一度可以拥有几乎无限的权力，但是他们甚至几乎并未以此为自己牟利。我说的并不是贵族的特权，最高法院的强制执行权，行会的特权，或是地方特权。这些权力一方面突破了专权的打击，另一方面保持了人民的反抗精神。尽管这些政治制度可能妨碍个人自由，却有助于保持人们内心对自由的热爱，而且这对自由的行使大有裨益。除了这些政治制度之外，国家的民情和舆论尽管并不起眼但是也带给皇权有力的束缚。宗教、臣民的爱戴、国王的仁德、荣誉

although they were less conspicuous. Religion, the affections of the people, the benevolence of the prince, the sense of honor, family pride, provincial prejudices, custom, and public opinion limited the power of kings, and restrained their authority within an invisible circle. The constitution of nations was despotic at that time, but their manners were free. Princes had the right, but they had neither the means nor the desire, of doing whatever they pleased.

But what now remains of those barriers which formerly arrested the aggressions of tyranny? Since religion has lost its empire over the souls of men, the most prominent boundary which divided good from evil is overthrown; the very elements of the moral world are indeterminate; the princes and the peoples of the earth are guided by chance, and none can define the natural limits of despotism and the bounds of license. Long revolutions have forever destroyed the respect which surrounded the rulers of the State; and since they have been relieved from the burden of public esteem, princes may henceforward surrender themselves without fear to the seductions of arbitrary power.

When kings find that the hearts of their subjects are turned towards them, they are clement, because they are conscious of their strength, and they are chary of the affection of their people, because the affection of their people is the bulwark of the throne. A mutual interchange of goodwill then takes place between the prince and the people, which resembles the gracious intercourse of domestic society. The subjects may murmur at the sovereign's decree, but they are grieved to displease him; and the sovereign chastises his subjects with the light hand of parental affection.

But when once the spell of royalty is broken in the tumult of revolution; when successive monarchs have crossed the throne, so as alternately to display to the people the weakness of their right and the harshness of their power, the sovereign is no longer regarded by any as the Father of the State, and he is feared by all as its master. If he be weak, he is despised; if he be strong, he is detested. He himself is full of animosity and alarm; he finds that he is as a stranger in his own country, and he treats his subjects like conquered enemies.

When the provinces and the towns formed so many different nations in the midst of their common country, each of them had a will of its own, which was opposed to the general spirit of subjection;

感、家门的荣耀、地方的特权、习惯和公共舆论共同将国王的权力限定在一个隐形的圈子之内。在那时，国家的制度是专制的，但是民情是自由的。国王拥有权力，但是他们既不能也不想行使所有的权力。

但是，曾经束缚暴政的屏障而今何在呢？在宗教失去对人类灵魂的控制之后，在善与恶的标准被颠倒之后，在道德世界的基本要素被模糊之后，国王和其臣民肆意妄为，再没有人能够分清专制的天然界限和放纵的界限。无休止的革命永远地摧毁了人们对国家统治者的尊重，而在他们放下了公众尊重的负担之后，国王们肆无忌惮地滥用权力。

当国王发现臣民的心倾向他的时候，他们是仁慈的，因为他们知道自己拥有力量，而且会珍惜臣民的爱戴，因为臣民的爱戴是王权的坚实壁垒。此时，君民感情融洽，就好像家人般亲密无间。臣民也许会对君主的法令发发牢骚，但当君主为此不快的时候他们也会感到难过；而君主则会像父亲惩罚孩子那样轻轻地拍上几巴掌。

然而，一旦在革命的骚乱中皇室的威信扫地，随后继位的君主一个不如一个，在人民面前表现出其权力的削弱和行为的残暴时，君主将不再被视为国父，而不过是令人畏惧的头头。如果他软弱，会被鄙视；如果他强硬，则会被憎恨。他本身充满着仇恨和惶恐，虽在自己的国家却感觉像个外国人，而且他对待臣民也如同对待被征服的敌人。

当一个国家中的各个省和城市成为许多不同的小国，它们会产生各自的意志，完全不同于原先服从的共同意志。但是，同一帝国的各个部分在失去它们各自的独立、习俗、成见、传统以及名称之后，既然要服从并习惯于同样的法律，那么，将它们合起来共同治

but now that all the parts of the same empire, after having lost their immunities, their customs, their prejudices, their traditions, and their names, are subjected and accustomed to the same laws, it is not more difficult to oppress them collectively than it was formerly to oppress them singly.

Whilst the nobles enjoyed their power, and indeed long after that power was lost, the honor of aristocracy conferred an extraordinary degree of force upon their personal opposition. They afford instances of men who, notwithstanding their weakness, still entertained a high opinion of their personal value, and dared to cope single-handed with the efforts of the public authority. But at the present day, when all ranks are more and more confounded, when the individual disappears in the throng, and is easily lost in the midst of a common obscurity, when the honor of monarchy has almost lost its empire without being succeeded by public virtue, and when nothing can enable man to rise above himself, who shall say at what point the exigencies of power and the servility of weakness will stop?

As long as family feeling was kept alive, the antagonist of oppression was never alone; he looked about him, and found his clients, his hereditary friends, and his kinsfolk. If this support was wanting, he was sustained by his ancestors and animated by his posterity. But when patrimonial estates are divided, and when a few years suffice to confound the distinctions of a race, where can family feeling be found? What force can there be in the customs of a country which has changed and is still perpetually changing, its aspect; in which every act of tyranny has a precedent, and every crime an example; in which there is nothing so old that its antiquity can save it from destruction, and nothing so unparalleled that its novelty can prevent it from being done? What resistance can be offered by manners of so pliant a make that they have already often yielded? What strength can even public opinion have retained, when no twenty persons are connected by a common tie; when not a man, nor a family, nor chartered corporation, nor class, nor free institution, has the power of representing or exerting that opinion; and when every citizen—being equally weak, equally poor, and equally dependent—has only his personal impotence to oppose to the organized force of the government?

The annals of France furnish nothing analogous to the condition in which that country might then

理，也并不会比原先分而治之更困难。

在贵族享受权力的时候，而且在其权力丧失后很长一段时间，贵族制度的荣誉会给予个人极大的反抗力量。尽管他们中很多人已经失势，但是他们依旧保持高尚的人格，敢于单枪匹马对抗国家。但是，如今当各个阶级越来越混为一体，个人渐渐淹没在群众之中而很容易变得默默无闻的时候，当君主制度的声誉扫地而又没有美德来补救，且没有任何东西能够让人上劲的时候，谁又能够说清强者的要求和弱者的服从会在何处停止呢？

只要家庭感一直存在下去，反抗压迫的人就不会感到孤单；他环顾身边，看到的是追随者、世交和至亲。如果没有这样的支持，他也会感到祖先对他的督促，子孙对他的鼓舞。但是当世袭的家产被分割，种族的差别几年后就会消失的时候，又有该到哪里去寻找家庭感呢？如果一个国家面貌已经发生改变或是正在改变之中，且所有暴政行为都有先例可循，每项罪行都是例行公事，没有任何古老的东西能够免遭毁灭，更没有什么新鲜事物是人们不敢涉足的，那么它的习惯法还有什么力量而言呢？如此驯服的民情一直以来不断地屈服，又能指望它进行怎样的抗争呢？当没有很多的人被一条共同的纽带连接起来，当既没有一个人，也没有一个家庭、一个团体、一个阶层、一个自由组织，有力量代表或是影响公共舆论的时候，而且当每个公民都同样的无能、同样的贫穷以及同样的孤独无依，且只能用个人的软弱与政府有组织的力量进行抗争的时候，公共舆论还能有什么力量呢？

对于类似的情况下国家也许会陷入何种状况，法国的年鉴并未能给出任何答案。但也许可以追溯一下古代的时候，和那些可怕的罗马暴政时代。那时候，社会风气堕落，传统

be thrown. But it may more aptly be assimilated to the times of old, and to those hideous eras of Roman oppression, when the manners of the people were corrupted, their traditions obliterated, their habits destroyed, their opinions shaken, and freedom, expelled from the laws, could find no refuge in the land; when nothing protected the citizens, and the citizens no longer protected themselves; when human nature was the sport of man, and princes wearied out the clemency of Heaven before they exhausted the patience of their subjects. Those who hope to revive the monarchy of Henry IV or of Louis XIV, appear to me to be afflicted with mental blindness; and when I consider the present condition of several European nations—a condition to which all the others tend—I am led to believe that they will soon be left with no other alternative than democratic liberty, or the tyranny of the Caesars.

And indeed it is deserving of consideration, whether men are to be entirely emancipated or entirely enslaved; whether their rights are to be made equal, or wholly taken away from them. If the rulers of society were reduced either gradually to raise the crowd to their own level, or to sink the citizens below that of humanity, would not the doubts of many be resolved, the consciences of many be healed, and the community prepared to make great sacrifices with little difficulty? In that case, the gradual growth of democratic manners and institutions should be regarded, not as the best, but as the only means of preserving freedom; and without liking the government of democracy, it might be adopted as the most applicable and the fairest remedy for the present ills of society.

It is difficult to associate a people in the work of government; but it is still more difficult to supply it with experience, and to inspire it with the feelings which it requires in order to govern well. I grant that the caprices of democracy are perpetual; its instruments are rude; its laws imperfect. But if it were true that soon no just medium would exist between the empire of democracy and the dominion of a single arm, should we not rather incline towards the former than submit voluntarily to the latter? And if complete equality be our fate, is it not better to be levelled by free institutions than by despotic power?

Those who, after having read this book, should imagine that my intention in writing it has been to propose the laws and manners of the Anglo-Americans for the imitation of all democratic

被忘却，习惯被摧毁，观念被动摇，自由也被法律驱逐已无容身之地，公民毫无保护而且也不再自我保护，人性成为游戏，国王不再仁慈而强迫公民逆来顺受。那些想要复兴亨利四世和路易十四君主统治的人，在我看来已完全神志不清。我对几个欧洲国家的现状进行思索，而这样的状况也是所有其他国家未来的发展趋势，我又确信不是民主自由就是恺撒的暴政，除此之外，他们别无他选。

而且这的确值得思考，难道人不是获得完全解放就是被完全奴役；不是所有权利平等就是被剥夺所有权利；如果社会的统治者不是将民众逐渐提高到与他们相同的水平就是将公民降低到人的水平之下，所以只要打消顾虑，坚定信心，并教育社会中的每一个人做出巨大牺牲，不就足够了吗？在这样的情况下，民主的民情和制度的不断发展会被认为哪怕不是最好，至少也是自由得以维护的唯一手段。而且，不喜欢民主政府，它也不大可能成为治愈当今社会顽疾的最适合、最佳的良药。

让人民参与政府工作困难重重，但是更难的是让人民积累管理经验并激发出将国家管理好的态度。我承认，民主一直反复无常，其手段尚显粗鲁，其法律也不完美。但是如果在民主的帝国和独夫统治之间不再有中间路可走成为事实，难道我们宁可主动屈从后者，而不向前者倒戈吗？如果完全平等是我们的命运，难道让自由将我们拉平不比暴政将我们拉平更好吗？

那些已经读过这本书的人，如果认为我写书的意图就是要让所有民主国家的人民效仿英裔美国人的法制和民情，那就大错特错了，他们一定只注意到我思想的外在，而没有认

peoples, would commit a very great mistake; they must have paid more attention to the form than to the substance of my ideas. My aim has been to show, by the example of America, that laws, and especially manners, may exist which will allow a democratic people to remain free. But I am very far from thinking that we ought to follow the example of the American democracy, and copy the means which it has employed to attain its ends; for I am well aware of the influence which the nature of a country and its political precedents exercise upon a constitution; and I should regard it as a great misfortune for mankind if liberty were to exist all over the world under the same forms.

But I am of opinion that if we do not succeed in gradually introducing democratic institutions into France, and if we despair of imparting to the citizens those ideas and sentiments which first prepare them for freedom, and afterwards allow them to enjoy it, there will be no independence at all, either for the middling classes or the nobility, for the poor or for the rich, but an equal tyranny over all; and I foresee that if the peaceable empire of the majority be not founded amongst us in time, we shall sooner or later arrive at the unlimited authority of a single despot.

识到我思想的内在。用美国的例子，我旨在说明，法制，而且特别是民情，能够让一个民主国家保持自由。但是我绝不认为我们应该效仿美国，照搬它实现目的采用的所有手段，因为我清楚地意识到一个国家的自然环境和以往的政治先例会对其政治制度产生怎样的影响。而且如果在全世界自由将以同样的形式存在，我会认为这是人类的大不幸。

　　但是我认为，如果我们没能成功地将民主制度逐渐引入法国，而且对向人民灌输那些为自由做准备及其以后便于人们享受自由的思想和情感失去信心，那么，无论是有产者还是贵族，穷人还是富人，都无法独立自主，到头来暴政会统治所有人。我料想如果我们无法及时建立多数的和平帝国，我们迟早会沦落到独夫绝对权力的统治之下。

Chapter XVIII: Future Condition Of Three Races In The United States

The Present And Probable Future Condition Of The Three Races Which Inhabit The Territory Of The United States

The principal part of the task which I had imposed upon myself is now performed. I have shown, as far as I was able, the laws and the manners of the American democracy. Here I might stop; but the reader would perhaps feel that I had not satisfied his expectations.

The absolute supremacy of democracy is not all that we meet with in America; the inhabitants of the New World may be considered from more than one point of view. In the course of this work my subject has often led me to speak of the Indians and the Negroes; but I have never been able to stop in order to show what place these two races occupy in the midst of the democratic people whom I was engaged in describing. I have mentioned in what spirit, and according to what laws, the Anglo-American Union was formed; but I could only glance at the dangers which menace that confederation, whilst it was equally impossible for me to give a detailed account of its chances of duration, independently of its laws and manners. When speaking of the united republican States, I hazarded no conjectures upon the permanence of republican forms in the New World, and when making frequent allusion to the commercial activity which reigns in the Union, I was unable to inquire into the future condition of the Americans as a commercial people.

These topics are collaterally connected with my subject without forming a part of it; they are

第十八章　美国境内三个种族的未来

美国境内三个种族的现状及其可能的未来

我为自己制定的任务的主要部分现在已经完成。我已尽我所能对美国的法制和民情进行说明。我本可在此告一段落，但是读者也许会觉得我没能达到他们的期望值。

民主的绝对优势并不是我在美国的所有见闻，还可以从许多不同的角度对新世界的居民加以研究。在这部分内容中，话题总是将我引到印第安人和黑人身上。但是我一直以来都无暇说明这两个种族在我所描述的民主国家中占据的地位。我已谈到英裔美国人是以什么样的精神和法制建立的联邦，但是我只是草草谈了谈有碍联邦存在的危险，而且除了民情和法制以外，也同样未能详细说明这个国家长治久安的条件。当谈到合众国的共和制度时，我不敢对共和制度在新世界的表现妄加推测，而且当不断谈及盛行联邦的商业活动时，我也无法对美国作为一个商业国家的未来妄加评论。

这些问题虽然都和我的主题有关，但我并未对其进行深入探讨。因为它们虽然都跟美国有关但是却与民主没有干系，而描摹美国的民主才是我的主要目的。因此，有必要先将

American without being democratic; and to portray democracy has been my principal aim. It was therefore necessary to postpone these questions, which I now take up as the proper termination of my work.

The territory now occupied or claimed by the American Union spreads from the shores of the Atlantic to those of the Pacific Ocean. On the east and west its limits are those of the continent itself. On the south it advances nearly to the tropic, and it extends upwards to the icy regions of the North. The human beings who are scattered over this space do not form, as in Europe, so many branches of the same stock. Three races, naturally distinct, and, I might almost say, hostile to each other, are discoverable amongst them at the first glance. Almost insurmountable barriers had been raised between them by education and by law, as well as by their origin and outward characteristics; but fortune has brought them together on the same soil, where, although they are mixed, they do not amalgamate, and each race fulfils its destiny apart.

Amongst these widely differing families of men, the first which attracts attention, the superior in intelligence, in power and in enjoyment, is the white or European, the man pre-eminent; and in subordinate grades, the negro and the Indian. These two unhappy races have nothing in common; neither birth, nor features, nor language, nor habits. Their only resemblance lies in their misfortunes. Both of them occupy an inferior rank in the country they inhabit; both suffer from tyranny; and if their wrongs are not the same, they originate, at any rate, with the same authors.

If we reasoned from what passes in the world, we should almost say that the European is to the other races of mankind, what man is to the lower animals;—he makes them subservient to his use; and when he cannot subdue, he destroys them. Oppression has, at one stroke, deprived the descendants of the Africans of almost all the privileges of humanity. The negro of the United States has lost all remembrance of his country; the language which his forefathers spoke is never heard around him; he abjured their religion and forgot their customs when he ceased to belong to Africa, without acquiring any claim to European privileges. But he remains half way between the two communities; sold by the one, repulsed by the other; finding not a spot in the universe to call by the

这些问题放在一边，留待本书结束的时候再做叙述。

美联邦现在占据或是宣称为其所有的领土从大西洋海岸一直延伸到太平洋海岸。无论是东面还是西面，这个大陆的天然边界就是美国疆土的边界。在南面，它的领土几乎延伸到热带；而在北面，则深入到冰冻地带。散居在这片大地的人们并没有像在欧洲那样，形成一脉相承的数个分支。一眼望去，在人们中间会看到三个天生不同，而且可以说互相仇视的民族。教育、法律以及血统和外貌特征在他们之间竖起了不可以逾越的障碍，但命运却将他们带到同一片土地，在这里尽管他们杂居一处，却从未融合，他们各自按照自己的命运发展。

在这些天差地别的种族之中，首先引起人们注意的是知识、力量和享受都高人一等的白人或者说欧洲人，他们都是出类拔萃的人，而在他们之下，则是黑人和印第安人。这两个不幸的种族丝毫没有共同之处，无论是出生地、外貌特征、语言还是习惯。他们唯一的相似之处就是他们的不幸。这两个种族在他们所居住的这个国家地位都很低下，都饱受暴政之苦，而且尽管他们所受的虐待并不相同，却都是被同样一些人虐待。

如果从世界上以往的情况来看，我们几乎可以说欧洲人对待其他人种就好似人类对待低等动物，他们奴役其他种族，而如果其他种族不愿服从，他们便要将其毁灭。欧洲人的压迫几乎一下子将非洲后裔所有的人权全部剥夺。美国的黑人已经失去了对故土的记忆，也不曾听过他们祖先曾经使用的语言；在他们离开非洲，他们放弃了自己的宗教，忘记了自己的习俗，却没有得到欧洲人那样的权利。他们游离于两个社会之间，被一个买卖，被

name of country, except the faint image of a home which the shelter of his master's roof affords.

The negro has no family; woman is merely the temporary companion of his pleasures, and his children are upon an equality with himself from the moment of their birth. Am I to call it a proof of God's mercy or a visitation of his wrath, that man in certain states appears to be insensible to his extreme wretchedness, and almost affects, with a depraved taste, the cause of his misfortunes? The negro, who is plunged in this abyss of evils, scarcely feels his own calamitous situation. Violence made him a slave, and the habit of servitude gives him the thoughts and desires of a slave; he admires his tyrants more than he hates them, and finds his joy and his pride in the servile imitation of those who oppress him: his understanding is degraded to the level of his soul.

The negro enters upon slavery as soon as he is born: nay, he may have been purchased in the womb, and have begun his slavery before he began his existence. Equally devoid of wants and of enjoyment, and useless to himself, he learns, with his first notions of existence, that he is the property of another, who has an interest in preserving his life, and that the care of it does not devolve upon himself; even the power of thought appears to him a useless gift of Providence, and he quietly enjoys the privileges of his debasement. If he becomes free, independence is often felt by him to be a heavier burden than slavery; for having learned, in the course of his life, to submit to everything except reason, he is too much unacquainted with her dictates to obey them. A thousand new desires beset him, and he is destitute of the knowledge and energy necessary to resist them: these are masters which it is necessary to contend with, and he has learnt only to submit and obey. In short, he sinks to such a depth of wretchedness, that while servitude brutalizes, liberty destroys him.

Oppression has been no less fatal to the Indian than to the negro race, but its effects are different. Before the arrival of white men in the New World, the inhabitants of North America lived quietly in their woods, enduring the vicissitudes and practising the virtues and vices common to savage nations. The Europeans, having dispersed the Indian tribes and driven them into the deserts, condemned them to a wandering life full of inexpressible sufferings.

另一个厌弃，茫茫宇宙间找不到一个可以称之为祖国的地方，只有主人为他安排的小屋成为他们对故乡的模糊记忆。

黑人没有家，女人不过是男人寻欢作乐的暂时伴侣，而他的孩子一出生地位就跟他同样卑微。我是应该把这种在某些州中出现的对人极端悲惨境遇的无动于衷，而且往往对其不幸的根源采用可鄙的态度，称为上帝对人类的仁慈还是对人类的斥责呢？堕入灾难深渊的黑人几乎没有察觉到自己的不幸处境。暴力让他们成为奴隶，而受奴役的习惯让他们养成奴隶的思想和愿望。他们对残暴主人的羡慕超过憎恨，并通过模仿压迫者来找到自己的快乐和骄傲。他们的智力已经下降到跟他们心灵同样的水平。

黑人从一出生就是奴隶，甚至还在娘胎中就被人买卖，可以说在出生之前就已经成为奴隶。他们既无需要也无享乐，这些对他们毫无用处。他们出生后最先知道的就是自己是别人的财产，要为这个人的利益奉献自己的一生，而照料自己的生活则不归他管，甚至用头脑思考的能力在他看来都是上帝赐予的无用的恩赐，而且他们对自己卑微的地位感到心悦诚服。如果他获得自由，独立自主往往会成为一个比奴役更沉重的负担。因为终其一生学到的是除了理性以外的绝对服从，而当理性前来指引他们的时候，他们却不知所措。太多新的要求困扰着他们，而他们却没有必要的知识和能力与之对抗。这些要求来自他们本应反抗的主人，而他们学到的只有屈服和顺从。简而言之，他们陷入一个如此悲惨的深渊，在这个深渊之中，奴役让他们失去理性，自由则会让他们灭亡。

压迫对于印第安人而言同样致命，但是结果却完全不同。在白人来到新世界之前，北美的居民平静地生活在密林之中，饱经沧桑，一直保留着蛮族的美德和恶习。欧洲人鄙视

Savage nations are only controlled by opinion and by custom. When the North American Indians had lost the sentiment of attachment to their country; when their families were dispersed, their traditions obscured, and the chain of their recollections broken; when all their habits were changed, and their wants increased beyond measure, European tyranny rendered them more disorderly and less civilized than they were before. The moral and physical condition of these tribes continually grew worse, and they became more barbarous as they became more wretched. Nevertheless, the Europeans have not been able to metamorphose the character of the Indians; and though they have had power to destroy them, they have never been able to make them submit to the rules of civilized society.

The lot of the negro is placed on the extreme limit of servitude, while that of the Indian lies on the uttermost verge of liberty; and slavery does not produce more fatal effects upon the first, than independence upon the second. The negro has lost all property in his own person, and he cannot dispose of his existence without committing a sort of fraud: but the savage is his own master as soon as he is able to act; parental authority is scarcely known to him; he has never bent his will to that of any of his kind, nor learned the difference between voluntary obedience and a shameful subjection; and the very name of law is unknown to him. To be free, with him, signifies to escape from all the shackles of society. As he delights in this barbarous independence, and would rather perish than sacrifice the least part of it, civilization has little power over him.

The negro makes a thousand fruitless efforts to insinuate himself amongst men who repulse him; he conforms to the tastes of his oppressors, adopts their opinions, and hopes by imitating them to form a part of their community. Having been told from infancy that his race is naturally inferior to that of the whites, he assents to the proposition and is ashamed of his own nature. In each of his features he discovers a trace of slavery, and, if it were in his power, he would willingly rid himself of everything that makes him what he is.

The Indian, on the contrary, has his imagination inflated with the pretended nobility of his origin, and lives and dies in the midst of these dreams of pride. Far from desiring to conform his habits to

印第安人并将它们驱赶到荒野，迫使他们过着难以言喻的痛苦的流离生活。

蛮族只受舆论和习俗的支配。当北美印第安人失去对故土的依恋，当他们的家庭分崩离析，传统被淡忘，记忆的链条被打破，当他们所有的习惯被改变，同时欲望不断增加却无法实现的时候，欧洲人的暴虐让他们比以前更加混乱，更加野蛮。这些部落的身心状况不断恶化，随着境遇越来越悲惨，他们变得越来越野蛮。然而，欧洲人未能改变印第安人的性格特点，而且尽管欧洲人曾经用国家的力量来毁灭他们，却从未能让印第安人屈服于文明社会的统治。

黑人的命运构筑在极端的奴役之上，而印第安人的命运则有赖于极度的自由。奴役对于前者并没有产生比独立自主对后者更为致命的影响。黑人没有财产，甚至本人也不属于自己，他们出卖自己就是犯了诈骗罪。但是野蛮人只要能行动就是自己的主人，他们甚至不知道什么是家长权，而且也从不会让自己的意志屈服于自己的部族，而且也弄不清自愿的遵守和屈辱的服从有什么不同，而且他们也不知道法律为何物。对他而言，自由就是不受任何社会枷锁的束缚。当他为这种野蛮的独立自主欣喜之时，宁可毁灭也不愿牺牲一丝一毫。文明对这样的人束手无策。

黑人为让自己融入那个排斥他们的社会做过无数徒劳的努力，他让自己的品位与压迫者保持一致，接受他们的观念，并希望通过模仿他们成为其中一分子。自打一出生，人们就告诉他自己的种族天生不如白人，于是他便认同这一观点并羞于自己的天性。他的每一个特点都带有奴隶的痕迹，而且如果自己有能力，他会很愿意丢弃让他成为现在这个自己的所有一切。

ours, he loves his savage life as the distinguishing mark of his race, and he repels every advance to civilization, less perhaps from the hatred which he entertains for it, than from a dread of resembling the Europeans. While he has nothing to oppose to our perfection in the arts but the resources of the desert, to our tactics nothing but undisciplined courage; whilst our well-digested plans are met by the spontaneous instincts of savage life, who can wonder if he fails in this unequal contest?

The negro, who earnestly desires to mingle his race with that of the European, cannot effect if; while the Indian, who might succeed to a certain extent, disdains to make the attempt. The servility of the one dooms him to slavery, the pride of the other to death.

I remember that while I was travelling through the forests which still cover the State of Alabama, I arrived one day at the log house of a pioneer. I did not wish to penetrate into the dwelling of the American, but retired to rest myself for a while on the margin of a spring, which was not far off, in the woods. While I was in this place (which was in the neighborhood of the Creek territory), an Indian woman appeared, followed by a negress, and holding by the hand a little white girl of five or six years old, whom I took to be the daughter of the pioneer. A sort of barbarous luxury set off the costume of the Indian; rings of metal were hanging from her nostrils and ears; her hair, which was adorned with glass beads, fell loosely upon her shoulders; and I saw that she was not married, for she still wore that necklace of shells which the bride always deposits on the nuptial couch. The negress was clad in squalid European garments. They all three came and seated themselves upon the banks of the fountain; and the young Indian, taking the child in her arms, lavished upon her such fond caresses as mothers give; while the negress endeavored by various little artifices to attract the attention of the young Creole.

The child displayed in her slightest gestures a consciousness of superiority which formed a strange contrast with her infantine weakness; as if she received the attentions of her companions with a sort of condescension. The negress was seated on the ground before her mistress, watching her smallest desires, and apparently divided between strong affection for the child and servile fear; whilst the savage displayed, in the midst of her tenderness, an air of freedom and of pride which was

相反，在印第安人的想象中，他们认为自己出身高贵，而且由生到死都坠在这样引以为傲的梦幻之中。他们把自己的野蛮生活方式当作自己种族的独特标志来热爱，根本不想让自己的民情与我们一致起来。他们抗拒接受文明，其原因并不是对文明本身的憎恨，而是害怕自己变得跟欧洲人一样。然而除了原始的武器和匹夫之勇以外，他们没有任何东西来对抗我们精良的武器和战术。当我们深思熟虑的计划碰到野蛮人的本能抵抗，有谁会对他们在这场力量悬殊的对抗中的失败感到奇怪呢？

黑人，真心地希望能够与欧洲人为伍，但却未能实现；而印第安人，尽管他们在一定程度上能够做到这一点，但是却对此嗤之以鼻。一个是奴性让自己注定为奴，而另一个的骄傲却让自己走向死亡。

我记得在我经过亚拉巴马州密林的时候，有一天路过一个拓荒者的小屋。我本不想进入这个美国人的居所，只想在不远处的溪边小憩片刻。而我刚在这个地方（这里离克里克部落的领地不远）坐下，来了一个印第安女人，领着一个五六岁的白人小女孩，应该是拓荒者的女儿，后面还跟着一个黑人女人。这个印第安女人极尽野蛮人的华丽装饰，鼻孔和耳朵都带着铜环，点缀着玻璃珠的头发松松地披在肩上。依我看，她还没结婚，因为她脖子上还带着贝壳项链，因为按照习俗新娘会将它放在婚床上。那个黑人女人身着一件脏脏的欧式服装。她们三人来到泉水边坐下，那个年轻的印第安女人将小女孩抱在怀中，像妈妈一样爱抚着她；而那个黑人女人也使出浑身解数逗孩子高兴。

在小女孩最漫不经心的举止中，表现出一种与其幼小年龄不相符的优越感，似乎对于

almost ferocious. I had approached the group, and I contemplated them in silence; but my curiosity was probably displeasing to the Indian woman, for she suddenly rose, pushed the child roughly from her, and giving me an angry look plunged into the thicket. I had often chanced to see individuals met together in the same place, who belonged to the three races of men which people North America. I had perceived from many different results the preponderance of the whites. But in the picture which I have just been describing there was something peculiarly touching; a bond of affection here united the oppressors with the oppressed, and the effort of nature to bring them together rendered still more striking the immense distance placed between them by prejudice and by law.

The Present And Probable Future Condition Of The Indian Tribes Which Inhabit The Territory Possessed By The Union

Gradual disappearance of the native tribes—Manner in which it takes place—Miseries accompanying the forced migrations of the Indians—The savages of North America had only two ways of escaping destruction; war or civilization—They are no longer able to make war—Reasons why they refused to become civilized when it was in their power, and why they cannot become so now that they desire it—Instance of the Creeks and Cherokees—Policy of the particular States towards these Indians—Policy of the Federal Government.

None of the Indian tribes which formerly inhabited the territory of New England—the Naragansetts, the Mohicans, the Pecots—have any existence but in the recollection of man. The Lenapes, who received William Penn, a hundred and fifty years ago, upon the banks of the Delaware, have disappeared; and I myself met with the last of the Iroquois, who were begging alms. The nations I have mentioned formerly covered the country to the sea-coast; but a traveller at the present day must penetrate more than a hundred leagues into the interior of the continent to find an Indian. Not only have these wild tribes receded, but they are destroyed; and as they give way or perish, an immense and increasing people fills their place. There is no instance upon record of so prodigious a

同伴的关注显得有点不屑一顾。黑人女人坐在女主人面前的地上，哪怕是她最微不足道的愿望也不敢怠慢，既有对小主人的爱也有源自奴性的畏惧。然而，在这个野蛮人流露出的温柔之中，表现出一种自由、骄傲甚至有点可怕的神气。我走过去，默默地注视者他们，但我的好奇心可能让这个印第安女人感到不快，因为她突然站了起来，粗鲁地将小女孩推开，朝我怒视一眼之后，便走进森林之中。我经常能看到北美三个种族的人聚在一处，通过多次不同的观察我注意到白人的优越感。但是在我刚才的描述中有某种特别感人的东西，一种压迫者和被压迫者之间的情感纽带，而大自然让她们彼此亲近的努力，则使得偏见和法制在她们之间构筑的巨大鸿沟更加醒目。

居住在联邦境内的印第安部落的现状和未来

土著部落逐渐消失——消失的方式——悲惨与印第安人的被迫迁徙相伴——北美的蛮人只有两条路可以摆脱灭亡的命运：战争或是文明——他们已无力进行战争——印第安人有能力文明时却表示拒绝的原因，以及他们无法文明时却想文明的原因——克里克部落和柴罗基部落的例子——个别州对待印第安人的政策——联邦政府的政策。

以前曾定居在新英格兰地区的印第安部落，如纳拉干、莫希干、佩科特，已经不复存在，只留存在人们的记忆中。150年前，曾经欢迎佩恩的位于特拉华沿岸的勒纳普部族也已经消失不见。我曾碰到几个仅存的易洛魁人，他们现在以讨饭为生。我所提到的这些部族

growth, or so rapid a destruction: the manner in which the latter change takes place is not difficult to describe.

When the Indians were the sole inhabitants of the wilds from whence they have since been expelled, their wants were few. Their arms were of their own manufacture, their only drink was the water of the brook, and their clothes consisted of the skins of animals, whose flesh furnished them with food.

The Europeans introduced amongst the savages of North America fire-arms, ardent spirits, and iron: they taught them to exchange for manufactured stuffs, the rough garments which had previously satisfied their untutored simplicity. Having acquired new tastes, without the arts by which they could be gratified, the Indians were obliged to have recourse to the workmanship of the whites; but in return for their productions the savage had nothing to offer except the rich furs which still abounded in his woods. Hence the chase became necessary, not merely to provide for his subsistence, but in order to procure the only objects of barter which he could furnish to Europe. Whilst the wants of the natives were thus increasing, their resources continued to diminish.

From the moment when a European settlement is formed in the neighborhood of the territory occupied by the Indians, the beasts of chase take the alarm. Thousands of savages, wandering in the forests and destitute of any fixed dwelling, did not disturb them; but as soon as the continuous sounds of European labor are heard in their neighborhood, they begin to flee away, and retire to the West, where their instinct teaches them that they will find deserts of immeasurable extent. "The buffalo is constantly receding," say Messrs. Clarke and Cass in their Report of the year 1829; "a few years since they approached the base of the Alleghany; and a few years hence they may even be rare upon the immense plains which extend to the base of the Rocky Mountains." I have been assured that this effect of the approach of the whites is often felt at two hundred leagues' distance from their frontier. Their influence is thus exerted over tribes whose name is unknown to them; and who suffer the evils of usurpation long before they are acquainted with the authors of their distress.

Bold adventurers soon penetrate into the country the Indians have deserted, and when they have

曾经遍布北美各地乃至沿海地区，但是如今的行者必须深入内陆一百多里才能看到印第安人的影子。这些野蛮部落不仅向内陆撤退，而且正在走向毁灭；而且随着印第安人的出走和死亡，不断有大量的居民占满他们的地盘。在人类历史上从未有如此惊人的发展和如此快速的灭亡。至于灭亡是如何发生的，这并不难解释。

当印第安人还是他们被驱逐出去的那片荒野的唯一居民时，他们的要求很少。他们自己制作武器，河水是他们唯一的饮料，而且以兽皮为衣，以兽肉为食。

欧洲人将火器、铁器和烈酒带到北美的原住民之中，教他们脱去原先用来满足其原始简朴需要的粗陋服装，换上人工纺织而成的衣服。印第安人在养成新的嗜好之后，并没有学会满足这些嗜好的技术，所以不得不依靠白人的手艺，作为对这些物品的回报，印第安人能拿出的除了森林中出产丰富的皮草外，什么也没有。从此，狩猎不仅是维持生活的必需，更是为了获得能跟欧洲人物物交易的东西。在土著人的需求不断增长的同时，他们的资源逐渐枯竭。

自从欧洲人在印第安人安居乐业之所不远居住下来之后，野兽都闻风而逃。而行走在森林之中居无定所的数以千计的野蛮人，却不会干扰到它们，只要在附近能够听到欧洲人持续不断的劳作声，它们便开始逃离，逃向西部，本能告诉它们在那里能找到无边无际的荒野。克拉克先生和卡斯先生在他们1829年的报告中写道："成群的野牛不断逃离，几年前它们还常常在阿勒格尼山脚下出没，而几年之后，甚至在沿着落基山脉延伸的广阔原野上也难觅其踪。"有人很肯定地告诉我，白人到来的影响往往在200里之外就能感觉到。他

advanced about fifteen or twenty leagues from the extreme frontiers of the whites, they begin to build habitations for civilized beings in the midst of the wilderness. This is done without difficulty, as the territory of a hunting-nation is ill-defined; it is the common property of the tribe, and belongs to no one in particular, so that individual interests are not concerned in the protection of any part of it.

A few European families, settled in different situations at a considerable distance from each other, soon drive away the wild animals which remain between their places of abode. The Indians, who had previously lived in a sort of abundance, then find it difficult to subsist, and still more difficult to procure the articles of barter which they stand in need of.

To drive away their game is to deprive them of the means of existence, as effectually as if the fields of our agriculturists were stricken with barrenness; and they are reduced, like famished wolves, to prowl through the forsaken woods in quest of prey. Their instinctive love of their country attaches them to the soil which gave them birth, even after it has ceased to yield anything but misery and death. At length they are compelled to acquiesce, and to depart: they follow the traces of the elk, the buffalo, and the beaver, and are guided by these wild animals in the choice of their future country. Properly speaking, therefore, it is not the Europeans who drive away the native inhabitants of America; it is famine which compels them to recede; a happy distinction which had escaped the casuists of former times, and for which we are indebted to modern discovery!

It is impossible to conceive the extent of the sufferings which attend these forced emigrations. They are undertaken by a people already exhausted and reduced; and the countries to which the newcomers betake themselves are inhabited by other tribes which receive them with jealous hostility. Hunger is in the rear; war awaits them, and misery besets them on all sides. In the hope of escaping from such a host of enemies, they separate, and each individual endeavors to procure the means of supporting his existence in solitude and secrecy, living in the immensity of the desert like an outcast in civilized society. The social tie, which distress had long since weakened, is then dissolved; they have lost their country, and their people soon desert them: their very families are obliterated; the names they bore in common are forgotten, their language perishes, and all traces of their origin

们对那些他们连名字都不知道的部落产生着影响，而且这些部落早在识得其苦难制造者的庐山真面之前很久就尝到了被掠夺的滋味。

胆大的冒险家不久后深入到印第安人已经遗弃的地方，他们越过白人居住区的边界向前深入15或20里，开始在印第安人遗弃的荒野建造文明人的居所。在这里他们并没有碰到什么困难，因为狩猎民族的领土边界并不清晰，而且领地属于整个部落而非个人所有，故而并没有人关心保护领地的任何部分。

一些迁到此处的欧洲的家庭，彼此居住的地方相隔很远；他们的到来不久便把那些出没在他们住所间得野兽吓走。随后，曾经在此过着丰衣足食生活的印第安人发现不但难以维持生计，而且更找不到可以用来进行物物交换的东西。

赶走印第安人的猎物就是剥夺他们生存的手段，就好像我们农民的土地变得寸草不生。如同饥饿的狼群一般，为了捕获猎物他们不得不在荒山野林中徘徊。对故土的本能热爱将印第安人与他们出生的土地紧紧相连，即使留在那里只有饥饿和死亡。最后，他们终于决心离开，跟随着大脚鹿、野牛和河狸的脚步，并在这些野生动物的指引下选定新的家园。因此，可以肯定地说，赶走美国土著人的并不是欧洲人，而是饥荒迫使他们逃离。这是以前诡辩家都没能发现的高论，我们真应感激现代的发现！

很难想象这些被迫迁徙带来的后续苦难。这些被迫离开家园的印第安人已经精疲力竭，衰败不堪，而他们选择的新家园居住着对新来者还有敌意的其他部落。前有饥饿后有战争，简直四面楚歌。为了避开众多的敌人，他们分开行动，每个人独自默默地努力寻找

disappear. Their nation has ceased to exist, except in the recollection of the antiquaries of America and a few of the learned of Europe.

I should be sorry to have my reader suppose that I am coloring the picture too highly; I saw with my own eyes several of the cases of misery which I have been describing; and I was the witness of sufferings which I have not the power to portray.

At the end of the year 1831, whilst I was on the left bank of the Mississippi at a place named by Europeans, Memphis, there arrived a numerous band of Choctaws (or Chactas, as they are called by the French in Louisiana). These savages had left their country, and were endeavoring to gain the right bank of the Mississippi, where they hoped to find an asylum which had been promised them by the American government. It was then the middle of winter, and the cold was unusually severe; the snow had frozen hard upon the ground, and the river was drifting huge masses of ice. The Indians had their families with them; and they brought in their train the wounded and sick, with children newly born, and old men upon the verge of death. They possessed neither tents nor wagons, but only their arms and some provisions. I saw them embark to pass the mighty river, and never will that solemn spectacle fade from my remembrance. No cry, no sob was heard amongst the assembled crowd; all were silent. Their calamities were of ancient date, and they knew them to be irremediable. The Indians had all stepped into the bark which was to carry them across, but their dogs remained upon the bank. As soon as these animals perceived that their masters were finally leaving the shore, they set up a dismal howl, and, plunging all together into the icy waters of the Mississippi, they swam after the boat.

The ejectment of the Indians very often takes place at the present day, in a regular, and, as it were, a legal manner. When the European population begins to approach the limit of the desert inhabited by a savage tribe, the government of the United States usually dispatches envoys to them, who assemble the Indians in a large plain, and having first eaten and drunk with them, accost them in the following manner: "What have you to do in the land of your fathers? Before long, you must dig up their bones in order to live. In what respect is the country you inhabit better than another? Are there no woods,

生存的手段，生活在一望无际荒野上的他们就好像文明社会的流浪汉一样。很久以前便已削弱的社会纽带，现今已经完全断裂。他们失去了自己的家园，同胞不久也将他们抛弃。他们的家族被摧毁，共同的族名被遗忘，语言也不复存在，他们起源的所有痕迹正在消失。作为一个民族他们已经消失，只是作为记忆留在美洲考古学家和一些欧洲饱学之士的脑海。

如果给读者留下夸大其词的印象我感到很遗憾，我所描述的一些悲惨情境乃是我亲眼得见，而且我所见证的苦难简直无法用言语描述。

1831年末，当时我在密西西比河左岸的一个欧洲人称之为孟菲斯的地方，那里来了一大群巧克陶部落的人（路易斯安那的法国人将他们称为夏克塔部落）。这些土著人背井离乡，想到密西西比河的右岸，希望在那里找到一处美国政府能够许可的栖身之地。当时正值隆冬季节，而且那年的冬天异常寒冷，土地上的雪冻得硬硬的，河面上漂浮着巨大的冰块。印第安人带领着他们的家人，后面跟随着一批老弱病残，既有刚出生的婴儿也有行将就木的老人。他们既没有帐篷也没有马车，只有一些武器和食物。我看到他们登船渡过这条大河时的情景，那场面之庄严简直令我终生难忘。没有呼喊，没有啜泣，这群人全都默不作声。他们的苦难由来已久，而且他们深知这些苦难无法救治。这些印第安人登上他们用来渡河的三桅帆船，却将狗留在了岸上。这些动物一发觉它们的主人最终将离岸而去，便开始凄凉地嚎叫，一起跳入刺骨的密西西比河水，跟在主人的船后。

今天，驱逐印第安人往往以一种正规合法的方式进行。当欧洲的白人开始进入印第安

marshes, or prairies, except where you dwell? And can you live nowhere but under your own sun? Beyond those mountains which you see at the horizon, beyond the lake which bounds your territory on the west, there lie vast countries where beasts of chase are found in great abundance; sell your lands to us, and go to live happily in those solitudes." After holding this language, they spread before the eyes of the Indians firearms, woollen garments, kegs of brandy, glass necklaces, bracelets of tinsel, earrings, and looking-glasses. If, when they have beheld all these riches, they still hesitate, it is insinuated that they have not the means of refusing their required consent, and that the government itself will not long have the power of protecting them in their rights. What are they to do? Half convinced, and half compelled, they go to inhabit new deserts, where the importunate whites will not let them remain ten years in tranquillity. In this manner do the Americans obtain, at a very low price, whole provinces, which the richest sovereigns of Europe could not purchase.

These are great evils; and it must be added that they appear to me to be irremediable. I believe that the Indian nations of North America are doomed to perish; and that whenever the Europeans shall be established on the shores of the Pacific Ocean, that race of men will be no more. The Indians had only the two alternatives of war or civilization; in other words, they must either have destroyed the Europeans or become their equals.

At the first settlement of the colonies they might have found it possible, by uniting their forces, to deliver themselves from the small bodies of strangers who landed on their continent. They several times attempted to do it, and were on the point of succeeding; but the disproportion of their resources, at the present day, when compared with those of the whites, is too great to allow such an enterprise to be thought of. Nevertheless, there do arise from time to time among the Indians men of penetration, who foresee the final destiny which awaits the native population, and who exert themselves to unite all the tribes in common hostility to the Europeans; but their efforts are unavailing. Those tribes which are in the neighborhood of the whites, are too much weakened to offer an effectual resistance; whilst the others, giving way to that childish carelessness of the morrow which characterizes savage life, wait for the near approach of danger before they prepare to meet it; some are unable, the others

部落的荒凉地界时，美国政府一般会让信使给他们送信，将印第安人召集到一块空场地，先跟他们大吃大喝一通，接着会这样跟他们说："你们在祖先留下的这片土地上做过些什么？不久以后，你们肯定会靠挖他们的骨头为生。你们现在住的地方哪里比别的地方好呀？除了你们住的地方，别的地方就没有森林、沼泽和大草原吗？除了这里你们就没别的地方可去了吗？在天边的那座大山后面，你们土地最西面那个湖的对岸，那里的土地上奔跑着大量的野兽。把你们的土地卖给我们，然后去那里幸福地生活吧。"说完这番话，便将火枪、毛呢服装、小桶的白兰地、玻璃项链、金属的镯子耳环以及镜子摆到他们面前。如果他们在看过这些宝贝之后仍然犹豫不决，便会含沙射影地告诉他们不要拒绝对他们提出的要求，而且政府也无力保护他们的权利。他们会怎么做呢？印第安人往往在威逼利诱之下离开，寻找新的荒野居住，而纠缠不休的白人也不会让他们在这里平静地过上十年。采用这种方式，美国人以低廉的价格获得最富有的欧洲君主也买不起的大片大片的土地。

这些就是他们的苦难，而且我必须补充一下，在我看来这些苦难根本无法挽救。我认为北美的印第安人注定要灭亡，而且无论何时只要欧洲人在太平洋沿岸立足，那里的印第安人也将不复存在。印第安人只有两个选择：战争或是文明。换句话说，他们要不就将欧洲人消灭，要不就变得跟欧洲人一样。

欧洲人在美洲建立第一个殖民地之初，印第安人本有可能团结起来，将这一小撮登上他们土地的外来人赶走。为此他们曾经做过几次尝试，而且一度接近成功，但是，如今彼此力量对比的悬殊让他们不再有这样的想法。然而，印第安人之中的一些有识之士能够预

are unwilling, to exert themselves.

It is easy to foresee that the Indians will never conform to civilization; or that it will be too late, whenever they may be inclined to make the experiment.

Civilization is the result of a long social process which takes place in the same spot, and is handed down from one generation to another, each one profiting by the experience of the last. Of all nations, those submit to civilization with the most difficulty which habitually live by the chase. Pastoral tribes, indeed, often change their place of abode; but they follow a regular order in their migrations, and often return again to their old stations, whilst the dwelling of the hunter varies with that of the animals he pursues.

Several attempts have been made to diffuse knowledge amongst the Indians, without controlling their wandering propensities; by the Jesuits in Canada, and by the Puritans in New England; but none of these endeavors were crowned by any lasting success. Civilization began in the cabin, but it soon retired to expire in the woods. The great error of these legislators of the Indians was their not understanding that, in order to succeed in civilizing a people, it is first necessary to fix it; which cannot be done without inducing it to cultivate the soil; the Indians ought in the first place to have been accustomed to agriculture. But not only are they destitute of this indispensable preliminary to civilization, they would even have great difficulty in acquiring it. Men who have once abandoned themselves to the restless and adventurous life of the hunter, feel an insurmountable disgust for the constant and regular labor which tillage requires. We see this proved in the bosom of our own society; but it is far more visible among peoples whose partiality for the chase is a part of their national character.

Independently of this general difficulty, there is another, which applies peculiarly to the Indians; they consider labor not merely as an evil, but as a disgrace; so that their pride prevents them from becoming civilized, as much as their indolence.

There is no Indian so wretched as not to retain under his hut of bark a lofty idea of his personal worth; he considers the cares of industry and labor as degrading occupations; he compares the

见到等待着他们族人的最终命运，并尝试团结所有的部落共同对付欧洲人，但是他们的努力徒劳无功。那些与白人毗邻的部落太虚弱已经无力进行有效的抵抗，而其他的一些部落则出于野蛮人的天性，对未来表现出幼稚的满不在乎，只是等待厄运一步步地逼近而不采取对策。一些人无力抗争，而另一些人不愿抗争。

不难预见印第安人无法顺应文明，或者说他们想这样做的时候已为时太晚。

文明是在同一地方社会长期发展的结果，而且代代相传，每一代都能从上一代人那里受益。在所有的民族中，最难以被文明征服的就是狩猎民族。尽管游牧部落居无定所，但是他们总是遵循同样的迁徙路线，而后往往会再次回到老地方，而狩猎部落的住所，也会随着他们捕猎动物栖息地的变化而变化。

有人曾多次尝试深入到印第安人中间传播知识，但并未试图改变他们游牧的习性，耶稣会会士在加拿大，清教徒在新英格兰，都做过这样的尝试，但是没有任何一次尝试取得长久的成功。文明始于小木屋，但是不久之后便在森林里灭亡。那些在印第安人中间传播知识的人所犯下的重大错误在于，他们不明白为了让一个民族接受文明的教化，必须要让他们先定居下来，而为了让他们能定居下来，就要教会他们农耕，所以印第安人应该首先适应农耕生活。但是印第安人不仅缺少这个不可或缺的文明前奏，而且他们甚至很难进入这个前奏。人一旦放任自己过着猎人四处游荡的冒险生活，便会对持续规律的农耕劳作感到难以克服的厌恶。这在我们的社会中也得到印证，而且在狩猎成为国民特征一部分的民族中，表现得更为明显。

husbandman to the ox which traces the furrow; and even in our most ingenious handicraft, he can see nothing but the labor of slaves. Not that he is devoid of admiration for the power and intellectual greatness of the whites; but although the result of our efforts surprises him, he contemns the means by which we obtain it; and while he acknowledges our ascendancy, he still believes in his superiority. War and hunting are the only pursuits which appear to him worthy to be the occupations of a man. The Indian, in the dreary solitude of his woods, cherishes the same ideas, the same opinions as the noble of the Middle ages in his castle, and he only requires to become a conqueror to complete the resemblance; thus, however strange it may seem, it is in the forests of the New World, and not amongst the Europeans who people its coasts, that the ancient prejudices of Europe are still in existence.

More than once, in the course of this work, I have endeavored to explain the prodigious influence which the social condition appears to exercise upon the laws and the manners of men; and I beg to add a few words on the same subject.

When I perceive the resemblance which exists between the political institutions of our ancestors, the Germans, and of the wandering tribes of North America; between the customs described by Tacitus, and those of which I have sometimes been a witness, I cannot help thinking that the same cause has brought about the same results in both hemispheres; and that in the midst of the apparent diversity of human affairs, a certain number of primary facts may be discovered, from which all the others are derived. In what we usually call the German institutions, then, I am inclined only to perceive barbarian habits; and the opinions of savages in what we style feudal principles.

However strongly the vices and prejudices of the North American Indians may be opposed to their becoming agricultural and civilized, necessity sometimes obliges them to it. Several of the Southern nations, and amongst others the Cherokees and the Creeks, were surrounded by Europeans, who had landed on the shores of the Atlantic; and who, either descending the Ohio or proceeding up the Mississippi, arrived simultaneously upon their borders. These tribes have not been driven from place to place, like their Northern brethren; but they have been gradually enclosed within narrow limits,

　　除了这个一般原因外，还有另外一个印第安人所特有的原因。在印第安人心中，劳动不但被视为坏事，而且被认为是不光彩的事情。因此与他们的惰性一样，荣誉感同样阻碍他们变得文明起来。

　　没有一个印第安人认为自己居住在树皮盖的茅草屋中便失去个人尊严，也不会因此而苦恼。他们认为勤奋劳动是下贱工作，还把耕田的人比作犁地的牛。而且在他们眼中，我们最精巧的手艺也不过是奴隶的劳作罢了。对于白人的高超智慧他们也并不是全无钦佩，但是尽管他们对我们努力的成果深表赞许，却又对我们的实现手段不屑一顾。他们在认可我们优势的同时依旧认为自己高高在上。在印第安人看来，战争和狩猎是唯一值得人孜孜追求的职业。印第安人在森林中过着沉寂的生活，跟中世纪生活在城堡中的贵族有着同样的思想和同样的观念，而且如果他们成为征服者就和那些贵族一般无二。所以，多么奇怪呀，古老的欧洲偏见依旧存在，但并不是出现在欧洲人聚居的沿岸地带，而是出现在新世界的森林深处。

　　在本书的写作过程中，我不止一次想要努力说明社会状况对法制和民情的巨大影响，而这里我还想再对此做一点儿补充说明。

　　当我意识到我们的祖先日耳曼人的政治制度和北美游牧部落的相似之处，以及塔西佗所描绘的日耳曼人的生活习惯和我所亲眼得见的印第安人生活习惯的共同之处，便不禁会想，同样的原因已促使两个半球产生同样的结果，所以，在显然纷繁不同的人类事务中找出几个能促使其他事实产生的主要事实也并非没有可能。那么，我认为一定能够在我们称

like the game within the thicket, before the huntsmen plunge into the interior. The Indians who were thus placed between civilization and death, found themselves obliged to live by ignominious labor like the whites. They took to agriculture, and without entirely forsaking their old habits or manners, sacrificed only as much as was necessary to their existence.

The Cherokees went further; they created a written language; established a permanent form of government; and as everything proceeds rapidly in the New World, before they had all of them clothes, they set up a newspaper.

The growth of European habits has been remarkably accelerated among these Indians by the mixed race which has sprung up. Deriving intelligence from their father's side, without entirely losing the savage customs of the mother, the half-blood forms the natural link between civilization and barbarism. Wherever this race has multiplied the savage state has become modified, and a great change has taken place in the manners of the people.

The success of the Cherokees proves that the Indians are capable of civilization, but it does not prove that they will succeed in it. This difficulty which the Indians find in submitting to civilization proceeds from the influence of a general cause, which it is almost impossible for them to escape. An attentive survey of history demonstrates that, in general, barbarous nations have raised themselves to civilization by degrees, and by their own efforts. Whenever they derive knowledge from a foreign people, they stood towards it in the relation of conquerors, and not of a conquered nation. When the conquered nation is enlightened, and the conquerors are half savage, as in the case of the invasion of Rome by the Northern nations or that of China by the Mongols, the power which victory bestows upon the barbarian is sufficient to keep up his importance among civilized men, and permit him to rank as their equal, until he becomes their rival: the one has might on his side, the other has intelligence; the former admires the knowledge and the arts of the conquered, the latter envies the power of the conquerors. The barbarians at length admit civilized man into their palaces, and he in turn opens his schools to the barbarians. But when the side on which the physical force lies, also possesses an intellectual preponderance, the conquered party seldom become civilized; it retreats,

之为日耳曼人的政治制度中发现野蛮人的习惯，并在我们所说的封建制度中看到野蛮人的观念。

无论北美印第安人反对农耕和文明的恶习和偏见多么强烈，但是有时候现实的需要也会迫使他们不得不如此。除去南方的几个部落外，还有柴罗基部落和克里克部落都被欧洲人围了起来，这些欧洲人蜂拥而至，他们中有些人来自大西洋沿岸，有些人沿俄亥俄河顺流而下，还有些人从密西西比河逆流而上。这些印第安人并没有像北方的那些部落一样被从一个地方赶到另一个地方，而是逐渐被压缩到一个有限的区域，就好像猎物被猎人围住，只待束手就擒。所以，对于不是文明就是灭亡的印第安人来说，他们必须像白人那样靠低贱的劳动生活。他们开始农耕，但并没有完全放弃他们古老的习惯和风俗，只是为了生存做出一些必要的牺牲。

柴罗基部落走得更远，他们创造了文字，确立了稳定的管理形式，而且因为新世界中的一切都发展得太快，他们在全体还过着衣不遮体生活的时候就创建了自己的报纸。随着混血儿的不断出现，欧洲人的习惯在印第安人中显然得到加速传播。从他们父亲那里继承的智慧，同时也不缺少来自母亲的野蛮人的习惯，使得混血儿们成为文明与野蛮的天然联系。但凡混血儿多的地方，野蛮的状况就有所改善，而且那里的民情也会发生很大的变化。

柴罗基部落的成功证明印第安人有能力变得文明，但是并不能证明他们能够成功地变成文明人。印第安人文明化进程的困难在于他们受到一个几乎无法逃脱的普遍原因的影响。认真地阅读一下历史可以看到，一般来说，野蛮部落是通过自身的努力逐步文明起

or is destroyed. It may therefore be said, in a general way, that savages go forth in arms to seek knowledge, but that they do not receive it when it comes to them.

If the Indian tribes which now inhabit the heart of the continent could summon up energy enough to attempt to civilize themselves, they might possibly succeed. Superior already to the barbarous nations which surround them, they would gradually gain strength and experience, and when the Europeans should appear upon their borders, they would be in a state, if not to maintain their independence, at least to assert their right to the soil, and to incorporate themselves with the conquerors. But it is the misfortune of Indians to be brought into contact with a civilized people, which is also (it must be owned) the most avaricious nation on the globe, whilst they are still semi-barbarian: to find despots in their instructors, and to receive knowledge from the hand of oppression. Living in the freedom of the woods, the North American Indian was destitute, but he had no feeling of inferiority towards anyone; as soon, however, as he desires to penetrate into the social scale of the whites, he takes the lowest rank in society, for he enters, ignorant and poor, within the pale of science and wealth. After having led a life of agitation, beset with evils and dangers, but at the same time filled with proud emotions, he is obliged to submit to a wearisome, obscure, and degraded state; and to gain the bread which nourishes him by hard and ignoble labor; such are in his eyes the only results of which civilization can boast: and even this much he is not sure to obtain.

When the Indians undertake to imitate their European neighbors, and to till the earth like the settlers, they are immediately exposed to a very formidable competition. The white man is skilled in the craft of agriculture; the Indian is a rough beginner in an art with which he is unacquainted. The former reaps abundant crops without difficulty, the latter meets with a thousand obstacles in raising the fruits of the earth.

The European is placed amongst a population whose wants he knows and partakes. The savage is isolated in the midst of a hostile people, with whose manners, language, and laws he is imperfectly acquainted, but without whose assistance he cannot live. He can only procure the materials of comfort by bartering his commodities against the goods of the European, for the assistance of his

来。当他们从外国汲取知识的时候，面对异族，总是处于征服者的地位，而不是被征服者的地位。若被征服的国家是文明的，而征服者处于半野蛮状态，就好像古罗马被北方民族和中国被蒙古入侵一样，胜利赋予野蛮人的力量足以使他们在文明人中举足轻重，并拥有与文明人同样的地位直到文明人能成为他们的对手。一方有力量在手，另一方则智慧在握；前者羡慕被征服者的知识和技艺，后者则嫉妒征服者的力量。最终，野蛮人将文明人请进他们的宫殿，而文明人则向野蛮人开放自己的学校。但是当具有物质力量的一方同时拥有智慧优势的时候，被征服的一方则难以走向文明，他们不是后退就是被毁灭。因此，大体上可以说，野蛮人是手持武器寻求知识，但当知识向他们袭来时却不愿接受。

现在居住在大陆中心地区的印第安人当初如果能够积聚起足够的能量尝试让自己变文明，他们也有可能取得成功。当时他们已经比周围的部族优越，并渐渐获得力量和经验，而当欧洲人出现在他们边界的时候，按照他们当时的状况，即使不能保持独立，至少能够让自己对土地的所有权得到认可，并与征服者相融合。但是印第安人的不幸在于跟他们打交道的文明人是地球上最贪婪的民族，而他们自己此时还处在半野蛮化状态。他们找到的导师却原来是暴君，学到知识的同时接受了压迫。自由生活在北美森林中的印第安人是贫困的，但是他们并不觉得自己比任何人卑微。然而，他们一旦想要进入白人的社会阶层，便成为社会的最底层，因为无知贫困的他们来到一个科学财富统治的世界。在经过一段时间的不安，灾难重重且危机四伏，同时又感到兴奋自豪的生活之后，他们必然会处于一种单调乏味浑浑噩噩的状态。为了获得生存必需的面包只能做着辛苦卑贱的工作，而在他们眼中，这就为人所

countrymen is wholly insufficient to supply his wants. When the Indian wishes to sell the produce of his labor, he cannot always meet with a purchaser, whilst the European readily finds a market; and the former can only produce at a considerable cost that which the latter vends at a very low rate. Thus the Indian has no sooner escaped those evils to which barbarous nations are exposed, than he is subjected to the still greater miseries of civilized communities; and he finds is scarcely less difficult to live in the midst of our abundance, than in the depth of his own wilderness.

He has not yet lost the habits of his erratic life; the traditions of his fathers and his passion for the chase are still alive within him. The wild enjoyments which formerly animated him in the woods, painfully excite his troubled imagination; and his former privations appear to be less keen, his former perils less appalling. He contrasts the independence which he possessed amongst his equals with the servile position which he occupies in civilized society. On the other hand, the solitudes which were so long his free home are still at hand; a few hours' march will bring him back to them once more. The whites offer him a sum, which seems to him to be considerable, for the ground which he has begun to clear. This money of the Europeans may possibly furnish him with the means of a happy and peaceful subsistence in remoter regions; and he quits the plough, resumes his native arms, and returns to the wilderness forever. The condition of the Creeks and Cherokees, to which I have already alluded, sufficiently corroborates the truth of this deplorable picture.

The Indians, in the little which they have done, have unquestionably displayed as much natural genius as the peoples of Europe in their most important designs; but nations as well as men require time to learn, whatever may be their intelligence and their zeal. Whilst the savages were engaged in the work of civilization, the Europeans continued to surround them on every side, and to confine them within narrower limits; the two races gradually met, and they are now in immediate juxtaposition to each other. The Indian is already superior to his barbarous parent, but he is still very far below his white neighbor. With their resources and acquired knowledge, the Europeans soon appropriated to themselves most of the advantages which the natives might have derived from the possession of the soil; they have settled in the country, they have purchased land at a very low rate or

称道的文明产生的唯一成果，而哪怕是这样的成果，他们也并不一定能得到。

当印第安人开始模仿他们的邻居欧洲人耕作土地的时候，立即遭遇非常可怕的竞争。白人精通农业种植技术，而印第安人不过是对这行一窍不通的新手。欧洲人能毫无困难地获得大丰收，而印第安人得克服重重困难才能让土地结出果实。

欧洲人生活在一群野蛮人中，并对他们的需要了若指掌，而且他们的生活需求也跟自己相同。野蛮人孤独地生活在敌视他们的白人中，尽管对白人的习俗、语言和法律不甚了解，但是又离不开白人。印第安人因为同族不能再给他们提供本就不充足的援助，只能通过跟欧洲人进行物物交换获得生活必需品。当印第安人想要出售他的劳动成果时，并不总能找到买主，而欧洲人的货则不愁销路。此外，印第安人要用更高的成本才能生产出白人以低价兜售的产品。因此，印第安人刚刚逃脱野蛮民族的厄运便遭遇文明社会更加悲惨的不幸。他们发现生活在我们的富裕社会中的困难不亚于他们在自己的森林之中。

印第安人并没有抛弃他们漂泊不定的生活习惯，祖先的传统和狩猎的热情依然在他们的体内存留。曾经在森林中享受的狂野的欢乐，只留在他们模糊的记忆中，而原先曾经历过的贫困也似乎不再那么强烈，原先的危险也不再那么可怕。他们曾经在彼此平等的人们中享有的独立和他们如今在文明社会中所处的奴隶地位形成鲜明的对比。另一方面，他们曾长期自由生活的荒野依旧近在咫尺，只要几个小时的路程就能旧地重游。如果白人用一笔在他们看来数目不菲的钱将其半荒的那块地买走，而且这笔钱足以让他们在更偏远的地方过上幸福安宁的生活，他们便会放下锄头，重新拿起原始的武器，永远回到荒野中。我

have occupied it by force, and the Indians have been ruined by a competition which they had not the means of resisting. They were isolated in their own country, and their race only constituted a colony of troublesome aliens in the midst of a numerous and domineering people.

Washington said in one of his messages to Congress, "We are more enlightened and more powerful than the Indian nations, we are therefore bound in honor to treat them with kindness and even with generosity." But this virtuous and high-minded policy has not been followed. The rapacity of the settlers is usually backed by the tyranny of the government. Although the Cherokees and the Creeks are established upon the territory which they inhabited before the settlement of the Europeans, and although the Americans have frequently treated with them as with foreign nations, the surrounding States have not consented to acknowledge them as independent peoples, and attempts have been made to subject these children of the woods to Anglo-American magistrates, laws, and customs. Destitution had driven these unfortunate Indians to civilization, and oppression now drives them back to their former condition: many of them abandon the soil which they had begun to clear, and return to their savage course of life.

In 1830 the State of Mississippi assimilated the Choctaws and Chickasaws to the white population, and declared that any of them that should take the title of chief would be punished by a fine of $1,000 and a year's imprisonment. When these laws were enforced upon the Choctaws, who inhabited that district, the tribe assembled, their chief communicated to them the intentions of the whites, and read to them some of the laws to which it was intended that they should submit; and they unanimously declared that it was better at once to retreat again into the wilds.

If we consider the tyrannical measures which have been adopted by the legislatures of the Southern States, the conduct of their Governors, and the decrees of their courts of justice, we shall be convinced that the entire expulsion of the Indians is the final result to which the efforts of their policy are directed. The Americans of that part of the Union look with jealousy upon the aborigines, they are aware that these tribes have not yet lost the traditions of savage life, and before civilization has permanently fixed them to the soil, it is intended to force them to recede by reducing them to despair.

前面已经提到的克里克部落和柴罗基部落的情况，是这幅悲惨图景的充分真实的写照。

印第安人，就其所做的少数事情上已表现出的与生俱来的才华，无疑跟欧洲人在最重大的事业上所表现的才华不相上下。但是无论是一个民族还是一个个人，也不论其智力多么高超，热情多么高涨，都需要时间去学习。野蛮人致力于文明开化，欧洲人则持续从四面八方朝他们围拢过来，将他们压缩在一个狭小的范围，两个种族不断接触，最终毗邻而居。印第安人已经比他们的祖先进步，但却远远落后于他们的白人邻居。靠着自己的资源和知识，欧洲人很快将大多数土著人因占有土地而取得的优势据为己有。他们在这个国家定居，或以低廉的价格购买土地或以武力占有，而印第安人则在他们无力抵御的竞争中败下阵来。印第安人孤独地伫立在自己国家，并被一个数量众多且占据统治地位的民族视为不安定的异族。

华盛顿曾在致国会的一篇咨文中说道："我们比印第安各部落更加文明而强大，因此要仁慈而慷慨地对待他们。"但是这种正直高尚的思想并没有得到遵从。移民的掠夺往往得到政府保证的支持。尽管柴罗基部落和克里克部落在欧洲移民到来之前就已经在这片土地上生活，尽管美国人总是像对待外来民族那样对待他们，但是他们周边的各州却不愿意将他们视为独立的民族，并试图让这些森林的孩子服从英裔美国人的行政管理、法律和习俗。贫困促使这些不幸的印第安人走向文明，现在压迫又促使他们回归野蛮。他们当中有许多人离开他们才刚刚开垦的土地，回归野蛮的生活。

1830年，密西西比州实行将巧克陶部和契克索部同化为白人的政策，并宣布带头反对的人将受到1000美元罚款和一年徒刑的惩罚。当密西西比州将这项法令应用到州境内的夏

The Creeks and Cherokees, oppressed by the several States, have appealed to the central government, which is by no means insensible to their misfortunes, and is sincerely desirous of saving the remnant of the natives, and of maintaining them in the free possession of that territory, which the Union is pledged to respect. But the several States oppose so formidable a resistance to the execution of this design, that the government is obliged to consent to the extirpation of a few barbarous tribes in order not to endanger the safety of the American Union.

But the federal government, which is not able to protect the Indians, would fain mitigate the hardships of their lot; and, with this intention, proposals have been made to transport them into more remote regions at the public cost.

Between the thirty-third and thirty-seventh degrees of north latitude, a vast tract of country lies, which has taken the name of Arkansas, from the principal river that waters its extent. It is bounded on the one side by the confines of Mexico, on the other by the Mississippi. Numberless streams cross it in every direction; the climate is mild, and the soil productive, but it is only inhabited by a few wandering hordes of savages. The government of the Union wishes to transport the broken remnants of the indigenous population of the South to the portion of this country which is nearest to Mexico, and at a great distance from the American settlements.

We were assured, towards the end of the year 1831, that 10,000 Indians had already gone down to the shores of the Arkansas; and fresh detachments were constantly following them; but Congress has been unable to excite a unanimous determination in those whom it is disposed to protect. Some, indeed, are willing to quit the seat of oppression, but the most enlightened members of the community refuse to abandon their recent dwellings and their springing crops; they are of opinion that the work of civilization, once interrupted, will never be resumed; they fear that those domestic habits which have been so recently contracted, may be irrevocably lost in the midst of a country which is still barbarous, and where nothing is prepared for the subsistence of an agricultural people; they know that their entrance into those wilds will be opposed by inimical hordes, and that they have

克塔部时，这个部落的印第安人曾集会对这个问题进行讨论。他们的酋长向他们揭穿了白人的意图，并号召人们反对白人要求他们服从的法律。于是野蛮人异口同声地宣称，他们宁愿重新回到森林里去。

只要看一下南方诸州立法机构采用的暴政、各州统治者的行径以及法院的判例，我们就不难发现，驱逐印第安人是这些州所有政策的共同的终极目标。居住在联邦这一地区的美国人用嫉妒的目光注视着这里的土著人，他们意识到这些部落还没有丢弃他们野蛮生活的传统，而且在文明开化之前会一直留在这片土地，只有让他们感到绝望才能迫使他们离开。受到所在州压迫的克里克人和柴罗基人忍无可忍，并向中央寻求帮助。联邦衷心希望能够保护残余的土著人，并保护他们对联邦赋予他们的土地的所有权。但是各州对这样的安排反应非常强烈，所以政府不得不同意将一些野蛮部落彻底消灭以避免联邦陷入危机。

无力保护印第安人的联邦政府后来曾设法减轻他们的苦难，出于这样的目的，联邦政府决定出资将这些印第安人迁往他处。

在北纬33°~37°之间，有大片的空旷地带，因一条大河在其境内流淌而过故称为阿肯色。阿肯色的一侧与墨西哥接壤，另一侧则是密西西比河，无数条河流在其境内纵横交错，这里气候温和，土地肥沃，却只有几个游牧部落在此居住。联邦政府希望将南方土著部落的残余迁到这个与墨西哥毗邻而远离美国白人的地方。

据说，1831年末已经有1万印第安人来到阿肯色，而且还有新的印第安人紧随其后源源不断地涌入。但是那些有待国会保护的人对此的反应并不一致。的确，有些人对能够摆脱被压迫的地位感到很高兴，但是其中的一些非常开化的印第安人则不愿放弃他们刚刚建

lost the energy of barbarians, without acquiring the resources of civilization to resist their attacks. Moreover, the Indians readily discover that the settlement which is proposed to them is merely a temporary expedient. Who can assure them that they will at length be allowed to dwell in peace in their new retreat? The United States pledge themselves to the observance of the obligation; but the territory which they at present occupy was formerly secured to them by the most solemn oaths of Anglo-American faith. The American government does not indeed rob them of their lands, but it allows perpetual incursions to be made on them. In a few years the same white population which now flocks around them, will track them to the solitudes of the Arkansas; they will then be exposed to the same evils without the same remedies, and as the limits of the earth will at last fail them, their only refuge is the grave.

The Union treats the Indians with less cupidity and rigor than the policy of the several States, but the two governments are alike destitute of good faith. The States extend what they are pleased to term the benefits of their laws to the Indians, with a belief that the tribes will recede rather than submit; and the central government, which promises a permanent refuge to these unhappy beings is well aware of its inability to secure it to them.

Thus the tyranny of the States obliges the savages to retire, the Union, by its promises and resources, facilitates their retreat; and these measures tend to precisely the same end. "By the will of our Father in Heaven, the Governor of the whole world," said the Cherokees in their petition to Congress, "the red man of America has become small, and the white man great and renowned. When the ancestors of the people of these United States first came to the shores of America they found the red man strong: though he was ignorant and savage, yet he received them kindly, and gave them dry land to rest their weary feet. They met in peace, and shook hands in token of friendship. Whatever the white man wanted and asked of the Indian, the latter willingly gave. At that time the Indian was the lord, and the white man the suppliant. But now the scene has changed. The strength of the red man has become weakness. As his neighbors increased in numbers his power became less and less,

好的房舍和刚刚播种的庄稼。他们认为文明的进程一旦被打断就无法再继续，他们担心最近才养成的那些生活习惯，将不可避免地消失在一个依旧荒夷且没有为务农的人提供任何物质准备的地方。他们知道进入这些荒凉地区会遭到一些游牧部落的敌视，而他们已经失去野蛮人的力量，也没有文明人的智谋去抵抗敌人。而且，印第安人已经发现，给他们所做的安排不过是暂时性的。谁能跟他们保证，他们能够在这片新的驻地可以一直宁静地生活下去？美国政府保证会为他们提供保护，但是美国政府也曾对他们现在居住的土地做过同样信誓旦旦地保证。美国政府的确没有掠夺印第安人的土地，但却任凭印第安人不断受到侵犯。几年之后，现在聚在他们身边的这群白人同样会追随他们来到荒凉的阿肯色，那时他们还会面对同样的无法改变的厄运，最终他们将无路可退，只有死路一条。

联邦对印第安人的政策与一些州相比，没有那么贪婪和苛刻，但是无论是联邦政府还是州政府都同样不守信用。那些州在施行它们称之为对印第安人有利的法律之时，就已经预料印第安部落宁可远走他乡也不愿服从；而中央政府承诺为这些不幸的人安排永久居留地的时候，也并非没有意识到自己的无能为力。

因此，州政府通过暴力赶走土著人，联邦则用它的承诺和财力帮助那些州赶走土著人，这些措施虽不相同，但结果出奇的一致。柴罗基部落在给国会的请愿书中写道："奉世界之主我们天上先祖之愿，美洲的红色人种已经变得弱小，而白色人种则变得强大而闻名。当这些美国人的祖先刚踏上美洲大陆的时候，他们看到红色人种很强大；尽管红色人种无知野蛮，但却热情地欢迎他们的到来，并提供干爽的土地让他们疲惫的双脚歇息。他们彼此握手言欢，和平相处。无论白人向印第安人要什么或是有所求，印第安人必会欣然

and now, of the many and powerful tribes who once covered these United States, only a few are to be seen—a few whom a sweeping pestilence has left. The northern tribes, who were once so numerous and powerful, are now nearly extinct. Thus it has happened to the red man of America. Shall we, who are remnants, share the same fate?"

"The land on which we stand we have received as an inheritance from our fathers, who possessed it from time immemorial, as a gift from our common Father in Heaven. They bequeathed it to us as their children, and we have sacredly kept it, as containing the remains of our beloved men. This right of inheritance we have never ceded nor ever forfeited. Permit us to ask what better right can the people have to a country than the right of inheritance and immemorial peaceable possession? We know it is said of late by the State of Georgia and by the Executive of the United States, that we have forfeited this right; but we think this is said gratuitously. At what time have we made the forfeit? What great crime have we committed, whereby we must forever be divested of our country and rights? Was it when we were hostile to the United States, and took part with the King of Great Britain, during the struggle for independence? If so, why was not this forfeiture declared in the first treaty of peace between the United States and our beloved men? Why was not such an article as the following inserted in the treaty:—'The United States give peace to the Cherokees, but, for the part they took in the late war, declare them to be but tenants at will, to be removed when the convenience of the States, within whose chartered limits they live, shall require it'? That was the proper time to assume such a possession. But it was not thought of, nor would our forefathers have agreed to any treaty whose tendency was to deprive them of their rights and their country."

Such is the language of the Indians: their assertions are true, their forebodings inevitable. From whichever side we consider the destinies of the aborigines of North America, their calamities appear to be irremediable: if they continue barbarous, they are forced to retire; if they attempt to civilize their manners, the contact of a more civilized community subjects them to oppression and destitution. They perish if they continue to wander from waste to waste, and if they attempt to settle they still

应允。那时候印第安人是施主，白人是乞讨者。而现在局面发生改变。红色人种的力量被削弱。随着邻居人数的增加，红色人种的力量不断变弱，曾经遍布美国的那些众多强有力的部落犹如瘟疫来袭一般已所剩不多。曾经人多势众的北方部落现在已经几乎灭绝。这就是美洲红色人种的遭遇。而我们这些幸存下来的人，也要经历相同的命运吗？

"我们拥有的这片土地是祖先留给我们的遗产，自古以来便属于我们的祖先，是天父馈赠给我们祖先的礼物。我们的先人又将它作为遗产留给自己的子孙，而我们庄重地将它保存下来，因为这里埋藏着先人的遗骸。我们既没有出让也不曾丧失继承权。恕我们冒昧地问一句：还有什么权利能够比继承权和最先占有权能更充分地让一个民族拥有一片国土呢？我们知道，如今佐治亚州政府和联邦政府却硬说我们已经丧失这一权利，那么我们的权利是何时丧失的呢？我们又犯了什么样的过错，以至于必须剥夺我们的国土和权利呢？难道是在独立战争时期，我们曾经协同英军与美国为敌的时候吗？如果是这样，为什么美国在与我们可敬的祖先签订第一份协议的时候没有指出剥夺这项权利呢？而为什么在这份条约中没有写明这样的条款：合众国愿同柴罗基部落和平共处，但是为了对其参战予以处罚，兹宣布将柴罗基部落仅视为土地的佃户，当与其接壤的各州感到有所不便的时候，必须离开。那时是一个合适的时机来宣布你们对土地的占有，但是没有人想到这一点，而我们的祖先也从未认可任何旨在剥夺他们权利和国家的条约。"

这就是印第安人的原话，而且他们所说的完全属实，他们的不祥之感也无可避免。无论从哪个角度来看北美土著人的命运，他们的灾难似乎无法补救。如果他们继续野蛮下去，就只有不断被驱赶；如果他们尝试走向文明，那么在与一个更加文明的社会的接触

must perish; the assistance of Europeans is necessary to instruct them, but the approach of Europeans corrupts and repels them into savage life; they refuse to change their habits as long as their solitudes are their own, and it is too late to change them when they are constrained to submit.

The Spaniards pursued the Indians with bloodhounds, like wild beasts; they sacked the New World with no more temper or compassion than a city taken by storm; but destruction must cease, and frenzy be stayed; the remnant of the Indian population which had escaped the massacre mixed with its conquerors, and adopted in the end their religion and their manners. The conduct of the Americans of the United States towards the aborigines is characterized, on the other hand, by a singular attachment to the formalities of law. Provided that the Indians retain their barbarous condition, the Americans take no part in their affairs; they treat them as independent nations, and do not possess themselves of their hunting grounds without a treaty of purchase; and if an Indian nation happens to be so encroached upon as to be unable to subsist upon its territory, they afford it brotherly assistance in transporting it to a grave sufficiently remote from the land of its fathers.

The Spaniards were unable to exterminate the Indian race by those unparalleled atrocities which brand them with indelible shame, nor did they even succeed in wholly depriving it of its rights; but the Americans of the United States have accomplished this twofold purpose with singular felicity; tranquilly, legally, philanthropically, without shedding blood, and without violating a single great principle of morality in the eyes of the world. It is impossible to destroy men with more respect for the laws of humanity.

Situation Of The Black Population In The United States, And Dangers With Which Its Presence Threatens The Whites

Why it is more difficult to abolish slavery, and to efface all vestiges of it amongst the moderns than it was amongst the ancients—In the United States the prejudices of the Whites against the Blacks seem to increase in proportion as slavery is abolished—Situation of the Negroes in the

中，则要受到压迫和贫困的困扰。如果他们继续从一个荒地漂泊到另一个荒地，必定会灭亡；然而，如果尝试定居下来，依然无法逃脱灭亡的厄运。印第安人只有在欧洲人的帮助下才能开化，但是与欧洲人的接触却让他们境遇更糟，并重返野蛮生活。只要荒野依然属于他们，印第安人就不会改变他们的生活习惯，而当他们不得不做出改变的时候却已为时已晚。

西班牙人像对待野兽一般，用猎狗驱赶印第安人，他们犹如暴风雨席卷城市一般，毫无怜悯地洗劫了新大陆，但是摧毁必定要停止，疯狂也不会永无休止；免受涂炭而幸存的印第安人与征服者融合，最终接受了他们的宗教和生活方式。联邦的美国人对待土著人的行事方式刚好相反，表现出一点对规矩和法律的拘泥。只要印第安人想要继续保持他们野蛮的生活状态，美国人也不会介入他们事务，并将他们视为独立的民族，而且除非有购买协议否则不会占据他们的猎场。如果一个印第安部落刚好因为某种不幸无法在原地继续生活，他们伸出兄弟般的友谊之手帮助他们迁徙到一个远离故土的地方。

西班牙人用给自己带来奇耻大辱的空前暴行也无法将印第安人种斩尽杀绝，甚至无法剥夺他们的所有权利。但是美联邦的美国人则一箭双雕，用平稳、合法、慈悲的手段，在不流血也不违反世人眼中伟大人类道德原则的前提下取得成功。只有用尊重人类的法律才能将人摧毁。

黑人在美国的处境以及给美国白人带来的威胁

为什么在现代比在古代更难以废除奴隶制和消除其所有残余——在美国，白人对黑人的偏见似乎随奴隶制的废除而日益加深——黑人在北方诸州和南方诸州的地位——让奴隶

Northern and Southern States—Why the Americans abolish slavery—Servitude, which debases the slave, impoverishes the master—Contrast between the left and the right bank of the Ohio—To what attributable—The Black race, as well as slavery, recedes towards the South—Explanation of this fact—Difficulties attendant upon the abolition of slavery in the South—Dangers to come—General anxiety—Foundation of a Black colony in Africa—Why the Americans of the South increase the hardships of slavery, whilst they are distressed at its continuance.

The Indians will perish in the same isolated condition in which they have lived; but the destiny of the negroes is in some measure interwoven with that of the Europeans. These two races are attached to each other without intermingling, and they are alike unable entirely to separate or to combine. The most formidable of all the ills which threaten the future existence of the Union arises from the presence of a black population upon its territory; and in contemplating the cause of the present embarrassments or of the future dangers of the United States, the observer is invariably led to consider this as a primary fact.

The permanent evils to which mankind is subjected are usually produced by the vehement or the increasing efforts of men; but there is one calamity which penetrated furtively into the world, and which was at first scarcely distinguishable amidst the ordinary abuses of power; it originated with an individual whose name history has not preserved; it was wafted like some accursed germ upon a portion of the soil, but it afterwards nurtured itself, grew without effort, and spreads naturally with the society to which it belongs. I need scarcely add that this calamity is slavery. Christianity suppressed slavery, but the Christians of the sixteenth century re-established it—as an exception, indeed, to their social system, and restricted to one of the races of mankind; but the wound thus inflicted upon humanity, though less extensive, was at the same time rendered far more difficult of cure.

It is important to make an accurate distinction between slavery itself and its consequences. The immediate evils which are produced by slavery were very nearly the same in antiquity as they

地位低下的奴役致使主人变得贫困——俄亥俄河左岸和右岸的差别——其差异产生的原因是什么——随着黑人向南方不断退缩，奴隶制也往南转移——这种现象出现的原因——南方奴隶制废除的困难所在——随之而来的危险——人们的普遍忧虑——在非洲黑人殖民地的建立——为什么南方的美国人在对奴隶制深感不安的同时加剧了这一制度的残酷性。

印第安人在孤独中生存，也在孤独中灭亡；但是黑人的命运则跟欧洲人的命运交织在一起。这两个种族既无法完全分割也无法完全融合。威胁联邦未来存亡的所有灾祸中最可怕的就是黑人在这片国土上的出现。在思索美国目前的尴尬状况和未来危险的原因时，所有的观察家都不约而同地归结到这一事实。

人类与日俱增的强烈追求往往会造成长期的灾难，但是有一种灾难却悄悄地来到这个世界，最初它混迹于常见的滥用权力之中几乎无法察觉，诞生于一个并未载入史册之人的手中，而后像某种遭人厌弃的病菌在大地上游荡，随后自我繁殖，肆意生长，并随其所在社会的壮大自然而然地传播。我几乎无须说明，这个灾难就是奴隶制。起初基督教废除了奴隶制，但16世纪的基督徒又将其恢复起来，作为社会的一种特例，只针对一个人类种族实施。尽管这个伤口不大，却刺痛人类，而且很难治愈。

对奴隶制本身和奴隶制的后果加以准确区分非常重要。奴隶制造就的直接罪恶无论是在古代还是现代几乎完全一样，但是这些罪恶产生的结果却有所不同。在古代，奴隶与其主人属于同一种族，而且奴隶的教育和知识水平往往比他的主人高。自由与否是两者的唯

are amongst the moderns; but the consequences of these evils were different. The slave, amongst the ancients, belonged to the same race as his master, and he was often the superior of the two in education and instruction. Freedom was the only distinction between them; and when freedom was conferred they were easily confounded together. The ancients, then, had a very simple means of avoiding slavery and its evil consequences, which was that of affranchisement; and they succeeded as soon as they adopted this measure generally. Not but, in ancient States, the vestiges of servitude subsisted for some time after servitude itself was abolished. There is a natural prejudice which prompts men to despise whomsoever has been their inferior long after he is become their equal; and the real inequality which is produced by fortune or by law is always succeeded by an imaginary inequality which is implanted in the manners of the people. Nevertheless, this secondary consequence of slavery was limited to a certain term amongst the ancients, for the freedman bore so entire a resemblance to those born free, that it soon became impossible to distinguish him from amongst them.

The greatest difficulty in antiquity was that of altering the law; amongst the moderns it is that of altering the manners; and, as far as we are concerned, the real obstacles begin where those of the ancients left off. This arises from the circumstance that, amongst the moderns, the abstract and transient fact of slavery is fatally united to the physical and permanent fact of color. The tradition of slavery dishonors the race, and the peculiarity of the race perpetuates the tradition of slavery. No African has ever voluntarily emigrated to the shores of the New World; whence it must be inferred, that all the blacks who are now to be found in that hemisphere are either slaves or freedmen. Thus the negro transmits the eternal mark of his ignominy to all his descendants; and although the law may abolish slavery, God alone can obliterate the traces of its existence.

The modern slave differs from his master not only in his condition, but in his origin. You may set the negro free, but you cannot make him otherwise than an alien to the European. Nor is this all; we scarcely acknowledge the common features of mankind in this child of debasement whom slavery has brought amongst us. His physiognomy is to our eyes hideous, his understanding weak,

一区别，当奴隶获得自由，便能轻而易举地跟主人混为一体。因此，古代人有一种很简单的办法避免奴隶制及其恶果的出现，那就是恢复自由。这种方法一经普遍采用便可取得成功。但是，在古代奴隶制的痕迹还会在其被废除后留存一段时间。有一种自然的偏见会促使人瞧不起长期以来比自己地位低下而今却与自己平起平坐的人。继财富和法律的真正不平等之后，常常会出现一种扎根于民情的想象的不平等。但是，在古代，奴隶制产生的次要后果有一定的限度，获得自由的奴隶跟生来自由的人完全没有差别，而且很快就无法再将他们区分开来。

在古代，最困难的事情就是改革法律；而在现代，最困难的事情则是改变民情。在我们看来，真正的障碍在于那些古代没有的问题。这个障碍源自现代社会将奴隶制抽象短暂的压迫与种族肤色的外在永久的不同致命地联系起来。奴隶制的传统会让某些种族蒙羞，特别是那些有着长期奴隶制传统的种族。从未有非洲人自愿移民到新大陆，由此可见，居住在新大陆的黑人不是奴隶就是获得解放的奴隶。因此，黑人将耻辱的外在标志传给所有的子孙后代。尽管法律已经废除奴隶制，而唯有上帝才能够抹去奴隶制的痕迹。

现代的奴隶不仅在处境上，而且在族源上，都与主人不同。你可以让黑人获得自由，但是你无法不让欧洲人视其为异类。不仅如此，奴隶生来地位卑微，并以这样的身份生活在我们中间，以至于我们几乎不愿承认他们具有人类的共同特征。在我们的眼中，他们的外貌丑陋、领悟力差、品位低，几乎将他们视为人与兽之间的生物。于是，在现代，当奴隶制被废除之后，还要与三个比奴隶制还要难以对付的偏见做斗争：奴隶主的偏见、种族

his tastes low; and we are almost inclined to look upon him as a being intermediate between man and the brutes. The moderns, then, after they have abolished slavery, have three prejudices to contend against, which are less easy to attack and far less easy to conquer than the mere fact of servitude: the prejudice of the master, the prejudice of the race, and the prejudice of color.

It is difficult for us, who have had the good fortune to be born amongst men like ourselves by nature, and equal to ourselves by law, to conceive the irreconcilable differences which separate the negro from the European in America. But we may derive some faint notion of them from analogy. France was formerly a country in which numerous distinctions of rank existed, that had been created by the legislation. Nothing can be more fictitious than a purely legal inferiority; nothing more contrary to the instinct of mankind than these permanent divisions which had been established between beings evidently similar. Nevertheless these divisions subsisted for ages; they still subsist in many places; and on all sides they have left imaginary vestiges, which time alone can efface. If it be so difficult to root out an inequality which solely originates in the law, how are those distinctions to be destroyed which seem to be based upon the immutable laws of Nature herself? When I remember the extreme difficulty with which aristocratic bodies, of whatever nature they may be, are commingled with the mass of the people; and the exceeding care which they take to preserve the ideal boundaries of their caste inviolate, I despair of seeing an aristocracy disappear which is founded upon visible and indelible signs. Those who hope that the Europeans will ever mix with the negroes, appear to me to delude themselves; and I am not led to any such conclusion by my own reason, or by the evidence of facts.

Hitherto, wherever the whites have been the most powerful, they have maintained the blacks in a subordinate or a servile position; wherever the negroes have been strongest they have destroyed the whites; such has been the only retribution which has ever taken place between the two races.

I see that in a certain portion of the territory of the United States at the present day, the legal barrier which separated the two races is tending to fall away, but not that which exists in the manners of the country; slavery recedes, but the prejudice to which it has given birth remains stationary.

的偏见和肤色的偏见。

我们有幸生在与我们样貌相同，且法律让我们平等的人们之中，所以我们很难想象在美国将黑人和欧洲人区别开的那些无法消除的不同。但是通过类比我们也许能够窥知一二。法国曾经是一个有众多不同阶层存在的国家，法律将人们分出高低贵贱。然而，这种纯法律制造出的尊卑最为虚妄，而且在显然同类的人之间构建起永久的区别也是对人性最大的忤逆。但是，这种差别却存在了几个世纪，并仍然在许多地方存在着，而且到处还残留着想象中的痕迹，只有时间才能将其抹去。既然根除纯法律造成的不平等都如此的困难，那么又该如何摧毁那些似乎基于不可动摇自然法则之上的不平等呢？

当我想起一些贵族团体，无论其性质如何，都难以同人民大众融合的时候，当我想起这些贵族团体为了保住自己社会地位的绝佳屏障而煞费苦心的时候，我感到想要看到高举鲜明而光辉旗帜的贵族制度的消失，已毫无希望。

那些希望欧洲人有朝一日能跟黑人混为一体的人，依我看完全是自欺欺人。而我之所以得出这样的结论靠的并非是理性分析，而是以事实为依据。

迄今为止，只要是白人强大的地方，黑人就一直处于卑微或是被奴役的地位；只要是黑人强大的地方，白人就会被消灭。这就是这两个种族之间的唯一结局。

我注意到，今天在美联邦的一些地方，将两个种族隔离开的法律壁垒正在摇摇欲坠，但民情上的壁垒依旧存在。奴隶制不断萎缩，但是由此而来的偏见依旧根深蒂固。只要是在美国生活过的人都一定会发现，在联邦那些黑人不再为奴的地区，黑人非但没有跟白人

Whosoever has inhabited the United States must have perceived that in those parts of the Union in which the negroes are no longer slaves, they have in no wise drawn nearer to the whites. On the contrary, the prejudice of the race appears to be stronger in the States which have abolished slavery, than in those where it still exists; and nowhere is it so intolerant as in those States where servitude has never been known.

It is true, that in the North of the Union, marriages may be legally contracted between negroes and whites; but public opinion would stigmatize a man who should connect himself with a negress as infamous, and it would be difficult to meet with a single instance of such a union. The electoral franchise has been conferred upon the negroes in almost all the States in which slavery has been abolished; but if they come forward to vote, their lives are in danger. If oppressed, they may bring an action at law, but they will find none but whites amongst their judges; and although they may legally serve as jurors, prejudice repulses them from that office. The same schools do not receive the child of the black and of the European. In the theatres, gold cannot procure a seat for the servile race beside their former masters; in the hospitals they lie apart; and although they are allowed to invoke the same Divinity as the whites, it must be at a different altar, and in their own churches, with their own clergy. The gates of Heaven are not closed against these unhappy beings; but their inferiority is continued to the very confines of the other world; when the negro is defunct, his bones are cast aside, and the distinction of condition prevails even in the equality of death. The negro is free, but he can share neither the rights, nor the pleasures, nor the labor, nor the afflictions, nor the tomb of him whose equal he has been declared to be; and he cannot meet him upon fair terms in life or in death.

In the South, where slavery still exists, the negroes are less carefully kept apart; they sometimes share the labor and the recreations of the whites; the whites consent to intermix with them to a certain extent, and although the legislation treats them more harshly, the habits of the people are more tolerant and compassionate. In the South the master is not afraid to raise his slave to his own standing, because he knows that he can in a moment reduce him to the dust at pleasure. In the North the white no longer distinctly perceives the barrier which separates him from the degraded race, and

走得更近；相反，在美国奴隶制被废除的州，人种的偏见比在奴隶制依然存在的州来得更加强烈。没有任何一个地方的种族偏见比那些不知奴隶制为何物的州更令人不堪忍受。事实上，在联邦北方的一些州法律规定黑人和白人可以通婚，但是公众舆论会给迎娶黑人女子的白人男子冠上无耻之名，所以很难看到这种通婚的例子。奴隶制被废除的几乎所有州都赋予黑人选举权，但是如果他们前来投票，生命就会受到威胁。如果受到压迫，黑人可以去告状，但是所有的法官无一例外都是白人，而且尽管法律上允许黑人担任陪审员，但是偏见却将他们拒之千里。同一所学校不会同时接收白人孩子和黑人孩子；在剧院，黑人即使有钱也买不到与昔日主人并肩而坐的位子；在医院里，黑人和白人也被分在不同的病房。尽管黑人可以崇拜白人崇拜的上帝，但却不能在同一所教堂礼拜，黑人有自己的教士和教堂。上帝之门并未向这些不幸的人关闭，但是他们卑微的地位依旧成为他们来世的束缚。当黑人死去时，他们的骸骨被丢在一边，身份的差别甚至造成死后的不平等。

黑人是自由的，但并未能分享那些在宣布平等后应分享到权利、享乐、劳动的机会，乃至死后都无法葬在同一处墓地。无论是生前还是死后，他们都没有得到公正的待遇。

在南方，那里的奴隶制依然存在，黑人并没有与白人严格地隔离。他们有时候同白人一起劳作娱乐，白人同意在一定程度上与他们混在一起。尽管法律对他们非常严厉，但是人们习惯上却更加宽容和富于同情心。在南方，主人并不担心让黑人与自己平起平坐，因为他知道自己可以随心所欲地将其投入垃圾堆。在北方，白人尽管不再将自己与低等人种之间的壁垒看得那样森严，但却更加执拗地回避与黑人的接触，唯恐某一天自己会与他们

he shuns the negro with the more pertinacity, since he fears lest they should some day be confounded together.

Amongst the Americans of the South, nature sometimes reasserts her rights, and restores a transient equality between the blacks and the whites; but in the North pride restrains the most imperious of human passions. The American of the Northern States would perhaps allow the negress to share his licentious pleasures, if the laws of his country did not declare that she may aspire to be the legitimate partner of his bed; but he recoils with horror from her who might become his wife.

Thus it is, in the United States, that the prejudice which repels the negroes seems to increase in proportion as they are emancipated, and inequality is sanctioned by the manners whilst it is effaced from the laws of the country. But if the relative position of the two races which inhabit the United States is such as I have described, it may be asked why the Americans have abolished slavery in the North of the Union, why they maintain it in the South, and why they aggravate its hardships there? The answer is easily given. It is not for the good of the negroes, but for that of the whites, that measures are taken to abolish slavery in the United States.

The first negroes were imported into Virginia about the year 1621. In America, therefore, as well as in the rest of the globe, slavery originated in the South. Thence it spread from one settlement to another; but the number of slaves diminished towards the Northern States, and the negro population was always very limited in New England.

A century had scarcely elapsed since the foundation of the colonies, when the attention of the planters was struck by the extraordinary fact, that the provinces which were comparatively destitute of slaves, increased in population, in wealth, and in prosperity more rapidly than those which contained the greatest number of negroes. In the former, however, the inhabitants were obliged to cultivate the soil themselves, or by hired laborers; in the latter they were furnished with hands for which they paid no wages; yet although labor and expenses were on the one side, and ease with economy on the other, the former were in possession of the most advantageous system. This consequence seemed to be the more difficult to explain, since the settlers, who all belonged to the

为伍。

在南方的美国人中，大自然有时会重申她的权利，暂时让白人和黑人重新变得平等，但是在北方，骄傲却束缚了人类情感的最自然的流露。在北方如果法律宣布黑人女人不可与白人男人同床共枕，那么北方的美国人可能会将黑种女人当作行乐的对象；但是在北方，法律允许她成为他的妻子，而这却令他畏缩不前。

因此，在美国，随着黑人获得自由，其遭受的偏见也逐渐增加，而且随着法律上不平等的消失，生活中的不平等则愈演愈烈。但是，如果居住在美国的两个种族的地位如我所述，为什么美国人要在北方废除奴隶制，而在南方保留奴隶制？他们又为什么让奴隶制造成的疾苦加剧呢？答案很容易找到。在美国之所以要采取废除奴隶制的措施并不是为黑人着想，而是为了白人的利益。

大约在1621年，第一批黑人被输送到弗吉尼亚。因此，与在世界其他地方一样，美国的奴隶制也始于南方。随后，向各地蔓延开来，但是奴隶的数量越往北则越少，而在新英格兰黑人的数量已经非常有限了。

从第一个殖民地的建立至今，已经有一个世纪了，一个奇怪的现象开始引起大家的注意。奴隶数量相对少的地方，其人口数量、财富积累和繁荣程度都比那些黑奴数量庞大的地区要高得多。可是，在非奴隶制的地区，人们要么自己耕作土地，要么雇人来干；而在奴隶制地区，人们无须付酬劳就有人手为他们干活。但是尽管前者出钱出力，后者省钱省力，前者却能比后者获得更丰厚的利益。这样的结果似乎难以解释，因为南方和北方的定

same European race, had the same habits, the same civilization, the same laws, and their shades of difference were extremely slight.

Time, however, continued to advance, and the Anglo-Americans, spreading beyond the coasts of the Atlantic Ocean, penetrated farther and farther into the solitudes of the West; they met with a new soil and an unwonted climate; the obstacles which opposed them were of the most various character; their races intermingled, the inhabitants of the South went up towards the North, those of the North descended to the South; but in the midst of all these causes, the same result occurred at every step, and in general, the colonies in which there were no slaves became more populous and more rich than those in which slavery flourished. The more progress was made, the more was it shown that slavery, which is so cruel to the slave, is prejudicial to the master.

But this truth was most satisfactorily demonstrated when civilization reached the banks of the Ohio. The stream which the Indians had distinguished by the name of Ohio, or Beautiful River, waters one of the most magnificent valleys that has ever been made the abode of man. Undulating lands extend upon both shores of the Ohio, whose soil affords inexhaustible treasures to the laborer; on either bank the air is wholesome and the climate mild, and each of them forms the extreme frontier of a vast State: That which follows the numerous windings of the Ohio upon the left is called Kentucky, that upon the right bears the name of the river. These two States only differ in a single respect; Kentucky has admitted slavery, but the State of Ohio has prohibited the existence of slaves within its borders.

Thus the traveller who floats down the current of the Ohio to the spot where that river falls into the Mississippi, may be said to sail between liberty and servitude; and a transient inspection of the surrounding objects will convince him as to which of the two is most favorable to mankind. Upon the left bank of the stream the population is rare; from time to time one descries a troop of slaves loitering in the half-desert fields; the primaeval forest recurs at every turn; society seems to be asleep, man to be idle, and nature alone offers a scene of activity and of life. From the right bank, on the contrary, a confused hum is heard which proclaims the presence of industry; the fields are covered

居者都是欧洲的移民，拥有同样的习惯、同样的文明、同样的法制，不过是在一些不显眼的细节上有些许不同而已。

然而，时间依旧向前，英裔美国人离开了大西洋沿岸，向着西部的荒野越走越深。在那里，他们找到了新的土地，适应了新的气候，遇到的困难也各种各样。在这里各方的人们交会，南方的居民从这里北上，而北方人则从这里南下。所有的这些因素，同时起作用催生出同一个结果。一般来说，没有奴隶的殖民地比那些奴隶制盛行的殖民地人口更加稠密，社会更加繁荣。殖民地越是发展，残酷的奴役奴隶的奴隶制度就越是对奴隶主有害。

当文明来到俄亥俄河沿岸的时候，这一事实越发的明显。印第安人称之为俄亥俄河或是美丽之河的这条大河流经人们曾居住过的最棒的河谷之一。绵延起伏的土地在俄亥俄河两岸延伸开来，成为这里居民取之不竭的宝藏。俄亥俄河两岸空气清新气候宜人，每一侧的河岸都是一个大州的边界：在蜿蜒曲折的俄亥俄河的左岸是肯塔基州，右岸则是以河为名的俄亥俄州。这两个州唯一的不同之处是：肯塔基州承认奴隶制，而俄亥俄州则在其境内不允许奴隶的存在。

因此，对从俄亥俄河顺流而下的来到汇入密西西比河河口的行者而言，简直就是航行在自由和奴役之间，只要对两岸稍作观察他就能确定哪一种对人类最有利。在河的左岸人烟稀少，时不时地能看到一群群的奴隶在半荒的土地上游荡，被伐后的原始森林又重获生机，社会似乎昏昏欲睡，人们优哉游哉地生活，唯有大自然呈现出一派欣欣向荣的景象。相反，在河的右岸，可以听到机器的轰鸣，说明工厂的存在，田地里的庄稼生长茂盛，漂

with abundant harvests, the elegance of the dwellings announces the taste and activity of the laborer, and man appears to be in the enjoyment of that wealth and contentment which is the reward of labor.

The State of Kentucky was founded in 1775, the State of Ohio only twelve years later; but twelve years are more in America than half a century in Europe, and, at the present day, the population of Ohio exceeds that of Kentucky by two hundred and fifty thousand souls. These opposite consequences of slavery and freedom may readily be understood, and they suffice to explain many of the differences which we remark between the civilization of antiquity and that of our own time.

Upon the left bank of the Ohio labor is confounded with the idea of slavery, upon the right bank it is identified with that of prosperity and improvement; on the one side it is degraded, on the other it is honored; on the former territory no white laborers can be found, for they would be afraid of assimilating themselves to the negroes; on the latter no one is idle, for the white population extends its activity and its intelligence to every kind of employment. Thus the men whose task it is to cultivate the rich soil of Kentucky are ignorant and lukewarm; whilst those who are active and enlightened either do nothing or pass over into the State of Ohio, where they may work without dishonor.

It is true that in Kentucky the planters are not obliged to pay wages to the slaves whom they employ; but they derive small profits from their labor, whilst the wages paid to free workmen would be returned with interest in the value of their services. The free workman is paid, but he does his work quicker than the slave, and rapidity of execution is one of the great elements of economy. The white sells his services, but they are only purchased at the times at which they may be useful; the black can claim no remuneration for his toil, but the expense of his maintenance is perpetual; he must be supported in his old age as well as in the prime of manhood, in his profitless infancy as well as in the productive years of youth. Payment must equally be made in order to obtain the services of either class of men: the free workman receives his wages in money, the slave in education, in food, in care, and in clothing. The money which a master spends in the maintenance of his slaves goes gradually and in detail, so that it is scarcely perceived; the salary of the free workman is paid in a round sum,

亮的房子证明了主人的品位和爱好，人们似乎很享受劳动带来的财富和满足感。

肯塔基州建于1775年，俄亥俄州则建于12年之后，但是在美国的12年胜过欧洲的半个世纪。现在，俄亥俄州的人口已经比肯塔基多出25万。奴隶制和自由造成的截然相反的结果并不难理解，而且也足以说明我们谈到的古代文明和现代文明的许多不同之处。

在俄亥俄河的左岸，劳动与奴役被混为一谈；而在河对岸，劳动则代表富裕和进步。在左岸，劳动是低贱的；在右岸，劳动则是光荣的。在河的左岸，看不到白人的劳动者，因为他们害怕自己与奴隶为伍；在河的右岸，根本找不到闲人，因为白人将自己的活力与智慧投入各种各样的劳作。因此，在肯塔基州的肥沃土地上耕作的人不但无知而且毫无热情，而那些有热情有知识的人不是什么都不干，就是过河来到俄亥俄州，在这里光荣地劳动。

实际上，在肯塔基州种植园主不用付报酬给他们工作的奴隶，但是奴隶劳动带来的利益也不大，而付给自由工人的工资，却可以让他们获得远超过其劳动价值的利益。自由工人需要酬劳，但活干得比奴隶快得多，工作效率是经济效益的重要因素之一。白人出卖自己的服务，但只有在其劳动有用的时候才有人购买；黑人不会为他们的劳动索取报酬，但得养活他们一辈子。也就是说，无论是在他们老年还是壮年，还是在他们无法创造收益的幼年或精力旺盛的青年时期，都得养活他们。所以无论是让这里两类人谁来提供服务，所付的酬劳实际上是一样的。自由工人得到的酬劳是金钱，奴隶得到的是教育、食物、照顾和衣服。主人花在养活奴隶上的钱是细水长流，不易察觉；付给自由工人的钱则是一整笔，似乎得到这笔钱的人就发笔小财一样。最终，养活奴隶的开销要比雇用自由工人大得

which appears only to enrich the individual who receives it, but in the end the slave has cost more than the free servant, and his labor is less productive.

The influence of slavery extends still further; it affects the character of the master, and imparts a peculiar tendency to his ideas and his tastes. Upon both banks of the Ohio, the character of the inhabitants is enterprising and energetic; but this vigor is very differently exercised in the two States. The white inhabitant of Ohio, who is obliged to subsist by his own exertions, regards temporal prosperity as the principal aim of his existence; and as the country which he occupies presents inexhaustible resources to his industry and ever-varying lures to his activity, his acquisitive ardor surpasses the ordinary limits of human cupidity: he is tormented by the desire of wealth, and he boldly enters upon every path which fortune opens to him; he becomes a sailor, a pioneer, an artisan, or a laborer with the same indifference, and he supports, with equal constancy, the fatigues and the dangers incidental to these various professions; the resources of his intelligence are astonishing, and his avidity in the pursuit of gain amounts to a species of heroism.

But the Kentuckian scorns not only labor, but all the undertakings which labor promotes; as he lives in an idle independence, his tastes are those of an idle man; money loses a portion of its value in his eyes; he covets wealth much less than pleasure and excitement; and the energy which his neighbor devotes to gain, turns with him to a passionate love of field sports and military exercises; he delights in violent bodily exertion, he is familiar with the use of arms, and is accustomed from a very early age to expose his life in single combat. Thus slavery not only prevents the whites from becoming opulent, but even from desiring to become so.

As the same causes have been continually producing opposite effects for the last two centuries in the British colonies of North America, they have established a very striking difference between the commercial capacity of the inhabitants of the South and those of the North. At the present day it is only the Northern States which are in possession of shipping, manufactures, railroads, and canals. This difference is perceptible not only in comparing the North with the South, but in comparing the several Southern States. Almost all the individuals who carry on commercial operations, or who

多，而劳动效率则低得多。

奴隶制的影响远比这要广泛，不但影响了奴隶主的性格，还左右了他们的思想和爱好。在俄亥俄河的两岸，居民都有着勇于进取、精力充沛的性格，但是在这两个州，这些共同点的运用却大不相同。俄亥俄州的白人居民，必须靠自己的努力生活，并将物质利益视为他的主要人生目标，而且因为他所在的州有取之不尽的资源供其辛勤劳作，层出不穷的诱惑让其欲罢不能，所以他贪婪的热情超越了人类贪欲的一般界限。他被发财致富的渴望折磨，敢于尝试任何一条通往财富的道路。无论是做水手还是开荒人抑或是手艺人，什么样的工作他都无所谓，他都能用坚韧的毅力来克服这些不同行业可能碰到的疲惫和危险；他惊人的智慧和追求成功的欲望造就出一种英雄主义。

但是肯塔基人不但鄙视劳动，而且鄙视劳动所促成的一切事业。他们的生活悠闲自在，与懒人臭味相投。在他们的眼中，钱失去了它的一部分价值，他们对财富的追求远不及对享乐和刺激的追求。邻人用来追求成功的劲头，被他们转化成为对狩猎和打仗的热爱。疯狂地使用体力让他们感到快乐，对从小就见惯决斗的他们而言，舞刀弄枪已经习以为常。因此，奴隶制不但未能让白人发财致富，反而让其失去了对发财致富的渴望。

这些相同的因素，在过去的两百年来在北美英国人的殖民地不断发挥截然不同的作用，从而造成南方和北方居民经商能力的巨大差异。今天，只有北方拥有航运业、制造业、铁路和运河。这些差别不但可以通过南北方的对比看到，而且通过南方各州的对比也能发现。在联邦南方的大部分州，几乎所有从事商业或努力从奴隶制中获利的人都来自北

endeavor to turn slave labor to account in the most Southern districts of the Union, have emigrated from the North. The natives of the Northern States are constantly spreading over that portion of the American territory where they have less to fear from competition; they discover resources there which escaped the notice of the inhabitants; and, as they comply with a system which they do not approve, they succeed in turning it to better advantage than those who first founded and who still maintain it.

Were I inclined to continue this parallel, I could easily prove that almost all the differences which may be remarked between the characters of the Americans in the Southern and in the Northern States have originated in slavery; but this would divert me from my subject, and my present intention is not to point out all the consequences of servitude, but those effects which it has produced upon the prosperity of the countries which have admitted it.

The influence of slavery upon the production of wealth must have been very imperfectly known in antiquity, as slavery then obtained throughout the civilized world; and the nations which were unacquainted with it were barbarous. And indeed Christianity only abolished slavery by advocating the claims of the slave; at the present time it may be attacked in the name of the master, and, upon this point, interest is reconciled with morality.

As these truths became apparent in the United States, slavery receded before the progress of experience. Servitude had begun in the South, and had thence spread towards the North; but it now retires again. Freedom, which started from the North, now descends uninterruptedly towards the South. Amongst the great States, Pennsylvania now constitutes the extreme limit of slavery to the North: but even within those limits the slave system is shaken: Maryland, which is immediately below Pennsylvania, is preparing for its abolition; and Virginia, which comes next to Maryland, is already discussing its utility and its dangers.

No great change takes place in human institutions without involving amongst its causes the law of inheritance. When the law of primogeniture obtained in the South, each family was represented by a wealthy individual, who was neither compelled nor induced to labor; and he was surrounded, as

方。北方各州的人不断来到美国的这一地区，因为在这里他们不用为竞争担心。他们发现这里的资源没有被当地人注意到，于是便利用他们本不赞成的制度，攫取比那些创立并一直维护这一制度的人更多的利益。

如果我继续比较，可以轻而易举地证明美国南方人和北方人的性格差异几乎都源自奴隶制，但这样做会让我偏离主题，我现在的目的并非要指出奴役造成的所有后果，而是要指出它对承认奴隶制的地区的繁荣昌盛所产生的影响。

奴隶制对创造财富的影响在古代一定无法被人们充分理解。那时候，奴隶制在文明世界普遍存在，对其一无所知的是蛮族。而且基督教通过替奴隶主张权利的方式将奴隶制废除，而今天人们能用奴隶主的名义去攻击奴隶制，因而在这一点上，利益和道德被调和起来。

随着这些事实在美国变得显而易见，奴隶制在经验的步步紧逼下节节败退。奴役始自南方，随后向北方蔓延，而如今它开始撤退了。自由，始于北方，现在正势不可当地向南方推进。在一些大州中，宾夕法尼亚州是实行奴隶制的最靠北的州，在这里奴隶制已经摇摇欲坠。紧挨着宾夕法尼亚州南面的马里兰州，也正在准备废除奴隶制；紧挨着马里兰州的弗吉尼亚州，则正在讨论奴隶制的功用和危险。

引起人类制度发生重大变化的众多因素之中，无一不涉及继承法。当长子继承法在南方施行的时候，每个家庭都有一个有钱的人为代表，他既不想也不用劳动，而在他的身边围绕着按照法律无法分享财产继承的其他家庭成员，他们好像寄生植物一样攀附着他，过

by parasitic plants, by the other members of his family who were then excluded by law from sharing the common inheritance, and who led the same kind of life as himself. The very same thing then occurred in all the families of the South as still happens in the wealthy families of some countries in Europe, namely, that the younger sons remain in the same state of idleness as their elder brother, without being as rich as he is. This identical result seems to be produced in Europe and in America by wholly analogous causes. In the South of the United States the whole race of whites formed an aristocratic body, which was headed by a certain number of privileged individuals, whose wealth was permanent, and whose leisure was hereditary. These leaders of the American nobility kept alive the traditional prejudices of the white race in the body of which they were the representatives, and maintained the honor of inactive life. This aristocracy contained many who were poor, but none who would work; its members preferred want to labor, consequently no competition was set on foot against negro laborers and slaves, and, whatever opinion might be entertained as to the utility of their efforts, it was indispensable to employ them, since there was no one else to work.

No sooner was the law of primogeniture abolished than fortunes began to diminish, and all the families of the country were simultaneously reduced to a state in which labor became necessary to procure the means of subsistence: several of them have since entirely disappeared, and all of them learned to look forward to the time at which it would be necessary for everyone to provide for his own wants. Wealthy individuals are still to be met with, but they no longer constitute a compact and hereditary body, nor have they been able to adopt a line of conduct in which they could persevere, and which they could infuse into all ranks of society. The prejudice which stigmatized labor was in the first place abandoned by common consent; the number of needy men was increased, and the needy were allowed to gain a laborious subsistence without blushing for their exertions. Thus one of the most immediate consequences of the partible quality of estates has been to create a class of free laborers. As soon as a competition was set on foot between the free laborer and the slave, the inferiority of the latter became manifest, and slavery was attacked in its fundamental principle, which is the interest of the master.

着跟他一样的生活。发生在所有南方家庭的同样事情也在某些欧洲国家的富裕家庭上演，也就是说，年幼的弟弟们一如他们的兄长一样无所事事，尽管他们没有他有钱。在欧洲和美国出现的这种同样的结果似乎源自完全类似的原因。在美国的南方，整个白人种族形成一个贵族集团，由一定数量的特权人物来领导，这些人的财产和悠闲生活都是辈辈相传。美国贵族的这些领导者们让白色人种的传统偏见在他们所代表的团体中持续存在，并继续维持着悠闲生活的骄傲。这些贵族中，有的人很穷但依然没有人去工作，他们宁可受穷也不工作。结果，就使得黑人劳工和奴隶不会碰到任何竞争，而且无论白人对他们的劳动效果怎么看，也只能雇用他们，因为没有其他人可用。

长子继承法一被废除，财富就开始分散变小，而且几乎所有的家庭都同时下降到必须靠工作才能维持生计的地步。有一些家庭已经消失，而所有的家庭都预见到一个人人都劳动才能维持生计时代的到来。富人们依然存在，但是他们不再是一个密不可分的世袭团体，也无法再采用他们惯有的并能够对社会各个阶层产生影响的一套行事方式。鄙视劳动的偏见首次遭到大家的一致抛弃。穷人数量的增加，使得穷人不再为自食其力而脸红。因此，财产平均分配的最直接的后果之一就是创造了一个劳动阶级。自由工人和奴隶之间一旦出现竞争，后者的劣势就变得明显起来，而奴隶制的基本原则，即奴隶主的利益，也受到攻击。

随着奴隶制的退败，黑人也跟随着奴隶制的脚步，退回到他们当初出走的热带地区。这一现象起初看起来反常，但不久人们就理解了。尽管美国人废除了奴隶制的原则，但并

As slavery recedes, the black population follows its retrograde course, and returns with it towards those tropical regions from which it originally came. However singular this fact may at first appear to be, it may readily be explained. Although the Americans abolish the principle of slavery, they do not set their slaves free. To illustrate this remark, I will quote the example of the State of New York. In 1788, the State of New York prohibited the sale of slaves within its limits, which was an indirect method of prohibiting the importation of blacks. Thenceforward the number of negroes could only increase according to the ratio of the natural increase of population. But eight years later a more decisive measure was taken, and it was enacted that all children born of slave parents after July 4, 1799, should be free. No increase could then take place, and although slaves still existed, slavery might be said to be abolished.

From the time at which a Northern State prohibited the importation of slaves, no slaves were brought from the South to be sold in its markets. On the other hand, as the sale of slaves was forbidden in that State, an owner was no longer able to get rid of his slave (who thus became a burdensome possession) otherwise than by transporting him to the South. But when a Northern State declared that the son of the slave should be born free, the slave lost a large portion of his market value, since his posterity was no longer included in the bargain, and the owner had then a strong interest in transporting him to the South. Thus the same law prevents the slaves of the South from coming to the Northern States, and drives those of the North to the South.

The want of free hands is felt in a State in proportion as the number of slaves decreases. But in proportion as labor is performed by free hands, slave labor becomes less productive; and the slave is then a useless or onerous possession, whom it is important to export to those Southern States where the same competition is not to be feared. Thus the abolition of slavery does not set the slave free, but it merely transfers him from one master to another, and from the North to the South.

The emancipated negroes, and those born after the abolition of slavery, do not, indeed, migrate from the North to the South; but their situation with regard to the Europeans is not unlike that of the aborigines of America; they remain half civilized, and deprived of their rights in the midst of a

没有给奴隶自由。我举一个纽约州的例子来证明我所说的话。1788年，纽约州禁止在其境内进行奴隶买卖，这是禁止奴隶输入的一种间接手段。从那时起，黑人的数量只是按照人口自然增长的比例增长。但是，8年之后纽约采取了更为果断的措施，根据这项法令的规定，1799年4月以后出生的黑人奴隶的子女，一律获得自由。自此以后，黑人奴隶的数量将不会再增加，尽管奴隶还依旧存在，但是奴隶制可以说已经被废除。

从北方的一个州禁止奴隶输入之时起，便没有奴隶再被从南方贩卖到北方。另外，因为北方的州禁止奴隶买卖，奴隶主无法再将他的奴隶处理掉（因而已经成为一种负担），除非将他们贩卖到南方。但是，当北方的州宣布奴隶的孩子生来就获得自由的时候，奴隶的市场价值就大大下降，因为他们的孩子不能再进行买卖，但如果把奴隶贩往南方，奴隶主还能获得丰厚的利润。所以，同一条法律，在阻止南方的奴隶来到北方的同时，却将北方的奴隶驱赶到南方。

随着奴隶数量的减少，自由劳动力的需求不断上升。但是，随着自由工人的出现，奴隶的生产效率变得越来越低，并成为无用的繁重的负担。但是，将奴隶输送到南方就无须担心这样的竞争。因此，奴隶制的废除并没有让奴隶获得自由，只不过是从一个主人转给另一个主人，从北方转到南方。

获得解放的黑人以及那些奴隶制废除后出生的黑人，虽然没有从北方迁到南方，但是他们在欧洲人中的地位与土著印第安人并没有什么不同。在财富和知识远在他们之上的人群中，他们依旧处于半开化状态，依旧毫无权利可言，他们遭受法律的暴政和人们的排

population which is far superior to them in wealth and in knowledge; where they are exposed to the tyranny of the laws and the intolerance of the people. On some accounts they are still more to be pitied than the Indians, since they are haunted by the reminiscence of slavery, and they cannot claim possession of a single portion of the soil: many of them perish miserably, and the rest congregate in the great towns, where they perform the meanest offices, and lead a wretched and precarious existence.

But even if the number of negroes continued to increase as rapidly as when they were still in a state of slavery, as the number of whites augments with twofold rapidity since the abolition of slavery, the blacks would soon be, as it were, lost in the midst of a strange population.

A district which is cultivated by slaves is in general more scantily peopled than a district cultivated by free labor: moreover, America is still a new country, and a State is therefore not half peopled at the time when it abolishes slavery. No sooner is an end put to slavery than the want of free labor is felt, and a crowd of enterprising adventurers immediately arrive from all parts of the country, who hasten to profit by the fresh resources which are then opened to industry. The soil is soon divided amongst them, and a family of white settlers takes possession of each tract of country. Besides which, European emigration is exclusively directed to the free States; for what would be the fate of a poor emigrant who crosses the Atlantic in search of ease and happiness if he were to land in a country where labor is stigmatized as degrading?

Thus the white population grows by its natural increase, and at the same time by the immense influx of emigrants; whilst the black population receives no emigrants, and is upon its decline. The proportion which existed between the two races is soon inverted. The negroes constitute a scanty remnant, a poor tribe of vagrants, which is lost in the midst of an immense people in full possession of the land; and the presence of the blacks is only marked by the injustice and the hardships of which they are the unhappy victims.

In several of the Western States the negro race never made its appearance, and in all the Northern States it is rapidly declining. Thus the great question of its future condition is confined within a

挤。在某些方面，他们比印第安人还可怜，因为他们无法忘怀曾经受到的奴役，而且他们也没有一点属于自己的土地。他们中的很多人悲惨地死去，而余下的人则挤在大城市里，做着最卑微的工作，过着朝不保夕的悲惨生活。

然而，尽管黑人的数量仍然按照奴隶制时的速度增长，但是自从奴隶制废除以来，白人的增速则是原来的两倍。因此，不久之后，黑人将置身于白人的包围之中。

一般来说，靠奴隶耕作的地方，人口比靠自由工人进行耕种的地方要稀少。此外，美国依旧是一个新兴国家，因此一个州在废除奴隶制的时候，尚有一半的土地无人居住。所以一个州在取消奴隶制之后，马上便感到自由工人的匮乏，于是一些胆大的冒险者立即从全国各地蜂拥而至，想要从刚刚对工业开放的新资源中谋取利益。土地不久之后就被他们瓜分一空，白人家庭占据了这里的每块土地。此外，欧洲的移民直接来到废奴州。穿越大西洋到新大陆追求幸福和安逸的贫苦移民，如果他们来到视劳动为低贱的地方，命运将会如何呢？

因此，白人的人口在自然增长的同时随着大量移民的涌入迅速攀升，而黑人的人口由于没有移民的补充呈现下降的趋势。这两个人种间的比例开始发生逆转。剩下的为数不多的黑人，成为贫困的流浪汉部落，消失在人口众多拥有所有土地的白人中间。黑人的存在只不过是不幸的牺牲者遭受的不公和苦难的标志。

在西部的一些州，至今没有黑人出现，而在所有的北方各州黑人的数量正迅速下降。因此，黑人未来的重大问题被限定在一个狭小的圈子。尽管解决起来并不容易，但也并不

narrow circle, where it becomes less formidable, though not more easy of solution.

The more we descend towards the South, the more difficult does it become to abolish slavery with advantage: and this arises from several physical causes which it is important to point out.

The first of these causes is the climate; it is well known that in proportion as Europeans approach the tropics they suffer more from labor. Many of the Americans even assert that within a certain latitude the exertions which a negro can make without danger are fatal to them; but I do not think that this opinion, which is so favorable to the indolence of the inhabitants of southern regions, is confirmed by experience. The southern parts of the Union are not hotter than the South of Italy and of Spain; and it may be asked why the European cannot work as well there as in the two latter countries. If slavery has been abolished in Italy and in Spain without causing the destruction of the masters, why should not the same thing take place in the Union? I cannot believe that nature has prohibited the Europeans in Georgia and the Floridas, under pain of death, from raising the means of subsistence from the soil, but their labor would unquestionably be more irksome and less productive to them than to the inhabitants of New England. As the free workman thus loses a portion of his superiority over the slave in the Southern States, there are fewer inducements to abolish slavery.

All the plants of Europe grow in the northern parts of the Union; the South has special productions of its own. It has been observed that slave labor is a very expensive method of cultivating corn. The farmer of corn land in a country where slavery is unknown habitually retains a small number of laborers in his service, and at seed-time and harvest he hires several additional hands, who only live at his cost for a short period. But the agriculturist in a slave State is obliged to keep a large number of slaves the whole year round, in order to sow his fields and to gather in his crops, although their services are only required for a few weeks; but slaves are unable to wait till they are hired, and to subsist by their own labor in the mean time like free laborers; in order to have their services they must be bought. Slavery, independently of its general disadvantages, is therefore still more inapplicable to countries in which corn is cultivated than to those which produce crops of a different kind. The cultivation of tobacco, of cotton, and especially of the sugar-cane, demands, on the other

十分可怕。

我们越往南走，废除奴隶制就变得越困难，之所以会出现这样的情况，是因为存在几个必须要说明的自然原因。

首先是气候原因。众所周知，欧洲人越是接近热带越感到劳动困难。许多美国人甚至断言在一定的纬度劳作会要了他们的命，然而黑人则可安然处之丝毫没有危险。但是我并不认为这个有利于南方人游手好闲的观点能够得到经验的证实。联邦的南方地区并不比意大利和西班牙的南方更热，而欧洲人为什么不能像在意大利和西班牙那样在这里工作呢？既然在意大利和西班牙奴隶制的废除并没有导致奴隶主的毁灭，为什么同样的事情不会在联邦出现呢？我不相信大自然会害怕欧洲人被累死而不让他们在佐治亚州和佛罗里达州耕田劳作，但是与新英格兰的居民相比，他们的劳动无疑会更艰苦，产量也更少。因此，随着自由工人在南方失去一部分对奴隶的优势，废除奴隶制的诱因更少了。

欧洲所有的作物都可以在联邦的北方生长，而南方则有其特殊的品种。人们注意到，用奴隶种植谷物的经营方式成本太高。在非奴隶制地区，种植谷物的农户一般长期雇用的工人数量并不多，而是在播种和收获季节额外雇用一些短工。而奴隶制地区的农场主，为了完成几个星期就能做完的播种收割的工作，却不得不养活一大帮的奴隶一整年。但是奴隶不能像自由工人那样能够靠自己的劳动养活自己的同时，等着别人雇用，所以为了能让他们为自己服务，只能将他们买下来。因此，除了奴隶制的一般缺陷外，与种植其他作物的地方相比，奴隶制更不适合谷物种植地区。此外，烟草、棉花，特别是甘蔗的种植需要

hand, unremitting attention: and women and children are employed in it, whose services are of but little use in the cultivation of wheat. Thus slavery is naturally more fitted to the countries from which these productions are derived. Tobacco, cotton, and the sugar-cane are exclusively grown in the South, and they form one of the principal sources of the wealth of those States. If slavery were abolished, the inhabitants of the South would be constrained to adopt one of two alternatives: they must either change their system of cultivation, and then they would come into competition with the more active and more experienced inhabitants of the North; or, if they continued to cultivate the same produce without slave labor, they would have to support the competition of the other States of the South, which might still retain their slaves. Thus, peculiar reasons for maintaining slavery exist in the South which do not operate in the North.

But there is yet another motive which is more cogent than all the others: the South might indeed, rigorously speaking, abolish slavery; but how should it rid its territory of the black population? Slaves and slavery are driven from the North by the same law, but this twofold result cannot be hoped for in the South.

The arguments which I have adduced to show that slavery is more natural and more advantageous in the South than in the North, sufficiently prove that the number of slaves must be far greater in the former districts. It was to the southern settlements that the first Africans were brought, and it is there that the greatest number of them have always been imported. As we advance towards the South, the prejudice which sanctions idleness increases in power. In the States nearest to the tropics there is not a single white laborer; the negroes are consequently much more numerous in the South than in the North. And, as I have already observed, this disproportion increases daily, since the negroes are transferred to one part of the Union as soon as slavery is abolished in the other. Thus the black population augments in the South, not only by its natural fecundity, but by the compulsory emigration of the negroes from the North; and the African race has causes of increase in the South very analogous to those which so powerfully accelerate the growth of the European race in the North.

In the State of Maine there is one negro in 300 inhabitants; in Massachusetts, one in 100; in New

持续的关注，女人和孩子们都能派上用场，但是在小麦种植上他们则没什么用武之地。所以，奴隶制自然更适合种植我所提到的那些作物的地区。烟草、棉花和甘蔗只能在南方生长，并成为南方诸州的主要财源之一。如果奴隶制被废除，南方的居民将不得不面临如下的抉择：不是改变原有的耕种模式，与更主动、更有经验的北方居民展开激烈的竞争，就是在没有奴隶帮助的情况下继续原有作物品种的耕种，不得不与仍然使用奴隶的其他南方州进行竞争。由此可见，南方存在北方所没有的保留奴隶制的特殊原因。

然而，还有一个比所有因素都更加强有力的动机，严格来说，南方本可以废除奴隶制，但是又该如何处置生活在这片土地上的奴隶呢？在北方，一条法律将奴隶和奴隶制同时驱除，可是在南方却无法指望能同时达到这两个目的。

我所述的奴隶制在南方比在北方更自然、更有利的观点足以证明奴隶的数量在南方一定非常多。输入第一批非洲人的正是南方，而奴隶输入量最大的也是南方。我们越往南行，崇尚悠闲自在的偏见就越强。在最接近热带地区的那些州里，没有一个白人劳力。结果，黑人的数量自然比北方多。而且，正如我已经说过的，这种不平衡还在日益加剧，因为北方的奴隶制一旦被废除，奴隶就向南方一带汇集。所以，南方黑人数量的增加不仅源于人口的自然繁殖，还源于北方黑人的被迫南迁。非洲人种在南方激增的原因与北方欧洲人种的迅速增长有着异曲同工之处。

在缅因州，每300个居民中只有1个黑人，在马萨诸塞州是100∶1，在纽约州是100∶2，在宾夕法尼亚州是100∶3，在马里兰州是100∶34，在弗吉尼亚州是100∶42，最

York, two in 100; in Pennsylvania, three in the same number; in Maryland, thirty-four; in Virginia, forty-two; and lastly, in South Carolina fifty-five per cent. Such was the proportion of the black population to the whites in the year 1830. But this proportion is perpetually changing, as it constantly decreases in the North and augments in the South.

It is evident that the most Southern States of the Union cannot abolish slavery without incurring very great dangers, which the North had no reason to apprehend when it emancipated its black population. We have already shown the system by which the Northern States secure the transition from slavery to freedom, by keeping the present generation in chains, and setting their descendants free; by this means the negroes are gradually introduced into society; and whilst the men who might abuse their freedom are kept in a state of servitude, those who are emancipated may learn the art of being free before they become their own masters. But it would be difficult to apply this method in the South. To declare that all the negroes born after a certain period shall be free, is to introduce the principle and the notion of liberty into the heart of slavery; the blacks whom the law thus maintains in a state of slavery from which their children are delivered, are astonished at so unequal a fate, and their astonishment is only the prelude to their impatience and irritation. Thenceforward slavery loses, in their eyes, that kind of moral power which it derived from time and habit; it is reduced to a mere palpable abuse of force. The Northern States had nothing to fear from the contrast, because in them the blacks were few in number, and the white population was very considerable. But if this faint dawn of freedom were to show two millions of men their true position, the oppressors would have reason to tremble. After having affranchised the children of their slaves the Europeans of the Southern States would very shortly be obliged to extend the same benefit to the whole black population.

In the North, as I have already remarked, a twofold migration ensues upon the abolition of slavery, or even precedes that event when circumstances have rendered it probable; the slaves quit the country to be transported southwards; and the whites of the Northern States, as well as the emigrants from Europe, hasten to fill up their place. But these two causes cannot operate in the same manner

后在南卡罗来纳州是100：55。这就是1830年白人人口和黑人人口的比例。而且这个比例随着北方黑人的减少和南方黑人的增加一直不断变化。

显然，联邦最靠南的各州在解决这些严重问题之前，无法废除奴隶制，而这些问题是北方在解放黑奴的时候无须考虑的问题。我们已经看到北方通过让现在一代的奴隶身份保持不变，而让其后代获得自由的办法，来确保奴隶制向自由的过渡。通过这种方式，黑人逐渐融入社会，同时有可能滥用自由的人依旧是奴隶之身，而那些已经获得解放的黑人会在自己当家做主前学会享用自由的技巧。但是这种方式在南方并不适用。宣布在某一特定时间之后出生的所有黑人为自由人即使将自由的原则和观念植入黑奴的内心，从而使那些根据法律规定依然身为黑奴的黑人在看到自己的孩子获得自由后，会惊叹命运如此的不公，而他们的惊叹又会成为焦躁和废奴的序曲。从此之后，在他们眼中，时间和习惯造就的那种奴隶制的道德力量将不复存在，而变身成为一种显而易见的暴力的滥用。北方的州就不用担心黑人的这种感觉对比，因为在北方黑人的数量很少，白人数量众多。但是，如果自由之光将照耀200万人，压迫者就有理由感到害怕。南方的欧洲人在给予黑奴的子女自由之后，很快就不得不将这样的好处带给全部黑色人种。

正如我所述，在北方，双重的移民确保奴隶制的废除，甚至是在奴隶制废除之前就已经开始。奴隶们离开北方被送往南方，而来自欧洲的白人移民在北方迅速取代了他们的位置。但是这两个因素无法同时出现在南方各州。一方面，奴隶的人数众多，以至于人们无法想象他们迁走以后会怎样；另一方面，北方的欧洲人和英裔美国人不愿前往劳动不受尊

in the Southern States. On the one hand, the mass of slaves is too great for any expectation of their ever being removed from the country to be entertained; and on the other hand, the Europeans and Anglo-Americans of the North are afraid to come to inhabit a country in which labor has not yet been reinstated in its rightful honors. Besides, they very justly look upon the States in which the proportion of the negroes equals or exceeds that of the whites, as exposed to very great dangers; and they refrain from turning their activity in that direction.

Thus the inhabitants of the South would not be able, like their Northern countrymen, to initiate the slaves gradually into a state of freedom by abolishing slavery; they have no means of perceptibly diminishing the black population, and they would remain unsupported to repress its excesses. So that in the course of a few years, a great people of free negroes would exist in the heart of a white nation of equal size.

The same abuses of power which still maintain slavery, would then become the source of the most alarming perils which the white population of the South might have to apprehend. At the present time the descendants of the Europeans are the sole owners of the land; the absolute masters of all labor; and the only persons who are possessed of wealth, knowledge, and arms. The black is destitute of all these advantages, but he subsists without them because he is a slave. If he were free, and obliged to provide for his own subsistence, would it be possible for him to remain without these things and to support life? Or would not the very instruments of the present superiority of the white, whilst slavery exists, expose him to a thousand dangers if it were abolished?

As long as the negro remains a slave, he may be kept in a condition not very far removed from that of the brutes; but, with his liberty, he cannot but acquire a degree of instruction which will enable him to appreciate his misfortunes, and to discern a remedy for them. Moreover, there exists a singular principle of relative justice which is very firmly implanted in the human heart. Men are much more forcibly struck by those inequalities which exist within the circle of the same class, than with those which may be remarked between different classes. It is more easy for them to admit slavery, than to allow several millions of citizens to exist under a load of eternal infamy and hereditary wretchedness.

重的地方定居。此外，他们有理由相信，在黑人数量等于或超过白人的州里，白人更容易受到威胁，因此他们不愿前往这一地区创业。

所以，南方的居民无法像北方的同胞那样通过让奴隶逐渐获得自由的方式废除奴隶制。显然他们没有办法缩减黑人人口，而且对黑人数量的持续增长无能为力。如此下去，几年之后，在一个白人国家中将存在与其数量同样庞大的自由黑人民族。

以滥用权力得以维持的奴隶制，是南方白人深感胆战心惊的严重的危险根源。目前，欧洲人的后裔是这片土地的唯一主人，是所有劳力的绝对主人，是唯一财富、知识和武力的拥有者。而所有这些优势黑人一无所有，但没有这些东西他们依然可以活下去，因为他们是奴隶。可如果他们是自由人，而且必须自食其力，没有这些东西他们还能维持生活吗？或者说，奴隶制存在时占有优势的白人采用的那些手段，会不会在奴隶制废除之后将他们置于重重危险之中呢？

只要黑人还是奴隶，他们的地位就和畜生没有多大的区别，但是，有了自由，他们就能获得一定程度的教育，就能意识到自己不幸，并找到根除这些不幸的方法。此外，还有一个相对公正的原则深植在人们心中。同一阶级中存在的不平等对人们的冲击远比不同阶级之间的不平等带来的冲击要大得多。跟让几百万公民身负永久的屈辱和世世代代的苦难生活下去相比，奴隶制似乎更容易为人们所接受。在北方，自由的黑人感受到了这些困难，并憎恨这样的屈辱，但是他们势单力薄，而在南方，他们则人多势众。

可以预见，只要将白人和获得解放的黑人安置在同一片土地，而且彼此之间视对方为

In the North the population of freed negroes feels these hardships and resents these indignities; but its numbers and its powers are small, whilst in the South it would be numerous and strong.

As soon as it is admitted that the whites and the emancipated blacks are placed upon the same territory in the situation of two alien communities, it will readily be understood that there are but two alternatives for the future; the negroes and the whites must either wholly part or wholly mingle. I have already expressed the conviction which I entertain as to the latter event. I do not imagine that the white and black races will ever live in any country upon an equal footing. But I believe the difficulty to be still greater in the United States than elsewhere. An isolated individual may surmount the prejudices of religion, of his country, or of his race, and if this individual is a king he may effect surprising changes in society; but a whole people cannot rise, as it were, above itself. A despot who should subject the Americans and their former slaves to the same yoke, might perhaps succeed in commingling their races; but as long as the American democracy remains at the head of affairs, no one will undertake so difficult a task; and it may be foreseen that the freer the white population of the United States becomes, the more isolated will it remain.

I have previously observed that the mixed race is the true bond of union between the Europeans and the Indians; just so the mulattoes are the true means of transition between the white and the negro; so that wherever mulattoes abound, the intermixture of the two races is not impossible. In some parts of America, the European and the negro races are so crossed by one another, that it is rare to meet with a man who is entirely black, or entirely white: when they are arrived at this point, the two races may really be said to be combined; or rather to have been absorbed in a third race, which is connected with both without being identical with either.

Of all the Europeans the English are those who have mixed least with the negroes. More mulattoes are to be seen in the South of the Union than in the North, but still they are infinitely more scarce than in any other European colony: mulattoes are by no means numerous in the United States; they have no force peculiar to themselves, and when quarrels originating in differences of color take place, they generally side with the whites; just as the lackeys of the great, in Europe, assume the

异类，他们的未来就只有两种：黑人和白人不是完全分离就是完全融合。在前面我已经表明过对后一种可能性的看法。我不能想象，白人和黑人有一天能平等地生活在一个国家。但是我相信这样的困难在美国比在其他地方要大得多。一个人也许可以跨越宗教、国家乃至种族的偏见，而如果这个人是国王，他可能给社会带来惊人的变化。但是，整个民族不可能超越自己。一个可以给美国人和他们原来的奴隶戴上同样枷锁的暴君，也许可以成功地让他们融为一体，但是只要美国人的民主是决定国家大事的主人，就没有任何人能够承担这样困难的任务，而且可以预见美国的白人越是自由，就会变得越是孤立。

前面我已经说过，混血人种是欧洲人和印第安人的真正纽带，混血儿也是白人和黑人之间的真正桥梁。只要是黑白混血儿多的地方，这两个种族的融合也并非不无可能。在美洲的一些地区，欧洲人和黑人相互交融，以至于几乎都找不到一个纯种的黑人或白人。当他们的融合到达这样一种程度的时候，可以说两个种族达到真正的融合，或者说形成了与原来的两个种族关系密切又完全不相同的第三个种族。

在所有的欧洲人中，英国人和黑人的联姻最少。在联邦南方，黑白混血儿比在北方更常见，但是，依然比欧洲人在美洲其他地方的殖民地要少得多。黑白混血儿在美国并不多，所以并没有什么力量，当有关肤色不同的争议出现的时候，他们往往站在白人的一边，就好像欧洲的大贵族的奴仆一般，以贵族自居，鄙视下层阶级。

英国人与生俱来的种族骄傲，又因为民主自由在美国人身上培育出的个人骄傲而得到进一步加强。在联邦的北方，美国的白人公民和黑人互不相融，但是为什么在南方他们

contemptuous airs of nobility to the lower orders.

The pride of origin, which is natural to the English, is singularly augmented by the personal pride which democratic liberty fosters amongst the Americans: the white citizen of the United States is proud of his race, and proud of himself. But if the whites and the negroes do not intermingle in the North of the Union, how should they mix in the South? Can it be supposed for an instant, that an American of the Southern States, placed, as he must forever be, between the white man with all his physical and moral superiority and the negro, will ever think of preferring the latter? The Americans of the Southern States have two powerful passions which will always keep them aloof; the first is the fear of being assimilated to the negroes, their former slaves; and the second the dread of sinking below the whites, their neighbors.

If I were called upon to predict what will probably occur at some future time, I should say, that the abolition of slavery in the South will, in the common course of things, increase the repugnance of the white population for the men of color. I found this opinion upon the analogous observation which I already had occasion to make in the North. I there remarked that the white inhabitants of the North avoid the negroes with increasing care, in proportion as the legal barriers of separation are removed by the legislature; and why should not the same result take place in the South? In the North, the whites are deterred from intermingling with the blacks by the fear of an imaginary danger; in the South, where the danger would be real, I cannot imagine that the fear would be less general.

If, on the one hand, it be admitted (and the fact is unquestionable) that the colored population perpetually accumulates in the extreme South, and that it increases more rapidly than that of the whites; and if, on the other hand, it be allowed that it is impossible to foresee a time at which the whites and the blacks will be so intermingled as to derive the same benefits from society; must it not be inferred that the blacks and the whites will, sooner or later, come to open strife in the Southern States of the Union? But if it be asked what the issue of the struggle is likely to be, it will readily be understood that we are here left to form a very vague surmise of the truth. The human mind may succeed in tracing a wide circle, as it were, which includes the course of future events; but within that

却可以呢？能否认为是这样一种情况，南方各州的美国白人处在身心均占据优势和黑人中间，所以想要和黑人结合？南方各州的美国人有两种强烈的情绪让他们保持孤立的状态。一是担心被黑人同化，与原来的黑奴平起平坐；二是害怕自己掉价儿，在白人邻居中抬不起头。

如果让我来预测未来可能会发生什么，我要说，奴隶制的废除在南方将同样会加深白人对有色人种的憎恨。这个观点是建立在我对北方所做的类似论断之上的。我说过，随着立法机构将种族隔离的法律壁垒废除，北方的白人居民会更加小心翼翼地避开黑人，然而为什么在南方也会产生同样的情况呢？在北方，白人之所以不与黑人融合是出于想象中的危险；在南方，危险是真实存在的，我不认为害怕的程度会下降。

如果，一方面已经看到（这一事实毋庸置疑）黑色人种不断向南方汇集，而且增加的速度远超白人；另一方面，黑人和白人相互交融同样能从社会得到好处的日子遥遥无期，难道就不能推断黑人和白人迟早要在联邦南方发生冲突吗？但是如果冲突，结果会怎样？不难理解我们所能做的只是做一个大概的推测。对于未来的进程，人类的头脑也许可以成功地画出一个大致的范围，但是在这个范围之内有上千种不同的可能和情况会直接将未来引入不同的轨道。在每一幅未来的蓝图中都有一个黑点，是智慧之眼无法看穿的东西。然而，似乎极有可能预见的是在西印度群岛白人注定要屈服，而在大陆上黑人注定要屈服。

在西印度群岛，白人种植园主的身边围绕着一大群的黑人；在大陆上，黑人处在大海和人口不计其数的民族之间。这个民族凌驾于他们之上，遍布从加拿大冰地到弗吉尼亚的

circle a thousand various chances and circumstances may direct it in as many different ways; and in every picture of the future there is a dim spot, which the eye of the understanding cannot penetrate. It appears, however, to be extremely probable that in the West Indian Islands the white race is destined to be subdued, and the black population to share the same fate upon the continent.

In the West India Islands the white planters are surrounded by an immense black population; on the continent, the blacks are placed between the ocean and an innumerable people, which already extends over them in a dense mass, from the icy confines of Canada to the frontiers of Virginia, and from the banks of the Missouri to the shores of the Atlantic. If the white citizens of North America remain united, it cannot be supposed that the negroes will escape the destruction with which they are menaced; they must be subdued by want or by the sword. But the black population which is accumulated along the coast of the Gulf of Mexico, has a chance of success if the American Union is dissolved when the struggle between the two races begins. If the federal tie were broken, the citizens of the South would be wrong to rely upon any lasting succor from their Northern countrymen. The latter are well aware that the danger can never reach them; and unless they are constrained to march to the assistance of the South by a positive obligation, it may be foreseen that the sympathy of color will be insufficient to stimulate their exertions.

Yet, at whatever period the strife may break out, the whites of the South, even if they are abandoned to their own resources, will enter the lists with an immense superiority of knowledge and of the means of warfare; but the blacks will have numerical strength and the energy of despair upon their side, and these are powerful resources to men who have taken up arms. The fate of the white population of the Southern States will, perhaps, be similar to that of the Moors in Spain. After having occupied the land for centuries, it will perhaps be forced to retire to the country whence its ancestors came, and to abandon to the negroes the possession of a territory, which Providence seems to have more peculiarly destined for them, since they can subsist and labor in it more easily that the whites.

The danger of a conflict between the white and the black inhabitants of the Southern States of the Union—a danger which, however remote it may be, is inevitable—perpetually haunts the imagination

边界，从密苏里河两岸到大西洋沿岸的广袤地区。如果北美的白人公民一直保持团结，可以肯定黑人将无法逃脱被毁灭的威胁，他们不是屈服于缺衣少穿就是洋枪大炮。但是，如果两个种族的冲突开始的时候，美联邦解散了，那么在墨西哥沿岸汇集起来的黑人则有机会幸免于难。如果联邦的纽带断裂，南方的白人公民就不能指望得到他们北方同胞的持续支援。北方的白人清楚地意识到危险永远不会降临到他们头上，然而如果他们出于义务前去支援南方，可以预见，种族的同情也不足以激发他们的斗志。

然而，无论这场冲突何时爆发，南方的白人，即使他们不得不独自战斗，依然可以凭借巨大的知识和武器的优势进入竞技场；黑人则依靠人数的优势和视死如归的精神进行战斗，而一旦黑人拿起武器，这些就会成为强大的战斗力。南方白人也会有着和西班牙摩尔人一样的命运。在占据这片土地数百年之后，他们也许被迫退回原处，将这片上帝注定留给黑人的土地还给他们，因为在这里他们能够比白人更轻松地生活劳作。

联邦南方各州的白人和黑人居民之间冲突的危险，尽管还很遥远但无法避免，会一直在美国人头脑中挥之不去。北方的居民尽管不会从这场斗争中受到直接伤害，但这会成为他们的日常谈资。他们努力想要找到一种可以避免他们所预见到的这一不幸的方法，却一无所获。在南方各州，人们对此避而不谈，种植园主从来不跟生人谈论未来，即使在亲朋好友之间也不会提及，他们把所有的话留在心里，但是南方的缄默不语比北方的高呼忧虑更为可怕。

这种普遍存在的忧虑促成一个鲜为人知的事业的诞生，这项事业可能会改变人类中一

of the Americans. The inhabitants of the North make it a common topic of conversation, although they have no direct injury to fear from the struggle; but they vainly endeavor to devise some means of obviating the misfortunes which they foresee. In the Southern States the subject is not discussed: the planter does not allude to the future in conversing with strangers; the citizen does not communicate his apprehensions to his friends; he seeks to conceal them from himself; but there is something more alarming in the tacit forebodings of the South, than in the clamorous fears of the Northern States.

This all-pervading disquietude has given birth to an undertaking which is but little known, but which may have the effect of changing the fate of a portion of the human race. From apprehension of the dangers which I have just been describing, a certain number of American citizens have formed a society for the purpose of exporting to the coast of Guinea, at their own expense, such free negroes as may be willing to escape from the oppression to which they are subject. In 1820, the society to which I allude formed a settlement in Africa, upon the seventh degree of north latitude, which bears the name of Liberia. The most recent intelligence informs us that 2,500 negroes are collected there; they have introduced the democratic institutions of America into the country of their forefathers; and Liberia has a representative system of government, negro jurymen, negro magistrates, and negro priests; churches have been built, newspapers established, and, by a singular change in the vicissitudes of the world, white men are prohibited from sojourning within the settlement.

This is indeed a strange caprice of fortune. Two hundred years have now elapsed since the inhabitants of Europe undertook to tear the negro from his family and his home, in order to transport him to the shores of North America; at the present day, the European settlers are engaged in sending back the descendants of those very negroes to the Continent from which they were originally taken; and the barbarous Africans have been brought into contact with civilization in the midst of bondage, and have become acquainted with free political institutions in slavery. Up to the present time Africa has been closed against the arts and sciences of the whites; but the inventions of Europe will perhaps penetrate into those regions, now that they are introduced by Africans themselves. The settlement of Liberia is founded upon a lofty and a most fruitful idea; but whatever may be its results with regard

部分人的命运。出于对我所描述的危险的恐惧，一些美国公民成立了一个协会，其目的是由该协会出资，将想要摆脱压迫的自由黑人送到几内亚海岸。1820年，我提到的这个协会在非洲北纬7°附近建立第一个定居点，取名为利比亚。据最新消息称，已有2500名黑人来到此处，他们将美国的民主制度带到他们祖先的土地。利比亚政府采用代议制，有黑人陪审员、黑人行政官和黑人牧师，并建立教堂，开办报社。在这里，唯一的不同就是白人不允许在此定居。

这的确是一场异想天开的运动。欧洲人强迫黑人背井离乡把他们运往北美沿岸贩卖，已经有200多年；如今，欧洲人又忙于将这些黑人的子孙运回他们原来被带走的地方。野蛮的黑人在被奴役的过程中接触到文明，并学会自由的政治制度。时至今日，非洲一直对白人的技术和科学采取闭关锁国的态度，而这些黑人自己带回的欧洲文明可能会在这里生根发芽。利比亚定居点建立在最美好崇高的理想之上，但是无论它会给非洲大陆带来怎样的变化，都无法成为新大陆的解药。

12年来，黑人移民协会已经将2500名黑人送回非洲，但在此期间，大约有70万黑人在美国出生。如果利比亚的殖民地每年能够接受数千名新居民，而且即使黑人能够在那里过上好日子，即使联邦每年都会给予该协会资金支持，将黑人装船运往非洲依旧无法抵消黑人人口的自然增长。而且，因为每年出生的黑人数量远大于送走的黑人数量，所以这无助于缓解在这个国家中黑人苦难的加剧。黑色人种永远不会从美洲大陆的海岸消失，而且只要新大陆存在，他们就不会从那里消失。美国的居民也许可以延缓他们所担心的灾难的发

to the Continent of Africa, it can afford no remedy to the New World.

In twelve years the Colonization Society has transported 2,500 negroes to Africa; in the same space of time about 700,000 blacks were born in the United States. If the colony of Liberia were so situated as to be able to receive thousands of new inhabitants every year, and if the negroes were in a state to be sent thither with advantage; if the Union were to supply the society with annual subsidies, and to transport the negroes to Africa in the vessels of the State, it would still be unable to counterpoise the natural increase of population amongst the blacks; and as it could not remove as many men in a year as are born upon its territory within the same space of time, it would fail in suspending the growth of the evil which is daily increasing in the States. The negro race will never leave those shores of the American continent, to which it was brought by the passions and the vices of Europeans; and it will not disappear from the New World as long as it continues to exist. The inhabitants of the United States may retard the calamities which they apprehend, but they cannot now destroy their efficient cause.

I am obliged to confess that I do not regard the abolition of slavery as a means of warding off the struggle of the two races in the United States. The negroes may long remain slaves without complaining; but if they are once raised to the level of free men, they will soon revolt at being deprived of all their civil rights; and as they cannot become the equals of the whites, they will speedily declare themselves as enemies. In the North everything contributed to facilitate the emancipation of the slaves; and slavery was abolished, without placing the free negroes in a position which could become formidable, since their number was too small for them ever to claim the exercise of their rights. But such is not the case in the South. The question of slavery was a question of commerce and manufacture for the slave-owners in the North; for those of the South, it is a question of life and death. God forbid that I should seek to justify the principle of negro slavery, as has been done by some American writers! But I only observe that all the countries which formerly adopted that execrable principle are not equally able to abandon it at the present time.

When I contemplate the condition of the South, I can only discover two alternatives which may be adopted by the white inhabitants of those States; viz., either to emancipate the negroes, and to intermingle with them; or, remaining isolated from them, to keep them in a state of slavery as long

生，但是无法摧毁灾难产生的根源。

我必须要说，我并不认为废除奴隶制是避免美国两个种族斗争的手段。黑人可以长期为奴而毫无怨言，但是他们一旦站起来成为自由人，用不了多久就会因为被剥夺所有的公民权而进行斗争，而当他们不能成为与白人平等的人时，便会立即成为白人的敌人。在北方，一切都有利于奴隶的解放，而且废除奴隶制并没有让黑人变得可怕，因为他们寡不敌众永远也不敢主张自己的权利。但是在南方，情况则不可同日而语。对北方的奴隶主而言，奴隶制的问题不过是一个商业和工业的问题；而对南方的奴隶主而言，则是事关生死存亡的问题。上帝不允许我像某些美国作者那样为奴役黑人的原则辩护。而我只是说，原先曾经采用这个可憎原则的地方，现在并不都能同样废除它。

当我观察南方诸州时，我发现那里的白人只有两条路可走：不是解放黑人并与他们融为一体，就是依旧孤立自身，并尽可能地让他们长期处于奴隶地位。所有折中的办法在我看来最后并很快就会导致可怕的内战，甚至两个种族中的一个会因此而毁灭。这就是南方美国人对这一问题的看法，而且他们也据此行事。只要他们决心不跟黑人融合，他们就不会解放黑人。

这并不是因为南方的居民将奴隶制视为种植园主发财致富必不可少的手段，而是因为在这一点上他们中的许多人和北方的同胞持相同的见解，承认奴隶制有悖于自己的利益，但是为了生活又不得不如此。现在，随着教育在南方的普及，居民认识到奴隶制对奴隶主

as possible. All intermediate measures seem to me likely to terminate, and that shortly, in the most horrible of civil wars, and perhaps in the extirpation of one or other of the two races. Such is the view which the Americans of the South take of the question, and they act consistently with it. As they are determined not to mingle with the negroes, they refuse to emancipate them.

Not that the inhabitants of the South regard slavery as necessary to the wealth of the planter, for on this point many of them agree with their Northern countrymen in freely admitting that slavery is prejudicial to their interest; but they are convinced that, however prejudicial it may be, they hold their lives upon no other tenure. The instruction which is now diffused in the South has convinced the inhabitants that slavery is injurious to the slave-owner, but it has also shown them, more clearly than before, that no means exist of getting rid of its bad consequences. Hence arises a singular contrast; the more the utility of slavery is contested, the more firmly is it established in the laws; and whilst the principle of servitude is gradually abolished in the North, that self-same principle gives rise to more and more rigorous consequences in the South.

The legislation of the Southern States with regard to slaves, presents at the present day such unparalleled atrocities as suffice to show how radically the laws of humanity have been perverted, and to betray the desperate position of the community in which that legislation has been promulgated. The Americans of this portion of the Union have not, indeed, augmented the hardships of slavery; they have, on the contrary, bettered the physical condition of the slaves. The only means by which the ancients maintained slavery were fetters and death; the Americans of the South of the Union have discovered more intellectual securities for the duration of their power. They have employed their despotism and their violence against the human mind. In antiquity, precautions were taken to prevent the slave from breaking his chains; at the present day measures are adopted to deprive him even of the desire of freedom. The ancients kept the bodies of their slaves in bondage, but they placed no restraint upon the mind and no check upon education; and they acted consistently with their established principle, since a natural termination of slavery then existed, and one day or other the slave might be set free, and become the equal of his master. But the Americans of the South, who do not admit that the negroes can ever be commingled with themselves, have forbidden them to be

没有好处，但同时他们也比以前更清楚地看到奴隶制的恶果没有办法可以消除。因此出现一种独特的对比，奴隶制越是受到质疑，法律就越是要加强它，而当奴隶制在北方被逐渐废除的时候，同样的原则却在南方产生越来越可怕的后果。

如今，南方诸州有关奴隶的立法呈现出史无前例的残酷，是对人类法律的极端歪曲，是对法制、对社会绝望群体的背叛。联邦这一地区的美国人并不是只加剧了奴隶制的残酷性，反过来，他们也改善了奴隶的物质条件。在古代，维护奴隶制的唯一手段就是枷锁和死亡，而南方的美国人则发现更加明智的方法来确保他们权利的持久。他们对人们的思想使用专制和暴力。在古代，奴隶主想方设法防止奴隶打破镣铐，今天，人们采取措施剥夺奴隶想要自由的愿望。古代的人给奴隶的身体戴上锁链，但并未限制他们思想的自由，也没有限制他们受教育，而且他们言行一致，因为那时奴役有结束的期限，奴隶迟早会获得自由，成为跟主人平起平坐的人。但是，南方的美国人从未想过黑人有一天会跟自己融为一体，他们禁止奴隶学习读书写字。他们不想把黑人提升到与自己相同的地位，所以尽可能地让他们保持原始状态。

一直以来，奴隶都希望自由能够改变他们悲惨的处境。但是南方的美国人已经充分意识到当获得自由的人无法与原来的主人平起平坐时，解放带来的就只有危险。让一个人获得自由，却无法让他摆脱贫困和屈辱，不过是为奴隶造反准备一个未来的领袖而已。此外，很早以前就有人指出，自由黑人的出现会在他不幸的同胞心中隐隐激起涟漪，并传达

taught to read or to write, under severe penalties; and as they will not raise them to their own level, they sink them as nearly as possible to that of the brutes.

The hope of liberty had always been allowed to the slave to cheer the hardships of his condition. But the Americans of the South are well aware that emancipation cannot but be dangerous, when the freed man can never be assimilated to his former master. To give a man his freedom, and to leave him in wretchedness and ignominy, is nothing less than to prepare a future chief for a revolt of the slaves. Moreover, it has long been remarked that the presence of a free negro vaguely agitates the minds of his less fortunate brethren, and conveys to them a dim notion of their rights. The Americans of the South have consequently taken measures to prevent slave-owners from emancipating their slaves in most cases; not indeed by a positive prohibition, but by subjecting that step to various forms which it is difficult to comply with. I happened to meet with an old man, in the South of the Union, who had lived in illicit intercourse with one of his negresses, and had had several children by her, who were born the slaves of their father. He had indeed frequently thought of bequeathing to them at least their liberty; but years had elapsed without his being able to surmount the legal obstacles to their emancipation, and in the mean while his old age was come, and he was about to die. He pictured to himself his sons dragged from market to market, and passing from the authority of a parent to the rod of the stranger, until these horrid anticipations worked his expiring imagination into frenzy. When I saw him he was a prey to all the anguish of despair, and he made me feel how awful is the retribution of nature upon those who have broken her laws.

These evils are unquestionably great; but they are the necessary and foreseen consequence of the very principle of modern slavery. When the Europeans chose their slaves from a race differing from their own, which many of them considered as inferior to the other races of mankind, and which they all repelled with horror from any notion of intimate connection, they must have believed that slavery would last forever; since there is no intermediate state which can be durable between the excessive inequality produced by servitude and the complete equality which originates in independence. The Europeans did imperfectly feel this truth, but without acknowledging it even to themselves. Whenever they have had to do with negroes, their conduct has either been dictated by their interest and their pride, or by

给他们一种模糊的权力观念。以至于南方的美国人在大多数情况下会采取措施阻止奴隶主解放他的奴隶。尽管不是明确禁止，而是运用各种方式使之无法有效。我曾在南方联邦碰到一个老头，他长期和一个女黑奴非法同居，并有了几个孩子，而这些孩子一出生就成了他们父亲的奴隶。他曾几次想要把自己的权利传给他们，至少让他们获得自由，但是几年过去了，依旧未能克服解放奴隶的法律障碍，而且在此期间，他逐渐老去，行将就木。他想象着他的孩子被从一个市场拖到另一个市场，从父母的关爱到陌生人的鞭挞，这些可怕的预感让老人本已衰退的想象力再度活跃起来。我看着被绝望痛苦折磨的他，感到大自然对那些违反她的法则的人们的惩罚是何等的残酷。

无疑这些灾难是可怕的，但却是可以预见的现代奴隶制原则的必然结果。当欧洲人从不同于他们自己的种族中掠夺奴隶的时候，许多人认为他们比其他人种低劣，害怕与他们有任何的瓜葛，并认定奴隶制必将永存，因为他们认为在奴役制造的极度不平等和源自独立的完全平等之间不可能存在持久的中间状态。欧洲人似乎觉得这是一个真理，但却并未令自己完全信服。所以当他们不得不和黑人打交道的时候，他们的行为不是受到利益和骄傲的驱使，就是受到同情心的左右。他们对待黑人，先是侵犯其所有人权，而后又告知其这些权利多么珍贵多么不可侵犯。他们向奴隶敞开他们的社会，但是当黑人想要进来的时候又会被他们喝退。他们一不小心不情不愿地承认自由取代奴役。他们既没有勇气丧尽天良，也没有勇气刚正不阿。

their compassion. They first violated every right of humanity by their treatment of the negro and they afterwards informed him that those rights were precious and inviolable. They affected to open their ranks to the slaves, but the negroes who attempted to penetrate into the community were driven back with scorn; and they have incautiously and involuntarily been led to admit of freedom instead of slavery, without having the courage to be wholly iniquitous, or wholly just.

If it be impossible to anticipate a period at which the Americans of the South will mingle their blood with that of the negroes, can they allow their slaves to become free without compromising their own security? And if they are obliged to keep that race in bondage in order to save their own families, may they not be excused for availing themselves of the means best adapted to that end? The events which are taking place in the Southern States of the Union appear to me to be at once the most horrible and the most natural results of slavery. When I see the order of nature overthrown, and when I hear the cry of humanity in its vain struggle against the laws, my indignation does not light upon the men of our own time who are the instruments of these outrages; but I reserve my execration for those who, after a thousand years of freedom, brought back slavery into the world once more.

Whatever may be the efforts of the Americans of the South to maintain slavery, they will not always succeed. Slavery, which is now confined to a single tract of the civilized earth, which is attacked by Christianity as unjust, and by political economy as prejudicial; and which is now contrasted with democratic liberties and the information of our age, cannot survive. By the choice of the master, or by the will of the slave, it will cease; and in either case great calamities may be expected to ensue. If liberty be refused to the negroes of the South, they will in the end seize it for themselves by force; if it be given, they will abuse it ere long.

What Are The Chances In Favor Of The Duration Of The American Union, And What Dangers Threaten It

Reason for which the preponderating force lies in the States rather than in the Union—The Union will only last as long as all the States choose to belong to it—Causes which tend to keep them united—Utility of the Union to resist foreign enemies, and to prevent the existence of foreigners in

　　既然无法预知美国南方白人何时能够跟黑人血脉相融，他们又怎会以自己的安危为代价换取奴隶的自由呢？而且既然他们可以为了挽救自己的种族而奴役另一个种族，那么他们现在为了达到这个目的而采用最有效的手段又有什么不可原谅的呢？在联邦南方各州发生的事情在我看来不过是奴隶制最可怕也是最自然的结果。当我看到自然的法则被颠覆，听到人类与自然法则徒劳对抗中的呼喊的时候，我不会将愤怒的矛头指向成为暴行工具的我们这个时代的人，而是去憎恨那些在一千年以后又再次将奴隶制带到这个世界的人。

　　无论南方的美国人做出何种努力来维护奴隶制，他们永远不会取得成功。曾经被基督教斥为不公，被政治经济学斥为有害，如今仅存在于文明世界的一个角落，与我们这个时代的民主自由和知识形成鲜明对比的奴隶制绝不可能幸存下去。它的终止是奴隶主的选择，是奴隶的意愿。无论是哪种情况，严重的灾祸都不可避免。如果拒绝赋予南方黑人自由，他们最终将通过暴力获得；如果赋予他们自由，他们又很快会滥用自由。

有利于美联邦长久存在的机遇，以及威胁其存在的危险

　　优势力量源于各州而不是联邦——只要各州选择归属联邦，联邦将会一直存在下去——促使各州继续联合下去的原因——联邦的存在不但能够抵御外敌，还能防止外敌入侵美国——美国各州之间没有天然屏障——不存在致使各州分裂的利益冲突——北方、南方和西部各州之间利益互惠——美国人联合的非物质利益纽带——舆论的一致性——联邦

America—No natural barriers between the several States—No conflicting interests to divide them—Reciprocal interests of the Northern, Southern, and Western States—Intellectual ties of union—Uniformity of opinions—Dangers of the Union resulting from the different characters and the passions of its citizens—Character of the citizens in the South and in the North—The rapid growth of the Union one of its greatest dangers—Progress of the population to the Northwest—Power gravitates in the same direction—Passions originating from sudden turns of fortune—Whether the existing Government of the Union tends to gain strength, or to lose it—Various signs of its decrease—Internal improvements—Waste lands—Indians—The Bank—The Tariff—General Jackson.

The maintenance of the existing institutions of the several States depends in some measure upon the maintenance of the Union itself. It is therefore important in the first instance to inquire into the probable fate of the Union. One point may indeed be assumed at once: if the present confederation were dissolved, it appears to me to be incontestable that the States of which it is now composed would not return to their original isolated condition, but that several unions would then be formed in the place of one. It is not my intention to inquire into the principles upon which these new unions would probably be established, but merely to show what the causes are which may effect the dismemberment of the existing confederation.

With this object I shall be obliged to retrace some of the steps which I have already taken, and to revert to topics which I have before discussed. I am aware that the reader may accuse me of repetition, but the importance of the matter which still remains to be treated is my excuse; I had rather say too much, than say too little to be thoroughly understood, and I prefer injuring the author to slighting the subject.

The legislators who formed the Constitution of 1789 endeavored to confer a distinct and preponderating authority upon the federal power. But they were confined by the conditions of the task which they had undertaken to perform. They were not appointed to constitute the government of a single people, but to regulate the association of several States; and, whatever their inclinations might be, they could not but divide the exercise of sovereignty in the end.

的危险来自各州公民的不同性格和爱好——南方和北方公民的性格——联邦的迅速扩张的最主要危险之一——人口向西北移动——势力被吸引到这一方向——形势的突然转变引发的热情——联邦目前的存在状态是会让政府变强大还是变软弱——政府内部的改革——荒地——印第安人——银行业——关税——杰克逊将军。

联邦各州现有制度的维护得益于联邦本身的存在。因此很有必要首先探讨一下联邦未来的命运。必须要肯定的一点是：如果目前的联邦解体，在我看来组成联邦的各州无疑不会再恢复原来的独立状态，届时会出现几个联邦来替代现在的一个联邦。我的目的并不是探究这些新联邦会建立在什么样的原则之上，而不过是想说明可能会导致现存联邦解体的原因。

为了达到这个目的，我必须再追溯一下已经走过的一些路，再探讨一下前面已经谈过的问题。我知道读者可能会说我啰唆，但是有待研究的问题的重要性是我不得不这样做的理由。我宁可多说，也不愿让读者难解其意，所以，我宁可自己挨批评也不要放过一个问题。

1789年宪法的制定者们努力赋予联邦政权一种独立且具有优势的权威。但是，他们受到所要解决的问题自身条件的限制。他们的任务不是组建单一国家的政府，而是让几个主权独立的州联合起来，而且无论其愿意与否，最终都要分享国家的主权。

为了能让读者理解分享国家主权产生的后果，有必要对国家事务加以简单区分。有一些事务究其本质而言具有全国性，也就是说，有关整个国家，只能委托给全权代表整个国

In order to understand the consequences of this division, it is necessary to make a short distinction between the affairs of the Government. There are some objects which are national by their very nature, that is to say, which affect the nation as a body, and can only be intrusted to the man or the assembly of men who most completely represent the entire nation. Amongst these may be reckoned war and diplomacy. There are other objects which are provincial by their very nature, that is to say, which only affect certain localities, and which can only be properly treated in that locality. Such, for instance, is the budget of a municipality. Lastly, there are certain objects of a mixed nature, which are national inasmuch as they affect all the citizens who compose the nation, and which are provincial inasmuch as it is not necessary that the nation itself should provide for them all. Such are the rights which regulate the civil and political condition of the citizens. No society can exist without civil and political rights. These rights therefore interest all the citizens alike; but it is not always necessary to the existence and the prosperity of the nation that these rights should be uniform, nor, consequently, that they should be regulated by the central authority.

There are, then, two distinct categories of objects which are submitted to the direction of the sovereign power; and these categories occur in all well-constituted communities, whatever the basis of the political constitution may otherwise be. Between these two extremes the objects which I have termed mixed may be considered to lie. As these objects are neither exclusively national nor entirely provincial, they may be obtained by a national or by a provincial government, according to the agreement of the contracting parties, without in any way impairing the contract of association.

The sovereign power is usually formed by the union of separate individuals, who compose a people; and individual powers or collective forces, each representing a very small portion of the sovereign authority, are the sole elements which are subjected to the general Government of their choice. In this case the general Government is more naturally called upon to regulate, not only those affairs which are of essential national importance, but those which are of a more local interest; and the local governments are reduced to that small share of sovereign authority which is indispensable to their prosperity.

But sometimes the sovereign authority is composed of preorganized political bodies, by virtue of

家的某个人或是某个集体。其中战争和外交事务就属于此类。还有一些其他事务本质上属于地方性质，也就是说只会影响到特定的地区，只能由地方政府进行妥善处理，例如地方预算的编制就属此类。最后，有一类具有混合性质的事务，既具有全国性质会影响到这个国家的所有公民，又具有地方性质不需要国家亲自出面处理。例如，调整公民民事和政治活动权利的问题。没有任何一个社会没有公民权利和政治权利。因此，这些权利关乎所有公民的利益，但又并不总是事关国家存亡兴衰而必须统一一致，因此没有必要由中央政府做出规定。

因此，有两类必要的事务，要服从国家主权的管辖。在所有组织健全的国家，无论其政治制度的基础如何，都会有这两大类事务。而在这两类事务之间，存在着我所说的混合性质事务。因为这些事务既不是完全国家性的也不是完全地方性的，而是根据达成协议的联邦的各个成员，在不破坏联邦约定的前提下，由全国或是地方政府处理。

一般来说，最高权力当局由几个人组成，进而成立国家。在最高权力当局设立的全国政府之下，只能由个体或集体的权力各自代表很小一部分主权。这样，全国政府自然而然不但要管理事关全国的事务，还要处理那些涉及地方利益的事务即具有混合性质的事务，而地方政府只拥有一小部分与自身繁荣密不可分的主权。

但是，有时候由于联合之前的既成事实，主权会由几个早已存在的政治团体组成。在这种情形下，地方政府不仅要管理地方专属事务，还要管理全部或部分有待明确规定的具有混合性质的事务。因为在联邦成立之前各自拥有独立主权的联邦只会同意让出一部分联

circumstances anterior to their union; and in this case the provincial governments assume the control, not only of those affairs which more peculiarly belong to their province, but of all, or of a part of the mixed affairs to which allusion has been made. For the confederate nations which were independent sovereign States before their union, and which still represent a very considerable share of the sovereign power, have only consented to cede to the general Government the exercise of those rights which are indispensable to the Union.

When the national Government, independently of the prerogatives inherent in its nature, is invested with the right of regulating the affairs which relate partly to the general and partly to the local interests, it possesses a preponderating influence. Not only are its own rights extensive, but all the rights which it does not possess exist by its sufferance, and it may be apprehended that the provincial governments may be deprived of their natural and necessary prerogatives by its influence.

When, on the other hand, the provincial governments are invested with the power of regulating those same affairs of mixed interest, an opposite tendency prevails in society. The preponderating force resides in the province, not in the nation; and it may be apprehended that the national Government may in the end be stripped of the privileges which are necessary to its existence.

Independent nations have therefore a natural tendency to centralization, and confederations to dismemberment.

It now only remains for us to apply these general principles to the American Union. The several States were necessarily possessed of the right of regulating all exclusively provincial affairs. Moreover these same States retained the rights of determining the civil and political competency of the citizens, or regulating the reciprocal relations of the members of the community, and of dispensing justice; rights which are of a general nature, but which do not necessarily appertain to the national Government. We have shown that the Government of the Union is invested with the power of acting in the name of the whole nation in those cases in which the nation has to appear as a single and undivided power; as, for instance, in foreign relations, and in offering a common resistance to a common enemy; in short, in conducting those affairs which I have styled exclusively national.

合不可或缺的权力给统一政府。

当全国政府，除本身性质所固有的特权之外，被赋予权力管理部分涉及总体部分涉及地方利益的事务时，便会具有优势权力。这样，它的权力不但得到扩充，而且所有它不具备的权力也会受其影响。这就是说地方政府可能会被剥夺其固有的必要的特权。

反之，当地方政府被赋予处理混合型事务的权力时，社会上就会出现截然相反的趋势。优势权力就会归属地方而不是国家。这样，全国政府最终有可能会失去其存在所必需的那些特权。

因此，各自独立的国家具有集中的自然趋势，而联邦国家则具有分裂的自然趋势。

现在，我们要做的是将这些通用的原则应用到美联邦上。联邦的各州拥有管理纯属地方事务的权力。此外，各州还保有决定公民民事行为能力和政治行为能力的权力，调整公民间关系的权力，以及对公民进行审判的权力。这些权利具有全国性质，但是也没有必要非归属全国政府。我们已经说过，联邦政府在国家必须以单一独立权力出现的情况下，有权以整个国家的名义发号施令。例如，对外关系和共同抵抗国家的共同敌人。简而言之，就是管理我所说的全国性事务。

这种主权的分享，乍看起来联邦分享的主权比各州的要大得多，但是深入研究后就会发现联邦分享的主权更少。联邦政府的承担的工作虽然非常重大，但是影响更不易为人们所察觉。而地方政府的工作虽然相对比较少，但却没完没了，不断提醒人们它们的存在。联邦政府关注的是国家的共同利益，但是一个国家的共同利益对于个人幸福的影响无法确

In this division of the rights of sovereignty, the share of the Union seems at first sight to be more considerable than that of the States; but a more attentive investigation shows it to be less so. The undertakings of the Government of the Union are more vast, but their influence is more rarely felt. Those of the provincial governments are comparatively small, but they are incessant, and they serve to keep alive the authority which they represent. The Government of the Union watches the general interests of the country; but the general interests of a people have a very questionable influence upon individual happiness, whilst provincial interests produce a most immediate effect upon the welfare of the inhabitants. The Union secures the independence and the greatness of the nation, which do not immediately affect private citizens; but the several States maintain the liberty, regulate the rights, protect the fortune, and secure the life and the whole future prosperity of every citizen.

The Federal Government is very far removed from its subjects, whilst the provincial governments are within the reach of them all, and are ready to attend to the smallest appeal. The central Government has upon its side the passions of a few superior men who aspire to conduct it; but upon the side of the provincial governments are the interests of all those second-rate individuals who can only hope to obtain power within their own State, and who nevertheless exercise the largest share of authority over the people because they are placed nearest to its level. The Americans have therefore much more to hope and to fear from the States than from the Union; and, in conformity with the natural tendency of the human mind, they are more likely to attach themselves to the former than to the latter. In this respect their habits and feelings harmonize with their interests.

When a compact nation divides its sovereignty, and adopts a confederate form of government, the traditions, the customs, and the manners of the people are for a long time at variance with their legislation; and the former tend to give a degree of influence to the central government which the latter forbids. When a number of confederate states unite to form a single nation, the same causes operate in an opposite direction. I have no doubt that if France were to become a confederate republic like that of the United States, the government would at first display more energy than that of the Union; and if the Union were to alter its constitution to a monarchy like that of France, I think

定；然而地方利益对居民的福利会产生最直接的影响。联邦政府确保国家的独立和强大，并不对公民个人产生直接影响，但是各州负责维护公民的自由、规范他们的权利、保护他们的财产和生命安全，并保障每个国民的未来幸福。

联邦政府远在天边，地方政府则近在眼前，而且人民会随时响应它最微不足道的号召。中央政府拥有的是几个希望领导它的杰出人物的热情，但在地方政府的身边则是一些二流人物的关注，他们只希望在本州掌权，而且因为最接近人民，所以能对人民施以最大程度的影响。因此，美国人对州的期待与恐惧要比对联邦更甚，而且从人心的自然趋势来说，美国人也更倾向于前者而不是后者。从这方面来看，美国人的习惯和情感与他们的利益完全一致。

当一个团结的国家将主权分割，并采用联邦制时，传统、风俗和人民的行事方式将会与立法长期对立，并往往会对中央政府施以法律所不允许的影响。当联邦的州联合起来形成一个单一的国家时，同样的因素会产生相反的作用。我丝毫不怀疑，如果法国成为一个像美国一样的联邦共和国，政府一定会比联邦政府更具活力；而如果联邦将政体改变成与法国一样的君主政体，我认为美国政府会需要很长一段时间才能像现在的法国政府一样强有力。在英裔美国人国家建立之初，他们的地方政府早已建立起来，乡镇和所在州公民个人之间的关系也已建立，人们已经习惯于用共同的观点去思考问题，并好像有关切身利益一样处理其他事务。

联邦是一个庞大的团体，只是给爱国主义提供一个不甚明确的对象。而州的形式和

that the American Government would be a long time in acquiring the force which now rules the latter nation. When the national existence of the Anglo-Americans began, their provincial existence was already of long standing; necessary relations were established between the townships and the individual citizens of the same States; and they were accustomed to consider some objects as common to them all, and to conduct other affairs as exclusively relating to their own special interests.

The Union is a vast body which presents no definite object to patriotic feeling. The forms and limits of the State are distinct and circumscribed; since it represents a certain number of objects which are familiar to the citizens and beloved by all. It is identified with the very soil, with the right of property and the domestic affections, with the recollections of the past, the labors of the present, and the hopes of the future. Patriotism, then, which is frequently a mere extension of individual egotism, is still directed to the State, and is not excited by the Union. Thus the tendency of the interests, the habits, and the feelings of the people is to centre political activity in the States, in preference to the Union.

It is easy to estimate the different forces of the two governments, by remarking the manner in which they fulfil their respective functions. Whenever the government of a State has occasion to address an individual or an assembly of individuals, its language is clear and imperative; and such is also the tone of the Federal Government in its intercourse with individuals, but no sooner has it anything to do with a State than it begins to parley, to explain its motives and to justify its conduct, to argue, to advise, and, in short, anything but to command. If doubts are raised as to the limits of the constitutional powers of each government, the provincial government prefers its claim with boldness, and takes prompt and energetic steps to support it. In the mean while the Government of the Union reasons; it appeals to the interests, to the good sense, to the glory of the nation; it temporizes, it negotiates, and does not consent to act until it is reduced to the last extremity. At first sight it might readily be imagined that it is the provincial government which is armed with the authority of the nation, and that Congress represents a single State.

The Federal Government is, therefore, notwithstanding the precautions of those who founded

范围则固定而明确，因为它代表的是被所有公民所熟悉和热爱的对象。它代表的是那片土地、财产的权利和家庭的热爱，以及对过去的记忆、现在的劳作和未来的希望。所以，爱国主义，往往不过是个人利己主义的外延，会指向州，而几乎不会涉及联邦。因此，人们的利益、习惯和情感趋向于将政治活动集中在州里，而不是联邦。

通过观察州和联邦各自履行职权的方式，不难发现两个政府力量的差别。每当州政府在与个人和一个群体讲话时，它的语言明确且具有强制性，而且联邦政府在与个人对话的时候语气也是如此，但是一旦开始与州打交道，就要开始采用谈判的口气，解释动机、证明行为得当、讨论商量，简而言之就是不能下命令。如果对任何一个政府的宪法规定的权力上限有所质疑，地方政府更敢于提出自己的主张，并立即采取有力行动维护自己的权利。与此同时，联邦政府则要晓之以理，并借助人民的良知、国家的利益和荣誉。它会伺机而动，与之谈判，不到迫不得已绝不采取行动。乍看起来，人们可能会认为州政府握有国家大权，而国会只是一个国家的代表。

因此，尽管联邦政府的缔造者们采取预防措施，但其依旧先天不足，特别需要被统治者的自愿支持来维系它的存在。不难察觉，联邦的目的是要让各州能够清楚地意识到他们继续联合的决心，只要这个初步条件具备，联邦政府就是有力、温和且有效的。这样的制度适合政府控制个人，并能轻易克服人们对公共决定的抵制，但是他们没有想到会有一个或几个州从联邦分离。

如果今天联邦的主权与各州分享的主权发生冲突，联邦的失败则是必然的，而且激烈

it, naturally so weak that it more peculiarly requires the free consent of the governed to enable it to subsist. It is easy to perceive that its object is to enable the States to realize with facility their determination of remaining united; and, as long as this preliminary condition exists, its authority is great, temperate, and effective. The Constitution fits the Government to control individuals, and easily to surmount such obstacles as they may be inclined to offer; but it was by no means established with a view to the possible separation of one or more of the States from the Union.

If the sovereignty of the Union were to engage in a struggle with that of the States at the present day, its defeat may be confidently predicted; and it is not probable that such a struggle would be seriously undertaken. As often as a steady resistance is offered to the Federal Government it will be found to yield. Experience has hitherto shown that whenever a State has demanded anything with perseverance and resolution, it has invariably succeeded; and that if a separate government has distinctly refused to act, it was left to do as it thought fit.

But even if the Government of the Union had any strength inherent in itself, the physical situation of the country would render the exercise of that strength very difficult. The United States cover an immense territory; they are separated from each other by great distances; and the population is disseminated over the surface of a country which is still half a wilderness. If the Union were to undertake to enforce the allegiance of the confederate States by military means, it would be in a position very analogous to that of England at the time of the War of Independence.

However strong a government may be, it cannot easily escape from the consequences of a principle which it has once admitted as the foundation of its constitution. The Union was formed by the voluntary agreement of the States; and, in uniting together, they have not forfeited their nationality, nor have they been reduced to the condition of one and the same people. If one of the States chose to withdraw its name from the contract, it would be difficult to disprove its right of doing so; and the Federal Government would have no means of maintaining its claims directly, either by force or by right. In order to enable the Federal Government easily to conquer the resistance which may be offered to it by any one of its subjects, it would be necessary that one or more of them should be specially interested

冲突的发生也并非不无可能。每当联邦政府遭遇持续的抵抗，便会做出让步。迄今为止的经验说明只要州有毅力有决心，要求必然能够达成，而如果一个州的政府确实想要拒绝服从，那也只好听之任之。

但是即使联邦政府本身拥有力量，国家的现实条件也难以让其力量得以发挥。美国疆土辽阔，各州相距甚远，人口分布在依然有一半是荒土的国土之上。如果联邦采用军事力量确保联邦各州的效忠，就意味着将陷入类似独立战争时期英国所处的境地。

无论一个政府如何强大，都无法轻易逃脱其曾经认可的作为其成立基础的一个原则的影响。联邦建立在资源的基础之上，而且在联合之时，并没有丧失各自的主权，也并没有形成一个单一的单民族的国家。如果其中的一个州选择将自己的名字从条约中取消，很难证明其无权这么做，而联邦政府无论是从力量还是权力上，都没有任何办法对其进行直接制止。为了能够让联邦政府可以轻而易举地战胜某个州的反抗，就要像世界联邦制度史上常见的那样，必须让一个或者更多的州的利益与联邦的存在息息相关。

如果假定联邦纽带联合起来的州中有一些能够享受到联合带来的巨大好处，或者其繁荣有赖于联邦的存在，毫无疑问它们会一直支持中央政府从而迫使其他的州服从。但是中央政府凭借的并不是自身的力量，而是源自一个与其本性相反的原则。各州之所以要结成联邦就是为了能够从联合中获取同等的利益，就像刚才所说的那种情况，联邦政府可以从各州利益分配的不平等中获得力量。

如果联邦的一个州取得大得足以取代中央政权的优势，必会将其他的州视为附庸，

in the existence of the Union, as has frequently been the case in the history of confederations.

If it be supposed that amongst the States which are united by the federal tie there are some which exclusively enjoy the principal advantages of union, or whose prosperity depends on the duration of that union, it is unquestionable that they will always be ready to support the central Government in enforcing the obedience of the others. But the Government would then be exerting a force not derived from itself, but from a principle contrary to its nature. States form confederations in order to derive equal advantages from their union; and in the case just alluded to, the Federal Government would derive its power from the unequal distribution of those benefits amongst the States.

If one of the confederate States have acquired a preponderance sufficiently great to enable it to take exclusive possession of the central authority, it will consider the other States as subject provinces, and it will cause its own supremacy to be respected under the borrowed name of the sovereignty of the Union. Great things may then be done in the name of the Federal Government, but in reality that Government will have ceased to exist. In both these cases, the power which acts in the name of the confederation becomes stronger the more it abandons the natural state and the acknowledged principles of confederations.

In America the existing Union is advantageous to all the States, but it is not indispensable to any one of them. Several of them might break the federal tie without compromising the welfare of the others, although their own prosperity would be lessened. As the existence and the happiness of none of the States are wholly dependent on the present Constitution, they would none of them be disposed to make great personal sacrifices to maintain it. On the other hand, there is no State which seems hitherto to have its ambition much interested in the maintenance of the existing Union. They certainly do not all exercise the same influence in the federal councils, but no one of them can hope to domineer over the rest, or to treat them as its inferiors or as its subjects.

It appears to me unquestionable that if any portion of the Union seriously desired to separate itself from the other States, they would not be able, nor indeed would they attempt, to prevent it; and that the present Union will only last as long as the States which compose it choose to continue members

并假借联邦主权的名义让自己的主权获得尊重。此时尽管许多大事依旧冠以联邦政府的名义，但实际上联邦政府已经名存实亡。在这两种情形中，以联邦名义行事的政权越强大，就越会置联邦的自然状态和公认的原则于不顾。

在美国，目前的联邦虽然对所有的州都有利，但也并非必不可少。一些州即使割断与联邦的纽带，也不会对其他州危害，尽管他们自身的繁荣会受到一定的影响。因为没有任何一个州的存在和福祉完全有赖于目前的联邦，所以也没有一个州会为了维护联邦而做出重大牺牲。另一方面，到目前为止似乎还没有一个州怀有控制现今联邦的野心。当然各州对联邦议会的影响不尽相同，但是没有任何一个州能对其他的州发号施令，或是将他们视为自己的下属或附庸。

因此，我可以肯定，如果联邦的某一部分真的想要脱离其他州，不仅无法阻止而且也没人想要阻止，而目前的联邦会一直存在下去，只要组成联邦的成员州选择继续联合下去。如果这一点得到认同，问题就变得不那么困难了，而我们的目的并不是研究目前联邦各州是否会分裂，而是他们是否会选择继续联合。

目前联邦能带给美国人好处的各种原因之中，有两个主要原因特别容易引起人们的注意。尽管美国人似乎独处在这片大陆，贸易让他们与所有与其有贸易往来的国家成为邻居。虽然他们表面上独处一隅，但依然需要保持一定程度的力量，而这样的力量只能通过联合才能获得。如果各州分裂，他们一致对外的力量就会削弱，而且不久就会招致外敌的入侵。分裂之后，届时还要建立一套内陆的关税制度，河流山谷会被视为领土的界限，并

of the confederation. If this point be admitted, the question becomes less difficult; and our object is, not to inquire whether the States of the existing Union are capable of separating, but whether they will choose to remain united.

Amongst the various reasons which tend to render the existing Union useful to the Americans, two principal causes are peculiarly evident to the observer. Although the Americans are, as it were, alone upon their continent, their commerce makes them the neighbors of all the nations with which they trade. Notwithstanding their apparent isolation, the Americans require a certain degree of strength, which they cannot retain otherwise than by remaining united to each other. If the States were to split, they would not only diminish the strength which they are now able to display towards foreign nations, but they would soon create foreign powers upon their own territory. A system of inland custom-houses would then be established; the valleys would be divided by imaginary boundary lines; the courses of the rivers would be confined by territorial distinctions; and a multitude of hindrances would prevent the Americans from exploring the whole of that vast continent which Providence has allotted to them for a dominion. At present they have no invasion to fear, and consequently no standing armies to maintain, no taxes to levy. If the Union were dissolved, all these burdensome measures might ere long be required. The Americans are then very powerfully interested in the maintenance of their Union. On the other hand, it is almost impossible to discover any sort of material interest which might at present tempt a portion of the Union to separate from the other States.

When we cast our eyes upon the map of the United States, we perceive the chain of the Alleghany Mountains, running from the northeast to the southwest, and crossing nearly one thousand miles of country; and we are led to imagine that the design of Providence was to raise between the valley of the Mississippi and the coast of the Atlantic Ocean one of those natural barriers which break the mutual intercourse of men, and form the necessary limits of different States. But the average height of the Alleghanies does not exceed 2,500 feet; their greatest elevation is not above 4,000 feet; their rounded summits, and the spacious valleys which they conceal within their passes, are of easy access from several sides. Besides which, the principal rivers which fall into the Atlantic Ocean—

会给美国人开发这片上帝赐予他们治理的广袤大陆带来无数的阻碍。现在，他们不必担心外来的入侵，所以不需要维持常备军，也没必要为此征税。如果联邦解散，所有这些会带来负担的措施不久便会必不可少。因此，联邦的维系对美国人有重大的利益。而且，目前并不存在任何物质利益会使联邦的某一部分想要脱离其他部分。

当我们将目光投向美国地图，会看到阿勒格尼山脉从东北贯穿西南，绵延近千英里国土，所以我们不禁想象上帝本想在密西西比河流域和大西洋沿岸之间设立一道天然屏障，阻隔人们的往来，并为不同国家划定界限。但是阿勒格尼山脉的平均高度不超过2500英尺，最高的海拔不过4000英尺，它们的圆形山顶以及山间空旷的谷地隐藏的路径，便于人们从四面八方汇集而来。汇入大西洋的几条大河，即赫德森河、萨斯奎哈纳河和波托马克河，都发源于阿勒格尼山脉与密西西比河山谷毗邻的高原。这些河流流淌过这一地区之后，穿过似乎要迫使它们流向西方的层峦叠嶂，在它们流经的山区给人们开辟出自然天成的道路。英裔美国人如今居住的各个地区之间并没有天然的屏障，阿勒格尼山脉远没有成为各州的阻隔，甚至都不曾成为州与州的界限。纽约州、宾夕法尼亚州和弗吉尼亚州将这条山脉围了起来，各自向西向东延伸出去。现在，联邦的24州以及虽有居民但尚未取得州资格的三大区所共同占据的国土面积为1002600平方英里，大约相当于法国领土的5倍。在这片领土上，拥有极为各异的土壤、不同的气候和多样的物产。英裔美国人的共和国覆盖的土地之广，都不禁使人怀疑他们的联邦能否维持下去。这里有一点需要说明，在这个广阔的帝国有时候的确会出现各州之间的利益冲突，甚至最后会导致彼此的冲突；于是，国

the Hudson, the Susquehanna, and the Potomac—take their rise beyond the Alleghanies, in an open district, which borders upon the valley of the Mississippi. These streams quit this tract of country, make their way through the barrier which would seem to turn them westward, and as they wind through the mountains they open an easy and natural passage to man. No natural barrier exists in the regions which are now inhabited by the Anglo-Americans; the Alleghanies are so far from serving as a boundary to separate nations, that they do not even serve as a frontier to the States. New York, Pennsylvania, and Virginia comprise them within their borders, and they extend as much to the west as to the east of the line. The territory now occupied by the twenty-four States of the Union, and the three great districts which have not yet acquired the rank of States, although they already contain inhabitants, covers a surface of 1,002,600 square miles, which is about equal to five times the extent of France. Within these limits the qualities of the soil, the temperature, and the produce of the country, are extremely various. The vast extent of territory occupied by the Anglo-American republics has given rise to doubts as to the maintenance of their Union. Here a distinction must be made; contrary interests sometimes arise in the different provinces of a vast empire, which often terminate in open dissensions; and the extent of the country is then most prejudicial to the power of the State. But if the inhabitants of these vast regions are not divided by contrary interests, the extent of the territory may be favorable to their prosperity; for the unity of the government promotes the interchange of the different productions of the soil, and increases their value by facilitating their consumption.

It is indeed easy to discover different interests in the different parts of the Union, but I am unacquainted with any which are hostile to each other. The Southern States are almost exclusively agricultural. The Northern States are more peculiarly commercial and manufacturing. The States of the West are at the same time agricultural and manufacturing. In the South the crops consist of tobacco, of rice, of cotton, and of sugar; in the North and the West, of wheat and maize. These are different sources of wealth; but union is the means by which these sources are opened to all, and rendered equally advantageous to the several districts.

The North, which ships the produce of the Anglo-Americans to all parts of the world, and brings

土的辽阔就可能对国家长治久安极为不利。但是如果这片广阔土地上的居民没有因为利益冲突而分裂，土地的辽阔就非常有利于国家的繁荣，因为统一的政府会有助于不同地区物产的交换，并通过促进流通来提高产品价值。

的确，很容易注意到在联邦的不同地区有各自不同的利益，但我并没有看到它们彼此间互有敌意。南方各州几乎清一色以农业为主，北方各州多工商业，而西部各州则兼有农业和制造业。在南方，作物主要有烟草、大米、棉花和蔗糖；在北方和西部主要是小麦和玉米。这些财源虽然不同，但是联邦却让这些财源能够向所有人开放并让不同地区具有同样的优势。

北方将英裔美国人的产品用船运往世界各地，并将全球的产品带回联邦，为了能够确保美国生产者和消费者保持在尽可能高的数量，显然北方希望联邦的现状能够维持下去。北方一方面是联邦南方和西部的最天然联络员，另一方面也是联邦与世界其他地方的中间人。因此，南方和西部的繁荣有利于北方，从而能够为其制造业提供源源不断的原材料，为其船舶运业带来货源。

南方和西部就其本身而言也能够从联邦的存在和北方的繁荣中获得更为直接的利益。一般来说，南方的产品通过海上出口，所以南方和西部自然需要北方的商业资源。它们都同样需要联邦能够拥有一支强大的舰队来有效地保护它们。南方和西部并没有船舶，但是它们也一定不会拒绝出钱支援海军建设，因为如果欧洲的舰队封锁南方口岸和密西西比河三角洲，那么卡罗来纳州的大米、弗吉尼亚州的烟草以及密西西比河谷的蔗糖和棉花要怎

back the produce of the globe to the Union, is evidently interested in maintaining the confederation in its present condition, in order that the number of American producers and consumers may remain as large as possible. The North is the most natural agent of communication between the South and the West of the Union on the one hand, and the rest of the world upon the other; the North is therefore interested in the union and prosperity of the South and the West, in order that they may continue to furnish raw materials for its manufactures, and cargoes for its shipping.

The South and the West, on their side, are still more directly interested in the preservation of the Union, and the prosperity of the North. The produce of the South is, for the most part, exported beyond seas; the South and the West consequently stand in need of the commercial resources of the North. They are likewise interested in the maintenance of a powerful fleet by the Union, to protect them efficaciously. The South and the West have no vessels, but they cannot refuse a willing subsidy to defray the expenses of the navy; for if the fleets of Europe were to blockade the ports of the South and the delta of the Mississippi, what would become of the rice of the Carolinas, the tobacco of Virginia, and the sugar and cotton which grow in the valley of the Mississippi? Every portion of the federal budget does therefore contribute to the maintenance of material interests which are common to all the confederate States.

Independently of this commercial utility, the South and the West of the Union derive great political advantages from their connection with the North. The South contains an enormous slave population; a population which is already alarming, and still more formidable for the future. The States of the West lie in the remotest parts of a single valley; and all the rivers which intersect their territory rise in the Rocky Mountains or in the Alleghanies, and fall into the Mississippi, which bears them onwards to the Gulf of Mexico. The Western States are consequently entirely cut off, by their position, from the traditions of Europe and the civilization of the Old World. The inhabitants of the South, then, are induced to support the Union in order to avail themselves of its protection against the blacks; and the inhabitants of the West in order not to be excluded from a free communication with the rest of the globe, and shut up in the wilds of central America. The North cannot but desire the maintenance of the Union, in order to remain, as it now is, the connecting link between that vast body and the other parts of the world.

么办呢？因此，联邦政府的每一部分预算都有利于维护各联邦州的共同物质利益。

除了商业上的作用外，联邦南方和西部还可以从与北方的联合中获得巨大的政治利益。南方奴隶人口庞大，已经产生威胁，而且未来的威胁会更加可怕。西部的各州位于一条大河的流域，流经这里的纵横交错的所有河流都发源于落基山脉或是阿勒格尼山脉，并汇入密西西比河，最终流入墨西哥湾。西部各州的地理位置将它们与传统欧洲和旧大陆的文明隔绝开。南方的居民之所以愿意支持联邦是要利用联邦政府保护自己免受黑人的威胁；而西部居民则是为了让自己不被排除在与其余世界的自由交流之外，不被封闭在美国的中部；北方之所以要维护联邦的存在，则是为了以联邦为纽带将这片广袤的土地与世界其他地方联系起来。

联邦所有各部分的现实利益紧密相连，而称之为非物质利益的人们的观念和情感方面也会出现共同的主张。

美国的居民总是谈到他们对祖国的热爱，但是恕我直言，我并不信赖这种建立在物质利益之上的爱国主义，一旦利益关系发生变化，爱国主义也会随之消失。而且对于美国人日常谈话中常常表示出的要将祖先采用联邦制度继续下去的意愿我也不以为意。一个政府要保持对大多数居民的统治，远不是出于大多数人的自愿和理性的认可，而更多是出于本能和一定程度上的被迫认同。这种认同往往来自情感的相似和观点的接近。我从不认为人们之所以能成为一个社会，仅仅是因为他们服从同一个领导和同样的法律。只有当大多数人对大多数事情持有相同的观点时，只有同样的事情会让他们产生同样的想法和印象时，

The temporal interests of all the several parts of the Union are, then, intimately connected; and the same assertion holds true respecting those opinions and sentiments which may be termed the immaterial interests of men.

The inhabitants of the United States talk a great deal of their attachment to their country; but I confess that I do not rely upon that calculating patriotism which is founded upon interest, and which a change in the interests at stake may obliterate. Nor do I attach much importance to the language of the Americans, when they manifest, in their daily conversations, the intention of maintaining the federal system adopted by their forefathers. A government retains its sway over a great number of citizens, far less by the voluntary and rational consent of the multitude, than by that instinctive, and to a certain extent involuntary agreement, which results from similarity of feelings and resemblances of opinion. I will never admit that men constitute a social body, simply because they obey the same head and the same laws. Society can only exist when a great number of men consider a great number of things in the same point of view; when they hold the same opinions upon many subjects, and when the same occurrences suggest the same thoughts and impressions to their minds.

The observer who examines the present condition of the United States upon this principle, will readily discover, that although the citizens are divided into twenty-four distinct sovereignties, they nevertheless constitute a single people; and he may perhaps be led to think that the state of the Anglo-American Union is more truly a state of society than that of certain nations of Europe which live under the same legislation and the same prince.

Although the Anglo-Americans have several religious sects, they all regard religion in the same manner. They are not always agreed upon the measures which are most conducive to good government, and they vary upon some of the forms of government which it is expedient to adopt; but they are unanimous upon the general principles which ought to rule human society. From Maine to the Floridas, and from the Missouri to the Atlantic Ocean, the people is held to be the legitimate source of all power. The same notions are entertained respecting liberty and equality, the liberty of the press, the right of association, the jury, and the responsibility of the agents of Government.

社会才能存在。

基于这一原则对美国现状进行考察的人,必然会发现美国的公民尽管分别居住在24个拥有主权的州,然而它们却形成一个单一的国家。他可能会据此认为英裔美国人联邦的社会状况,与欧洲一些只有一个立法机构并只服从一个人的特定国家的社会状况相比,更为合理。

尽管英裔美国人的教派不尽相同,但他们对所有的教派一视同仁。在何种方式最有利于政府管理的问题上他们的观点并不总是一致,并会时常改变方式来适应政府的工作,但是他们在治理人类社会的普遍原则上是一致的。从缅因州到佛罗里达州,从密苏里州到大西洋,人们都认为人民是所有权力的立法源泉。而且,在自由和平等、出版自由、结社权、陪审制度以及公务人员责任上,各州人民也都持有相同的看法。

如果我们从政治宗教的观点转向规范人们日常行为和指导其行动的道德和哲学思想,依然可以发现同样的一致性。英裔美国人承认公认的道理是道德权威,这就如同他们承认全体公民的政治权威一样。而且他们还认为,对于什么合法,什么被禁止,什么是真,什么是假,公共舆论才是最令人信服的仲裁者。大多数人都相信,一个人只要真正认清自己的利益,就会被引向公正和至善。他们认为人生来就具有自我管理的权利,而且任何人都无权强迫他人追求幸福。他们都相信人可以达到至善,并认定知识的传播必然会带来好的结果,而无知则是致命的。他们都把社会视为一个不断进步的有机体,人性作为不断变换的画面,在这里没有任何东西是或者应该是一成不变的,而且他们承认今天对他们有益的

If we turn from their political and religious opinions to the moral and philosophical principles which regulate the daily actions of life and govern their conduct, we shall still find the same uniformity. The Anglo-Americans acknowledge the absolute moral authority of the reason of the community, as they acknowledge the political authority of the mass of citizens; and they hold that public opinion is the surest arbiter of what is lawful or forbidden, true or false. The majority of them believe that a man will be led to do what is just and good by following his own interest rightly understood. They hold that every man is born in possession of the right of self-government, and that no one has the right of constraining his fellow-creatures to be happy. They have all a lively faith in the perfectibility of man; they are of opinion that the effects of the diffusion of knowledge must necessarily be advantageous, and the consequences of ignorance fatal; they all consider society as a body in a state of improvement, humanity as a changing scene, in which nothing is, or ought to be, permanent; and they admit that what appears to them to be good to-day may be superseded by something better-to-morrow. I do not give all these opinions as true, but I quote them as characteristic of the Americans.

The Anglo-Americans are not only united together by these common opinions, but they are separated from all other nations by a common feeling of pride. For the last fifty years no pains have been spared to convince the inhabitants of the United States that they constitute the only religious, enlightened, and free people. They perceive that, for the present, their own democratic institutions succeed, whilst those of other countries fail; hence they conceive an overweening opinion of their superiority, and they are not very remote from believing themselves to belong to a distinct race of mankind.

The dangers which threaten the American Union do not originate in the diversity of interests or of opinions, but in the various characters and passions of the Americans. The men who inhabit the vast territory of the United States are almost all the issue of a common stock; but the effects of the climate, and more especially of slavery, have gradually introduced very striking differences between the British settler of the Southern States and the British settler of the North. In Europe it is generally believed that slavery has rendered the interests of one part of the Union contrary to those of another part; but I by no means remarked this to be the case: slavery has not created interests in the South contrary to those of

东西也许明天就会被某种更好的东西取代。我并不是说他们所有的观点都正确，而是通过引用这些观点说明美国人的特性。

英裔美国人一方面在这些共同观念的作用下团结起来，另一方面他们又因共同的骄傲而让自己与其他民族隔离开来。过去的50年来，有人不遗余力地让美国居民相信他们是世界上信仰最虔诚、文明最开化和最自由的国家。他们认为，至今只有他们自己的民主制度获得成功，而其他国家均告失败。所以他们自视甚高，以至于他们差不多认为自己是人类的一个独特种族。

威胁着美联邦的危险并不是源自利益和观念的千差万别，而是存在于美国人各种各样的性格和激情。居住在美国广阔土地上的人们几乎都出自同一民族，但是气候，特别是奴隶制的影响渐渐使北方和南方的英国移民出现明显的性格差异。在欧洲，人们普遍认为奴隶制使得联邦一部分地区的利益与另一部分产生对立。而我并不这么认为，奴隶制并没有让南方和北方产生利益冲突，但的确改变了南方居民的性格和习惯。

我已经说过奴隶制对美国南方人商业能力的影响，而这样的影响同样波及民情。奴隶是永远不会反抗的奴仆，他们会毫无怨言地服从。他们也许有时候会刺杀主人，但从不公开反抗。在南方没有一个家庭穷得没有奴隶。联邦南方各州的公民从小就拥有一种家庭独裁的权力。他人生中获得的第一个观念就是他生来就要发号施令，而他养成的第一个习惯就是奴隶的无条件服从。因此，他的教育让他成为一个暴躁傲慢的人，他穷奢极欲，遇到障碍便不耐烦，一旦遭到失败就灰心丧气。

the North, but it has modified the character and changed the habits of the natives of the South.

I have already explained the influence which slavery has exercised upon the commercial ability of the Americans in the South; and this same influence equally extends to their manners. The slave is a servant who never remonstrates, and who submits to everything without complaint. He may sometimes assassinate, but he never withstands, his master. In the South there are no families so poor as not to have slaves. The citizen of the Southern States of the Union is invested with a sort of domestic dictatorship, from his earliest years; the first notion he acquires in life is that he is born to command, and the first habit which he contracts is that of being obeyed without resistance. His education tends, then, to give him the character of a supercilious and a hasty man; irascible, violent, and ardent in his desires, impatient of obstacles, but easily discouraged if he cannot succeed upon his first attempt.

The American of the Northern States is surrounded by no slaves in his childhood; he is even unattended by free servants, and is usually obliged to provide for his own wants. No sooner does he enter the world than the idea of necessity assails him on every side: he soon learns to know exactly the natural limit of his authority; he never expects to subdue those who withstand him, by force; and he knows that the surest means of obtaining the support of his fellow-creatures, is to win their favor. He therefore becomes patient, reflecting, tolerant, slow to act, and persevering in his designs.

In the Southern States the more immediate wants of life are always supplied; the inhabitants of those parts are not busied in the material cares of life, which are always provided for by others; and their imagination is diverted to more captivating and less definite objects. The American of the South is fond of grandeur, luxury, and renown, of gayety, of pleasure, and above all of idleness; nothing obliges him to exert himself in order to subsist; and as he has no necessary occupations, he gives way to indolence, and does not even attempt what would be useful.

But the equality of fortunes, and the absence of slavery in the North, plunge the inhabitants in those same cares of daily life which are disdained by the white population of the South. They are taught from infancy to combat want, and to place comfort above all the pleasures of the intellect or the heart. The imagination is extinguished by the trivial details of life, and the ideas become

北方的美国人从小身边就没有奴隶，甚至都不曾被雇用的奴仆服侍，通常都是自食其力。他一进入社会，匮乏的概念就从四面八方向他发起攻击。不久，他便知道了自己权利的天然界限，他从不曾想通过武力迫使反抗他的人屈服，而且他知道获得同胞支持最有效的办法是引得他们的喜爱。因此，他有耐心、心思缜密、对人宽容、行动从容不迫，而且一旦定出计划就坚持到底。

在南方各州，人们生活中的迫切需要总能得到满足，所以住在这里的居民并不需要为生计忙碌，因为会有其他人为他们劳作，因此他们的想象力被用在华而不实的活动上。南方的美国人喜好盛大奢华，沽名钓誉，寻欢作乐，尤其是悠闲自在。没有什么会让他们为生活操劳，而且因为他们无须工作，所以他们好逸恶劳，对有用的事情想都不想。

但是，在北方，机会的平等，以及奴隶制的不复存在，促使人们终日为那些南方白人所不齿的工作忙碌。他们从小就知道要为自己的需要努力奋斗，并将生活的舒适放在所有精神和心灵的享乐之上。他们的想象力被生活的琐事消磨，想法越来越少，越来越窄，但却更为实际和明确。因为发财致富是他们的唯一目标，所以人们全力以赴。大自然和人力被用来创造财富，社会被巧妙地利用为每个社会成员造福，同时个人的利己主义是普遍幸福的来源。

北方公民不但有经验，而且有知识。然而他们并不将学习知识视为乐趣，而是将其视为达成目的的手段，只希望它能够得到更丰富的应用。南方的公民行事易于冲动，而且更聪明，更坦白，更慷慨，更智慧也更有才华。前者更具活力，富于常识，消息灵通，普遍

less numerous and less general, but far more practical and more precise. As prosperity is the sole aim of exertion, it is excellently well attained; nature and mankind are turned to the best pecuniary advantage, and society is dexterously made to contribute to the welfare of each of its members, whilst individual egotism is the source of general happiness.

The citizen of the North has not only experience, but knowledge: nevertheless he sets but little value upon the pleasures of knowledge; he esteems it as the means of attaining a certain end, and he is only anxious to seize its more lucrative applications. The citizen of the South is more given to act upon impulse; he is more clever, more frank, more generous, more intellectual, and more brilliant. The former, with a greater degree of activity, of common-sense, of information, and of general aptitude, has the characteristic good and evil qualities of the middle classes. The latter has the tastes, the prejudices, the weaknesses, and the magnanimity of all aristocracies. If two men are united in society, who have the same interests, and to a certain extent the same opinions, but different characters, different acquirements, and a different style of civilization, it is probable that these men will not agree. The same remark is applicable to a society of nations. Slavery, then, does not attack the American Union directly in its interests, but indirectly in its manners.

The States which gave their assent to the federal contract in 1790 were thirteen in number; the Union now consists of thirty-four members. The population, which amounted to nearly 4,000,000 in 1790, had more than tripled in the space of forty years; and in 1830 it amounted to nearly 13,000,000. Changes of such magnitude cannot take place without some danger.

A society of nations, as well as a society of individuals, derives its principal chances of duration from the wisdom of its members, their individual weakness, and their limited number. The Americans who quit the coasts of the Atlantic Ocean to plunge into the western wilderness, are adventurers impatient of restraint, greedy of wealth, and frequently men expelled from the States in which they were born. When they arrive in the deserts they are unknown to each other, and they have neither traditions, family feeling, nor the force of example to check their excesses. The empire of the laws is feeble amongst them; that of morality is still more powerless. The settlers who are constantly peopling

很有才干，这些都是中产阶级的品质特征。后者的品位、偏见、弱点以及慷慨大方都是贵族的特点。如果为了让两个人联合，使他们的利益趋同，观点在一定程度上一致，但是因为性格的不同、知识的差异，以及文明程度的区别，有可能他们不会同意。这样的观点同样适用于国家和民族的联合。奴隶制并没有对美联邦的利益构成直接打击，但却间接伤害到民情。

1790年，有13个州在联邦公约上签字表示同意。现在联邦有34个成员。1790年时人口将近400万，40年来联邦人口已经增加了2倍多，到1830年时，人口总量已达近1300万。这样的巨大变化必然会伴随某种危险。

由不同国家组成的社会，与由个人组成的社会一样，长久存在的主要机遇来自其成员的智慧、成员个体的软弱和成员数量的有限。离开大西洋沿岸涌入西部荒野的美国人都是些冒险家，他们不堪忍受束缚，贪财，而且往往是被他们出生的州所驱逐。他们来到这片荒野，彼此互不相识，而且他们既没有传统也无家庭感，更没有先例供他们效仿。帝国的法律对他们而言虚弱不堪，道德也丝毫没有约束力。因此，不断迁来密西西比河谷生活的居民在各个方面都不及居住在联邦原来13个州的美国人。然而，他们却对西部的乡镇产生巨大的影响，并在学会自我管理之前就着手建立起管理公共事务的政府。

缔结条约加入联邦的个体成员越是弱小，联邦长治久安的可能性就越大，因为各成员州的安全完全仰仗他们的联邦。1790年的时候美国各州的人口最多的也不超过50万，那时每个州都觉得自己不够强大成为一个独立国家，这种想法让他们更容易服从联邦的权威。

the valley of the Mississippi are, then, in every respect very inferior to the Americans who inhabit the older parts of the Union. Nevertheless, they already exercise a great influence in its councils; and they arrive at the government of the commonwealth before they have learnt to govern themselves.

The greater the individual weakness of each of the contracting parties, the greater are the chances of the duration of the contract; for their safety is then dependent upon their union. When, in 1790, the most populous of the American republics did not contain 500,000 inhabitants, each of them felt its own insignificance as an independent people, and this feeling rendered compliance with the federal authority more easy. But when one of the confederate States reckons, like the State of New York, 2,000,000 of inhabitants, and covers an extent of territory equal in surface to a quarter of France, it feels its own strength; and although it may continue to support the Union as advantageous to its prosperity, it no longer regards that body as necessary to its existence, and as it continues to belong to the federal compact, it soon aims at preponderance in the federal assemblies. The probable unanimity of the States is diminished as their number increases. At present the interests of the different parts of the Union are not at variance; but who is able to foresee the multifarious changes of the future, in a country in which towns are founded from day to day, and States almost from year to year?

Since the first settlement of the British colonies, the number of inhabitants has about doubled every twenty-two years. I perceive no causes which are likely to check this progressive increase of the Anglo-American population for the next hundred years; and before that space of time has elapsed, I believe that the territories and dependencies of the United States will be covered by more than 100,000,000 of inhabitants, and divided into forty States. I admit that these 100,000,000 of men have no hostile interests. I suppose, on the contrary, that they are all equally interested in the maintenance of the Union; but I am still of opinion that where there are 100,000,000 of men, and forty distinct nations, unequally strong, the continuance of the Federal Government can only be a fortunate accident.

Whatever faith I may have in the perfectibility of man, until human nature is altered, and men wholly transformed, I shall refuse to believe in the duration of a government which is called upon to hold together forty different peoples, disseminated over a territory equal to one-half of Europe in

当联邦州中某个州，好像拥有200万人口面积相当于四分之一法国的纽约州，便会开始自恃强大，尽管它可能会为了自身的繁荣继续支持联邦但已不再觉得联邦必不可少。不久，它便开始想要在联邦中占据主导地位。随着联邦成员数量的增加，各州的一致性也在降低。今天，联邦不同地区的利益虽然差别不大，但是，对于一个每天都有新城市出现、每年都有新的州成立的国家，谁能够预见它未来的各种变化呢？

自从第一个英国殖民地的建立，居民的数量每22年大约翻一番。我注意到，在未来的100年中，没有任何因素有可能减缓英裔美国人人口的激增。而且我认为在未来不到100年的时间里，美国的国土或属地的人口将超过1亿，形成40多个州。我认为这1亿人不会有什么不同的利益，相反他们都能从联邦的存在中获得同等的好处，但是我也认为这1亿人划分而成的40多个不同的州不会同样的强大，所以联邦政府的存在不过是幸运的偶然。

无论我对人类的至善多有信心，但只要人不改变自己的性格，不做彻底的改变，我依然会拒绝承认，一个管理着面积相当于大半个欧洲由40个不同的州组成的政府能够长期存在。这个政府不但要避免州与州之间的对抗和斗争，防止他们的野心，还要指导他们各自的行动完成共同的事业。

但伴随着联邦日益扩大的最大危险是其内部势力的不断变化。从苏必利尔湖到墨西哥湾直线距离超过1200英里，美国长长的边疆沿这条线蜿蜒开来，有时候往回缩一点，但大多时候是向外延伸到荒野。根据计算，美国白人每年沿这条边界向外侧荒地挺进约17英里。他们时常会碰到诸如不毛之地、湖泊和突然出现的印第安人之类的障碍。这时，前进

extent; to avoid all rivalry, ambition, and struggles between them, and to direct their independent activity to the accomplishment of the same designs.

But the greatest peril to which the Union is exposed by its increase arises from the continual changes which take place in the position of its internal strength. The distance from Lake Superior to the Gulf of Mexico extends from the 47th to the 30th degree of latitude, a distance of more than 1,200 miles as the bird flies. The frontier of the United States winds along the whole of this immense line, sometimes falling within its limits, but more frequently extending far beyond it, into the waste. It has been calculated that the whites advance every year a mean distance of seventeen miles along the whole of his vast boundary. Obstacles, such as an unproductive district, a lake or an Indian nation unexpectedly encountered, are sometimes met with. The advancing column then halts for a while; its two extremities fall back upon themselves, and as soon as they are reunited they proceed onwards. This gradual and continuous progress of the European race towards the Rocky Mountains has the solemnity of a providential event; it is like a deluge of men rising unabatedly, and daily driven onwards by the hand of God.

Within this first line of conquering settlers towns are built, and vast States founded. In 1790 there were only a few thousand pioneers sprinkled along the valleys of the Mississippi; and at the present day these valleys contain as many inhabitants as were to be found in the whole Union in 1790. Their population amounts to nearly 4,000,000. The city of Washington was founded in 1800, in the very centre of the Union; but such are the changes which have taken place, that it now stands at one of the extremities; and the delegates of the most remote Western States are already obliged to perform a journey as long as that from Vienna to Paris.

All the States are borne onwards at the same time in the path of fortune, but of course they do not all increase and prosper in the same proportion. To the North of the Union the detached branches of the Alleghany chain, which extend as far as the Atlantic Ocean, form spacious roads and ports, which are constantly accessible to vessels of the greatest burden. But from the Potomac to the mouth of the Mississippi the coast is sandy and flat. In this part of the Union the mouths of almost all the rivers are obstructed; and the few harbors which exist amongst these lagoons afford much shallower water to

的队伍就要耽搁一会儿，等到落在后面的人马跟上后再继续前进。欧洲人逐渐持续地向落基山脉挺进好像出自神意一般，人们如潮水一般一波波涌来，在上帝的指引下不断前进。

在第一线征服者的身后，新的城镇建立起来，一个个的大州相继出现。1790年时，只有零星的几千名拓荒者散布在密西西比河河谷，现在，这里的居民已经接近1790年整个联邦的人口数量。人口总数接近400万。华盛顿市成立于1800年，当时几乎是联邦的正中心，但是随着不断变化的出现，现在几乎处于联邦的一极。而西部最远的几个州的议员不得不走过从维也纳到巴黎那么远的路程才能前来参加国会。

所有的州都同时走向富强，当然它们发展繁荣的速度并不相同。在联邦的北方，阿勒格尼山脉的分支延伸向大西洋，形成多条宽阔的道路和能够容纳巨大船舶的港口。但从波托马克到密西西比河河口，沿岸平坦多沙。在联邦的这一地区，几乎所有大河的河口都被泥沙阻塞，为数不多的沿着这条浅水岸分布的口岸浅得无法停靠船舶，与北方相比几乎没有一点商业优势。

除了自然条件的劣势外，还有另一个法制劣势。我们已经看到在北方已被废除的奴隶制，在南方依然存在，而且我也已经指出过为种植园主带来财富的奴隶制的致命后果。

因此，北方无论在商业还是制造业上都超过南方。因此，北方的人口和财富比南方增长得迅速也是自然而然的事情。位于大西洋沿岸的各州人口已达半饱和状态。大多数的土地已经有主，因此这里无法再像有着广阔待开发土地的西部那样接收那么多的移民。密西西比河谷的土地远比大西洋沿岸肥沃。这个原因，再加上所有其他的原因，促使欧洲人向

vessels, and much fewer commercial advantages than those of the North.

This first natural cause of inferiority is united to another cause proceeding from the laws. We have already seen that slavery, which is abolished in the North, still exists in the South; and I have pointed out its fatal consequences upon the prosperity of the planter himself.

The North is therefore superior to the South both in commerce and manufacture; the natural consequence of which is the more rapid increase of population and of wealth within its borders. The States situate upon the shores of the Atlantic Ocean are already half-peopled. Most of the land is held by an owner; and these districts cannot therefore receive so many emigrants as the Western States, where a boundless field is still open to their exertions. The valley of the Mississippi is far more fertile than the coast of the Atlantic Ocean. This reason, added to all the others, contributes to drive the Europeans westward—a fact which may be rigorously demonstrated by figures. It is found that the sum total of the population of all the United States has about tripled in the course of forty years. But in the recent States adjacent to the Mississippi, the population has increased thirty-one-fold, within the same space of time.

The relative position of the central federal power is continually displaced. Forty years ago the majority of the citizens of the Union was established upon the coast of the Atlantic, in the environs of the spot upon which Washington now stands; but the great body of the people is now advancing inland and to the north, so that in twenty years the majority will unquestionably be on the western side of the Alleghanies. If the Union goes on to subsist, the basin of the Mississippi is evidently marked out, by its fertility and its extent, as the future centre of the Federal Government. In thirty or forty years, that tract of country will have assumed the rank which naturally belongs to it. It is easy to calculate that its population, compared to that of the coast of the Atlantic, will be, in round numbers, as 40 to 11. In a few years the States which founded the Union will lose the direction of its policy, and the population of the valley of the Mississippi will preponderate in the federal assemblies.

This constant gravitation of the federal power and influence towards the northwest is shown every ten years, when a general census of the population is made, and the number of delegates which each State sends to Congress is settled afresh. In 1790 Virginia had nineteen representatives in Congress.

西部进发，这一事实有数据为证。在过去的40年，美国人口的总数增加了2倍多，而临近密西西比河流域的各州，在这40年来增长了30倍。

联邦权力中心的相对位置不断变换。40年前，联邦大多数公民居住在大西洋沿岸，即今天的华盛顿附近的地区，但是随着大批人口开往内陆并向北挺进，无疑20年后美国大部分人口将居住在阿勒格尼山脉西侧。如果联邦继续存在下去，密西西比盆地将凭借其富饶广阔异军突起，成为未来联邦的中心。三四十年之内，密西西比河地区将获得其应有的地位。不难算出，到那时这里的人口与大西洋沿岸人口之比将达到40∶11。再过几年，联邦成立之初的那些州将会失去对联邦的主导，密西西比河流域的人口将在联邦议会中占据优势。

联邦权力和影响力不断向西北转移的趋势每10年就会有所表现。因为在每10年进行一次的人口普查之后，每个州入选国会的议员数量都会更新。1790年，弗吉尼亚州在国会有19名代表，而且这个人数还在一直增长，直到1831年达到23人。自此之后，人数开始下降，1833年弗吉尼亚州的代表人数回落至21人。同期纽约州的代表数量则呈现相反的趋势。1790年时在国会有10名代表，1813年时达到27名，1823年为34名，1833年则为40名。而俄亥俄州1803年时只有1名代表，而1833年时已增加到19人。

无法想象，一个富强的州能够跟一个贫弱的州长期结成联邦，即使已经证明一个的富强并不是导致另一个贫弱的原因。但是当一方正在变弱而另一方不断变强的时候，联邦依旧难以维系。某些州快速且不合比例的发展威胁到其他州的独立。拥有200万人口和40名众议院的纽约州也许可以成功地在国会中压倒其他各州。但即使强大的州并不想压迫

This number continued to increase until the year 1813, when it reached to twenty-three; from that time it began to decrease, and in 1833 Virginia elected only twenty-one representatives. During the same period the State of New York progressed in the contrary direction: in 1790 it had ten representatives in Congress; in 1813, twenty-seven; in 1823, thirty-four; and in 1833, forty. The State of Ohio had only one representative in 1803, and in 1833 it had already nineteen.

It is difficult to imagine a durable union of a people which is rich and strong with one which is poor and weak, even if it were proved that the strength and wealth of the one are not the causes of the weakness and poverty of the other. But union is still more difficult to maintain at a time at which one party is losing strength, and the other is gaining it. This rapid and disproportionate increase of certain States threatens the independence of the others. New York might perhaps succeed, with its 2,000,000 of inhabitants and its forty representatives, in dictating to the other States in Congress. But even if the more powerful States make no attempt to bear down the lesser ones, the danger still exists; for there is almost as much in the possibility of the act as in the act itself. The weak generally mistrust the justice and the reason of the strong. The States which increase less rapidly than the others look upon those which are more favored by fortune with envy and suspicion. Hence arise the deep-seated uneasiness and ill-defined agitation which are observable in the South, and which form so striking a contrast to the confidence and prosperity which are common to other parts of the Union. I am inclined to think that the hostile measures taken by the Southern provinces upon a recent occasion are attributable to no other cause. The inhabitants of the Southern States are, of all the Americans, those who are most interested in the maintenance of the Union; they would assuredly suffer most from being left to themselves; and yet they are the only citizens who threaten to break the tie of confederation. But it is easy to perceive that the South, which has given four Presidents, Washington, Jefferson, Madison, and Monroe, to the Union, which perceives that it is losing its federal influence, and that the number of its representatives in Congress is diminishing from year to year, whilst those of the Northern and Western States are increasing; the South, which is peopled with ardent and irascible beings, is becoming more and more irritated and alarmed. The citizens reflect upon their

弱小的州，危险依然存在。因为压迫的可能性和现实性同样存在。弱者往往无法信任强者的正义和逻辑。所以那些发展得不够快速的州对那些幸运的州总是持嫉妒和怀疑的态度。因此，南方地区表现出的深深苦恼和难以名状的不安与联邦其他地区普遍呈现出的自信和欣欣向荣形成鲜明的对比。我认为，南方最近所采取的敌对态度原因就在于此。在所有美国人中，南方的居民最需要联邦的存在，一旦脱离联邦肯定损失也最大，而他们也是联邦存在的最大威胁。不难发现，南方曾出过华盛顿、杰斐逊、麦迪逊和门罗四位美国总统，然而如今他们已在联邦失势，国会中代表数量也是逐年减少，同时北方和西部的代表人数则不断增长。居住在南方的暴躁易怒的居民变得越来越不安，越来越惊恐。思索现在的处境，回顾过去的影响，南方的公民每天都在怀疑是否受到压迫。如果他们发现联邦的法律并不是明显有利于自己，便会抗议滥用职权。如果他们的激烈抗议未被采纳，则威胁退出联邦，声称联邦只让他们承担义务，而剥夺他们应得的利益。1832年卡罗来纳州的居民声称："关税富裕了北方，毁了南方。因为如果不是关税，是什么使得气候寒冷土地贫瘠的北方的财富和权势不断增加，而堪称美国花园的南方又何以迅速衰落呢？"

如果我所说的变化是渐进的，以至于每一代人至少无法目睹秩序的变化给他们带来的影响，危险可能就不会那么大，但是美国社会的发展突如其来，甚至是革命性的。一个公民一生之中既见证了本州曾经在联邦中的领先，又看到其随后在联邦议会中的失势。一个英裔美国人的共和国可以成长得非常迅速，从诞生到成年只用30年的时间。然而，不要认为已经失势的州，其人口和财富也会随之减少。它们的繁荣不会就此止步，甚至还会比任

present position and remember their past influence, with the melancholy uneasiness of men who suspect oppression: if they discover a law of the Union which is not unequivocally favorable to their interests, they protest against it as an abuse of force; and if their ardent remonstrances are not listened to, they threaten to quit an association which loads them with burdens whilst it deprives them of their due profits. "The tariff," said the inhabitants of Carolina in 1832, "enriches the North, and ruins the South; for if this were not the case, to what can we attribute the continually increasing power and wealth of the North, with its inclement skies and arid soil; whilst the South, which may be styled the garden of America, is rapidly declining?"

If the changes which I have described were gradual, so that each generation at least might have time to disappear with the order of things under which it had lived, the danger would be less; but the progress of society in America is precipitate, and almost revolutionary. The same citizen may have lived to see his State take the lead in the Union, and afterwards become powerless in the federal assemblies; and an Anglo-American republic has been known to grow as rapidly as a man passing from birth and infancy to maturity in the course of thirty years. It must not be imagined, however, that the States which lose their preponderance, also lose their population or their riches: no stop is put to their prosperity, and they even go on to increase more rapidly than any kingdom in Europe. But they believe themselves to be impoverished because their wealth does not augment as rapidly as that of their neighbors; any they think that their power is lost, because they suddenly come into collision with a power greater than their own: thus they are more hurt in their feelings and their passions than in their interests. But this is amply sufficient to endanger the maintenance of the Union. If kings and peoples had only had their true interests in view ever since the beginning of the world, the name of war would scarcely be known among mankind.

Thus the prosperity of the United States is the source of the most serious dangers that threaten them, since it tends to create in some of the confederate States that over-excitement which accompanies a rapid increase of fortune; and to awaken in others those feelings of envy, mistrust, and regret which usually attend upon the loss of it. The Americans contemplate this extraordinary

何欧洲王国的增长更为迅速。但是它们自己却认为自己穷了，因为它们的财富没有邻居增长得快，而且它们认为自己的力量变弱了，因为它们突然与一个比自己强大的力量发生碰撞。因此，它们在感性和热情上受到的伤害远比利益上要大得多。但这足以对联邦的存亡构成危险。如果自开天辟地以来，各国的国王和人民都能只关注他们的真正利益，人类将不会有战争。

因此，威胁美国的最可怕的危险正是其自身的繁荣，因为繁荣会让某些联邦州因财富的迅速增长而大喜过望，同时还会激起其他州的嫉妒、怀疑和失去财富的遗憾。美国人得意地注视着这种感觉奇特迅速的变化，但如果他们够聪明就会感到悲伤和恐惧。无疑，美国会成为世界上最强大的国家之一，他们的后代也将遍布整个北美，他们居住的土地也会由他们来统治而且不会从他们手中丢掉。是什么让他们如此迅速地占据了这里？财富、权力和名誉迟早都会属于他们，但他们却冲向他们的宝藏似乎晚一分钟就什么都没有了似的。

我认为我已经充分证明目前联邦的存在完全依赖于所有联邦州一直以来的认同，而从这一原则出发，我得到会诱导一些州脱离联邦的一些因素。但是，只有两种方式会导致联邦的毁灭：一是联邦州选择退出联盟公约，粗暴地打断联邦纽带，我前面所说的大部分适用于这种假设；二是联邦政府的权威会因加盟的各州同时要求恢复独立而不断受到侵犯。中央政府的特权被相继剥夺，只能默认无能，最终无法再实现自己的目标。而第二个联邦也会像第一个一样在无力中衰亡。联邦纽带的不断削弱最终会导致联邦的解体，而且在导致如此剧烈的变化之前还会制造各种各样的次要后果。即使其政府已经软弱无力使国家处

and hasty progress with exultation; but they would be wiser to consider it with sorrow and alarm. The Americans of the United States must inevitably become one of the greatest nations in the world; their offset will cover almost the whole of North America; the continent which they inhabit is their dominion, and it cannot escape them. What urges them to take possession of it so soon? Riches, power, and renown cannot fail to be theirs at some future time, but they rush upon their fortune as if but a moment remained for them to make it their own.

I think that I have demonstrated that the existence of the present confederation depends entirely on the continued assent of all the confederates; and, starting from this principle, I have inquired into the causes which may induce the several States to separate from the others. The Union may, however, perish in two different ways: one of the confederate States may choose to retire from the compact, and so forcibly to sever the federal tie; and it is to this supposition that most of the remarks that I have made apply: or the authority of the Federal Government may be progressively entrenched on by the simultaneous tendency of the united republics to resume their independence. The central power, successively stripped of all its prerogatives, and reduced to impotence by tacit consent, would become incompetent to fulfil its purpose; and the second Union would perish, like the first, by a sort of senile inaptitude. The gradual weakening of the federal tie, which may finally lead to the dissolution of the Union, is a distinct circumstance, that may produce a variety of minor consequences before it operates so violent a change. The confederation might still subsist, although its Government were reduced to such a degree of inanition as to paralyze the nation, to cause internal anarchy, and to check the general prosperity of the country.

After having investigated the causes which may induce the Anglo-Americans to disunite, it is important to inquire whether, if the Union continues to subsist, their Government will extend or contract its sphere of action, and whether it will become more energetic or more weak.

The Americans are evidently disposed to look upon their future condition with alarm. They perceive that in most of the nations of the world the exercise of the rights of sovereignty tends to fall under the control of a few individuals, and they are dismayed by the idea that such will also be

于瘫痪状态，造成无政府状态，并对国家的繁荣造成阻碍，联邦也许依然可以存在。

在对诱使英裔美国人分裂的原因进行分析之后，有必要探寻一下，如果联邦继续存在下去，其政府的活动半径是会扩大还是缩小，是会变得更强大还是更虚弱？

显然，美国人对他们的未来忧心忡忡。他们注意到，世界上大多数国家的主权往往控制在几个人手中由他们来行使，而他们很担心同样的事情会落到他们的国家，甚至政客们都有这样的恐惧感，至少是假装如此。因为在美国，中央集权不得民心时，抨击中央政府来取悦多数是最佳的办法。美国人没有注意到，存在中央集权危险倾向的国家的居民都是单一民族，而联邦则由不同的民族组成，这一点足以推翻由类比而做出的所有推测。我承认，在我看来许多美国人的这种恐惧纯属想象，而且我非但不认同他们所害怕的联邦主权的加强，反而认为联邦政府的力量显然正在减弱。

要证明我的这个论断，无须求助于古代的例子，只用我所目睹的我们这个时代的例子就可以。

仔细考察美国的现状，我们会很容易发现在这个国家有两种相反的趋势存在，就好像同一条河道流淌着方向相反的两股水流。如今联邦已经存在45年，在这段时间里，最初反对联邦的大多数地方偏见已经消失。美国人对本州的爱国主义情感已经变得不那么狭隘，联邦不同地区的联系越来越紧密，彼此越来越了解。邮政，人们彼此联系最伟大工具，如今已经深入到边远地区。轮船每天来往于各口岸之间，内陆的货物以空前的速度沿内河运往上游和下游。除了自然和人为的便利条件外，无尽的渴望、孜孜不倦的追求和对发财致富的

the case in their own country. Even the statesmen feel, or affect to feel, these fears; for, in America, centralization is by no means popular, and there is no surer means of courting the majority than by inveighing against the encroachments of the central power. The Americans do not perceive that the countries in which this alarming tendency to centralization exists are inhabited by a single people; whilst the fact of the Union being composed of different confederate communities is sufficient to baffle all the inferences which might be drawn from analogous circumstances. I confess that I am inclined to consider the fears of a great number of Americans as purely imaginary; and far from participating in their dread of the consolidation of power in the hands of the Union, I think that the Federal Government is visibly losing strength.

To prove this assertion I shall not have recourse to any remote occurrences, but to circumstances which I have myself witnessed, and which belong to our own time.

An attentive examination of what is going on in the United States will easily convince us that two opposite tendencies exist in that country, like two distinct currents flowing in contrary directions in the same channel. The Union has now existed for forty-five years, and in the course of that time a vast number of provincial prejudices, which were at first hostile to its power, have died away. The patriotic feeling which attached each of the Americans to his own native State is become less exclusive; and the different parts of the Union have become more intimately connected the better they have become acquainted with each other. The post, that great instrument of intellectual intercourse, now reaches into the backwoods; and steamboats have established daily means of communication between the different points of the coast. An inland navigation of unexampled rapidity conveys commodities up and down the rivers of the country. And to these facilities of nature and art may be added those restless cravings, that busy-mindedness, and love of pelf, which are constantly urging the American into active life, and bringing him into contact with his fellow-citizens. He crosses the country in every direction; he visits all the various populations of the land; and there is not a province in France in which the natives are so well known to each other as the 13,000,000 of men who cover the territory of the United States.

热爱，不断刺激美国人积极地生活，促进他们与同胞的交流。他们走遍全国各地，拜访各地居民，而在法国，没有一个省份的居民能够像1300万美国人那样相互之间如此熟悉。

但是随着美国人的相互融合，他们彼此之间变得越来越像。气候、原籍和制度的不同带来的差异越来越小，他们越来越接近同一类型。每年，成千上万的人离开北方前往联邦的其他地方定居，与他们一起前来的还有他们的信仰、观念和民情，而且因为他们比他们要住下来的地方的原有居民更加文明，所以不久就主管其当地的事务，并把社会塑造成有利于自己的样子。北方向南方的不断移民特别有利于把不同地方的特点融合为全国一致的特点。北方的文明似乎注定有一天要将全国上下同化，成为整个国家的共同标准。

联结各联邦州的商业纽带随美国制造业的发展变得越来越强。最初由于观念一致而开始的联邦，逐渐成为现实的需要。随着时间的流逝，曾经困扰1789年时人们的想象中的恐惧被一扫而光。联邦当局没有成为压迫者，没有摧毁各州的独立，也没有让联邦州服从君主制度，而且联邦也没有让弱小的州成为大州的附庸，但联邦的人口、财富和力量一直以来持续增长。因此，我确信阻碍美联邦存在下去的自然条件的障碍现在已经不像1789年那样强大，而联邦的敌人如今也没有那时那么多了。

然而，仔细研究美国最近45年的历史肯定会发现联邦的力量在不断被削弱，解释这种现象出现的原因也不是什么难事。当1789年宪法颁布的时候，全国还处于无政府状态，随后成立的联邦激起了更大的恐惧和仇视，但却因为能够满足各州迫切的需要而受到热烈的欢迎。因此，尽管联邦受到的攻击比现在多，但其力量很快达到最高峰，就好像一个政

But whilst the Americans intermingle, they grow in resemblance of each other; the differences resulting from their climate, their origin, and their institutions, diminish; and they all draw nearer and nearer to the common type. Every year, thousands of men leave the North to settle in different parts of the Union: they bring with them their faith, their opinions, and their manners; and as they are more enlighthned than the men amongst whom they are about to dwell, they soon rise to the head of affairs, and they adapt society to their own advantage. This continual emigration of the North to the South is peculiarly favorable to the fusion of all the different provincial characters into one national character. The civilization of the North appears to be the common standard, to which the whole nation will one day be assimilated.

The commercial ties which unite the confederate States are strengthened by the increasing manufactures of the Americans; and the union which began to exist in their opinions, gradually forms a part of their habits: the course of time has swept away the bugbear thoughts which haunted the imaginations of the citizens in 1789. The federal power is not become oppressive; it has not destroyed the independence of the States; it has not subjected the confederates to monarchial institutions; and the Union has not rendered the lesser States dependent upon the larger ones; but the confederation has continued to increase in population, in wealth, and in power. I am therefore convinced that the natural obstacles to the continuance of the American Union are not so powerful at the present time as they were in 1789; and that the enemies of the Union are not so numerous.

Nevertheless, a careful examination of the history of the United States for the last forty-five years will readily convince us that the federal power is declining; nor is it difficult to explain the causes of this phenomenon. When the Constitution of 1789 was promulgated, the nation was a prey to anarchy; the Union, which succeeded this confusion, excited much dread and much animosity; but it was warmly supported because it satisfied an imperious want. Thus, although it was more attacked than it is now, the federal power soon reached the maximum of its authority, as is usually the case with a government which triumphs after having braced its strength by the struggle. At that time the interpretation of the Constitution seemed to extend, rather than to repress, the federal sovereignty;

府在斗争获胜之后所做的一样迅速获得力量。那时，对宪法的解释似乎是对联邦主权的扩大，而不是约束。所以，联邦在很多方面呈现出一个统一国家的面貌，对内对外也由一个政府领导。但是为了达到这一目的，人民的地位被抬高到几乎凌驾于联邦之上。

宪法没有破坏各州的地方主权，而且所有的州无论其性质如何都受到某种倾向的驱使要维护自身的独立。这种趋势在像美国这样的国家更加坚决，因为在这里每个乡镇就好像一个已经习惯于自我管理的小共和国。所以，必须付出一番努力才能让各州服从联邦的权威。然而无论所做的努力取得何等的成功，都必然会随着这种努力所产生的原因的减弱而渐弱。

随着联邦政府巩固自己的权威，美国的国际地位得到恢复，边疆的和平重现，政府的信任得以重建。混乱被稳定所取代，特别有利于勤奋的人充分自由地施展。正是这样的繁荣让美国人忘记繁荣正是这个原因。一旦危险过去，让他们勇敢起来的活力和爱国主义精神便被忘得一干二净。他们一摆脱曾经困扰他们的恐惧，便立即回到习惯的老路，完全听凭自己的喜好为所欲为。当不再需要一个强有力的政府时，便立刻觉得它令人生厌。各州在联邦的鼓励下共同富裕起来，没有谁想要放弃联邦，但却希望代表联邦的当局尽可能少管事情。联邦的普遍原则易被认可，但是却很少被人应用，以至于联邦政府在建立秩序与和平的同时也走向衰败。

人们这样的情绪暴露出来之后，专靠人民激情生活的各党派领袖，便开始利用它为自己牟利。联邦政府的地位随之变得岌岌可危。而它的敌人则赢得了普遍的支持，并企图向

and the Union offered, in several respects, the appearance of a single and undivided people, directed in its foreign and internal policy by a single Government. But to attain this point the people had risen, to a certain extent, above itself.

The Constitution had not destroyed the distinct sovereignty of the States; and all communities, of whatever nature they may be, are impelled by a secret propensity to assert their independence. This propensity is still more decided in a country like America, in which every village forms a sort of republic accustomed to conduct its own affairs. It therefore cost the States an effort to submit to the federal supremacy; and all efforts, however successful they may be, necessarily subside with the causes in which they originated.

As the Federal Government consolidated its authority, America resumed its rank amongst the nations, peace returned to its frontiers, and public credit was restored; confusion was succeeded by a fixed state of things, which was favorable to the full and free exercise of industrious enterprise. It was this very prosperity which made the Americans forget the cause to which it was attributable; and when once the danger was passed, the energy and the patriotism which had enabled them to brave it disappeared from amongst them. No sooner were they delivered from the cares which oppressed them, than they easily returned to their ordinary habits, and gave themselves up without resistance to their natural inclinations. When a powerful Government no longer appeared to be necessary, they once more began to think it irksome. The Union encouraged a general prosperity, and the States were not inclined to abandon the Union; but they desired to render the action of the power which represented that body as light as possible. The general principle of Union was adopted, but in every minor detail there was an actual tendency to independence. The principle of confederation was every day more easily admitted, and more rarely applied; so that the Federal Government brought about its own decline, whilst it was creating order and peace.

As soon as this tendency of public opinion began to be manifested externally, the leaders of parties, who live by the passions of the people, began to work it to their own advantage. The position of the Federal Government then became exceedingly critical. Its enemies were in possession of

人民承诺会减少它的影响来获得执政的权力。从那时起，联邦政府不断和各州政府发生争执，并不可避免地节节败退。而当涉及对联邦宪法的解释时，做出的解释往往不利于联邦而是有利于州。

宪法赋予联邦政府关心全国性利益的权力，其初衷是让联邦成为监督涉及整个国家繁荣的国内项目的最适合的权威当局，例如开凿运河。但是各州却很警惕可以处置其境内部分领土的这样一股外来的力量，它们害怕中央政府会通过这种方式喧宾夺主，在自己的境内发号施令夺走它们留给自己人的权力。一直以来反对加强联邦权力的民主党指责国会滥用职权，总统野心勃勃。中央政府被这样的反对吓住，不久便承认自己的错误，并承诺未来会将自己的势力限定在规定的范围之内。

宪法赋予联邦对外交涉的权力。生活在美国的边境地区的印第安部落也被视为此类。只要这些野蛮部落同意向文明的居民让步，联邦就不会提出任何异议，但是只要印第安部落想在一个地方定居下来，周边的州就会宣称对这片土地的所有权，并对居住在这里的人行使主权。中央政府会很快认可州所宣称的这两项权利，随后将印第安部落视为一个独立的共和国与之缔结条约，并任凭州的立法机构对印第安人实施暴政。

建立在大西洋沿岸的一些州，不断向西扩张，深入到欧洲人不曾踏足的荒野深处。而那些边界已经勘定的州则用嫉妒的眼光盯着它们的邻州未来等待开垦的无垠的土地。于是，后者出于安抚的目的，同时也便于联邦行事，同意划定它们的边界，放弃边界以外的全部土地的所有权并移交给联邦政府。从此以后，联邦政府成为最初加盟联邦的13个州之

the popular favor; and they obtained the right of conducting its policy by pledging themselves to lessen its influence. From that time forwards the Government of the Union has invariably been obliged to recede, as often as it has attempted to enter the lists with the governments of the States. And whenever an interpretation of the terms of the Federal Constitution has been called for, that interpretation has most frequently been opposed to the Union, and favorable to the States.

The Constitution invested the Federal Government with the right of providing for the interests of the nation; and it had been held that no other authority was so fit to superintend the "internal improvements" which affected the prosperity of the whole Union; such, for instance, as the cutting of canals. But the States were alarmed at a power, distinct from their own, which could thus dispose of a portion of their territory; and they were afraid that the central Government would, by this means, acquire a formidable extent of patronage within their own confines, and exercise a degree of influence which they intended to reserve exclusively to their own agents. The Democratic party, which has constantly been opposed to the increase of the federal authority, then accused the Congress of usurpation, and the Chief Magistrate of ambition. The central Government was intimidated by the opposition; and it soon acknowledged its error, promising exactly to confine its influence for the future within the circle which was prescribed to it.

The Constitution confers upon the Union the right of treating with foreign nations. The Indian tribes, which border upon the frontiers of the United States, had usually been regarded in this light. As long as these savages consented to retire before the civilized settlers, the federal right was not contested: but as soon as an Indian tribe attempted to fix its dwelling upon a given spot, the adjacent States claimed possession of the lands and the rights of sovereignty over the natives. The central Government soon recognized both these claims; and after it had concluded treaties with the Indians as independent nations, it gave them up as subjects to the legislative tyranny of the States.

Some of the States which had been founded upon the coast of the Atlantic, extended indefinitely to the West, into wild regions where no European had ever penetrated. The States whose confines were irrevocably fixed, looked with a jealous eye upon the unbounded regions which the future would

外所有未开垦土地的主人，并有权分配和出售这些土地，由此获得的所有收入全部归入联邦国库，以便利用这笔收入向印第安人购买土地，开辟通向偏远定居点的道路，以及尽快加速文明的传播。可是，随着大西洋沿岸居民的进驻，新的州在此期间已经在新的荒地上建立起来。但是为了国家的利益，国会依然会出售新成立的州占据的土地。但后者却宣称因为新州已经成立，所以它们应该独享出售其土地的收益，供自己使用。当它们的要求越来越具威胁性时，国会便开始考虑让联邦放弃迄今为止所享受的这一部分特权，并最终在1832年通过一项法令，规定允许西部各共和国获得出售土地的绝大部分收入并供其使用，但是这些土地本身并不属于它们。

只要对美国稍作观察就会发现银行制度给这个国家带来的优势。优势有很多，但其中有一个特别引人注目。美国的纸币在边远地区的价值与在银行所在地费城的价值一般无二。

但是，合众国银行却成为主要的憎恨对象。银行的董事们公开宣布反对总统，而他们被指控滥施影响力妨碍总统选举也并非空穴来风。因此，带着个人的敌意。总统全力攻击这些人所代表的银行。因为相信得到多数的秘密支持，总统的报复受到大大的鼓舞。银行可以看作是联邦最大的金融纽带，就如同国会是立法纽带一样，促使州独立的那股热情也想让银行倒台。

合众国银行一直拥有大量地方银行发行的流通券，并可以随时迫使地方银行将其兑换为现金。但对合众国银行而言，则没有这样的担忧，因为其巨额的流动资金足以应付所有的提款要求。但是地方银行的生存则因此受到威胁，活动受到限制，因为它们只能按其资

enable their neighbors to explore. The latter then agreed, with a view to conciliate the others, and to facilitate the act of union, to lay down their own boundaries, and to abandon all the territory which lay beyond those limits to the confederation at large. Thenceforward the Federal Government became the owner of all the uncultivated lands which lie beyond the borders of the thirteen States first confederated. It was invested with the right of parcelling and selling them, and the sums derived from this source were exclusively reserved to the public treasure of the Union, in order to furnish supplies for purchasing tracts of country from the Indians, for opening roads to the remote settlements, and for accelerating the increase of civilization as much as possible. New States have, however, been formed in the course of time, in the midst of those wilds which were formerly ceded by the inhabitants of the shores of the Atlantic. Congress has gone on to sell, for the profit of the nation at large, the uncultivated lands which those new States contained. But the latter at length asserted that, as they were now fully constituted, they ought to enjoy the exclusive right of converting the produce of these sales to their own use. As their remonstrances became more and more threatening, Congress thought fit to deprive the Union of a portion of the privileges which it had hitherto enjoyed; and at the end of 1832 it passed a law by which the greatest part of the revenue derived from the sale of lands was made over to the new western republics, although the lands themselves were not ceded to them.

The slightest observation in the United States enables one to appreciate the advantages which the country derives from the bank. These advantages are of several kinds, but one of them is peculiarly striking to the stranger. The banknotes of the United States are taken upon the borders of the desert for the same value as at Philadelphia, where the bank conducts its operations.

The Bank of the United States is nevertheless the object of great animosity. Its directors have proclaimed their hostility to the President: and they are accused, not without some show of probability, of having abused their influence to thwart his election. The President therefore attacks the establishment which they represent with all the warmth of personal enmity; and he is encouraged in the pursuit of his revenge by the conviction that he is supported by the secret propensities of the majority. The bank may be regarded as the great monetary tie of the Union, just as Congress is the great legislative tie; and the same passions which tend to render the States independent of the central

本的一定比例发行一定量的流通券。于是它们只能不耐烦地忍受这种有意的控制。受到地方银行收买的报纸和出于自身利益而沦为其工具的总统一起对合众国银行发起猛攻。他们煽动起地方情绪和盲目的民主本能来助自己一臂之力。他们断言,银行的董事们已经形成一个贵族集团,最终将会对政府施以影响,而且必然会破坏美国社会所依据的平等原则。

合众国银行与其反对者之间的斗争只是在美国上演的地方权力和中央权力斗争,以及民主独立精神和等级服从精神斗争的一个例子。我并不认为,合众国银行的敌人与在其他问题上攻击联邦政府的完全一样。但我要说,指向合众国银行的攻击和对联邦政府的抵制都是源自同一种倾向,而合众国银行众多的反对者恰好是后者声势渐微的可悲征兆。

联邦的软弱在关税问题上表现得最为明显。法国革命战争和1812年英美战争,切断了美国与欧洲的一切自由来往,并促使联邦北方制造业兴起。随着和平的恢复,欧洲产品输送到新大陆的航道重启,美国人认为是时候建立关税制度,达到一箭双雕的目的,既可以保护尚处萌芽阶段的本国制造业,又可以偿还战争时期欠下的大量外债。南方各州没有有待振兴的制造业,只有农业,所以不久便开始对这项措施颇有微词。事实就是如此,这里我也不想探讨它们的不满是有根有据还是信口雌黄。

早在1820年,南卡罗来纳州在给国会的请愿书中声称,关税是违宪的、压迫的和不公正的。随后,佐治亚州、弗吉尼亚州、北卡罗来纳州、亚拉巴马州以及密西西比州相继表示不同程度的强烈反对。但是,国会对此根本置之不理,分别在1824年和1828年两次提

power, contribute to the overthrow of the bank.

The Bank of the United States always holds a great number of the notes issued by the provincial banks, which it can at any time oblige them to convert into cash. It has itself nothing to fear from a similar demand, as the extent of its resources enables it to meet all claims. But the existence of the provincial banks is thus threatened, and their operations are restricted, since they are only able to issue a quantity of notes duly proportioned to their capital. They submit with impatience to this salutary control. The newspapers which they have bought over, and the President, whose interest renders him their instrument, attack the bank with the greatest vehemence. They rouse the local passions and the blind democratic instinct of the country to aid their cause; and they assert that the bank directors form a permanent aristocratic body, whose influence must ultimately be felt in the Government, and must affect those principles of equality upon which society rests in America.

The contest between the bank and its opponents is only an incident in the great struggle which is going on in America between the provinces and the central power; between the spirit of democratic independence and the spirit of gradation and subordination. I do not mean that the enemies of the bank are identically the same individuals who, on other points, attack the Federal Government; but I assert that the attacks directed against the bank of the United States originate in the same propensities which militate against the Federal Government; and that the very numerous opponents of the former afford a deplorable symptom of the decreasing support of the latter.

The Union has never displayed so much weakness as in the celebrated question of the tariff. The wars of the French Revolution and of 1812 had created manufacturing establishments in the North of the Union, by cutting off all free communication between America and Europe. When peace was concluded, and the channel of intercourse reopened by which the produce of Europe was transmitted to the New World, the Americans thought fit to establish a system of import duties, for the twofold purpose of protecting their incipient manufactures and of paying off the amount of the debt contracted during the war. The Southern States, which have no manufactures to encourage, and which are exclusively agricultural, soon complained of this measure. Such were the simple facts, and I do not pretend to examine in this place whether their complaints were well founded or unjust.

高税率，并对关税征收的原则再次加以肯定。于是，南方提出或者不如说是恢复一个名为"拒绝执行联邦法令"的主张。

我在讲述联邦宪法的时候已经指出，联邦宪法的目的并不是建立一个联盟，而是建立一个全国政府。只有在宪法特别规定的情形下，美国才是一个单一的不可分割的国家。而且只有在这些情况下，才会像在所有立宪国家那样，由多数来表达国家的意志。当多数做出决定后，少数只有服从的义务。这是合理的法条，是唯一一个符合宪法条文及宪法制定者公认意图的学说。

南方的"拒绝执行联邦法令派"坚称美国人联合起来的意图不是成立一个单一的民族国家，而是结成独立州的联盟，所以每个州都拥有各自主权，即使不是实际上，至少应该是法律上有权对国会颁布的法令加以解释，此外，还有权在本州内停止执行那些自认为违宪和不公正的法令。

"拒绝执行联邦法令派"的整个主张可以用南方的领袖副总统卡尔霍斯1833年在参议院的一番讲话来概括。他说："宪法是一份契约，参与其中的各州均具有主权地位。当缔约各方对契约的解释发生分歧的时候，各方有权对其性质、范围和义务做出自己的判断。"显然，这一原则破坏了联邦宪法的基础，致使美国人已经摆脱的旧邦联时期的所有问题重现。

当南卡罗来纳州看到国会对其抗议不闻不问的时候，便威胁将"拒绝执行联邦法令

As early as the year 1820, South Carolina declared, in a petition to Congress, that the tariff was "unconstitutional, oppressive, and unjust." And the States of Georgia, Virginia, North Carolina, Alabama, and Mississippi subsequently remonstrated against it with more or less vigor. But Congress, far from lending an ear to these complaints, raised the scale of tariff duties in the years 1824 and 1828, and recognized anew the principle on which it was founded. A doctrine was then proclaimed, or rather revived, in the South, which took the name of Nullification.

I have shown in the proper place that the object of the Federal Constitution was not to form a league, but to create a national government. The Americans of the United States form a sole and undivided people, in all the cases which are specified by that Constitution; and upon these points the will of the nation is expressed, as it is in all constitutional nations, by the voice of the majority. When the majority has pronounced its decision, it is the duty of the minority to submit. Such is the sound legal doctrine, and the only one which agrees with the text of the Constitution, and the known intention of those who framed it.

The partisans of Nullification in the South maintain, on the contrary, that the intention of the Americans in uniting was not to reduce themselves to the condition of one and the same people; that they meant to constitute a league of independent States; and that each State, consequently retains its entire sovereignty, if not de facto, at least de jure; and has the right of putting its own construction upon the laws of Congress, and of suspending their execution within the limits of its own territory, if they are held to be unconstitutional and unjust.

The entire doctrine of Nullification is comprised in a sentence uttered by Vice-President Calhoun, the head of that party in the South, before the Senate of the United States, in the year 1833: could: "The Constitution is a compact to which the States were parties in their sovereign capacity; now, whenever a compact is entered into by parties which acknowledge no tribunal above their authority to decide in the last resort, each of them has a right to judge for itself in relation to the nature, extent, and obligations of the instrument." It is evident that a similar doctrine destroys the very basis of the Federal Constitution, and brings back all the evils of the old confederation, from which the Americans were supposed to have had a safe deliverance.

派”的主张应用于联邦关税法。国会坚持自己原先的立场，最终一场风暴爆发了。1832年间，南卡罗来纳州的公民成立一个国民代表会议，商讨他们将不得不采用的非常举措。同年的11月24日，此次会议颁布一条法令，并以此为依据宣布联邦关税法无效，禁止征收该法律规定的税款，并拒绝接受可能向联邦法院提出的诉讼。这一法令将于次年的2月生效，并同时宣布，如果国会在此期间对关税做出调整，南卡罗来纳州有可能不再采取接下来的措施。随后，南卡罗来纳州模糊地表示愿将这一问题提交有联邦所有成员州组成的特别委员会处理。

与此同时，南卡罗来纳州磨刀霍霍，积极备战。然而对百姓的恳求置之不理的国会，看到他们拿起武器后，立即倾听了他们的不满。随后，国会通过一项法律规定，关税将在十年内逐步递减，直到不超过政府开支的所需。因此，国会完全放弃关税的原则，并用单纯的财政税款取代保护性的关税体制。联邦政府为了掩盖自己的失败，采用了软弱的政府通常使用的权宜之计，即在事实上做出让步，却在原则上毫不退让。国会在对关税法进行修改的同时，还通过另一项法案，授予总统特别的权力，使之可以动用武力镇压那时实际上已经不存在的反抗。

但是，南卡罗来纳州甚至不同意让联邦享受这个仅有的胜利。宣布关税法无效的国民会议再次召开后，接受了联邦提出的让步，但同时宣布将继续坚持“拒绝执行联邦法令派”主张。而且为了证明言行一致，它宣布总统获得的特别权力无效，尽管它明知这项法

When South Carolina perceived that Congress turned a deaf ear to its remonstrances, it threatened to apply the doctrine of nullification to the federal tariff bill. Congress persisted in its former system; and at length the storm broke out. In the course of 1832 the citizens of South Carolina, named a national Convention, to consult upon the extraordinary measures which they were called upon to take; and on November 24th of the same year this Convention promulgated a law, under the form of a decree, which annulled the federal law of the tariff, forbade the levy of the imposts which that law commands, and refused to recognize the appeal which might be made to the federal courts of law. This decree was only to be put in execution in the ensuing month of February, and it was intimated, that if Congress modified the tariff before that period, South Carolina might be induced to proceed no further with her menaces; and a vague desire was afterwards expressed of submitting the question to an extraordinary assembly of all the confederate States.

In the meantime South Carolina armed her militia, and prepared for war. But Congress, which had slighted its suppliant subjects, listened to their complaints as soon as they were found to have taken up arms. A law was passed, by which the tariff duties were to be progressively reduced for ten years, until they were brought so low as not to exceed the amount of supplies necessary to the Government. Thus Congress completely abandoned the principle of the tariff; and substituted a mere fiscal impost to a system of protective duties. The Government of the Union, in order to conceal its defeat, had recourse to an expedient which is very much in vogue with feeble governments. It yielded the point de facto, but it remained inflexible upon the principles in question; and whilst Congress was altering the tariff law, it passed another bill, by which the President was invested with extraordinary powers, enabling him to overcome by force a resistance which was then no longer to be apprehended.

But South Carolina did not consent to leave the Union in the enjoyment of these scanty trophies of success: the same national Convention which had annulled the tariff bill, met again, and accepted the proffered concession; but at the same time it declared it unabated perseverance in the doctrine of Nullification: and to prove what it said, it annulled the law investing the President with extraordinary powers, although it was very certain that the clauses of that law would never be carried into effect.

Almost all the controversies of which I have been speaking have taken place under the Presidency

律永远不可能付诸实践。

我所谈到的几乎所有争议都出现在杰克逊将军的总统任期内，而且不可否认在关税问题上，他曾对联邦的主张巧妙地给予大力支持。然而，在我看来，今天联邦政府的领导者会将他的行为看作威胁联邦存在的一个隐患。

在欧洲，一些人对杰克逊将军对美国事务可能产生的影响形成一种看法，他们的看法在曾经到美国进行亲自考察的人看来显得非常荒谬。人们告诉我们杰克逊将军打过各种各样的胜仗，精力充沛，生性和习惯诉诸武力，并贪图权力，是个十足的暴君。这些说法也许都对，但是据此做出的推断则极其错误。人们推测，杰克逊将军致力于在美国建立独裁统治，推崇尚武精神，要将中央政权的影响力扩大到足以危害地方自由的程度。但是，在美国做这样的事情的时机和出现这样人物的时代，都还没有到来。如果杰克逊将军想要用这样的方式进行统治，他必然会丧失其政治地位，乃至生命。因此，他不会贸然采取这样的行动。

杰克逊总统非但不想扩大联邦的权力，而且其所在的党派反而想要将其权力控制在宪法明文规定的范围之内，并从未要对宪法做出有利于联邦的解释。杰克逊将军绝不是中央集权的斗士，而是唯恐失去权力的地方政府的代理人。将他推到高高在上地位的是人们地方分权的热情，只有不断迎合这样的热情，他才能保住自己的地位和声望。杰克逊将军是多数的奴仆，他服从多数的愿望、爱好以及要求，也许说他自己就期待并鼓动这样的情绪

of General Jackson; and it cannot be denied that in the question of the tariff he has supported the claims of the Union with vigor and with skill. I am, however, of opinion that the conduct of the individual who now represents the Federal Government may be reckoned as one of the dangers which threaten its continuance.

Some persons in Europe have formed an opinion of the possible influence of General Jackson upon the affairs of his country, which appears highly extravagant to those who have seen more of the subject. We have been told that General Jackson has won sundry battles, that he is an energetic man, prone by nature and by habit to the use of force, covetous of power, and a despot by taste. All this may perhaps be true; but the inferences which have been drawn from these truths are exceedingly erroneous. It has been imagined that General Jackson is bent on establishing a dictatorship in America, on introducing a military spirit, and on giving a degree of influence to the central authority which cannot but be dangerous to provincial liberties. But in America the time for similar undertakings, and the age for men of this kind, is not yet come: if General Jackson had entertained a hope of exercising his authority in this manner, he would infallibly have forfeited his political station, and compromised his life; accordingly he has not been so imprudent as to make any such attempt.

Far from wishing to extend the federal power, the President belongs to the party which is desirous of limiting that power to the bare and precise letter of the Constitution, and which never puts a construction upon that act favorable to the Government of the Union; far from standing forth as the champion of centralization, General Jackson is the agent of all the jealousies of the States; and he was placed in the lofty station he occupies by the passions of the people which are most opposed to the central Government. It is by perpetually flattering these passions that he maintains his station and his popularity. General Jackson is the slave of the majority: he yields to its wishes, its propensities, and its demands; say rather, that he anticipates and forestalls them.

Whenever the governments of the States come into collision with that of the Union, the President is generally the first to question his own rights: he almost always outstrips the legislature; and when the extent of the federal power is controverted, he takes part, as it were, against himself; he conceals his official interests, and extinguishes his own natural inclinations. Not indeed that he is naturally

更为合适。

只要州政府与联邦政府发生冲突，总统往往首先质疑自己的权力，总是跑在立法机构的前面，而且当联邦职权范围有所争议时，还总是站在反对联邦的一方。他隐藏自己的政治立场，突出自己的天然爱好。这并不是因为他天性软弱或与联邦为敌，因为当多数表示反对南方的"拒绝执行联邦法令派"时，他便立即站到多数的前面，明确坚定地表达多数的主张，并首先提议使用武力。但是，在我看来，如果允许我用美国人的话来说，杰斐逊将军爱好上是联邦主义者，务实上是共和主义者。

杰克逊将军向多数低头并获得他们的支持，但是当他觉得自己的地位稳固的时候，会排除一切障碍，实现获得多数认可或多数尚有怀疑的目标。他拥有前任所没有的强大支持，并利用任何一位前任总统不曾有过的便利条件践踏自己的敌人。他为自己采取的从没有人敢采取的措施负责，他甚至用近乎侮辱的蔑视态度对待全国的议员。他拒绝批准国会的法案，而且不断对强大立法机构的质问置之不理。他就是一个有时候粗暴对待主人的幸运儿。因此杰克逊将军的威望不断加强，而总统的权力不断被削弱。杰斐逊手中的联邦政府强大而有力，但是留给他继任者手中的政府则羸弱不堪。

如果我说的没有大错，美国联邦政府会不断削弱下去，管理的公务越来越少，活动范围会变得越来越窄。联邦政府天生软弱，而现在甚至放弃了貌似强大的外表。另一方面，我也认为在美国，人们的独立感在各州表现得日益明显，对地方政府的爱也日益强烈。人

weak or hostile to the Union; for when the majority decided against the claims of the partisans of nullification, he put himself at its head, asserted the doctrines which the nation held distinctly and energetically, and was the first to recommend forcible measures; but General Jackson appears to me, if I may use the American expressions, to be a Federalist by taste, and a Republican by calculation.

General Jackson stoops to gain the favor of the majority, but when he feels that his popularity is secure, he overthrows all obstacles in the pursuit of the objects which the community approves, or of those which it does not look upon with a jealous eye. He is supported by a power with which his predecessors were unacquainted; and he tramples on his personal enemies whenever they cross his path with a facility which no former President ever enjoyed; he takes upon himself the responsibility of measures which no one before him would have ventured to attempt: he even treats the national representatives with disdain approaching to insult; he puts his veto upon the laws of Congress, and frequently neglects to reply to that powerful body. He is a favorite who sometimes treats his master roughly. The power of General Jackson perpetually increases; but that of the President declines; in his hands the Federal Government is strong, but it will pass enfeebled into the hands of his successor.

I am strangely mistaken if the Federal Government of the United States be not constantly losing strength, retiring gradually from public affairs, and narrowing its circle of action more and more. It is naturally feeble, but it now abandons even its pretensions to strength. On the other hand, I thought that I remarked a more lively sense of independence, and a more decided attachment to provincial government in the States. The Union is to subsist, but to subsist as a shadow; it is to be strong in certain cases, and weak in all others; in time of warfare, it is to be able to concentrate all the forces of the nation and all the resources of the country in its hands; and in time of peace its existence is to be scarcely perceptible: as if this alternate debility and vigor were natural or possible.

I do not foresee anything for the present which may be able to check this general impulse of public opinion; the causes in which it originated do not cease to operate with the same effect. The change will therefore go on, and it may be predicted that, unless some extraordinary event occurs, the Government of the Union will grow weaker and weaker every day.

I think, however, that the period is still remote at which the federal power will be entirely

们想要联邦，但只把它作为一个影子。有些时候，人们希望联邦强大，而其他时候又希望它弱小。在战争时期，人们愿意将全国所有的人力物力集中到联邦政府手中，而在和平时期，人们不想感受到它的存在，这种忽而软弱、忽而强大的变化很自然也很合理。

我并不认为现在有什么能够阻碍人们思想的这种普遍的冲动，造成这种冲动的原因也一直没有停止发挥作用。所以，变化将继续下去，可以预见，除非出现非常事件，否则联邦政府将会日益衰弱。

可是，我认为联邦当局完全无力自保，维护国内和平，最终灭亡的日子还远未到来。联邦是民情民愿之所向，而且联邦的成就显著，带来的好处有目共睹。当人们发觉联邦政府的软弱会危及联邦的存在时，我丝毫不怀疑会出现加强联邦力量的反应。

在迄今为止成立的所有联邦政府中，美国政府是最按照联邦天性来行事的政府。只要不受到法律解释的直接打击，只要本质不发生根本变化，舆论的变化，国内的危机或战争，可以重新恢复联邦应具有的全部活力。我想指出的是，特别是在法国，许多人认为，在美国人们的观念正在向有利于中央集权的方向发生变化，人们主张将权力交给总统和国会。然而，我认为美国出现的趋势刚好与此相反。我并不是说联邦政府因日益老化而变得越来越虚弱，对各州主权的威胁越来越大，而是想说，联邦变得越来越虚弱，而且只有它的主权受到威胁。这就是现状。这种趋势的未来无法预见，会阻止、推迟和加速我所说的这种变化的偶然事件也未可知，而且我也无法假装可以揭开挡在我们眼前的那层面纱。

extinguished by its inability to protect itself and to maintain peace in the country. The Union is sanctioned by the manners and desires of the people; its results are palpable, its benefits visible. When it is perceived that the weakness of the Federal Government compromises the existence of the Union, I do not doubt that a reaction will take place with a view to increase its strength.

The Government of the United States is, of all the federal governments which have hitherto been established, the one which is most naturally destined to act. As long as it is only indirectly assailed by the interpretation of its laws, and as long as its substance is not seriously altered, a change of opinion, an internal crisis, or a war, may restore all the vigor which it requires. The point which I have been most anxious to put in a clear light is simply this: Many people, especially in France, imagine that a change in opinion is going on in the United States, which is favorable to a centralization of power in the hands of the President and the Congress. I hold that a contrary tendency may distinctly be observed. So far is the Federal Government from acquiring strength, and from threatening the sovereignty of the States, as it grows older, that I maintain it to be growing weaker and weaker, and that the sovereignty of the Union alone is in danger. Such are the facts which the present time discloses. The future conceals the final result of this tendency, and the events which may check, retard, or accelerate the changes I have described; but I do not affect to be able to remove the veil which hides them from our sight.

Of The Republican Institutions Of The United States, And What Their Chances Of Duration Are

The Union is accidental—The Republican institutions have more prospect of permanence— A republic for the present the natural state of the Anglo-Americans—Reason of this—In order to destroy it, all the laws must be changed at the same time, and a great alteration take place in manners—Difficulties experienced by the Americans in creating an aristocracy.

The dismemberment of the Union, by the introduction of war into the heart of those States which are now confederate, with standing armies, a dictatorship, and a heavy taxation, might, eventually, compromise the fate of the republican institutions. But we ought not to confound the future prospects

美国共和制度及其持久存在的机遇

联邦的出现具有偶然性——共和制最具前途——目前，共和制最适合英裔美国人的自然状态——其原因何在——要破坏共和制，必须同时改变所有法律，改造整个民情——美国人建立贵族制度的困难。

如果加盟的各州之间发生战争，并因此而拥有常备军队，实行独裁统治并加重赋税，进而导致联邦解体，最终也将危害共和制度的命运。但我们不应该将共和的前途和联邦的未来混为一谈。联邦的出现具有偶然性，只要环境对其有利，会一直存在下去。但是，共和制在我看来符合美国人的自然状态，除非有相反因素持续发挥作用，否则君主制不会出现。联邦的存在依靠的主要是组建联邦的法律，一场革命，舆论的改变，就会让它永远消失。但共和制度却有着根深蒂固的基础。

在美国，人们认为共和是社会自身缓慢和平的活动，是真正建立在人民意愿之上的常规状态。在这样一种管理制度下，一项决定需要长时间地酝酿，有针对性地讨论，成熟后方能实施。美国的共和主义者非常看重道德，尊重宗教信仰，承认权利的存在。他们公开表示，越是道德、虔诚、温和的民族就越是自由。在美国，所谓的共和就是多数的和平统治。多数在自我审视后，让人们认可自己的存在，并成为国家一切权力之源。但是多数的权力就其本身而言也并非是无限的。在道德世界，人性、公正和理性享有不可撼动的至高

of the republic with those of the Union. The Union is an accident, which will only last as long as circumstances are favorable to its existence; but a republican form of government seems to me to be the natural state of the Americans; which nothing but the continued action of hostile causes, always acting in the same direction, could change into a monarchy. The Union exists principally in the law which formed it; one revolution, one change in public opinion, might destroy it forever; but the republic has a much deeper foundation to rest upon.

What is understood by a republican government in the United States is the slow and quiet action of society upon itself. It is a regular state of things really founded upon the enlightened will of the people. It is a conciliatory government under which resolutions are allowed time to ripen; and in which they are deliberately discussed, and executed with mature judgment. The republicans in the United States set a high value upon morality, respect religious belief, and acknowledge the existence of rights. They profess to think that a people ought to be moral, religious, and temperate, in proportion as it is free. What is called the republic in the United States, is the tranquil rule of the majority, which, after having had time to examine itself, and to give proof of its existence, is the common source of all the powers of the State. But the power of the majority is not of itself unlimited. In the moral world humanity, justice, and reason enjoy an undisputed supremacy; in the political world vested rights are treated with no less deference. The majority recognizes these two barriers; and if it now and then overstep them, it is because, like individuals, it has passions, and, like them, it is prone to do what is wrong, whilst it discerns what is right.

But the demagogues of Europe have made strange discoveries. A republic is not, according to them, the rule of the majority, as has hitherto been thought, but the rule of those who are strenuous partisans of the majority. It is not the people who preponderates in this kind of government, but those who are best versed in the good qualities of the people. A happy distinction, which allows men to act in the name of nations without consulting them, and to claim their gratitude whilst their rights are spurned. A republican government, moreover, is the only one which claims the right of doing whatever it chooses, and despising what men have hitherto respected, from the highest moral obligations to the vulgar rules of common-sense. It had been supposed, until our time, that despotism

地位；在政治世界，既得权力获得同样的尊重。多数承认在这两方面受到限制，而且如果多数偶尔破坏了它们，也是因为像人一样多数也有激情，而且也像人一样会好心办坏事。

但是，欧洲蛊惑人心的政客却有不同的发现。在他们眼中，共和并不是人们一直认为的那样是多数的统治，而是依靠多数取得权势的几个党派分子的统治。在这样的政府中处于优势的不是人民，而是那些最了解人民作用的人。其特点在于可以不经人民的同意以人民的名义行事，在人民的权利遭到践踏时依旧让人民对他们感恩戴德。此外，共和制政府是唯一一个有权肆意妄为的政府，鄙视人们迄今为止所尊重的一切的政府，从至高无上的道义责任到通俗的常识规范。他们一直以来都认为无论什么形式的独裁都令人憎恨。但是，现在他们有了新发现，即以人民名义实行的立法暴政和神圣的不公。

美国人对于共和制度的看法让他们能够更便于采用共和制度，并能保证其长久存在。在这里，即使共和制度实际成果往往并不尽如人意，但至少其理论初衷是好的，所以，最终人民还是会按其原则行事。

在美国，无论是联邦建立之初还是现在乃至未来都难以建立中央集权制度。美国的居民分布得太广，彼此间还有无数的天然屏障，所以一个人无法对他们进行事无巨细的管理。所以，美国是一个地地道道的由州政府和乡镇政府管理的国家。除了这个所有新大陆的欧洲居民已感到的原因外，英裔美国人还加上了几个他们特有的原因。

北美殖民地建立之初，乡镇自由的精神就已经深入英国人的法律和民情。英国的移民

was odious, under whatever form it appeared. But it is a discovery of modern days that there are such things as legitimate tyranny and holy injustice, provided they are exercised in the name of the people.

The ideas which the Americans have adopted respecting the republican form of government, render it easy for them to live under it, and insure its duration. If, in their country, this form be often practically bad, at least it is theoretically good; and, in the end, the people always acts in conformity to it.

It was impossible at the foundation of the States, and it would still be difficult, to establish a central administration in America. The inhabitants are dispersed over too great a space, and separated by too many natural obstacles, for one man to undertake to direct the details of their existence. America is therefore pre-eminently the country of provincial and municipal government. To this cause, which was plainly felt by all the Europeans of the New World, the Anglo-Americans added several others peculiar to themselves.

At the time of the settlement of the North American colonies, municipal liberty had already penetrated into the laws as well as the manners of the English; and the emigrants adopted it, not only as a necessary thing, but as a benefit which they knew how to appreciate. We have already seen the manner in which the colonies were founded: every province, and almost every district, was peopled separately by men who were strangers to each other, or who associated with very different purposes. The English settlers in the United States, therefore, early perceived that they were divided into a great number of small and distinct communities which belonged to no common centre; and that it was needful for each of these little communities to take care of its own affairs, since there did not appear to be any central authority which was naturally bound and easily enabled to provide for them. Thus, the nature of the country, the manner in which the British colonies were founded, the habits of the first emigrants, in short everything, united to promote, in an extraordinary degree, municipal and provincial liberties.

In the United States, therefore, the mass of the institutions of the country is essentially republican; and in order permanently to destroy the laws which form the basis of the republic, it would be necessary to abolish all the laws at once. At the present day it would be even more difficult for a party to succeed in founding a monarchy in the United States than for a set of men to proclaim that France should

不仅将其视为必不可少的东西，而且视为极具价值的东西保留下来。我们已经说过殖民地是如何建立起来的。在每个地方，几乎每个教区，都被一些彼此陌生或出于不同目的聚集起来的人们割据。因此，美国的英国居民很早就意识到他们被分成许许多多各自为政的小社区，每个小社区都需要自行管理自己的事务，因为似乎并不存在任何中央当局应当或是可以轻易对它们进行治理。因此，这个国家的自然条件，英国殖民地建立的方式，第一批移民的习惯，简而言之就是所有一切，共同作用促成乡镇和地方自由的惊人发展。

因此，在美国，国家的所有制度本质上都是共和制，而如果想要永远摧毁共和制度建立的法律基础，必须同时废除所有的法律。今天，如果一个党派想要在美国建立君主专制，要比在法国建立共和还要难上加难。法国的王权在建立之前并没有拟定一套立法制度，所以只是实际上被共和制度包围起来的君主政体。所以，君主政体的原则在向美国民情渗透时也遭遇同样的困难。

在美国，人民主权并不是一个孤立的学说，并非与人民中盛行的民情和观念毫无关联，相反应该被视为联系整个英裔美国世界的最后一环。上帝赋予每一个人必要的一定理性以处理与自己息息相关的事务。美国的市民社会和政治社会就是建立在这样的伟大准则之上。一家之长将其用于子女，主人用于奴仆，乡镇用于官员，县用于乡镇，州用于县，联邦用于各州，而当它被扩大到整个国家的时候，就成为人民主权学说。

所以，在美国，共和的基本原则与制约人类行为的大部分原则相同。共和的观念在

henceforward be a republic. Royalty would not find a system of legislation prepared for it beforehand; and a monarchy would then exist, really surrounded by republican institutions. The monarchical principle would likewise have great difficulty in penetrating into the manners of the Americans.

In the United States, the sovereignty of the people is not an isolated doctrine bearing no relation to the prevailing manners and ideas of the people: it may, on the contrary, be regarded as the last link of a chain of opinions which binds the whole Anglo-American world. That Providence has given to every human being the degree of reason necessary to direct himself in the affairs which interest him exclusively—such is the grand maxim upon which civil and political society rests in the United States. The father of a family applies it to his children; the master to his servants; the township to its officers; the province to its townships; the State to its provinces; the Union to the States; and when extended to the nation, it becomes the doctrine of the sovereignty of the people.

Thus, in the United States, the fundamental principle of the republic is the same which governs the greater part of human actions; republican notions insinuate themselves into all the ideas, opinions, and habits of the Americans, whilst they are formerly recognized by the legislation: and before this legislation can be altered the whole community must undergo very serious changes. In the United States, even the religion of most of the citizens is republican, since it submits the truths of the other world to private judgment: as in politics the care of its temporal interests is abandoned to the good sense of the people. Thus every man is allowed freely to take that road which he thinks will lead him to heaven; just as the law permits every citizen to have the right of choosing his government.

It is evident that nothing but a long series of events, all having the same tendency, can substitute for this combination of laws, opinions, and manners, a mass of opposite opinions, manners, and laws.

If republican principles are to perish in America, they can only yield after a laborious social process, often interrupted, and as often resumed; they will have many apparent revivals, and will not become totally extinct until an entirely new people shall have succeeded to that which now exists. Now, it must be admitted that there is no symptom or presage of the approach of such a revolution. There is nothing more striking to a person newly arrived in the United States, than the kind of tumultuous agitation in which he finds political society. The laws are incessantly changing, and at

得到立法认可的同时，早已深入到美国人的所有思想、看法和习惯之中，而想要改变其法律，必须先要改变所有这一切。在美国，甚至大多数公民信仰的宗教也是共和的，因为宗教让来世的真理服从个人的判断，就好像政治对个人现实私利的关心要服从人民的判断。因此，每个人都可以自由选择他认为会将自己引向天堂的道路，就好像法律允许每个公民有权选择自己的政府一样。

显而易见，只有一连串具有同样倾向的事件共同发生作用才能用一套相反的观念、民情和法律取代现在的这套观念、民情和法律。

如果共和的原则在美国覆灭，也只有在经过时胜时败的长期反复斗争之后才有可能，而且，共和的许多原则还会反复，不会完全灭绝，直到一个全新的民族取代现有的民族。现在，必须承认并没有这样一场革命到来的征兆或预示。在美国，最令初来乍到的人大吃一惊的是政治社会的动荡不安。法律不断地变化，以至于乍看起来这样一个人们信念不断变化的国家无可避免地将很快被另一个全新的政府所取代。然而，这样的看法很不成熟。政治制度的不稳定有两种情形，不能将两者混淆起来。第一种是不断对次要法律进行修改，但并不会影响社会的稳定；第二种会动摇宪法的基础，破坏立法的基本原则。这样的不稳定往往会导致动乱和革命接踵而来，而深受其害的国家也将处于动荡之中。

经验告诉我们立法的这两种不稳定性并没有必然的联系，因为随着时间和情况的不同，它们彼此之间有时密不可分，有时互不相干。而我们在美国普遍看到的是第一种而不

first sight it seems impossible that a people so variable in its desires should avoid adopting, within a short space of time, a completely new form of government. Such apprehensions are, however, premature; the instability which affects political institutions is of two kinds, which ought not to be confounded: the first, which modifies secondary laws, is not incompatible with a very settled state of society; the other shakes the very foundations of the Constitution, and attacks the fundamental principles of legislation; this species of instability is always followed by troubles and revolutions, and the nation which suffers under it is in a state of violent transition.

Experience shows that these two kinds of legislative instability have no necessary connection; for they have been found united or separate, according to times and circumstances. The first is common in the United States, but not the second: the Americans often change their laws, but the foundation of the Constitution is respected.

In our days the republican principle rules in America, as the monarchical principle did in France under Louis XIV. The French of that period were not only friends of the monarchy, but they thought it impossible to put anything in its place; they received it as we receive the rays of the sun and the return of the seasons. Amongst them the royal power had neither advocates nor opponents. In like manner does the republican government exist in America, without contention or opposition; without proofs and arguments, by a tacit agreement, a sort of consensus universalis. It is, however, my opinion that by changing their administrative forms as often as they do, the inhabitants of the United States compromise the future stability of their government.

It may be apprehended that men, perpetually thwarted in their designs by the mutability of the legislation, will learn to look upon republican institutions as an inconvenient form of society; the evil resulting from the instability of the secondary enactments might then raise a doubt as to the nature of the fundamental principles of the Constitution, and indirectly bring about a revolution; but this epoch is still very remote.

It may, however, be foreseen even now, that when the Americans lose their republican institutions they will speedily arrive at a despotic government, without a long interval of limited monarchy. Montesquieu remarked, that nothing is more absolute than the authority of a prince who immediately

是第二种。尽管美国人时常改变其法律，但是宪法的基础却一直受到尊重。

在我们这个时代，共和主义原则在美国的统治，就如同路易十四时期君主制原则在法国的统治一般。那一时期的法国人不但热爱君主制，而且认为没有什么可以将其取代。君主政体之于他们，就好像我们接受阳光的沐浴和四季的轮回一般自然。那时的法国人之中，既没有王权的积极拥护者，也没有激烈反对者。就跟如今在美国的共和政府一样，是一种默认的，consensus universalis（一致认可）的存在，既没有争议反对，也无须证明反驳。然而，我认为，美国居民如果总像他们对行政管理制度那样改来改去，共和政府未来的稳定性必会受到影响。

可以理解，由于立法的不稳定性而计划不断受挫的人们必然会将共和体制视为一种不方便的社会形式。那么，次级立法不稳定引发的不良后果也许会引起对宪法基本原则本质的质疑，并间接导致革命的发生。但是这个时代还远未到来。

可是，即使现在我们也能预见，当美国人放弃共和制度后，将经历一个短暂的君主政体后，迅速进入独裁统治。孟德斯鸠曾经说过，再没有比继共和之后建立的君主政体更独裁的了，因为原先毫不担心的交给民选首脑的所有权力，此时全部落入世袭君主的手中。这是一个普遍的真理，而且特别适用于一个民主共和国。在美国，立法官员并不是公民中的特定阶级，而是由国家的多数选出，他们是大众热情的直接代表，而且因为他们完全依赖于多数的喜好，所以人们既不憎恨也不害怕他们。因此，正如我已经说过的那样，人们

succeeds a republic, since the powers which had fearlessly been intrusted to an elected magistrate are then transferred to a hereditary sovereign. This is true in general, but it is more peculiarly applicable to a democratic republic. In the United States, the magistrates are not elected by a particular class of citizens, but by the majority of the nation; they are the immediate representatives of the passions of the multitude; and as they are wholly dependent upon its pleasure, they excite neither hatred nor fear: hence, as I have already shown, very little care has been taken to limit their influence, and they are left in possession of a vast deal of arbitrary power. This state of things has engendered habits which would outlive itself; the American magistrate would retain his power, but he would cease to be responsible for the exercise of it; and it is impossible to say what bounds could then be set to tyranny.

Some of our European politicians expect to see an aristocracy arise in America, and they already predict the exact period at which it will be able to assume the reins of government. I have previously observed, and I repeat my assertion, that the present tendency of American society appears to me to become more and more democratic. Nevertheless, I do not assert that the Americans will not, at some future time, restrict the circle of political rights in their country, or confiscate those rights to the advantage of a single individual; but I cannot imagine that they will ever bestow the exclusive exercise of them upon a privileged class of citizens, or, in other words, that they will ever found an aristocracy.

An aristocratic body is composed of a certain number of citizens who, without being very far removed from the mass of the people, are, nevertheless, permanently stationed above it: a body which it is easy to touch and difficult to strike; with which the people are in daily contact, but with which they can never combine. Nothing can be imagined more contrary to nature and to the secret propensities of the human heart than a subjection of this kind; and men who are left to follow their own bent will always prefer the arbitrary power of a king to the regular administration of an aristocracy. Aristocratic institutions cannot subsist without laying down the inequality of men as a fundamental principle, as a part and parcel of the legislation, affecting the condition of the human family as much as it affects that of society; but these are things so repugnant to natural equity that they can only be extorted from men by constraint.

并不关心对他们的权力加以限制，而是留给他们很大一部分的专制权力。这样的状况催生了一些比起自身更具生命力的习惯。美国的立法官员，在国会休会或是离职之后，依然拥有影响力，而且很难说暴政将在何时何地终止。

我们欧洲的一些政客希望美国出现贵族政体，他们甚至已经预测贵族政府将在什么时期驾驭政府。前面我已经说过，这里我还要再重复一遍，美国社会目前的趋势，在我看来，正变得越来越民主。然而，我并不断言未来美国人将不会为政治权力划定范围，或不将这些权力没收而为一人所独享。但是我无法想象，他们会让社会中某一特权阶级独享这些权力，或者换句话说，他们将建立贵族政体。

贵族集团由一定数量的公民组成，他们尽管并未远离大众，但是永远凌驾于他们之上；是一个可以轻易触及却无法达到的集团；人们天天与之打交道，却永远无法与之融合。无法想象，还能有什么比这种服从更加有违人类天性和内心的隐秘倾向。而随心所欲的人们宁可服从国王的专制也不愿屈服于贵族的正规管理。贵族制度的存在要以不平等为基础原则，并作为立法的一部分，不但影响人们的家庭状况而且影响社会状况。但是，这些与天生平等相矛盾的东西，只有通过强制手段才能强加于人。

我并不认为，自人类社会存在以来，出现过一个国家根据自己的自由意志自行建立起贵族政体的例子。所有中世纪的贵族政体都是军事征服的产物，征服者是贵族，被征服者成为奴隶。于是，不平等通过武力得以实现，随后成为民情，用于维护自己的统治，并被

I do not think a single people can be quoted, since human society began to exist, which has, by its own free will and by its own exertions, created an aristocracy within its own bosom. All the aristocracies of the Middle Ages were founded by military conquest; the conqueror was the noble, the vanquished became the serf. Inequality was then imposed by force; and after it had been introduced into the manners of the country it maintained its own authority, and was sanctioned by the legislation. Communities have existed which were aristocratic from their earliest origin, owing to circumstances anterior to that event, and which became more democratic in each succeeding age. Such was the destiny of the Romans, and of the barbarians after them. But a people, having taken its rise in civilization and democracy, which should gradually establish an inequality of conditions, until it arrived at inviolable privileges and exclusive castes, would be a novelty in the world; and nothing intimates that America is likely to furnish so singular an example.

Reflection On The Causes Of The Commercial Prosperity Of The Of The United States

The Americans destined by Nature to be a great maritime people—Extent of their coasts—Depth of their ports—Size of their rivers—The commercial superiority of the Anglo-Americans less attributable, however, to physical circumstances than to moral and intellectual causes—Reason of this opinion—Future destiny of the Anglo-Americans as a commercial nation—The dissolution of the Union would not check the maritime vigor of the States—Reason of this—Anglo-Americans will naturally supply the wants of the inhabitants of South America—They will become, like the English, the factors of a great portion of the world.

The coast of the United States, from the Bay of Fundy to the Sabine River in the Gulf of Mexico, is more than two thousand miles in extent. These shores form an unbroken line, and they are all subject to the same government. No nation in the world possesses vaster, deeper, or more secure ports for shipping than the Americans.

The inhabitants of the United States constitute a great civilized people, which fortune has placed in the midst of an uncultivated country at a distance of three thousand miles from the central point

法律所承认。一些社会，由于在其之前发生过的一些事件，成为天生的贵族社会，并随着时间的流逝，变得越来越民主。这就是罗马人和继其之后的强大的蛮族的命运。但是，一个已经文明和民主的国家，在逐步确立身份不平等后，最终出现不可侵犯的特权和唯我独尊的种姓，这才是世界的一大奇闻。而且没有任何暗示表明美国有可能成为这样的第一个例子。

美国商业兴盛的原因

美国人的天性注定其要成为一个伟大的海洋民族——美国漫长的海岸线——港口的水深——庞大的河流——但是，自然因素对英裔美国人商业优势的贡献不及道德和智力因素——原因何在——英裔美国人作为商业民族的未来——联邦的解体不会阻碍美国的海上活力——其原因何在——英裔美国人自然而然要满足南美居民的需求——像英国人一样，美国人会成为世界上大部分地区的代理人。

美国的海岸线，从芬迪湾到墨西哥湾的萨宾河，全长超过2000英里。这条绵延不断的海岸线全部归属同一政府管理。世界上，没有任何一个国家拥有比美国更大、更深和更可靠的港口。

美国的居民组建了一个伟大的文明国家，命运将他们安置在一片荒地之中，与文明的

of civilization. America consequently stands in daily need of European trade. The Americans will, no doubt, ultimately succeed in producing or manufacturing at home most of the articles which they require; but the two continents can never be independent of each other, so numerous are the natural ties which exist between their wants, their ideas, their habits, and their manners.

The Union produces peculiar commodities which are now become necessary to us, but which cannot be cultivated, or can only be raised at an enormous expense, upon the soil of Europe. The Americans only consume a small portion of this produce, and they are willing to sell us the rest. Europe is therefore the market of America, as America is the market of Europe; and maritime commerce is no less necessary to enable the inhabitants of the United States to transport their raw materials to the ports of Europe, than it is to enable us to supply them with our manufactured produce. The United States were therefore necessarily reduced to the alternative of increasing the business of other maritime nations to a great extent, if they had themselves declined to enter into commerce, as the Spaniards of Mexico have hitherto done; or, in the second place, of becoming one of the first trading powers of the globe.

The Anglo-Americans have always displayed a very decided taste for the sea. The Declaration of Independence broke the commercial restrictions which united them to England, and gave a fresh and powerful stimulus to their maritime genius. Ever since that time, the shipping of the Union has increased in almost the same rapid proportion as the number of its inhabitants. The Americans themselves now transport to their own shores nine-tenths of the European produce which they consume. And they also bring three-quarters of the exports of the New World to the European consumer. The ships of the United States fill the docks of Havre and of Liverpool; whilst the number of English and French vessels which are to be seen at New York is comparatively small.

Thus, not only does the American merchant face the competition of his own countrymen, but he even supports that of foreign nations in their own ports with success. This is readily explained by the fact that the vessels of the United States can cross the seas at a cheaper rate than any other vessels in the world. As long as the mercantile shipping of the United States preserves this superiority, it will not only retain what it has acquired, but it will constantly increase in prosperity.

中心相距3000英里之遥。所以，美国的日常需要完全仰赖欧洲。毫无疑问，美国人最终成功地在本土生产制造出大部分他们所需的物品，但是这两块大陆永远不可能完全对立互不相干，在它们之间存在着需求、思想、习惯和民情上的众多天然纽带。

联邦生产的一些特别商品已经成为我们的必需，因为这些东西不是无法在欧洲培育，就是所需成本太高。美国人只能消费这些产品的一小部分，所以他们很乐意卖给我们。因此，欧洲成为美国的市场，就像美国是欧洲的市场一样，而为了能够将美国的原材料运往欧洲，并将欧洲的成品运回美国，海上贸易必不可少。所以，美国不是像墨西哥的西班牙人迄今一直做的那样，放弃贸易而转向为海洋国家工业提供大量原材料，就是成为世界上的一流贸易强国。

英裔美国人一直以来都对海洋表现出一种明确的喜好。独立宣言在打破它与英国的贸易纽带的同时给予他们的航海天才一个新鲜有力的刺激。自此之后，联邦的船舶增长速度几乎与居民的增长速度同样快。现在，美国人消耗的十分之九的欧洲产品都是由他们自己的船只运输。而且他们还将四分之三的新大陆的出口货物运送给欧洲的消费者。美国的船只遍布哈佛和利物浦的码头，而英国和法国来到纽约的船只则相对较少。

因此，美国商人不但面对着自己同胞的竞争，还敢于与外国商人一较高下。这一点很好解释，因为美国船只的运费比世界上任何地方的都便宜。只要美国的海上商业运输保持这一优势，它不但可以保持现在的成就，而且还能变得越来越繁荣。

It is difficult to say for what reason the Americans can trade at a lower rate than other nations; and one is at first led to attribute this circumstance to the physical or natural advantages which are within their reach; but this supposition is erroneous. The American vessels cost almost as much to build as our own; they are not better built, and they generally last for a shorter time. The pay of the American sailor is more considerable than the pay on board European ships; which is proved by the great number of Europeans who are to be met with in the merchant vessels of the United States. But I am of opinion that the true cause of their superiority must not be sought for in physical advantages, but that it is wholly attributable to their moral and intellectual qualities.

The following comparison will illustrate my meaning. During the campaigns of the Revolution the French introduced a new system of tactics into the art of war, which perplexed the oldest generals, and very nearly destroyed the most ancient monarchies in Europe. They undertook (what had never before been attempted) to make shift without a number of things which had always been held to be indispensable in warfare; they required novel exertions on the part of their troops which no civilized nations had ever thought of; they achieved great actions in an incredibly short space of time; and they risked human life without hesitation to obtain the object in view. The French had less money and fewer men than their enemies; their resources were infinitely inferior; nevertheless they were constantly victorious, until their adversaries chose to imitate their example.

The Americans have introduced a similar system into their commercial speculations; and they do for cheapness what the French did for conquest. The European sailor navigates with prudence; he only sets sail when the weather is favorable; if an unforseen accident befalls him, he puts into port; at night he furls a portion of his canvas; and when the whitening billows intimate the vicinity of land, he checks his way, and takes an observation of the sun. But the American neglects these precautions and braves these dangers. He weighs anchor in the midst of tempestuous gales; by night and by day he spreads his sheets to the wind; he repairs as he goes along such damage as his vessel may have sustained from the storm; and when he at last approaches the term of his voyage, he darts onward to the shore as if he already descried a port. The Americans are often shipwrecked, but no trader crosses the seas so rapidly. And as they perform the same distance in a shorter time, they can perform it at a

很难说是什么原因让美国人的海上运营成本低于其他国家。有人主张，这首先应归功于美国人得天独厚的物质自然条件，但是这样的见解并不正确。美国船只的制造成本几乎与我们的完全一样，而且船造得也不好，一般用不了很长时间。美国人给水手的工资远高于欧洲船只，这就解释了为什么总是能够在美国商船上看到大量的欧洲人。所以，依我之见，他们的真正优势并非是物质优势，而应完全归功于他们的道德和智力特质。

下面的比较将证明我的看法。法国人在大革命期间，将一套新的战斗技巧用于军事艺术，令许多老将晕头转向，几乎摧毁了大多数的欧洲古老的王国。首先他们精简了一些一直被认为打仗必不可少的东西，并要求军队做出文明国家从未想过的新的努力。因此，他们在相对较短的时间内更多地行动，令他们的士兵能够毫不迟疑地冒着生命危险达成既定目标。法国人并不像他们的敌人那样财力雄厚人员充足，他们的物力远远处于劣势。然而，他们却能够不断取得胜利，直到敌人开始采用他们的战术。

美国人在商业方面采用了类似的战术，法国人为了取得战争胜利所做的一切，都被美国人用到降低航运成本上。欧洲的水手做事谨慎，只有天气有利的情况下才起航，要是有什么突发事故降临到他们头上，便会掉头回港，夜里，船员还会收起一部分船帆；而当白色的浪花泛起预示着陆地将近时，他会观察太阳小心调整路线。但是美国人则不会如此小心翼翼，敢于冒险行事。他们敢在剧烈的风暴中拔锚起航，不论是白天还是黑夜他们都全帆对风。他们一路航行，一路修理暴风雨给船只造成的损伤。当他们最终接近航程的终点

cheaper rate.

The European touches several times at different ports in the course of a long voyage; he loses a good deal of precious time in making the harbor, or in waiting for a favorable wind to leave it; and he pays daily dues to be allowed to remain there. The American starts from Boston to go to purchase tea in China; he arrives at Canton, stays there a few days, and then returns. In less than two years he has sailed as far as the entire circumference of the globe, and he has seen land but once. It is true that during a voyage of eight or ten months he has drunk brackish water and lived upon salt meat; that he has been in a continual contest with the sea, with disease, and with a tedious existence; but upon his return he can sell a pound of his tea for a half-penny less than the English merchant, and his purpose is accomplished.

I cannot better explain my meaning than by saying that the Americans affect a sort of heroism in their manner of trading. But the European merchant will always find it very difficult to imitate his American competitor, who, in adopting the system which I have just described, follows not only a calculation of his gain, but an impulse of his nature.

The inhabitants of the United States are subject to all the wants and all the desires which result from an advanced stage of civilization; but as they are not surrounded by a community admirably adapted, like that of Europe, to satisfy their wants, they are often obliged to procure for themselves the various articles which education and habit have rendered necessaries. In America it sometimes happens that the same individual tills his field, builds his dwelling, contrives his tools, makes his shoes, and weaves the coarse stuff of which his dress is composed. This circumstance is prejudicial to the excellence of the work; but it powerfully contributes to awaken the intelligence of the workman. Nothing tends to materialize man, and to deprive his work of the faintest trace of mind, more than extreme division of labor. In a country like America, where men devoted to special occupations are rare, a long apprenticeship cannot be required from anyone who embraces a profession. The Americans, therefore, change their means of gaining a livelihood very readily; and they suit their occupations to the exigencies of the moment, in the manner most profitable to themselves. Men are to be met with who have successively been barristers, farmers, merchants, ministers of the gospel, and

时，会继续扬帆前进，好像港口近在眼前似的急于靠岸。美国的船只常常在海上失事，但也没有哪个国家的船只能够像他们的船只那样迅速漂洋过海。因为他们能用更短的时间走完同样的距离，所以能够降低航运的成本。

欧洲船只在一次长途航行中需要多次停靠不同的港口。寻找靠岸的码头和等待有利时机起航让他们失去了宝贵的时间，而且每天还要支付停泊的费用。美国的商船从波士顿出发前往中国购买茶叶，到达广州后只停留数日便启程回国。不到两年的时间，航行的里程就能绕地球一圈，而且往复的途中只各靠岸一次。在一次八到十个月的航程中，船员喝的是咸水，吃的是腌肉，要不断跟大海、疾病和厌倦做斗争，但是只要他一回来就可以按每磅比英国商人便宜半便士的价格出售茶叶，这样他的目的就达到了。

除了说美国人在经商方面表现出一种英雄气概之外，没有更好的语言来表达我的意思。但是，欧洲商人永远也无法仿效他们的竞争对手。美国人之所以用我所描述的方式经商，并不是出于精打细算，而是天性使然。

美国的居民正在体验文明前进进程中的所有苦乐。但是他们并没有置身于一个如同欧洲那样的所有要求都能得到满足的社会，他们往往不得不靠自己去获得教育和习惯上必不可少的各种物品。在美国，有时候一个人既能耕地又能建屋，还能制造工具、做鞋，织布做衣。这虽不利于生产的进步，但却可以强有力地激发个人的才智。再没有什么比细致的分工能更令人变蠢，更能剥夺人们的匠人巧思的了。在一个像美国这样的国家，专门人才

physicians. If the American be less perfect in each craft than the European, at least there is scarcely any trade with which he is utterly unacquainted. His capacity is more general, and the circle of his intelligence is enlarged.

The inhabitants of the United States are never fettered by the axioms of their profession; they escape from all the prejudices of their present station; they are not more attached to one line of operation than to another; they are not more prone to employ an old method than a new one; they have no rooted habits, and they easily shake off the influence which the habits of other nations might exercise upon their minds from a conviction that their country is unlike any other, and that its situation is without a precedent in the world. America is a land of wonders, in which everything is in constant motion, and every movement seems an improvement. The idea of novelty is there indissolubly connected with the idea of amelioration. No natural boundary seems to be set to the efforts of man; and what is not yet done is only what he has not yet attempted to do.

This perpetual change which goes on in the United States, these frequent vicissitudes of fortune, accompanied by such unforeseen fluctuations in private and in public wealth, serve to keep the minds of the citizens in a perpetual state of feverish agitation, which admirably invigorates their exertions, and keeps them in a state of excitement above the ordinary level of mankind. The whole life of an American is passed like a game of chance, a revolutionary crisis, or a battle. As the same causes are continually in operation throughout the country, they ultimately impart an irresistible impulse to the national character. The American, taken as a chance specimen of his countrymen, must then be a man of singular warmth in his desires, enterprising, fond of adventure, and, above all, of innovation. The same bent is manifest in all that he does; he introduces it into his political laws, his religious doctrines, his theories of social economy, and his domestic occupations; he bears it with him in the depths of the backwoods, as well as in the business of the city. It is this same passion, applied to maritime commerce, which makes him the cheapest and the quickest trader in the world.

As long as the sailors of the United States retain these inspiriting advantages, and the practical superiority which they derive from them, they will not only continue to supply the wants of the producers and consumers of their own country, but they will tend more and more to become, like the

很少，从事任何职业也不需要长期的学习。因此，美国人能随时改变他们的谋生之道，随时找最有利可图的行业来做。有些人一生之中当过律师，种过地，经过商，做过教士和医生。如果说美国人在每一行上都没有欧洲人高超，但至少没有什么是他一窍不通的。他的能力一般，但知识范围很广。

美国的居民从不会让行业的清规戒律束手束脚，也没有任何职业偏见，既不厚此薄彼也不尚古轻今。他们没有根深蒂固的习惯，很容易摆脱外国习惯对他们的精神可能产生的影响。他们的情况堪称史无前例。美国是一片神奇之地，在这里一切都在变化之中，而且每次的变化都似乎是在进步。在这里，新奇的思想和改良的思想紧密结合。人的努力似乎也无止境，在他们看来，没有做的事情不过是他们还没来得及尝试。

美国的不断变化，运气的好坏无常，以及不可预见的私人财富和公共财富的起起落落，让人们的精神始终处于一种狂热的状态，让他们奋发图强，不甘落后。美国人的一生就好像一场赌博，一次革命，一场战斗。因为相同因素的在整个国家持续发挥作用，最终国民性被打上了不可抑制的冲动的烙印。美国人随时随地都热心追求，积极进取，热爱冒险，尤其是锐意革新的人。他们的这种嗜好体现在他们所做的所有事情上，他们把这种爱好带入政治法律、宗教信条、社会经济学说以及个人职业活动。他们将这种爱好带到森林深处，繁华的城市。正是应用到海上贸易的这股同样的激情，让他们拥有世界上最快最经济的商船。

English, the factors of all other peoples. This prediction has already begun to be realized; we perceive that the American traders are introducing themselves as intermediate agents in the commerce of several European nations; and America will offer a still wider field to their enterprise.

The great colonies which were founded in South America by the Spaniards and the Portuguese have since become empires. Civil war and oppression now lay waste those extensive regions. Population does not increase, and the thinly scattered inhabitants are too much absorbed in the cares of self-defense even to attempt any amelioration of their condition. Such, however, will not always be the case. Europe has succeeded by her own efforts in piercing the gloom of the Middle Ages; South America has the same Christian laws and Christian manners as we have; she contains all the germs of civilization which have grown amidst the nations of Europe or their offsets, added to the advantages to be derived from our example: why then should she always remain uncivilized? It is clear that the question is simply one of time; at some future period, which may be more or less remote, the inhabitants of South America will constitute flourishing and enlightened nations.

But when the Spaniards and Portuguese of South America begin to feel the wants common to all civilized nations, they will still be unable to satisfy those wants for themselves; as the youngest children of civilization, they must perforce admit the superiority of their elder brethren. They will be agriculturists long before they succeed in manufactures or commerce, and they will require the mediation of strangers to exchange their produce beyond seas for those articles for which a demand will begin to be felt.

It is unquestionable that the Americans of the North will one day supply the wants of the Americans of the South. Nature has placed them in contiguity, and has furnished the former with every means of knowing and appreciating those demands, of establishing a permanent connection with those States, and of gradually filling their markets. The merchants of the United States could only forfeit these natural advantages if he were very inferior to the merchant of Europe; to whom he is, on the contrary, superior in several respects. The Americans of the United States already exercise a very considerable moral influence upon all the peoples of the New World. They are the source of intelligence, and all the nations which inhabit the same continent are already accustomed to consider

只要美国的水手保持这种精神上的优势，以及由此而来的实际优势，他们不但能够满足国内生产者和消费者的需要，而且能够越来越像英国人一样成为世界其他国家的商务代理人。人们已经开始注意到这样的预示。我们发觉美国的商人正在充当几个欧洲国家商业的直接代理人，而且美国将给他们的事业提供更为广阔的天地。

西班牙和葡萄牙在南美建立的一些大的殖民地已经成帝国。内战和压迫让这片广阔的土地被浪费。人口没有增长，住在这里的为数不多的居民每天为自保而惶惶不可终日，根本没有心思改善他们的状况。然而，情况不会永远如此。欧洲经过自己的努力已经成功地打破了黑暗的中世纪。南美有同我们一样的基督教的法律和民情，拥有所有的在欧洲及其子孙之中生长的文明萌芽，以及我们的例子可供借鉴，那么，为什么它依旧如此蒙昧呢？显然，这只是一个时间问题，在或近或远的未来，南美的居民将成为文明繁荣的民族。

但是当南美的西班牙人和葡萄牙人感到文明国家的共同需要的时候，他们依然无法自己满足这些需要。作为文明最年幼的孩子，他们必须承认大哥们的优势。在他们学会工业生产和商业之前，还要做很长一段时间的农民。他们需要外国人做中介，将他们的产品运往海外销售以换取他们生产所需的东西。

毋庸置疑，北美的美国人总有一天将要为南美人的需求提供满足。大自然让他们毗邻而居，并赋予前者了解调查后者需求的手段，与之建立永久的来往，并逐渐占领他们的市场。美国的商人除非比欧洲商人差得远，否则不会错失这样得天独厚的天然优势，而且他

them as the most enlightened, the most powerful, and the most wealthy members of the great American family. All eyes are therefore turned towards the Union; and the States of which that body is composed are the models which the other communities try to imitate to the best of their power; it is from the United States that they borrow their political principles and their laws.

The Americans of the United States stand in precisely the same position with regard to the peoples of South America as their fathers, the English, occupy with regard to the Italians, the Spaniards, the Portuguese, and all those nations of Europe which receive their articles of daily consumption from England, because they are less advanced in civilization and trade. England is at this time the natural emporium of almost all the nations which are within its reach; the American Union will perform the same part in the other hemisphere; and every community which is founded, or which prospers in the New World, is founded and prospers to the advantage of the Anglo-Americans.

If the Union were to be dissolved, the commerce of the States which now compose it would undoubtedly be checked for a time; but this consequence would be less perceptible than is generally supposed. It is evident that, whatever may happen, the commercial States will remain united. They are all contiguous to each other; they have identically the same opinions, interests, and manners; and they are alone competent to form a very great maritime power. Even if the South of the Union were to become independent of the North, it would still require the services of those States. I have already observed that the South is not a commercial country, and nothing intimates that it is likely to become so. The Americans of the South of the United States will therefore be obliged, for a long time to come, to have recourse to strangers to export their produce, and to supply them with the commodities which are requisite to satisfy their wants. But the Northern States are undoubtedly able to act as their intermediate agents cheaper than any other merchants. They will therefore retain that employment, for cheapness is the sovereign law of commerce. National claims and national prejudices cannot resist the influence of cheapness. Nothing can be more virulent than the hatred which exists between the Americans of the United States and the English. But notwithstanding these inimical feelings, the Americans derive the greater part of their manufactured commodities from England, because England

们在其他方面也具备优势。美国人已经对所有新大陆的居民产生强大的精神影响。他们是知识之源，生活在这片大陆上的所有民族都已经习惯于将他们视为最文明、最强大、最富有的美洲大家庭的成员。因此，所有的眼光都投向它，一有机会就尽力仿效住在这里的居民，他们借鉴美国的政治理论和法制。

美国人在南美人面前的地位如同他们的祖先英国人在意大利人、西班牙人、葡萄牙人乃至所有欧洲民族面前的地位一样，因为它们在文化和工业上都不及英国，所以这些国家所有日常消费品都要仰仗英国。今天，英国是几乎所有与其有往来的国家的天然商业中心。美联邦将在另一个半球扮演起相同的角色。在新大陆建立或发展起来的每一个国家，其建立和发展都对英裔美国人有利。

如果联邦解体，各州的发展无疑将会在一段时间内放缓，但其后果必然不会如人们想象的那么严重。显而易见，无论发生什么，各州的商业联合将会保持下去。他们彼此相邻，观念、利益和民情一致，而且只有他们能够形成一个海洋强国。即使联邦的南方脱离北方独立，它依然需要北方的帮助。我已经说过，南方不是一个商业地区，而且也没有什么东西预示它会成为这样的地区。所以，美国的南方人不得不长期依靠外人将货物运出去再将他们所需要的东西带给他们。而无疑，北方州会扮演起比所有其他商人更物美价廉的中间代理商的角色。因此，他们自己也会找上北方，因为低价才是商业的至高法则。国家的主权和偏见都顶不住低价的影响。什么也比不上美国人和英国人之间的憎恨更强烈。然而，尽管存在这种敌对的情感，但是美国人的很大一部分制成品都来自英国，因为英国的

supplies them at a cheaper rate than any other nation. Thus the increasing prosperity of America turns, notwithstanding the grudges of the Americans, to the advantage of British manufactures.

Reason shows and experience proves that no commercial prosperity can be durable if it cannot be united, in case of need, to naval force. This truth is as well understood in the United States as it can be anywhere else: the Americans are already able to make their flag respected; in a few years they will be able to make it feared. I am convinced that the dismemberment of the Union would not have the effect of diminishing the naval power of the Americans, but that it would powerfully contribute to increase it. At the present time the commercial States are connected with others which have not the same interests, and which frequently yield an unwilling consent to the increase of a maritime power by which they are only indirectly benefited. If, on the contrary, the commercial States of the Union formed one independent nation, commerce would become the foremost of their national interests; they would consequently be willing to make very great sacrifices to protect their shipping, and nothing would prevent them from pursuing their designs upon this point.

Nations, as well as men, almost always betray the most prominent features of their future destiny in their earliest years. When I contemplate the ardor with which the Anglo-Americans prosecute commercial enterprise, the advantages which befriend them, and the success of their undertakings, I cannot refrain from believing that they will one day become the first maritime power of the globe. They are born to rule the seas, as the Romans were to conquer the world.

产品比其他国家的都便宜。因此，美国变得越来越繁荣，不管美国人愿意与否，都会给英国的制造业带来好处。

理性告诉我们，而且经验也向我们证明，不联合就不会有持久的商业繁荣，而且必要的时候，还需要武力的支援。跟其他国家一样，美国也深深懂得这个道理。美国已经能够让它的旗帜在世界上获得尊重，过不了几年，它会令人感到畏惧。我肯定，联邦的解体不会削弱美国人的海上力量，反而会大大促进它的增长。今天，商业州与那些非商业州联合，彼此没有共同的利益，所以后者只是勉强同意提高与它们并无直接关系的海军力量。相反，如果联邦的所有商业州成立一个独立的国家，商业将成为它们最首要的国家利益，所以，它们会非常乐于为了保护航运而做出巨大牺牲，而且什么也不能阻止他们实现这一目标。

国家同人一样，几乎总是在年幼时就暴露出其未来命运最显著的特征。当我思索英裔美国人对商业的那股狂热劲儿、他们的优势以及所取得的成功时，我不禁相信他们有一天必然会成为世界上的第一海上强国。他们生来就要统治海洋，就好像罗马人生来就要征服世界一样。

Conclusion

I have now nearly reached the close of my inquiry; hitherto, in speaking of the future destiny of the United States, I have endeavored to divide my subject into distinct portions, in order to study each of them with more attention. My present object is to embrace the whole from one single point; the remarks I shall make will be less detailed, but they will be more sure. I shall perceive each object less distinctly, but I shall descry the principal facts with more certainty. A traveller who has just left the walls of an immense city, climbs the neighboring hill; as he goes father off he loses sight of the men whom he has so recently quitted; their dwellings are confused in a dense mass; he can no longer distinguish the public squares, and he can scarcely trace out the great thoroughfares; but his eye has less difficulty in following the boundaries of the city, and for the first time he sees the shape of the vast whole. Such is the future destiny of the British race in North America to my eye; the details of the stupendous picture are overhung with shade, but I conceive a clear idea of the entire subject.

The territory now occupied or possessed by the United States of America forms about one-twentieth part of the habitable earth. But extensive as these confines are, it must not be supposed that the Anglo-American race will always remain within them; indeed, it has already far overstepped them.

There was once a time at which we also might have created a great French nation in the American wilds, to counterbalance the influence of the English upon the destinies of the New World. France formerly possessed a territory in North America, scarcely less extensive than the whole of Europe. The three greatest rivers of that continent then flowed within her dominions. The Indian tribes which

结论

现在，我的叙述即将结束。到目前为止，在探讨美国未来命运时，我努力将题目分成几个不同的部分，以便于专心研究每个题目。现在我要做的就是要从总体进行通观，接下来我的表述会更加宏观，但也更准确。我对每个问题的分析可能不如原来清晰，但却更能准确把握事实。一个刚刚走出大都市围墙的旅行者爬上附近的小山，但他离城市越来越远，看到的行人越来越稀少，房舍也模糊不清；他无法再看清公共场所的模样，也看不出街道的位置，但是却可以一眼看清城市的轮廓，他第一次看到这个城市的整体。这个就是我眼中北美英国人的未来命运，这个巨幅画作的细节也许还不够清晰，但我已对它的全貌有了清晰的概念。

美国占据并拥有的土地大约占整个地球可居住土地的二十分之一。尽管土地如此辽阔，但绝不要以为英裔美国人种会一直停留于此，实际上，他们现在就已经远远超出这个范围。

曾经有一个时期，我们也有可能在美洲的荒野上建立一个伟大的法兰西国家，与英国人对新大陆命运的影响分庭抗礼。法国曾经在北美占据的土地并不比整个欧洲小。

dwelt between the mouth of the St. Lawrence and the delta of the Mississippi were unaccustomed to any other tongue but ours; and all the European settlements scattered over that immense region recalled the traditions of our country. Louisbourg, Montmorency, Duquesne, St. Louis, Vincennes, New Orleans (for such were the names they bore) are words dear to France and familiar to our ears.

But a concourse of circumstances, which it would be tedious to enumerate, have deprived us of this magnificent inheritance. Wherever the French settlers were numerically weak and partially established, they have disappeared: those who remain are collected on a small extent of country, and are now subject to other laws. The 400,000 French inhabitants of Lower Canada constitute, at the present time, the remnant of an old nation lost in the midst of a new people. A foreign population is increasing around them unceasingly and on all sides, which already penetrates amongst the ancient masters of the country, predominates in their cities and corrupts their language. This population is identical with that of the United States; it is therefore with truth that I asserted that the British race is not confined within the frontiers of the Union, since it already extends to the northeast.

To the northwest nothing is to be met with but a few insignificant Russian settlements; but to the southwest, Mexico presents a barrier to the Anglo-Americans. Thus, the Spaniards and the Anglo-Americans are, properly speaking, the only two races which divide the possession of the New World. The limits of separation between them have been settled by a treaty; but although the conditions of that treaty are exceedingly favorable to the Anglo-Americans, I do not doubt that they will shortly infringe this arrangement. Vast provinces, extending beyond the frontiers of the Union towards Mexico, are still destitute of inhabitants. The natives of the United States will forestall the rightful occupants of these solitary regions. They will take possession of the soil, and establish social institutions, so that when the legal owner arrives at length, he will find the wilderness under cultivation, and strangers quietly settled in the midst of his inheritance.

The lands of the New World belong to the first occupant, and they are the natural reward of the swiftest pioneer. Even the countries which are already peopled will have some difficulty in securing themselves from this invasion. I have already alluded to what is taking place in the province of

美洲大陆三条最大的河流穿过我们管辖的这片土地。居住在圣劳伦斯河口以及密西西比三角洲的印第安部落曾经只听过我们的语言，散居在这片辽阔土地上的所有欧洲移民都会令人想起我们法国的传统。路易堡（Louisbourg）、蒙莫朗西（Montmorency）、迪凯纳（Duquesne）、圣路易（Saint-Louis）、万森（Vincennes）、新奥尔良（Nouvelle-Orkans），这些都是法国人听起来最亲切熟悉的字眼。

但是，一连串不胜枚举的情况，让我们失去了这笔巨大的遗产。在法国移民本就不多，而且也没有很好开发的地方，现在连法国人的影子也看不到了。仅剩的为数不多的法国人聚居在一个狭小的地区，正在接受别人的法律的管辖。现在，加拿大有法裔居民40万人，是一个古老民族在新民族汪洋中的残余。在他们的身边和四面八方，外国人的数量不断增长，取代了这片土地原来的主人，统治了他们的城市，破坏了他们语言。这些人就是来自美国的居民。所以，我所说的英国人种已经走出联邦是事实，因为他们已经向东北蔓延。

在西北，只有几个不太重要的俄国定居点，而在西南，墨西哥人成为英裔美国人的障碍。因此，确切地说，西班牙人和英裔美国人这两个种族分占新大陆。双方已经签订条约划定分界线。但是，尽管这个条约对英裔美国人极为有利，但是我丝毫不怀疑，他们很快就会破坏这个条约。在联邦与墨西哥的边界外侧，有大片大片依旧无人居住的地区。美国人抢在有权占领这片荒地的人之前来到这里。他们占据了这里的土地，建立起乡镇，而当这里的合法拥有者最终到来的时候，发现这边荒地已经被开发，外来的陌生人已经悄悄地在他们的遗产上定居下来。

Texas. The inhabitants of the United States are perpetually migrating to Texas, where they purchase land; and although they conform to the laws of the country, they are gradually founding the empire of their own language and their own manners. The province of Texas is still part of the Mexican dominions, but it will soon contain no Mexicans; the same thing has occurred whenever the Anglo-Americans have come into contact with populations of a different origin.

It cannot be denied that the British race has acquired an amazing preponderance over all the other European races in the New World; and that it is very superior to them in civilization, in industry, and in power. As long as it is only surrounded by desert or thinly peopled countries, as long as it encounters no dense populations upon its route, through which it cannot work its way, it will assuredly continue to spread. The lines marked out by treaties will not stop it; but it will everywhere transgress these imaginary barriers.

The geographical position of the British race in the New World is peculiarly favorable to its rapid increase. Above its northern frontiers the icy regions of the Pole extend; and a few degrees below its southern confines lies the burning climate of the Equator. The Anglo-Americans are, therefore, placed in the most temperate and habitable zone of the continent.

It is generally supposed that the prodigious increase of population in the United States is posterior to their Declaration of Independence. But this is an error: the population increased as rapidly under the colonial system as it does at the present day; that is to say, it doubled in about twenty-two years. But this proportion which is now applied to millions, was then applied to thousands of inhabitants; and the same fact which was scarcely noticeable a century ago, is now evident to every observer.

The British subjects in Canada, who are dependent on a king, augment and spread almost as rapidly as the British settlers of the United States, who live under a republican government. During the war of independence, which lasted eight years, the population continued to increase without intermission in the same ratio. Although powerful Indian nations allied with the English existed at that time upon the western frontiers, the emigration westward was never checked. Whilst the enemy laid waste the shores of the Atlantic, Kentucky, the western parts of Pennsylvania, and the States of

新大陆的土地归属于最先占据那里的人，是对最迅捷开拓者的奖赏。即使是那些已经有人居住的地方都很难让自己免受这样的侵犯。我已经说过在德克萨斯发生的事情。美国的居民不断向德克萨斯迁移，他们在这里购买土地，尽管他们服从当地的法律，但是渐渐地他们的语言和民情占据统治地位。德克萨斯依旧属于墨西哥的管辖，但是这里不再有墨西哥人。只要英裔美国人与不同种族的人发生接触，就会发生同样的事情。

不能否认，英裔人在新大陆已经获得超越所有其他欧洲人种的巨大优势，而且在文化、工业和力量上都远胜于他们。只要在他们的周围有荒地或是人烟稀少的地方，只要在他们前进的道路上没有人口稠密无法逾越的地方，他们就要不断扩张下去。条约标识出的界限不能让他们停下脚步，他们会逾越所有这些不真实的障碍。

英裔人种在新大陆的地理位置特别有利于他们的快速扩张。北方的边界外是北极的寒冷地带；南方的边界向下几个纬度就是灼热难耐的赤道地区。因此，英裔美国人位于这片大陆气候最温和宜人的地带。

一般来说，人们认为美国人口的飞速增长始于独立宣言之后。但是这是个错误看法。在这里，殖民时期的人口增长速度跟现在一样快速，也就是说，人口大约每22年翻一番。只不过现在的人口增长以百万计，而那时以几十万计罢了。一个世纪以前，同样的现象不易被人察觉，而现在所有人都能看得清清楚楚。

在加拿大，隶属同一国王管辖的英国臣民增长和扩张的速度几乎与生活在共和政府下的美国的英国移民一样快。在持续了8年的独立战争期间，人口依然按照原有的速率上涨，

Vermont and of Maine were filling with inhabitants. Nor did the unsettled state of the Constitution, which succeeded the war, prevent the increase of the population, or stop its progress across the wilds. Thus, the difference of laws, the various conditions of peace and war, of order and of anarchy, have exercised no perceptible influence upon the gradual development of the Anglo-Americans. This may be readily understood; for the fact is, that no causes are sufficiently general to exercise a simultaneous influence over the whole of so extensive a territory. One portion of the country always offers a sure retreat from the calamities which afflict another part; and however great may be the evil, the remedy which is at hand is greater still.

It must not, then, be imagined that the impulse of the British race in the New World can be arrested. The dismemberment of the Union, and the hostilities which might ensure, the abolition of republican institutions, and the tyrannical government which might succeed it, may retard this impulse, but they cannot prevent it from ultimately fulfilling the destinies to which that race is reserved. No power upon earth can close upon the emigrants that fertile wilderness which offers resources to all industry, and a refuge from all want. Future events, of whatever nature they may be, will not deprive the Americans of their climate or of their inland seas, of their great rivers or of their exuberant soil. Nor will bad laws, revolutions, and anarchy be able to obliterate that love of prosperity and that spirit of enterprise which seem to be the distinctive characteristics of their race, or to extinguish that knowledge which guides them on their way.

Thus, in the midst of the uncertain future, one event at least is sure. At a period which may be said to be near (for we are speaking of the life of a nation), the Anglo-Americans will alone cover the immense space contained between the polar regions and the tropics, extending from the coasts of the Atlantic to the shores of the Pacific Ocean. The territory which will probably be occupied by the Anglo-Americans at some future time, may be computed to equal three-quarters of Europe in extent. The climate of the Union is upon the whole preferable to that of Europe, and its natural advantages are not less great; it is therefore evident that its population will at some future time be proportionate to our own. Europe, divided as it is between so many different nations, and torn as it has been

丝毫没有减缓。尽管那时在西部的边界有与英国结盟的强有力的印第安部落存在，但是向西部的移民丝毫没有受到影响。当敌人洗劫大西洋沿岸的时候，肯塔基、宾夕法尼亚西部、佛蒙特州和缅因州已经住满人。战后的不稳定也并没有阻碍人口的增加，或是人们向荒野的挺进。因此，不同的法律，战争和平与否，秩序还是混乱，对于英裔美国人不断发展的影响微乎其微。这一点不难理解，因为没有任何因素具有足以影响整个如此辽阔的地域的力量。这个国家总是能给受到灾难影响的地方提供一个安全的避难所，而且，无论灾难有多大，总是能有更好的补救办法。

所以，不要以为新大陆英裔商人的飞速发展可以被抑制。联邦的解体，必然的敌视，共和制度的废除，以及随之而来的暴政，也许可以减缓他们的发展，但无法阻止他们最终完成他们的使命。世界上没有任何力量能够阻碍移民进驻到为勤奋的人准备的这片肥沃的荒野，也无法阻止受难的人前往可供他们休养生息的地方。无论未来发生什么样的事情都无法夺走美国的气候、内海、大河以及沃土。糟糕的法律，革命和无政府状态，都不能磨灭似乎已经成为这个民族特性的对财富的热爱和进取精神，也无法摧毁引领他们走上这条道路的知识。

因此，在未来发生的无可预知的诸多事情之中，至少有一件可以肯定：在即将到来的时代（因为此处我们谈的是一个国家的生命），英裔美国人将独占从北极到热带的这片广大区域，从大西洋沿岸一直延伸到太平洋之滨。英裔美国人占据的这片土地，在未来的某个时候，会达到整个欧洲面积的四分之三。联邦的气候总体来说也要好于欧洲，自然条件

by incessant wars and the barbarous manners of the Middle Ages, has notwithstanding attained a population of 410 inhabitants to the square league. What cause can prevent the United States from having as numerous a population in time?

Many ages must elapse before the divers offsets of the British race in America cease to present the same homogeneous characteristics: and the time cannot be foreseen at which a permanent inequality of conditions will be established in the New World. Whatever differences may arise, from peace or from war, from freedom or oppression, from prosperity or want, between the destinies of the different descendants of the great Anglo-American family, they will at least preserve an analogous social condition, and they will hold in common the customs and the opinions to which that social condition has given birth.

In the Middle Ages, the tie of religion was sufficiently powerful to imbue all the different populations of Europe with the same civilization. The British of the New World have a thousand other reciprocal ties; and they live at a time when the tendency to equality is general amongst mankind. The Middle Ages were a period when everything was broken up; when each people, each province, each city, and each family, had a strong tendency to maintain its distinct individuality. At the present time an opposite tendency seems to prevail, and the nations seem to be advancing to unity. Our means of intellectual intercourse unite the most remote parts of the earth; and it is impossible for men to remain strangers to each other, or to be ignorant of the events which are taking place in any corner of the globe. The consequence is that there is less difference, at the present day, between the Europeans and their descendants in the New World, than there was between certain towns in the thirteenth century which were only separated by a river. If this tendency to assimilation brings foreign nations closer to each other, it must a fortiori prevent the descendants of the same people from becoming aliens to each other.

The time will therefore come when one hundred and fifty millions of men will be living in North America, equal in condition, the progeny of one race, owing their origin to the same cause, and preserving the same civilization, the same language, the same religion, the same habits, the

也同样比欧洲强，所以显然，未来这里的人口一定能够与欧洲抗衡。分裂成为众多国家的欧洲在不断地经受战争的折磨和中世纪的野蛮统治之后，每平方公里约的人口依然能达到410人。所以，有什么因素能够阻止联邦的人口最终达到这样一个水平呢？

只有几个世纪之后，英裔美国人的子孙才会不再呈现同样的特征，而且我们无法预见他们会在什么时候在新大陆建立永久的不平等制度。无论英裔美国人大家庭的不同分支会出现什么样的不同，从和平到战争，从自由到压迫，从繁荣到落魄，他们至少能保持相同的社会状况，以及他们出生的那个社会共同的习俗和观念。

在中世纪，宗教的纽带足以将欧洲所有不同国家的人民联合在同一文明之下。新大陆的英国人之间有着千丝万缕的联系，而且他们生活在一个所有人趋于平等的时代。中世纪是一个分裂的时代，当时，每个民族，每个省，每个城市，乃至每个家庭，都呈现出很强的维护自身独立的趋势。如今，一个相反的趋势盛行，各国好像都走向联合。各国之间的文化交流将地球上最遥远的地方联系起来。人们再也无法彼此互不相识，或对地球任何角落发生的事情一无所知。结果，今天欧洲和他们新大陆的后裔之间的差别还没有13世纪仅有一河之隔的两个乡镇之间的差别大。如果这种同化的趋势让互为外国的人民越来越相近，必然能够更有力地阻止同一民族的后裔彼此成为异族他邦。

因此，这样一个时代必将会来临。那时，北美将拥有1.5亿人口，他们彼此平等，系出同宗，而且由于拥有共同的起源，会具有同样的文明、同样的语言、同样的宗教、同样的习惯、同样的民情，以及同样的观念和同样的肤色。尽管其他还无法确定，但有一点可以

same manners, and imbued with the same opinions, propagated under the same forms. The rest is uncertain, but this is certain; and it is a fact new to the world—a fact fraught with such portentous consequences as to baffle the efforts even of the imagination.

There are, at the present time, two great nations in the world which seem to tend towards the same end, although they started from different points: I allude to the Russians and the Americans. Both of them have grown up unnoticed; and whilst the attention of mankind was directed elsewhere, they have suddenly assumed a most prominent place amongst the nations; and the world learned their existence and their greatness at almost the same time.

All other nations seem to have nearly reached their natural limits, and only to be charged with the maintenance of their power; but these are still in the act of growth; all the others are stopped, or continue to advance with extreme difficulty; these are proceeding with ease and with celerity along a path to which the human eye can assign no term. The American struggles against the natural obstacles which oppose him; the adversaries of the Russian are men; the former combats the wilderness and savage life; the latter, civilization with all its weapons and its arts: the conquests of the one are therefore gained by the ploughshare; those of the other by the sword. The Anglo-American relies upon personal interest to accomplish his ends, and gives free scope to the unguided exertions and common-sense of the citizens; the Russian centres all the authority of society in a single arm: the principal instrument of the former is freedom; of the latter servitude. Their starting-point is different, and their courses are not the same; yet each of them seems to be marked out by the will of Heaven to sway the destinies of half the globe.

肯定，世界将出现一个想象力最丰富的人也无法想象的全新局面。

今天，世界上有两大民族，尽管彼此的起点不同，但似乎都正朝着同一目标前进。他们就是俄国人和美国人。当人类的注意力投向他处的时候，他们已经神不知鬼不觉地崛起，突然之间他们已跻身世界的前列，而且全世界几乎同时承认了他们的存在和强大。

所有的其他国家似乎已经到达它们发展的天然极限，只能努力保持原状；但是这两个国家依然在成长。其他的国家不是原地踏步，就是步履维艰地前进；而它们正沿着一条人们一眼望不到头的道路轻松快速地大步向前。美国人跟与其为敌的自然障碍做斗争，而俄国的敌人则是人。前者与荒野和野蛮战斗，后者则与全副武装的文明作战。因此，一个的征服靠的是劳动者的犁，另一个则靠的是士兵的剑。英裔美国人靠个人利益的驱动来实现目标，给予个人力量和智慧的发挥充分自由的空间；俄国人则将所有的社会权力集中到一人之手。前者的主要手段是自由，而后者是奴役。他们的起点不同，道路各异，但是每个国家似乎都受到天意的指派，注定要各自主宰半个世界。